HISTORY OF
THE SECOND WORLD WAR
UNITED KINGDOM MILITARY SERIES

Edited by SIR JAMES BUTLER

The authors of the Military Histories have been given full access to official documents. They and the editor are alone responsible for the statements made and the views expressed.

The Submission of the Italian Navy, 10th September, 1943

Top. H.M.S. *Valiant* leading two battleships and five cruisers to Malta (taken from
H.M.S. *Warspite*).
Middle (left to right): the *Vittorio Veneto, Duca D'Aosta, Eugenio di Savoia* and *Italia*
at the rendezvous with the Mediterranean Fleet.
Bottom. Italian submarines in Sliema Harbour, Malta.

THE WAR AT SEA
1939–1945

BY

CAPTAIN S. W. ROSKILL, D.S.C., R.N.

VOLUME III

THE OFFENSIVE

Part I

1st June 1943–31st May 1944

This edition of The War at Sea: Volume Three – Part I
first published in 2004
by The Naval & Military Press Ltd

Published by
The Naval & Military Press Ltd
Unit 10 Ridgewood Industrial Park,
Uckfield, East Sussex,
TN22 5QE England
Tel: +44 (0) 1825 749494
Fax: +44 (0) 1825 765701
www.naval–military–press.com

Printed and bound by Antony Rowe Ltd, Eastbourne

CONTENTS

APPENDICES

LIST OF MAPS

LIST OF TABLES

LIST OF ILLUSTRATIONS

THE WAR AT SEA
Vol. III Part I

ERRATUM

Page 96 lines 10–11. *Delete* reference to U.345 being sunk by an air-laid mine on 13th December. This U-boat was damaged in an American air raid on Kiel on that date and was never repaired. In Appendix D Table I (p. 369) opposite U.345 *delete* present entries under 'Name and Task of Killer' and 'Area', and *substitute* 'U.S. Army air raid—bombing' and 'Kiel'. In Appendix D Table IV (p. 375) *amend* the figures under 'German, 1943' to add one to 'Bombing raids' and subtract one from 'Mines laid by shore-based aircraft'. In Index (p. 411) *delete* reference to U.345.

LONDON: HER MAJESTY'S STATIONERY OFFICE:
1960

AUTHOR'S PREFACE

THE decision to offer the final volume of 'The War at Sea' to the public in two parts has been due to several causes. In the first place it became obvious to me well before the whole book was finished that my original assumption that, having covered the first twenty-seven months of the war in one volume, I could compress the events of the last twenty-six within a similar compass was fallacious; for there was far more fighting at sea, and in more theatres, during the latter period than there had been during the former, and the material available to the historian was correspondingly greater. I thus came to realise that only by reducing the whole scale of the canvas on which I was endeavouring to depict events could I adhere to the original decision; and that I was unwilling to accept, as it would have distorted the proportions of the last part of my story compared with the earlier parts. Secondly I was aware that the size of my first volume had about reached the limit of easy handling for the reader, and it seemed undesirable to produce an even bulkier one. Thirdly I had completed the story up to the middle of 1944 before the basic research into the records of the last year of the war had been completed in the British Service Departments and in the United States; and there seemed no good reason to withhold publication of the first part while awaiting the material needed to complete the story. This applied particularly to the last phase of the Pacific War, to deal with which I was bound to depend greatly on the help of the United States Navy Department and of its own historian, Rear-Admiral S. E. Morison, U.S.N.R. (Ret'd); and there were obvious perils in a British historian producing an account of great sea fights, such as Leyte Gulf, without benefit of the fruits of the research carried out by and on behalf of the nation which provided the great majority of the forces which took part on the Allied side. Finally I felt that the reader might prefer to have two smaller, cheaper and more easily handled volumes, produced at comparatively short intervals, than one over-large and more expensive book, whose production could not take place until at least a year after this first part was ready. After I had discussed these, and other considerations which affected the issue, with the Editor of the whole series, Professor Sir James Butler, he took the decision which I myself felt to be greatly preferable from the point of view both of the public of to-day and of the future student of the maritime war of 1939–45.

I have here, as in my previous volumes, told the story of combined operations mainly from the point of view of the Allied maritime

xiii

services involved in them; and it may thus happen that the historians of the Mediterranean and Pacific campaigns working under Major-Generals I. S. O. Playfair and S. W. Kirby will not accept all the conclusions I have drawn with regard to them. In historical research there can, of course, be no finality; and it may therefore well come to pass that the further research of my colleagues, especially in British and enemy Army records, will discover new material which will affect the conclusions. As the poet Pope put it:

> ' 'Tis with our judgements as our watches—none
> Go just alike—yet each believes his own.'

None the less, I have thought it justifiable, and even necessary for posterity's sake, to state what seem to me to be the outstanding lessons of those great undertakings; and I am encouraged in that belief by the fact that nothing has so far come to light which necessitates revision of the conclusions drawn in my first two volumes.

I feel that I must in this volume make a fuller acknowledgement of the help I have received from the officers of the Admiralty's Historical Section under Lieutenant-Commander P. K. Kemp, and from Mr J. C. Nerney's staff in the Air Historical Branch of the Air Ministry; for without their constant advice and sustained interest in my work it would have been quite impossible for me to cover an ever-widening field of increasingly intricate maritime operations. The officers of the Admiralty who have given me that indispensable assistance, and the subjects which have been their particular study, are Captains L. M. Shadwell (Submarine operations) and R. S. D. Armour (Fleet Air Arm operations); Commanders L. J. Pitcairn-Jones (Arctic Convoys and detailed accounts of many battles), G. A. Titterton (Mediterranean campaigns), W. B. Rowbotham (Home waters, Atlantic and statistics), F. Barley and Lieutenant-Commander D. W. Waters (Sea, air and mine warfare against merchant shipping) and Major C. S. Goldingham, R.M. (Indian Ocean and Pacific). For the Royal Air Force's contribution to the maritime war I owe a similar debt to Captain D. V. Peyton-Ward (Home Command operations) and Squadron-Leader W. M. Gould (Mediterranean air operations). I have also received the most cordial co-operation from Rear-Admiral S. E. Morison, U.S.N.R. (Ret'd) and his assistant Rear-Admiral Bern Anderson, U.S.N. (Ret'd), particularly with regard to the predominantly American operations in the Pacific; and Rear-Admiral E. M. Eller, U.S.N., head of the Navy Department's Office of Naval Records and History and his colleagues have not only been kind enough to read and comment on this volume while it was in draft, but have invariably met my many requests to check British records with their own. Though there are, as the reader will readily detect, certain problems which British and American historians are always likely to view differently, it has been a very happy experience to continue in this work my long collaboration with the U.S. Navy, which began in London when Admiral Ghormley's mission arrived in 1940 and lasted throughout my service at sea in the South Pacific theatre from 1941 to 1944 and in Washington during the last eighteen months of the war.

To the foregoing acknowledgements I must add my thanks to my unflagging and enthusiastic assistant, Commander Geoffrey Hare, to Mr G. H. Hurford of the Admiralty Historical Section's Information Room, to Commander M. G. Saunders and the staff of the same department's Foreign Documents Section, whose help in comparing German records with our own has been invaluable; and to Mr H. H. Ellmers and his successor Mr J. C. Gardner of the Admiralty's Record Office. Once again I have importuned many senior officers of all the Services who were concerned with particular operations; and they have invariably responded generously to my request that they should read and criticise my drafts, and give me the benefit of their recollections. For permission to reproduce illustrations I am indebted firstly to the Imperial War Museum. The United States Navy Department has very kindly provided me with those dealing with the Pacific war, the Director of the National Maritime Museum has allowed me to use certain of the Admiralty war artists' paintings and drawings, while Captain H. J. Reinicke and Mr Franz Selinger have found me some interesting German photographs. Finally I would thank Colonel T. M. Penney, who has directed the production of all my maps, and Messrs D. K. Purle and M. J. Godliman, who have produced the finished articles from my rough sketches.

S. W. ROSKILL.

Cabinet Office, *London*
October 1960

'By the mastery of the sea . . ., by her persistent enmity to the spirit of aggression . . ., by her own sustained and unshaken strength, she [Britain] drove the enemy into the battlefield of the Continental system, where his final ruin was certain'.

A. T. Mahan. *The Influence of Sea Power on the French Revolution and Empire*, Vol. II, pp. 400–401.

CHRONOLOGICAL SUMMARY
OF PRINCIPAL EVENTS
JUNE 1943–DECEMBER 1943

CHRONOLOGICAL SUMMARY OF PRINCIPAL EVENTS, JUNE 1943 – DECEMBER 1943

1943	Atlantic	Arctic	Mediterranean	Indian Ocean	Pacific	Europe
June	U-boats withdraw from North Atlantic to the west of the Azores, and to more distant areas after their defeat on the North Atlantic routes in May				30 Allied landings in New Georgia (Solomon Islands)	
July	Intensification of the Bay of Biscay air offensive		10 Invasion of Sicily	Increased U-boat activity causes heavier shipping losses	13 Battle of Kolombangara	German offensive on Russian fronts is held, and Russians start counter-offensive
August	U-boat activity subsides		3–17 Axis evacuation from Sicily	25 Admiral Lord Louis Mountbatten appointed Supreme Commander, South-East Asia	15 Allied landings on Vella Lavella	5 Russians recapture Orel 17 First Quebec Conference begins 23 Russians recapture Kharkov

September	U-boats return to the attack on North Atlantic convoys	22 Tirpitz damaged by midget submarine attack in Altenford	3 Allies invade Italian mainland 8 Italian armistice 9 Allies land at Salerno 10–17 Allies occupy Cos, Leros, and other Dodecanese Islands 19 Axis evacuate Sardinia	Eastern Fleet moves back from Kilindini to Ceylon Shipping losses decline	Allies recapture Huon Gulf ports in New Guinea	Germans on the retreat towards the Dnieper
October	8 Bases granted the Allies in the Azores Many U-boat sinkings. Second victory on the convoy routes		1 Allies enter Naples 3 Germans recapture Cos 4 Allies land in Corsica		7 Battle of Vella Lavella	3 Russians cross the Dnieper near Kiev
November		Arctic convoys resumed 15–24 JW.54A 22–2 Dec. JW.54B	16 Germans recapture Leros Allied advance in Italy halted on the Garigliano River		1 Allied landing on Bougainville 20 Allied landings in the Gilbert Islands, Central Pacific	6 Kiev recaptured 28–1 Dec. Teheran Conference
December		12–20 JW.55A 20–29 JW.55B 26 Scharnhorst sunk		19 The second offensive on the Arakan begins	26 Allied landings in New Britain	3–7 Cairo Conference

CHAPTER I

THE BACKGROUND TO THE
MARITIME OFFENSIVE

'We want an Army to *attack*, not one to
defend . . . We want a sea-going Army that
we can launch forth anywhere *at an hour's
notice*. Not 6 months!'
Admiral Sir John Fisher to
Edward A. Goulding, November 1908.

B Y June 1943, when we resume our story, there was no longer
any serious likelihood that the Axis powers ·would gain the
final victory; and the broad shape of the offensive strategy
which America and Britain intended to prosecute had become
plainer. Although agreement on the next move after clearing North
Africa was not easily reached, there was never any doubt that the
strategy of the western Allies would take full advantage of the
capacity to land the Army in theatres of our own choice which
maritime power conferred.[1]

It was true that the Americans, conscious of the vast industrial
capacity, the almost unlimited manpower, and the throbbing
dynamism of a young nation scarcely touched by the war, viewed
the matter differently from ourselves. They believed that a cross-
Channel invasion in 1943 was not only practicable, but the only way
to achieve the quick victory they desired. We, on the other hand,
were deeply aware of the effects of the continuing shortage of shipping, and of the fact that sufficient trained men and modern equipment could not yet be found; and memories of the price paid in the
past, when troops had been pitted against carefully prepared and
strongly defended coastal positions, had made us determined not to
accept risk of failure on a scale which might prove a parallel to the
Paschendaele offensive of 1917. At Casablanca in January 1943 it
had been comparatively easy to obtain American agreement to the
invasion of Sicily; but at the second Washington conference in the
following May it proved very much harder to convince them that
the next move should be against the mainland of Italy, with the
object of knocking that country finally out of the war. The Americans
only accepted the British purpose reluctantly, and it was plain that,

---

[1] See Vol. I, pp. 11–12.

as soon as the forces which our Ally could put into the field out-numbered our own, they would insist on their own strategy being adopted.[1]

Even after the passage of more than a decade it is as difficult to explain the American mistrust of the British Mediterranean strategy as it is hard to avoid the conclusion that post-war developments in central and western Europe might have been happier had it been carried through in the manner we desired. Anti-imperialism, anti-colonialism, anti-monarchism, and the sheer ancient prejudices of a people taught a myopic interpretation of history, and brought up to believe that they could grow rich in isolation from the rest of the world, probably all played a part. The broad result was that although vital American aid, especially in the air, continued to be given to the combined operations in the central Mediterranean, the British leaders became increasingly aware that many influential Americans regarded such commitments as 'diversions' from the invasion of western Europe; and that we could not expect whole-hearted co-operation from our principal Ally should a strategic opportunity arise in the eastern section of that theatre.

While the Americans mistrusted long-term British intentions in the Mediterranean, the British authorities, and especially those re-sponsible for the maritime war, had become increasingly conscious of the fact that not a few American eyes were concentrated mainly on the Pacific theatre, to which an ever-growing proportion of their resources was being allocated. The principal protagonist of the Pacific strategy was the U.S. Navy, under the direction of Admiral E. J. King; and a sympathetic understanding of his outlook and pur-poses was not aided by his rugged exterior and his forthright manner of expressing himself at inter-Allied conferences. The view that King was anti-British, though very prevalent at the time, is certainly an over-simplification of his attitude, and possibly an unfair stigmatism of a man who did, after all, repeatedly send help to the Royal Navy. It is probably nearer the truth to say that in his heart he admired the other service's traditions and fighting record, but was deter-mined that it should not deprive the United States Navy, in whose creation he himself had played such a great part, of the glory of victories which he felt to be its right. Be that as it may, King's attitude certainly did not help to smooth over the difficulties which inevitably arise between Allies, nor tend to eliminate the increasing doubts felt in Britain whether the United States Navy's Pacific strategy was not being carried to a point where it violated the long-standing governmental decision that the defeat of Germany should take priority over the defeat of Japan. In fact, of course, such fears

[1] See *Grand Strategy*, Vol. IV (in preparation), for a full discussion of the Casablanca and Washington conferences.

proved groundless; for the European grand strategy was successfully implemented, though not in the manner that some British leaders would have preferred. The impartial historian must therefore conclude that there was not much wrong with King's allocation of resources between the Pacific and European theatres. Moreover the speed with which America could build up her total strength, and so meet the material and human needs of both theatres, was almost certainly not fully realised in Britain. Finally it will surely be agreed that for sheer imaginative conception, and tactical brilliance in execution, the Pacific offensives, which the power and skill of the United States Navy made possible, have never been equalled; and it may be regretted that in Britain as a whole, and in the Royal Navy in particular, far too little attention has been paid to the operations in that theatre, rich though they are with lessons on every aspect of maritime warfare.

Though the differences over the Mediterranean strategy were both real and important, there were many other matters on which British and American views coincided. Thus there were no doubts that the continued strengthening of our control over the Atlantic convoy routes, first made secure by the victories of May 1943[1], was an essential preliminary to victory in the west; there was full agreement that the bombing offensive against Germany should continue with the three-fold purpose of reducing the enemy's productive capacity, of weakening his will to resist, and of gaining command of the air over Europe to the degree which was essential to a successful re-entry of the Allied armies on to the continent; and we were also agreed in the determination to supply and support the Russian armies, on which we entirely depended to halt the great German drive towards the Mesopotamian and Persian oil fields and India.

Perhaps the most remarkable fact about the joint conduct of the war by Britain and America was not that differences of strategic outlook and purpose arose, but that, after full and free discussions, the various inter-Allied conferences invariably achieved agreements which both parties were prepared to accept. Those agreements, though inevitably involving compromise and concessions, were themselves outstanding achievements; and they owed a great deal to the two heads of governments, who were always determined that agreement should be reached. Perhaps the greatest weakness of the Axis powers, leading to all their gravest strategic errors, arose from the fact that they possessed no organisation comparable to that of the British and American Joint and Combined Chiefs of Staffs' Committees. Thus decisions affecting the whole conduct of the war were generally arrived at either by a simple *ad hoc* process or through one

---

[1] See Vol. II, Chapter XIV.

man's 'intuitions', rather than by careful and logical discussion and reasoning. Nor did our Russian Allies, when they came to join the high-level discussions, fit into the well-tried and proven Anglo-American system; for compromise must ever be difficult to dictators. Thus we never came to achieve any real strategic co-ordination with the Russians, and east and west continued to a considerable extent to fight separate wars.

From the Royal Navy's point of view the implementing of its share in the prosecution of Allied strategy presented formidable difficulties at this time. While the need to maintain and strengthen its hold in the Atlantic was paramount, and placed a continuous strain on that service and its partners of Coastal Command, the Home Fleet was required to fight the Arctic convoys through, and also to reinforce the combined offensives in the Mediterranean; and the Admiralty was also endeavouring all the time to build up the Eastern Fleet to a point at which it could take the offensive against Japan. Furthermore an increasing proportion of the maritime effort, including ship-building and training of warship crews, had to be devoted to preparations for the new combined operations. The crux of the service's difficulties lay in the fact that, although the very severe losses which had been suffered during nearly four years of war had been replaced either by new British construction or by American ships transferred under 'Lend-Lease', it was becoming increasingly difficult to man the fleet.[1] Throughout 1943–44 no subject caused the Admiralty greater anxiety, nor was more frequently discussed, than the shortage of manpower. It was, moreover, plain that as we had started the war with a large proportion of over-age or obsolescent ships in the fleet[2], and our war construction programmes had generally been of a short-term or emergency nature, the post-war prospects for the Navy were grim indeed. All Lend-Lease ships would have to be returned to the United States, and the remainder of the once great British fleet might well prove quite inadequate to meet her world-wide commitments. Such considerations as these were, of course, regarded as very secondary to the winning of the war; but naval building is such a long-term process, and the consequences of neglecting regular replacement can be so serious, that the steady process of attrition from which the Royal Navy proper was obviously suffering could but cause apprehensions regarding the more distant future; for the proportion of the British nation's capital represented by the maritime services had obviously wasted substantially.

Of equal, if not greater consequence, were the heavy casualties suffered by the regular service. The above table shows how the

---

[1] See Table 1 (p. 9).
[2] See Vol. I, Appendix D.

Table 1. The British Empire's Naval Strength and Losses, 3rd September, 1939, to 1st October, 1943

Class of Ship	Strength on 3rd Sept., 1939	Losses 3rd Sept., 1939 to 1st Oct., 1943	Strength on 1st October, 1943 (includes Lend-Lease ships)
Battleships and Battle Cruisers .	15	5	15
Fleet and Light Fleet Aircraft Carriers	6	5	6
Escort Aircraft Carriers . .	Nil	3	25 (23 Lend-Lease)
Cruisers (all types) . . .	63	26	62
Destroyers and Escort Destroyers .	191	120	288 (75 *Hunt*-class)
Escort Vessels (cutters, sloops, frigates, corvettes) . . .	43	40	325 (37 Lend-Lease)
Fleet Minesweepers . . .	42	19	222 (19 Lend-Lease)
Submarines	69	67	98

NOTES: (1) British ships manned by Allied crews are included in the above table, but Allied warships are not included.
(2) A large proportion of the escort vessels and fleet minesweepers belonged to the Commonwealth Navies, and especially to the Royal Canadian and Australian Navies.

greatest losses of ships had been among the destroyers, escort vessels and submarines; and in almost every one of those sunken ships a number of experienced officers and long-service ratings had lost their lives. These were the tested and war-hardened men needed to command and man the new ships, and to train the great influx of temporary officers and 'hostilities only' ratings. By the 30th of June, 1943, when the Royal Navy's strength had grown from the pre-war 10,000 officers and 109,000 men to 57,682 and 604,248 respectively[1], the casualties had amounted to 4,280 officers and 38,164 men killed and missing.[2] In replacing the regular service's losses, and at the same time making possible the great war-time expansion, it was largely the reserve officer who came to the rescue. As so often before in her history, Britain was able to tap the hidden resources of her people's maritime skill and experience. Among all the various naval reserves the expansion was by far the greatest in the Royal Naval Volunteer Reserve, whose tiny pre-war nucleus could hardly have foretold the prodigious progeny which it was to beget. There were still a number of Royal Naval Reserve (ex-Merchant Navy) officers

[1] These latter figures exclude the W.R.N.S. who numbered 2,622 officers and 50,709 ratings, and also about 11,000 Merchant Navy officers and men serving in the Royal Navy under special contracts.
[2] Of the missing, 604 officers and 4,166 ratings were prisoners-of-war.

and men serving in the Navy, but because more could not be taken without weakening the Merchant Navy unacceptably, the Admiralty had virtually ceased to recruit from that source.

The R.N.V.R. officers brought to the Navy qualities which were peculiarly their own. Because they had not been moulded by the long education and apprenticeship of the regular officer, they had less respect for the authority of rank; but they also had fewer inhibitions against indulging in novel experiments in organisation, equipment and procedure. Indeed some of their experiments were so novel that they affronted (and may have been designed to affront) their more conventional-minded superiors. Yet they quickly developed, and were astute enough to show, a genuine respect for what was admirable and timeless in naval tradition; and because they were always ready to listen to the counsels of experience, they gained the confidence and affection of the regular officers. Furthermore they brought to their new tasks an infectious enthusiasm and a boundless sense of humour. Into a service in which conservatism was not the least common characteristic they blew a strong, fresh wind of unconventionality and non-conformity; and the regulars for their part returned the respect shown to their professionalism with a sympathetic understanding of the R.N.V.R's open-minded approach to every problem, and a tolerance of their occasional idiosyncrasies. Indeed the regular and reserve officers soon found that they could each learn from the other, to the advantage of the Service as a whole. Even the citadels of the Naval Staff were not immune from the invasion of wavy stripes; and there too the newcomers more than justified the growing responsibilities placed on them. A large proportion of the new ideas conceived during the war, and many of the novel weapons and devices which proliferated, must have originated from the 'Special Branch' officers and the civilian technicians and scientists who joined every Admiralty department. If their methods were sometimes deeply shocking to a service accustomed to seeking 'Board approval' for any considerable innovation, and (still more) prior 'Treasury approval' for any expenditure of public funds, their superiors quickly realised that they had among them some men of outstanding ability, and that to insist on conventional procedures might not be the best way of winning a war.

It was, however, at sea that the R.N.V.R. officer really gained his laurels. Before the war it had been considered unthinkable that any of His Majesty's ships should be commanded by them; yet after four years so many had worked their way with distinction through the lower ranks that it would plainly have been grossly unjust to deny them the ultimate responsibility of the sea officer. Now, in 1943, many destroyers, frigates and corvettes, a few submarines, and the majority of the special craft commissioning for combined operations were commanded by reserve officers, many of whom had regulars serving under them; and the greatly expanded Fleet Air Arm included not a few squadrons commanded by officers of the same reserve.[1] Never was confidence better justified than in giving these young men the responsibilities to which their experience and enthusiasm entitled them. Furthermore in order to maintain the ever-increasing demand for junior officers, promotion from the lower deck was thrown open to both regulars and reservists to an extent which could not have been imagined in 1939. Young 'hostilities only' ratings were accepted in large numbers, on recommendations from sea, for training as temporary officers; and many ratings from the Commonwealth and colonies qualified in the same way, and volunteered to serve in the Royal Navy. Of all the war-time training centres which contributed to keeping the fleet manned, none played a greater part than that at Hove (with off-shoots in other parts of Sussex), named H.M.S. *King Alfred*, where candidates for temporary commissions in the R.N.V.R. did their basic training. Starting from virtually nothing in September 1939[2], Captain J. N. Pelly built up an organisation which, in the course of the next five and a half years, qualified 22,508 young men from all walks of life as Sub-Lieutenants R.N.V.R.[3]

Another establishment which should be remembered was H.M.S. *Europa* at Lowestoft, where men for the Royal Naval Patrol Service were trained. The Corporation's concert hall was taken over just before war broke out (while a concert was actually in progress), and the small nucleus of ex-fishermen who dumped their kit on the stage that night, as the audience was leaving, swelled to a total of no less than 57,000 men. For the greater part of the war the *Europa* was commanded by Captain B. H. Piercy, R.N. (Ret'd), and the men whom he and his staff trained played an important part in manning the enormous variety of small ships and craft which joined the fleet during the war.

The training of the great influx of reserve officers and conscript ratings was, in the main part, carried out by the regular Navy; and it was here that retired officers and pensioner ratings made a big contribution to the efficient manning of the fleet. Every pre-war

---

[1] Two books which vividly recount the war experiences of R.N.V.R. officers who achieved command are *One of our Submarines* by Edward Young (Hart-Davis, 1952) and *Escort* by D. A. Rayner (Kimber, 1955).

[2] An account of the commissioning of H.M.S. *King Alfred* on 11th September 1939 and of the great programme of training accomplished by the establishment is to be found in *The R.N.V.R.* by Kerr and Granville (Harrap, 1957).

[3] Of the total qualified in the *King Alfred* 3,528 were entered as officers under a variety of schemes, while 18,080 were promoted from the lower deck. Nearly 15,000 of the officers qualified for the executive branch. The remainder were mainly 'special branch' (i.e. technical), accountant, and Royal Marine officers. All the Dominion Navies and many Allied Navies were also supplied with reserve officers by the *King Alfred*.

naval training establishment had by this time thrown off several new off-shoots; and schools where naval aviation, gunnery, radar, anti-submarine warfare, minelaying and minesweeping, and indeed every ancient as well as a good many new techniques were taught, abounded all over the country. It was these schools and establishments which kept the expanding fleet manned by trained crews, in spite of the ever-growing complexity of the equipment installed and the constant appearance of new types of ship to fulfil new, and sometimes strange, functions.

As to the fleet itself, its composition, and also the functions of different classes of ship, had altered considerably since 1939. The fleet carrier had displaced the battleship as the main arbiter of defeat or victory at sea; but the battleships had found a new function as the primary means of neutralising coastal defences with their heavy guns before an assault was made from the sea. Convoy escorts still carried out their traditional function, but carrier-borne and shore-based aircraft had added immensely to the effectiveness of the convoy strategy. Cruisers still supported the lighter warships when interference by enemy surface ships was possible, and they too were being used to support combined operations. It was, however, in the technique of landing armies on a hostile coast that the developments had been most marked. It had been the reversion to a maritime strategy, forced on Britain by her total expulsion from the continent in 1940, which had given real prominence to the need; and it may well puzzle posterity to understand or explain how it came to pass that between the wars so little attention was given by the British services to developing the techniques required to exploit what has always been one of the historic functions of maritime power.[1] The expensive failure at the Dardanelles in 1915 and the claim that air power had made assaults from the sea impossible were certainly contributory causes.

Though a few specialised craft had been produced in time for the Norwegian campaign of 1940, and had proved themselves then and in coastal operations in the Channel, no very great effort was devoted to the matter until Mr Churchill created the post of Director (later Chief) of Combined Operations in June 1940. Thereafter, and especially under the energetic direction of Admiral Lord Louis Mountbatten, the Combined Operations Headquarters acted as an

---

[1] See Rear-Admiral L. E. H. Maund, *Assault from the Sea* (Methuen, 1949), pp. 19–21, for a full account of the early developments in amphibious warfare. 'In April 1939' the author states 'a report was written to show up our unpreparedness . . . we should need two years to prepare for a landing by a brigade with the object of occupying territory.' This report resulted in the first considerable order for specialised landing craft being placed. None the less on the outbreak of war the Inter-Service Training and Development Centre, the only body which had been working on the subject, was disbanded. Its members were told that 'there would be no combined operations in this war'.

incubator of new ideas, its experimental establishments tried them out, and its training bases instructed officers and men of all services in the use of the craft and weapons which we had decided to adopt for service. All the developments made in Britain were given to the Americans, even before they had entered the war. But in November 1941, when meetings to discuss production of landing craft took place in Washington, the U.S. Navy finally declared that they could foresee no use for them in a war with Germany, that their building yards were already working to capacity, and that as the funds voted under 'Lend-Lease' were already fully committed it was impossible to include any in the current programme. The Americans, however, radically modified their views as soon as they found themselves at war, and in January 1942 an order for 200 L.S.Ts (Landing Ships Tank) was accepted on British account, and a like number ordered for their own use. The building of large numbers of L.C.Ts (Landing Craft Tank) was also soon put in hand, and in May 1942 the Americans gave absolute priority to the construction of the ships and craft needed for combined operations. None the less it remains true that the shortage of such vessels was a controlling factor in all Allied offensive plans, in all theatres, almost to the end of the war; and it seems possible that, had the Americans accepted earlier our views on the importance of the part they had to play, the shortages would at least have been mitigated. Be that as it may, if it was mainly British fertility of ideas, and our own early experiments and improvisations, which produced the first versions of, for example, the L.C.T. and L.S.T., it was the Americans who made the great combined operations of 1943 and 1944 possible by building them in large numbers. The combined result of the two nations' efforts was to create within the organisation of the conventional navies what amounted to a new and highly specialised branch, whose squadrons and flotillas were led by men who had made that aspect of maritime war their particular province; and it was those crews who played perhaps the greatest part in the Offensive Phase to be described in this volume.

In terms of strategy the greatest interest of the period here described lies in the fact that it saw the full exploitation of maritime power, aided and supported on every occasion by its new associate of air power, to land the Allied armies in assaults on one enemy's continental citadel in Europe, and on the other enemy's island fortresses in the Pacific. We had passed through the Defensive Phase, maintaining our home and overseas bases inviolate, gaining time to switch our economy from a peace to a war footing, and preserving all the while the world-wide maritime control on which our survival depended[1];

See Vol. I, Chapter I.

we had come through hard times, grievous defeats and desperate anxieties to see the balance gradually tilt in our favour. Now, in the middle of 1943, we and our new-world Ally were ready to reap the vast benefits conferred by the patient pursuit of a maritime strategy; for in all theatres we were ready to take the offensive.

CHAPTER II

THE BATTLE OF THE ATLANTIC

1st June–31st August, 1943

The Bay of Biscay Offensive

'In fact . . . the result of the convoy system, in this and other instances, warrants the inference that, when properly systematised and applied, it will have more success . . . than hunting for individual marauders which, even when most thoroughly planned, still resembles looking for a needle in a haystack.'

A. T. Mahan. *The Influence of Sea Power on the French Revolution and Empire, 1793–1812.* Vol. II, p. 217 (Samson Low, Marston and Co., 1892).

I T was told in the second volume of this history how, after the severe defeat suffered on the convoy routes in May 1943, the U-boats were withdrawn from the North Atlantic.[1] Their losses had risen from about thirteen per cent of those at sea to thirty per cent, which could not be sustained. In the middle of that fateful month, before he even knew the full extent of his defeat, Dönitz reported to Hitler that 'we are facing the greatest crisis in submarine warfare, since the enemy, by means of new location devices . . . makes fighting impossible, and is causing us heavy losses. . . . Furthermore at the present time the only outward route for submarines is a narrow lane in the Bay of Biscay. This passage is so difficult that it now takes a submarine ten days to get through.' It will thus be seen that Dönitz[2] attributed his discomfiture mainly to the inability of the

---

[1] See Vol. II, p. 377.

[2] Although Dönitz had been Commander-in-Chief of the German Navy since 30th January 1943 (see Vol. II, p. 354), he had retained his former title of Commander, U-boats (*Befehlshaber der U-boote*, or B.d.U. for short). He thus remained responsible for their general policy and broad dispositions. The day-to-day control of the U-boats was now conducted by Rear-Admiral E. Godt, the Chief of Staff to B.d.U. As, however, Dönitz continued to take the liveliest interest in everything concerning the U-boats, and it was by no means always clear where his responsibilities ended and Godt's began, it has been thought preferable in this narrative to regard him as the authority for the conduct of the Atlantic Battle on the German side.

search receivers then fitted in his U-boats to detect the transmissions of our new radar sets, and to the harassing action by Coastal Command's aircraft on the Bay of Biscay transit routes. Up to a point he was correct in both opinions, for the radar developments had undoubtedly restored the initiative to our surface escorts and air patrols, and the latter were making the passages to and from the operational U-boat bases increasingly hazardous. Moreover the German scientists believed at that time that we could not have overcome the technical difficulties involved in producing a centimetric radar set. But the Allied successes in fact stemmed from wider causes than these, and had Dönitz known about them his anxieties would certainly not have been diminished. In the first place recent reinforcements had enabled us to organise far stronger surface escorts, and far more regular air cover over and around the convoys. Support groups were constantly available to reinforce threatened convoys; and escort carriers had begun to accompany them throughout their passages, and were providing air cover in waters to which the shore-based aircraft could not yet reach. Equally important was the fact that Allied intelligence was now working with great speed and accuracy. This enabled convoys to be diverted clear of dangerous waters, and surface vessels or aircraft to be directed to the positions where they were most likely to find their quarry. Indeed the Admiralty's Submarine Tracking Room and the equivalent organisations, built to the British model, on the other side of the Atlantic had now reached the peak of efficiency. Though no details of the methods employed can be given, a large share of our success can confidently be attributed to the combination of the intuition of certain experienced individuals with the most modern technical resources. In that room, whose work throughout the entire war was directed by Commander Rodger Winn, R.N.V.R., a barrister by peace-time profession, intelligence of the utmost value to the ships and aircraft escorting our convoys or patrolling the seas was collected, interpreted and disseminated. Moreover the new and more deadly weapons now available, and the greatly improved standard of training achieved by the users of them, enabled those forces to strike with far more lethal effect than formerly. It was therefore not surprising that early in June Dönitz withdrew his U-boats to the west of the Azores, to try to find less-well-protected convoys running between America and Gibraltar, or to yet more distant waters where he hoped that they would be freed from the constantly searching eyes of the patrolling aircraft. His hopes of restoring the balance rested mainly on the introduction of a more efficient warning receiver, able to detect the transmissions from our centimetric radar sets. Pending the arrival of such instruments a radar decoy device was the only amelioration possible. He was also fitting more numerous close-range anti-aircraft

*The sinking of U.106 on 2nd August, 1943 by Sunderlands M/461 Squadron (R.A.A.F.)
and N/228 Squadron*

Top. The first attack by M/461 (taken by N/228).
Middle. Attack by N/228. Depth-charge plumes subsiding.
Bottom. The U-boat sinking by the stern.

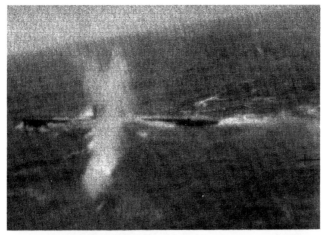

*The sinking of U.643 on
8th October, 1943 by
Liberators T/120 Squadron
and Z/86 Squadron*

Depth charges entering
the water.

The U-boat sinking with
her crew clustered in
the conning tower.

H.M.S. *Orwell* picking
up survivors.

weapons in all U-boats; and he set great store by the acoustic torpedo, which he hoped to have in service by the autumn, and to use
with deadly effect against our escorts. Finally he pressed Hitler for
better long-range air reconnaissance in the Atlantic, and for stronger
air cover on the transit routes. Because his relations with Hitler were
far more cordial than his predecessor's, Dönitz was in a stronger
position than Raeder had ever been to overcome the blustering
monomania of Göring, and so obtain the air co-operation which he
needed. 'Support from our Air Force is totally inadequate' he told
the Führer. 'Even now it is not too late to give our Navy an Air
Force.' Britain has indeed cause to be thankful that the Germans
never developed a system of intimate collaboration between sea and
air forces, such as characterised the work of the Royal Navy and
Coastal Command at this time. As longer-term measures Dönitz
obtained approval to increase U-boat production from thirty to forty
per month, and to give the highest priority to submarines capable of
greater speed under water. The 'Walter' boat, driven by the com-
bustion of diesel fuel with hydrogen peroxide[1], was still in the experimental stage; and although seven small boats (320 tons) of that class
were completed, and two large prototype boats (1,600 tons) had been
ordered for training and experimental purposes, the operational
version (850 tons) could not be expected before 1945. In fact the
technical troubles encountered were so serious that no Walter boat
was sent on active service before the end of the war. As an interim
measure, pending arrival of the Walter boats, Dönitz planned to
build a number of submarines with the streamlined hull of the
Walter design, and with electric batteries of far greater capacity than
the earlier boats. These, called Type XXI boats, would have a
bigger cruising range when submerged, and would be capable of
short bursts at speeds up to seventeen knots under water.[2] In July
Hitler gave top priority to the construction of this type. They were
to be pre-fabricated in eight sections and mass-produced in assembly
yards at Hamburg, Bremen and Danzig. A smaller version (230 tons)
was designed for work in the Mediterranean and Black Sea, to which
they were to be transported overland.[3] When the decision was taken
to build these types no more 'conventional' submarines were ordered.
The 250 already under construction were to be completed, but
deliveries would gradually taper off, until the last ones had entered
service during 1944. The programme of construction of the new types
(originally 288 Type XXI by February 1945 and 140 Type XXIII
by October 1944) was started at the end of 1943. First deliveries of the

---

[1] See Vol. II, p. 207.

[2] Full particulars of the Type XXI boats, including numbers constructed, will be
given in Appendix X to Part II of this volume.

[3] Called Type XXIII.

larger class were expected in April 1944, and production should have reached the formidable rate of thirty-three per month in September of that year. It cannot be doubted that even this interim design, on which the enemy relied to regain the initiative, or even to turn the tide in the U-boat war, was a serious threat to Allied control of the sea routes. Happily, and in spite of the most energetic and ruthless measures taken by the Germans, shortages of labour and materials, changes in priorities, and Allied bombing combined to cause the programme to fall badly in arrears. By the middle of 1944 only one large and two small boats had been delivered for trial; and before the end of that year it had become plain that few, if any, of the new types could be ready for operational use in the foreseeable future.

Another improvement by which Dönitz set considerable store was the 'Schnorkel' air intake and diesel exhaust mast. In 1940 the Germans had captured two Dutch submarines fitted with such a device, but they attached no great importance to its development until the heavy losses of April and May 1943 forced them to search for means to improve the survival prospects of their submarines.[1] Successful trials took place in July 1943, and by the middle of the following year thirty operational boats had been fitted. The Schnorkel enabled the U-boats to charge their electric batteries while remaining at periscope depth, it reduced the likelihood of being sighted or detected by radar while charging batteries, and it permitted operations to be restarted in waters which had recently been made prohibitively dangerous by our air patrols. On the other hand it did reduce the mobility of the submarines when submerged, it accentuated the problem of fatigue among the crews, and it tended towards making the U-boat commanders' outlook more defensive.

The survivors from the May defeat by the convoy escorts, about sixteen U-boats in all, were formed into a new group in the following month, and ordered to concentrate some 600 miles west of the Azores. But the sudden quiet in the North Atlantic had caused the Admiralty and Coastal Command to review the enemy's most probable action. On his own initiative Air Marshal Sir John Slessor, Commander-in-Chief, Coastal Command, had already concentrated seventy medium-range aircraft to reinforce the patrols flying on the U-boat

---

[1] The Schnorkel equipment had been invented by a Dutch naval officer as long ago as 1927, and four new submarines which escaped to England in an incomplete state in 1940 had it installed. The British authorities, however, saw no use for it at that time, and as it had certain disadvantages it was removed from the Dutch submarines before they operated under British control. Not until the arrival of ten-centimetre radar had so greatly increased the danger to a surfaced submarine did the Schnorkel come into its own. (Information from K. W. L. Bezemer, historian of the Royal Netherlands Navy.)

transit routes across the Bay of Biscay and around the north of Scotland, accepting that other forces would be weakened temporarily.[1] In addition American escort carriers were sent to work on the New York–Gibraltar route, and British surface forces were allocated to co-operate with Coastal Command's Bay of Biscay patrols.

In June no convoys were attacked on the north Atlantic convoy routes (north of 31 degrees N.); and in spite of Dönitz having left only a few U-boats there, with orders to use their wireless deceptively to simulate a much larger number of boats, our aircraft working in support of the convoys sank three enemies. Nor did the group off the Azores fare any better. Aircraft from the American escort carrier *Bogue* found their patrol line, and on the 5th of June they sank U.217. The convoy which was passing east at the time slipped through safely.

It is now plain that the difficulties experienced by the U-boats in locating and intercepting our convoys at this time derived largely from the fact that the highly skilled German cryptographers were no longer able to read Allied messages dealing with control of shipping. At the end of May 1943 we introduced a new cypher, and thereafter (except for a short period at the end of the year) the Germans were deprived of what had been their most valuable source of intelligence.[2]

Dönitz now tried harder than ever to find 'soft spots' in the more remote waters, and in particular off West Africa and Brazil. But the days had long since passed when he could rely on surface ships for replenishing his submarines, and he now had to employ special U-boats for the purpose. To see how his plans fared it will be best to turn first to the patrols by Coastal Command in the Bay of Biscay.

The sailing of U-boats in groups, which Dönitz had ordered because his single boats had suffered such heavy losses in May[3], started early in June. Their orders still were to stay submerged in the Bay at night, but to come to the surface by day and fight back against our attacking aircraft. Though an inward-bound boat (U.418) was sunk by a rocket-firing Beaufighter on the 1st, the outward-bound groups at first fared fortunately. No. 19 Group's patrols were increasing as more aircraft became available, but the German Air Force was also showing more activity, and attacks by Ju.88s on our anti-submarine aircraft were becoming much more common. To mention one such fight, on the 2nd of June Sunderland N. of No. 461 Royal Australian Air Force Squadron, commanded by Flight Lieutenant C. B. Walker,

---

[1] Appendix B gives the establishment of Coastal Command for the period covered by this volume.

[2] See also Vol. I, pp. 267 and 469–470, and Vol. II, pp. 112 and 207–208, regarding the earlier successes of the German cryptographers.

[3] See Vol. II, p. 371.

R.A.A.F., engaged eight Ju.88s for nearly an hour. Although his air-craft was badly damaged and his crew suffered several casualties Walker shot down three enemies, flew back 350 miles on three engines, and then beached his flying boat safely in Cornwall. To protect our anti-submarine aircraft against these marauders No. 19 Group's Beaufighter squadron (No. 248), and also Mosquitos from No. 10 Group of Fighter Command, started to fly interception patrols in the Bay, and they helped greatly to subdue the Luftwaffe.

By the 5th of June the convoy routes were so quiet that it was decided to reinforce Coastal Command's Bay patrols; but although many U-boats were crossing those waters at the time, few sightings and no attacks took place during the first days of the month. Then on the 12th, a group of five enemies was sighted, and two days later Air Marshal Slessor introduced a fresh scheme of search and attack. New patrol areas were established, and Nos. 15 and 19 Groups were ordered to devote their maximum effort by day and night to the Bay. Fighter cover was to be provided by Mosquitos, and an air-craft which sighted a U-boat was either to attack immediately, or shadow and 'home' reinforcements to the scene.

Success did not, however, come at once; for the next Sunderland to sight the U-boat group was shot down. But she damaged U.564, which turned for home with another U-boat as escort. The damaged boat was then sunk by a Whitley of No. 10 O.T.U.[1]; but the attacker crashed and was lost with all hands. The next series of engagements was against a group of three boats which left La Pallice on the 12th. Little damage was done, and two aircraft suffered badly from the U-boats' accurate anti-aircraft gunfire. A third group, of five boats, left Brest and Lorient on the same day, and were soon attacked by Mosquitos on fighter-interception duties. Their gun-fire forced two enemies to return; but the three survivors, though attacked several times more, crossed the Bay in safety. The record of sightings by our aircraft had been good; but the execution of the actual attacks plainly still left much to be desired by way of accuracy. None the less the U-boats suffered such heavy casualties among the exposed members of their crews that, on the 17th of June, Dönitz ordered them in future to cross the Bay submerged, and to surface only if it was necessary to charge batteries. If surprised by aircraft they were, however, still to fight back; and since many of them were caught in that manner the new orders made no substantial difference to our air patrols. More sightings, of inward- as well as outward-bound U-boats, took place between the 17th and 23rd; but no attack was successful.

On the 20th the famous 2nd Escort Group, commanded by

---

[1] This was a Bomber Command Operational Training Unit (O.T.U.) which was lent to Coastal Command from 12th August 1942 to 19th July 1943.

Captain F. J. Walker in the sloop *Starling*, arrived to co-operate with the Coastal Command patrols.[1] The cruiser *Scylla* was also sent south to support the small ships, in case the six big German destroyers known to be in La Pallice tried to molest them. But as Walker had come from Liverpool and had not called at Plymouth, under whose naval Commander-in-Chief he was now to work, he had no opportunity to familiarise himself with No. 19 Group's patrol system; and this vitiated his ability to co-operate to the best effect during the present cruise. None the less he followed up an aircraft sighting of an inward-bound group, and early on the 24th obtained asdic contact. Depth-charge attacks forced U.119 to the surface, and Walker promptly rammed and sank her. She was actually a minelaying U-boat detailed to act as reserve tanker for Dönitz's operations in distant waters. Two hours later the *Wren* obtained another contact. A long succession of attacks was made by the whole group except the leader, whose asdic had been put out of action by the earlier ramming, and in spite of the U-boat diving very deep she was destroyed after five hours of persistent counter-attacks, by charges set to explode between 500 and 750 feet. This was U.449.

Between the 24th of June, when these two quick successes were obtained, and the end of the month several U-boats passed inward and outward, but no more were sunk. Among those coming home was U.180, which had taken the nationalist leader Chandra Bose out on the first lap of his trip to India[2], and was now returning with two tons of gold on board. Although searched for by many aircraft and a new escort group of four destroyers, and attacked by one of our submarines off the Gironde, she reached harbour safely.

On the 28th Captain Walker's group returned to harbour, having been relieved by the 30th Escort Group. An inter-service conference now took place at Plymouth, and measures were introduced to improve communications, and so enable the senior naval officer afloat and the shore headquarters to be kept continuously and accurately informed of what was happening out in the patrol areas. It was also decided to give the senior officer's ship a special aircraft as his personal link with the Area Combined Headquarters on shore.[3]

While No. 19 Group was thus doing all it could to intensify and improve its patrols over the Bay of Biscay, Nos. 15 and 18 Groups were doing their best to cover the more stormy and much more extensive U-boat transit routes to the north-east of Scotland, and between Iceland and the Shetland Islands. Now that the convoy

---

[1] See Vol. I, pp. 478–479, and Vol. II, p. 367, regarding Captain Walker. At this time his group consisted of the sloops *Starling*, *Woodpecker*, *Wild Goose*, *Wren* and *Kite*.

[2] See Vol. II, p. 406.

[3] See Vol. I, pp. 19 and 36, regarding the establishment and functions of the Area Combined Headquarters.

routes were quiet more attention could be given to these patrols, and they were often combined with sweeps made in support of convoys on passage. It was not long before better results were accomplished. On the 11th of June a Fortress flown by No. 206 Squadron's commander, Wing-Commander R. B. Thomson, working from a station in the Hebrides attacked and sank U.417, but was severely damaged herself. The pilot had to come down only a few miles from where the U-boat's survivors were already in the water. The Fortress's crew took to their dinghy but, as they were in the middle of our own defensive minefield, rescue by surface vessel was impossible. Later in the day they were sighted by a U.S. Navy Catalina, but she herself crashed in attempting rescue, and her crew also took to their dinghy. For the next two days a gale hampered all rescue work; but provisions were dropped, and on the 14th a specially lightened Catalina landed and picked up Thomson and his men. Those from the American Catalina were not so lucky. They were not found until two days later, by which time all but one man had died of exposure.

The Germans were now sailing U-boats in groups on this route as well as in the Bay. The first three boats got out into the Atlantic safely; but on the 24th of June two of them (U.200 and U.194) were sunk by aircraft on convoy duty to the south of Iceland. Dönitz erroneously attributed these losses to our transit patrols, and thereupon cancelled group sailings. In consequence the northern air patrols were for some time searching an empty sea.

The successes achieved by the sea and air patrols in the Bay (four U-boats sunk and six damaged) and on the northern route (one sunk and one damaged) in June were not the whole story for that month. Off the Azores aircraft from the American escort carrier *Bogue* sank another of the reserve tankers (U.118) on the 12th. This success, taken with the loss of her sister U.119, seriously jeopardised the enemy's distant operations.

Air Marshal Slessor now planned to increase the pressure of the air patrols as quickly as possible. He asked the R.A.F. at Gibraltar and the American air forces in Morocco, neither of which were under his control, to co-operate[1]; and he also tried to persuade the Americans to release aircraft from their own side of the Atlantic to strengthen his forces. In the latter instance, however, it proved hard to get what was needed. It was told in our last volume how, in the previous April, the Americans had agreed to provide more 'Very Long Range' aircraft for the Battle of the Atlantic.[2] By early June, in spite of the Combined Chiefs of Staff having received a full statement of the results achieved in the Bay, none of these reinforcements

---

[1] See Vol. II, pp. 359–360, regarding control of these aircraft.
[2] Ibid. p. 364.

had arrived. On the 5th the urgency of the need was stressed to the Cabinet Anti-U-boat Committee by the Secretary of State for Air. Nor did the despatch of one U.S. Navy Catalina and one Ventura squadron to Iceland meet the need; for we only had one Liberator squadron (No. 120) stationed there for convoy work, and it was obviously impossible to transfer it to reinforce the Bay patrols. Meanwhile General Marshall had enquired privately whether several U.S. Army squadrons could be accommodated in England, and on the 15th the American Chiefs of Staff reported that they were prepared to transfer two Army Liberator squadrons to British control until the end of August—an offer which was at once accepted. Air Marshal Slessor now went to America himself, saw Admiral King and reached a large measure of agreement with him. The U.S.N. Catalina squadron already mentioned was to move from Iceland to southern England at once, the arrival of the two U.S. Army squadrons at St Eval in Cornwall was to be hastened, and further reinforcements up to the total of the promised seventy-two aircraft were to follow as soon as possible. But this intention was not fulfilled until September, by which time the climax of the Bay operations had passed; nor was the agreed total ever reached.

To turn now to the distant U-boat operations, in actual sinkings the seven boats in the western Atlantic accomplished little in June, and one of them (U.521) was sunk off Cape Hatteras by an American surface escort. Nor did West African waters prove more fruitful to the enemy, for in an attack on convoy TS.42 (Takoradi–Sierra Leone) only one ship was damaged—a very different result from that obtained against TS.37 a few weeks previously.[1] Off the Cape of Good Hope a few independents were sunk early in the month, and then the seven U-boats working in those waters withdrew to the south-east of Madagascar to refuel from the tanker *Charlotte Schliemann*.[2] On the 9th of June Dönitz detailed nine more boats and two supply submarines for the Indian Ocean. They were to work as far afield as Aden and Ceylon; but the outward movement started badly when U.200, the first one to leave Germany, was sunk by an air escort south of Iceland on the 24th, as already told.[3]

Meanwhile German U-boat strength inside the Mediterranean had been steadily declining. No reinforcements had got through since the preceding April and May, when four boats made the passage successfully.[4] At the end of May two more started out from France to make the attempt, but one of them, U.594, was sunk in the

---

[1] See Vol. II, pp. 371–372.

[2] Ibid. pp. 178–182, 265 and 267 for further details of this supply ship's career.

[3] See p. 22.

[4] See Vol. II, p. 429, where the number of U-boats which passed successfully into the Mediterrenean in May 1943 should read two instead of three.

approaches to Gibraltar by a rocket-firing Hudson on the 4th of June. The other was severely harried by the air patrols, but finally got through safely. No more reinforcements were sent to run the gauntlet in those dangerous waters until late in September.

If, taking the whole Atlantic struggle together, the month of June 1943 was a very poor one for the U-boat Command, the following month was to prove disastrous.

In July thirty U-boats sailed outward-bound, and they were very severely handled. Signs had not been lacking that the enemy was avoiding the direct routes from the Biscay bases out into the Atlantic, and was sending his U-boats to creep along the north coast of Spain to Cape Finisterre. The Commander-in-Chief, Coastal Command, asked for a special effort from the Gibraltar and Morocco aircraft, and early in the month we had for the first time two surface escort groups (B5 Group and Captain Walker's 2nd Escort Group) to work with the Coastal Command patrols. The cruiser *Bermuda* was also there to support the little ships against the German destroyers which were based on Biscay ports. The first success came on the 2nd of July, when the 'milch cow' U.462, which was destined for South African waters, was damaged by air attack shortly after leaving Bordeaux, and forced to return. In the small hours of the next morning a Leigh-Light Wellington of No. 172 Squadron attacked and sank U.126 outright. That same afternoon a Liberator of No. 224 Squadron sank U.628, but was herself severely hit by anti-aircraft fire. On the 5th three enemies were sighted inward-bound, and one of them (U.535) was mortally injured by another Liberator. Two days later U.514, one of the group of seven large boats outward-bound to the Indian Ocean, was sunk off the north of Spain. This success is of particular interest because the Liberator of No. 224 Squadron which achieved it was the first to be fitted with rocket projectors. She employed them, as well as depth charges and a new type of acoustic torpedo[1], to overwhelm the enemy. Between the 7th and 9th of July Air Marshal Slessor's request to the R.A.F. at Gibraltar and the American air forces at Port Lyautey in Morocco to co-operate with No. 19 Group achieved striking results. Three of a group of U-boats stationed off the coast of Portugal (U.951, 232 and 435) were sunk on successive days, and several others were damaged.[2] The U-boat command now told all boats to keep clear of those waters, and began to show serious alarm over the effectiveness of the combined sea and air blockade of its Biscay bases.

Typical of the fierce air fighting now taking place over those waters was an encounter between three Beaufighters of No. 248

---

[1] For security reasons this weapon was then known as the Mark 24 mine.
[2] See Map 1.

Squadron and a specially equipped anti-aircraft U-boat (U.441) on the 12th of July. The enemy 'whose bridge and casing were crammed with men serving the many guns' suffered heavy casualties, and had to return to Brest; but a flight of Ju. 88s came on the scene and shot down a patrolling Sunderland and a Whitley. That same day the U.S. Army Air Force accounted for another Cape-bound enemy (U.506) west of Finisterre. Next, on the 13th, the outward-bound U.607 was destroyed by the joint efforts of a Sunderland and a Halifax. The sloop *Wren*, of Captain Walker's group, picked up the German survivors, but his ships then had to return to Plymouth to fuel. Fighting on the transit route subsided somewhat between the middle and the end of July, but an action fought between the air patrols and U.558 merits special mention. The U-boat Captain had taken great trouble to train his crew in anti-aircraft defence, and during the first part of his homeward passage from a patrol off Portugal he reaped his reward by not only surviving several attacks, but also damaging the attackers. On the 20th of July however, when he was almost through the zone covered by our air patrols, he was attacked by a U.S. Army Liberator and damaged it; but his boat was severely injured by another aircraft from the same squadron. Then an R.A.F. Halifax arrived, joined in the fight and finished off the enemy. Her fight had been a gallant one.

On the 19th of July Bomber Command's No. 10 Operational Training Unit[1] was withdrawn from the fray. The First Sea Lord signalled his appreciation of 'the alertness and gallantry of the crews under training' who 'in all weathers have maintained their patrols in the Bay'. Three days later the Commander-in-Chief, Coastal Command, issued new orders to all his groups designed to speed up initial attacks, to improve wireless communications and navigation, and to ensure that the waters near any enemy were flooded with air reinforcements as quickly as possible. The orders provide a fine example of Air Marshal Slessor's strategy of relentless and increasing pressure on the enemy; and they were backed by his capacity to inspire his aircrews with determination to press home their attacks even in the face of heavy opposition. Perhaps an incident remembered by the Admiralty's representative on the Prime Minister's Anti-U-boat Committee may be quoted to illustrate the strength of Air Marshal Slessor's determination. A scientist asked him one day what would happen when the U-boats' anti-aircraft weapons forced our aircraft up, and reminded him how in 1940 we had made the Luftwaffe abandon low attacks on our convoys by using far less lethal weapons than those now being fitted in the U-boats. Slessor replied 'the one thing we want to see is the U-boat on the surface.

---

[1] See p. 20.

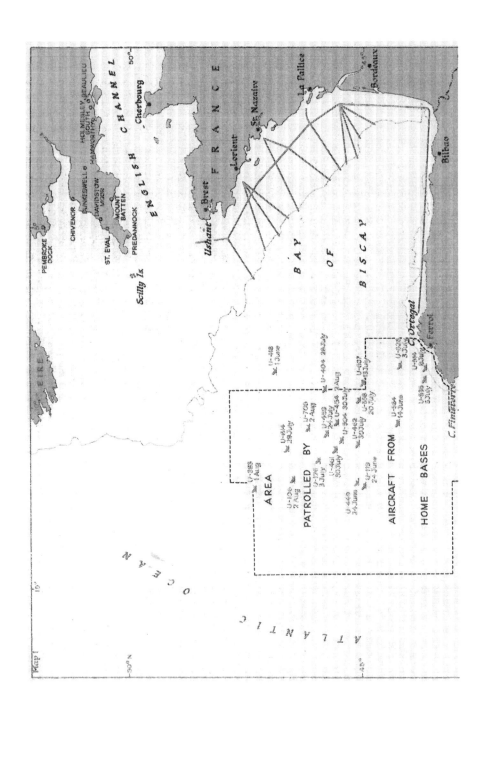

Map 1

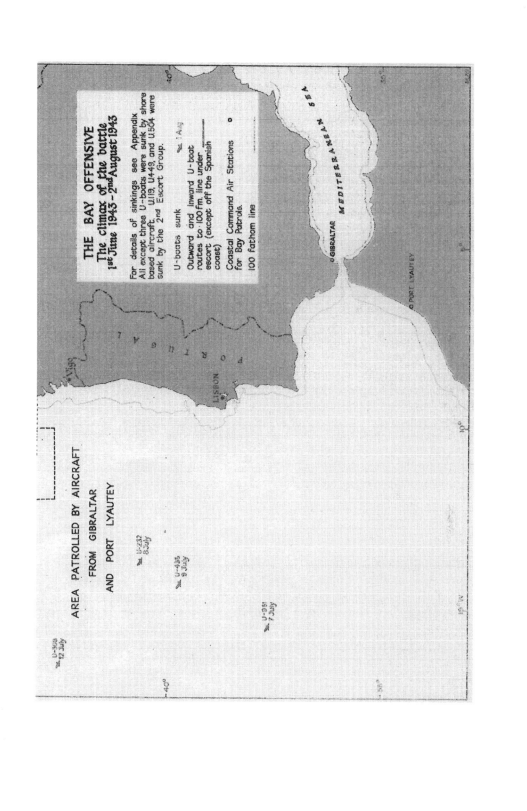

THE BAY OFFENSIVE
The climax of the battle
1st June 1943 - 2nd August 1943

For details of sinkings see Appendix
All except three U-boats were sunk by shore
based aircraft. U119, U449, and U504 were
sunk by the 2nd Escort Group.

U-boats sunk   1 Aug

Outward and inward U-boat
routes to 100 fm. line under
escort (except off the Spanish
coast)

Coastal Command Air Stations   o
for Bay Patrols.

100 fathom line

MEDITERRANEAN SEA

GIBRALTAR

PORTUGAL

LISBON

Vigo

PORT LYAUTEY

AREA PATROLLED BY AIRCRAFT
FROM GIBRALTAR
AND PORT LYAUTEY

U-232
8 July

U-435
9 July

U-951
7 July

U-508
12 July

We shall not be forced up.' It was precisely in that spirit that the Coastal Command aircrews were now sweeping the Bay.

At about the time when the new orders were issued from Coastal Command headquarters, B5 Escort Group, with its Senior Officer (Captain H. T. T. Bayliss) now in the escort carrier *Archer*, reappeared in the Bay, with four destroyers, three corvettes and the cruiser *Glasgow* in support. Another force, consisting of three Canadian destroyers, was on patrol at the same time. On the 24th of July No. 172 Squadron obtained another success. Flying Officer W. H. T. Jennings in his Wellington sighted the 'milch cow' U.459, and at once attacked in face of very heavy fire. His depth charges damaged the enemy, but his aircraft was severely hit and crashed right on top of the U-boat, whose crew thereupon abandoned ship. Only one man survived from the Wellington, but forty-one Germans were picked up by one of the patrolling destroyers. Two more successes fell to the air patrols on the 28th and 29th of July. On the former date U.404 was sunk by the combined efforts of three Liberators— two British and one American; and on the latter date another of No. 172 Squadron's Wellingtons avenged Flying Officer Jennings' death by sinking U.614.

These heavy blows struck by Coastal Command's air patrols followed hard on the heels of a remarkable series of successes achieved by the American escort carrier groups, which were working in support of the large troop and supply convoys then passing between the United States and Gibraltar. It has already been told how the *Bogue* had appeared in the waters off the Azores in June.[1] In the following month two more groups, comprising the escort carriers *Core* and *Santee*, each accompanied by about three destroyers, arrived there at a very opportune moment; for no less than sixteen U-boats, including several 'milch cows', were passing through the area, patrolling, or waiting to replenish with fuel. Acting on excellent intelligence the carrier air crews struck hard and effectively. Between the 13th and 16th the *Core* and *Santee* groups sank four enemies, including the 'milch cow' U.487. On the 23rd the *Bogue's* group scored a double success when her aircraft sank U.527 and one of the destroyers of her escort despatched U.613. On the 30th the *Santee's* aircraft increased the score of the carrier groups to seven U-boats in one month by sinking U.43, which had been on a minelaying mission and was then acting as an additional supply submarine. It will be told later how these successes by the carrier air groups were continued in the following month.[2]

During the last four days of July eleven U-boats, including two

[1] See p. 19.
[2] See pp. 31–32.

'milch cows' (U.461 and 462), which Dönitz was particularly anxious to get safely to sea[1], left western France to cross the Bay of Biscay. The U-tankers were given special escort by a third submarine (U.504), and this group of three was sighted by a Liberator early on the 30th. The position reported was, however, eighty miles in error, and contact might well have been lost but for a chance re-sighting by a Sunderland of No. 228 Squadron, and then by a Catalina attached to the 2nd Escort Group, which had recently returned to the Bay. An American Liberator and a Halifax next joined up, and thus there were four aircraft circling the U-boat group, while Captain Walker's sloops were hastening to the scene at maximum speed. Poor communications, however, prevented the aircraft making co-ordinated attacks, and the first attempt, made by the Halifax, failed. Reinforcements in the shape of another of No. 502 Squadron's Halifaxes and another Sunderland next arrived, and the first damage was done by the former to U.462 with anti-submarine bombs. The Liberator went in next, but was herself so badly mauled that she had to make a forced landing in Portugal. Then Sunderland U. of No. 461 Squadron attacked and sank U.461 with depth charges—a curious coincidence of numbers. Her already damaged colleague (U.462), who was unable to dive, was next attacked once more; but again she inflicted considerable damage on the aircraft with her gunfire. Meanwhile the 2nd Escort Group had signalled its arrival on the scene by opening fire, and the third enemy, U.504, promptly dived. Asdic conditions were poor, but contact was gained at about 1.50 p.m., and deep depth-charge patterns fired about two hours later destroyed that enemy. Meanwhile U.462 had also sunk. According to the recollections of her captain his damaged boat, as well as U.504, was fired on by Walker's ships, and he thereupon scuttled her. Whether the air attacks on U.462, as well as on U.461, were lethal thus remains uncertain; but the surface ships unquestionably picked up survivors from them both. This destruction of a complete group had been a splendid example of a combined sea and air operation; but fortune had favoured our side, and this undoubtedly offset the consequences of inaccurate air navigation and poor communications. Once again was the need for the most careful training in these specialised tasks emphasised by Coastal Command Headquarters.

After this battle eight of the original eleven U-boats which had sailed during the last four days of July were still in the Bay, and on the 1st of August six more left Lorient and St Nazaire. The offensive against them continued unremittingly. On the afternoon of the 1st of August the Catalina attached to Captain Walker's group made

---

[1] U.462 had been damaged on 2nd of July and forced to return. See p. 24.

a sighting, and called the surface ships to the scene. Two hours later a Sunderland of No. 10 Squadron (R.A.A.F.) sighted U.454 six miles ahead of the 2nd Escort Group. She at once attacked and sank her, though not without receiving such severe damage herself that she crashed into the sea, killing both pilots. The *Wren* rescued six of the Sunderland's crew and fourteen Germans, and then continued the search for other U-boats. Meanwhile further north another Sunderland (of No. 228 Squadron) sighted and mortally wounded U.383. She sank the next night, while the damaged aircraft just managed to struggle home. Next morning a U.S. Army Liberator accounted for another enemy, U.706. The morning of the 2nd of August found many Allied aircraft and two escort groups searching the western part of the patrol area for enemies; several U-boats were seeking their damaged colleagues, and the Germans had sent out three torpedo-boat destroyers to help them. There were many indecisive attacks and gun duels between aircraft and U-boats; but late in the evening U.106, which had been very persistently hunted, was finished off by two Sunderlands. The enemy T.B.Ds having been reported as large destroyers the Commander-in-Chief, Plymouth, now sent out reinforcements to the escort groups; but inaccurate sighting reports prevented a junction being made, and the German ships thus rescued U.106's survivors and reached harbour safely. Four U-boats had, however, been sunk in two days. This, coming so soon after the heavy losses of the preceding month, caused Dönitz to recall the last six boats to leave, and to cancel all group sailings. His inward-bound boats were ordered to make Cape Finisterre, and then use Spanish territorial waters to reach home.

During the whole of July the northern transit route was, in fact, almost clear of U-boats. Although the air patrols had been stepped up, and in the middle of the month Home Fleet destroyers were sent to work with No. 18 Group, no successes were achieved in the area. The Germans did, however, try to get one large 'U-cruiser' out by the Denmark Strait; but she hit an iceberg and had to return.

On the last day of July Dönitz gave Hitler a summary of the new measures and equipment by means of which he hoped to mitigate his difficulties. These included the new Walter boat, the Schnorkel, a better radar warning receiver, the acoustic torpedo and the pressure-operated mine; but for the time being he admitted that he had been forced on the defensive. 'The enemy' he concluded 'is directing his main efforts against the exit lanes of our submarines— the Shetland Strait and the Bay of Biscay. Consequently our losses in those waters are still very high.' He reported how our surface groups had been co-operating with the air patrols; 'and' he concluded 'against this combination we have as yet no defence'. Sailings had been stopped pending the fitting of more anti-aircraft weapons;

and until the acoustic torpedo was available, the U-boats would only be used for minelaying. For that purpose the co-operation of the German air force was essential; but Hitler was very nervous that the Luftwaffe would reveal the secret of the new pressure-operated mines by dropping them on land. 'If the British should lay these mines in the Baltic' he warned 'we are finished'—perhaps the first admission by Hitler that the defeat of Germany was possible.

The period between the 1st of July and the 2nd August marks the climax of the air operations by the Bay of Biscay patrols, and was the period of their greatest success. We now know that eighty-six U-boats crossed the Bay during those weeks. Fifty-five of them were sighted, sixteen were sunk by aircraft and one by a surface ship, while six others were forced to turn back. In addition, the air patrols off Cape Finisterre and the coast of Portugal sank three more enemies, and damaged a fourth.[1] Losses to our anti-submarine aircraft were, however, heavy. Fourteen did not return.

It had been the quiet prevailing on the convoy routes which had enabled us to transfer sea and air forces to the Bay; and the rapid switch effected provides an excellent example of flexibility in maritime strategy. But it must be emphasised that the safety of the convoys was the all-important requirement, and it would never have been sound to divert strength to patrolling had the U-boats been offering themselves as targets to our convoy escorts. The latter had repeatedly shown their ability to inflict heavy losses by determined counter-attacks, and had forcibly demonstrated it once again as recently as May 1943.[2] Taking the war as a whole they inflicted far heavier losses than patrols—or indeed than all the other measures taken against U-boats combined. We will return to this matter when the comparative results of convoy and patrolling are analysed for the whole war; but to point it out here detracts nothing from the credit due to the aircrews, mainly from Coastal Command of the Royal Air Force, who achieved such high success during the period recently described.

To return once more to the Bay of Biscay, by keeping close to the Spanish coast the U-boats had found a reasonably safe, if longer, route across the disputed waters. After the first five had got through safely in August, the enemy ordered all those bound to and from southerly latitudes to pass that way; and they introduced a mid-Bay route for single boats destined for more northerly waters. On that route the U-boats were now ordered to dive by day and charge their batteries only at night. Co-operation by the Luftwaffe was also much improved. German fighters were more frequently engaging

[1] See Map 1.
[2] See Vol. II, pp. 375–377.

our anti-submarine aircraft, and Coastal and Fighter Commands' long-range aircraft were constantly needed to keep them in check. The new long-range He.177 bombers appeared in August and replaced the older Ju.88s. Combats increased, and our losses rose to seventeen anti-submarine aircraft and six fighters in that month. Meanwhile sightings of U-boats on transit virtually ceased, even after night patrols by Leigh-Light aircraft had been intensified. Towards the end of August we realised that the U-boats were probably using Spanish waters, the westerly air patrols were cancelled and new ones were ordered to be flown between Cape Ortegal and Vigo, by night as well as by day[1]; while the Commander-in-Chief, Plymouth, sent two escort groups and a supporting cruiser to the same waters. On the 24th of August the first success since the beginning of the month was achieved by a Leigh-Light Wellington from Gibraltar, which sank U.134. Then the enemy struck at our surface patrols. The 1st Support Group (Senior Officer's ship *Egret*) relieved the 40th Escort Group on the 25th, and two days later the destroyers *Grenville* and *Athabaskan* (R.C.N.) joined. A sweep was started to the south of Finisterre, but shortly after noon on the 27th eighteen enemy aircraft attacked, using a new type of glider bomb.[2] One or two of these weapons, which had a wing span of eleven feet, could be carried under the wings of a heavy bomber such as the Do.217 or He.177. They had small jet engines which started after release, and the parent aircraft then guided them by radio control towards the target. Their speed was 300–400 knots and the explosive heads weighed 1,100 lbs. To lightly protected ships they were unpleasant weapons; but the escorts soon developed a technique for dealing with them by concentrated close-range A-A gunfire. On this occasion the *Egret* and *Athabaskan* were however both hit, and the former blew up. It was a set-back, but not a sufficient one to reverse the trend of the Atlantic battle.

After the first few days the month of August thus produced few successes to our sea and air patrols, and considerable losses were suffered by the latter. Dönitz had at least regained a large measure of safety on the Biscay transit routes, and never again did our patrols accomplish such good results as they had achieved in July.

On the northern route two events of importance took place in August. U.647 was sunk, probably by a mine on about the 3rd. She is the only U-boat believed to have been destroyed in the Iceland–Faeroes mine barrier, which now appears to have been a singularly unproductive and wholly defensive enterprise.[3] On the

---

[1] See Map 1.

[2] These were known as Hs.293 bombs.

[3] See Vol. I, pp. 264, 334 and 390, regarding the laying of this minefield.

4th yet another 'milch cow' U.489, which had only just entered service, was sunk by a Sunderland of No. 423 R.C.A.F. Squadron west of the Faeroes; but the flying boat was herself badly damaged and had to come down in the sea. A destroyer picked up five of her crew and the whole of the U-boat's company. This loss, coming on top of the recent destruction of three supply U-boats in the Bay[1], and of another to the west of the Azores[2], destroyed Dönitz's hopes of building up a formidable offensive in distant waters. The Germans only built ten submarines of this class (Type XIV), and seven of them had now gone.

Although July was such a catastrophic period for Dönitz, the first wave of U-boats sent to the distant waters arrived during the month; and for a time they achieved considerable successes against ships sailing independently off Brazil, in the West Indies, and off the west and south-east coasts of Africa. Between the 1st and 9th we lost twenty-one ships in those waters, and no retribution was exacted from the U-boats. Then the shore-based aircraft started to hit back hard, especially off Brazil, shipping losses decreased sharply during the remainder of the month, and ten U-boats were destroyed. Off West Africa, in spite of a heavy concentration of U-boats between Freetown and Lagos, we lost only one ship during the second half of July; and on the 15th the surface escorts of convoy OS.51 sank U.135 in the Canary Islands Channel after a spirited action which included depth charging the enemy at about 800 feet, engaging with gunfire when she surfaced, and finally ramming by the corvette *Mignonette*. Only in the southern Indian Ocean did appreciable shipping losses continue.[3]

Early in August the impossibility of replenishing his distant boats caused Dönitz to recall them from the western Atlantic. Then came the sinking of the tanker U.489 on the 4th, already mentioned. Next the U.S.S. *Card's* aircraft sank a reserve tanker (U.117) off the Azores on the 7th, and damaged U.66 which was caught in the act of refuelling from her. The Germans now realised that only by using outward-bound operational boats to replenish those running low of fuel could they get the latter back at all. The redoubtable aircrews of the *Card* drove home the enemy's precarious position still more forcibly by destroying U.664 on the 9th, and the emergency supply boat U.525 two days later. There were now a number of U-boats almost empty of fuel seeking non-existent supplies to the west of the Azores. A boat detailed for the Indian Ocean had to go to their rescue.

---

[1] U.459 (24th July), U.461 and U.462 (30th July). See pp. 26–27.

[2] U.487 (13th July). See p. 26.

[3] See pp. 219–221 regarding U-boat operations in the Indian Ocean between June and August 1943.

Shipping losses in the Atlantic were insignificant in August. Off the whole coast-line of North and South America only two ships were sunk, while an equal number of U-boats were destroyed by American forces. In West African waters we lost only one ship; U.403 was sunk off Dakar by British and French aircraft, and U.468 by a Liberator of No. 200 Squadron. Her captain, Pilot Officer L. A. Trigg, attacked in the face of intense fire, was mortally wounded and crashed in flames. The evidence of his gallantry was provided by survivors from the U-boat, who were picked up by a corvette, and Trigg was awarded a posthumous Victoria Cross. This must be one of the very rare occasions in history when a high award for gallantry has been made solely on evidence provided by the enemy. Finally the American escort carriers located the last remaining Atlantic U-boats, and completed their rout. On the 24th the *Core's* aircraft sank U.185 and U.84, and three days later U.847 fell to those of the *Card*. Next day the surface escorts of convoy OG.92 (the *Wanderer* and *Wallflower*) sank U.523, and on the 30th the *Stork* and *Stonecrop* did the same to U.634 while escorting SL.135.

During the three months June–August 1943 in all waters excluding the Mediterranean German U-boats sank no more than fifty-eight Allied merchantmen (totalling 327,081 tons); and nearly half those sinkings took place off South Africa and in the Indian Ocean. It cost the enemy seventy-four U-boats to achieve those very moderate results; and the great majority of those losses occurred, as Table 2 (p. 33) shows, in the Bay of Biscay, the North Atlantic and in waters remote from Europe. A remarkable feature is that no less than fifty-eight of the sunk U-boats (plus one shared with surface vessels) met their end at the hands of carrier-borne or shore-based aircraft. Though this owed something to the fact that few convoy battles took place during the period, the figures leave no room for doubt regarding which men and weapons gained this second major victory over the U-boats. Furthermore, except in the Indian Ocean the campaign in remote waters had been decisively defeated.

When he came to sum up his recent experiences at the end of August Dönitz found little to console him for the heavy losses suffered and the poor results accomplished. He attributed the successes of our aircraft mainly to the radiations emitted by the search receivers fitted in the U-boats, and hoped for better results when a new model became available. But in fact the conclusions at which he had arrived were quite wrong; for he had been misled by the scepticism of his own scientists regarding the possibility that we might be using centimetric radar, mentioned earlier, and by false information given by the pilot of a Coastal Command aircraft which had crashed. That officer told his interrogators that our aircraft were able to 'home' themselves on to U-boats by means of the emissions from the German

A Type XIV 'milch cow' (probably U.464, 1,690 tons) returning to Bordeaux, 1943.

U.441 (A Type VII C, 770-ton Atlantic boat) fitted with special A.A. armament, armoured conning tower, and radar search receiver for work in the Bay of Biscay.

One of U.441's quadruple 2-cm. A.A. guns.

(Photos. Franz Selinger)

'The sinking of a U-boat', by Norman Wilkinson.

Table 2. *Allied Merchant Ship and German U-boat Losses*
June–August 1943

Month	Allied Merchant Ships Sunk	German U-boats Sunk				
		In Bay of Biscay Offensive and Associated Operations	On Northern Transit Route	On North Atlantic Convoy Routes	In Remote Waters (see Note 2)	In Other Theatres
June . .	10	4	2	8	2	—
July . .	38	16	—	8	9	1 (Norway)
August .	10	5	2	8	6	2 (Baltic) 1 (Arctic)
TOTALS .	58	25	4	24	17	4

NOTES: (1) Allied merchant ship losses include one ship sunk by mines laid by a U-boat.
(2) Remote waters include the Caribbean, off the east coast of North America, off Brazil, off West Africa, and the South Atlantic and Indian Oceans.

search receivers; and, after ascertaining that this was in fact technically possible, the Germans accepted the pilot's assurances as gospel. In reality many factors had contributed to the achievements of the Allied anti-submarine forces, but detection of U-boats in the manner suggested was not one of them. The enemy's error led, moreover, to much effort being wasted on trying to reduce the radiation from the original ($1\frac{1}{2}$-metre) search receivers, instead of seeking the wave-length on which the new Allied radar sets actually worked. Not till the beginning of 1944 did it dawn on the Germans that our sets were working on the ten centimetre wave band. The weakness of the German Navy's technical intelligence service, exemplified by this incident, certainly played a part in bringing about the defeat of the U-boats. Not until the end of 1943 was a first-rate scientist put in charge of such work, and by the time that he had drawn the correct conclusions regarding Allied radar developments it was too late to reverse the trend of the Atlantic battle.

Only in the Indian Ocean had the U-boats achieved any significant measure of success[1], and the heavy casualties we had inflicted on the supply submarines had finally curtailed operations in that theatre, as in other remote waters. Nor was it likely that Dönitz could renew the campaign; for he had only two more 'milch cows' in western France ready for service. Finally, in the minelaying operations undertaken as substitute for the torpedo attacks on convoys,

[1] See pp. 219–221.

which had been proved prohibitively dangerous, the enemy accomplished very little and once more suffered losses. The four minefields actually laid off Dakar, Halifax, Norfolk (Virginia) and Charleston (South Carolina) only caused the loss of one ship. As to the future, Dönitz reported to his master that he intended to renew convoy attacks late in September, by which time an efficient acoustic torpedo, a new radar decoy and the improved search receiver would all be available.

The brief account in this chapter of the distinguished achievements of the American escort carriers in the central Atlantic in the summer of 1943 provides an opportunity to review a matter which, at the time, generated rather strong feelings in both the British Admiralty and the American Navy Department, and regarding which the conclusions of the historians of the two countries may well differ. The Board of Inquiry into the loss of the Lend-Lease escort carrier *Dasher* by a petrol explosion in March 1943[1] had concluded that safety arrangements were 'by our [i.e. British] standards practically non-existent'. This and the fact that, according to expert British opinion and experience, ships of her class needed between 1,200 and 2,000 tons of extra ballast to make them stable, determined the Admiralty to modify the later ships before they entered service.[2] The Admiralty also desired to make all the escort carriers transferred to Britain under Lend-Lease 'capable of full fighter operation, and not merely fit for anti-submarine work'. The reasons were that we intended to employ them on the Arctic route, where the operation of fighters was often as important to the convoys as anti-submarine protection[3], and also to provide fighter cover in combined operations carried out beyond the range of shore-based aircraft.[4] For the latter purpose fighter-direction radar sets and a good deal of special equipment were absolute necessities. Other modifications, such as extending the flight deck and rendering the ships more suitable for work in the Arctic, in which waters the American escort carriers were never called on to operate, were carried out only if they could be done in the time needed to modify the petrol systems and fit fighter-direction arrangements; but the essential work entailed placing the ships in dockyard hands for about seven weeks. After the alterations had been

---

[1] See Vol. II, p. 367.

[2] The U.S. Navy accepted the admission of salt water into empty fuel tanks to achieve stability.

[3] See, for example, Vol. II, pp. 280–285, regarding the work of the *Avenger* with PQ.18. For the work of the later escort carriers in the same waters see this volume, pp. 270–273 and 280–281.

[4] See pp. 173–174 regarding the use of escort carriers in the Salerno landings of September 1943.

completed a further five or six weeks were needed to 'work up' the ships, which might therefore play no part in the war for three months after their arrival in Britain. Towards the end of August the mission in Washington warned the Admiralty that there was 'strong and increasing criticism' by certain American naval officers over the lapse of time between the escort carriers being handed over to us and their entry into service. The Americans assessed that delay at six to eight months; but in fact about half of the interval was attributable to causes for which the Admiralty was by no means solely responsible. All the escort carriers were building on the American Pacific coast, and British crews were sent out to take the ships over at Seattle or San Francisco. Trials had to be carried out before they set off on the long journey through the Panama Canal to Norfolk, Virginia; and five or six weeks thus elapsed between taking the ships over and their arrival on the American east coast. Then they had to embark as many aircraft as possible, sometimes for the American forces in North Africa (in which case they were routed via Casablanca), but more commonly to meet British requirements. For the Atlantic crossing the ships were thus not in operational condition, and they generally had to proceed to New York to join a suitable convoy. It thus happened that almost three weeks elapsed between reaching Norfolk and arriving in Britain. It would have been hard to reduce the two to three months which had so far elapsed since commissioning; but the Americans added that interval to the period subsequently spent in British dockyards and in working up, and it was the aggregate delay of some six months which produced the criticisms already mentioned.

Nevertheless on the 27th of August the Allied Anti-Submarine Survey Board[1] reported to Admiral King that 'at the present stage of the war these delays are not considered acceptable', and proposed that, if they could not be reduced, the U.S. Navy should consider taking over the next seven ships allocated to Britain. Admiral King, however, very reasonably suggested that it was preferable to cut the delays rather than accept the confusion which would be caused by altering the allocations. In the Admiralty it seems to have been realised that, even if it was true that 'the United States Navy has no conception of the congestion and restriction on building and repair facilities in the United Kingdom at this time', and even though our Allies were not universally familiar with the exceptional difficulties involved in working carrier aircraft on the Arctic convoy route, it behoved the British authorities to do all that they could to eliminate the grounds for American complaints by getting the ships into service quicker. For the next six months they worked with that object, and

---

[1] See Vol. II, p. 360, regarding the composition of this body.

the small storm which blew up in August 1943 gradually subsided until the splendid work done by British escort carriers in the following year dissipated it for good. As is so often the case in a disagreement between Allies, it now seems that there was a certain amount of truth in the arguments used by both sides. If the Americans were more prepared to accept what we regarded as undue hazards, it was certainly unfair to compare the conditions which normally prevailed in the central Atlantic with those generally encountered in the far north, where British escort carriers were often required to work.[1]

---

[1] S. E. Morison, *The History of United States Naval Operations* (Little Brown, Boston, hereafter referred to as 'Morison'), Vol. X, p. 39 fn. (13) and p. 307, gives the American side of this story.

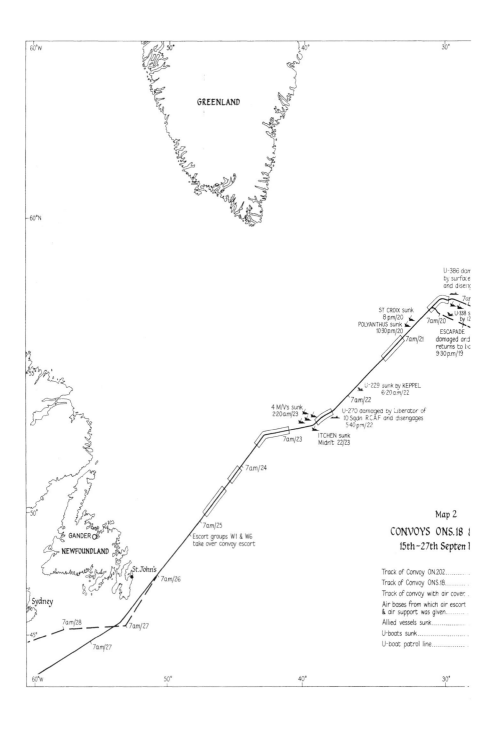

GREENLAND

60°N

55°m

U-386 dam
by surface
and diseng

7a

ST CROIX sunk
8 p.m/20   U-338 s
POLYANTHUS sunk   7a.m/20   by 12
10:30 p.m/20   ESCAPADE
                    7a.m/21   damaged and
                               returns to b
                               9:30 p.m/19

U-229 sunk by KEPPEL
6:20 a.m/22

4 M/V's sunk   7a.m/22
2:20 a.m/23   U-270 damaged by Liberator of
                   10 Sqdn. R.C.A.F. and disengages
              7a.m/23   5:40 a.m/22
                   ITCHEN sunk
                   Midn't 22/23

7a.m/24

50°

GANDER   7a.m/25
                Escort groups W1 & W6
NEWFOUNDLAND   take over convoy escort

St.John's
                               7a.m/26
Sydney

7a.m/28   7a.m/27
45°

7a.m/27

60°W   50°   40°   30°

Map 2

CONVOYS ONS.18 {
15th~27th Septen l

Track of Convoy ON.202............
Track of Convoy ONS.18............
Track of convoy with air cover: .
Air bases from which air escort
& air support was given.............
Allied vessels sunk.................
U-boats sunk.......................
U-boat patrol line.................

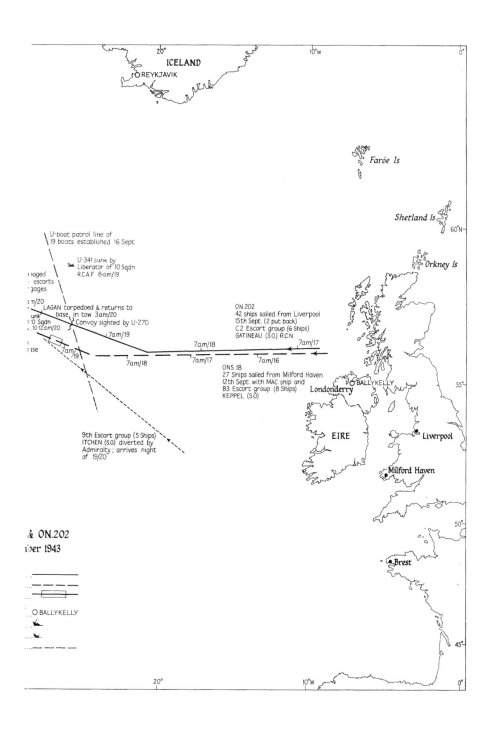

ICELAND

○REYKJAVIK

Faröe Is

Shetland Is

60°N

Orkney Is

U-boat patrol line of
19 boats established 16 Sept

U-341 sunk by
Liberator of 10 Sqdn
R.C.A.F. 8 a.m/19

naged
escorts
gages

n/20
unk
:0 Sqdn   LAGAN torpedoed & returns to
.10·12 a.m/20   base, in tow 3 a.m/20
                  Convoy sighted by U-270

ise   7 a.m/19

7am/
19   7am/18

7am/18

ON.202
42 ships sailed from Liverpool
15th Sept. (2 put back)
C.2. Escort group (6 Ships)
GATINEAU (S.O.) R.C.N

7a.m/18   7a.m/17   7a.m/16   7a.m/17

ONS.18
27 Ships sailed from Milford Haven
12th Sept. with MAC ship and
B3. Escort group (8 Ships)
KEPPEL (S.O.)

○O BALLYKELLY

Londonderry

55°

9th Escort group (5 Ships)
ITCHEN (S.O.) diverted by
Admiralty ; arrives night
of 19/20

EIRE

Liverpool

Milford Haven

50°

& ON.202
ber 1943

O BALLYKELLY

Brest

45°

20°   10°W   0°

CHAPTER III

THE BATTLE OF THE ATLANTIC

1st September–31st December, 1943

The Final Defeat of the 'Wolf Packs'

> 'We, an island Power, . . . dependent on the
> sea, can read the lesson and understand our
> own fate had we failed to master the
> U-boats.'
> W. S. Churchill, *The Second World
> War*, Vol. VI, p. 559.

EARLY in September the Naval Staff noted that 'this week, for the first time in the war, the U-boats have not sunk a merchant ship'; but they hastened to dispel the false optimism which this fact aroused in political circles by pointing out that we had sunk very few U-boats in the same period, and that all the signs pointed to a renewal of attacks on our Atlantic convoys. In fact nine U-boats and a supply submarine fitted with the improved radar search receiver[1], acoustic homing torpedoes and strengthened anti-aircraft armaments had sailed for the Atlantic late in August. They were followed early in September by thirteen more from Biscay ports, and six from Norway or Germany. All except U.669, which was sunk in the Bay by a Leigh-Light Wellington on the night of the 6th–7th of September, got out safely. Because the U-boats were again travelling submerged as much as possible, our patrolling aircraft now achieved only occasional successes. Moreover the surface forces which had been co-operating with Coastal Command had been withdrawn from the Bay to prepare for the expected renewal of the battle on the convoy routes. It was becoming plain that neither air nor surface ship patrols could alone stop the passage of U-boats through those waters. A combination of the two was needed; but now that the Germans had adopted the tactics of maximum submergence, were only surfacing to charge their batteries by night, and were hugging the Spanish coast as much as possible, the methods employed during the preceding months were no longer likely to achieve substantial successes. During the whole of September our Biscay air patrols only

---

[1] See p. 32.

sank two U-boats, while one other (U.760) was so damaged that she was forced to seek internment in Vigo; and we lost thirteen anti-submarine aircraft to various causes.

The Atlantic U-boats fuelled in mid-ocean from U.460, and by the 16th of September twenty of them had formed a patrol line designed to catch our slow outward-bound (ONS) convoys. Dönitz's orders now were to make the escorts the primary targets. But for all the enemy's endeavours to maintain strict secrecy regarding his new concentration, it had been detected in the ever-watchful Submarine Tracking Room; and on the same day that the U-boats formed their new patrol line the Admiralty diverted the 9th Escort Group, which had been destined for the Bay of Biscay, to reinforce convoy ONS.18.[1] That convoy, consisting of twenty-seven ships, including a Merchant Aircraft Carrier[2], sailed from Milford Haven on the 12th. The escort of eight ships was under Commander M. J. Evans in the destroyer *Keppel*. Three days later a faster convoy, ON.202, originally of forty-two ships, left Liverpool in charge of six escort vessels under Commander P. W. Burnett in the Canadian destroyer *Gatineau*.[3]

At noon on the 18th of September the slow convoy was in 56° North 23° West, with the faster one about 120 miles astern of it. The weather had so far frustrated air escort. That afternoon there were indications of U-boats ahead of ONS.18, and the Admiralty diverted it to the north-west. Liberators from Britain and Iceland reached the convoy soon after dawn next day, and one of them, belonging to No. 10 R.C.A.F. Squadron, actually drew first blood by sinking U.341 about 160 miles from the convoy early on the 19th. The following night what Commander Evans called 'a very mild attack' on ONS.18 by two U-boats took place, but the escorts were prevented from pressing home the counter-attack by a serious accident to the destroyer *Escapade's* 'Hedgehog'.[4] A premature explosion caused many casualties, and she had to be sent back. Meanwhile the 9th Escort Group, whose diversion to reinforce ONS.18 has been mentioned, was coming up from astern.[5]

By the morning of the 20th the faster convoy was only some thirty miles to the north-east of ONS.18, and at 2 a.m. its position was reported by a U-boat. The enemy at once unleashed his forces, and attacks started an hour later. Two merchantmen were sunk, and the frigate *Lagan* was so badly damaged by an acoustic torpedo that she had to be towed home. All that day the well-tried Liberators of

---

[1] See Map 2. Volume II, Appendix F, gives the meaning of the code letters identifying all Allied convoys.

[2] See Vol. II, p. 201, regarding M.A.C. ships.

[3] Although serving in an R.C.N. ship Commander Burnett was a Royal Navy Officer.

[4] See Vol. I, p. 480, regarding this weapon.

[5] See Map 2.

No. 120 Squadron from Iceland were with the convoys, and at 10.12 one of them sank U.338 with one of the new acoustic aerial torpedoes[1]—weapons which worked on similar principles to those which the Germans were now using for the first time. By noon the two convoys were so close together that the Commander-in-Chief, Western Approaches, ordered them to join together. Commander Evans took charge of the combined escort, which was soon strengthened by the arrival of the 9th Escort Group. But eight more U-boats had also reached the scene, and many encounters took place with them. During the afternoon the Liberators damaged one enemy and the surface escorts another.

Unfortunately the signal from Liverpool ordering ON.202 to join the slower convoy was received in very mutilated form, and the course to steer was omitted. The result was that, in Evans's words, 'the two convoys gyrated majestically about the ocean, never appearing to get much closer, and watched appreciatively by a growing swarm of U-boats'. During these manœuvres the *Keppel* sighted 'a yard and a half of periscope' a few yards off her starboard beam and attacked, though unsuccessfully; but by 8.20 p.m. the convoys had settled on a south-westerly course under the wing of twelve escorts. That night there were three attacks on the combined convoy, and all were frustrated. Astern of it, however, a fierce action developed. The Canadian destroyer *St. Croix* was torpedoed at about 8 p.m., and was sunk an hour later by another torpedo. The corvette *Polyanthus* was also sunk. Both fell victim to acoustic torpedoes, and survivors from both ships were picked up by the frigate *Itchen*. It was during these encounters that the destroyer *Icarus* rammed the Canadian corvette *Drumheller*, but so slightly that no damage was done. The Canadian at once came up on his signal lamp with the mildly protesting enquiry 'Having no submarines?'

Early on the 21st fog descended on the convoys, and when it temporarily lifted that afternoon ONS.18 was almost in station on the starboard beam of ON.202. Evans described this as 'a masterly manœuvre', but on enquiry he found out that it had happened accidentally—perhaps (he suggested) 'organised by a Higher Authority'. While in clear weather, the M.A.C. ship's Swordfish was flown off. Then the fog closed down again and the pilot landed safely on to the flight deck 'in absolutely dense fog'—which was considered little short of miraculous.

During the following night, that of the 21st–22nd, enemy intelligence was pouring in, but with fourteen escorts forming an extended as well as a close screen, the Senior Officer felt confident of his ability to deal with attacks. From 9 p.m. until 5 a.m. U-boat contacts were

---

[1] See p. 24 and fn. 1.

almost continuous. At least seven were in touch, but no attack got home on the merchantmen, and the *Keppel* herself successfully followed up a wireless bearing to ram and sink U.229 astern of the convoy. From dawn on the 22nd until the afternoon the fog was again very dense, and when it lifted 'the air was filled with Liberators'—actually R.C.A.F. aircraft from Newfoundland. Two attacks were made by them, but neither was decisive. At 6 p.m. a U-boat report caused Evans to form ONS.18 astern of ON.202, with the object of avoiding the enemy; but he later considered this action to have been mistaken, because it gave the combined convoys a depth of six or seven miles, and made them harder to protect. The night produced many attacks and counter-attacks, and the *Itchen* was hit by an acoustic torpedo. By a tragic chance she had on board all the survivors of the *St. Croix* and *Polyanthus*; and only three men from the three ships' companies were rescued. At 2.40 a.m. on the 23rd the U-boats at last managed to penetrate the screen, and sank three merchantmen. Four hours later another was torpedoed. She was abandoned prematurely, and was ultimately sunk. Daylight brought yet stronger air escorts, and the convoys changed back to their previous formation on a broad front. The escorts were re-fuelled, and by night-fall the convoys were well defended by inner and outer screens. The enemy had, however, by then abandoned the operation. The total results accomplished by nineteen U-boats in five days of battle amounted to six merchantmen (36,422 tons) and three escorts sunk, while one other escort was damaged. On our part three U-boats were sunk, and a like number damaged. The Germans claimed far greater successes against both the convoys and the escorts, and Dönitz considered the result 'very satisfactory'. Once again he had been misled by the exaggerated claims of the U-boat commanders.

The first use by the Germans of acoustic homing torpedoes thus was against ONS.18 and ON.202 in September 1943. To the Admiralty, however, this development was no surprise; for they had in fact expected it for some time. As we ourselves had by that time produced similar weapons it was natural that attention should also have been given to developing the necessary counter-measures. The latter were thus ready, though in a somewhat rudimentary form, at the moment when they were first needed. In essentials the antidote consisted of noise-making machines towed astern of the ship. This 'Foxer', as it was called, attracted the acoustic torpedo to itself instead of to the ships' propellers, and detonated it at a safe distance from the ship. It had the disadvantage that, in the case of the first models, it could not be towed at speeds in excess of fifteen knots, and the ships thus remained vulnerable to the torpedoes if, as was the usual practice, they followed up a wireless report or radar contact at high speed. Moreover when the 'Foxer' was working it vitiated the performance of a ship's own asdic. For these reasons the gear was not popular with escort commanders; but by February 1944 a better model, which could be towed at twenty knots, had been introduced, and the Admiralty was able to tell the fleet that 'escort vessels with Foxer operating should be immune from Gnats [acoustic torpedoes]'. Simultaneously with the development of these counter-measures, tactical instructions were issued with the object of minimising the risk to which escort vessels now had to expose themselves. Nor was it long before our intelligence services provided accurate knowledge of the performance of the new enemy weapon, thus enabling the antidote to be simplified and made more efficient. Finally the recovery of acoustic torpedoes from a sunken U-boat in June 1944 revealed their secrets with certainty. In sum, therefore, it can confidently be asserted that the weapon by which Dönitz had set such store did not fulfil his expectations. It caused us the loss of several valuable escort vessels, and of many of their experienced, hard-driven crews; but it never seriously impeded the steady passage of our convoys, nor came near to reversing the trend of the Atlantic battle. The initiative remained firmly in the hands of the Allied escorts.

The U-boat Command now re-formed the boats to await the next west-bound convoys (ON.204 and ONS.19); but their patrol line was located by aircraft, and the convoys were safely diverted to the north of it. Meanwhile an east-bound convoy (HX.258) was also passing through the danger area, and was given strong air escort until the 2nd of October, when the aircraft were switched to the position in which the patrol line of U-boats had been sighted earlier. The Iceland-based air squadrons seized the opportunity with vigour, and deployed their full strength. On the 4th they sank U.279 and U.336, and next day U.389 fell victim to a rocket-firing Hudson of No. 269 Squadron. Moreover the enemy accomplished absolutely no return for his heavy losses.

Convoy SC.143, of thirty-nine merchantmen and a M.A.C. ship, sailed from Halifax on the 28th of September, with an escort of nine ships and a support group of four more in the offing. The enemy sent eighteen U-boats against it. Early on the 8th of October the Polish destroyer *Orkan* was sunk, probably by an acoustic torpedo. Air escorts had joined early that day, and the Liberators searched astern of the convoy, where targets had already been found. They were rewarded with the destruction of two enemies (U.419 and U.643). That afternoon a German long-range flying boat appeared over the convoy with the object of 'homing' the U-boats towards their quarry, but with no success. Finally in the evening a Sunderland of No. 423 Squadron made a quick attack on an enemy sighted some thirty-five miles from the convoy, and sank U.610. That night for the first time in history a Leigh-Light aircraft stayed with the convoy after dark.[1] It was one more favourable development in air co-operation in the Atlantic battle; but no relief aircraft was available, and after the solitary night air escort had returned to base one merchantman was sunk. Apart from sinking the *Orkan* that was the only return obtained by the enemy for the loss of three U-boats. On the 9th the U-boat Command cancelled the operation.

The successes scored by the air escorts during the passage of convoy SC.143 provide an opportunity to review the development of anti-submarine tactics by Coastal Command. On the 12th June, 1943, Air Marshal Slessor issued revised instructions, and by the following autumn they were in general use by all aircraft employed on escort or patrol duties, by night as well as by day. In clear weather they would normally fly at 5,000 feet; but advantage was to be taken of low cloud to gain concealment, and so improve the chances of surprising the enemy. As soon as a U-boat was sighted, or a radar contact gained, the aircraft would lose height quickly and go in to the attack, aiming to place its 'stick' of 250-pound depth charges, which were set to explode at a depth of twenty-five feet, so as to straddle the conning tower.[2] If the enemy dived at once the attack had to be completed within thirty seconds of total submergence, or the shallow-set charges would probably be ineffective. Thus the first important need was to attack quickly. Secondly came accuracy. Although a low-level bomb sight was coming into service, it was still the common practice to aim the depth charges by eye. To achieve the desired standard of accuracy Air Marshal Slessor laid down that Liberators were to attack at heights between fifty and a hundred feet, and all other types at fifty feet. If the aircraft was armed with the new acoustic homing torpedo[3], however, she would wait until the enemy had dived before releasing them. After October 1943 some U-boats, confident in their new radar search receivers and strengthened anti-aircraft armaments, stayed on the surface to fight it out. If that happened the orders laid down that the aircraft was to go straight in 'irrespective of the accuracy of the gunfire'. Having thus placed strong emphasis on speed and accuracy, and on resolution in accepting the very real dangers involved in low attacks, Air Marshal Slessor stressed the vital importance of alertness, in order to sight the enemy as early as

---

[1] See Vol. I, p. 358, regarding the introduction of this device.

[2] The long-range and 'Very Long-Range' Liberators carried 4–6 depth charges. Shorter range aircraft might carry as many as twelve. The lethal range of the charges was considered to be 19 feet, and if six or less were carried they were all released in one 'stick'.

[3] See p. 24. These came into operational use in May 1943.

possible, and on the constant training and practice necessary to produce perfect team work between the various members of the crew. The principles laid down in mid-1943 remained in force, with only minor variations, until the end of the war.

To return to the waters north of the Azores, on the 4th of October the American escort carrier *Card* achieved a double success by sinking firstly U.422 and then, in the same position, the 'milch cow' U.460. This made the refuelling of the fifteen U-boats still in the Atlantic acutely difficult. The escort carrier next moved further north, and on the 13th her skilful and experienced aircrews sank U.402. Meanwhile two other American escort carriers had arrived in the waters north-west of the Azores, and they proceeded still further to imperil the enemy's refuelling programme. On the 20th the *Core's* aircraft sank U.378, and eight days later the emergency tanker U.220 fell victim to those of the *Block Island*. On the last day of October the *Card* obtained yet another success, when her aircraft caught two U-boats on the surface and sank U.584. Only one tanker (U.488) now remained to Dönitz, and he sent her far to the south-west, away from the waters which were being so effectively scoured by the American carrier-borne aircraft.

Meanwhile German U-boat strength inside the Mediterranean had again been seriously reduced by losses, and by September only thirteen remained. This and the submission of the Italian fleet, including thirty-four of their submarines[1], caused Dönitz to try once more to get reinforcements through the Gibraltar Straits; but after U.617 had been attacked by Leigh-Light Wellingtons on the 11th of September, driven ashore in Spanish Morocco and subsequently destroyed, and U.667 had been so severely harried by our air patrols that she was forced to return, he abandoned the attempt until the middle of October. Then five U-boats sailed for the Straits. U.566 was sunk by aircraft off Vigo on the 24th of October on the way south, while two others (U.340 and U.732) suffered such unrelenting pursuit by Gibraltar aircraft and surface ships that they both scuttled themselves. Thus only two of the original five reached the Mediterranean.

To turn to the operations in remote waters, the reader will remember how, by the end of August, the sinking of the supply submarines had destroyed Dönitz's hopes of intensifying that campaign.[2] In September there were no more than half-a-dozen U-boats in the distant Atlantic waters, and their only successes were obtained

---

[1] See pp. 166–169 and Appendix F.
[2] See p. 33.

off the Brazilian coast, where U.161 sank three ships, but was then sunk herself by a U.S. Navy Catalina. In October a steady trickle of U-boats left outward-bound but, because they could not be re-fuelled, their cruises were bound to be short. Mines were laid off St John's, Newfoundland, and the Panama Canal, but accomplished very little; and single marauders off South America, West Africa, the east coast of America and in the Caribbean only sank four ships between them. Two of the big (1,600-ton) 'U-cruisers' (U.848 and U.849) were sunk in the South Atlantic during November by American aircraft working from Ascension Island.

December produced similar results to the preceding months, namely occasional sinkings by the widely dispersed U-boats, gener-ally of ships sailing independently. Of the seven Allied ships lost, three fell victim to a U-boat which had moved from the waters off Freetown, which she had found unproductive, to the Gulf of Guinea. A reinforcement of three boats left for the Indian Ocean in November but two of them (U.172 and U.850) were sunk by the U.S.S. *Bogue's* aircraft off the Azores in the following month. Thus the Indian Ocean offensive, the most distant of all Dönitz's lunges, was also doomed. Because the submarines could no longer be refuelled in the remote theatres of operations, most of them had been forced to set course for their base at Penang by the end of the year.[1]

In the North Atlantic the next battle took place over and around convoys ON.206 and ONS.20, both of which were receiving the Liberator escort which had now become a regular feature of convoy passages. Although the U-boats had been ordered to fight back with their guns, and two Liberators were shot down, the highly experi-enced aircrews of Nos. 59, 86 and 120 Squadrons and Commander P. W. Gretton's redoubtable B7 Escort Group, which was supporting the convoys[2], hit the enemy hard.

Commander Gretton's ships left Londonderry on the 12th of October and met convoy ON.206, which was escorted by B6 Group under Commander R. A. Currie in the destroyer *Fame*, next day. During the night of the 15th–16th at least one enemy was driven below by the escorts before he could do any damage. Next forenoon two Liberators sank U.844 about fifteen miles from the convoy, and that evening three of our aircraft disposed of U.470 still further from the merchantmen. On the following night (16th–17th) quick action by the *Duncan* and *Vidette* frustrated more attacks, but the next actual success fell once more to the Liberators, two of which sank U.540 to the north of the convoy on the evening of the 17th. Then, after

---

[1] See pp. 219–221 regarding U-boat operations in the Indian Ocean.

[2] See Vol. II, pp. 373–375, regarding the earlier exploits of B7 Group. It now consisted of the destroyers *Duncan* (Senior Officer) and *Vidette*, and the corvettes *Sunflower*, *Loose-strife* and *Pink*.

dark, when B7 Group was steaming in line abreast towards ONS.20, which was some 150 miles away to the north-east, the *Sunflower* got a radar contact at 3,400 yards. The U-boat dived at once, but the corvette picked her up by asdic, blew her to the surface and sank her at the second attack. Her victim was U.631. The support group now transferred to the slower convoy, ONS.20. The one merchantman already sunk from that convoy had been quickly avenged by the sinking of U.964 by one of No. 86 Squadron's Liberators, and of U.841 by the frigate *Byard* on the 17th of October. The support group guarded the slow convoy until the 20th, by which time it was no longer in danger, and was then detached to meet the next convoy, ON.207. During the five-day battle around ON.206 and ONS.20 four U-boats were thus sunk by air escorts, and two more by the surface ships. As only one merchantman was lost it was a clear set-back for Dönitz; but the endurance of the escort groups had been severely taxed during the long ordeal. Commander Gretton's group was at sea for twenty-five days, during most of which the Atlantic produced its customary autumn gales. Fifteen years later one of the *Duncan's* company, who had been an Ordinary Seaman at the time, sent his recollections to the author. 'The conditions inside the ship' he wrote 'were almost indescribable. She often rolled between fifty and sixty degrees, and water several inches deep swirled continuously around on the mess decks. We were at "Action Stations" with scarcely a break, and no one had a stitch of dry clothing left. Towards the end we were living off little more than bully beef and ship's biscuit.' The memory of that member of the *Duncan's* crew may be taken to epitomise the conditions in which the Atlantic battle was fought by all the escort vessels.

In spite of the heavy losses suffered in the attack on ON.206 and ONS.20 Dönitz had no intention of giving up the struggle yet. With the arrival of fifteen fresh boats he formed a patrol line of a score of them about 500 miles east of Newfoundland. None the less the next four convoys to cross the ocean (ON.207, ONS.21, HX.263 and ON.208) suffered no losses at all; and the searching aircraft, the surface escorts and the omnipresent support groups, all of them vigorously on the offensive, sank between them U.274, U.420 and U.282. These successes provide a classic example of the effective integration of all arms in the defence of convoys, and of the way offensive opportunities were continuously sought for and, when found, were exploited to the uttermost by the escort and support forces. ON.207 not only received shore-based air cover, but was accompanied by the escort carrier *Tracker*, and when the Senior Officer of the escort knew that U-boats were in the vicinity he stationed her inside the convoy 'to give the support group more freedom of movement and to hide the air striking force from the enemy until more

U-boats should concentrate'. In other words he was offering the enemy a bait, and biding his time to seize the offensive opportunity when it came—the essence of sound strategy. It is not surprising that this convoy had a safe passage; for apart from its original escort group C1, it was supported by Gretton's B7 and Walker's 2nd Escort Group. A Liberator of No. 224 Squadron and Gretton's *Duncan* and *Vidette* shared in the sinking of U.274 on the 23rd of October; three days later an R.C.A.F. Liberator sank U.420, and on the 29th the *Duncan*, *Vidette* and *Sunflower* accounted for U.282. So accurate were B7 Group's attacks that they were now using their Hedgehogs in preference to depth charges, which could not be so precisely placed.

Towards the end of October Dönitz collected a new group of eight boats to work in conjunction with the newly co-operating Luftwaffe on the Gibraltar route. On the 27th a convoy of sixty ships (SL.138 and MKS.28 combined[1]) was reported by a Focke-Wulf aircraft off Portugal, and the U-boats were ordered to sweep south to intercept. The convoy received air cover from Gibraltar and from home bases for the next two days, and on the 30th a Fortress from the Azores joined up. This was the first instance of air escort being provided from the recently acquired bases in those islands, about which more will be said shortly. Not until dawn on the 31st did the U-boats gain touch with the convoy, and their experiences were not happy. First the destroyer *Whitehall* ran down the bearing on which the sighting U-boat's signals had been intercepted, and she and the corvette *Geranium* sank U.306. Soon afterwards a merchantman was torpedoed, but in the ensuing counter-attack another U-boat was badly damaged. The enemy then called off the attackers, and ordered them to form a patrol line between Cape Finisterre and the Azores. The U-boat command War Diary commented at this time on the first appearance of Allied aircraft from those new bases.

Actually the British and Portuguese Governments had been negotiating on the matter for two years. Plans had been made for an occupation by force or by invitation, but the British Government strongly hoped that force would not have to be used against our ancient ally. The negotiations thus dragged on until Dr Salazar's fears of German retaliation gradually receded. His reluctance to permit the landing of American as well as British forces, however, proved a serious obstacle, and American insistence on sharing any facilities gained very nearly caused a breakdown of the negotiations. Finally, on the 18th August, 1943, an Anglo-Portuguese agreement was signed. In return for the despatch of war materials and a guarantee against German aggression, we were promised the use of air bases on Fayal and Terceira islands from the 8th of October.

[1] See Volume II, Appendix F, for the identification of these and all other convoy code symbols.

The plans were now finalised, and a squadron consisting of the escort carrier *Fencer*, three destroyers and the necessary merchantmen, oilers, anti-submarine trawlers and landing craft was organised to carry to the Azores the men and stores needed to open and organise the sorely-needed bases. A new air group (No. 247) was formed under Air Vice-Marshal G. R. Bromet, who was made responsible to the Commander-in-Chief, Coastal Command, and arrangements were made to establish an Area Combined Headquarters on Fayal. At the same time control of the R.A.F. at Gibraltar at last reverted to Coastal Command.[1] Only the continued independence of the American Moroccan Sea Frontier command prevented the new pattern for the efficient control of maritime aircraft over the whole eastern Atlantic being perfected.[2]

The expedition for the Azores sailed from Britain under Commodore (Vice-Admiral, Retired) R. V. Holt on the last day of September in three small convoys, and arrived on the 8th of October. Meanwhile the Fortress aircraft, which were to fly from Gibraltar to the Lagens airfield on Terceira, had been delayed by bad weather. The *Fencer* therefore put to sea again on the 11th, and flew off nine Swordfish to the shore airfield. For the next week, in spite of the rudimentary facilities then available at Lagens, they carried out dawn and dusk searches of the adjacent waters, and anti-submarine patrols. Their work provides a good example of the mobility and adaptability of carrier-borne air forces. On the 18th the first of the Fortresses arrived; and they started operations on the following day. Thus, after more than four years of war, could reliable air cover at last be provided over the whole Atlantic north of 30° North; while the escort carriers looked after convoys using the more southerly routes. Though it was not until 1944 that the use of the Azores bases by American aircraft was finally resolved to the satisfaction of the Portuguese Government—by disguising them as part of Coastal Command's No. 19 Group—the prosecution of the Atlantic struggle had been transformed, and the U-boats quickly suffered further and drastic discomfiture.

To sum up the results of the first two months of the second campaign on the convoy routes, in September and October 1943 we lost nine merchant ships out of 2,468 which had sailed in sixty-four North Atlantic convoys. Twenty-five U-boats were sunk in mid-ocean, five by surface escorts, six by American carrier aircraft and thirteen by shore-based aircraft working with and around the convoys, while one was shared between warships and shore-based aircraft.[3] The immediate result of this heavy defeat was that Dönitz gave up

---

[1] See Vol. II, p. 360.

[2] Ibid.

[3] See Appendix D, Table I, for details of these U-boat sinkings.

working the U-boats in large mobile groups, and dispersed his forces more widely.

In the Admiralty this second victory on the convoy routes, for all that it was most welcome, produced some misgivings; for it encouraged a belief in certain circles that the campaign had been finally won. Such a belief, unless checked, could lead to a relaxation of our efforts and vigilance, so giving the enemy the opportunity to seize the initiative once again. The Naval Staff therefore pointed out that, in their estimate, some 300 operational U-boats still remained to the Germans, and that they would probably renew the battle as soon as their improved equipment, and especially the new radar sets, were available. That these fears were not groundless is shown by the great difficulty experienced in dealing with the 'Schnorkel' U-boats when they started operations in the middle of 1944.[1]

In November the enemy had five small groups of two or three U-boats to the east of Newfoundland, in waters where the escort carrier *Tracker* and Captain Walker's 2nd Escort Group were now working in support of convoys. The month opened with a full gale, which for some days prevented carrier aircraft from flying. The *Tracker* recorded rolling as much as fifty-two degrees, which 'put more aircraft out of action in five minutes than in two weeks flying at sea'. Not until the 5th did the weather moderate, and that day the carrier's aircraft sighted a U-boat. Walker at once started to search in her direction. At 2 a.m. on the 6th the *Kite* obtained a radar contact and illuminated. The U-boat at once dived; but Walker hurried over with the *Starling* and *Woodcock*, while the *Tracker*, escorted by the other two sloops, was sent clear of the danger area. The *Starling* and *Kite* were soon in contact, but Walker decided not to risk losing the quarry on a dark night through the inevitable disturbances made by depth charge explosions. He therefore stationed himself 1,500 yards astern of the enemy (who had gone very deep), and for four hours, with a sloop on either quarter, he steamed slowly south-west 'in close attendance on the U-boat'. It was a grim *cortège*, for the relentless tapping of the asdics must have told the U-boat crew that their hour had come. At 7 a.m. Walker directed the *Woodcock* to make a 'creeping attack'—his favourite tactics at a deep enemy. Twenty-six depth charges brought the remains of U.226 to the surface. That same afternoon a wireless report led to another search, the *Wild Goose* gained contact and, again directed by the *Starling*, she destroyed U.842. This was the fourth time Walker's group had made a 'creeping attack' of this type, and no enemy had so far survived to describe the experience. His method was to station a 'directing ship' about 1,000 yards astern

[1] See p. 262.

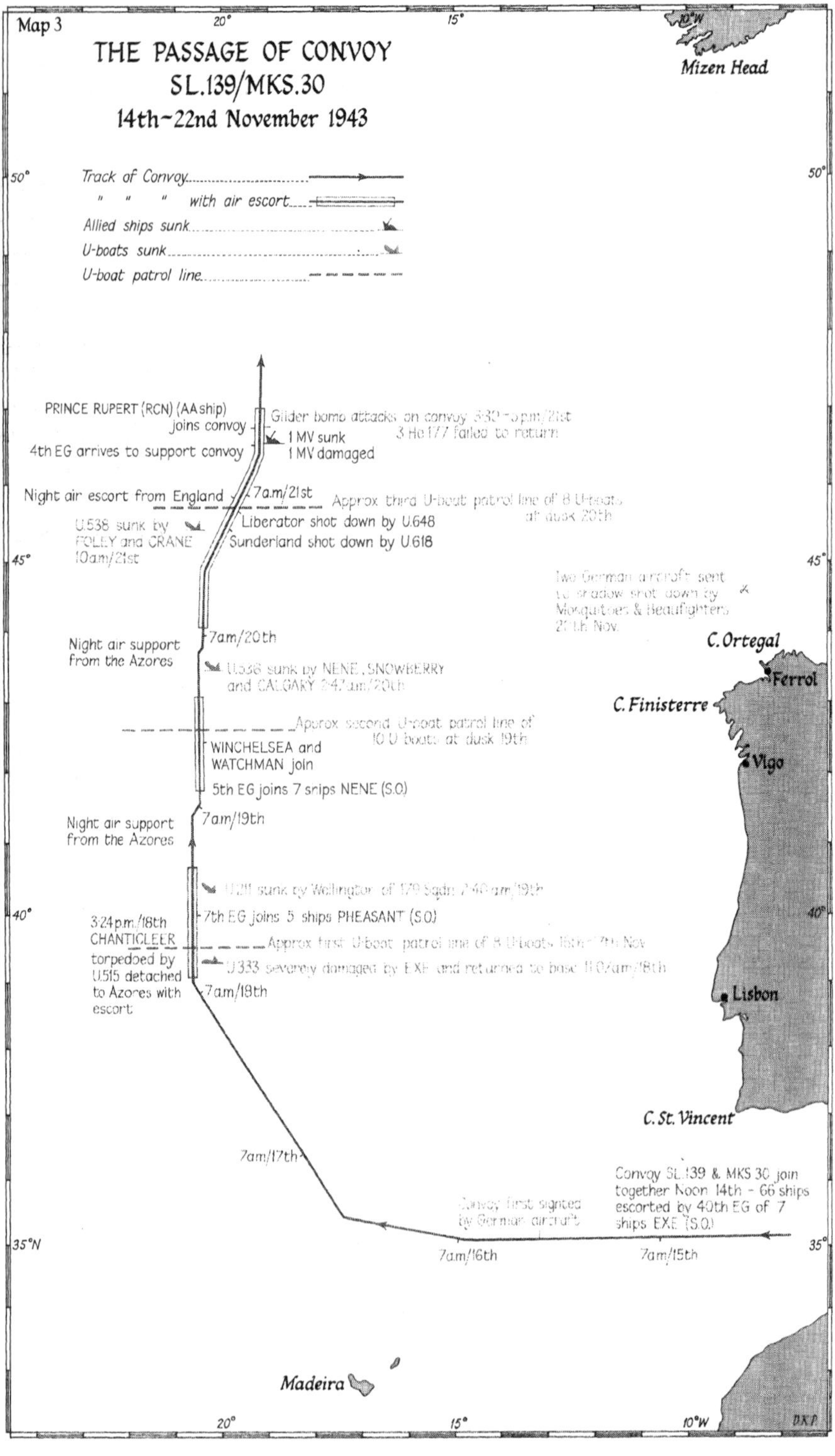

Map 3

THE PASSAGE OF CONVOY
SL.139/MKS.30
14th~22nd November 1943

20° 15° 10°W

Mizen Head

50° 50°

Track of Convoy...................................→

" " " with air escort......⊨⊨⊨⊨⊨

Allied ships sunk....................................↘

U-boats sunk.......................................∴↘

U-boat patrol line.................— — — —

PRINCE RUPERT (RCN) (AA ship)
joins convoy
4th EG arrives to support convoy

Glider bomb attacks on convoy 3.30~5 p.m/21st
3 He 177 failed to return
1 MV sunk
1 MV damaged

Night air escort from England — 7a.m/21st

Approx third U-boat patrol line of 8 U-boats
at dusk 20th

U.538 sunk by
FOLEY and CRANE
10 a.m/21st

Liberator shot down by U.648
Sunderland shot down by U.618

45° 45°

Two German aircraft sent
to shadow shot down by
Mosquitoes & Beaufighters
20th Nov.

C. Ortegal

Night air support
from the Azores

7am/20th

Ferrol

U.536 sunk by NENE, SNOWBERRY
and CALGARY 2.47 a.m/20th

C. Finisterre

Vigo

Approx second U-boat patrol line of
10 U-boats at dusk 19th

WINCHELSEA and
WATCHMAN join

5th EG joins 7 ships NENE (S.O.)

Night air support
from the Azores

7am/19th

U.211 sunk by Wellington of 179 sqdn 7.40 a.m/19th

7th EG joins 5 ships PHEASANT (S.O.)

40° 40°

3.24 p.m./18th
CHANTICLEER
torpedoed by
U.515 detached
to Azores with
escort

Approx first U-boat patrol line of 8 U-boats 16th ~ 7th Nov.
U.333 severely damaged by EXE and returned to base 11.07 a.m/18th

7am/19th

Lisbon

C. St. Vincent

7am/17th

Convoy first sighted
by German aircraft

Convoy SL.139 & MKS 30 join
together Noon 14th – 66 ships
escorted by 40th EG of 7
ships EXE (S.O.)

35°N 35°

7am/16th 7am/15th

Madeira

20° 15° 10°W D.K.P.

of the U-boat, to keep in contact all the time by asdic, while another ship, not using her asdic, meanwhile steamed very slowly (at perhaps five knots) up the enemy's track. The U-boat commander was thus lulled into a false sense of security; for he could only hear the comparatively distant asdic transmissions of the directing ship, and would not pick up the approach of the slowly moving attacking ship on his hydrophones. He would thus get no warning such as would enable him to take drastic avoiding action before the arrival of the depth charges. The directing ship ranged on the attacking ship while the latter steamed over and beyond the U-boat. When that range exceeded the asdic range of the enemy by the distance he would travel during the descent of the depth charges, the signal was made to the attacker to start releasing depth charges. She then dropped or fired about twenty-six charges in pairs at nine-second intervals, all set to explode between 500 and 740 feet, whilst continuing to creep ahead over the hapless and helpless enemy. A carpet of charges was thus laid directly on the U-boat's course, and he, unaware of what was coming, probably steered straight into it. If the enemy was already taking evasive action by frequently altering course Walker had an alternative way of outwitting him. Three ships would then be sent in to attack instead of only one, and they were stationed close abeam of each other to lay a 'creeping barrage' simultaneously. Whichever way the enemy might turn while the charges were descending, he would thus probably be caught by one of the three patterns. The tactics originated by Walker were promulgated by the Admiralty to all escort commanders, and they now became the standard method of dealing with an enemy who had dived very deep. Successes such as those recounted above were splendid demonstrations of the experience, confidence and deadly precision which groups such as Walker's were now displaying.

After destroying U.842 the group next supported convoy HX.264, and then set course for Argentia. On the way an acoustic torpedo was fired at the *Tracker*, but this 'indignity' (as Walker called it) could not be avenged because the sloops were short of fuel. After heaving-to during another gale the group reached Argentia on the 12th of November.

Dönitz had meanwhile stationed his twenty-two surviving boats in twos and threes off Cape Farewell, the southern tip of Greenland; but even such small groups could not evade the watchful aircraft.

On the Gibraltar route the U-boats had been severely handled in the battle around SL.138 and MKS.28 at the end of October[1], but were still in the fight. On the 7th of November a Focke-Wulf reported convoy MKS.29A, and Dönitz sent eight U-boats against

---

[1] See p. 46.

it. They did not, however, find their quarry until early on the 9th, and the only result was the sinking of U.707 by an Azores-based Fortress. The powerful surface escort, which had formed an outer as well as an inner screen, frustrated all attacks, and damaged another enemy; while the convoy passed safely home.

On the 12th of November Dönitz's staff despondently complained that 'the enemy holds all the trump cards. Far-reaching air cover using location methods against which we have no warning . . .' enabled our convoys to avoid their concentrations; 'the air menace has curtailed the mobility of the U-boats . . . as they can no longer be fuelled at sea they can spend far less time on patrol. The enemy knows all our secrets, and we know none of theirs . . .' The last remark echoed that made by Admiral Forbes to the Admiralty in June 1940—'it is most galling that the enemy should know just where our ships . . . always are, whereas we generally learn where his major forces are when they sink one or more of our ships.' [1] In the procurement and dissemination of intelligence the tables had certainly been completely turned; and the benefits which that brought to our sea and air forces working far out in the ocean spaces cannot be over-estimated.

The admission of defeat in the North Atlantic contained in the U-boat staff's words quoted above, which may well be compared to the similar sentiments expressed by Dönitz after his first crushing defeat on the convoy routes in May of the same year[2], was soon translated into action by the rest of the northern U-boats being transferred to the Gibraltar route. On the 16th of November, as though to hasten their departure, a Liberator of No. 86 Squadron escorting convoy HX.265 sank U.280, which was on her way to the new station.

The Sierra Leone convoy SL.139 joined company with MKS.30 from North African ports and Gibraltar about 100 miles south of Cape St Vincent at noon on the 14th of November.[3] The combined convoy, of sixty-six ships in fourteen columns, was originally protected by the seven escort vessels of the 40th Group under Commander G. V. Legassick, R.N.R., in the frigate *Exe*. Late on the 15th its position was reported by a German aircraft, and Dönitz ordered three groups totalling no less than twenty-six U-boats to attack; but the enemy's wireless traffic had warned the Admiralty of the need to reinforce the surface escort; and strong air support, by night as well as by day, was also quickly organised from home bases, Gibraltar and the Azores. Both sides suffered the first damage within a few hours of each other. At 11 a.m. on the 18th of November the *Exe*

---

[1] See Vol. I, p. 198.
[2] See Vol. II, p. 377.
[3] See Map 3 (facing p. 49).

attacked and then rammed U.333; but the U-boat got back to base safely, though with part of the frigate's propeller embedded in her hull. That afternoon the sloop *Chanticleer* had her stern blown off by an acoustic torpedo, and had to be towed to the Azores. By the evening, however, her departure had been more than made good by the arrival of the five ships of the 7th Escort Group under Commander L. F. Durnford-Slater.[1] All that day Hudsons, Fortresses and Catalinas escorted the convoy, and when night fell the Leigh-Light Wellingtons from the Azores replaced the day air escorts. It was one of the Wellingtons that attacked and sank U.211, which was pursuing the convoy, that night. On the 19th further reinforcements in the shape of the seven ships (four of them R.C.N.) of the 5th Escort Group and two more destroyers arrived, so that the convoy was now massively protected by no less than nineteen escorts formed in a double screen. Air cover was again continuous all that day. A German long-range aircraft having reported the convoy in the evening, Dönitz organised a night attack. The night was a busy one for the escorts, with many radar or asdic contacts and attacks. In the early hours of the 20th the frigate *Nene* and the Canadian corvettes *Calgary* and *Snowberry* despatched U.536 after blowing her to the surface with depth charges, and then engaging with great spirit and all their gun armaments. Later that day Coastal Command's Beaufighters retaliated against the German shadowing aircraft by intercepting and shooting two of them down off Cape Ortegal.[2] The convoy was still given very strong air cover, but U.618 shot down one of No. 422 Squadron's Sunderlands. The next night, that of 20th–21st, was as busy as the preceding one. At least four U-boats were sighted, and two of them were attacked; but one of No. 53 Squadron's escorting Liberators fell victim to U.648's gunfire. Just after midnight on the 21st the *Crane* and *Foley* were detached to search for a U-boat fixed by directional wireless on the port quarter of the convoy. At 4.35 a.m. the searching ships obtained a radar contact, followed it up, and then illuminated with star shell. A large U-boat was seen on the surface; but she dived immediately. Asdic contact followed, and a long series of attacks was made on the enemy. He released asdic decoys, went very deep, and used every evasive trick he knew; but it was of no avail. The tenacious escorts held on, and were finally rewarded, after six hours of patient pursuit, by the destruction of U.538. That same day Dönitz called off the attack. Thirty-one U-boats had actually taken part, yet all they had accomplished was to damage the *Chanticleer* and shoot down two aircraft.

---

[1] This group must not be confused with B7 Group, which has also appeared many times in this narrative. The North Atlantic forces were given the letters A (American), B (British) and C (Canadian). Other British escort groups were allotted numbers only, and were known as EG.7, EG.40, etc.

[2] See Map 3.

But the battle was not quite over. On the afternoon of the 21st, by which time the convoy was in 46° 46′ N., 18° 21′ W., two dozen bombers—about half of them new 4-engined He.177s—appeared, and glider bomb attacks started. The Canadian anti-aircraft ship *Prince Robert* joined at the height of the attacks and zig-zagged across the wake of the convoy, adding her gunfire to the heavy barrage put up by the smaller escorts. Many of the sixteen bombs released were aimed at a straggler three-and-a-half miles behind the convoy, and she was finally hit and abandoned. One other merchantman was damaged, but managed to reach harbour. Three He.177s were lost to the enemy.

The heavy calls of the preceding days left Coastal Command with only two Liberators available on the 22nd, and when Air Vice-Marshall B. E. Baker, commanding No. 19 Group, asked for help from the U.S. Naval Liberator Squadron which was operating from Dunkeswell under his control, the request was refused on the grounds that (to quote the squadron commander's words) his 'superiors . . . conceived his mission in Bay operations as an offensive mission against submarines on a planned basis'; and that 'departure therefrom to enter into the plan for the routine coverage of Gibraltar convoys by U.S.N. forces becomes a matter for Cominch [i.e. Admiral King] to decide'. The issue was at once taken up by Air Marshal Slessor with Admiral Stark, U.S.N., and was satisfactorily resolved; but it showed how necessary it was to achieve a clear understanding regarding the operational control of all Allied aircraft working in the eastern Atlantic, and how, even at this late date, the misconception that convoy work was 'defensive' had not yet been eliminated in some quarters.[1] In fact the control of maritime aircraft was being discussed in Washington at the time of this convoy battle, and, although Admiral King's intention to remove all U.S. Naval aircraft from the eastern Atlantic was not proceeded with, no satisfactory scheme for unified control of all Allied aircraft in the theatre was ever evolved.

Convoy SL.139–MKS.30 was not in fact molested again. On the 23rd the support forces were sent about other duties, and all the remaining merchantmen reached harbour safely.

'This convoy' wrote the Admiralty on the report of its passage 'was routed through a concentration of U-boats, but the faith placed in the escort was fully justified.' The victory of the sea and air escorts

---

[1] The American side of this controversy is mentioned in Morison, Vol. X, p. 102 fn. (25); but British records lend no support to the statement therein that Air Marshal Slessor 'acquiesced' in the line taken by the commander of the U.S.N. Liberator Squadron. Without making the case official he represented very strongly to Admiral Stark that the prosecution of the U-boat war was bound to suffer if the American aircraft operating under his control did not comply with his command's requests; and he was successful in preventing a recurrence of such an incident.

had indeed been resounding, and the long-awaited co-operation of the Luftwaffe with the U-boats had not achieved the results hoped for by Dönitz. The truth now seems to be that it came too late to restore the balance, let alone tip the scales in the German favour. By the autumn of 1943 Allied maritime air strength had gained such a long lead, and the training and experience of our aircrews was so greatly superior, that the enemy had little hope of overtaking us either in numbers or in quality. What the Luftwaffe failed to contribute to the Atlantic battle in 1942 could not be won back at the end of the following year. If Göring's megalomania contributed nothing else to the final defeat of his country, his long and stubborn refusal to co-operate with the German Navy, and his recurrent strife with Raeder, must have contributed a good deal towards the Allied victory in the Atlantic.

Dönitz now reformed his forces into a new group of sixteen U-boats to attack the south-bound convoys on the same route; but the Admiralty had already diverted the 4th Escort Group from the last convoy to protect OS.59 and KMS.30, which we believed the enemy to be seeking. Many U-boats thus ran right into the escort group, and some very long hunts were rewarded by the destruction of U.648 on the night of 22nd–23rd of November by the combined efforts of three frigates. The convoy was routed further west than usual, and passed safely on its way well shielded by aircraft from the Azores. The enemy never found it. He thereupon switched to the next north-bound convoy, and again the U-boats ran into ships of the 4th Escort Group. The frigates *Bazely* and *Blackwood* sank U.600 early on the 25th—their second success in two days. The battle now swung across to the big homeward convoy SL.140–MKS.31 of sixty-eight ships. The 4th Escort Group and the American carrier *Bogue* were moved to reinforce its original escort of the seven ships of B1 Group, while Azores aircraft flew continuously in support. On the 26th the 4th Escort Group severely damaged U.618 after a long series of attacks. The following night there were many sea and air actions, though none was conclusive: but the arrival of Captain Walker's 2nd Escort Group on the afternoon of the 27th boded ill for the U-boats. He at once took command of all the sixteen escort vessels present. The next success fell, however, to a Leigh-Light Wellington of No. 179 Squadron which sank U.542 that night, when the main battle between the escorts and U-boats developed. Throughout the dark hours there were dozens of wireless reports indicating the enemy's presence; many radar contacts were promptly illuminated, at least six U-boats were sighted or picked up by asdic, and they were all effectively harried by the unresting escorts. One enemy did, however, penetrate the screen; but her torpedoes missed and the corvette *Dahlia* promptly attacked and damaged her. On the 29th the hard-hitting aircraft from the *Bogue* sank U.86, and Dönitz then cancelled the attack. He attributed the total failure of his plan to the strength of the double screen, to the night air escorts, and to the deceptive use of flares and star shell—which was actually one of Walker's favourite stratagems.

Meanwhile a large number of fresh U-boats had come out by the northern route. Sixteen in all concentrated to the south of Iceland with orders to attack west-bound Atlantic convoys; but clever evasion enabled ON.214 to slip through their patrol line undetected. By the middle of December the enemy's strength in mid-ocean had risen to two dozen U-boats; but they sighted nothing until two of them intercepted the fast tanker convoy TU.5, bound from Trinidad to Britain, on the 23rd. Both were quickly harried by the air and surface convoy escorts. There next took place a series of confused actions spread over a wide area; for the U.S.S. *Card* was in the offing, and convoy OS.62–KMS.36 with the escort carrier *Striker* was just to the north of her. As the U-boats appeared to be making for the *Card* two British ships were diverted to reinforce her screen. U.645 was sunk by an American escort, but the U.S.S. *Leary* and the British destroyer *Hurricane* were both sunk by acoustic torpedoes. Next two more American escort carriers and many Azores aircraft swept this battle ground some 400 miles north-east of the Azores, but without any decisive success. It was however by now plain to Dönitz that the waters between the Azores and Portugal were altogether too unhealthy for big groups of U-boats to work there. Henceforth only scattered enemies appeared in the north-eastern Atlantic; but they too were constantly pursued by the air and surface escort and support forces.

The autumn of 1943 thus saw the second victory over the U-boats on the convoy routes, and the final defeat of the 'wolf pack' strategy which, since its introduction in the winter of 1940–41, had caused us such grievous losses.[1] The full extent of the U-boat's discomfiture can best be illustrated by quoting a few figures. In the single fateful month of March of this same year, before the enemy had suffered his first defeat, the Allies lost 108 ships of 627,377 tons to submarine attack.[2] In the four months between the beginning of September and the end of December our total losses caused by submarines amounted to only sixty-seven ships of 369,800 tons, an average of seventeen ships and 92,450 tons per month—less than one sixth of the March losses.[3] During those same four months the Germans lost sixty-two U-boats. The victory was most marked during the last two months

---

[1] See Vol. I, pp. 131 and 254–360.

[2] See Vol. II, p. 368, where the figure of 107 ships sunk in the North Atlantic during the first twenty days of March 1943 should read 67.

[3] See Appendix K for details of these losses.

of the year, and in the North Atlantic. In that period seventy-two ocean convoys totalling 2,218 ships reached their destinations without suffering any losses at all.

When Dönitz, having failed against the North Atlantic convoys, transferred his main strength to the north–south traffic from Sierra Leone and Gibraltar, the same pattern was reproduced. These latter successes owed a great deal to the long-awaited air cover from the Azores; and because we had suffered such cruel losses on that route in 1940–41 the transformation which had now taken place seemed all the more astonishing. But in telling the story of the victorious passages of the convoys in the summer and autumn of 1943, often with a double screen of a score of escort vessels, with shore-based aircraft constantly watching and searching all around them, and support groups almost always at call, it is right to remember that we had come through much darker days; and that the victories here described could not have been won but for the devotion of the merchantmen and of the one or two escorts who had struggled to defend the convoys at the beginning—and all too often saw their hapless charges blown up or sunk.

On the transit routes the year closed quietly, because the U-boats were again travelling submerged, and our air patrols were only occasionally detecting them. The need now was for long-endurance aircraft, capable of flying by night as well as by day, and fitted with ten centimetre radar. But the third victory of 1943 against the Atlantic U-boats was won around the convoys—exactly as the first one had been.

CHAPTER IV

HOME WATERS AND THE ARCTIC

1st June–31st December, 1943

'In the great epic of the sea war one of the most outstanding chapters was those magnificent exploits, the northern convoys.'

M. Maisky. Speech at the London Embassy of the U.S.S.R., quoted in *The Times*, 21st April, 1943.

THE Home Fleet's main base at Scapa Flow was extremely busy in the middle of 1943. But although that great expanse of sheltered water was generally full of large and small warships, many of them had only come there temporarily; and the effective strength available to the Commander-in-Chief, Admiral Sir Bruce Fraser, was in fact barely adequate to meet his responsibilities.[1] Moreover shortage of destroyers, or the lack of aircraft carriers, often deprived his fleet of the balance essential to the effective prosecution of maritime operations. New ships and those which had recently re-commissioned, or had completed refit or repairs, generally came to Scapa to 'work up' efficiency; but this placed an extra strain on the base, which had to provide them with targets, arrange exercises for them, and also give anti-submarine protection while they were at sea. Then, as the maritime war passed out of the defensive phase, totally new requirements arose, such as training crews for the parts they were to play in combined operations. Thus all the heavy ships of Force H (the battleships *Nelson*, *Rodney*, *Warspite* and *Valiant* and the fleet carrier *Indomitable*, under Vice-Admiral A. U. Willis) came from the western Mediterranean to Scapa during June to prepare for the invasion of Sicily and, in particular, to practise heavy gun bombardments in support of an army recently flung ashore on a hostile coast. When they returned to their normal station towards the end of the month the new battleships *King George V* and *Howe* were detached from the Home Fleet to the Mediterranean. This reduced Admiral Fraser's 2nd Battle Squadron to the *Duke of York* (fleet flagship), *Anson* and *Malaya*; and because of her unmodernised

---

[1] Admiral Fraser had succeeded Admiral Tovey as Commander-in-Chief, Home Fleet, on the 8th of May 1943. See Vol. II, p. 403.

state the last-named ship had little fighting value.[1] In July she left the fleet to reduce to 'Care and Maintenance', and so release her crew for more modern ships. To offset the obvious inadequacy of the remaining heavy ships of the Home Fleet to deal with the powerful German squadron (the *Tirpitz*, *Scharnhorst* and *Lützow*) based in Norway which, in Admiral Fraser's words, 'effectively blocked our route to north Russia, and threatened us with the possibility of a destructive break-out into the Atlantic', the Admiralty arranged with the U.S. Navy Department for the battleships *South Dakota* and *Alabama* and five destroyers under Rear-Admiral O. M. Hustvedt, U.S.N., to be transferred from Argentia in Newfoundland to Scapa, and to be placed under Admiral Fraser. To cover the Atlantic convoys against another surface-ship foray a battleship and two cruisers, or alternatively Admiral Hustvedt's task force, were normally stationed at Hvalfiord in Iceland. But the likelihood of the enemy making such an attempt was recognised to be decreasing, and after the *Tirpitz* had been damaged and immobilised[2], Admiral Fraser was able to reduce the covering force.

In August the two American battleships already mentioned were transferred to the Pacific, but to compensate for their departure the heavy cruisers *Augusta* and *Tuscaloosa* and the light fleet carrier *Ranger* then came to Scapa. The loan of the *Ranger* was particularly welcome at that time, for the *Victorious* had not yet returned from the Pacific, to which theatre she had been sent in December 1942 to reinforce American carrier strength at a difficult moment[3], and the recent departure of the *Illustrious* for the Mediterranean had left Admiral Fraser only the old *Furious*; and she was actually refitting.

In cruisers the Home Fleet was rather better off; for the 1st Cruiser Squadron consisted of five 8-inch ships of the *Kent* and *London* classes, while the 10th Cruiser Squadron nominally comprised five modern 6-inch ships and two smaller light cruisers; but after the middle of the year several cruisers and destroyers were generally on loan to the Commander-in-Chief, Plymouth, to cover our southbound convoys against the powerful German destroyers based on Bordeaux, and to work with Coastal Command's aircraft in the Bay of Biscay against enemy blockade-runners.[4]

There were theoretically three flotillas of destroyers (the 3rd, 8th and 17th, each of about nine ships) and one flotilla of the smaller *Hunt*-class in the fleet; but we have already seen how many of the

---

[1] The outbreak of war in 1939 prevented the *Malaya* ever being taken in hand for modernisation and reconstruction, as was done to her sister-ships *Warspite*, *Valiant* and *Queen Elizabeth*.

[2] See pp. 65–69 below.

[3] See Vol. II, pp. 415–416.

[4] See pp. 74–75.

former had to be taken to reinforce the Atlantic convoy escorts at a critical time[1], and when they returned from that vital duty one-and-a-half flotillas had to be detached to the Mediterranean. The shortage of destroyers thus continued to be one of the Commander-in-Chief's most chronic difficulties, as had been the case since the earliest days of the war.

The first fleet operation of the present phase was designed to relieve and supply the Norwegian force in Spitzbergen, to send stores and mail by destroyer to the ships which had been marooned in Kola Inlet since the preceding March, when the last west-bound convoy (RA. 53) had been run[2], and to bring back two corvettes from the same distant base. The cruisers *Cumberland*, *Bermuda* and two destroyers sailed from Iceland on the 7th of June, and landed men and stores in Spitzbergen three days later. The battle squadron covered the movement, and all the objects were accomplished without incident.

At the end of June Admiral Fraser wrote to the First Sea Lord reviewing the possibility of restarting the Arctic convoys in September. He considered that the general situation was little different from that which had prevailed at the end of March, when the convoys had been temporarily stopped.[3] Although German air striking power was reduced, their reconnaissance was still efficient, U-boat strength was 'diminished but sufficient for successful operation in those restricted waters', and their surface squadron was more powerful than ever before. He did not regard the attempt to run a convoy as justifiable unless the flow of supplies to Russia by that route was essential to the successful prosecution of the war, or it would 'enable the German surface forces to be brought successfully to action'. He did not personally consider the northern supply route vital, and he did not expect the German squadron to put to sea unless it saw the chance to attack a convoy which lacked powerful cover, or the British heavy units had suffered damage. In the latter event the situation of the convoy and its local escort and covering ships might become critical. 'In my view' concluded the Commander-in-Chief 'the effort required is not justified by the results to be expected; but if the decision is otherwise it is essential that adequate forces . . . should be provided.' It will be told later how the decision was taken to restart the convoys, how the necessary forces to ensure their safe passages were collected, and how a far greater degree of success than Admiral Fraser had anticipated was achieved.

The next call on the fleet was to simulate a large-scale combined

---

[1] See Vol. II, pp. 366–367.

[2] Ibid. p. 400.

[3] Ibid. pp. 348, 401.

operation against southern Norway, in order to divert German attention from the Mediterranean during the final preparations for the assault on Sicily. The whole available strength of the Home Fleet sailed towards Norway on the 8th of July, and Admiral Fraser trailed his coat only 150 miles off the coast 'inviting the enemy to investigate'. German records do not, however, suggest that the ruse caused them to redeploy any substantial forces. Perhaps the most interesting lesson derived from the operation was that the fleet, including the carrier *Furious*, could now work safely close off the enemy-held coast. At the end of the month the operation was repeated. Martlet fighters from the *Illustrious* and the air escort of Coastal Command Beaufighters then dealt severely with enemy shadowing aircraft, no less than five of which were shot down.

On the 5th of August the liner *Queen Mary* sailed from the Clyde with the Prime Minister and Chiefs of Staff on board for Halifax, to attend the 'Quadrant' conference at Quebec.[1] She was powerfully escorted by the *Illustrious*, three cruisers, and several destroyers from the Home Fleet. After the conference the battle cruiser *Renown* was sent to Halifax to bring home the British representatives. While in America the First Sea Lord, Admiral of the Fleet Sir Dudley Pound, suffered a stroke, and forthwith tendered his resignation to the Prime Minister. He returned to England in the *Renown*, but was soon struck by a second and more severe stroke, which left him totally paralysed. He died in hospital on Trafalgar Day, 1943. Since 1939 he had borne a tremendous burden with unshakable resolution and calm confidence in face of many set-backs and disasters. His character, though immensely firm, was so reserved that few except those who constantly worked close to him penetrated to its depths. He shunned the limelight, and this combined with his natural modesty kept his accomplishments veiled from the public eye, and perhaps also resulted in their being insufficiently recognised in naval circles; for he was not the type of leader whose personality made an impact on the service as a whole. His greatest achievement lay perhaps in the steadying influence he exerted in high places at times of difficulty and danger. Again and again did he successfully apply a brake to schemes which, by dissipating our slender maritime strength, might have led to irremediable disaster. Yet he won the Prime Minister's confidence from the beginning, and retained it to the last. He undoubtedly overworked himself; but that may have been made inevitable by the fact that the Admiralty, unlike the War Office or Air Ministry, was an operational headquarters as well as an administrative department. It may be that the sheer weight of this double burden contributed to his too frequent interventions in the conduct of operations, over the

---

[1] See Churchill, Vol. V, Chapter V.

heads of Commanders-in-Chief—a matter which has several times been commented on in these volumes.[1] None the less his contribution to the final victory at sea was immense, and we may be glad that he at any rate lived long enough to see the tide turn. His finest epitaph is, perhaps, Mr Churchill's remark that 'he was a true comrade to me'.[2]

Mr Churchill has told how it came to pass that the vacant office of First Sea Lord was first offered to Admiral Fraser, in spite of the First Lord having proposed Admiral Sir Andrew Cunningham as 'an obvious choice'; and how Fraser replied with dignity, and in words with which the whole Navy agreed, that whereas he believed he had the confidence of his own fleet 'Cunningham has that of the whole Navy'.[3] The result was that Admiral Cunningham was recalled from the Mediterranean, in which theatre he was succeeded by Admiral Sir John H. D. Cunningham[4], and took over his new responsibilities on the 15th of October. Sir Andrew Cunningham has himself re-counted the misgivings with which he accepted the post[5], and just as it seems clear that Mr Churchill was initially reluctant to approve the appointment of so powerful a personality to the Admiralty, the Admiral entertained some doubts regarding the reception he would receive from the Prime Minister[6]; for some of the signalled replies sent by him as Commander-in-Chief, Mediterranean, had been strongly worded and forthright, and were doubtless remembered. None the less it is plain from the records left by both these great men that closer contact produced better mutual understanding.

In September 1943 the Home Fleet's 1st Minelaying Squadron was at last disbanded and its ships were put to more profitable uses. It had been formed in 1940 to strengthen the east coast mine barrier and to lay the vast defensive minefield between the Faeroes and Iceland.[7] During the three-and-a-quarter years of its existence the squadron had laid no less than 110,500 mines, the great majority of them in the northern barrier. Admiral Fraser, in recording the decision to pay off the squadron, stated it as his view that 'the small

---

[1] See Vol. I, pp. 26–27 and Vol. II, pp. 139–140.

[2] Churchill, Vol. V, p. 146.

[3] Ibid. p. 145.

[4] Admirals Sir Andrew and Sir John Cunningham were not related to each other.

[5] Viscount Cunningham of Hyndhope, *A Sailor's Odyssey* (Hutchinson, 1951), pp. 573–575 and 577–582.

[6] Lord Cunningham's private diary records that on 19th February 1946 the First Lord (Mr A. V. Alexander) told him that the Prime Minister's reluctance to accept his appointment as First Sea Lord had stemmed from a feeling that with him in office the Admiralty would prove less malleable to his wishes. It seems likely that Mr Churchill had not forgotten the circumstances which led to Admiral Lord Fisher's resignation as First Sea Lord in May 1915, and to his own supersession as First Lord. See Marder, *Fear God and Dread Nought, The Correspondence of Admiral of the Fleet Lord Fisher of Kilverstone,* Vol. III, Chapter II (Cape, 1959).

[7] See Vol. I, pp. 263–264, 334, 390.

contribution to Atlantic security made by the northern minefields no longer justified . . . the retention on a defensive commitment of such a large number of men and amount of material'; which conclusion can hardly be disputed. What seems more surprising today is that the squadron was not disbanded much earlier; for we had long known that the minefields were of little hindrance to the enemy, and of some danger to our own ships. Whereas throughout the entire war the only success attributable to the northern mine barrier was the sinking of one U-boat[1], no less than nine Allied merchantmen and one escort vessel were lost when, owing to navigational errors, convoys inadvertently entered the danger area. Indeed the whole project was, from the Allied point of view, as unprofitable as the vast barrier laid across the North Sea in the 1914–18 war; and it seems that the lessons of the earlier venture cannot have been remembered when the later one was embarked on.[2] The Admiralty also decided at this time to discontinue all minelaying in the east coast barrier[3]; for the time when resources could justifiably be devoted to that defensive measure had also plainly passed.

During the latter part of 1943 heavy pressure was applied by the Cabinet on all the service departments to reduce or abolish all commitments which could reasonably be regarded as strategically defensive, and thereby release men and materials for offensive purposes. In the Admiralty's case not only was the laying of defensive minefields discontinued, but a start was made with paying off ships which were absorbing unreasonably large numbers of men in relation to the value of the services performed. In such circumstances it was natural for the department's attention to be directed towards the remaining Armed Merchant Cruisers. Many of these ships, of which fifty had originally been converted[4], had already transferred to service as troop-carriers, and before the end of the year orders were given for nearly all the remainder to be withdrawn from naval service. Their crews were urgently needed to commission the new escort carriers then completing in the United States. It would be easy, in the context of the summer of 1943, to dismiss the work carried out by the Armed Merchant Cruisers since the beginning of the war as unimportant, or even to regard the substantial effort needed to convert about fifty liners to this purpose as having been unprofitable. It is true that, by the stage now reached, they had become almost an anachronism; and it is also the case that no ship of that class ever fought a successful action with an enemy raider. None the less it

---

[1] U.647, on about 3rd August 1943. See p. 30.

[2] See Newbolt, *Naval Operations*, Vol. V, Chapter X (Longmans, 1931), and in particular pp. 342–343, regarding the ineffectiveness of the northern mine barrier of 1917–18.

[3] See Vol. I, pp. 45, 90, 96–97 and 125–126 and Map 10.

[4] See Vol. I, p. 46.

should be remembered that in the early days they played a substantial part in making the blockade of Germany by the Northern Patrol effective, and that they repeatedly guarded ocean convoys on their long sea passages to and from the remote theatres of war. Up to the middle of 1943 they had rendered important help in the Indian Ocean, and had defended troop convoys running from Australia and New Zealand to the Pacific Islands. Their work was always unobtrusive, and rarely received any appreciation; but as long as we lacked sufficient proper cruisers for ocean escort duty there was no alternative to the employment of converted auxiliaries. The only lesson to be drawn is that very many more cruisers are required to defend British trade in remote waters than is realised in times of peace. Finally we should remember that two British Armed Merchant Cruisers—the *Rawalpindi* and the *Jervis Bay*—gained immortality by their single-handed combats with vastly superior enemies.[1]

To return to northern waters, the month of September 1943 produced the rare event of a sortie by the German squadron from Altenfiord. The *Tirpitz*, *Scharnhorst* and ten destroyers sailed on the 6th, approached Spitzbergen unobserved, and bombarded the Allied shore installations. The news was received by wireless in London early on the 8th, and the Home Fleet put to sea that same day; but there was little possibility of catching the enemy, for he returned at once to the shelter of his fiord, and the fleet was then recalled. It is an interesting fact that, for all her considerable influence on Allied maritime strategy, the shells fired by the *Tirpitz* on this occasion were the only rounds she can be said to have fired from her main armament at an enemy. Wireless communication with Spitzbergen was restored on the 22nd, when a Catalina flew there with new equipment.

Readers of our second volume will remember how, after convoys JW.52 and JW.53 had made successful passages to Murmansk in January and February 1943, the lengthening days and the threat of attack by the *Tirpitz*, *Scharnhorst* and *Lützow*, all of which were based on Altenfiord in north Norway, caused Admiral Tovey to represent that the risks were too great to justify sending more convoys for the present.[2] Then the Atlantic battle rose to its climax in March, and every possible destroyer and escort vessel had to be detached from the Home Fleet to strengthen the convoy escorts.[3] This settled the issue whether the Arctic convoys should continue during the spring, since it was plainly impossible to run them until the Home Fleet flotillas had returned from the Atlantic. The convoys to Murmansk were accordingly postponed indefinitely, and the full effort of the British maritime services was concentrated on grappling with the

---

[1] See Vol. I, pp. 82–88 and 288–290, respectively.

[2] See Vol. II, pp. 399–401.

[3] Ibid. pp. 367 and 373–377.

U-boats, which were then making their most dangerous and determined attempt to sever the Atlantic life-line. The May victory on the convoy routes, however, enabled the next urgent problem to be tackled—to eliminate, or at any rate reduce, the threat from the German surface ships in the far north. This was no simple matter, for Altenfiord was about 900 miles from the nearest air bases in Britain, and neither heavy bombers nor torpedo-bombers could at that time strike at such a range and return to their home bases; the Home Fleet had no modern carriers, and even had such ships been transferred to Admiral Fraser it was doubtful whether the risk of taking them within 200 miles of the enemy coast to launch their torpedo striking forces could have been justified. Moreover the strike aircraft and their escort of Fleet Air Arm fighters would have been outclassed by the high-performance shore-based enemy fighters which would almost certainly be encountered over the targets. The alternative of operating torpedo-bombers from bases in north Russia had been tried in the summer of 1942, and the attempt had proved expensive.[1] Nor could conventional submarines emulate the exploits of those which had penetrated such powerfully defended waters as the Dardanelles and Baltic harbours in the 1914–18 war; for anti-submarine defences and devices had become vastly more effective. It was therefore plain that if we were to reduce the threat from the *Tirpitz* and her consorts, some more original form of attack must be devised. The problem was, in its essentials, nothing new to the Royal Navy. Many times in history has a need arisen to strike at enemy warship squadrons or merchant ships ensconced within strongly defended harbours; and one frequently used method had been to force the harbours, and then send in fireships to wreak havoc among the enemy vessels. The midget submarine, or X-craft, whose development was therefore put in hand, can reasonably be regarded as the descendant of the Elizabethan fireship. They were fifty-one feet long and weighed about thirty-five tons; they could make six-and-a-half knots on the surface, could dive to 300 feet, and propel themselves at five knots while submerged. Their operational range was limited by the endurance of their crews, which consisted of three officers and one engine-room artificer, all of whom were volunteers. After special training we believed that the crew might be able to live ten or even fourteen days in their craft, and cover 1,500 miles at four knots. Their only weapons consisted of two detachable charges, each containing two tons of explosive, which could be dropped on the sea-bed under the target, and were then fired by clockwork time fuses. The prototype of this class had completed trials in 1942, and an order was then placed by the Admiralty to build six of them.[2] On the

---

[1] See Vol. II, pp. 278–279.
[2] These six midget submarines were given numbers X5 to X10.

17th of April 1943 the 12th Submarine Flotilla (Captain W. E. Banks) was formed to train midget crews, and develop their weapons and equipment; and the first six midgets and a depot ship were attached to that flotilla. Throughout the summer the crews trained hard in Loch Cairnbawn in western Scotland, and made themselves expert at penetrating anti-submarine booms, nets and other defences.[1] The best method of transporting the X-craft to distant waters was investigated while training was in progress, and it was finally decided that each should be towed by a parent 'conventional' submarine.

Meanwhile the staff of the Rear-Admiral, Submarines (Rear-Admiral C. B. Barry), was working out detailed plans for the penetration of any of the Norwegian harbours where the enemy ships might be found. Last-minute photographic air reconnaissance took an important place in the plan, and at the end of August a special unit was sent by destroyer to north Russia for the purpose. Three Spitfires fitted for photography followed to Vaenga, near Murmansk, early in September; and arrangements were also made for Catalinas to fly the photographs back to England. Taking account of the hours of darkness needed, and the state of the moon and tide, it was decided that 'D-Day'—that on which the X-craft would be slipped from their parent submarines—should be the 20th of September.

The plan provided for the parent submarines, with the X-craft in tow, passing through a point seventy-five miles west of the Shetlands, and then proceeding by separate routes, about twenty miles apart, to a position 150 miles from Altenfiord.[2] From there they would steer inshore and make their landfalls. The operational crews of the X-craft would meanwhile have taken over from the passage crews. On 'D-Day' the X-craft were to be slipped a few miles outside the German minefield, across which they would proceed on the surface during the following night. They were to submerge during daylight on the 21st, and arrive at dawn on the 22nd off the entrance to the fiords in which the German ships were lying. The parent submarines would stay on patrol during the attack, and the returning X-craft would rendezvous with them in one of several positions specially established for their recovery.

Between the 30th of August and 1st of September the submarines *Thrasher*, *Truculent*, *Stubborn*, *Syrtis*, *Sceptre* and *Seanymph*, all specially fitted for towing, arrived at Loch Cairnbawn. After carrying out final trials, adjustments and preparations, the six submarines sailed

---

[1] An account of the training of the crews of the X-craft and of the actual attack on the *Tirpitz* is contained in C. E. T. Warren and J. Benson, *Above us the Waves* (Harrap, 1953), Chapters XIV to XVII. The despatches of Rear-Admiral (Submarines) on the operation against the *Tirpitz*, dated 8th November 1943 and 26th July 1945, were published as the Supplement to the London Gazette No. 38204 of 10th February 1948 (H.M.S.O.).

[2] See Map 4.

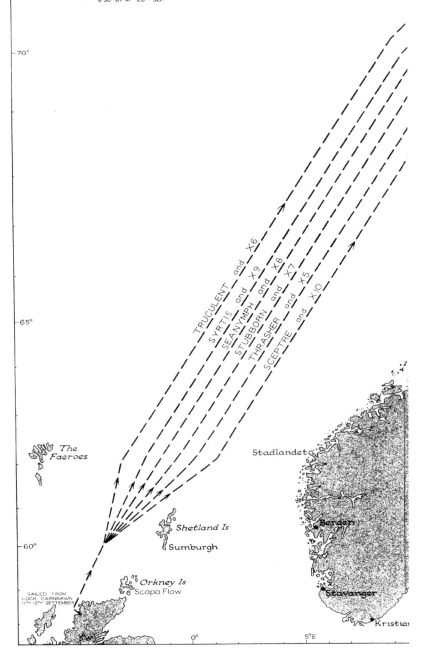

MAP 4

THE ATTACK ON THE TIRPITZ
BY MIDGET SUBMARINES
22nd September 1943

POSITIONS OF RELEASE OF
MIDGET SUBMARINES
6.30-8P.M 20TH SEP.   O

5 E°

—70°

—65°

TRUCULENT and X6
SYRTIS and X9
SEANYMPH and X8
STUBBORN and X7
THRASHER and X5
SCEPTRE and X10

The
Faeroes

Stadlandet

Shetland Is

Sumburgh

Bergen

—60°

SAILED FROM
LOCH CAIRNBAWN
11TH-12TH SEPTEMBER

Orkney Is
Scapa Flow

Stavanger

Kristia

0°   5°E

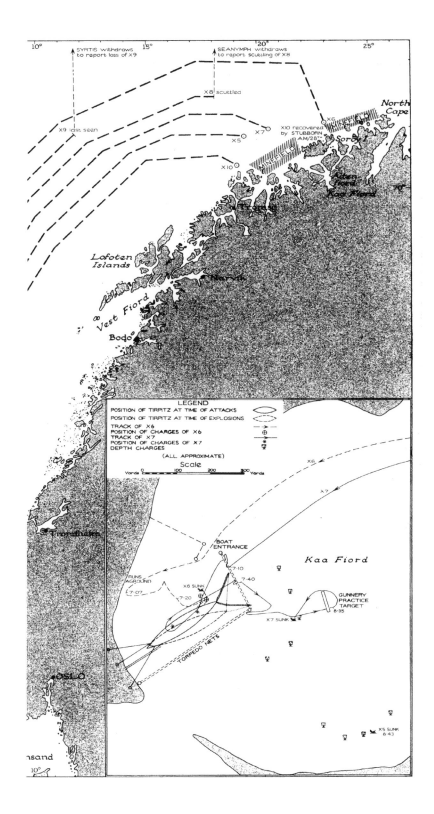

10° 15° 20° 25°

SYRTIS withdraws
to report loss of X9

SEANYMPH withdraws
to report scuttling of X8

North
Cape

X8 scuttled

X9 last seen

X6

X10 recovered
by STUBBORN
AM/28ᵗʰ

X7

Soroy I.

X5

Altan
Fiord
Kaa Fiord

X10

Lofoten
Islands

Narvik

Vest Fiord

Bodø

Trondheim

LEGEND
POSITION OF TIRPITZ AT TIME OF ATTACKS
POSITION OF TIRPITZ AT TIME OF EXPLOSIONS
TRACK OF X6
POSITION OF CHARGES OF X6
TRACK OF X7
POSITION OF CHARGES OF X7
DEPTH CHARGES
(ALL APPROXIMATE)

Scale
Yards 0   100   200   300 Yards

X6

X7

BOAT
ENTRANCE

Kaa Fiord

7·10

RUNS
AGROUND
7·07

7·40

X6 SUNK

7·20

GUNNERY
PRACTICE
TARGET
8·35

X7 SUNK

OSLO

TORPEDO NETS

X5 SUNK
8·43

nsand

10°

north, each with a midget in tow, between 4 p.m. on the 11th and 1 p.m. on the 12th. They did not yet know which base was to be attacked, but the most likely one was Altenfiord. From the 11th to the 14th the weather stayed fine and calm, and all went well. On the latter date the Spitfire's photographs reached Britain, and Admiral Barry made the pre-arranged signal ordering that X5, X6 and X7 should attack the *Tirpitz*, X9 and X10 the *Scharnhorst*, both of which were in Kaa fiord, while X8 attended to the *Lützow* in nearby Langefiord, another narrow inlet running into Altenfiord.

In the early hours of the 15th the tow between the *Seanymph* and X8 parted, and the two lost touch with each other. That afternoon X7 broke adrift from the *Stubborn*, which was on the adjacent route; and, while passing the auxiliary tow, they were joined by the vagrant X8. The three boats remained in company while endeavours were made to find the *Seanymph*. Unhappily X8 received the course to steer during the night wrongly, and she lost touch; but she was none the less found again by her own parent submarine, and by 8 p.m. on the 16th was once more in tow and heading north. Meanwhile disaster had overtaken X9, which was in tow by the *Syrtis*. She dived in the early hours of the 16th, and was never seen again. When the tow was hauled in it was found to have parted; and after vainly searching for her charge the *Syrtis* went further north, to a position whence it was permissible for her to report by wireless what had happened.

The *Thrasher* and *Truculent*, with X5 and X6, made their landfalls correctly on the 17th, but X8 unfortunately encountered further troubles. Owing to air escapes she could not maintain trim, and finally she had to jettison her charges and scuttle the craft. The *Seanymph* picked up her crew; but the assault force was thus reduced to four X-craft.

By the early hours of the 20th of September the operational crews had successfully transferred to X5, X6, X7 and X10; but early that morning the *Stubborn* and X7 had the alarming experience of getting caught up with a moored mine which impaled itself on the bows of the X-craft. It was finally cleared by 'the deft footwork' of her Captain. In the afternoon the weather improved, accurate fixes were obtained, and the stage was set for the attack. Between 6.30 and 8 p.m. that evening X5 (Lieutenant H. Henty-Creer, R.N.V.R.), X6 (Lieutenant D. Cameron, R.N.R.), X7 (Lieutenant B. C. G. Place) and X10 (Lieutenant K. R. Hudspeth, R.A.N.V.R.) slipped from their parent submarines and headed inshore towards Soröy Sound. Their crews were 'in great spirits and full of confidence'. The story of their subsequent adventures has been pieced together from the recollections of the survivors of X6 and X7 after their release from internment at the end of the war, and from the enemy's records.

There were no survivors from X5. She was last seen by X7 late on the 20th, and was probably destroyed by the enemy two days later. X.10 underwent a series of misadventures; but as the *Scharnhorst* had left her normal berth on the 21st in order to carry out exercises further down the fiord, she could not in any case have found her target.

X5, X6 and X7, all of whom were detailed to attack the *Tirpitz*, crossed the minefields safely during the night of the 20th-21st and the two latter reached their waiting positions on the evening of the 21st. The night was spent charging batteries and remedying defects whose development promised to add further danger to an already desperate venture. Between 1 and 2 a.m. on the morning of the 22nd both set course for the heavily defended Kaa fiord anchorage, with X7 leading. Lieutenant Place penetrated the anti-submarine boom at the entrance, but was then forced to dive by an enemy motor launch. He next became entangled in an unoccupied section of anti-torpedo nets, and took some two hours to get clear. Lieutenant Cameron in X6 was meanwhile having serious trouble with his periscope, and finally had to raise and lower it by hand, the motor having burnt out. None the less at 7 a.m. he had got through the entrance to the *Tirpitz's* net defences, and was within striking distance of his target. Five minutes behind him came Lieutenant Place's X7. So far nothing had aroused the enemy's suspicions. Then, at 7.7 a.m. a 'long black submarine-like object' was sighted from the *Tirpitz*. It was actually X6, which had inadvertently broken surface after running aground.[1] Things now began to happen very fast. Cameron's craft was blind, for his periscope was completely out of action, and his compass had failed. None the less he managed to grope his way close to the battleship, surfaced under grenade and small-arms fire, released his charges and scuttled his vessel. The whole crew was picked up by motorboat and taken on board the *Tirpitz*. The enemy ship's log and accounts of the next minutes as given by members of her crew who were captured when the *Scharnhorst* was sunk three months later, suggest that considerable alarm and confusion had set in on board the battleship. Not for a quarter of an hour after the sighting of X6 were A-A guns' crews closed up and watertight doors closed. Nor were the enemy's apprehensions reduced when, at 7.40, another object (actually X7) was sighted. This caused the Germans to cancel their intention to proceed to sea, close the gate in the nets, and shift the ship on her cable as far as possible from the position where X6 had sunk.

Meanwhile Lieutenant Place had also carried out his attack. As he approached he became entangled in the nets under which he was

---

[1] See Map 4.

trying to pass, and finally broke surface—much to his surprise only thirty yards from the *Tirpitz*. He promptly dived again, struck the battleship's side, passed right under her and released one of his charges. He then worked his way further aft, where he released the other charge. Place next tried to get out through the nets, but again got entangled. In spite of his compass having failed, and his high-pressure air running low, he got clear of the first nets—only to run into others. He was still held in these latter when, at 8.12, a violent explosion took place. It caused such damage to his craft that she could no longer be controlled. Constantly breaking surface, and under heavy fire, X7 finally ran alongside a gunnery practice target, on to which Place himself transferred safely. Unfortunately the X-craft then sank. The third officer, Sub-Lieutenant Aitken, R.N.V.R., got to the surface by using his Davis Escape Apparatus, but the other two members of the crew lost their lives.

On board the *Tirpitz* the explosion caused 'the whole great ship to heave several feet out of the water'. Lights went out, doors jammed and loose gear fell about everywhere; but the most serious damage was to the main turbines, all three sets of which were put out of action. The ship was thus completely immobilised, and the German Naval Staff later reported that April 1944 was the earliest date by which she could be made fit for service again.

It seems probable that all the four charges placed by X6 and X7 detonated, but that by moving herself on her cables the *Tirpitz* escaped the worst consequences of all except X7's second charge.[1] As the battleship finally brought up with that charge right under her engine rooms, the most serious damage can confidently be attributed to it.

As to the other two X-craft, little is known of the fate of X5 (Lieutenant Henty-Creer). The Germans claimed to have sunk one midget by gunfire at 8.43 a.m. outside the nets, and it may well have been her. X10 (Lieutenant Hudspeth) met such misfortunes on her way in that she was left without compass or periscope. She approached Kaa fiord, and lay on the bottom all day on the 22nd, trying to remedy her defects. The explosion of her colleagues' charges was heard; and knowing that in his boat's present condition he had no hope of getting in his attack, Hudspeth finally abandoned the operation and put out to sea again. Not until the small hours of the 28th did he find one of the parent submarines, the *Stubborn*. After a very long and difficult passage to within 400 miles of the Shetlands, with many parted towing wires, the last surviving X-craft finally had to be scuttled when a gale threatened on the 3rd of October. The six parent submarines all returned safely to base, and so ended a most

---

[1] See Map 4.

gallant penetration into the enemy's heavily-defended fleet anchorage. If the damage done to the *Tirpitz* was less than had been hoped, she was soon known to be incapable of steaming, and that knowledge brought important strategic consequences. The exploit of the X-craft was justly described by Admiral Barry as 'a daring attack which will surely go down to history as one of the most courageous acts of all time'. Lieutenants Cameron and Place were both awarded the Victoria Cross for their share in the operation.

As soon as the results of the midget submarine attack were known the strategic situation was reviewed in London and in the Home Fleet. In Admiral Fraser's view it had been 'considerably altered . . . allowing the Home Fleet to change from a waiting to a more offensive rôle by attacking shipping off the Norwegian coast and restarting the convoys to Russia. But while the *Scharnhorst* 'remained at large' substantial forces would still have to be allocated to each operation, and it would therefore only be possible to undertake one of his two main purposes at a time. Preparations were therefore immediately put in hand to run a new series of convoys to Russia, and the decision to do so certainly underlines the far-reaching influence exerted by the single powerful enemy battleship throughout the twenty-one months which had passed since she first arrived in Norway.[1] With our present knowledge of the highly restrictive conditions placed by Hitler on her employment, and of the enemy's reluctance to expose her to carrier-borne aircraft or destroyer torpedo attack, it may seem that her potentialities were over-estimated; but we should remember that, had she and her consorts ever been used with skill and determination, they could easily have overwhelmed the escorts and covering cruisers during the latter part of the convoys' long, outflanked journeys to Murmansk or Archangel.

Before the end of September the threat from the German surface ships was further reduced by the return of the *Lützow* to the Baltic to refit. Between the 21st and 25th several intelligence reports had suggested to the Admiralty that a southward movement by a heavy ship was imminent. We knew that enemy fighters had been sent to Bodo, while the stationing of others near Bergen indicated that the movement would be to the Baltic, and not merely to Trondheim; a tanker was also known to have arrived at Altenfiord from Kiel. The *Lützow* actually left Altenfiord on the 23rd of September. From the 24th to the 26th, when she sailed south again, bound for Gdynia, she was at anchor near Narvik.

Shortly after noon on the 26th the Admiralty promulgated an intelligence report, not graded as very reliable, that at 8 a.m. that

---

[1] See Vol. II, p. 116.

morning the pocket-battleship had been sighted off the entrance to Vestfiord, steering south. Though the agent's report was in fact accurate, nearly twenty-four hours elapsed before it was confirmed by air reconnaissance. The possibility of attacking the ship was, however, at once investigated; but it was clear that no Coastal Command striking force could reach her until the 27th. Admiral Fraser considered the possibility of sending the U.S.S. *Ranger* to a position whence she could launch her aircraft at the pocket-battleship off Stadlandet; but, assuming the intelligence report to be correct, it was plainly impossible for the carrier to reach such a position in time. As nothing could be done on that day, plans for the 27th were discussed between the Commander-in-Chief, Home Fleet, and No. 18 Group of Coastal Command. Owing to a chain of unfortunate circumstances, the strength available to the latter was very small. To use the slow and obsolete Hampden torpedo-bombers of Nos. 455 and 489 Squadrons was considered unjustifiable, and the Strike Wing[1] stationed at North Coates in Lincolnshire had been temporarily weakened by losses and damage suffered in an operation off the Dutch coast two days earlier. Another squadron (No. 144) was out of action while re-equipping with torpedo-Beaufighters ('Torbeaus'); and, lastly, very few modern long-range fighters were available in No. 18 Group.

By a lucky chance No. 832 Fleet Air Arm Squadron, equipped with Tarpon torpedo-bombers, had just disembarked from the *Victorious*, which had recently returned from the Pacific and was about to refit.[2] They landed at Hatston in the Orkneys on the 26th of September, and Admiral Fraser had them rapidly equipped with torpedoes. Early next day they were transferred to the Coastal Command station at Sumburgh in the Shetlands, where they were to be joined by the available Beaufighters. The whole operation was to be conducted by Air Vice-Marshal Ellwood, commanding No. 18 Group. At 6.24 a.m. that morning a reconnaissance aircraft sighted the *Lützow*, and Admiral Fraser arranged with his colleagues of Coastal Command to send out the striking force; but only six Beaufighters could be collected from various sources to escort the torpedo-bombers. No. 18 Group Headquarters warned the Admiral that, in their view, this was inadequate, and that in any case the Beaufighters would not provide any protection against single-engined fighters, but could only smother the enemy ship's anti-aircraft gunfire. Another handicap was that the naval and R.A.F.

---

[1] See Vol. II, pp. 259 and 388–390, regarding the composition and functions of the Strike Wings of Coastal Command.

[2] The Tarpon was the original name given to the American Avenger torpedo-bomber. The *Victorious* had been equipped with them for service in the Pacific. See Vol. II, pp. 415–416.

aircrews had never worked together, and time was too short to allow a proper tactical plan to be worked out. None the less Admiral Fraser held that, provided there was reasonable cloud cover over the target, the opportunity justified acceptance of the risks. Next it became known that even the anticipated total of six Beaufighters would not be available. It had been necessary to send two of them on the early morning reconnaissance, and Air Vice-Marshal Ellwood insisted that fresh crews should take over before the same aircraft made new sorties. The relief crews which were to have been flown to Sumburgh were, however, delayed. When the reconnaissance aircraft reported only six- to eight-tenths cloud over the target, No. 18 Group declared the weather conditions to be unsuitable for the attack. Admiral Fraser however disagreed; and he pressed his view so strongly that the striking force was ordered to take off at 10.10 a.m. Meanwhile No. 18 Group had consulted Coastal Command Headquarters, and the Commander-in-Chief held that the air escort was inadequate, the prospects of success were poor, and heavy losses were likely to be suffered. Air Vice-Marshal Ellwood thereupon cancelled the attack. On hearing this decision the Commander-in-Chief, Home Fleet, pointed out that the naval aircrews were highly trained, and that they would have been sent from a carrier without even such escort as the few Beaufighters could provide. Coastal Command thereupon withdrew their ban, and No. 18 Group gave orders for the striking force to take off at 10.40. Admiral Fraser and Air Vice-Marshal Ellwood had agreed that there was a good chance of catching the *Lützow* off Stadlandet until 3 p.m. At 12.16 p.m. the Tarpons were airborne; but the Beaufighter escort had suffered a further reduction of strength, and only three of them actually went with the torpedo-bombers. The striking force made its landfall off Norway at 1.42, and then searched to the north. It appears that the *Lützow* was actually about forty miles to the south at the time. Finding nothing, and lacking any considerable cloud cover, the torpedo-bombers returned to base.

Further reconnaissance flights were made during the afternoon and at 5.40 p.m. a Mosquito re-sighted the enemy squadron, and photographed it. Meanwhile a new striking force, with an escort of Wildcat fighters from the U.S.S. *Ranger*, was being arranged for the 28th. Actually the *Lützow* left the shelter of 'the Leads' at 10 p.m. on the 27th, reached Kristiansand, where she was met by a fighter escort, early next morning, and then passed by the Sound into the Baltic. On the 1st of October, after repeated sweeping of the channel against our airlaid mines, she arrived safely at Gdynia.

It was natural that the escape of this important ship without being attacked, let alone damaged, should have been the subject of close investigation by the Admiralty and Air Ministry. Issues of high policy governing the control and operation of forces of both services, as well as their tactical training, were involved. In November the joint committee rendered its report. The main conclusions were that Coastal Command's strike strength, which successive Commanders-in-Chief had long regarded as quite inadequate[1], should be built up to three Strike Wings, each composed of twenty torpedo-bombers and a like number of twin-engined fighters; and that the question of the single-engined fighter protection which would normally be necessary in operations such as the recent abortive attempt on the *Lützow* should be discussed with Fighter Command. The Naval Staff stressed the need for air reconnaissance to be flown as far to the north as possible during the period when an important enemy movement was anticipated, and the Air Staff sought earlier warning of special requirements involving a change of priorities for Coastal Command. The desirability of a tactical doctrine common to both services was accepted, and the recommendations of a special committee appointed to consider that matter were adopted. In general the discussions showed an earnest desire on both sides to eliminate the causes of the recent failure. They did not cover, and were not intended to cover, any investigation of responsibility such as took place after the escape of the *Scharnhorst* and *Gneisenau* up-Channel in February 1942.[2] In consequence no evidence is available on which the historian might fairly record an opinion. None the less it may well puzzle posterity how it came to pass that, after almost exactly four years of war, a German pocket-battleship was still able to steam from Vestfiord to the Baltic in complete immunity. In terms of strategy her removal from north Norway at least had the advantage of reducing the threat to the Arctic convoys; but once again the enemy may be credited with a tactical success.[3]

It could not, of course, then have been forecast that the *Lützow's* arrival in her home waters in order to refit would actually mark the end of her part in the war in the open seas. In 1944 she returned to active service, but was only used in the Baltic to support the seaward flank of the German armies; and on the 16th of April 1945 she was completely wrecked by heavy bombs dropped in air attacks on Swinemunde.

Towards the end of November 1943 the American squadron which had been attached to the Home Fleet (the *Ranger*, *Augusta*, *Tuscaloosa* and five destroyers[4]) sailed from Iceland for the United States. Their presence in the eastern Atlantic had been most welcome during the period when the German squadron in north Norway had

---

[1] See Vol. I, pp. 338, 503 and 508–509.

[2] See Vol. II, pp. 159–161.

[3] Compare Vol. II, p. 159.

[4] See p. 58.

been at the peak of its strength, while the Home Fleet, owing mainly to detachments sent to the Mediterranean for the invasion of Sicily, had been exceptionally weak. But Admiral Fraser's fleet had now recovered something like its normal strength, as several important ships had returned to him from refitting or repairing damage; and this, combined with the damage to the *Tirpitz* and the return home of the *Lützow*, eliminated the need to keep United States ships in British waters.

Among the reinforcements to reach the Home Fleet at this time was the French battleship *Richelieu*, which arrived at Scapa from Oran on the 20th of November. She had been at Dakar, and had passed into Allied hands at the time of the North African landings in November 1942[1], after which she was refitted in America. Admiral Sir John Cunningham reported home from the Mediterranean that she was 'a very remarkable ship and a potentially fine fighting unit', and that her company was in good spirit; all of which made happy reading to those British officers who had never ceased to regret that, after she had made a gallant escape from France in June 1940[2], cruel circumstances had forced British warships to attack her in Dakar later in that same year.[3] Her arrival in the Royal Navy's main base was a sign that the two services had once more joined hands in full accord against the common enemy.

Throughout the summer months of 1943 Coastal Command kept a constant watch on the French Atlantic ports, whence blockade-runners to the Far East always sailed. By the beginning of September seven ships were known to be ready or preparing to leave. Our intelligence had also reported that five ships with a carrying capacity of some 38,000 tons were available to bring cargoes home from the east, and by mid-October three of these were known to be loaded and ready in Saigon. Taken together all this information strongly suggested that a renewal of blockade-running, of which there had been none except by a trickle of submarines since the previous April[4], was imminent. Early in November the Admiralty issued a warning to that effect. Coastal Command prepared powerful forces of Halifaxes and Liberators to search for and attack the ships as they approached or left the Bay of Biscay, and surface forces were organised to work under the orders of the Commander-in-Chief, Plymouth (Admiral Sir Ralph Leatham), in the same waters.

The first sign of activity came on the 26th of November when the Italian ship *Pietro Orseolo*, which was known to be loaded for the Far East, moved from Bordeaux to an anchorage near Concarneau on the

---

[1] See Vol. II, pp. 314 and 331.

[2] See Vol. I, pp. 233–234 and 240.

[3] Ibid. pp. 245 and 317–320.

[4] See Vol. II, pp. 408–411 and Appendix N.

south coast of Brittany. The first air attack, made on the 1st of December, failed; but by the 18th Coastal Command had a powerful force of 'Torbeaus'[1] and cannon-fitted Beaufighters ready. They attacked under cover of an escort of Typhoons, and damaged the *Orseolo* so badly that she foundered off Lorient soon afterwards. Five days after this attack aircraft from the American escort carrier *Card* sighted a suspicious ship, which was actually the inward-bound *Osorno*, some 500 miles south-west of Ushant. German surface warships were sighted soon afterwards steaming to the west; but the carrier aircraft could not keep the blockade-runner under observation. Coastal Command sent out searches and striking forces, and on the 24th and 25th of December there was heavy air fighting around the ship and her escort; but no damage was done. She reached the Gironde safely, but struck a wreck at the entrance and had to be beached. On the night of the 29th–30th of December twelve Stirlings of Bomber Command carried out a special minelaying mission with the object of impeding the discharge of her cargo of raw rubber; but it achieved no success, and the greater part of the cargo was safely removed by the enemy.

As we believed another blockade-runner besides the *Osorno* to be in the offing the air searches were continued, and early on the 27th of December a Sunderland sighted the *Alsterufer*. She shadowed successfully, but failed with her attack. Liberators had meanwhile been sent out, and aircraft H of 311 (Czech) Squadron, commanded by Pilot Officer O. Dolezal, made a most determined low-level attack with rockets and bombs. The ship was set on fire and abandoned. Many of her crew were later picked up by the 6th Escort Group. Knowing that German destroyers were on the way to meet and bring in the blockade-runner, Admiral Leatham had organised cruisers to intercept them. He now directed the *Glasgow* (Captain C. P. Clarke) and *Enterprise* (Captain H. T. W. Grant, R.C.N.) to a position in which they might catch the enemy at dawn on the 28th of December.

At 9.20 that morning an American Liberator sighted two groups, consisting of four and six enemy destroyers, steering west. The *Glasgow* and *Enterprise* were some distance to the south at the time, and increased speed to twenty-eight knots to close. By 11 a.m. our aircraft reported that the two groups of destroyers had joined up, and had reversed course to the east. Early in the afternoon Coastal Command sent out fighters to protect the cruisers, and a score of strike aircraft to attack the enemy; but the surface forces got their blows in first. At 1.35 p.m., in rough weather, they sighted the enemy, and opened fire at 18,000 yards. Some rather half-hearted glider-bomb attacks did no harm to our ships, nor did the torpedoes fired by the

---

[1] These were Beaufighters converted to carry a torpedo. See Vol. II, pp. 84, 165 and 259.

German destroyers. As the cruisers pressed in at thirty knots to try and close the range the enemy force divided once again. Four destroyers turned north-west, while the other six made off to the south under cover of smoke. The cruisers pursued the former group, and by 4 p.m. had sunk the large destroyer Z.27 (2,688 tons) and also the two fleet torpedo-boats T.25 and T.26 of 1,318 tons. As the *Glasgow* was now running low of ammunition and the *Enterprise* had developed defects, they were unable to pursue the group fleeing to the south. More air attacks on our ships followed, but did no damage. By the evening of the 29th they were safely back at Plymouth after what Admiral Leatham called 'an excellent day's work'.

The next three homeward-bound blockade-runners (the *Weserland*, *Burgenland* and *Rio Grande*) were all caught by American warships in the south Atlantic between the 3rd and 5th of January 1944, and thus ended the last enemy attempt to bring home cargoes from the Far East. Out of the 33,095 tons which the five ships had loaded, only 6,890 tons were landed in France. At Hitler's conference on the 18th Dönitz proposed to cancel the departure of all the outward-bound ships. Hitler approved, and the eight ships made ready for the purpose were finally all scuttled in ports of western France in August 1944.

The enemy's three-year blockade-running campaign can conveniently be summarised here. In all it cost him twenty ships, of which fifteen were sunk or captured by surface ships, or scuttled themselves when intercepted by them.[1] Two were sunk by R.A.F. aircraft, two by the enemy's own submarines, while one was destroyed by explosion in harbour. Out of twenty-one ships which left France for the Far East with 69,300 tons of cargo, fifteen with 57,000 arrived safely. Of thirty-five which started out from the east with 257,770 tons of cargo only sixteen with 111,490 tons arrived. By far the greatest proportion of successful journeys took place between January 1941 and May 1942[2], before our counter-measures were properly organised. Once we held a firm grip on the central and south Atlantic, with air bases on the African and South American coasts, in the Azores and on Ascension Island, the prospects of successful evasion declined greatly. But it was clearly shown how only by the use of aircraft and surface ships in close conjunction was it possible to achieve a high proportion of successful interceptions. In addition to the surface blockade-runners the enemy employed about a score of German and nine Italian submarines on such journeys; and the cargoes they carried, though small in tonnage, were very valuable to the German armament industry. A special class of U-boat (Type XX) capable of embarking 750 tons of rubber, tin and

[1] This figure includes the *Elbe*, sunk by aircraft from the carrier *Eagle*. (See Vol. II, p. 183.)

[2] See Vol. II, pp. 182–184 and Appendix N.

concentrates of minerals, such as wolfram and molybdenum, was designed; but none ever reached the oceans. In fact, as our control of the seas in all theatres tightened, even blockade-running by submarine became unprofitable.

To return to the Arctic convoys, the Admiralty had undertaken to send forty ships a month to north Russia; but Admiral Fraser shared his predecessor's opinion that this was far too many to include in a single convoy[1], particularly during the winter months when the constant gales were all too likely to scatter the merchantmen far and wide, and so leave them easy prey to the U-boats and bombers. The Admiralty therefore decided to run the new convoys in two approximately equal sections, about a week apart. Each section was to be taken right through by a powerful escort, while cruisers covered their progress during the most dangerous part of the journey south of Bear Island, and heavy ships afforded more distant cover from a position some 200 miles to the south-west of that island. The re-starting of these hazardous and exacting convoy operations was not made easier by what Admiral Fraser described as 'the persistently intransigent attitude of the Russians towards granting the necessary visas for [sending] additional British service personnel to north Russia, and ameliorating the conditions of those already there'. Mr Churchill, remembering no doubt earlier Russian accusations of bad faith when, in January 1943, we had sent rather fewer ships than we had hoped[2], now made it plain to Stalin that our present intentions constituted 'no contract or bargain, but rather a declaration of our solemn and earnest resolve'.[3]

The Germans now had two U-boat flotillas, each of about a dozen boats, based at Bergen and Trondheim, where they had constructed bomb-proof shelters for them. Two repair ships were allocated for maintenance purposes, thus making the flotillas comparatively self-supporting. The U-boats employed in the north were generally Type VIIC (surface displacement 769 tons[4]), which could cruise for six to nine weeks. Co-operation with the Luftwaffe squadrons based in Norway was satisfactory, but after the end of 1943 the diversion of aircraft to other theatres greatly reduced its effectiveness. Apart from air reconnaissance the Germans gained a good deal of intelligence regarding our convoy movements from our wireless traffic, and U-boats often carried specially trained men to listen to and interpret such messages. When they knew that an eastbound convoy was at sea their usual strategy was first to establish a patrol line, about 200 miles

---

[1] See Vol. II, pp. 135–136.

[2] Ibid. pp. 397–398.

[3] See *Churchill*, Vol. V, pp. 234–235, regarding the Prime Minister's representations to Stalin at this time.

[4] See Vol. II, Appendix K, for particulars of these U-boats.

long, to the east of Jan Mayen Island. A second concentration, in the Bear Island passage, was ordered after the convoy had passed the first patrol line; and finally they would station a semi-circle of U-boats off the entrance to Kola Inlet. The Germans had a poor opinion of Russian anti-submarine tactics and procedure, and rarely suffered much inconvenience, let alone losses, from their air or surface ship patrols; but Russian motor torpedo-boats and submarines did better against the shipping which carried important German supplies to Petsamo. U-boats sometimes also worked in the Kara Sea against Russian traffic to the Pacific by the Behring Strait, and during the summer of 1943 the enemy laid no less than twenty-five minefields in the shallow waters north of Murmansk and in the Kara Sea. It was these minefields which forced us to maintain a flotilla of sweepers in the north, and to sweep all convoys in and out of the approaches to Kola Inlet. Though the mines never caused serious losses they did add to the strain and difficulty of running the Arctic convoys.

The first convoy of the new series (RA.54A) consisted of thirteen empty ships, which had been languishing in Archangel since the previous spring. They sailed on the 1st of November in charge of an escort specially sent out from Iceland; and, shielded for much of the time by thick fog, they all arrived safely in British ports. The first outward convoy, JW.54A of eighteen loaded merchantmen, left Loch Ewe on the 15th of November, followed a week later by the second section (JW.54B of fourteen ships). The usual close escort of about a dozen flotilla vessels accompanied both sections, the cruisers *Kent*, *Jamaica* and *Bermuda* under Rear-Admiral A. F. E. Palliser provided close cover, while Vice-Admiral Sir Henry Moore in the battleship *Anson* with one cruiser formed the more distant covering force. Neither convoy suffered any loss or damage, and thus the decision to restart this traffic appeared to have been amply justified.

In December the next group of convoys, this time run in two sections in both directions, started out. JW.55A sailed from Loch Ewe on the 12th, escorted and covered in the same manner as the preceding convoys, and like them, arrived unmolested. It was, how-ever, reported by enemy aircraft, and this suggested to Admiral Fraser that an attempt to retaliate, probably with surface ships, was likely in the near future. He accordingly extended the normal battleship cover by going right through to Kola Inlet himself in the *Duke of York*—the first time that a Home Fleet capital ship had appeared in those waters. While there from the 16th to 18th of December Admiral Fraser met the Russian Commander-in-Chief, Admiral Golovko, and made himself fully informed regarding local conditions. He then returned to Iceland in his flagship.

The enemy had in fact meanwhile been considering the possibility of renewing attacks on the Arctic convoys with his surface ships.

Early in 1943 Dönitz had managed to persuade Hitler to allow him authority to decide whether and when the remaining big ships should be committed to action in the north. German records make it plain that, even though the views of other authorities and individuals may have influenced Dönitz, responsibility for the orders now to be discussed rested with him and the German Naval Staff, and not, as has since been claimed by German writers, with Hitler or the German Supreme Command (O.K.W.).[1] As early as the 24th of March the German Naval Staff had issued a new directive describing the *Scharnhorst* as 'a significant reinforcement for attacking convoys running to north Russia'. 'This task', it continued, was 'to be given priority' over the 'secondary consideration of the defence of Norway'. The record of the discussions between Dönitz, the Flag Officer Group North (Admiral Schniewind) and the commander of the Northern Task Force (Admiral Kummetz) shows that all three senior officers were determined that, if the ships were sent to sea, they should not hesitate to engage in combat.[2] The causes of the timidity which had frustrated earlier sorties appeared to be understood.[3] Throughout the summer of 1943, when the Arctic convoys were stopped—a fact which the enemy attributed, with some reason, to the presence of his powerful squadron in the north—the future employment of his forces was not again discussed. But after the enemy discovered that two convoys (JW.54A and RA.54A) had got through unmolested in November, their Naval Staff issued 'a directive for operations of fleet forces in the winter of 1943–44'. In the north, stated those orders, 'the functions of the ships remain unaltered . . . Against this traffic [i.e. convoys to Russia] both the Northern Task Force and the U-boats are to be employed.' In spite of the categorical nature of this statement the Naval Staff seems to have entertained doubts regarding the wisdom of committing the battle cruiser; for the orders of the 20th of November continued with the cautious statement that 'although operations must be compatible with our small strength, the use of the *Scharnhorst* during the winter is to be considered'. Admiral Kummetz seems to have inferred from this that nothing more ambitious than a foray by destroyers would be attempted, at any rate until the *Tirpitz* had completed her repairs in March 1944. He certainly knew, from first-hand experience in the abortive attack on convoy JW.51B on the 31st of December

---

[1] Compare for example Fritz Otto Busch, *The Drama of the Scharnhorst* (English translation, Robert Hale, 1956), pp. 42–46.

[2] At the meeting with Schniewind on 16th April Dönitz said 'In all circumstances we are ready to fight . . .' and his colleague replied 'All commanding officers of the Northern Task Force are in no doubt that the main purpose of their ships is to fight'.

[3] See Vol. II, pp. 291–299, regarding the actions of the *Lützow* and *Hipper* on 31st December 1942.

1942[1], that British radar was superior to his own; and he must have realised that this advantage might well prove decisive in the long nights of the Arctic winter. Furthermore he can have had few illusions regarding the danger of exposing heavy ships to the powerful torpedo armaments of our escorts. That he was allowed to proceed on 'prolonged leave' early in November seems to show that his superiors accepted the view that the early employment of the *Scharnhorst* was unlikely. His command devolved temporarily on Rear-Admiral Bey, who had been in charge of the destroyer group in the north.

On the 22nd of November Bey set out his own views on the situation. They corresponded generally with those of Admiral Kummetz—namely that nothing more than a destroyer raid against the convoys was practicable; but he ended his report on an optimistic and somewhat contradictory note. 'The chances of success' he wrote 'will depend largely on good luck . . . Experience in this war which, despite our weakness, has produced many favourable situations for us, justifies the hope that we have luck on our side.' This report may have influenced the Naval Staff to modify their view somewhat; for on the 2nd of December they stated, still cautiously, 'that it may be expedient to employ the *Scharnhorst*, despite the experiences of 31st December 1942'. Finally, on the 19th of December, Dönitz informed Hitler that the *Scharnhorst* and destroyers would attack the next Arctic convoy 'if a successful operation seems assured'. It seems strange that Admiral Kummetz was not recalled from leave at that time. In their report on the operation, after it was all over, the German Naval Staff laid a good deal of stress on the importance they had attributed to easing pressure on the eastern front by interrupting the stream of supplies being carried to the Russians by the Arctic route; and Dönitz himself mentioned this purpose in his final signal to Admiral Bey.[2] It therefore seems clear that the need to help the Army played a part in Dönitz's decision, even though the Supreme Command never put pressure on him to that end.

On the 20th of December JW.55B (nineteen ships) left Loch Ewe, and three days later RA.55A (twenty-two ships) sailed from Kola Inlet, each with an escort of ten destroyers and three or four smaller vessels. The double movement was covered by Vice-Admiral R. L. Burnett with the cruisers *Belfast*, *Sheffield* and *Norfolk*, while Admiral Fraser sailed from Iceland to provide the usual distant cover with the battleship *Duke of York*, the cruiser *Jamaica* and four destroyers.

---

[1] See Vol. II, pp. 291–299.

[2] Since the previous August the Russians had been on the offensive in the Smolensk, Kharkov and Kiev sectors of the eastern front, and in November they struck new blows west of Leningrad.

The east-bound convoy was sighted by enemy reconnaissance planes on the 22nd, but their report that it consisted of 'forty troop transports' with powerful warship escort misled them into expecting a raid on the Norwegian coast; and the U-boats were therefore ordered to concentrate off Vestfiord. Later the enemy realised that it was probably a normal Arctic convoy that had been sighted, cancelled those instructions, and sent eight U-boats to the Bear Island passage. On the morning of Christmas Eve JW.55B was continuously shadowed from the air, and Admiral Fraser, who had 'felt very strongly that the *Scharnhorst* would come out and endeavour to attack', ordered the convoy, which was then only 400 miles from Altenfiord and completely unsupported, to reverse course for three hours.[1] He also increased the speed of his own force to nineteen knots. As it was suggested elsewhere in this history that in certain other operations wireless silence may have been too rigidly maintained by British forces, with the result that widely dispersed units were unable to co-ordinate their movements to the best advantage[2], it is interesting to remark that Admiral Fraser used his wireless to pass the aforementioned order to the convoy, and acted similarly on several occasions during the operations now to be described. Though it can never be easy to strike the right balance between concealment of intentions and co-ordination of movements, it is certain that on the present occasion the benefits derived from breaking wireless silence far outweighed the disadvantages incurred by revealing the presence of our forces.

By Christmas morning it seemed clear that, whereas the west-bound convoy had not been detected and would soon be clear of danger, the constant shadowing of the east-bound ships indicated that it was against them that the enemy's effort would be made. Admiral Fraser accordingly signalled for four fleet destroyers to be detached from RA.55A to join JW.55B, and at the same time diverted the latter convoy further north to move it clear of the danger area south of Bear Island. This brought JW.55B's escort up to fourteen destroyers, which was enough to drive off the *Scharnhorst*, or perhaps to damage her sufficiently to enable the Commander-in-Chief to come to grips.

At 2 p.m. on Christmas Day the German Admiralty gave orders for the operation to proceed, and five hours later Admiral Bey with the *Scharnhorst* and five destroyers put to sea and headed north.[3] The 32,000-ton battle cruiser had nearly 2,000 men on board, including

---

[1] See Supplement to the London Gazette No. 38038 dated 5th August 1947, which contains Admiral Fraser's despatch on these operations, dated 28th January 1944 (H.M.S.O.).

[2] See Vol. I, pp. 399, 404–405 and 565–568.

[3] See Map 5.

The *Tirpitz* inside net defences in Kaa fiord (off Altenfiord) 1943.

(*Photograph Captain H. J. Reinicke*)

Air reconnaissance photograph of Kaa fiord after the midget submarine attack of
22nd September, 1943, showing the *Tirpitz* (left) with a repair ship alongside.

A British midget submarine or X-craft.

A British human torpedo or 'Chariot' under way.

forty naval cadets sent to her for training.[1] The eight U-boats waiting
to the south of Bear Island had been ordered to form a patrol line
further west, while the German Air Force, whose strength in Norway
was now too weak to undertake mass attacks such as those made
against earlier convoys[2], had been asked to provide the essential
reconnaissance.

Soon after the German squadron left harbour Dönitz's final instructions were received by wireless. Although they included a
definite order to attack the convoy, and emphasis was placed on
'exploiting the tactical situation skilfully and boldly', Admiral Bey
was also told to 'disengage if heavy units are encountered'. Thus, in
spite of all the good resolutions expressed earlier, the old tendency to
cramp a commander by giving detailed and in this instance somewhat contradictory orders, and the old tendency to try to achieve
success without accepting risks, re-asserted themselves in the German
camp.

At about 9 a.m. on Christmas Day U.601 reported JW.55B in
about 73½° North 12½° East, and thereafter the U-boat shadowed the
convoy, thus acting as substitute for the reconnaissance aircraft
which, because of the stormy weather, remained grounded. She
reported the composition of the escort force fairly correctly; but,
in spite of Admiral Fraser having already broken wireless silence,
the enemy received no indication that heavy ships were also in the
offing.

It soon became plain that in the heavy seas then running, the
German destroyers could not keep up with the battle cruiser; but
when Admiral Bey signalled to ask whether in these conditions he
should go on alone Dönitz decided, in spite of the apprehensions of
the shore authorities in Norway regarding the risks involved, that he
might do so. He left the final decision in Bey's hands.

During the night of the 25th–26th the British heavy squadron
steamed east, through a rising and unpleasant sea, at seventeen
knots. At 3.39 a.m. on the 26th the Admiralty signalled that the
Scharnhorst was probably at sea. Once again British intelligence had
worked fast and accurately. It is interesting to learn from the enemy's
records that, because the preceding convoys had got through unmolested, they expected us to be less alert on this occasion. In fact the
exact opposite was the case; for it was the immunity of the recent
convoys, combined with good intelligence, which had caused
Admiral Fraser to anticipate attack by surface ships, and dispose his
forces in readiness to meet it.

---

[1] See Vol. I, pp. 52, 58 and Appendix G regarding the true displacement of the
Scharnhorst, and her armaments.

[2] See for example Vol. II, p. 131, regarding the air attacks on PQ.16.

It will help the reader to follow what happened if the situation at 4 a.m. on the 26th of December is first described. In 72° North on that day 'nautical twilight' (i.e. when the sun was twelve degrees or less below the horizon) lasted from 8.27 a.m. to 3.34 p.m. During those seven hours there might be some slight glimmer of daylight, but the stormy weather made it certain that it would never be much. For the rest of the day virtually total darkness would prevail. The home-bound convoy (RA.55A) was about 220 miles west of Bear Island, and the enemy appeared to be unaware of its presence. In fact we now know that it was late on the 26th before the enemy received any

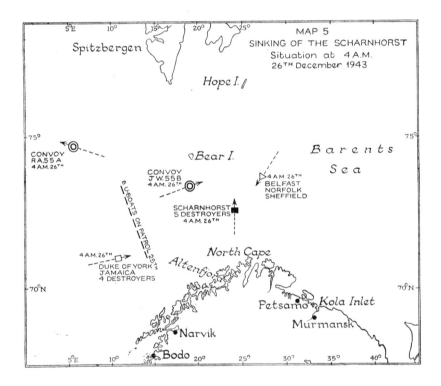

MAP 5
SINKING OF THE SCHARNHORST
Situation at 4 A.M.
26TH December 1943

inkling that there was a west-bound as well as an east-bound convoy at sea. RA.55A was scattered by a gale that day, but re-formed successfully, and all its ships arrived safely in Loch Ewe on New Year's Day 1944. At 4 a.m. on the 26th of December JW.55B was fifty miles south of Bear Island steering about ENE at eight knots. It was escorted by fourteen destroyers and three smaller vessels, all commanded by Captain J. A. McCoy in the *Onslow*. Admiral Burnett with his three cruisers was about 150 miles to the east of the convoy, steering south-west on a course which would very probably intercept the German squadron if it came north from Altenfiord.

About 210 miles to the south-west of the convoy was Admiral Fraser's heavy squadron, the battleship *Duke of York* (Captain Hon. G. H. E. Russell), the cruiser *Jamaica* (Captain J. Hughes-Hallett) and four screening destroyers. They were steering slightly north of east at twenty-four knots. The wind was blowing strongly from the south-west, and there was a heavy following sea, which made the handling of the destroyers very difficult. Though he still needed to make more distance to the east to be sure of cutting off the *Scharnhorst*, Admiral Fraser could see from his plot that the stage was well set. He decided that 'the safety of the convoy must be the primary object', which was a departure from the traditional view that in such circumstances the destruction of the enemy's main forces took precedence over any other purposes.[1] To further his tactical intention, at 4.01 a.m. the Commander-in-Chief ordered Admiral Burnett and Captain McCoy to report their positions, and at the same time gave them his own. Thus, at the price of again breaking wireless silence, he reduced or even eliminated what must always be a source of doubt and confusion in complicated operations. Each of our own forces now knew where the others were.[2] To make it more difficult for the enemy to find the convoy, at 6.28 a.m. the Commander-in-Chief ordered it to alter course further to the north, and told Admiral Burnett to close it in support.

At about 7.30 a.m. Admiral Bey spread his destroyers ahead to search to the south-west; but confusion in signalling resulted in the *Scharnhorst* losing touch with them soon afterwards, and the destroyers never rejoined the flagship. Nor did they play any significant part in the battle now pending.

At 8.15 Admiral Burnett hauled round to the north-west towards the convoy and increased speed to twenty-four knots. Twenty-five minutes later the cruiser flagship *Belfast* (Captain F. R. Parham) picked up the enemy by radar at 25,000 yards, bearing slightly north of west. At the time the *Scharnhorst* was only about thirty miles from the convoy.[3] As the two forces were on intercepting courses, the range now closed rapidly. At 9.21 the *Sheffield* (Captain C. T. Addis) reported 'enemy in sight, range 13,000 yards'. Three minutes later the *Belfast*, which was leading Admiral Burnett's squadron, fired star shell, and at 9.29 the Admiral gave the order to engage with main armaments, and turned towards to close the range. Actually the *Norfolk* (Captain D. K. Bain) was the only ship to get into action in

---

[1] Compare Admiral Tovey's views regarding the relative importance of the destruction of the *Tirpitz* and the safety of convoys PQ.12 and QP.8. (See Vol. II, p. 124.) Admiral Fraser's orders, however, corresponded to the view which the Admiralty had pressed on Admiral Tovey on the earlier occasion.

[2] Compare with the account of the defence of convoy JW.51B, Vol. II, pp. 291–299.

[3] See Map 6 (Phase 1, facing p. 85).

this phase[1], because the quarter-line disposition of the squadron resulted in the other two ships' lines of fire being masked. The enemy did not reply. Instead he hauled round to the south, while the British cruisers turned in the same direction to chase[2]; but the battle cruiser quickly drew away from them at about thirty knots. The *Scharnhorst* had, however, certainly received one hit, and possibly two from the *Norfolk*. At 9.55 Bey altered course to the north-east and, realising that this probably indicated an intention to work round to the north for a second attempt at the convoy, Admiral Burnett, who was still tracking his adversary by radar, decided that he must place himself between the enemy and his quarry. Since, in the prevailing sea, his best speed was evidently some five knots less than the enemy's there was no time to be lost in accomplishing this purpose. At 10 o'clock he accordingly returned to the north-west, and soon afterwards lost contact with his adversary. Thus ended the first phase of the battle.[3]

At 9.30 the Commander-in-Chief diverted the convoy still further to the north, and ordered Captain McCoy to detach four of his destroyers to join Admiral Burnett. At 10.24 the 36th Division (*Musketeer*, *Opportune*, *Virago* and *Matchless*) under Commander R. L. Fisher accordingly joined the cruiser Admiral. A few minutes later the Commander-in-Chief told the convoy to resume its north-easterly course. Admiral Burnett had meanwhile closed the convoy, and successfully placed himself between it and the enemy. By 10.50 he was in station ten miles ahead of the merchantmen, with his newly-joined destroyers disposed to screen the cruisers. The re-dispositions had, considering the weather conditions, been brilliantly carried out.

Admiral Fraser now had two main anxieties. Firstly he could not hope to bring the enemy to action unless the cruisers regained contact. At 10.44 he received Admiral Burnett's signal reporting that he had lost touch, and fourteen minutes later he told the cruiser Admiral that 'unless touch can be regained there is no chance of my finding the enemy'. In his report, however, the Commander-in-Chief stated that Admiral Burnett 'rightly considered it undesirable to split his force . . . to search', because he felt confident 'that the enemy would

---

[1] The *Norfolk's* main armament was eight 8-inch guns, while the *Belfast* and *Sheffield* each mounted twelve 6-inch. (See Vol. I, Appendix D, for fuller particulars.) The *Scharnhorst* mounted nine 11-inch and twelve 5·9-inch weapons.

[2] See Map 6 (Phase 1).

[3] In the subsequent analysis of the action made in the Admiralty the question whether Admiral Burnett would have been better advised to continue to shadow the enemy by radar was fully discussed. To keep in touch with a superior enemy in order to bring our main forces into contact is, of course, the core of cruiser tradition; but in the circumstances then prevailing—and bearing in mind the enemy's superiority in speed—it seems unlikely that the British cruisers could have accomplished such a purpose. Criticism of Admiral Burnett's actions can therefore hardly be sustained.

MAP 6

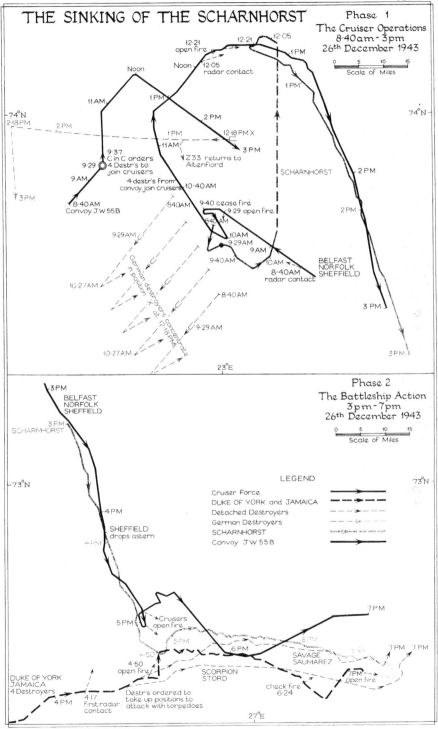

THE SINKING OF THE SCHARNHORST

Phase 1
The Cruiser Operations
8·40am – 3pm
26th December 1943

Scale of Miles
0   5   10   15

Phase 2
The Battleship Action
3pm – 7pm
26th December 1943

Scale of Miles
0   5   10   15

LEGEND

Cruiser Force	
DUKE OF YORK and JAMAICA	
Detached Destroyers	
German Destroyers	
SCHARNHORST	
Convoy JW 55B	

Labels on Phase 1:
- 12·21 open fire
- 12·21
- 12·05
- 1 PM
- Noon
- 12·05 radar contact
- 1 PM
- 2 PM
- SCHARNHORST
- 2 PM
- 2 PM
- 11 AM
- 1 PM
- 74°N 2·18 PM
- 2 PM
- 12·18 PM X
- 1 PM
- 11 AM
- 3 PM
- 74°N
- 9·37 C in C orders 4 Destr's to join cruisers
- 9·29
- Z33 returns to Altenfiord
- 9 AM
- 4 destr's from convoy join cruisers 10·40 AM
- 3 PM
- 8·40 AM Convoy JW 55B
- 8·40 AM
- 9·40 cease fire
- 9·29 open fire
- 8·40 AM
- 9·29 AM
- 10 AM
- 9·29 AM
- 9 AM
- 10·27 AM
- German destroyers in position
- 9·40 AM
- 10 AM
- 8·40 AM radar contact
- BELFAST NORFOLK SHEFFIELD
- 10·27 AM
- 8·40 AM
- 2 PM
- 2 PM
- concentrate at 12·18 PM
- 9·29 AM
- 3 PM
- 3 PM
- 10·27 AM
- 23°E

Labels on Phase 2:
- 3 PM BELFAST NORFOLK SHEFFIELD
- 3 PM SCHARNHORST
- 73°N
- 4 PM
- SHEFFIELD drops astern
- 4 PM
- 7 PM
- 73°N
- 5 PM Cruisers open fire
- 5 PM
- 5 PM
- 6 PM
- 8 PM
- SAVAGE SAUMAREZ
- 7 PM 7 PM
- 4·50 open fire
- 4·50 open fire
- SCORPION STORD
- 7 PM open fire
- DUKE OF YORK JAMAICA 4 Destroyers
- check fire 6·24
- 4 PM
- 4·17 First radar contact
- Destr's ordered to take up positions to attack with torpedoes
- 27°E

return to the convoy from the north or north-east'. The second of Admiral Fraser's anxieties arose from the fact that the destroyers with the heavy squadron were running low in fuel, and he would soon have to decide whether to take his ships right on to Kola Inlet to replenish or whether to turn back. As Fraser had no chance of catching the *Scharnhorst* if she had, as was quite likely, already set course for home, there might well be no object in accepting the risks involved in going on to Kola. Happily the dilemma was resolved when, shortly after noon, the *Belfast* regained radar contact, and Burnett's anticipations were shown to have been correct. Hopes rose correspondingly in the fleet flagship, now only about 160 miles to the south-west; for it was obvious that there was an excellent chance of cutting the enemy off from his base.

It was again Captain Addis's *Sheffield* which, at 12.21 p.m., made the traditional and cheering signal 'Enemy in sight'.[1] Admiral Burnett already had his ships favourably disposed, and they quickly opened fire at about 11,000 yards. The destroyers were ordered to attack with torpedoes; but as the Admiral's turn to the east towards the enemy had left them on the port bow of the cruiser squadron, and the *Scharnhorst* turned sharply away in the other direction, they were unable to reach a firing position, and the opportunity was lost. The gun action lasted about twenty minutes, and all three British ships almost certainly obtained hits; but we have no accurate knowledge of the damage they caused.

On our side the *Norfolk* had a turret and all her radar sets except one put out of action by 11-inch shells, and the *Sheffield* suffered slight damage. As the enemy was removing himself as fast as possible from the vicinity of the convoy, at 12.41 Admiral Burnett checked fire and ordered all his ships to shadow by radar from just outside visibility range; for he knew that the *Scharnhorst's* southerly course was taking her straight towards Admiral Fraser. For the next three hours she unwittingly steamed steadily in the direction most desired by her adversaries.

Meanwhile the five powerful German destroyers were supposed to be searching for the convoy. They seem actually to have passed within as little as ten miles of it at 1 p.m.; but they sighted nothing and accomplished nothing. At 2.18 Admiral Bey ordered them to break off the operation and make for the Norwegian coast. They thus pass out of the story, after playing a fruitless and ineffective part in these events. Though the poor sea-keeping qualities of the German destroyers, compared with their British counterparts, and also their lack of advanced technical equipment (such as modern radar sets) may have played a part, there does seem to have been a lack of

---

[1] See Map 6 (Phase 1).

vigour and determination in their handling on this occasion, as well as in the action on New Year's Eve 1942.[1] But the division of his forces must be laid mainly at Admiral Bey's door; and it probably contributed to his doom.

Admiral Fraser had, of course, been intercepting the shadowing cruisers' reports, to whose accuracy he paid warm tribute in his despatch, and at 4.17 p.m. the *Duke of York's* radar picked up the *Scharnhorst* when she was about twenty-two miles away to the NNE.[2] The range closed rapidly, and the destroyers *Savage* (Commander M. D. G. Meyrick), *Saumarez*, *Scorpion* and the Norwegian *Stord* were next ordered to take up positions to attack with torpedoes. But, surprisingly, they were told not to attack until ordered to do so. Admiral Fraser's tactical plan, as he had made clear before the action, was to close to within 12,000 yards of the enemy battle cruiser, and then to engage with his heavy guns, as well as releasing his destroyers to attack with torpedoes. He has since stated that he imposed the restriction on the destroyers because the single enemy ship had complete freedom of manœuvre and, should she turn away as soon as he opened fire, their torpedoes might all be wasted. He considered that he himself was in the best position to judge when the enemy was pinned down; and that depended partly on the position reached by the cruisers on the opposite quarter of the *Scharnhorst*. None the less the order given to the destroyers resulted in the *Savage* and *Saumarez* losing a favourable opportunity, which was not to recur until one-and-a-half hours later. Admiral Fraser meanwhile adjusted his course to bring all his guns to bear; and when star shell from the *Belfast* and from the fleet flagship illuminated the enemy at 4.50, the *Duke of York* and *Jamaica* opened fire at 12,000 yards. The *Scharnhorst* was taken completely by surprise, and it was some minutes before she replied. An officer in the control tower of the destroyer *Scorpion* described this dramatic moment in these words. 'When the starshell first illuminated the *Scharnhorst* I could see her so clearly that I noticed her turrets were fore-and-aft; and what a lovely sight she was at full speed. She was almost at once obliterated by a wall of water from the *Duke of York's* first salvo . . . When she re-appeared her turrets wore a different aspect.'

As soon as she came under fire the German battle cruiser hauled round to the north.[3] Admiral Fraser followed; and when the enemy next turned east he again conformed to her movements. The cruiser squadron, now reduced by shaft trouble in the *Sheffield* to two ships, opened fire from the north and thus prevented the enemy breaking

[1] See Vol. II, pp. 298–299.

[2] See Map 6 (Phase 2).

[3] See Map 6 (Phase 2).

away in that direction; while the *Duke of York* and *Jamaica* pursued
and engaged from the south, though at ranges which the German
ship's superior speed caused steadily to open. Both divisions of
British destroyers were meanwhile struggling to 'gain bearing', and
so reach a position of torpedo advantage. At 5.24 p.m. Admiral Bey
signalled 'Am surrounded by heavy units'. We cannot be sure which
ships scored the hits now seen on the enemy, but it is likely that the
Duke of York's 14-inch shells put one turret out of action and caused
the underwater damage which reduced her speed in this phase. The
Scharnhorst's gunnery was at first erratic, possibly owing to the shock
and surprise of the totally unexpected contact with our heavy forces;
but she soon steadied down, frequently straddled the *Duke of York* at
17,000 to 20,000 yards, and put 11-inch shells through both her
masts. Happily neither exploded. By 5.40 the battle had settled down
to a gun duel between the two heavy ships; for the *Jamaica* had
ceased fire, and the other cruisers were out of range. At 6.20 the
enemy's guns fell silent and her speed dropped. Four minutes later
the British flagship checked fire, and turned to the south-east.[1] The
final phase was now at hand, for the enemy battle cruiser's condition was clearly becoming desperate. She had just signalled to
Hitler 'We shall fight to the last shell'.

The British destroyers were meanwhile still struggling eastwards;
but until the enemy's speed dropped they had not looked like gaining
an attacking position. At 6.20, however, they started to forge ahead,
and in the next twenty minutes the *Savage, Saumarez, Scorpion* and
Stord closed to within five miles.[2] The two first-named moved in from
the north-west under heavy fire, while their consorts came up,
apparently unseen, on the *Scharnhorst's* starboard side. Star shell fired
by the *Savage* and *Saumarez* were bursting between the enemy and
the other two destroyers, and blinded the latter; but the illuminants
probably also obscured the enemy's view of the *Scorpion* and *Stord*, and
so saved them from coming under fire as they closed to within 3,000
yards of their formidable adversary. At that range she looked
enormous to the destroyers' crews, and her silhouette more than
filled the field of the control officers' binoculars. At this moment a
sailor in the *Scorpion* was heard to remark 'Get out wires and fenders.
We're going alongside the bastard!' At about 6.49 p.m. the *Scharnhorst* suddenly sighted these destroyers, and put her wheel hard over
to starboard to turn away; but quick re-calculations by the control

---

[1] The *Duke of York* had by then fired fifty-two broadsides, of which thirty-one were
reported as straddles, and sixteen as falling within 200 yards of the enemy. This was
remarkable shooting, even when allowing for the efficiency of her radar control and
spotting. But at such comparatively short ranges her 14-inch shell were unlikely, due to
the flatness of the trajectory, to penetrate the enemy's main armoured deck and so do her
lethal injury.

[2] See Map 7 (facing p. 89).

crews enabled the *Scorpion* and *Stord* to place their torpedoes right across the enemy's new track. At least one of the *Scorpion's* salvo hit; but the *Stord* was less well placed at the critical moment, and hers probably missed. Had the *Scharnhorst* held on and obliterated these two small adversaries with her powerful secondary armaments she might have gained at least a temporary reprieve; for there were at the moment no other ships on that side of her—which was, moreover, in the direction of the Norwegian coast. As it was, her turn away gave the *Savage* and *Saumarez* their chance. They pressed in and, of the twelve torpedoes fired, it is likely that three hit. The *Saumarez* was herself damaged, and only got off half of her outfit of eight torpedoes. This attack, however, sealed the enemy's fate; for her speed was further reduced, and her damage was all the time mounting.

While the four destroyers which had just attacked drew off to the north, the *Duke of York* and *Jamaica* came up from the south-west, and re-opened fire at about 10,400 yards.[1] Admiral Burnett's cruisers, which were now on their way to join the Commander-in-Chief, also joined in. The repeated hits, fires and explosions showed that the enemy was being reduced to a shambles; and by 7.30 her speed had dropped to five knots. The cruisers were then told to 'finish her off with torpedoes'. They closed in from both sides, and obtained several more hits. Then Commander Fisher's four destroyers arrived on the scene, and they also divided and attacked from both sides. Through the dense smoke nothing could now be seen of the *Scharnhorst* except a dull glow; but she probably sank at about 7.45 p.m. in 72° 16′ North 28° 41′ East. For the next hour most of the cruisers and destroyers searched the icy, wreck-strewn water for survivors; but only thirty-six were found.

Whatever we may think of the faulty planning, weak intelligence and uncertain leadership which led to her doom the *Scharnhorst* had, like the *Bismarck* before her, fought gallantly to the end against over-whelmingly superior forces. And, again like the *Bismarck*, the amount of punishment she withstood without blowing up and before she sank was remarkable. She probably received at least thirteen heavy shell hits from the *Duke of York*, and perhaps a dozen from the smaller weapons of the cruisers; and of the fifty-five torpedoes fired at her it is likely that eleven hit. Once again the ability of the Germans to build tremendously stout ships had been demonstrated.[2] On our own side there was ample cause for satisfaction over the conduct of the whole operation, as well as the final result. It was accurate intelligence which had made all else possible; but the control exercised by Admiral Fraser over his numerous, and originally widely-separated

---

[1] See Map 7.

[2] Compare Vol. I, pp. 415–418, on the sinking of the *Bismarck*.

MAP 7

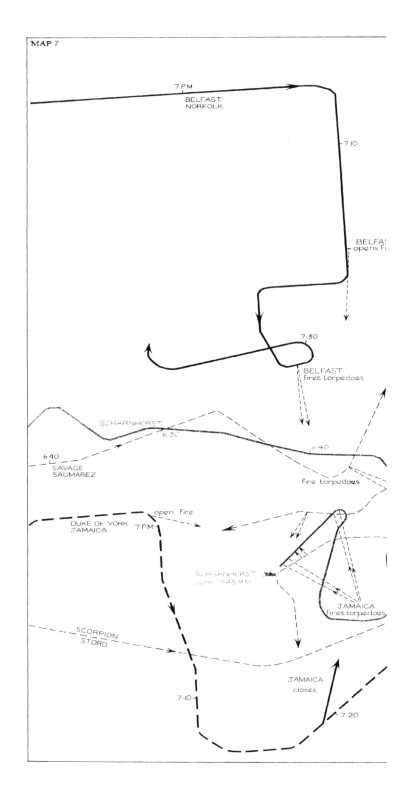

7 PM
BELFAST
NORFOLK

7·10

BELFAS
opens fi

7·30

BELFAST
fires torpedoes

SCHARNHORST
6·30

6·40

6·40
SAVAGE
SAUMAREZ

fire torpedoes

open fire

DUKE OF YORK
JAMAICA   7 PM

SCHARNHORST
sunk 7·45 PM

JAMAICA
fires torpedoes

SCORPION
STORD

JAMAICA
closes

7·10

7·20

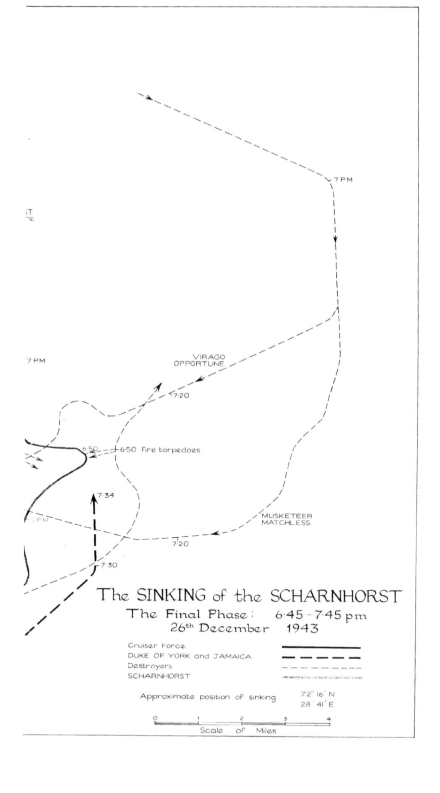

7 PM

7 PM

VIRAGO
OPPORTUNE

7·20

6·50 — 6·50 fire torpedoes

7·34

7 PM

MUSKETEER
MATCHLESS

7·20

7·30

The SINKING of the SCHARNHORST
The Final Phase : 6·45 - 7·45 pm
26ᵗʰ December 1943

Cruiser Force
DUKE OF YORK and JAMAICA
Destroyers
SCHARNHORST

Approximate position of sinking   72° 16′ N
                                    28° 41′ E

0   1   2   3   4
Scale   of   Miles

forces had been masterly; the vigour shown in the handling of Admiral Burnett's cruisers, whether they were shadowing a superior enemy or engaging him, is to be admired, and the destroyers had played their part in a manner typical of their class. But, in the Commander-in-Chief's words, it was the *Duke of York* which was 'the principal factor in the battle. She fought the *Scharnhorst* at night, and she won.'

Little more remains to be told. All the Home Fleet forces arrived at Kola Inlet on the 27th of December, while convoy JW.55B continued its voyage safely and unmolested.[1] So ended the last attempt by the German Navy to interfere with our Arctic convoys with surface forces. With the *Tirpitz* damaged and immobilised, the *Lützow* back in Germany for repairs, and the *Scharnhorst* sunk, the long-standing threat against the traffic to Murmansk and Archangel had been eliminated—at least temporarily. 'The strategic picture had', wrote Admiral Fraser, 'changed once again.' Not only was it now acceptable to reduce the Home Fleet's strength to reinforce the Eastern Fleet, but his ships had won for themselves far greater freedom of movement. Continuous offensive operations could henceforth be carried out off the Norwegian coast, and a heavy attack on the *Tirpitz* with naval aircraft was soon being planned.

---

[1] Part II of this volume will contain an Appendix giving full details of Arctic convoys for the whole war.

CHAPTER V

COASTAL WARFARE

1st June–31st December, 1943

'I hope we shall be able as usual to get so close to our Enemies that our shot cannot miss their objects'.

Nelson to Captain Sir Edward Berry,
9th March 1801

THE first operations against enemy shipping by the Strike Wing of Coastal Command's No. 16 Group were described in our preceding volume, and the reader will remember that the Wing was withdrawn from active service from November 1942 until April 1943 to improve the co-ordination of its work with other forces and the tactical training of the aircrews.[1] In the spring of 1943 it re-entered the fray, and quickly obtained a few successes against powerfully escorted convoys moving along the North Sea coast of Holland.[2] This contributed to the sharp decline in the traffic to and from Rotterdam, which the Admiralty noticed at the time. That port was by far the most convenient for the discharge of the Norwegian and Swedish iron ore needed by the Ruhr industries; but to avoid the increasing danger to ships coming so far west, and to allay the anxiety of the Swedes regarding the exposure of their merchantmen to air attacks and mines, the Germans were forced to make greater use of Emden, at the cost of increasing the strain on their inland transport system.

At the start of the period covered by this volume the Strike Wing consisted of sixty Beaufighters formed into three first-line squadrons. Its weapons were the torpedo, the bomb and the 20 mm. cannon; and to them was soon added the new rocket projectile. Co-ordination with Fighter Command's short-range air escorts, and with the Coastal Forces of the Nore and Dover naval commands, consisting of motor torpedo-boat and motor gunboat flotillas, had now greatly improved. In June three sorties by the Strike Wing took place. On the 13th a heavily escorted convoy was attacked off Den Helder, and

---

[1] See Vol. II, p. 259.
[2] Ibid. pp. 389–390.

one large merchantman and an escort vessel were sunk; but the next attack, on the 22nd, was less successful. Although thirty-six Beaufighters, armed with torpedoes, rockets and cannon took part, and they achieved complete surprise, the enemy convoy of five merchantmen protected by thirteen escorts passed on its way unharmed. Five days later another sortie in similar strength also accomplished nothing. Nor did the one sortie made in July produce better results; and in that operation two Beaufighters were shot down and three others damaged. It was now obvious that the accomplishments of the Strike Wing were not coming up to expectations. Since it had re-started work in mid-April all but one of the fifty-six German convoys known to have been run between the Elbe and the Hook of Holland had been sighted[1], but only nine had been attacked. This low figure was attributed mainly to inadequate or faulty reconnaissance, and to the difficulty of arranging with Fighter Command for the protection of the attacking aircraft. Heavy calls were being made at the time for fighters to escort the American bombers making daylight raids in Germany, and to cover our anti-submarine patrols in the Bay[2], and it was difficult for Fighter Command to meet them as well as the needs of the Strike Wing. Moreover things moved so fast in these attacks that very accurate timing was essential if the single-seater fighters were to be over the target during the few minutes when the Strike Wing most needed their protection.

The results accomplished in the southern North Sea were so slender that Air Marshal Slessor, the Commander-in-Chief, Coastal Command, raised the question whether the Strike Wing, on which so much time, labour and material had been expended, should continue.[3] The chief reason why the number of sorties actually carried out had only been about half that intended was the difficulty experienced by Fighter Command in providing escorts for the Beaufighters; but faulty navigation, resulting in enemy convoys being missed by the striking forces, had also been a contributory cause. For a time the very existence of the Strike Wing was threatened; but at a meeting held on the 20th of August the Admiralty and Ministry of Economic Warfare urged that its operations should not be abandoned, but should rather be regarded as part of a great, integrated campaign against enemy shipping, to which the Coastal Force flotillas, the daylight and night bombing raids, and the air and surface mine-layers were all contributing. The conference held that the entire campaign might be imperilled by the withdrawal of one of the arms taking part, and therefore decided that the Strike Wing should con-

---

[1] See Map 8.

[2] See pp. 19–20.

[3] Appendix B gives the establishment of Coastal Command's anti-shipping squadrons for the period covered by this volume.

THE ENGLISH CHANNEL AND NORTH SEA

Map 8

tinue. None the less the results continued disappointing right to the end of the year, in spite of a great effort in flying hours being devoted to the purpose.

While No. 16 Group was thus passing through a difficult and trying period in its attempts to interfere with enemy traffic in the southern North Sea, No. 18 Group's Hampdens and Mosquitos were endeavouring to conduct a similar campaign off the Norwegian coast, while No. 19 Group's aircraft watched for any signs of an increase in the iron ore traffic from northern Spain to France.[1] In July No. 18 Group were reinforced by a special unit composed of Beaufighters, analogous to No. 16 Group's Strike Wing; but we soon found that fighter protection was essential to air striking forces working off Norway, and the only suitable aircraft for such missions was the Mustang, none of which could be spared by Fighter Command.

In the English Channel Fighter Command's shorter-range aircraft worked in conjunction with the Navy's surface vessels in operations against enemy convoys, which generally moved by night and in short stages from harbour to harbour in both directions. In June we expected that the Germans would try to transfer merchant ships from the west of France to the North Sea ports, to ease the shortage of tonnage in the Baltic and Scandinavian trades. The expectation was in fact correct; but attempts to stop such movements were at first not at all successful. Though numerous small enemy vessels were sunk or damaged in fighter attacks, successes against larger ships were comparatively rare until the autumn. By that time the scale of air operations was steadily mounting. In day time Typhoons (both fighters and those fitted to carry small bombs[2]), Whirlwinds[3], and American Mitchell bombers were employed; and Spitfire escorts were normally provided for them. By night we generally employed 'Hurribombers'[4] and Fleet Air Arm Albacores. One squadron equipped with the latter type of aircraft had been lent by the Admiralty to the R.A.F., and worked under Fighter Command throughout nearly the whole of 1943. To give an idea of the scale on which these operations were now conducted, in October Fighter Command aircraft made 112 attacks on shipping. Two ships totalling 1,225 tons were sunk and a former blockade-runner, the *Munsterland*, was damaged in Cherbourg harbour. Ten of our aircraft were lost during the month on these operations. The rising tempo of the air offensive against enemy shipping is shown in the next table, and readers of our earlier volumes will be interested to remark how

---

[1] See Vol. I, pp. 551–552 and Vol. II, p. 391.

[2] These latter were called 'Bomphoons'.

[3] These were long-range fighter-bombers, able to carry a 500-pound bomb. Only two squadrons were commissioned by the R.A.F., and in 1943 they were replaced by Typhoons.

[4] These were Hurricane fighters converted to carry small bombs.

the aggregate results in tonnage sunk by the Royal Air Force's direct attacks at sea overtook the losses inflicted by our air-laid mines in this phase.[1] The reasons appear to be that German shipping now almost always sailed in convoy, and that at this stage of the war the enemy's minesweeping service had achieved a high degree of efficiency. It is also interesting to find that most of our aircraft losses were caused by anti-aircraft fire from the numerous and well handled light weapons mounted in the German merchantmen and escorts. These were

Table 3. The Air Offensive against Enemy Shipping by Direct Attacks at Sea

(All Royal Air Force Commands, Home Theatre only)

June–December 1943

Month 1943	Aircraft Sorties	Attacks Made	Enemy Vessels Sunk		Enemy Vessels Damaged		Aircraft Losses
			No.	Tonnage	No.	Tonnage	
June .	1,450	222	4	6,885	Nil		20
July .	1,788	104	1	548	2	4,294	19
August .	1,341	155	6	3,676	Nil		11
September.	1,535	320	8	4,594	1	5,485	18
October .	1,419	147	2	1,225	2	23,409*	13
November.	1,681	162	4	8,884	2	1,785	25
December .	1,058	89	3	9,410	Nil		13
TOTALS .	10,272	1,119	28	35,222	7	34,973	119

* Includes liner *Strasburg* (ex-Dutch *Balderan*) attacked while grounded after being mined (see also Table 5, p. 96).

Table 4. German Air Attacks on Allied Shipping and Royal Air Force Sorties in Defence of Shipping

(Home Theatre only)

June–December 1943

Month 1943	Estimated German Day and Night Sorties for (1) Direct Attack (2) Minelaying		Allied Shipping Sunk by Direct Attacks, Day and Night		Royal Air Force Sorties in Defence of Shipping (Day and Night)	Royal Air Force Losses
	(1)	(2)	No.	Tonnage		
June . .	527	25	Nil		784	1
July . .	611	70	Nil		585	2
August .	626	30	Nil		314	1
September .	548	180	Nil		335	1
October .	484	120	Nil		304	Nil
November .	513	20	Nil		404	Nil
December .	449	5	Nil		207	3
TOTALS .	3,758	450	Nil		2,933	8

[1] See Tables 3 and 5. Compare Vol. I, Tables 10 and 11, 15 and 17, and 18. Also Vol. II, Tables 12 and 14, 18 and 20, 34 and 35.

manned by specially trained crews, who travelled in the coastal convoys in exactly the same manner as the 'Channel Guard' which we ourselves had formed to meet a similar threat in 1940.[1]

In the enemy's air attacks on our own shipping the statistics for this period show a widely different trend from the increasing successes achieved by the Royal Air Force; for the Luftwaffe inflicted no losses at all. In consequence the calls on Fighter Command for defensive sorties decreased sharply, and greater effort could therefore be devoted to offensive purposes. On the coastal shipping routes the tables had indeed now been turned on the enemy.

We saw earlier how, in April 1943, Coastal Command ceased to carry a share of the air minelaying campaign in enemy waters, and the whole burden thereafter fell on Bomber Command.[2] Throughout the second half of 1943 a big effort was devoted to mining the approaches to the U-boat bases in the Bay of Biscay. On an average the bombers laid no less than 480 mines in those waters during each month; but we now know that no U-boats were sunk at this time. The varied firing mechanisms used undoubtedly put a heavy strain on the German minesweepers; but they surmounted their formidable difficulties, and continued to sweep the U-boats in and out of the harbours safely. Several enemy sweepers were, however, themselves sunk by mines in the process. The Admiralty now wished to devote more attention to the Baltic, where newly-commissioned U-boats carried out their training; but our bombers could not infest those waters until the nights had lengthened.

The decision of the Casablanca Conference in January 1943 to devote a special bombing effort to the enemy's U-boat bases had not, we now realised, justified itself.[3] In fact the results achieved had been small. The desirability of devoting more aircraft to minelaying against U-boats was therefore discussed at this time, but was opposed by the Air Ministry if it meant any reduction in the bombing of Germany. This view was certainly reasonable, since air-laid mines had not so far achieved marked successes against U-boats, to which the enemy always gave special protection. In the whole war only seventeen U-boats were sunk by mines laid by our shore-based aircraft, and four of them fell victim right at the end, when the German minesweeping organisation had at last broken down.[4]

---

[1] See Vol. I, pp. 324–325.

[2] See Vol. II, pp. 392–394.

[3] Ibid. pp. 351–353.

[4] See Vol. I, Appendix K, Table III, and similar tables in Vol. II, Appendix J and this volume, Appendix D. Quite apart from the U-boats actually sunk, our air minelaying caused severe dislocation to the training of new U-boat crews in the Baltic towards the end of the war. (See Part II of this volume.)

The short nights of summer limited Bomber Command's minelay-ing sorties to the coastal waters between the Bay of Biscay and the North Sea coasts of Holland and Germany. The aircraft employed were Wellingtons, Halifaxes, Stirlings and Lancasters, drawn from no less than six bomber groups. During the summer a considerable number of small enemy vessels was sunk or damaged by mines. As the nights lengthened in the autumn it was possible to extend mine-laying to the more distant waters, and in October the Command turned its attention again to the Baltic shipping routes, and to the waters where new U-boats carried out their training. ~~U-345 was sunk off Warnemunde by an air-laid mine on the 13th of December.~~   *see ERRA*

The effort entailed by all these operations and the results achieved are shown in the next table.

Table 5. The R.A.F's Air Minelaying Campaign
(Home Theatre only)
June–December 1943

Month 1943	Aircraft Sorties	Mines Laid	Enemy Vessels Sunk		Enemy Vessels Damaged		Aircraft Lost
			No.	Tonnage	No.	Tonnage	
June .	426	1,174	14	10,103	1	4,969	8
July . .	313	927	22	7,086	2	1,629	7
August .	501	1,103	4	256	3	1,901	11
September.	396	1,188	7	1,438	3	21,437*	5
October .	367	1,076	7	3,662	1	44	5
November .	352	976	7	919	3	6,944	9
December .	256	800	8	2,287	Nil		8
TOTALS .	2,611	7,244	69	25,751	13	36,924	53

* Includes liner *Strasburg* (17,001 tons) damaged on mine and grounded.

In addition to the mines laid by Bomber Command, the Nore and Dover Coastal Force flotillas made frequent sorties to place mines in the enemy's swept channels, and in the entrances to his harbours; but it has proved impossible to assess the results achieved by them. As the number of mines laid by these vessels was far fewer than were laid by aircraft, it seems unlikely that a very substantial proportion of the enemy's losses can be attributed to them.[1] They must, how-ever, have added to the burden of his minesweeping, and to the difficulty of keeping his coastal traffic moving.

The air operations so far described were by no means the only offensive measures taken against the enemy's coastal shipping at this time. The motor torpedo-boats and motor gunboats of the Nore and Dover Commands made repeated forays against the convoys; but,

[1] In July 1943 Coastal force craft laid 81 mines, and in September 92 off various ports on the Dutch coast. This was less than one-tenth of the number laid by Bomber Com-mand during the same months (see Table 5).

'The end of the *Scharnhorst*', by Charles Pears.

Survivors of the *Scharnhorst* landing in Britain.

Top. H.M. King George VI with Flag Officers of the Home Fleet on board H.M.S. *Duke of York*, 12th August, 1943. (Left to right: Rear-Admirals I. G. Glennie, L. H. K. Hamilton, R. L. Burnett, Vice-Admiral Sir Henry Moore, the King, and Admiral Sir Bruce Fraser, Commander-in-Chief.)

Middle. The U.S.N. battleships *South Dakota* and *Alabama* with H.M.S. *Furious* (right) and other units of the Home Fleet, June 1943 (taken from H.M.S. *Duke of York*).

Bottom. Convoy JW.57 to North Russia, February 1944. (Note escorting aircraft from H.M.S. *Chaser*.)

just as Coastal Command's Strike Wing had found it very difficult to inflict appreciable losses in day attacks, so did the light craft find that their night attacks often failed to produce the desired results. It is interesting to remark how closely the enemy's methods of defending coastal shipping corresponded to those which we had first adopted in the crisis of 1940, and had constantly improved ever since[1]; and his experiences were, moreover, very similar to our own. The records of both sides leave no doubt at all that well-organised convoys, closely escorted by numerous well-armed small craft, could provide a very effective defence against both air and surface vessel attacks.

The strength and disposition of the British coastal forces allocated to the southern naval commands at this time is shown in the next table.

Table 6. Operational Strength of Coastal Forces, September 1943
(Southern Commands at home only. Training craft excluded.)

I. *Portsmouth Command*

Portsmouth	10	Motor torpedo or Motor gunboats
	20	Motor launches
Newhaven	11	Motor torpedo-boats
	6	Motor gunboats
	6	Steam gunboats
	24	Motor launches
Portland	4	Motor gunboats
	12	Motor launches
Weymouth	9	Motor torpedo-boats
	4	Motor gunboats

II. *Plymouth Command*

Plymouth	13	Motor launches
Dartmouth	8	Motor torpedo-boats
	21	Motor gunboats
Falmouth	12	Motor launches

III. *Dover Command*

Dover	24	Motor torpedo-boats
	13	Motor gunboats
	9	Motor launches

VI. *Nore Command*

Felixstowe	16	Motor torpedo-boats
	7	Motor gunboats
	4	Motor launches
Lowestoft	8	Motor torpedo-boats
	20	Motor gunboats
	16	Motor launches
Yarmouth	15	Motor torpedo-boats
	20	Motor gunboats
	12	Motor launches

---

[1] See Vol. I, Chapters VI, VIII and XVI.

In July Admiral Sir John Tovey, who had recently taken over the Nore Command, stressed that new tactics must be developed by the Coastal Forces 'if we are to succeed in sinking ships in convoy—the over-riding object in all these operations'. But results none the less continued disappointing, and successes were, we now know, considerably less than we believed at the time. It is probably misleading, however, to estimate the effects of the unremitting sweeps and attacks by our Coastal Forces solely in terms of tonnage sunk. The War Diary of the German E-Boat[1] command for the latter part of 1943 contains many rueful comments on the effective way in which the Coastal Force operations were forcing their own flotillas on to the defensive; and the difficulty experienced in attacking British convoys in face of their numerous and heavily armed escorts is also frequently stressed.

In addition to the destroyers of the 16th and 21st Flotillas, which had escorted the east coast convoys between the Thames and Forth ever since the early months of the war, there were now about half-a-dozen destroyers, mostly of the *Hunt*-class, in the Portsmouth and Plymouth naval commands. The '*Hunts*' were normally employed as convoy escorts, but they were also used to support the light coastal craft on their offensive sweeps. As they carried no torpedoes and had a maximum speed of only twenty-nine knots they were not very suitable for this latter work; but it was rare for more than two of the larger and faster 'fleet' destroyers, which had powerful torpedo armaments, to be available. We knew that, in addition to the six large (2,700 tons) destroyers based on the Bay of Biscay ports, the Germans had six of their smaller (1,300 tons) ships and also five torpedo-boats (800–900 tons) at the western end of the English Channel.[2] To give greater support to our light forces against these ships, in October we tried the experiment of sending a light cruiser out with the Plymouth destroyers; but the only result was, as will be told shortly, to give the enemy torpedo-boats one of their most notable successes.

In July and August there were many fierce clashes between our light craft and the enemy's convoy escorts, patrols and minesweepers off the Dutch coast and in the Channel. The destroyers from

---

[1] Strictly speaking the expression 'E boat', frequently used in these volumes, should only refer to the German motor torpedo-boats. During the war the British authorities applied it to all the many types of small enemy coastal warships, which we were sometimes unable to identify more accurately.

[2] In contemporary British documents the large German destroyers are often referred to as '*Narvik*' class and the smaller ones as '*Elbings*'. Neither definition has, however, any historical validity. The first misnomer probably arose through Hitler having commemorated the destroyers lost at Narvik on 10th and 13th April 1940 (see Vol. I, pp. 172 and 177–178) by ordering a flotilla to be commissioned as the 'Narvik flotilla'. The smaller destroyers (Numbers T22–T36) were all built at Elbing, but the Germans always referred to them as fleet torpedo-boats.

Plymouth often swept close inshore off the Brittany coast, and on the 10th of July they engaged enemy torpedo-boats and minesweepers, damaging several of them. Most of these fast-moving night encounters consisted of a confused series of individual fights, often lasting for several hours and spread over a wide area. Sometimes one or two enemy escort craft were sunk or seriously damaged, sometimes a British motor torpedo-boat or motor gunboat was overwhelmed. Rarely was a substantial advantage gained by either side, and still more rarely did an M.T.B's torpedoes find the enemy merchant ships in the centre of the close ring of escorts. On the 27th of July four of our steam gunboats, which were more heavily armed than the M.G.Bs, fought about a dozen enemy trawlers and patrol craft off Cherbourg, and went so close inshore that they were heavily engaged by the coastal defences; but little damage was suffered on either side. In the following month the E-boats returned to our east coast convoy route, and sank a patrol trawler off Harwich on the 5th. As radar cover of our inshore swept channels had now improved, the slow and weakly armed trawlers were gradually being withdrawn from the duty of patrolling them; and by October we were using corvettes to keep watch at the danger points by night. Though they lacked sufficient speed to pursue the E-boats they carried heavier armaments than the trawlers, and so could better defend themselves and any merchant-men in their vicinity. The fights off Ijmuiden, the Texel and Ter-schelling continued throughout the summer.[1] One M.T.B. and one M.G.B. flotilla from the Nore Command Coastal Force bases usually worked together; but the general trend of the battles was no different from those fought in the preceding months. In the Dover Straits the same type of engagement was common, and the heavy gun batteries on the Dover cliffs and on Cape Gris Nez often added their thunder to the fray—though rarely with any effect.

In the early hours of the 4th of October a force of five British destroyers was sweeping close inshore off the Brittany coast, when they encountered five enemy destroyers. In a chasing action damage was suffered by both sides. On the evening of the 22nd a squadron consisting of the light cruiser *Charybdis*, two fleet destroyers and four of the *Hunt*-class sailed from Plymouth to try to intercept the mer-chantman *Munsterland*, a former blockade runner, which was expected to move from Brest to Cherbourg.[2] The British force comprised ships of several different types and widely varying performance. Moreover they had done no tactical training together, and the *Hunt*-class destroyers were not only slower than the 'fleets' but they lacked tor-pedoes. Their normal duty had been to escort convoys in the western

---

[1] See Map 8.

[2] See p. 93 regarding bomb damage suffered by this ship while in Cherbourg.

Channel. The squadron was thus ill-fitted to act as substitute for a properly organised and well-trained night striking force.

The *Munsterland* actually left Brest on the afternoon of the 22nd of October with eight small vessels as escort. Five of the German 1,100-ton destroyers joined her as outer screen that evening, and took station to the north of the convoy, but within sight of it. Shortly after midnight the British searching force reached a position seven miles off the north coast of Brittany, and started to sweep west at thirteen knots. We now know that at half-past twelve next morning the German shore radar station picked up our ships, and soon afterwards gave the alarm. On our side the *Hunt*-class destroyers had meanwhile intercepted enemy voice-radio transmissions and passed them to the *Charybdis*, which was not herself fitted to receive them; nor does she appear to have appreciated their probable significance. At 1.30 a.m. the *Charybdis* herself obtained a radar contact ahead at 14,000 yards. She increased speed, but did not warn the destroyers that contact appeared imminent. Fifteen minutes later, when the range had closed to 4,000 yards, she fired star shell; but the enemy destroyers had already sighted her. They turned quickly, and fired torpedoes to such good effect that the cruiser was hit several times, and sank with heavy loss of life. The destroyer *Limbourne* was also hit and sunk, and the enemy's rapid success caused some confusion among the surviving British ships, which took no retaliatory action. The Germans watched the rescue operations, but luckily did not interfere further. Had they pressed home their advantage they might well have caused us further losses. The *Munsterland* and her escort proceeded on their way unimpeded.

Admiral Sir Ralph Leatham, the Commander-in-Chief, Plymouth, ruefully admitted that the Germans had completely turned the tables on our force, and caught it by surprise. He attributed the unhappy outcome of the encounter mainly to lack of opportunity to exercise the ships of his command in the new technique of night fighting by radar control. Nor can it be doubted that the British ships lacked the mutual confidence which only intensive training can give[1]; but perhaps the most surprising aspect of the operation is that, at so late a stage in the war, no air co-operation should have been requested. The lessons of the encounter were, however, at once digested; and we took steps to build up a more suitable force for such operations, composed of light cruisers and fleet destroyers, and to give it such training as would enable the command of the western Channel to be effectively disputed.

Two nights after this enemy success in the Channel, one of the

---

[1] The reader may usefully compare this action with that fought by Force K from Malta in November 1941 (see Vol. I, pp. 532–533), and on the other side, with the Japanese success at the Battle of Savo Island in August 1942 (see Vol. II, pp. 224–225).

biggest E-boat battles of the war took place on the east coast route. No less than twenty-eight boats from Ijmuiden—almost the whole strength deployed by the enemy in the narrow seas—attacked convoy FN.1160 off Cromer. They were heavily engaged by the destroyers and coastal craft of the escort, and in a long series of running fights two enemies were sunk and one other was damaged. Except for a trawler, which had straggled astern of the convoy and was sunk, little damage was suffered on our side, and the convoy passed on its way unharmed. It is interesting to find that the tactical plan employed by the enemy on this occasion was based on material captured from one of our M.G.Bs, which had been sunk a short while previously.

Early in November an attack on the Channel convoy CW.221 by nine E-boats from Boulogne brought the Germans greater success than the big east coast foray just described. For eighteen months these convoys had been immune from such attacks, and there seems little doubt that the escorts were taken by surprise. Three merchantmen totalling 3,957 tons were sunk between Dungeness and Beachy Head. Next night, that of the 4th–5th of November, another east coast convoy, FN.1170, was attacked between Cromer and Yarmouth by about twenty enemies, which were actually out on a mine-laying mission. Two ships were torpedoed, but both made harbour safely, and one E-boat was sunk by Coastal Command Beaufighters on its way back to Ijmuiden. The enemy surface craft were actually still laying a large number of mines in our coastal channels at this time, including a proportion with a new magnetic-acoustic firing mechanism; but, thanks to the unceasing work of the sweepers, mine casualties were comparatively rare events. In November two merchantmen were, however, mined off Harwich; and in the following month the destroyers *Holderness* and *Worcester* were both damaged. In 1943 the Nore Command minesweepers swept 373 ground mines and eighty-six moored mines.

The last month of the year brought no reduction in the number of encounters which took place up and down the enemy's and our own coasts; and, if it was plain that the German forays were now unlikely to cause us serious harm, it was equally true that, in spite of the fine offensive spirit in our Coastal Forces, we had by no means yet mastered the defences sufficiently to deny the enemy reasonable control of his own coastal waters. The Commanders-in-Chief of the naval commands in the south all insisted that to achieve the desired mastery more destroyers were essential; but in face of the heavy demands coming from the combined operations in the Mediterranean the Admiralty could not make any more available. Even though the forces allocated to defend our own coastal traffic were doubtless not always ideal to the purpose their achievement remains remarkable. During the whole of this phase the E-boats only sank four ships totalling 8,538 tons, and losses from all causes in British home waters amounted to no more than eleven ships of 19,362 tons.[1] In the whole of 1943 the shipping which passed safely in and out of the Thames reached the prodigious figure of 36,033,847 tons.

The operations of Coastal Command's No. 18 Group off Norway, already described, were by no means the only offensive conducted against enemy inshore shipping in those waters. In fact so many different arms and organisations were now involved that, towards the end of May, the Admiralty ordered that the Admiral Commanding, Orkneys and Shetlands (Admiral Sir Lionel Wells), should direct and co-ordinate them all. Thenceforth he became responsible for the raids by the 30th (Norwegian-manned) motor torpedo-boat flotilla into 'the Leads', where they laid mines and often lay up in a lonely fiord during the night, to attack when a promising target next appeared. Though the losses inflicted were not very heavy, the constant threat was a substantial irritant to the enemy and, moreover, helped to encourage his belief that a large-scale invasion of Norway was planned by the Allies. It was part of our policy of strategic deception to do everything possible to encourage this obsession.[2]

We have already remarked how the damage done by the midget submarines to the *Tirpitz* on the 22nd of September enabled forces to be diverted to offensive purposes.[3] Admiral Fraser, the Commander-in-Chief, Home Fleet, was quick to take advantage of this, and on the 2nd of October he sailed with his main strength to a position 140 miles off the Norwegian port of Bodo. There thirty strike aircraft (Dauntless dive-bombers and Avenger torpedo-bombers), all armed with bombs, flew off from the U.S.S. *Ranger* on the morning of the 4th. Fourteen of the carrier's fighters went with them as escort. Admiral Fraser had originally intended to send the *Formidable's* aircrews to attack shipping in another harbour farther south; but that part of the plan had to be cancelled because the weather was unfavourable. At Bodo the American naval aircrews, sixty per cent of whom were making their first operational sortie, scored an outstanding success. They attacked in two waves, at very low heights, and sank or destroyed five ships totalling 20,753 tons, including a loaded troop transport. Another seven ships were damaged, among them a large tanker. The results were a striking vindication of their dive- and low-level bombing techniques. Only three of the attackers were lost, and they were avenged later in the day when the *Ranger's* fighters shot down two enemy shadowing planes. On the 6th all our forces were safely back at Scapa.

---

[1] See Appendix K for particulars.
[2] See Vol. II, pp. 116, 124 and 176.
[3] See p. 69.

The next operation in Norwegian waters was an original one by four one-man submarines, called 'Welman' craft, which were carried over by M.T.Bs and tried to penetrate into Bergen harbour.[1] The attack failed, one 'Welman' was captured by the enemy, and the other three had to be scuttled. After various unsuccessful attempts, the crews of these latter craft were finally rescued and brought safely back by M.T.B. in February 1944. In this, and indeed in most of the operations on the Norwegian coast, the people of that country played an essential and gallant part by saving our men from falling into the enemy's clutches, by providing intelligence about enemy movements and, once they had been supplied with arms and equipment, by themselves attacking German ships and installations. The Norwegian resistance movement was, indeed, a most important factor in the increasing struggle for control of the coastal shipping routes off Scandinavia.

To sum up the present phase of coastal warfare, the many-pronged Allied offensive was gaining in momentum, but had not yet achieved such successes as would stop the enemy's coastal traffic. The Germans for their part were being forced increasingly on the defensive; but they still possessed the ability and the will to strike suddenly and hard at any point they might choose on our east coast or in the Channel. Although, with certain important exceptions, their successes were rare, there was as yet no justification for relaxing the constant watch which the little ships and patrolling aircraft had maintained around our shores for over four years.

---

[1] These crafts were named after their inventor, an Army officer. A description will be found in F. W. Lipscomb, *The British Submarine* (A. and C. Black, 1954), p. 188. They must not be confused with the 'human torpedoes' or 'Chariots' which have appeared elsewhere in this narrative (see Vol. II, pp. 258, 342–343, etc.), nor with the midget submarines or 'X-craft' (see pp. 65–68). After the abortive attack on Bergen it was decided not to continue the development of the Welman craft, but to concentrate on the other two types of small submersibles.

CHAPTER VI

THE MEDITERRANEAN CAMPAIGNS

1st June–15th August, 1943

The Invasion of Sicily

> 'And what made this expedition to Sicily so famous was not only its astonishing daring, and the brilliant show that it made, but also . . . the fact that this voyage . . . was being undertaken with hopes for the future which . . . were of the most far-reaching kind.'
>
> Thucydides. *Peloponnesian War*, Book VI. 31.6. (Trans. Rex Warner, Penguin Books).

THE second volume of this trilogy closed at the moment when the through-Mediterranean sea route had at last been re-opened, and regular traffic was once more beginning to flow direct from Gibraltar to Egypt. Though hundreds of mines had been swept from the shallow channels south of Malta, and the threat of surface ship attack had declined, the convoys were by no means freed from all dangers, and considerable naval and air strength still had to be deployed for the protection of each one of them. There were seventeen German U-boats in the Mediterranean at the beginning of this period, and one more got through the Straits of Gibraltar early in June; but they were suffering from a steady attrition and, as reinforcement had become increasingly difficult, by the beginning of September their numbers had declined to thirteen. Although fifteen more were ordered out in the last four months of the year, only six ran the gauntlet of our sea and air patrols in the Straits successfully. At the start of this phase the German U-boat commander in Italy expressed his anxiety over the increasing density and skill of the Allied sea and air escorts and patrols; and he admitted that the prospects of 'waging effective U-boat warfare' had decreased. It will be seen later how the losses we inflicted before the end of the year offset the reinforcements which got through.

In spite of their small numbers the German U-boats were a serious threat to the troopships and supply vessels, whose routes could be varied but little. Between the start of this phase and the end of 1943 Allied and neutral shipping losses in the Mediterranean amounted to eighty ships of 397,710 tons—an average of about twelve ships and 57,000 tons in each month. German submarines contributed thirty-one ships of 136,071 tons to the total figure. In June there were still about forty-five Italian submarines in fit condition for operations; but in the short time now remaining to their country as junior partner in the once-vaunted Axis they did us very little harm. In the whole of 1943 not one Allied merchantman was sunk by an Italian submarine; and, as will be told later, they continued to suffer heavy losses themselves.

The second serious threat to our shipping came from the enemy's aircraft, which still had the use of well-sited bases in Sardinia, Sicily, southern Italy and Crete, from which it was easy to attack the convoys moving slowly along the 2,000-mile route from Gibraltar to the ports of the Levant. In all we lost forty-one ships of 225,450 tons to air attacks at sea and in harbour between June and December 1943. Considering the scale on which combined operations were carried out in Sicily and Italy, involving scores of valuable ships anchoring close off enemy-held coasts, it is remarkable that losses from air attacks were not much heavier.[1] Attacks on ships in convoy and in the many ports of discharge were generally kept well in check by the five Air Commands which shared the responsibility for the protection of shipping in the whole Mediterranean theatre. It will be convenient to consider here the organisation of those commands in further detail. A convoy entering the Mediterranean from the west would first come under the protection of aircraft operated by Air Headquarters, Gibraltar, whose responsibility extended as far as the longitude of Oran. This command had been placed under the orders of the Allied Commander-in-Chief (General Eisenhower) for operation 'Torch', and did not return to the control of Coastal Command Headquarters until October 1943.[2] On passing Oran the convoy would enter the area for which the North-West African

---

[1] The monthly losses of Allied shipping to air attacks were as follows:

	No. of ships	Tons	
June	1	813	
July	8	54,306	(Invasion of Sicily)
August	3	5,537	
September	3	15,770	(Landings at Salerno)
October	3	15,504	
November	6	58,047	(includes *M. Van St. Aldegonde*, 19,335 tons)
December	17	75,471*	
TOTAL	41	225,448	tons

* All except one of the ships lost in December were destroyed by fires and explosions following on an air raid on Bari on 2nd December (see p. 210).

[2] See Vol. II, p. 360.

Coastal Air Force (Air Vice-Marshal H. P. Lloyd) was responsible. This command formed part of the North-West African Air Forces, which were under Lieutenant-General Carl Spaatz, U.S.A.A.F. It undertook the defence of shipping up to the Tunis–Tripoli frontier, but excluding the waters within fifty miles of Malta for which Air Vice-Marshal Sir K. R. Park's Air Headquarters, Malta, was responsible. On passing through 'the Narrows' our convoy would therefore be protected for a short time by Malta-based aircraft. In the eastern basin of the Mediterranean, from the Levant coast up to the Tripoli–Tunis frontier, No. 201 Naval Co-operation Group (Air Vice-Marshal T. A. Langford-Sainsbury) protected all shipping outside forty miles from the North African coast and fifty miles from Malta, while convoys passing closer in shore were shielded by fighters controlled by the headquarters of the Air Defences, Eastern Mediterranean Command, which was directly under Royal Air Force Headquarters, Middle East. For the purposes of this narrative we are concerned mainly with the work of the North-West African Coastal Air Force and No. 201 Naval Co-operation Group; but the other commands mentioned also bore a share in the protection of our warships, and of our troop and supply convoys. The strengths of the five air commands in July 1943 are shown in Table 7 (p. 108).

As to the enemy's strength, the Germans reinforced their air flotillas in the central and eastern Mediterranean at this time, at the expense of the Russian front and of western Europe, to the tune of no less than 440 aircraft. By the beginning of July there were 975 German aircraft of all types in the central Mediterranean, and a further 305 at airfields around the eastern basin. The allocation of so much strength to the latter theatre, where it could play little part in the great events now pending in the central basin, suggests that the Allies' deceptive measures, designed to mislead the enemy into expecting a combined operation against the Balkans, achieved considerable success.[1] Of the German aircraft allocated to the central Mediterranean only about 300 were, however, long-range bombers; and on the 10th of July 1943 no more than some 200 of them were fit for operations. The great majority of these were stationed in Sicily, in central and southern Italy and in Sardinia; and it was they who most frequently attacked our convoys. Compared with German air strength the Regia Aeronautica formations available to contest control of the sea routes were weak and ill-equipped. On the 12th of June serviceable Italian bombers and fighters totalled only seventy and about 300 respectively; many of them were of obsolescent types, and no more than about a score of bombers were stationed at airfields whence they could work against our convoys. The Germans already realised that they could not rely on the Italian navy and air

---

[1] See p. 126.

Table 7. Air Commands associated with the War at Sea—Mediterranean Theatre, July 1943 [Strength in Squadrons]

	Air Headquarters, Gibraltar			North-West African Coastal Air Force			Air Headquarters, Malta			No. 201 Naval Co-operation Group			Air Defences, Eastern Mediterranean		
	R.A.F.	F.A.A.	Allied and Commonwealth	R.A.F.	F.A.A.	Allied and Commonwealth	R.A.F.	F.A.A.	Allied and Commonwealth	R.A.F.	F.A.A.	Allied and Commonwealth	R.A.F.	F.A.A.	Allied and Commonwealth
Day Fighters	½	—	—	4	—	9 U.S. 2 French	8½	—	1 S.A.A.F.	3 (Day or Night)	—	—	13	—	3 S.A.A.F. 1 R.A.A.F.
Night Fighters	—	—	—	3	—	—	2	—	—	—	—	—	3	—	—
General Reconnaissance	—	—	—	4	—	—	2	—	—	4	—	2 R.A.A.F. 1 S.A.A.F. 1 Greek	—	—	—
Anti-Shipping and Anti-Submarine	5½	1	—	6	2½	1 R.A.A.F.	—	½	—	—	2	—	—	—	—

NOTES: 1. Squadrons have been listed in their primary roles. If the occasion arose, general reconnaissance squadrons could be switched to anti-shipping or anti-submarine duties.

2. American squadrons were generally larger than British squadrons. For single-seater fighters the establishments were 16 aircraft for British squadrons and 25 for American. For simplicity, no account is taken of the variation in establishment between different types of aircraft in this table.

force to carry an appreciable share of the burden of the war—not even if their homeland was threatened with invasion. Mistrust and tactlessness on the part of the Germans, divided counsels in the Fascist hierarchy, and low morale in the Italian fighting services aggravated difficulties caused by the serious shortage of fuel and the rising tempo of Allied air attacks on Italian towns and industry. In mid-July Dönitz complained bitterly to Hitler about the 'infamous' attitude of Admiral Riccardi, the head of the Italian Naval Staff (Supermarina). He wanted to abolish that organisation and to substitute a German command staff working under Italian officers of his own choice. Nor was it long before the senior partner of the Axis began to scent 'treachery' in the unwillingness of his Ally to fall in with German plans and intentions. But the Italian Navy managed to preserve its independence to the end.

In June 1943 the most important Allied purpose was, therefore, to bring in the convoys carrying the reinforcements and enormous quantities of vehicles and stores needed for the projected invasion of Sicily. The planning of that great undertaking will be described shortly, but as the whole operation depended on the safe arrival of the convoys from Britain and America it will be logical first to discuss their organisation and defence.

The main threats lay, as has been said, with the German U-boats and aircraft; but the convoys had to pass within easy striking distance of Italian naval bases in Sicily and southern Italy, and it was therefore necessary to protect them against surface ship interference as well. On the 1st of June the eastern limit of Admiral Sir Andrew Cunningham's command was shifted still further east, to the 20th meridian, at the expense of Admiral Sir John Cunningham's Levant Command.[1] By this decision the movements of the invasion convoys coming towards Sicily from the east as well as from the west came under Sir Andrew Cunningham's control well before the approach to the assault areas. It was told in our second volume how the forces destined to move on Sicily from the eastern Mediterranean had started to build up by the long Cape route long before the Axis armies had been cleared out of Africa.[2] Now the reinforcements and stores for the Middle East, as well as for the assault forces training and assembling in Tunisia, were passing straight through the narrow seas. To defend these convoys Sir Andrew Cunningham commanded substantial naval strength, both British and American.

To turn now to the movements of Allied shipping, the normal practice was for the KM convoys, which sailed from Britain to Gibraltar under the care of the Western Approaches command, to

---

[1] See Vol. II, Map 31. Admiral Sir John Cunningham took over the Levant Command from Admiral Sir Ralph Leatham on 6th June 1943.

[2] See Vol. II, p. 444.

join with the UG convoys from America, which the U.S. Navy brought across to Gibraltar.[1] After passing that base the convoys became a British responsibility, but the surface escorts generally included American as well as British ships. In between the passages of these large military convoys smaller 'intermediate' ones, called GTX if eastbound or XTG if westbound, were run. Convoy GTX.1 sailed from Gibraltar on the 24th of May, and reached Alexandria safely on the 4th of June; and no less than four of the large convoys followed through in that same month. This great acceleration of the traffic entering the Mediterranean produced the largest convoy of the war up to that date. UGS.8A, originally of fifty-eight ships from Casablanca, combined with KMS.15, originally of seventy-four from Britain; and, after three ships had been detached at Gibraltar, no less than 129 entered the Mediterranean together on the 2nd of June. They covered over sixty-eight square miles of sea, and were screened by nineteen escorts. Eighty-six ships were soon detached to Oran and Algiers, but a few new ones joined. Smaller sections broke off for other North African ports and for Malta, and the rest of the convoy reached Tripoli safely on the 8th of June. On this occasion the enemy's reaction was slight; but it was not to be expected that he would allow such vast Armadas again to enjoy complete immunity. On our side the successful protection of the first through convoys greatly enhanced the confidence of the naval and air commands, and justified the decision to continue building up the forces for the invasion of Sicily by the shortest route. The later June convoys were strongly escorted by surface ships, and were provided with virtually continuous air cover, sent out from successive Allied bases as they passed slowly along the North African coast. To give an idea of the scale on which this protection was provided, and its effectiveness, we will briefly follow the progress of an important convoy which left Gibraltar on the 22nd of June. Under strong air cover it reached 'the Narrows' safely on the 26th, by which time its numbers had risen to forty-one merchantmen and twelve surface escorts. Soon after rounding Cape Bon and turning south for Tripoli nearly 200 fighter-bombers attacked; and after dark they were followed by about a score of Ju.88 torpedo-bombers. The standing air patrols were quickly reinforced, and generally engaged the attackers well before they reached the convoy. Not many enemies were actually shot down in the air fighting, but the Allied fighters broke up the attacking formations and harassed them so severely that not a ship was lost from the convoy. The operation was a fine success to the North-West African Coastal Air Force, and provided a splendid example of what could be done for coastal shipping by

---

[1] See Vol. II, pp. 315–317 and Appendix F regarding the nomenclature and routes of these convoys.

shore-based fighters, directed by an efficient system of control based on radar warning of the enemy's approach.

On the 12th of June King George VI arrived by air at Algiers, where he spent some busy days visiting and inspecting Allied ships. A week later he embarked in the cruiser *Aurora* for Malta. No more appropriate ship could have been named to carry out that duty; for she had led the original 'Force K' of cruisers and destroyers, which had struck from Malta at Italian convoys in the difficult autumn of 1941, and was still commanded by Commodore W. G. Agnew, who had led the earlier force so brilliantly.[1] The King arrived in the Grand Harbour early on the 20th. 'The entry of the *Aurora* flying the Royal Standard, with the battlements black with Maltese, was an unforgettable sight' wrote Sir Andrew Cunningham to the First Sea Lord. The King toured the dockyard and service establishments 'and received ovations wherever he went'. After a very full day in Malta he sailed again for Tripoli to inspect the Eighth Army.

While the June convoys were making their passages almost unharmed by U-boats and aircraft, the decision to capture Pantelleria and other small islands lying between the Tunisian coast and Sicily was put into effect. Preliminary bombing and bombardments had started in the middle of May[2], and they continued with rising intensity until the assault forces, commanded by Rear-Admiral R. R. McGrigor, sailed from Sfax and Sousse between 1 p.m. on the 10th and the early hours of the 11th of June. Heavy final bombardments from sea and air were followed by a summons to surrender, and when no answer to this was received the assault forces landed. Little resistance was encountered, and after a message was received from the garrison commander 'Beg to surrender through lack of water' all further military action was stopped. On the 12th the smaller island of Lampedusa, which had been subdued by prolonged bombing and bombardments, also surrendered. Another step towards ensuring full Allied control of the Sicilian Channel was thus completed. Though the Italian naval historian considers that Sicily could have been invaded without capturing Pantelleria[3], and suggests that, if it was necessary to capture the island, a quite excessive effort was expended by the Allies, to have left even a small base in the enemy's possession so close off the ports where about half of the invasion army for Sicily was assembling, and from which it would soon sail, would have been to court avoidable losses. Moreover by far the most important reason for capturing the island was that its airfield was badly needed for use by our own fighters during the early stages of the invasion of Sicily. Malta alone could not operate and maintain sufficient aircraft,

[1] See Vol. I, pp. 532–533.
[2] See Vol. II, p. 444.
[3] See M. A. Bragadin, *Che ha fatto la Marina?* (Garzanti, 1949), pp. 436–445.

and the Tunisian airfields were too far away to enable continuous cover to be provided from them. Finally it is not the case that the capture of Pantelleria and its smaller neighbour Lampedusa 'involved . . . the loss of a month's valuable time'. The selection of 'D-Day' for the invasion of Sicily depended on quite other factors than the seizure of those islands—the chief one being the assembly of the necessary forces, shipping and landing craft. Whether excessive strength was used in the reduction of the islands is another matter and, if today it seems that the large civil population might have been spared some suffering, it is at least fair to point out that the garrison did not surrender until after the assault forces had landed.

We must now retrace our steps to the beginning of the year to review the preparation of plans for the next Allied offensive. The reader who desires to follow in detail the British–American negotiations which culminated in the decision to invade Sicily must be referred to the volume of this series dealing with Allied Grand Strategy.[1] But without some knowledge of the discussions which preceded the launching of the operation it will be difficult to understand the problems which faced the Admiralty and Air Ministry and the naval and air commands concerned in the detailed planning and preparation. It therefore seems justifiable to give here an outline of the high-level discussions which took place between the Casablanca Conference in January 1943 and the approval of the final plan by the Combined Chiefs of Staff on the 13th of May.

The American Chiefs of Staff had come to the Casablanca Conference determined to press for the cross-Channel invasion of Europe in 1943; but their British colleagues were convinced that no such operation was practicable until the following year, and that a new offensive should be launched in the Mediterranean theatre as soon as possible after the conquest of Tunisia. The British view having prevailed on the main issue, alternative plans for the Mediterranean offensive were next discussed. Because an attack on Sardinia could be mounted as early as May, the British Chiefs of Staff at first proposed making that island the next objective. At the time they believed that, because the invasion of Sicily was a much more formidable venture, it would be impossible to undertake it until August. The British preference for Sardinia, however, received no American support. The outcome of the discussions was that, on the 19th of January, the Combined Chiefs of Staff agreed to the invasion of Sicily, and ordered that planning should at once be put in hand. The strategic purposes of the operation were, firstly, to make our Mediterranean shipping more secure; secondly, to divert enemy strength from Russia, and thirdly to increase the pressure on Italy

---

[1] *Grand Strategy*, Vol. IV, October 1942–August 1943 (in preparation).

decisively. It was next agreed that, provided Tunisia had been cleared of enemies, and that certain of its ports were made available for the assembly of British instead of American forces, the need to mount a large part of the expedition from Britain could be reduced. This enabled the date to be advanced to the period of the July moon. The final date was not, however, fixed until the 13th of May.

In February a special planning staff was set up at Algiers, and this formed the nucleus from which ultimately grew the headquarters of the Fifteenth Army Group, which was to carry out the operation. Certain very important strategic considerations quickly became apparent to the planners. In the first place it was obvious that the enemy could reinforce Sicily across the two-mile-wide Messina Straits much faster than the Allies could bring in troops from the Middle East, or even from North African ports. Secondly, although it was plain that the capture of Messina itself was the most important Allied object, it lay beyond the range of our single-seater fighter aircraft. As strong fighter cover over the landing beaches was considered absolutely essential to success, an assault at Messina, or on the north coast of Sicily, or on the greater part of the east coast was ruled out. This left only the beaches stretching from a point south of Syracuse round to Trapani in the west as possible sites for the initial landings; and on that part of the Sicilian coast there existed no ports through which an army could be kept adequately supplied.[1] Hence, from the naval point of view the rapid capture of Syracuse and Augusta, if not of Catania itself, assumed great importance. But there were other considerations than these which had to be taken into account. To provide the necessary air cover and support, the early capture of enemy airfields was essential. There were three groups of these—in the east of the island around Gerbini, in the southeast at Gela, and in the west at Castelvetrano. It was thus plain that the initial assaults had to be made where there were good prospects of quickly seizing at any rate some of the airfields. The first outline plan therefore provided for the British forces to land on both sides of Cape Passero, and the Americans in the far west of the island. On the 13th of March this plan was approved by General Eisenhower and by the three Service Commanders-in-Chief, Admiral Sir Andrew Cunningham, General Alexander and Air Chief Marshal Tedder; but it was at once rejected by General Montgomery, who was to command the military forces in the eastern assaults, on the ground that the strength allotted to the landings north of Cape Passero was inadequate to ensure the early capture of the adjacent airfields, and of the all-important seaports further north. In General Montgomery's view another division was needed for that assault.

---

[1] See Map 9.

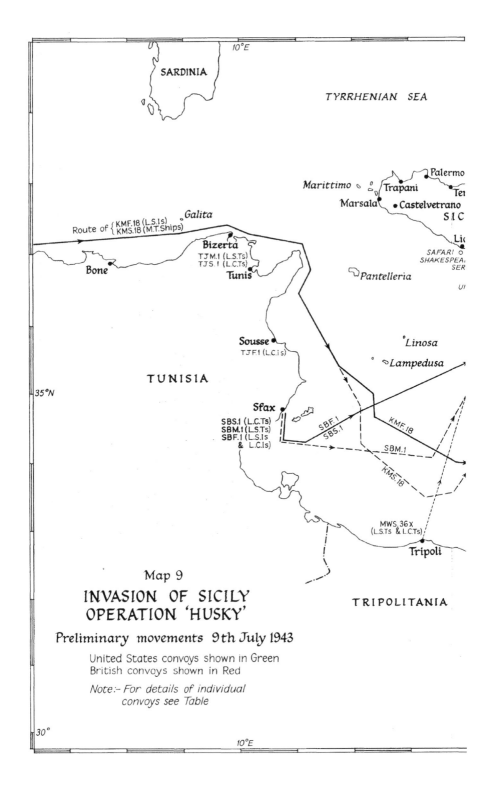

SARDINIA

TYRRHENIAN SEA

10°E

Marittimo

Palermo

Trapani

Te

Marsala

Castelvetrano

SIC

Li

SAFARI O.
SHAKESPEA.
SER

Pantelleria

UI

Route of { KMF.18 (L.S.Is)
            KMS.18 (M.T.Ships)

Galita

Bizerta
TJM.1 (L.S.Ts)
TJS.1 (L.C.Ts)

Tunis

Bone

Linosa

Lampedusa

Sousse
TJF1 (L.C.Is)

TUNISIA

35°N

Sfax

SBS.1 (L.C.Ts)
SBM.1 (L.S.Ts)
SBF.1 (L.S.Is
   & L.C.Is)

SBF.1
SBS.1

KMF 18

SBM.1

KMS.18

MWS.36 X
(L.S.Ts & L.C.Ts)

Tripoli

Map 9

INVASION OF SICILY
OPERATION 'HUSKY'

Preliminary movements 9th July 1943

United States convoys shown in Green
British convoys shown in Red

Note:- For details of individual
       convoys see Table

TRIPOLITANIA

30°

10°E

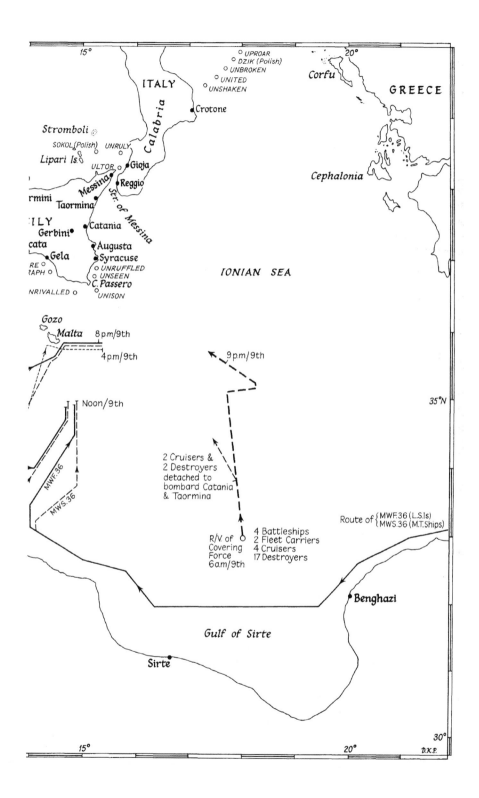

His opinion was accepted by General Alexander, and it was decided that, as the additional strength would have to be transferred from the western forces to the eastern, the assaults by the former on the south-west coast would have to be abandoned. Objections to this change were, however, soon voiced by the British Chiefs of Staff, because the main purpose of the western assault had been to capture the group of airfields around Castelvetrano, and if that were not accomplished the attack on Palermo itself, which we hoped to launch about four days after the initial landings, could not be safely undertaken. It was finally agreed that the additional division needed by General Montgomery should be provided from the Middle East, instead of by robbing the western task force, and that by embarking some of its men and equipment in Malta the increased needs for shipping and landing craft could be accepted. This plan, which appeared to meet all the requirements stated by the service representatives, was approved by General Eisenhower on the 7th of April. The Supreme Commander, however, was anxious regarding the possibility that the Germans might be able to reinforce Sicily quickly, and about the possible consequences of loss of surprise. Supported by General Alexander and Admiral Cunningham he told the Combined Chiefs of Staff that he considered that the operation should be abandoned if both unfavourable circumstances (large German reinforcements and loss of surprise) should materialise. The Combined Chiefs of Staff, however, took a more optimistic view, and on the 10th of April replied that in no circumstances would they consider such a proposal. This, however, did not at once stabilise the Allied plan.

Before the middle of May Tunisia had been cleared of Axis forces[1], and the Eighth Army Commander was able to study his part in the Sicilian invasion more closely. This led to further objections from General Montgomery, who felt that enemy opposition was likely to be stronger than had been allowed for, and that his army should not be divided by assaulting on both sides of Cape Passero. His new purpose was to concentrate his troops to the north of that promontory; but because this meant abandoning the early capture of the south-eastern group of airfields it was rejected by Admiral Cunningham and Air Chief Marshal Tedder. The former now told the First Sea Lord that 'we are arriving at a state of deadlock over "Husky" . . . the seriousness of it all is that we are with no agreed plan, just over two months off D Day . . . and even if we do get final agreement someone will be operating a plan he doesn't agree with'. The crux of the matter was that, to give the Eighth Army good prospects of success, both seaports and airfields had to be captured quickly; and at one time those two needs appeared to be mutually

---

[1] See Vol. II, pp. 441–442.

conflicting. General Montgomery's solution was to abandon the intended early capture of Palermo, and to throw the American army in immediately on his left; but this would involve reliance on maintaining the two armies over the beaches to an extent that had never before been deemed acceptable. The dilemma, which at one time appeared virtually insoluble, was in fact solved by the arrival from America of the new amphibious vehicles called DUKWS[1], whose remarkable performance in carrying men and stores direct from the assault ships and up the landing beaches reduced the need for the very early capture of a major port. As Admiral Vian wrote later of his experiences in the western assault 'the DUKWS first and last were the outstanding success of the operation'.

The final plan thus brought into being was approved by the Combined Chiefs of Staff on the 13th of May. It met General Montgomery's call to concentrate all the Army's strength at the south-eastern corner of the island, it provided for the seizure of the much-needed adjacent airfields, and it gave hopes of the reasonably early capture of Syracuse, Augusta and Catania as needed by the Navy. The planning staff at Algiers was now able to make real progress, and a start was made with framing the operation orders.

The British Eighth Army consisted of two Army Corps, the XIIIth and the XXXth. The former was to land on beaches on both sides of Avola (called 'Acid North' and 'Acid South') with the object of capturing Syracuse quickly, while the latter would attack in three sectors (called 'Bark East', 'Bark South' and 'Bark West') stretching around Cape Passero, and capture the airfield at Pachino.[2] The troops for the 'Acid North', 'Acid South' and 'Bark East' sectors were to be transported from the Middle East; those for 'Bark South' would come from Tunisian ports and Malta, while the 1st Canadian Division would be sent out from Britain to carry out the assault in 'Bark West'. The American Seventh Army was to land in three sectors on the south coast of Sicily adjoining the most westerly of the British assaults. These were called (from east to west) 'Cent', 'Dime' and 'Joss'. Forces for 'Cent' were to come from the United States, while those for 'Dime' and 'Joss' would embark in North African ports. The initial object of the American assaults was to capture the three south coast airfields of Ponte Olivo, Biscari and Comiso, and the small port of Licata. Heavy air attacks, especially against enemy airfields and communications, were to precede the assaults; but preliminary air and naval bombardments of the beach defences were sacrificed in order to increase the probability of achieving surprise.

---

[1] These amphibious craft, colloquially known as 'Ducks', derived their name from the factory serial letters of the firm producing them, viz.: D—year of origin (1942, fourth year of war); U—utility; K—front-wheel drive; W—six-wheeled.

[2] See Map 10.

The date and time of the assault were fixed for the 10th of July at 2.45 a.m., which was about three hours before dawn.[1] From the purely naval point of view the timing of the assault was not ideal. As the moon was in the first quarter, and set at 12.31 a.m., the final approach of the convoys would be made in darkness. Moreover the fact that the moon was waxing until the night of the 17th–18th, when it became full, meant that the defence of the assault anchorages might be handicapped during the critical period of building up the Army's strength. These conditions were accepted by the Navy in the interests of the paratroops, whom we had originally intended to drop shortly before the landings in order to soften the beach defences. In the event they were used in a different manner, as will be told later[2]; but by the time that decision was taken it was too late to alter the date and hour of the assault. Although Sir Andrew Cunningham commented later that the Navies were thus forced to accept unnecessarily disadvantageous conditions, it does not seem that their handicap was really appreciable. It may even be that Admiral Ramsay was correct in attributing the achievement of surprise partly to the acceptance of unfavourable conditions for an assault from the sea.[3]

After gaining its initial objects, the Eighth Army was to push north as fast as possible to capture Augusta and Catania and the group of airfields at Gerbini, while the Seventh Army would protect the British left flank. When the necessary ports and airfields were in Allied hands, the final stage of the operation—the complete clearance of the island—would be undertaken. The achievement of agreement on the best way of launching so vast and important an operation, when at one time the requirements of each of the three services had appeared irreconcilable, must always stand as an excellent example of the working of the British–American system of planning.

We will next briefly outline the Air and Naval Plans, on which the execution of the maritime side of operation 'Husky' depended.

The total air strength expected to be available amounted to $113\frac{1}{2}$ British and 146 American squadrons, comprising some 4,000 aircraft of all types. These included the North African Strategic and Tactical Air Forces, with whose part we need not here deal in detail, as well as the air commands mainly concerned with the maritime war, whose organisation was outlined earlier.[4]

Unlike the Naval Plan the Air Plan named no primary object, such as the safe arrival and disembarkation of the expeditionary

---

[1] Sunrise on the morning of the 10th of July was at 5.46 a.m. local time (Zone-2).

[2] See pp. 129–130 and 134.

[3] Supplement to the London Gazette No. 38895 of 25th April 1950. (H.M.S.O.). Admiral Cunningham's despatch para. 8, and Admiral Ramsay's report para. 3.

[4] See pp. 106–107 and Table 7.

force, and this omission may have provided fuel to those who later criticised the conduct of the air operations as having been unrelated to the needs of the other services. With regard to bombing policy the Air Plan laid down that 'the greater part of our effort will be directed with the object of gaining and maintaining air supremacy. With this in view most of the available bombing effort will be developed against enemy airfields in Sicily by day and night. . . . Air action will also be needed in support of the assaulting forces.' Though the relative priority of these two main purposes can perhaps be argued, it seems beyond doubt that together they stated the correct and proper employment of Allied air power. 'For the Western Task Force' continued the orders 'fighter-bombers will be available for close support and, in emergency, bombers can be diverted from their other tasks. . . . To be effective it normally will be necessary for bombing attacks in support of our ground forces to be pre-arranged.'

Certain American criticisms of the Air Plan, made after the operation, will be discussed later, and an attempt will then be made to assess their fairness.[1] Here we may remark that some highly-placed Royal Air Force officers later admitted that co-ordination of the Air Plan with those of the other services was shown by events to have been imperfect, particularly in the matter of close support of the assault forces; but the Air Plan itself was produced under very difficult conditions. The pressure of current operations in Tunisia prevented the senior officers who were to direct the air side of the invasion of Sicily from themselves supervising the planning; the changes in the outline plan demanded by the Army necessitated completely re-casting the Air Plan, and the physical separation of the planning staff in Algiers from the headquarters of the Seventh and Eighth Armies, which were to carry out the invasion, made matters yet more difficult.

After the arrival of the assault forces off the beaches and until the airfields in Sicily had been captured, fighter cover for the eastern assaults was to be provided by the R.A.F. from Malta. Congestion on that island's few airfields was acute, and although priority was given to stationing fighters on them, it was realised that their numbers would be insufficient to enable constant cover of the assault beaches to be afforded by day and by night. The rapid construction by the Americans of an airfield on the small neighbouring island of Gozo did, however, appreciably ease this problem. The western assault forces would be protected by R.A.F. and U.S.A.A.F. squadrons working from Tunisia and Pantelleria, as well as from Malta. In addition to these important responsibilities the Air Plan provided for strategic bombing of targets such as the ports of Naples,

See pp. 139–140.

Messina and Palermo, to hinder the build-up of enemy reinforcements and their despatch to Sicily. For the last week before the landings, it was intended to strike so heavily at the enemy's airfields that interference with the landings by the Axis air forces would not be serious. Lastly in the long list of duties required of the Air Forces came the need to watch for any sign of movement by the Italian fleet in the Ionian and Tyrrhenian Seas, and to attack both warships and supply vessels whenever opportunities occurred.

The Naval Plan for the operation was issued by Sir Andrew Cunningham on the 20th of May. Though it comprised a substantial volume it was in essence very simple. The capture of the island of Sicily was, said the preamble, 'a large and complicated operation involving . . . the movement of some 2,500 ships and major landing craft'. Landings were to be made in two separate but adjoining sectors on the south-east and south coasts; the former by British forces from the Middle East, Tunisia and Britain, and the latter by American forces from the United States and North Africa. The British, or Eastern, Naval Task Force was to be commanded by Admiral Sir Bertram Ramsay, who was also Admiral Cunningham's deputy, while Vice-Admiral H. K. Hewitt, U.S.N., commanded the American, or Western, Naval Task Force. The main naval covering forces were to be under Vice-Admiral Sir A. U. Willis, the commander of 'Force H' in the western Mediterranean. Rear-Admiral T. H. Troubridge was to command the assaults in the 'Acid North', 'Acid South' and 'Bark East' sectors already mentioned, all of which would sail from the Middle East. Rear-Admiral R. R. McGrigor had charge of the landings in 'Bark South', which were to be mounted in Tunisia, while Rear-Admiral Sir Philip Vian would bring out from Britain the forces which were to land in 'Bark West'. The three American landings in the 'Cent', 'Dime' and 'Joss' sectors were commanded by Rear-Admirals A. G. Kirk, J. L. Hall and R. L. Conolly, U.S.N., respectively. Within all these eight sectors separate beaches were allocated to each of the assault units comprising the larger forces.[1]

The three British and three American subordinate flag officers were, under their Task Force Commanders' directions, responsible for bringing the assault convoys safely to their destinations, for landing their troops, and for giving the soldiers the initial support needed. To each of them was therefore allocated a substantial number of warships, the types of which varied according to the probable needs of each individual force. It would be tedious to give these in full detail, but the senior officers flew their flags in ships which had, in greater or lesser degree, been converted and equipped

---

[1] See Vol. II, pp. 322–324 and Map 33, regarding the normal British practice and procedure in a combined operation at this time.

to fulfil the function of Combined Operations Headquarters ships[1], and their forces included destroyers and smaller vessels for convoy escort work, minesweepers to clear the approach channels, heavily-armed monitors, small gunboats and special landing craft to give fire support. A.A. ships would help keep the skies clear, motor launches were to lead in the first waves of assault landing craft, and vessels such as netlayers were included to protect the ports which we hoped to capture.[2]

In each of the British sectors a 'Senior Naval Officer Landing' was appointed to carry the responsibility for the naval side of the actual assaults. They were officers of Captain's rank who had, of recent years, specialised in the organisation and execution of combined operations. They and their staffs sailed in Landing Ships Infantry (L.S.Is) with the first assault convoys. During the period of preparation for the invasion of Sicily they had carried out all the training of their landing craft crews, and had established the intimate understanding with the senior officers of the Army units whom they were to put ashore, on which so much depended. The creation of this highly specialised body of experts had been a gradual evolution since the early days of the war, and the need had been reinforced by the experiences of the Dieppe raid.[3] Latterly every effort had been made to keep together the staffs of all three services who were trained and experienced in combined operations, and to leave them in the same ships, thus making their experience in one assault fully profitable to the next. Another aspect of the organisation of combined operations to which considerable attention had been given since the North African landings of November 1942 was the provision of trained parties of specialists drawn from all three services, but principally from the Army and Navy, to control the landing of vehicles, stores and ammunition. These were colloquially known as 'Beach Bricks', and included the naval Beach Commandos. In operation 'Husky' the parties detailed for the British sector alone numbered some 2,600 officers and men; and their work in producing order out of the inevitable confusion arising from the simultaneous arrival and discharge of large numbers of landing craft was commended on all sides.

Though the Eastern Task Force was preponderantly British and the Western Task Force American, each included some ships belonging to the other nation; but the organisation of the two forces was not identical. The Americans repeated the practice, which had served

---

[1] The *Ancon*, flagship of Admiral Kirk, U.S.N., was the first of the specially designed headquarters ships. All the remainder, both British and American, had been converted to that purpose; and some were still far from fully equipped. Admiral Conolly's flagship was a partially converted U.S. Coast Guard cutter.

[2] A summary of these naval forces is given in Table 8 (p. 121).

[3] See Vol. II, pp. 240–252.

them well in Operation 'Torch'[1], of placing the troop transports, store ships and all the multitude of auxiliary and landing vessels under the assault force commanders from the beginning[2]; while the British assault convoys had separate identities from the naval forces with which they were to be associated in the actual invasion, and only came under the force commanders when they approached the assault area. Apart from national preference for one or other system, it was the greater distances over which many of the British convoys had to sail, with their escorts frequently changing, that decided the organisation of the forces destined for the eastern assaults.

Turning to the opposition which might be encountered, the plan stated that although the Italian fleet still possessed considerable strength its past record of inactivity and lack of success were considered to account for its present low morale. 'It must, however, be recognised' continued the orders 'that if it is ever going to fight, it must fight now in defence of its country . . . and that it is strategically well placed to do so'.[3] Hence arose the need to provide strong covering forces, especially for the more exposed Eastern Task Force.

Sir Andrew Cunningham's objects were tersely described as 'the safe and timely arrival of the assault forces at their beaches, the cover of their disembarkation, and subsequently their support and maintenance'. Strong escort and covering forces, both naval and air, would protect the convoys during their progress along the African coast and during the actual assaults. The heavy covering force was to assemble to the north of the Gulf of Sirte during the day before the actual landings[4], and lighter forces would protect the exposed northern and western flanks of the assault areas. Enemy reserves were to be 'contained' by the ruse of a demonstration off western Sicily; arrangements for the protection of follow-up and return convoys were laid down; and, finally, the Naval Commander would 'continue to support and maintain our armies to the full extent of their requirements'. The preliminary dispositions, which were worked out in great detail for every port from Gibraltar to Haifa and Port Said, showed exactly where every unit taking part was to

---

[1] See Vol. II, pp. 312–337.

[2] See Morison, Vol. IX, Appendix, I for details of the Western Task Force's organisation.

[3] The strength of the Italian fleet (effective ships only) was at the time as follows:

Battleships	6
Cruisers	7
Destroyers	32
Torpedo-boats	16
Escort Vessels	27
Submarines	48
M.T.Bs and M.G.Bs	About 115

[4] See Map 9.

The Invasion of Sicily, operation 'Husky', 10th July, 1943
Above. The main assault convoy KMF.18 from Britain passes through the
Mediterranean.
Below. Convoy MWF.36 from the Middle East bound for the 'Acid South' sector.
(Note barrage balloons flown from some ships.)

The Invasion of Sicily, 10th July, 1943

Above. Landing craft leaving Sousse.

Below. Approaching the beaches.

The Invasion of Sicily, 10th July, 1943

Above. A 'Bark South' beach: the 51st Division landing.

Below. Troops landing in 'Bark West' sector.

The capture of the
Italian Submarine
Bronzo off Syracuse
12th July, 1943. She is
shown in tow by
H.M.S. *Seaham*.

Left and below. The
crossing of the Messina
Straits, operation 'Bay-
town', 3rd September,
1943. DUKWS
approaching the Italian
coast and Eighth Army
units disembarking near
Reggio.

be located for the last eight days before the assault. The order to 'carry out operation "Husky" ', would be the executive signal to set the whole of the vast organisation in motion. Control of all forces would remain centralised in the hands of the Commander-in-Chief until they entered the two assault areas, when it would pass to the Eastern and Western Naval Task Force Commanders.

The Naval Commander's intention was, then, 'to bring the assaulting troop convoys intact within sufficient distance of the island' to enable the two Task Force Commanders to accomplish their objects. The actual assaults would be conducted according to the orders of Admirals Ramsay and Hewitt and were 'to be pressed home with relentless vigour, regardless of loss or difficulty'. The strength of the naval forces allocated to the operation is shown in the table below.

Table 8. Naval Forces for Operation 'Husky'

Class	British	American	Other Nations
Battleships . . .	6	—	—
Fleet Carriers . .	2 (97 F.A.A. aircraft)	—	—
Cruisers . . .	10	5	—
A-A Ships . . .	4	—	—
Fighter Direction Ships .	2	—	—
Monitors . . .	3	—	—
Gunboats . . .	3	—	2 Dutch
Minelayers . . .	1	3	—
H.Q. Ships . . .	5	4	—
Destroyers . . .	71	48	6 Greek, 3 Polish
Escort Vessels . .	35 (2 R.I.N.)	—	1 Greek
Minesweepers . .	34	8	—
Landing Ships Infantry .	8	—	—
Major Landing Craft .	319	190	—
Minor Landing Craft .	715	510	—
Coastal Craft. . .	160	83	—
Submarines . . .	23	—	1 Dutch, 2 Polish
Miscellaneous Vessels .	58	28	
Merchant Ships, Troop Transports and M.T. Ships	155	66	7 Dutch, 4 Polish, 1 Belgian, 4 Norwegian
TOTALS . . .	1614	945	31

From the foregoing brief summary of Allied plans and intentions the reader will realise that the invasion of Sicily which, in its first stage, involved landing some 115,000 British Empire troops and over

66,000 Americans on a comparatively small stretch of the east and south coasts of the island, necessitated far-reaching maritime movements, starting not only from the Middle East and North Africa but from the distant ports of Britain and the United States. All the military forces concerned were to be either afloat or concentrated in the shore zones allotted to them five days before the actual assault. The first convoy bringing troops and stores from America to the 'Cent' sector of the western assault area sailed as early as the 28th of May. Six assault and follow-up convoys were to be formed from these ships and others which were to assemble at Oran and Algiers (called NCF.1 and 2 and NCS. 1, 2, 3, and 4), and together they would transport General Patton's Seventh Army and all its assault craft and supplies to Sicily. Convoy NCS.1 was to sail from Algiers on the 4th of July, and would be quickly followed by the main assault convoy NCF.1 of Admiral Hewitt's Western Task Force.[1]

The ships coming from Britain, which carried the 1st Canadian Division and comprised the assault and follow-up convoys for 'Bark West', were to sail in four convoys (called KMF.18 and 19 and KMS.18 and 19) between the 20th of June and the 1st of July, the slower convoys starting several days before the faster ones. The main movement of XIII and XXX Corps of the Eighth Army from the Middle East would also be made in four convoys (called MWF.36 and 37 and MWS.36 and 37), which would set out from Port Said and Alexandria for the 'Acid North', 'Acid South' and 'Bark East' sectors between the 3rd and 9th of July. The landing craft convoys, which were to carry the 51st (Highland) Division from Bizerta, Sousse and Tunis to the 'Bark South' sector, would not sail until the 8th and 9th of July.[2] Last to sail were convoys SBF.2 and 3, composed of Landing Craft Infantry, carrying assault troops from Malta for the 'Bark South' assault. These convoys had the shortest distance to travel, and only left harbour at 3 p.m. on the 9th and early on the 10th respectively. The composition of all the assault and follow-up convoys which took part in the invasion of Sicily, together with a summary of the troops they carried, is set out in the next table.

Surface escorts had, of course, to be provided for all these convoys, during the ocean journeys and also for the passages along the North African coast; and complex arrangements for relieving and refuelling

---

[1] See Map 9.

[2] It is interesting to recall that when, in 255 B.C., after the Roman fleet had been destroyed in a violent storm, the Carthaginians sent an expedition to invade Sicily, the elephants, which were the contemporary armoured fighting vehicles, must have been embarked in one or more of the harbours from which this twentieth-century mechanised army sailed. *Polybius* (I.38) records that 'The Carthaginians . . . at once despatched Hasdrubal to Sicily, giving him the troops they previously had and a force which had joined them from Heraclea, together with 140 elephants . . . Hasdrubal having crossed safely to Lilybaeum (Marsala) occupied himself in drilling unopposed his elephants and the rest of his force'. (*Trans. Loeb Classical Library*, Heinemann, 1922.)

Table 9. Operation 'Husky' Assault and Follow-up Convoys

I. BRITISH

[A] FROM BRITAIN. TROOPS CARRIED:

1st, 2nd, 3rd Canadian Infantry Brigades (1st Canadian Division).
1st Canadian Army Tank Brigade.
Nos. 40 and 41 Royal Marine Commandos.
73rd A.A. Brigade, Royal Artillery.

Convoy Designation	Port and Date of Departure	Speed (Knots)	Composition	Assault Sector
KMS.18A	Clyde 20/6	8	8 L.S.T. 1 L.S.G. 1 Petrol Carrier	Bark West
KMS.18B	Clyde 24/6	8	17 M.T. Store Ships 1 L.S.G. (Joined by 7 L.S.Ts from Algiers)	Bark West
KMS.19	Clyde 25/6	7	31 M.T. Store Ships 6 L.S.Ts 5 Petrol Carriers 1 Collier (Joined by 9 M.T. Store Ships for Western Task Force from Algiers)	Bark West
KMF.18	Clyde 28/6	12	1 H.Q. Ship 3 L.S.Ts 8 L.S.Is	Bark West
KMF.19	Clyde 1/7	12	9 Troop Transports 1 L.S.I. (Joined by 4 Troop Transports for Western Task Force. See NCF.2)	Bark West

[B] FROM MIDDLE EAST. TROOPS CARRIED:

13th, 15th, 17th Infantry Brigades (5th Infantry Division).
69th, 151st, 168th Infantry Brigades (50th Infantry Division).
231st Independent Infantry Brigade.
No. 3 Commando.
4th Armoured Brigade.

Convoy Designation	Port and Date of Departure	Speed (Knots)	Composition	Assault Sector
MWS.36	Alexandria 3/7	8	30 M.T. Store Ships 15 L.S.Ts (Joined MWS.36X, q.v.) 2 L.S.Gs 3 Oilers (Joined from Malta)	Acid North Acid South Bark East
MWS.37	Alexandria 6/7	7	30 M.T. Store Ships 2 Petrol Carriers (Joined from Malta)	Acid North Acid South Bark East

Table 9 (continued)

Convoy Designation	Port and Date of Departure	Speed (Knots)	Composition	Assault Sector
MWF.36	Port Said 5/7	12	1 H.Q. Ship 17 L.S.Is (4 L.C.Is joined from Tripoli)	}Acid North Acid South Bark East
MWF.37	Alexandria 9/7	12	12 L.S.Is	{Acid North Acid South

[C] FROM NORTH AFRICA AND MALTA. TROOPS CARRIED:
152nd, 153rd and 154th Infantry Brigades (51st Division).
23rd Armoured Brigade.

Convoy Designation	Port and Date of Departure	Speed (Knots)	Composition	Assault Sector
SBS.1	Sfax 7/7	6	1 L.S.T. 29 L.C.Ts	Bark South
SBM.1	Sfax 8/7	8	26 L.S.Ts	Bark South
SBF.1	Sfax 8/7	13	1 H.Q. Ship 4 L.S.Is (6 L.C.Is joined from Malta)	Bark South
MWS.36X	Tripoli 8/7	6	15 L.S.Ts (see MWS.36) 48 L.C.Ts	All Eastern Task Force Sectors
SBF.2	Malta 9/7	12½	23 L.C.Is	Bark South
SBF.3	Malta 10/7	12½	14 L.C.Is	Bark South

NOTE: Each of the above groups of British convoys carried a proportion of Divisional and Army artillery, Divisional Royal Engineers, Royal Army Service Corps, and Army Troops such as Airfield Construction Groups.

II. AMERICAN

TROOPS CARRIED: 1st, 3rd, 9th and 45th Infantry Divisions.
1st, 3rd, 9th and 4th Infantry Divisions.
2nd Armoured Division.
2nd Paratroop Regiment.

Convoy Designation	Port and Date of Departure	Speed (Knots)	Composition	Assault Sector
NCF.1	Oran 5/7 Algiers 6/7	13	1 H.Q. Ship 22 Combat Loaders (cf. British L.S.I.) 7 M.T. Store Ships	}Cent Dime
NCF.2	Algiers 9/7	12	4 Troop Transports (joined KMF.19, q.v.)	Reserve
TJF.1	Bizerta 5/7 via Sousse 9/7	12½	106 L.C.Is	}Cent 6 Joss 54 Dime 19 Reserve 27

Convoy Designation	Port and Date of Departure	Speed (Knots)	Composition	Assault Sector
TJS.1	Bizerta and Tunis 8/7	6½	100 L.C.Ts 16 L.C.Ts (British)	Cent 8 Joss 85 Reserve 7
TJM.1	Bizerta and Tunis 8/7	8	76 L.S.Ts 2 L.S.Ts (British)	Cent 14 L.S.Ts Dime 16 L.S.Ts Joss 40 L.S.Ts Reserve 6 L.S.Ts
NCS.1	Oran 4/7 (via Tripoli)	8	7 M.T. Store Ships	Reserve
NCS.2	Oran 9/7	8	17 M.T. Store Ships	Cent Dime

Abbreviations:

M.T.   Mechanical Transport.
L.S.I.   Landing Ship Infantry (includes Landing Ships Personnel).
L.S.T.   Landing Ship Tank.
L.S.G.   Landing Ship Gantry (includes Landing Ships Carrier).
L.C.T.   Landing Craft Tank.
L.C.I.   Landing Craft Infantry.
    Sub-classifications of Landing Ships and Craft are omitted.

the escorts were included in the plans. Once inside the Mediterranean, day and night air cover was to be continuously provided by the air commands mentioned earlier. But the organisation of the assault and follow-up convoys did not, of course, mark the end of the work of the planning staffs on the maritime side of the operation; for arrangements had to be made to clear ships which had landed their troops and equipment as quickly as possible from the assault area, and to assemble them into return convoys. These would start to sail in various directions long before the last follow-up convoy had arrived; and the return convoys also had to be protected. The burden of servicing the heavy traffic passing in both directions through the Mediterranean was mainly borne by the bases at Gibraltar, Algiers and Alexandria.

The success which attended the careful arrangements made for the protection and routeing of the numerous convoys is best demonstrated by anticipating events and mentioning here that only one convoy from the east and one from the west was attacked. The three ships in KMS.18B sunk by German U-boats on the 4th and 5th of July off Cape Tenez and one from MWS.36 torpedoed off Derna on the 6th by U.453 were the only losses inflicted by the enemy before the ships reached the assault areas.[1]

Very careful plans were laid to mislead the enemy about the date and the destination of the assaults. The convoys were to conform as long as possible to the movements of normal through-Mediterranean

[1] The attacks on 4th July were made by U.409 and U.375, but it is uncertain which sank which ship. U.593 sank one ship on 5th July. U.409 and U.375 were themselves sunk before the end of the month (see p. 138).

shipping, and concentration in the central basin was to be delayed until the last moment. This, and the appearance of strong naval forces in the Ionian Sea would, it was hoped, suggest an attack on Crete and Greece; while similar measures taken in the west were intended to produce the impression that the American forces in North Africa were about to attack Sardinia and Corsica, followed by landings in southern France. But, because of the size of the shipping movements involved, we did not expect that complete strategical or tactical surprise would be achieved. Rather did we hope to delay the reinforcement of Sicily, to reduce the air threat to the great concourse of Allied ships, and to keep the main Italian naval forces to the east of Sicily. Finally among the deceptive measures employed mention must be made of the macabre ruse of placing in the sea off the Spanish coast a disguised corpse bearing faked letters from high officers so worded as to give the impression that the attack, when it came, would be against Greece and Sardinia.[1] The corpse was washed ashore and the letters were recovered and sent to the German High Command by an agent in Spain, exactly as had been hoped. Though Hitler and his intimate advisers were certainly deceived, the local German and Italian commanders seem to have been less gullible, and additional reinforcements were in fact moved into Sicily towards the end of June.

Having briefly described the organisation of the invasion convoys we must now turn to the other maritime forces involved in the operation. These were mostly British, and consisted of Admiral Willis's covering force and of a support force commanded by Rear-Admiral C. H. J. Harcourt. The former (Force H) comprised the battleships *Nelson*, *Rodney*, *Warspite* and *Valiant*, the fleet carriers *Indomitable* and *Formidable*, the 12th Cruiser Squadron of six light cruisers, and three flotillas totalling eighteen destroyers. This powerful fleet was to operate to the east of Sicily to cover the assaults from interference by the Italian Navy. Two more battleships (the *Howe* and *King George V*), with six destroyers for screening, were retained in the western basin to cover the eastward movement of the assault convoys, to carry out the deceptive demonstration off western Sicily mentioned earlier, and to reinforce Admiral Willis should casualties be suffered by him.

Admiral Harcourt's four cruisers and six destroyers were to work close inshore with the assault forces, protecting them against attack by enemy light forces which might make lightning raids from the Messina Straits, and providing the initial close gun support which the Army was certain to need. The supporting and covering forces for the Western Naval Task Force were divided between the three

---

[1] See Ewen Montagu, *The Man Who Never Was* (Evans Bros., 1953).

Attack Force Commanders, and included five American six-inch cruisers and the British monitor *Abercrombie*. Lastly there were forty-seven submarines (including six French, four Greek, two Polish, one Dutch and one Yugo-Slav) based on Malta, Algiers and Oran. Seven were allocated to the assault forces to act as navigational beacons during the final approach, three were to land small raiding parties in the enemy's rear, while about a dozen others were sent on offensive patrols in the Tyrrhenian Sea, off the northern entrance to the Messina Straits and off Taranto, with the object of intercepting enemy warships which might put to sea.

At the end of May preliminary exercises were carried out in the Gulf of Aqaba and Red Sea, and in mid-June rehearsals for the Eastern Task Force took place with troops embarked. By the beginning of July loading of the assault and follow-up convoys was virtually complete, and on the 1st Admiral Ramsay and his staff transferred from Alexandria to Malta. There, as had been expected, the assembly and loading of the additional landing craft for the extra division which had been included at General Montgomery's request produced many difficult problems. They were, however, all dealt with successfully by the Vice-Admiral, Malta (Vice-Admiral A. J. Power) and his staff.

Meanwhile the whole vast and intricate organisation, on which so many months of thought and planning had been expended, was set in motion on the morning of the 4th of July by Admiral Sir Andrew Cunningham's laconic order to 'carry out Operation Husky'. He also sent a general message to all his forces telling them that 'We are about to embark on the most momentous enterprise of the war —striking for the first time at the enemy in his own land', and emphasising that 'great risks must be and are to be accepted'.[1] The American General Bedell Smith, Chief of Staff to the Supreme Commander, had this message framed and hung in his office at Algiers as a reminder to all who visited him that in a combined operation the hazards were immense, and that success depended, as Cunningham said, on the sense of duty by which every individual officer or man was inspired. Meanwhile, in the Admiralty, Admiral Pound was anxiously watching the start of the far-reaching naval movements for which he held so great a share of the responsibility. On the 3rd of July he wrote to Admiral Cunningham to wish him 'the best of luck in your great endeavour'. 'The result' continued the First Sea Lord 'will be the determining factor in our plans'.

The assault forces from the Middle East, which included 65,000 men, 10,000 vehicles and 60,000 tons of stores, now made their way towards a rendezvous in 35° North 14° 45′ East (about fifty miles

---

[1] For the full text of this message see Viscount Cunningham of Hyndhope, *A Sailor's Odyssey*, pp. 550–551 (Hutchinson, 1951).

south of Malta), which they had been ordered to reach by noon on the 9th of July; ships and craft from Malta were sailed to join their convoys at sea; Admiral McGrigor's landing craft convoys left North African ports for the assault in 'Bark South', as did the corresponding American convoys for the western assaults; Admiral Vian was bringing the 1st Canadian Division along the North African coast, and Admiral Hewitt's ships for the 'Dime' and 'Cent' assaults had left Oran and Algiers and were steering the same course as Admiral Vian towards the Tunisian War Channel, spaced at comfortable intervals from each other.[1]

We will next follow the fortunes of the Eastern Naval Task Force. Early on the 9th Admiral Ramsay sailed from Malta in the *Antwerp*[2], to witness the concentration of the convoys from Britain and the Middle East and their junction with the landing craft coming from North African ports and Malta. At noon on that day, the datum time for the main assault convoys to reach the rendezvous south of Malta, Admiral Ramsay assumed command of the whole of the Eastern Naval Task Force.

After passing through the rendezvous position the ships and craft for the eastern assaults were to steer towards their several 'release positions'.[3] The fast assault convoys were to arrive first, two and a half hours before 'H-hour', followed by the gun support craft and the first L.C.Ts. Next to arrive were the slow assault convoys, and finally, three hours after 'H-hour', came the L.S.Ts. The ships and craft for the western assaults, and Admiral Vian's ships for 'Bark West', were all routed to pass through a position five miles west of Gozo between 4 and 7.20 p.m. on the 9th, whence they would proceed towards their release positions in a similar manner to the ships taking part in the eastern assaults.

One part of the covering force (*Warspite, Valiant, Formidable,* and nine destroyers) left Alexandria on the 7th and steered to the west, to concentrate with the *Nelson, Rodney, Indomitable,* two light cruisers and six destroyers from Algiers in a position 240 miles south-east of Malta early on the 9th. That day the cruisers *Aurora* and *Penelope* and two destroyers, which had escorted convoy KMS.18 through the Tunisian War Channel and then joined the covering force, were detached to bombard Catania and Taormina, and then protect the exposed flank of the most northerly assault. While carrying out these bombardments the cruiser flagship intercepted a message from Taormina telling the Italians in Cagliari (Sardinia) that 'there is a war on here'. The Sicilian station was very soon to discover that the

---

[1] See Map 9.

[2] The *Antwerp* was a converted cross-Channel steamer, which was actually too small to serve as a satisfactory headquarters ship.

[3] See Vol. II, pp. 322–324 and this volume, Map 10.

night's disturbance did indeed signify that the war had arrived on their doorstep.

On the evening of the 9th the rest of the fleet first made a deceptive movement to the east and then, after dark, steered for a position a few miles off Cape Passero whence it could effectively cover the eastern assault area. Dawn on the 10th found this great body of war-ships manœuvring as though taking part in a peace-time exercise right in the middle of the waters which Mussolini had once unwisely claimed as '*mare nostrum*'. The day was undisturbed by enemy sub-marine or air activity—let alone by any appearance of the Italian fleet. Thereafter a succession of ships was detached in turn to patrol close inshore on the northern flank of the assault, and on the 12th the main force returned to Malta to fuel. It was the first time since December 1940 that British battleships had moored in the Grand Harbour, and it was singularly appropriate that the *Warspite*, which had made the 1940 visit as Admiral Cunningham's flagship, should have been present on this later occasion.[1]

Meanwhile the reserve squadron of the covering force (the *Howe*, *King George V*, two light cruisers and six destroyers) sailed from Algiers on the 9th to carry out the diversion off western Sicily, in-cluding shore bombardments of Trapani and Marsala.

Dawn on the 9th of July, the day before the assaults, broke over a calm sea; but the north-westerly wind freshened considerably in the afternoon and set up a nasty enough lop to cause the troops in the landing craft severe discomfort, and slow down the convoys. This produced 'considerable anxiety' at command headquarters; but it was by then 'manifestly too late for postponement', and matters had to be allowed to take their course.[2] From 11.30 p.m. onwards, to Admiral Cunningham's relief, 'the wind mercifully started to ease', and in the Eastern Task Force 'daylight on the 10th saw the begin-ning of a perfect day with a clear blue sky and steadily decreasing swell'. Admiral Hewitt's ships, whose beaches were more exposed than those of the eastern assault forces, were not, however, at the end of the trouble caused by the sea and swell. None the less the un-favourable weather prevailing on the afternoon and evening of the 9th did probably contribute to the achievement of surprise. As Admiral Cunningham put it, the enemy considered that 'tonight at any rate they can't come', and relaxed his vigilance. 'But' continues the Naval Commander's report 'they came.'[3]

The assaults in the eastern sectors started with airborne landings just before daylight on the 10th of July. About 1,600 men of the

---

[1] See Vol. I, p. 304.

[2] Admiral Cunningham's despatch. Supplement to the London Gazette No. 38895 of 25th April 1950, paras 22–23 (H.M.S.O.).

[3] Ibid., para. 23.

1st British Airborne Division were embarked in North Africa in 137 gliders towed by Dakotas and other aircraft and were to seize strategic points south of Syracuse. Unfortunately faults in the planned timing of the operation were accentuated by the strong head winds encountered, and no less than sixty-nine gliders came down in the sea in consequence. Losses among the airborne troops were heavy; but the few who landed at or near the correct place did help to make the early capture of Syracuse possible.

In the 'Acid' sectors, although some of the personnel ships did not reach the correct release position at the intended time of fifteen minutes after midnight and there was still enough swell to make the lowering of the assault landing craft (L.C.As) hazardous and the embarkation of the troops in the L.C.Is difficult, the first waves managed to 'touch down' nearly on time, though by no means all at the correct spot. Admiral Ramsay considered that the landing craft crews acquitted themselves well; but the commander of 50th Division was critical of the organisation for the embarkation of the assault troops, of the delay in forming up the landing craft and despatching them inshore, and of the navigational errors which arose on the way in, which resulted in some of them touching down on the wrong beaches. No doubt there was a good deal to be said for both points of view; but at the time of operation 'Husky' we still had a long way to go towards perfecting inter-service organisation, and the weather certainly provided a severe test for the crews of the landing craft. In the event, and perhaps fortunately, resistance in the 'Acid' sectors was slight, and some desultory shelling of the beaches was quickly stopped by the supporting ships' gunfire. At 5 a.m. all shipping moved closer inshore, and just over an hour later the 50th Division reported 'All troops [of the assaults brigade] landed. Capture and mopping up of beach defences completed'. The slow convoy MWS.36 anchored off the beaches an hour later, and unloading continued steadily throughout the day. By the afternoon the large personnel ships had been cleared, and sailed in convoy to Malta.

As the landing ships and craft which had taken part in the assault were unloaded they were sent back to Malta or to North African ports, where they were reloaded and joined the ferry service running to and from the assault area. Because more L.S.Ts and landing craft were actually serviceable at the time of the assault than had been anticipated, it proved possible to start sending loaded craft out from Malta before any had returned from the beaches. No less than fifty-six L.S.Ts, thirty-six L.C.Ts and thirty-three L.C.Is left Malta fully loaded during the week following the invasion.

The departure of the large personnel ships from the 'Acid' sectors took place just in time to escape the first air attacks, which started at 1 p.m. on the 10th and continued intermittently, sometimes in considerable strength, until dark. The only serious casualty was the sinking, with heavy loss of life, of the hospital ship *Talamba*, which was lying, fully illuminated, five miles off the beaches. After dark enemy air raids were generally frustrated by the smoke screen put up by specially equipped craft, and by Allied night fighters. Before nightfall on the 10th British troops had entered Syracuse.

The assault force for the 'Bark East' sector was commanded by Captain Lord Ashbourne in the *Keren*. His ships had sailed from Egypt in convoy MWF.36, and carried the 231st Infantry Brigade. At 12.30 a.m. his three Landing Ships Infantry reached their release position. A confused sea made the lowering of the assault craft difficult, but they got away safely, though in somewhat ragged formation, and touched down nearly on time. The ships of the slow convoy then arrived, and the empty personnel ships were sent out of harm's way in convoy. Enemy aircraft attacked intermittently during the day but did no damage. The troops encountered little resistance on landing, and the support ships quickly subdued an enemy battery which opened fire on the beaches.

To the 'Bark South' sector Rear-Admiral McGrigor, whose head-quarters ship was the *Largs*, was carrying troops of the 51st Division to make a 'shore to shore' assault from North African ports and from Malta.[1] Apart from those embarked in the four medium-sized Landing Ships Infantry (L.S.Is) sailing in convoy SBF.1, the troops were all embarked in landing craft, and they had the most difficult time of any in the Eastern Task Force. The Tank Landing Craft convoy SBS.1 in particular was severely buffeted by the heavy seas prevailing on the afternoon and evening before D-Day. Several craft broke down and had to be taken in tow; but they all managed eventually to disembark their loads. The convoy was, however, two hours late in arriving.

When the leading ships reached the release position just after 12.30 a.m. the assault craft were quickly lowered and sent in. Although head seas and an unpleasant swell on the beaches produced difficulties, resistance was slight, and the troops got ashore with only light casualties. The L.C.Ts were ordered inshore as soon as they arrived, thus ensuring that tanks and anti-tank guns were available in time to meet the expected counter-attack. At daylight the beaches were surveyed, and then the Landing Ships Tank (L.S.Ts) were signalled to come inshore as soon as possible; but a 'false beach', or shingle reef offshore, caused trouble; and it was by unloading stores from L.S.Ts which had grounded on it that the

---

[1] A 'shore to shore' assault was one in which the troops landed from the craft in which they had embarked at their points of departure. In the more common 'ship to shore' assault the troops were carried by ship to the offshore lowering position, where they transferred to landing craft to make their assaults.

DUKWS first showed their remarkable versatility. In the afternoon of D-Day Convoy SBF.2 of twenty Landing Craft Infantry (L.C.Is) arrived and disembarked 4,000 men almost simultaneously. The L.S.Is and L.S.Ts were sent back to Malta as fast as they were unloaded, and by dark the 51st Division was well established on shore. Intermittent air attacks took place during the night, but did little damage.

Meanwhile Admiral Vian, in the headquarters ship *Hilary*, had reached the 'Bark West' sector at about 1 a.m. with the big convoy KMF.18, which had brought the 1st Canadian Division and two Royal Marine Commandos out from Britain. The L.C.Ts for this assault had come from Tripoli in a special convoy (called MWS.36X); but they had suffered from the weather on passage and were half-an-hour late.

We knew that the coast in this sector was by no means ideal for an assault from the sea, because of the reefs which lay close offshore; but this had been accepted in order to achieve the rapid capture of the adjacent airfield of Pachino and to support the left flank of XXX Corps, which had landed in the adjacent 'Bark South' sector.

The Royal Marine Commandos moved inshore in L.C.As immediately Admiral Vian's assault convoy had anchored; but the need to provide an alternative means of landing the troops in L.C.Ts, in case use of the L.C.As proved impracticable, caused some confusion and delay. However, in spite of the swell making the transfer of men from ships to landing craft very difficult, by 3.15 a.m. the assault troops had all got away, and by 5.30 'success signals' had been received in the headquarters ship from all beaches. The slow convoy KMS.18 arrived at about the same time, and unloading proceeded throughout the day. By nightfall empty ships were being sent back to Malta and Tripoli under escort. Resistance to the landings had been slight, and the only enemy battery to fire on the landing craft was quickly silenced by the 15-inch shells of the monitor *Roberts*. The troubles of the day in this sector were caused chiefly by the swell in the anchorage, by the heavy surf breaking on the shore, which caused landing craft to broach to, and by the 'false beaches' which prevented the big L.S.Ts unloading as intended. The American-invented 'pontoon causeways', which were towed across by L.S.Ts, helped later to unload craft which had grounded on the false beaches; but they were not available in time for the initial assaults. In the 'Bark West' sector the DUKWS once again proved invaluable in unloading the larger vessels, which were unable to reach the shore.

The beaches in 'Bark South' were so superior to those used in the 'Bark West' sector that on the 11th Admiral Ramsay decided to close the latter, and to concentrate all unloading through the former. The follow-up convoys KMF.19 and KMS.19 were therefore diverted to 'Bark South', and arrived there early on the 13th.

Meanwhile Admiral Hewitt's three American forces had made their assaults further to the west, and it is to them that we must now briefly turn.[1] Some 26,000 troops, most of them destined for Admiral Kirk's 'Cent' force, had crossed the Atlantic in two large convoys, and arrived at Oran on the 22nd of June. Admiral Hall's 'Dime' force had loaded 19,250 troops at Algiers, while Admiral Conolly's 'Joss' force had assembled and embarked 27,650 men, mainly in landing ships and craft, in Bizerta. To each sector commander were allocated warships for the same manifold duties as were needed in the British landings. By the early hours of the 7th of July the main American assault convoy (NCF.1) was off Algiers, steaming to the east along the same coastal route as was used by Admiral Vian's 'Bark West' assault force.[2] On the 8th it rounded Cape Bon, and made a wide sweep to the south before turning towards the rendezvous off Gozo, through which all the American assault forces were to pass at carefully regulated intervals. The movement of all the L.S.Ts, L.C.Is and L.C.Ts, the majority of which were allocated to Admiral Conolly's 'shore to shore' assault in the 'Joss' sector, also started on the 8th. They were formed into separate convoys according to class, and the L.C.I. convoy (TJF.1) was staged through Sousse in order to reduce congestion in Tunis harbour. The L.S.Ts and L.C.Ts sailed from Tunis and Bizerta on the 8th, and formed into convoys TJM.1 and TJS.1 respectively. After rounding Cape Bon they followed the routes which had been designed to bring them to the rendezvous at their appointed times on the evening of the 9th.

The landing craft of the Western Task Force were, like those of the Eastern Force, subjected to a severe buffeting by the short, steep seas raised by the north-west wind on the afternoon of the 9th; but they managed to keep to the times laid down in the orders. After passing through the position off Gozo, which the American historian has aptly described as 'a maritime marshalling yard'[3], the 'Joss' forces formed up for the approach, the assault convoy NCF.1 divided and set course for the 'Cent' and 'Dime' sectors, and the L.S.Ts and L.C.Is which were to take part in the two latter landings split off from their original convoys to join their own particular assault forces. To keep to the planned intention of making the initial landings at 2.45 a.m. the ships had to press ahead regardless of the weather, and it is a tribute to the seamanship of the landing craft crews that the severe conditions experienced during the approach

---

[1] See Morison, Vol. IX, Chapters IV–VII, for a full account of the assaults by the Western Naval Task Force.

[2] See Map 9.

[3] Morison, Vol. IX, p. 65.

did not seriously dislocate any part of the plans. Land was picked up by radar at 10 p.m., and the beacon submarines enabled final navigational checks to be made. The 'Cent' and 'Dime' forces reached their initial positions for the assault at about forty-five minutes after midnight—almost exactly at the time intended—and the lowering of the assault craft at once began.[1] But the earlier troubles caused by the weather, and the choppy sea still running in the transport anchorage, now caused delays; and 'H-hour' for the 'Cent' landings therefore had to be postponed until 3.45 a.m. Nor was that the end of Admiral Kirk's troubles, for when landing craft started to go inshore the heavy surf and the 'false beaches' off-shore, combined with indifferent handling of landing craft by some inexperienced crews, caused almost as heavy losses of craft as had been experienced in the Moroccan landings in operation 'Torch'.[2] Luckily bombardments by warships just before the touch-down had subdued the weak enemy forces in the locality, and resistance was slight. The first air attack took place at 4.30 a.m. and added to the confusion in the sector, though no ships were seriously damaged. But in spite of all these troubles the assault troops made good progress on shore and by the evening of D-Day had reached their initial objectives.

The centre American assault, in the 'Dime' sector, was to take place at the mouth of the Gela River, near the small town of the same name.[3] At first light on D-Day an American airborne division, consisting of some 2,800 men from North Africa, was to be dropped from 226 Dakotas inland of the assault beaches, to seize important points and hold up counter-attacks until the assault troops had consolidated their beach-heads. The troop carriers became very dispersed during the outward flight, with the result that the paratroops landed in widely scattered places; but the few who did reach their intended positions certainly helped to disorganise the enemy defences. Only eight troop carriers were lost, and although the operation was not a complete success it certainly fared better than the British airborne landings near Syracuse or an American reinforcement operation carried out two nights later.

The 'Dime' assault forces under Rear-Admiral Hall reached their allotted anchorage only about half an hour late, but the weather delayed the L.C.Is and L.S.Ts by two or three hours. Assault craft were lowered from the troop transports (which included two British L.S.Is), and carried inshore the U.S. Rangers (the equivalent to British Commandos) for the initial landings. Here the beaches were heavily mined, and enemy resistance was the strongest encountered anywhere in operation 'Husky'. Unloading difficulties on shore,

---

[1] See Map 10.
[2] See Vol. II, pp. 312-337, and Morison, Vol. IX, pp. 137-142.
[3] See Map 10.

enemy air attacks, gunfire from shore emplacements and counter-attacks by German as well as Italian forces combined to produce a difficult situation. In particular, tanks and anti-tank guns were not got ashore nearly as fast as had been intended. This and the lack of close tactical air support for the assault forces (a subject on which more will be said later), resulted in the task of stopping the enemy counter-attacks falling on the divisional artillery and supporting war-ships. It was indeed very fortunate that the naval gunfire available for the purpose proved adequate to the occasion.[1]

In the 'Dime' and in the adjacent 'Joss' sector attacks by German aircraft were at first heavier and more frequent than in the British sectors, and a few losses were suffered by the ships. The very sus-tained bombing to which the Axis airfields in Sicily had been sub-jected for several days before the invasion had not prevented the enemy reacting quite strongly. It is furthermore hard to avoid the conclusion that the arrangements made for the fighter protection of the American invasion fleet, and of the beaches in the western assault area, did not prove adequate. As the day progressed and losses to air attacks mounted, the demands for stronger fighter cover grew more insistent. Then when the fighters did turn up there was a great deal of wild firing by the ships, and several of our own aircraft were damaged. Bearing in mind that the enemy had been making low fighter-bomber attacks on the beaches and the ships, the breakdown in aircraft identification is easily to be understood, even if in certain cases it cannot be entirely excused. In spite of the troubles encoun-tered, by the morning of the 12th of July the American army had, however, captured the three airfields inland from the assault beaches; and thereafter matters steadily improved on shore.

On the night of the 11th–12th July the Americans made a second airborne operation with the object of dropping a complete division ahead of the forward troops in the 'Dime' sector. The various authorities concerned had been given adequate warning of the inten-tion, but at a late hour the plan was postponed one day, and the change of date probably did not reach all naval and military units in time. The result was that the transport planes, which flew along the actual battle front for many miles, came under heavy fire from Army guns. To avoid this they turned out to sea and crossed the shipping anchorage at a low height, exactly when an enemy air raid was in progress. It was hardly surprising that twenty-three of the 144 transport aircraft taking part were destroyed—mostly by Ameri-can ship and shore gunfire. Co-ordination with the other services of

---

[1] Both General Eisenhower in his Despatch (pp. 45–46) and General Patton, com-mander of the U.S. Seventh Army in his 'Notes on the Sicilian Campaign' commended in very warm terms the work of the supporting warships on this occasion. Morison (Vol. IX, p. 112) dates General Patton's 'conversion to the value of naval gunfire support' to the experiences of 11th July 1943 off Gela.

what must always be a hazardous and intricate operation had failed badly. This tragedy, and a somewhat similar chain of events when another airborne operation was carried out on the night of the 13th–14th of July to seize important points in the British sector near Catania, led to an enquiry by Allied Force Headquarters into the whole conduct of the airborne operations in 'Husky'.[1] Though better training in aircraft recognition and tighter control over guns' crews could undoubtedly have saved many lives, it could not be denied that the ships were within their rights in firing at unidentified aircraft which approached them closely, and with apparently hostile intent. The main lessons were that in combined operations much longer warning of the passage of airborne forces must be given, that more attention should be devoted to accurate navigation to prevent aircraft straying from the 'safe lanes', and that the means available to aircraft to establish their identity should be improved. The principle that 'ships must and will fire without warning' at aircraft which had not been identified as friendly was, however, firmly maintained.

The 'Joss' assault forces were to make two landings on each side of the small port of Licata.[2] In spite of the swell running in the off-shore anchorages and heavy surf on the beaches, the assaults took place very much in the manner planned. The careful and realistic rehearsals which Admiral Conolly had carried out in Africa now reaped their reward. The supporting ships' gunfire was again very effective, local opposition was quickly overcome, and by noon on D-Day Licata was in American hands. The comparatively new technique of the 'shore to shore' assault was strikingly successful both here and under Admiral McGrigor in the British 'Bark South' sector.

Once the American Seventh Army had consolidated its beachheads and, with the help of naval gunfire, repelled a dangerous enemy counter-attack at Gela on the 11th of July, its advance was very rapid. The western half of Sicily was quickly overrun, and Palermo was captured on the 22nd. Five days later the port was opened to shipping, and thereafter the American warships remaining on the station were reorganised into a new Task Force, whose purpose was to support and assist the Seventh Army, part of which now turned east to fight its way along the north coast of Sicily towards Messina.[3]

To return to the British assault area, the rapid collapse of the powerful defences of Syracuse on the day of the landings was a very important success to the Eighth Army. Next day, the 11th, after the approach channel had been swept for mines, Admiral Troubridge

[1] See Supplement to the London Gazette No. 38895 of 25th April 1950, paras. 30–32 (H.M.S.O.).
[2] See Map 10.
[3] See Map 9.

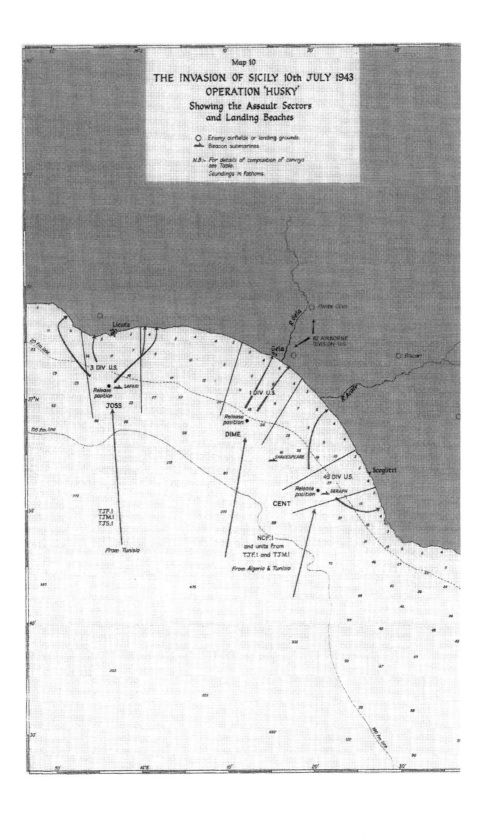

Map 10

THE INVASION OF SICILY 10th JULY 1943
OPERATION 'HUSKY'
Showing the Assault Sectors
and Landing Beaches

○ Enemy airfields or landing grounds.
⚓ Beacon submarines.

N.B :- For details of composition of convoys
see Table.
Soundings in fathoms.

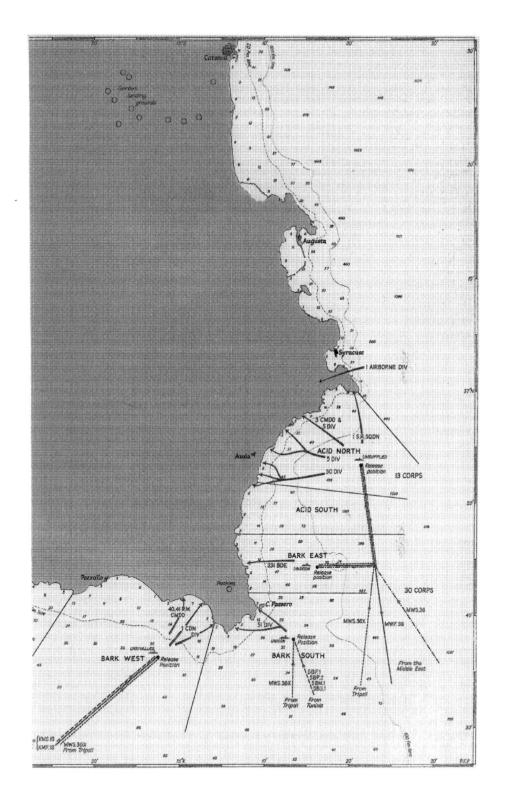

entered the port. He found its facilities virtually undamaged, and at once made arrangements to unload a proportion of the Army's supplies there rather than over the beaches. Two days later the follow-up convoy MWF.37 entered the port, and was berthed and unloaded so efficiently that its ships were all cleared that same evening. On that day, the 13th, Admiral McGrigor transferred to Syracuse, and took over responsibility for the whole naval shore organisation in the eastern assault area with the title of Flag Officer, Sicily. Admiral Vian now assumed command of the offshore forces in all 'Bark' sectors.

After the capture of Syracuse the next important objective was Augusta, some fifteen miles to the north. At 7.30 p.m. on the 12th the L.S.I. *Ulster Monarch*, escorted by a destroyer and two motor gun-boats, entered the port and landed the Special Raiding Squadron; but the town was still under heavy enemy fire, and the naval port party had to withdraw temporarily half an hour later. During the night, however, troops of the 5th Division arrived, and by daylight on the 13th Augusta was firmly in our hands. Here Allied bombing had caused more damage than at Syracuse; and, because it was a naval base rather than a commercial port, it was much less suitable for the rapid unloading of stores. Only some 1,600 tons of cargo could be discharged daily at Augusta, compared with 5,000 tons in Syracuse, and the latter therefore remained the more important supply port for the Eighth Army. Admiral Troubridge's first attempts to enter Augusta were met by heavy gunfire, and he had to make two hasty withdrawals; but by the 14th all enemy resistance had been quelled, and the task of re-opening the port could be pressed ahead. The enemy, however, now switched his main air effort from the American assault sectors to the British Army's beaches and ports of discharge, which were nearer to the airfields in southern Italy from which his bombers were working. In these attacks the enemy was aided by the clear nights and by the nearly full moon; but the smoke screens put up by specially equipped landing craft were very effective, and the offshore shipping did not suffer severely. Thus on th night of 14th–15th there was a good deal of enemy air activity off the 'Bark South' beaches. Circling torpedoes as well as bombs were used, but no damage was suffered by any ship.[1]

As the Eighth Army's supplies and reinforcements began to flow more freely through Syracuse and Augusta, unloading over the beaches steadily declined until, on the 23rd, the last ships of convoy KMS.19 sailed homewards, and the 'Bark' sectors were then finally closed. The 'Acid' sectors remained in use longer, mainly because it was decided to disembark the 78th Division, which was urgently

---

[1] See Vol. II, pp. 437–438, regarding circling torpedoes, which had first been used against shipping in Algiers harbour in November 1942 during operation 'Torch'.

needed to reinforce the Eighth Army, over the beaches. This was accomplished between the 25th and 29th of July, and on the 6th August all remaining ships left the northern assault area.

From D-Day onwards the guns of the bombarding ships were available to meet the Army's many calls for support. The 15-inch monitors *Roberts* and *Erebus* served the British sectors as well as their sister-ship the *Abercrombie* served the Americans; while the smaller warships frequently engaged targets along the coastline. In all some 200 calls for gun support were answered by the British bombarding ships in 'Husky', and if some contemporary claims to have knocked out gun positions by direct hits are now known to have been optimistic, it is certain that the effect of this gunfire from the sea was as helpful to our own troops as it was demoralising to the enemy's. In spite of frequent air attacks little damage was caused to the warships, but on the 23rd of July the cruiser *Newfoundland*, flagship of Rear-Admiral Harcourt's support force, was torpedoed by the Italian submarine *Ascianghi*, which was herself promptly sunk by the destroyers *Laforey* and *Eclipse*. The Axis submarines did remarkably little damage to the 'Husky' convoys, either during the approach or after the actual landings; and they suffered heavily themselves. On the 12th of July the destroyer *Inconstant*, which was escorting a return convoy of empty troopships, sank U.409 off the Algerian coast after a three-hour hunt. That same night M.T.B.81, while on patrol in the Straits of Messina, torpedoed U.561 at very close range and sank her, and on the 30th an American patrol vessel destroyed U.375 off Pantelleria. The Italian submarines suffered even heavier losses than the Germans. The *Flutto* was sunk on the 11th after a running fight with British M.T.Bs off Catania, the *Bronzo* was captured by British escort vessels off Syracuse next day, and the *Nereide* fell to the destroyers *Ilex* and *Echo* off Augusta on the 13th. On the same day the submarine *Unruly* destroyed the *Acciaio* with a torpedo in the northern approaches to the Messina Straits, and the *Argento* was sunk in the early hours of the 3rd of August by an American destroyer, which was escorting a convoy from the 'Joss' sector to Oran. Nor were these losses of operational boats the end of the story, for three large Italian submarines, specially built to run cargoes from the Far East through the Allied blockade, were ordered from Taranto to Naples on D-Day; and all three were sunk on the way. Two (the *Remo* and *Pietro Micca*) fell victims to British submarines, while an R.A.F. aircraft accounted for the *Romolo*.[1] In the three weeks following the invasion of Sicily three German and nine Italian submarines were thus destroyed or captured; and in return the total losses they inflicted on the entire Allied expedition amounted to only four British merchantmen and

---

[1] See Appendix D for details of all these sinkings of enemy submarines.

two American L.S.Ts sunk, while three merchantmen and the cruisers *Cleopatra* and *Newfoundland* were damaged.

The enemy's air attacks caused far more trouble and dislocation, and heavier losses, than his submarines; and it was again the Eastern Task Force which suffered the more heavily. Between D-Day and the end of July three of its coastal or landing craft and six merchantmen or auxiliaries (totalling 41,509 tons) were sunk by air attacks in or near the assault area. A number of important warships, including the fleet carrier *Indomitable*, the monitor *Erebus*, two destroyers and four landing craft were damaged in the same period, as were three merchantmen. The corresponding figures for the Western Task Force were a destroyer, a minesweeper, two L.S.Ts and one merchantship (7,176 tons) sunk, and a few transports, minesweepers and L.S.Ts damaged—mostly superficially by near-misses.

Thus ended the assault phase of the invasion of Sicily. Although the battle for the island was still far from won, and the enemy was in fact already reinforcing the defenders by flying in paratroops and shipping a whole German armoured division across the Messina Straits, all the initial aims of the Allies had been achieved, and at a comparatively small cost in ships and lives. The need for a major port through which to supply the Eighth Army had been met by the capture of Syracuse and Augusta within seventy-two hours of the first landings. All the airfields in south-east Sicily were in Allied hands, and the movement on to them of our own aircraft had started. The assault troops had all established satisfactory beach-heads, and the follow-up forces and supplies were pouring ashore. The Allied Navies had accomplished the first part of their great task with complete success, and the Eighth Army were well placed to press on with the second part of the strategic plan—to capture Catania and the group of airfields around Gerbini. The maritime forces now had to divert a large proportion of their efforts to the vital, if subordinate, rôle of supporting and supplying the military arm—and, if called on to do so, to re-embark troops and land them wherever the High Command might order. But before we deal with the maritime side of the next phase an attempt must be made to assess the effectiveness of the Tactical and Strategical Air Forces' contribution to the success of the assaults. It has been mentioned that Admiral Kirk was critical of the lack of tactical bomber support in the 'Cent' sector, and of what he considered to have been a failure to integrate the Air Plan with the needs of the other forces engaged in the combined operation.[1] His views were expanded and enlarged upon in Admiral Hewitt's

---

[1] See Morison, Vol. IX, p. 142.

report, which blamed the Air Plan in general, the U.S. Army Air
Force in particular and, by implication, the Strategic and Tactical
Air Force commanders, for many of the difficulties and troubles
experienced by the Western Naval Task Force. Though such views
found no echoes in Admiral Ramsay's reports on events in the
eastern sectors, nor in Admiral Cunningham's despatch on the whole
operation[1], it is fair to emphasise that the American assault forces
encountered the more difficult conditions on the beaches and the
stiffer initial opposition on shore. On the other hand, after the first
few days the main weight of the enemy's counter-action from the air
fell on Admiral Ramsay's ships which, as was said earlier, suffered
considerably heavier losses than Admiral Hewitt's. Though the
American naval historian has accepted and enlarged upon the view
of his service's commanders[2], to this writer it seems that the matter
must be viewed through a wider lens than could possibly be available
to an individual assault commander, or even to the senior officer of
a Task Force. Though it now seems to be the case that the Air Plan
suffered through lack of co-ordination with those of the other services, the accomplishments of the Air Forces—many of which could
not possibly be seen from the assault beaches—none the less remain
impressive. The North African Coastal Air Force certainly contributed enormously to the safe arrival of the convoys, and the Malta
Air Force, even if fighter protection for the Western Task Force could
have been better, played a big part in gaining the comparative
immunity from air attacks which the naval forces enjoyed during the
approach and the actual assaults. Losses of ships from bombing were
far less than had been expected; and it is certainly undeniable that,
out of the hundreds of ships taking part, few were lost.[3] To Admiral
Cunningham who, as he said in his despatch, 'had fought through
the Mediterranean campaign from the beginning', it appeared
'almost magical that great fleets of ships could remain anchored on
the enemy's coast, within forty miles of the main aerodromes, with
only such slight losses . . . as were incurred.' [4] In a combined operation it is inevitable that the crews of warships and of merchantmen,
who know that they have many tons of highly explosive cargo beneath their feet, should demand continuous fighter protection; and
it is equally certain that assault troops, who have survived the
hazards of an opposed landing only to find themselves held up by
enemy strong-points, will demand that tactical bombers should at
once be sent to neutralise the opposition. We ourselves had repeatedly experienced these phenomena in the early days of the war,

---

[1] Supplement to the London Gazette No. 38895 of 25th April 1950 (H.M.S.O.).
[2] Morison, Vol. IX, pp. 21–23.
[3] See p. 139.
[4] Despatch, para. 29.

when from Norway to Dunkirk and from the Central Mediterranean to Crete, our ships and troops had been the targets of virtually unopposed attacks by enemy bombers. But we had gradually learnt that it was impossible to assess the effectiveness of the work of the Air Forces by what could be seen from the deck of a ship; and we had come to realise that, for example, more effective protection might well be gained from an enemy airfield being put out of action by our bombers, or by our fighters intercepting a formation far away over the horizon, than by a few aircraft constantly patrolling overhead. Moreover we had learnt that continuous fighter cover in appreciable strength demanded a prodigious number of sorties, and that unless numerous good airfields were available close at hand it was impossible to provide it for a protracted period. Though it anticipates events which will be recounted later, it may be mentioned here that when, in the following September off Salerno, we tried the new experiment of employing carrier-borne fighters to provide the necessary air cover, we found that the effective strength of their patrols declined rapidly.[1] A fair and final judgement on the matter can, it is suggested, only be reached by careful study of the results achieved by the Air Forces in operation 'Husky'; and supreme among them stand the incontrovertible facts that the success of the expedition was achieved at far less cost than we had anticipated, and that even the troublesome enemy counter-attacks from the air never came near to wrecking the undertaking. If the controversy be viewed in that light it must surely be admitted that discussion on whether better results might have been achieved by a different tactical plan, or by a different allocation of air strength, can only be of academic interest.

We must now continue the story of the invasion of Sicily from the end of the assault phase up to the completion of the final object of the operation, namely the clearance of the enemy from the rest of the island. The American Seventh Army had shown great dash and determination in the rapid advance in the west, had captured Palermo on the 22nd of July, and then turned east towards Messina; but whereas the Italian Army's resistance in this part of the island had been feeble, General Montgomery's Eighth Army was now coming up against far more resolute German forces, as it approached the Catania plain. The key to Catania was the two river bridges carrying the coastal road; and it was therefore decided to use Commandos to seize one bridge and airborne forces the other. On the night of 13th–14th July 105 Dakotas and thirty R.A.F. Albemarles

---

[1] See p. 173.

and Halifaxes, some of which towed gliders, set out from Africa to drop a parachute brigade. The outward-bound aircraft passed over a convoy which was itself under air attack at the time, and so came under heavy gunfire from friendly ships. Fourteen aircraft were lost, and although many of the remainder dropped their troops correctly, and they managed to seize the bridge, by nightfall German reinforcements had forced them back. The Commandos landed successfully, but suffered a similar experience to the airborne troops, and were forced to retire. The intended rush on Catania was thus frustrated, and the enemy had gained time to reinforce and re-group. Admiral Cunningham was meanwhile watching the situation on the Catania front anxiously. He had ample heavy ships available to support the Army by their gunfire, and was holding certain landing ships ready at the call of the Flag Officer, Sicily, should the Army ask to be re-embarked and carried further up the coast. Calls for gun support from the warships were received and complied with on several occasions. On the evening of the 17th the battleship *Warspite* was sent up at full speed from Malta and fired fifty-seven 15-inch shells at the batteries defending Catania. This ship, completed in 1915, had been Admiral Cunningham's flagship in 1940 and 1941, until she was severely damaged off Crete. Her long service, and the many actions in which she had fought, including Jutland, the 2nd Battle of Narvik, Calabria and Matapan, had earned her a special place in the affections of the Commander-in-Chief.[1] On her return from Catania Admiral Cunningham signalled 'Operation well carried out. There is no question when the old lady lifts her skirts she can run.' But *Warspite's* bombardment did not weaken the enemy's hold on Catania, and that same night a frontal attack by the 50th Division was repulsed with heavy losses. General Montgomery now decided to abandon the direct thrust towards Catania, on the grounds that it would be too costly.[2] General Alexander accepted his views, and issued new orders directing that the advance towards Messina should be made by circling around the great massif of Mount Etna to the west, instead of fighting straight up the coastal road. The necessary re-grouping produced a lull on the Catania front until the end of July. To the Naval Commander-in-Chief this decision appeared surprising. 'There were doubtless sound military reasons' wrote Admiral Cunningham 'for making no use of this . . . priceless asset of sea power, and flexibility of manœuvre; but it is worth considering . . . whether much time and costly fighting could not be saved by even minor flank attacks, which must necessarily be unsettling to the enemy. It must always be for the General to decide. The Navy can

---

[1] See Roskill, *H.M.S. Warspite, The Story of a Famous Battleship* (Collins, 1957).

[2] Viscount Montgomery of Alamein, *El Alamein to the River Sangro*, pp. 86–92 (Hutchinson, 1946).

only provide the means, and advise on the practicability . . . of the projected operation. It may be' he modestly concluded 'that, had I pressed my views more strongly, more could have been done.'[1] Admiral McGrigor had meanwhile made all preparations to lift a proportion of the Eighth Army up the coast. He later wrote to an officer of the Commander-in-Chief's staff that he had 'twice had a big Commando force actually embarked, and once even sailed to cut the very vulnerable [enemy] communications by road and rail along the coast to the north; but each time the Army . . . called it off'.

Turning to the American Army's advance along the north coast of Sicily towards Messina, small outflanking operations were three times executed by the special naval task force of Rear-Admiral L. A. Davidson, U.S.N.; but we now know that in fact they made little difference to the enemy's carefully planned retreat by stages to the east.[2] Though one may justly admire the speed with which these operations were mounted, and the resolution with which they were carried out, it is clear that they were too small to cut the enemy's line of retreat to Messina, and in some cases took place too late even to have any local effect.[3]

During the first week of August the pressure on the retreating enemy exerted by the Americans along the north coast of Sicily, and by the Canadians against the south-west flank of Mount Etna, continued. On the 5th of August the Germans abandoned Catania, and the 5th and 50th Divisions entered the city without encountering any serious opposition. On the 4th and 5th of August naval forces bombarded the coast road near Taormina with the object of impeding the enemy's retreat towards Messina from the south; but German records do not indicate that even the 15-inch shells fired by the monitor *Roberts* caused more than a temporary dislocation of traffic. On the 16th a more ambitious attempt to cut the coastal communications was carried out at a point about fifteen miles north of Taormina, where two L.S.Is, covered by the *Roberts* and seven destroyers, landed a Commando in the early hours of the morning. It was, however, by that time too late to influence events on land by cutting the coastal communications; for on the 17th American troops, shortly followed by British Commandos, entered Messina—to find that the evacuation of the Axis armies had been completed twenty-four hours earlier.

It will be appropriate now to retrace our steps by three or four

---

[1] Despatch, para. 40.

[2] See Morison, Vol. IX, pp. 197–199, for the landing at St Agata (7th–8th August), pp. 204–205 for the landing at Brolo (11th–12th August) and pp. 207–208 for the landing at Spadafora.

[3] Compare Admiral Cunningham's despatch, para. 38.

weeks, and to survey how it came to pass that the enemy accomplished this withdrawal with such a high degree of success.

On the 25th of July Mussolini fell from power and was taken into custody. Marshal Badoglio, who succeeded him, declared his intention of continuing the war alongside his German allies; but the latter were under no illusions regarding the intention of the new Italian government to seek an armistice. The political situation in Italy and the military situation in Sicily were frequently discussed at Hitler's conferences at this time, and although the German naval authorities in Italy were told to evacuate Sicily if necessary, no executive decision to carry it out had been taken by the 27th of July. However General Jodl, the head of the operations section of the German High Command, had meanwhile sent verbal instructions to General Hube, who had been given command of all German troops in Sicily, that he was at all costs to extricate the three excellent German divisions in the island.[1] Hube's first intention was to start the movement across to the mainland on the 1st of August; but the Allied advance forced a postponement. An efficient ferry service across the Straits of Messina had, however, been organised previously by Captain von Liebenstein; and all the men who could be dispensed with were already crossing steadily by day and by night. The German Army plan was to retreat gradually to five successive defensive positions, holding each for a short time, and disengaging a proportion of the troops at each stage. The evacuation was supposed to last five nights. Actually it was spread out over five days and six nights. On the 2nd of August Field-Marshal Kesselring, who commanded the German troops in the southern theatre, told the naval authorities that evacuation could start on the 6th; but the American advance along the north coast caused another postponement, and it did not actually begin until 6 p.m. on the 11th of August.

The Italian evacuation, which was organised quite separately, had started in a small way as early as the 3rd of August, and proceeded quietly until the 9th, by which time 7,000 troops had been removed. The tempo was then increased in order to lift the whole of their XVI Army Corps. Rear-Admiral P. Barone, commander of the Italian naval forces in Sicily, was in charge, and the success achieved by the two Axis navies was mainly due to his and Captain von Liebenstein's careful and thorough preparations. The Italian troops were taken across the straits by three main routes, one of which ran from Messina itself and the other two from small ports to the north of that town.[2] A mixed flotilla which included two train ferries,

---

[1] Kesselring in his *Memoirs*, p. 165 (Kimber, 1953) states that he gave the order for the evacuation on his own initiative; but a letter written by Jodl on 16th August states that he (Jodl) gave the order to Kesselring.

[2] See Map 11.

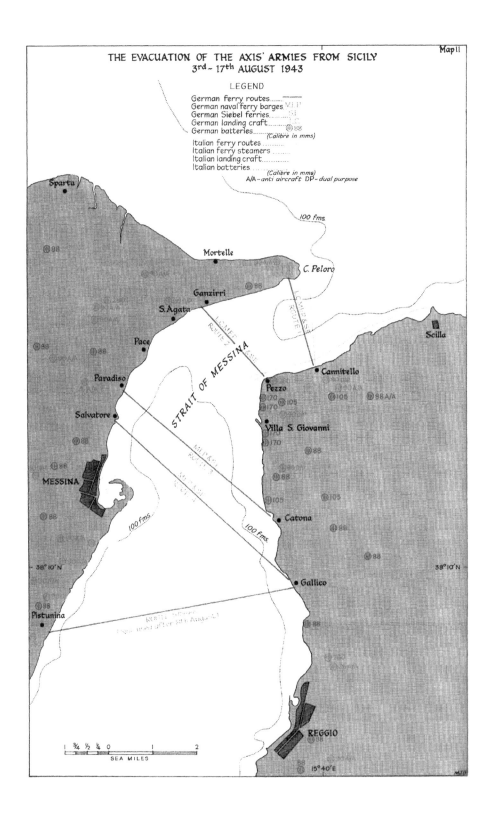

THE EVACUATION OF THE AXIS' ARMIES FROM SICILY
3rd - 17th AUGUST 1943

LEGEND

German ferry routes......
German naval ferry barges
German Siebel ferries......
German landing craft......
German batteries......
      (Calibre in mms)

Italian ferry routes......
Italian ferry steamers......
Italian landing craft......
Italian batteries......
      (Calibre in mms)
A/A – anti aircraft DP – dual purpose

100 fms

Sparta

Mortelle

C. Peloro

Ganzirri

S.Agata

Pace

Scilla

Paradiso

Cannitello

Pezzo

Salvatore

Villa S. Giovanni

MESSINA

STRAIT OF MESSINA

Catona

100 fms.

100 fms.

38°10'N

38°10'N

Gallico

Pistunina

Reggio

REGGIO

15°40'E

SEA MILES
¾ ½ ¼ 0   1   2

three small steamers (250–480 tons) and about a dozen landing craft was employed. The Germans used 'Siebel ferries' [1], landing craft, naval ferry barges and miscellaneous small craft. All vessels were very heavily armed with anti-aircraft guns, and some flew balloons.

Though it is certainly the case that in the early stages of the Sicily campaign Axis troops and supplies were moved across by routes far south of Messina, including one to and from Taormina, the evacuations definitely took place at the narrowest part of the straits, where no more than two-and-a-half to five miles of water separated Sicily from the Italian mainland. The Germans and Italians each organised four routes, all of which started from Messina harbour or points to the north of it.[2] There was a fifth German route just south of Messina, which was to be brought into force only in emergency and was never actually used. This matter is important because the shortness of the routes contributed enormously to the difficulties experienced by the Allies in stopping the traffic.[3] The second biggest factor was the strength of the coastal gun defences. Covering the straits themselves were four batteries of 280-mm. (11·2-inch) and two of 152-mm. (6-inch) Italian guns, to which the Germans had added four batteries of 170-mm. (6·8-inch) weapons on the Calabrian coast. In addition very large numbers of mobile dual-purpose weapons

---

[1] These were motor-propelled craft about 80 feet long and 50 feet in the beam. Their draught was small, and they were highly manœuvrable. Their speed was 9 knots, and they could mount three 88 mm. (3·5-inch) guns and a number of smaller A.A. weapons. About 450 men or 10 vehicles could be embarked. The Germans built them by mass-production methods, and designed them for transport overland in sections, and for assembly by their crews wherever they were needed. They were named after an aircraft designer called Fritz Siebel who, in the 1920s, had befriended an unemployed aviator of the 1914–18 war called Göring. In 1940 that same Göring employed him to study seized French aircraft factories, which led to an interest in designing barges for the invasion of Britain.

[2] See Map 11, which only shows the defences at the narrowest part of the Straits of Messina. The positions of the Italian batteries have been taken from an Italian map dated 14th July 1943 and those of the German batteries from a German map dated 28th July 1943. Thus changes in the dispositions of mobile guns may have taken place by the time that the actual evacuation was carried out in August. Enemy records do not give the actual dispositions of guns at that time. Italian dual-purpose and A.A. batteries were normally of three or four guns, and German ones of four or six guns; but German records are not clear regarding which of their batteries were dual purpose and which purely A.A. The map does not show batteries of guns below 76-mm. (3-inch), of which a large number were present; nor does it take account of the 88-mm. (3·5-inch) guns mounted in Siebel ferries.

[3] Morison, Vol. IX, pp. 209–218 and his map on p. 211 state that the Axis armies were evacuated from points far south of Messina, as well as across the narrowest parts of the straits. However the War Diary of Colonel Baade, the German Army's 'Commandant of the Messina Straits', and the records kept by Captain von Liebenstein of the German Navy make it quite plain that, once the evacuation (operation 'Lehrgang') had started, the whole of the German traffic passed across the four routes in the Straits of Messina shown on Map 11. The fifth route, which was just south of Messina, was an emergency route; and although there is evidence that some traffic passed across it before the main evacuation started, it is certain that it was never used during operation 'Lehrgang'. Colonel Baade's records are held in Washington, U.S.A., under U.S. Army Adjutant General's Reference Nos. 35746/1 –/2 and –/3. They were borrowed in 1956, very thoroughly scrutinised, and translated by official historical staffs in London.

(3- to 4-inch) were mounted on both shores. Admiral Barone states that the total reached about 150 guns at the height of the evacuation, and his estimate is probably conservative. The number of smaller weapons cannot easily be computed, but it was certainly very large. The concentrated fire which these defences could bring to bear on warships operating only a mile or two off-shore made it suicidal to attempt to keep patrols in the straits for protracted periods; and to put the coastal guns out of action by air bombardment was extremely difficult; for they were small targets, and our low-flying aircraft were subjected to a tremendous volume of fire whenever they approached the straits.

Turning now to Allied plans and intentions, on the 31st of July the Joint Intelligence Committee of the theatre reported that 'at present time there is no sign that the enemy intends an evacuation of Sicily'. Traffic across the straits had not actually increased at that date, and stubborn resistance still continued before Catania, which did not fall until the 5th of August. During the first week of August signs of the enemy's intention were, however, not lacking. Air reconnaissance reported that some two score landing craft or Siebel ferries were in the straits, and General Patton's staff had gauged the purpose of the enemy's staged withdrawals with accuracy. The Joint Intelligence Committee followed up its first report with a review of 'the enemy's capability to evacuate Sicily', which concluded that 'at the present time [i.e. the 4th of August] there is no sign that the enemy intends to evacuate the island'. But on the day before that report was issued General Alexander had signalled to Admiral Cunningham and Air Chief Marshal Tedder that 'indications suggest that Germans are making preparations for withdrawal to the mainland'. 'We must' he continued 'be in a position to take advantage of such a situation by using [the] full weight of navy and air power. You have no doubt co-ordinated plans to meet this contingency.' The Naval Commander replied that light craft were already operating in the straits by night, and 'this will be intensified'. When the enemy's retreat began the Air Force should, he suggested, operate 'without let or hindrance north of 38 degrees North [i.e. over the whole of the Messina Straits] and east of Milazzo on the north coast'.[1] Regarding the employment of warships, Admiral Cunningham said that 'as the coast batteries are mopped up it will be possible for surface forces to operate further into the straits'. Air Chief Marshal Tedder replied accepting his naval colleague's proposals, and suggested that they should be 'put into operation at once'. The Naval Commander agreed, and General Spaatz (commanding the North-West African Air Forces) was informed accordingly. The

---

[1] See Map 12 (facing p. 149).

air commands primarily concerned were the North-West African Tactical and Strategic Air Forces, and the correspondence of Air Vice-Marshal Coningham, who commanded the former, makes plain not only that he discussed plans with his subordinate commanders, but co-ordinated his intentions with General Doolittle's Strategic Air Force. Thus on the 4th of August Coningham wrote to Air Vice-Marshal Broadhurst, the commander of the Desert Air Force, that 'Strategic Air Force representatives are reporting to me on 5th August, as an effective day effort to stop evacuation should include full-out attack on the other side of the straits by P.38s etc.[1], in addition to all that we can do. But the night is our problem, and though the increasing moon will help the air, only a positive physical barrier, such as the Navy can provide, would be effective. The difficulty of operating naval surface forces in the narrow part of the strait is obvious, and I do not see how we can hope for the same proportion of success as at Cape Bon'.[2]

The critical question was whether the Navy could supply such a 'positive physical barrier' as would stop the enemy traffic across the straits. Ever since Syracuse and Augusta had been captured we had stationed light coastal forces (M.T.Bs and M.G.Bs) in those ports; and they had carried out frequent sweeps by night in the Messina Straits. An 'Inshore Squadron' composed of two monitors, a few gunboats, minesweepers, destroyers, and specially equipped landing craft had also been formed under Admiral McGrigor to work in support of the Army. These ships were not, however, suitable for offensive patrols in the straits; for they were mostly too slow, and too vulnerable to shore gunfire. From the middle of July the coastal craft were out every night, and after the beginning of August destroyers were regularly sent to support them. But they found very few targets, the light craft frequently came under heavy fire from the enemy's shore guns, and they lost one M.G.B. and three M.T.Bs on these patrols. A number of running fights took place in the glare of the enemy searchlights, but they had little effect on the evacuation traffic.

On the 6th Air Marshal Coningham issued an operational instruction to his subordinate commands. Daily reconnaissances were to be flown to give warning of the start of evacuation, which he expected to take place mostly by night; and he anticipated that considerable air opposition would be encountered over the straits. Events were to prove both these premises wrong; for in fact a great part of the traffic crossed by day, and the enemy's air opposition was negligible. By an order issued on the 2nd of August the heavy bombers of General Doolittle's Strategic Air Force were not to be used; but this

---

[1] These were Lightning twin-engined fighters.

[2] That is to say, in the surrender in Tunisia, operation 'Retribution', see Vol. II, p. 441.

embargo was modified a few days later by a decision to permit the diversion of bombers and fighter-bombers at the discretion of the Strategic Air Force commander, on being requested to do so by his Tactical Air Force colleague at twelve hours' notice. Between the 5th and 9th, Fortresses actually attacked Messina harbour three times by day, while the Wellingtons made night attacks on the northern ferry terminals. Regarding the rest of the Strategic Air Force's considerable strength, the Lightning fighters made ground attacks on communications in Calabria, the three squadrons of War-hawks were attacking installations in Sardinia, and the 278 medium bombers (Mitchells and Marauders) were attacking airfields and communications in Italy. These operations were all preliminaries to the intended invasion of the Italian mainland. The total strength available to the Strategic and Tactical Air Forces at this time is set out below.

Table 10. The North-West African Air Force's Strength, August 1943

	Strategic Air Force		Tactical Air Force	
	R.A.F.	U.S.A.F.	R.A.F.	U.S.A.F.
Heavy Bombers . .	—	181	—	—
Medium Bombers . .	130	278	—	112
Light Bombers . .	—	—	94	43
Fighter-Bombers and Fighters . . .	—	280	344	377
TOTALS . . .	130	739	438	532

The fact that so large a proportion of the Strategic Air Force played no part in the attempts to trap the Axis armies in Sicily may be attributed to the erroneous belief that crossings would be made mainly by night, and to confidence in the ability of the Tactical bombers and fighters to cope with day traffic. It is certain that at no stage did the three Allied Commanders-in-Chief represent to the Supreme Commander that an emergency, such as would justify the diversion of all available air strength, had arisen. The enemy later expressed his astonishment that the Allies had not used their overwhelming air superiority to greater effect.

Not until the afternoon of the 13th did the Tactical Air Force receive orders that 'evacuation is held to have begun', and that all sorties were to be directed against ships, barges and beaches; and, as we have already seen, Rome had ordered the Italian movements to be accelerated on the 9th, while General Hube had started his main evacuation on the 11th, and was transporting across the straits some 7,000 men daily, with their vehicles and supplies. On the day that the main German withdrawal to Italy started, Air Vice-Marshal

Map12   THE CENTRAL MEDITERRANEAN

Coningham reported to his Commander-in-Chief that the enemy's decision now appeared plain, 'but that there was no sign of large-scale shipping movements by day.' He considered that should 'withdrawal develop on a big scale . . . we can handle it with our own resources and naval assistance'. He therefore recommended the release of the Strategic Air Force from its commitment to attack the traffic across the straits by day, if requested to do so, but asked that the maximum effort of the Wellingtons should continue by night. On the 14th, the third day of the German evacuation, General Alexander signalled to Air Chief Marshal Tedder that 'it now appears German evacuation has really started'; and in fact by that time the enemy had shifted mainly to day-time crossings. But the heavy bombers were deployed against Rome, Naples and other targets in Italy, and were not available to deal with that traffic. Captain von Liebenstein wrote in his War Diary on the 15th that 'it is astonishing that the enemy has not made stronger attacks in the past days. . . . High level attacks have been practically non-existent. It is only during the night that raids are frequently incessant'. In fact the strategic bombers' attacks, carried out from the night of the 5th–6th to that of the 12th–13th, after which they were diverted to targets in southern Italy, contributed to the enemy changing from night-time to daylight crossings. The Tactical Air Force's daytime effort had meanwhile been steadily increasing, and rose steeply to 270 fighter-bomber and forty-seven medium bomber sorties on the 16th. Several enemy vessels were sunk, and others damaged; but we now know that contemporary claims regarding the effectiveness of the Allied counter-measures bore little relation to the truth.[1] The losses and damage caused to the German and Italian evacuation fleets never sufficed to interfere seriously with the traffic. At 6 a.m. on the 17th of August the last German ferry left Messina, by which time Allied troops were about to enter the town. The enemy's accomplishment, compiled from his own records, is set out in Table 11 (p. 150).

In conclusion it now seems plain that the enemy's success was achieved by a skilfully conducted retreat, supported by excellent naval organisation. His gun concentration in the straits successfully inhibited both low-flying air attacks and protracted raids by surface ships. On our side it appears that the Intelligence services were late in drawing the correct conclusions; but even when the enemy's intention was plain the action taken suffered from lack of inter-service co-ordination. The naval effort made was weak, and the air effort lacked concentration. Though it is true that, until the enemy batteries had been subdued, protracted surface operations in the straits

---

[1] For example, the *Chronology of the Second World War* published in 1947 by the Institute of International Affairs states (p. 203) that '306 Axis ships evacuating troops were sunk between August 5th and 17th'.

Table 11. The Axis Evacuations from Sicily

	Italian 3rd–16th Aug.	German 11th–16th Aug.
Men	62,000	39,569
Vehicles . . .	227	9,605
Tanks . . .	Not recorded	47
Guns	41	94
Stores and Ammunition	Not recorded	17,000 tons
Losses of craft used in	8 sunk	7 sunk
evacuation . .	5 damaged (all scuttled at end of operation)	1 damaged

NOTE. The German figures are those reported by Field-Marshal Kesselring.

could only have been undertaken at prohibitive cost, the possibility of carrying out heavy ship bombardments from the north does not appear to have been seriously considered at the time. It would, however, have been necessary to send battleships or heavy cruisers; and for such ships to have engaged the enemy batteries with any chance of success, daylight bombardments with air spotting would have been essential. It seems unlikely that, in the conditions then prevailing, the slow and vulnerable spotting aircraft could have survived for long. Though the gains from such an undertaking must therefore be considered doubtful, it none the less now seems that more might have been attempted; and Admiral Cunningham himself has admitted some perplexity on that score to the author. The release of the Strategic Air Force from its commitment to attack the evacuation traffic by day certainly now seems to have been premature. But perhaps the biggest lesson to be learnt was that to defeat the enemy's intention demanded as carefully co-ordinated inter-service planning as an offensive combined operation. It was in fact, from the Allied point of view, a combined operation in reverse; and if that view be accepted it may reasonably be asked why the Supreme Commander took no steps to bring his service commanders together with the object of quickly producing a joint plan. The difficulties of doing so were, however, increased by the physical separation of the three Allied Service Commanders-in-Chief from each other and from the Supreme Commander; for while General Alexander was in Sicily, Admiral Cunningham's headquarters were at Malta, Air Chief Marshal Tedder's were in North Africa, near Tunis, and General Eisenhower's planning staff was at Algiers. The reader will recollect that the wide dispersal of the Service staffs produced difficulties in planning the invasion of Sicily[1], and it is likely that the same cause contributed to the failure to produce a fully integrated effort against

---

[1] See p. 117.

the enemy's evacuation traffic from Sicily. Moreover all the Commanders-in-Chief were at the time deeply involved in preparing for the invasion of Calabria and the landing at Salerno. The importance of the prize to be gained from blocking the Straits of Messina may, it now seems, not have been fully realised at the time; and it appears undeniable that, had all three services set themselves jointly to the task, a higher degree of success could have been achieved. As the Allied purpose could only prosper if our surface ships gained firm control of the narrow waters, and it was the enemy's shore guns which inhibited their work, the primary need plainly was to neutralise the batteries by any and every means possible; and it is difficult not to believe that concentrated and continuous blows from the air could have reduced the ferry terminals to a shambles. None of those purposes was, however, accomplished.

The question whether we made the best use of our maritime power after the initial landings in Sicily merits examination. To the naval commanders it seemed that the Eighth Army's swing inland, after it had been held up before Catania, took it away from the element by which a rapid advance to the key point of Messina could best be furthered. But in the middle of July 1943, when the issue was first debated, it would certainly have been no simple matter to carry out a major combined operation further up the east coast of Sicily. In the first place the troops already landed could hardly have disengaged themselves and re-embarked with their equipment in a short time; secondly, to the north of Catania the coast becomes so precipitous, and the few beaches have such poor exits, that it was scarcely possible to land or deploy a substantial assault force; and thirdly, the strength of the enemy's gun defences in the straits would have made it very hazardous to try to pass large troop and supply convoys up those narrow waters. What could perhaps have been done —and the Navy expected to be done—was to land comparatively small forces to harass and disorganise the traffic on the coastal road and railway; and there is no doubt that the Axis commanders were very apprehensive about the vulnerability of their line of retreat to such landings. The plans prepared to carry out such a purpose in mid-July and again early in August were, however, cancelled by the military authorities; and the one landing which actually took place (on the night of 15th–16th August[1]) was too late to hinder the retreat of the Axis forces towards Messina.

As to the larger strategic issues, the difficulty of arriving at a fair judgment is enhanced by the fact that, whereas in July 1943 the

---

[1] See p. 143.

escape of the Axis armies from Sicily may have seemed a possible though unlikely eventuality, we know that, in spite of the Allies possessing overwhelming preponderance on the sea and in the air, it actually happened. It is thus reasonable to enquire whether there existed an alternative to the strategy actually adopted, which stood a better chance of frustrating the enemy's withdrawal to the Italian mainland. The anxiety of the naval leaders to exploit our sea power in traditional manner can easily be understood; as can the possible reluctance of the soldiers to commit themselves once more to an element at whose hands they had recently received none too kindly treatment; but to this historian it seems that the only way in which the trap might have been firmly closed on the enemy was by making a new landing on the southern shore of the Calabrian peninsula. As, however, the threat of such a landing would have been abundantly plain to the enemy, and a strong reaction was therefore virtually certain, it would have been dangerous as well as futile to put ashore only weak forces. Finally it seems reasonable to suppose that, had the Supreme Commander and the service leaders agreed on such a strategy in the middle of July, by which time the success of the landings in Sicily was assured, the Navies could have assembled the ships and craft needed to carry it out early in August; and that would have been in time to stop the withdrawal of the major part of the Axis armies across the Messina Straits.

CHAPTER VII

THE MEDITERRANEAN
CAMPAIGNS

16th August–31st December, 1943

'Be pleased to inform Their Lordships that
the Italian battle fleet now lies at anchor
under the guns of the fortress of Malta.'
Admiral Sir Andrew Cunningham to
the Admiralty, 11th September, 1943.

THE three weeks following the enemy's withdrawal from Sicily
provided a short breathing space in which the hundreds of
ships and craft used in the invasion were sorted out and repaired, completed with stores and ammunition, and made ready for
the next combined operation.

Plans for a landing on the enemy's flank some distance up the west
coast of Italy had been under consideration since the previous June,
when General Eisenhower had discussed with the Combined Chiefs
of Staff the alternative possibilities of making an assault in the Gulf
of Gioja or of invading Sardinia.[1] On the 16th of July the First Sea
Lord told Admiral Cunningham that the British Chiefs of Staff were
considering the possibility of making assaults on either side of the
'toe' of Italy—at Crotone as well as in the Gulf of Gioja—and asked
the Commander-in-Chief to give an estimate of the naval requirements for such a dual operation, as well as for a single landing on the
west coast. In the same signal Admiral Pound hinted that escort
carriers might be sent out to provide fighter cover. On the day that
this message was sent from London the Combined Chiefs of Staff
sought General Eisenhower's views on the possibility of mounting an
assault from the sea against Naples, instead of invading Sardinia.
This was the first mention of Naples as the possible object of the next
operation. It was a far bolder, and considerably more hazardous plan
than the landings further south. On the 18th the Supreme Commander reported to Washington and London that he and his three
Commanders-in-Chief expected Sicily to be cleared by the middle of
August, and said that they were all agreed that the mainland of Italy
should then be invaded. The site of the landings was, continued

[1] See Map 12.

General Eisenhower, not yet decided; but the Gulf of Gioja was still the most favoured of the various alternative possibilities. A direct assault on Naples had, he went on to say, not yet been considered, firstly because it would demand more landing craft than he was likely to have available, and secondly because it would take place at the extreme range of fighter aircraft working from Sicilian airfields; and the use of aircraft carriers to provide fighter cover had so far been considered too hazardous. The end of July was thus approaching before any serious consideration had been given to the possibility of invading Italy by the shortest route, let alone striking directly at Naples. The poor resistance put up by the Italian army in Sicily, and the comparatively light losses of landing craft which we had suffered in operation 'Husky', probably influenced the decision to invade the mainland much sooner than had at first been considered feasible.

The Admiralty next considered ways and means of building up the necessary big ship force for the Naples operation. The *Illustrious* was to be sent out to replace the recently damaged *Indomitable*[1], and Admiral King was asked to send across the U.S.S. *Ranger* to replace her in the Home Fleet.[2] Four escort carriers were also to go to the Mediterranean, which left only one for the North Atlantic convoys; but the Admiralty was prepared to accept the weakening of convoy escorts, because the U-boat threat had recently been far less serious. They did, however, ask the Americans whether they could replace the departed escort carriers should the U-boats suddenly become more active again.

While the next moves were being discussed the British Chiefs of Staff became anxious that General Eisenhower's resources should not be run down by the release of the landing ships which, in accordance with a decision taken at the Washington Conference in the previous May, were due to leave for India to take part in the projected Arakan offensive.[3] On the 21st of July Admiral Cunningham accordingly asked the C-in-C, Levant, to hold the ships in question: but he warned the Admiralty that this action contradicted the orders already received from Washington. On the same day the Combined Chiefs of Staff approved the invasion of the Italian mainland; but they told the Supreme Commander that no more long-range fighters could be sent to him, because all were required to escort the strategic bomber raids on Germany. The extra troops required would, however, be sent from America, and his naval needs would be met. In London, opinion now hardened in favour of the landing near Naples, to which the name 'Avalanche' had been given; but as its success

[1] See p. 139.

[2] See p. 58.

[3] See p. 344.

would depend largely on the provision of the aircraft carriers, and the most favourable date appeared to be the end of August, the British Chiefs of Staff pressed for an early decision, and urged that no forces should meanwhile be moved away from the Mediterranean. The Americans, however, disagreed with the latter request, and insisted that the new operation should be carried out with the forces which, by the decision of the Washington Conference, were to be left in the theatre after the clearance of Sicily. Their reasons were that the British proposal was bound to delay the build-up of forces in the Pacific and also cause a postponement of the Arakan operation.

On the 24th of July the British Chiefs of Staff returned to the charge, and stressed that the Washington Conference had definitely stated that the early elimination of Italy was one of the Allies' objects; they claimed that operation 'Avalanche' was the best way to accomplish that purpose. They again urged that a 'stand still' order should be given to ships and craft in the Mediterranean, at any rate until such time as General Eisenhower had estimated his needs. The Americans, however, would not yield on the disputed question of the movement of ships away from the Mediterranean, so the British Chiefs of Staff went ahead with their intention to send out the aircraft carriers, and took steps to mitigate the thinness of the forces left to General Eisenhower as best they could from British resources. On the 25th the Admiralty told Admiral Cunningham that the *Illustrious* would definitely be sent to join the covering force needed for 'Avalanche', and that the *Unicorn*, *Attacker*, *Battler*, *Hunter* and *Stalker* would also be sent to join his fleet.[1] The aircraft carriers should, they said, be able at first to keep thirty-five fighters continuously over the assault area in daylight. Next day they ordered ten large troop-ships which had come home after operation 'Husky' to return to the Mediterranean. It may here be remarked that the build-up for 'Avalanche', the slowness of which later caused anxiety, would have been very much slower had·not these ships been made available to carry in American as well as British troops.

The detailed planning of the operation was meanwhile going ahead, though not without difficulties. Because of the large number of ships and craft needed, every major port in North Africa, from Oran to Alexandria, had to play a part in mounting the assault; and this meant that the forces started off from widely separated points. Secondly the senior officers of all three services were strenuously engaged in the day-to-day conduct of operations in Sicily, and the officers appointed to command the various forces in 'Avalanche' were

---

[1] The *Formidable* was already in the Mediterranean (see p. 126). The *Unicorn* was an aircraft repair ship, but as she had a flight deck she could operate aircraft, and was therefore classed alternatively as a light fleet carrier. The other four ships were all escort carriers.

widely scattered between Sicily, Malta and various places in Africa. There is no doubt that this caused serious difficulties in the planning and execution of the new undertaking. The ideal arrangement would have been to separate future planning from current operations, and to bring all the commanders appointed for a new operation into one headquarters; but in the Mediterranean this never proved feasible. One staff had to undertake both duties, and physical problems of accommodation and communications even prevented full integration of the various service headquarters concerned. On the last day of July Vice-Admiral H. K. Hewitt, U.S.N., was appointed to command the naval forces in 'Avalanche', with the title of Naval Commander, Western Task Force. The two naval assault forces had already been placed under Commodore G. N. Oliver (Northern) and Rear-Admiral J. L. Hall, U.S.N. (Southern). The planning problems were further complicated by the need to prepare concurrently for the transport of the Eighth Army across the Straits of Messina, and for the landings in the Gulf of Gioja and at Crotone mentioned earlier. Furthermore a 'cover plan', designed to mislead the enemy into expecting an attack in the Peloponnese, was also being prepared.

Meanwhile the situation inside Italy had been transformed by the dismissal and arrest of Mussolini on the 25th of July, and the formation of a new government under Marshal Badoglio. He, however, announced his intention to continue the war alongside Germany, and it was not until the bombing of Italian towns had been renewed in mid-August that emissaries arrived in Madrid to open negotiations for an armistice. The details were worked out at Syracuse, and the terms were finally signed on the 3rd of September; but this was kept secret until a few hours before the new landing.[1] We will return later to the naval clauses of the treaty, and to the transfer of the greater part of the Italian fleet to Allied control.

On the 13th of August the 'Quadrant' Conference opened in Quebec. With the clearance of the Axis armies from Sicily and the fall of Mussolini the long-desired elimination of Italy from the war, which at the time of El Alamein had seemed little more than a remote mirage, had suddenly become practicable. Discussion on the best means of accomplishing this was, however, still very active. Ships and landing craft were now being loaded, but their destination was not yet decided. On the 16th, however, the landing near Naples was given priority over that in the Gulf of Gioja, and at the same time the date for the former operation was tentatively fixed for the 9th of September. The choice of date was governed chiefly by the phase of the moon[2]—for the Army wished to make the initial land-

---

[1] See p. 166.

[2] On the 8th September off Salerno the moon, which was in the first quarter, set at 10.57 p.m. Sunrise on the 9th was at 4.36 a.m. and sunset at 5.34 p.m.

ings in darkness in order to improve the prospects of achieving surprise—and by the need to ensure that landing craft were available in sufficient numbers. From the naval point of view to make the approach and assault in darkness was by no means ideal, but the disadvantages were accepted.

By the middle of August the shape of future operations had become clearer. The Eighth Army was to be carried across the Straits of Messina to the Italian mainland (operation 'Baytown') early in September, and a few days later a full-scale assault was to be made in the Gulf of Salerno ('Avalanche'). To aid the advance of the Eighth Army up the 'toe' of Italy small landings were to be made at various points in the enemy's rear. But before this stage had been reached the Supreme Commander and the Naval Commander-in-Chief had expressed their anxiety over the adequacy of the forces available to them. General Eisenhower and Air Chief Marshal Tedder wanted to mitigate the comparatively weak fighter cover, which was all that could be kept over the beaches, by making heavy attacks on enemy airfields in Italy; but requests for the loan of Fortress bombers from Britain, and to retain the three groups of Liberators lent for operation 'Husky', were both refused by the Combined Chiefs of Staff. Admiral Cunningham for his part had asked for the two fleet carriers and four escort carriers mentioned earlier, for two cruisers to replace the ships damaged in the invasion of Sicily, and to retain the modern battleships *Howe* and *King George V* until the forthcoming operations were over. All these requests the Admiralty was able to meet, and the naval C-in-C was also allowed to retain a number of L.C.Ts which had been due to return home. In passing it may be remarked here that had the Admiralty not met the naval needs so fully the narrow margin by which operation 'Avalanche' was finally successful might well have disappeared. In spite of the fulfilment of most of his requests Admiral Cunningham remained anxious over the tendency 'to whittle away our resources now to build up "Overlord" [the invasion of north-west France]', and over the probable consequences of the removal of the heavy bombers. The Combined Chiefs of Staff had, however, confirmed at Quebec that the Mediterranean operations should in the main be carried out with the forces allocated at the Washington Conference. In consequence on the 20th of August ten American L.S.Ts, which had been detained at Oran, were ordered to sail for India, and the 'stand-still' imposed by Admiral Cunningham on British shipping movements away from the Mediterranean was revoked. These decisions were to produce unfortunate consequences on operations in the Aegean, to be discussed later.[1]

---

[1] See pp. 190–191.

It was not until the conquest of Sicily had been completed in the middle of August that the naval, military and air commanders and their staffs could give most of their attention to the plans for 'Avalanche'. Yet at the end of that month General Eisenhower was able to submit his proposals to the Combined Chiefs of Staff. After considering the possible alternatives of landing north of Naples and in the Gulf of Naples itself, he recommended an assault at Salerno, thirty miles south of that port, largely because it was the nearest point which could be covered by fighters working from Sicilian airfields. The assault was to be carried out by the Fifth Army under General Mark Clark, with VI Corps (American) on the right and X Corps (British), which included two Commandos and three U.S. Ranger battalions, on the left. The dividing line between the two assaults was the River Sele.[1] The British forces, which were stronger than the American, were to make a mainly 'shore to shore' assault from bases in North Africa, and had as their initial objects the port of Salerno and Montecorvino airfield. The American assaults were to be chiefly 'ship to shore'[2], and aimed at the early capture of the high ground which commanded the coastal plain. It was originally intended that paratroops should be dropped to capture an important bridge north of Naples, and so delay the southward progress of enemy reinforcements; but this part of the plan was not carried out. Naval forces were to stage a diversion off the coast to the north of Naples; Allied bombers were to neutralise the airfields from which the enemy might launch attacks on the beaches, while shore-based fighters (which were available in greater strength than had been anticipated), and also those operating from the escort carriers, were to cover the actual landings. We expected that thirty-six shore-based and twenty-two carrier-borne fighters could be kept constantly on patrol over the assault area at the time of the landings ; and Spitfires were to fly to Montecorvino airfield as soon as it was captured—which we hoped to accomplish on D-Day. In British circles anxiety continued over the possibility of the enemy reinforcing his troops faster than we could build up our own; and, in spite of the fact that the Americans had continually refused to increase the number of ships available for the undertaking, they too finally became uneasy on that score. As late as the 7th of September the First Sea Lord, who was still in America, signalled to the Vice Chief of Naval Staff to stress that Admiral Cunningham should have all that he needed, even at the expense of other theatres.

Up to almost the last moment changes were made in the orders; and with planning proceeding simultaneously at General Eisenhower's headquarters, by Admiral Hewitt's staff, and in the flagships

---

[1] See Map 13.

[2] See p. 131 f.n. 1 for definitions of the two types of assaults.

of the two Naval Task Force Commanders, it was inevitable that some confusion should arise. Bearing in mind the late hour at which the major decisions were taken this was perhaps unavoidable; but dislocation such as was caused by General Clark advancing 'H-Hour' by thirty minutes on the 24th of August, which necessitated alterations in the convoy orders, certainly might have been avoided. The late discovery of enemy minefields in the Gulf of Salerno also caused alterations to the assault plan, and revision of the intricate time-tables for the various waves of landing craft. Lastly landing craft had to be released to carry the Eighth Army across the Straits of Messina only a few days before the assault at Salerno. The consequence of all these difficulties is clearly revealed by the final state of the orders for the operation. Admiral Cunningham's are heavily amended in manuscript, and the amendments sometimes differ from those made in Admiral Hewitt's orders. The latter appear indeed never to have been finally completed. In such circumstances much reliance had to be placed on briefing verbally the senior officers of convoys, the captains of ships, and the commanders of the groups of landing craft. That very few misunderstandings actually arose is a tribute to the care and skill with which this was done; but the completion and issue of Commodore Oliver's own orders on the 29th of August had called for 'superhuman efforts by all concerned', and he hoped that 'a combined operation will never again have to be concerted in such conditions'.

Because the Army laid so much stress on the need to achieve surprise, no preliminary naval or air bombardments of the assault area were permitted. A very detailed plan was, however, made for bombardments in support of the Army after it had landed; but the effectiveness of the warships' gunfire depended greatly on the establishment of observer posts on shore, which could hardly be accomplished until some hours after the actual assault. Air spotting was recognised to be preferable, but we suffered from a shortage of suitable aircraft. In the British sector arrangements were made for close support of the troops by a large number of special landing craft, fitted to fire mortars and rockets as well as guns; but no such close support was provided for the American troops.

The convoy organisation and time-tables were exceedingly complex, mainly because all the landing craft and small escort vessels had to refuel on the way from North African ports to Salerno. British craft were therefore staged through Termini, and American craft through Castellamare, both on the north coast of Sicily.[1] Although the naval forces taking part in the northern assault were mainly British, and those for the southern assault mainly American, each

---

[1] See Map 12.

Table 12. Operation 'Avalanche'—Assault and Follow-up Convoys

Convoy Designation	Speed (knots)	Port, Time and Date of Departure	Initial Composition	Initial Escort	Special Orders
TSF.1	11	Tripoli, 5.0 p.m. 6th September	H.Q.Ship *Hilary* 9 L.S.Is	1 A.A. Cruiser 6 Destroyers 5 Minesweepers	To R/V with 15th Cruiser Squadron 5.30 a.m. 8th September
TSF.1(X)	8	Palermo, 3.0 a.m. 8th September	3 L.S.Is 8 L.C.Is	2 Destroyers 2 Minesweepers	To R/V with FSS.2 7.30 a.m. 8th September
TSS.1	5	Tripoli, 6.0 a.m. 3rd September	29 L.C.Ts 10 Support Landing Craft	6 Minesweepers 9 M.Ls	To stage through Termini, where 24 L.C.Is joined from TSM.1. Then became TSS.1(X)
TSS.2	8	Tripoli, 5.0 a.m. 6th September	20 L.S.Ts 3 M.T. Ships 1 Tanker 1 Tug 1 Petrol Carrier	1 A.A. Ship 1 Destroyer 10 Trawlers	To R/V with TSM.1 11.30 a.m. 8th September
TSS.3	8	Tripoli, 6.0 a.m. 7th September	17 L.S.Ts	2 Trawlers 4 M.Ls	To R/V with FSS.3
TSM.1	10 (8 after Termini)	Tripoli, 6.30 a.m. 6th September	36 L.C.Is	1 Destroyer 16 M.Ls	To stage through Termini. See TSS.1 and 2 above
FSS.2	8	Bizerta, 5.30 a.m. 7th September	H.Q.Ship *Biscayne* 1 Monitor 2 M.T. Ships 2 Petrol and Water Carriers 2 Coasters 2 Tugs 20 L.S.Ts	2 Destroyers 6 Minesweepers 9 Patrol Craft (U.S.N.)	To R/V with TSF.1(X) 7.30 a.m. 8th Se tember (see above)

FSS.2(X)	8	Bizerta, 6.30 a.m. 7th September	1 Monitor / 2 L.S.Cs / 2 Tugs / 18 L.S.Ts / 20 L.C.Is	2 Destroyers (U.S.N.) / 12 Minesweepers (U.S.N.) / 8 Patrol Craft (U.S.N.)	To R/V with FSS2(Y) 4.0 p.m. 8th September
FSS.2(Y)	8	Termini, 5.0 a.m. 8th September	16 L.S.Ts / 23 L.C.Is	As for FSS.2(X)	To R/V FSS.2(X) (see above)
FSM.1	10	Bizerta, 1.0 p.m. 6th September	44 L.C.Is (U.S.N. and R.N.)	10 Patrol Craft (U.S.N.) / 6 Minesweepers (U.S.N.)	To stage through Castellamare
FSS.1	5	Bizerta, 12.30 p.m. 4th September	37 L.C.Ts / 9 Support Landing Craft	1 Destroyer / 5 Patrol Craft (U.S.N.) / 3 Minesweepers (U.S.N.)	To stage through Castellamare
FSS.3	8	Bizerta, 1.15 p.m. 7th September	18 L.S.Ts / 1 Water boat	6 Patrol Craft (U.S.N.)	To R/V with TSS.3 (see above)
FSM.1(X)	10	Bizerta, 1.0 p.m. 6th September	1 Destroyer (U.S.N.) / 1 Gunboat (Dutch) / 4 M.T.Bs / 17 M.T.Bs (U.S.N.) / 4 Patrol Craft (U.S.N.) / 6 M.Ls	—	Part of Control Force, directly under Admiral Hewitt. To stage through Palermo.
NSF.1	13	Oran, 3.0 p.m. 5th September	9 Attack Tranports (U.S.N.) / 4 M.T. Store Ships (U.S.N.) / 3 L.S.Is / 3 L.S.Ts	3 Cruisers (U.S.N.) / 1 Fighter Direction Ship / 12 Destroyers (U.S.N.) / 8 Minesweepers (U.S.N.)	To R/V with NSF.1(X) 10.0 a.m. 6th September
NSF.1(X)	13	Algiers, 7.30 a.m. 6th September	H.Q. Ship *Ancon* (U.S.N.)	1 Fighter Direction Ship / 3 Destroyers (U.S.N.)	To R/V with NSF.1 (see above).

NOTES: (1) British and American L.S.Ts, L.C.Is and L.C.Ts cannot be distinguished. All other ships were R.N. unless shown above as belonging to another conutry.

(2) In the convoy designations letter T stood for Tripoli, F for Bizerta and N for Oran. The second letter (S) stood for the destination (Salerno), while the third letter (F, M, S) stood for Fast, Medium or Slow respectively.

contained some ships and craft belonging to the other nation. More-over American troops sometimes sailed in British vessels, and British troops in American vessels. In all some 700 large and small warships, merchantmen and landing craft, of a great multiplicity of types, took part. The complete organisation of the assault and follow-up convoys is shown in Table 12 (pp. 160–161). It will be seen that the plans provided for three groups of convoys, bearing the initial letters T, F and N respectively. The 'T' convoys, which started from Tripoli, carried the Northern Attack Force and its equipment; the 'F' convoys assembled at Bizerta and were also mainly destined for the northern assault, while the 'N' convoys sailed from Oran and Algiers with the greater part of the Southern Attack Force. In several instances the routes laid down for the various convoys crossed each other, thus necessitating very accurate timing of their progress towards the assault area. Apart from the close escorts provided to each convoy (as shown in the Table 12) their passages were to be covered by Vice-Admiral Willis's powerful Force H, of four battle-ships and two fleet carriers from Malta. The plans provided for Commodore W. G. Agnew's 12th Cruiser Squadron of four ships to join Force H; but in the event they were diverted to Taranto when the opportunity arose to seize that important base, and they did not therefore appear off Salerno until later.[1] Rear-Admiral C. H. J. Harcourt's 15th Cruiser Squadron of three cruisers as well as the A.A. ship *Delhi*, the monitor *Roberts* and a number of destroyers, were allocated for fire support in the northern assault area, while a Task Force commanded by Rear-Admiral L. A. Davidson, U.S.N., consisting of the British monitor *Abercrombie* and four American cruisers, was to provide the same service for the southern assault force.

In addition to the assault convoys so far discussed the plans provided for a long series of follow-up convoys, the first of which consisted of fifteen mechanical transport (MT) ships, and was due to arrive on the 11th. We hoped that the first troop convoy, of thirteen ships, which was expected at its destination on the 21st, could be unloaded in Naples; but all its ships actually had to discharge over the Salerno beaches. Apart from all these regular convoys, L.S.Ts and L.C.Is were to run a shuttle service, ferrying troops and vehicles continuously from Sicily and from North Africa.

The Air Plan laid down that, as in the invasion of Sicily, the Malta and North-West African Coastal Air Forces would protect the convoys during their outward passages until the evening before the assaults.[2] Thereafter the North-West African Tactical Air Force would take over responsibility when the convoys were within fifty

---

[1] See p. 170.
[2] See p. 117.

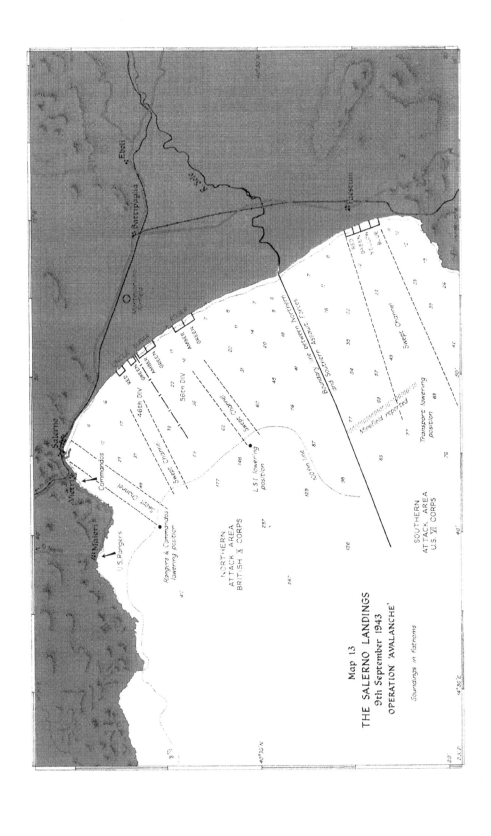

Map 13
THE SALERNO LANDINGS
9th September 1943
OPERATION 'AVALANCHE'

Soundings in Fathoms

miles of the coast; but outside that distance the Coastal Air Force would remain responsible. Protection of the beaches themselves, and close support of the Army, were to be carried out by the 12th Air Support Command of the Tactical Air Force, supplemented by fighters from Rear-Admiral Vian's squadron of aircraft carriers which, as has already been told, had been sent specially out from Britain for the purpose.

Let us now look at the topography of the coastal district on which the first major Allied landing on the mainland of Europe was to be carried out. From the northern promontory of the Bay of Naples to the south of the Gulf of Salerno the coast is mountainous, and the narrow valleys offered few opportunities for assaults from the sea; but in the Gulf of Salerno itself there existed a continuous stretch of coast some twenty miles long on which landings were perfectly practicable. Though the points of assault selected were reasonably satisfactory from the naval point of view, the narrowness of the exits from them was likely to delay a rapid build-up, and both the beaches themselves and the flat plain inland of them could easily be commanded from the high ground five to ten miles away. The only airfield within easy reach of the assault area was at Montecorvino, though there was an inferior landing strip at Paestum.[1] The early capture of the heights from which enemy guns could fire on the beaches and of Montecorvino airfield were therefore the primary tasks of the American VI Corps and the British X Corps respectively. Three American Ranger battalions and two British Commandos were to land on the left of X Corp's assault, with the object of cutting the road and rail communications from Naples where they passed through the hills and of seizing the small port of Salerno. Intelligence indicated that six good divisions of German troops were in various positions south of Rome; so the need to land the two British and two American assaulting divisions quickly, to secure and develop the beach-heads with the least possible delay, and to build up our strength by the rapid arrival and disembarkation of the troops and vehicles in the follow-up convoys needed no emphasis. The contemporary estimate of the Luftwaffe's strength and dispositions was that some 700 aircraft, of which 480 were bombers or fighter-bombers, were stationed within range of the assault area[2]; but the effectiveness of the enemy's counter-action from the air depended greatly on the accomplishments of the Strategic Air Force, which was to deploy its main strength against his airfields and communications from the 2nd of September.

The short time allowed for planning the operation, and the fact that many landing craft were refitting, or repairing damage received

---

[1] See Map 13.
[2] The actual figures were 558 and 323 respectively.

in the invasion of Sicily, prevented any comprehensive rehearsals being carried out; but the two British Divisions involved (the 46th and 56th) did manage to fit in some valuable combined exercises in North Africa in August; and some American units also went through an intensive course in amphibious warfare. The American transports started loading at Oran on the 19th of August, and the manner in which the loading was carried out gave rise to some severe criticisms from Admiral Hewitt. On the British side fewer errors seem to have been made in the matter of 'tactical loading' of ships and craft; but improper stowage of ammunition did lead to an explosion in Tripoli harbour and caused the loss of the services of four L.C.Ts, which could ill be spared. In spite of the late issue of the operation orders and the complications caused by the many amendments made to them almost at the eleventh hour, only one mistake of any consequence occurred in the loading and sailing of the convoys. Six American L.S.Ts, which by Admiral Cunningham's orders should have arrived at Milazzo in north-east Sicily to load Royal Air Force stores and equipment, did not turn up. Landing craft had therefore to be diverted from ferrrying the Eighth Army across the Messina Straits to replace the errant L.S.Ts. As, however, Montecorvino airfield could not be used by Allied aircraft as early as we had hoped, the consequences were not actually serious.

By the 1st of September all preparations for operation 'Avalanche' had been completed, and Admiral Cunningham made a general signal ordering it to be carried out on the 9th. 'H-Hour' was to be at 3.30 a.m.—just over an hour before sunrise. But, before the main movements towards the Gulf of Salerno began, the Allied Navies had to carry the Eighth Army across the Straits of Messina to the Italian mainland. As a first step large and small warships several times bombarded the land defences on the Italian side of the straits. On the last day of August Admiral Willis took the *Nelson* and *Rodney*, the cruiser *Orion* and a number of destroyers right up to the southern entrance to the narrows to attack the defences of Reggio[1]; and on the 2nd of September the *Warspite* and *Valiant* carried out a similar operation. These heavy bombardments possibly contributed to the ease with which the Army's crossing was carried out on the 3rd. The three 15-inch monitors *Abercrombie*, *Roberts* and *Erebus*, the cruisers *Mauritius* and *Orion*, six destroyers and two gunboats were in support, and they and the artillery of the Eighth Army laid down a heavy preliminary barrage. Then the troops and their equipment were ferried across the straits in twenty-two L.S.Ts and some 270 landing craft of various types. The landings were unopposed, the port of Reggio was soon brought into use, and thereafter a steady stream of

---

[1] See Map 12.

vessels kept the Army supplied as it advanced north. Some destroyers and a few landing craft remained in the vicinity of Messina to forestall any attempt to interfere with our traffic, and to land small forces on the seaward flank of the retreating enemy. A few warships also worked off the coast to give fire support to the Army whenever it was needed; but the majority of the ships moved at once to the stations where they were needed to prepare for the Salerno landing. The only considerable combined operation carried out to help the Army's advance was the landing of one brigade near Vibo Valentia in the early hours of the 8th of September.[1] It coincided unexpectedly with the passage of the retreating German army, and encountered considerable resistance. By the evening the assault had, however, been successfully completed, and the troops disembarked from the sea soon linked up with those advancing by land. It will be told later how, on the 16th of September, the advance patrols of the Eighth Army gained touch with the Fifth Army in Salerno Bay, for we must now return to the movements of warships and convoys prior to operation 'Avalanche'.

The main naval strength in the Mediterranean (Force H) sailed from Malta on the afternoon of the 7th. It consisted of the *Nelson*, *Rodney* and *Illustrious* escorted by destroyers of the 4th and 24th flotillas, and the *Warspite*, *Valiant* and *Formidable* escorted by the 8th destroyer flotilla. After steering initially to the south of Malta, in order to give the impression that the intention merely was to carry out exercises in the usual waters, the fleet passed through the Sicilian channel to enter the Tyrrhenian Sea by a circuitous route. Its main function was, for a battle fleet, unusual; for it was required 'to provide fighter cover over an escort carrier force which in turn was providing cover over the assault beaches and shipping'.

On the night of the 8th–9th some thirty German torpedo-bombers attacked the big ships. Although the *Warspite* and *Formidable* had narrow escapes, they suffered no damage; and substantial losses were inflicted on the enemy by the dense A.A. barrage put up by the fleet, and by night fighters. Enemy records suggest that the attacks had been intended for the invasion convoys, and not for the battle fleet. By daylight on the 9th fighters from the two fleet carriers were in the air, and thereafter they shielded Admiral Vian's squadron of escort carriers very successfully until the evening of the 11th. On the same day that Force H sailed from Malta the battleships *Howe* and *King George V* left Algiers for Augusta escorted by six destroyers. This squadron was to be held in reserve during the landings at Salerno; but its next operation, to be recounted shortly, actually proved a very unusual one.

---

[1] See Map 12.

The first 'Avalanche' convoy to sail was TSS.1, mainly composed of L.C.Ts, which left Tripoli early on the 3rd for Termini. Convoy FSS.2 was heavily attacked by about 80 German aircraft while in Bizerta roads on the night of the 6th–7th, but suffered little damage. While the assault convoys were on their way to the various rendezvous more air attacks took place; but they achieved remarkably few successes. One L.S.T. was torpedoed and beached, and one L.C.T. was sunk; but some of the enemy's effort had been dissipated by the fruitless attacks on Force H, already mentioned.

The staging of the assault convoys through Sicilian ports went smoothly except at Castellamare, where a swell necessitated fuelling the craft in an adjacent bay. As night closed down on the 8th all convoys were correctly in position, and steering for the assault area. Aided by mark boats and beacon vessels they all arrived on time shortly after midnight.

While the scores of vessels in the assault convoys were converging on Salerno under a bright moon on a typically calm Mediterranean evening, a very mixed force of British, American and Dutch small warships and coastal craft had sailed from Palermo to carry out raids and bombardments against islands off Naples and in the Gulf of Gaeta.[1] We hoped that this force's activities would divert the enemy's attention from Salerno; but German records give no indication that any appreciable results of that nature were achieved. After the assault, the diversionary force was reorganised, and its M.T.Bs did valuable service by capturing various islands close off the Italian coast, including Capri, which then became the base for Allied coastal craft operating off the Bay of Naples.

Meanwhile the news that an armistice had been signed with Italy had been broadcast from London on the evening before the assaults. The naval commanders' reports state that, in spite of the efforts of senior officers to emphasise that this did not reduce the likelihood of stiff opposition being encountered from German troops, the broadcast produced an undesirable complacency among the assault forces. Be that as it may, the news produced the immediate need to meet the Italian fleet at sea, and to escort it to Malta.

The armistice terms included 'the immediate transfer of the Italian fleet and Italian aircraft to such points as may be designated by the Allied Commander-in-Chief . . .', and for the requisitioning of Italian merchant shipping. The warships, most of which were at Spezia, were instructed to sail after dark on the 8th and steer a pre-arranged route. Admiral Cunningham meanwhile gave orders to all British and American ships on his station to carry out an operation

---

[1] See Map 12.

for their reception called 'Gibbon'. Evidently someone on his staff had recalled an earlier 'Decline and Fall'. At 1.30 p.m. on the 8th the *Warspite* and *Valiant*, escorted by five British, one French and one Greek destroyer, were accordingly detached from Force H under Rear-Admiral A. W. la T. Bisset to meet their erstwhile enemies twenty miles to the north of Bone early on the 10th. It was a disappointment to Admiral Willis that he and the rest of his force (the *Nelson*, *Rodney*, *Illustrious* and *Formidable*) were still needed off Salerno, and could not be spared to undertake a duty in which they justly felt entitled to play a major part.

At 3 a.m. on the 9th the main body of the Italian fleet, including the battleships *Roma*, *Vittorio Veneto* and *Italia* (formerly the *Littorio*), six cruisers and eight destroyers left Spezia under the command of Admiral Bergamini, and steamed down the west coast of Corsica. Soon after daylight they were sighted by our reconnaissance aircraft, and were seen to be following the route we had prescribed. On the previous day, however, Admiral de Courten, the Italian Chief of Naval Staff, had considered requesting Allied permission for the fleet to go to Maddalena instead of Malta, because at that time the Italian Government hoped to move to Sardinia. In fact no such request was ever made, but it is possible that Admiral Bergamini was told by telephone that it was under consideration. It must therefore have been on the Italian Commander-in-Chief's own initiative that, on the afternoon of the 9th, the fleet altered course to pass between Corsica and Sardinia, as though to proceed to Maddalena.[1] Our reconnaissance aircraft reported this change of route, which came as a complete surprise to the Allied authorities.[2] Meanwhile the Germans had taken over control of all the ports and bases in Corsica and Sardinia, and this decided the Italian Government to move to Brindisi. Shortly before 4 p.m. Admiral Bergamini altered to the west again, as though to resume the course prescribed by the Allies. He had probably heard from Rome that the Germans were in possession of Maddalena. Almost simultaneously his fleet was attacked by eleven Do. 217s flown from the south of France, and equipped to use

---

[1] This account is based mainly on information received from the Italian Naval Historical Section (1956), but there is no documentary evidence of the orders given to Admiral Bergamini. Commander M. A. Bragadin, who was serving in the Italian Admiralty at the time, gives in *Che ha fatto la Marina?* (pp. 538–548) an account of the events leading up to the transfer of the Italian fleet, reconstructed from his recollections, and from post-war discussions with the Italian Chief of Naval Staff and his Deputy.

[2] Admiral Cunningham (*A Sailor's Odyssey*, p. 563) records his bewilderment over the Italian fleet's alteration to the east, and suggests that the delay which it caused gave the Germans the chance to attack. He was, however, under the impression that the fleet had sailed from Spezia on the evening of the 8th, and that they should therefore have been outside the range of the German bombers by the following afternoon. In fact, not having sailed until 3 a.m. on the 9th the fleet was bound to be within bomber range all that day. Nor could it be protected by shore-based fighters from North Africa until it reached the latitude of southern Sardinia.

the new wireless-controlled bombs.[1] The Italians, believing the air-craft to be Allied, offered no resistance. The *Roma* was hit, caught fire and blew up, and the *Italia* was slightly damaged. Most of the flagship's crew, including the Commander-in-Chief, were lost. Apart from a cruiser and some destroyers, which stayed behind to pick up the *Roma's* survivors, the rest of the force then proceeded on its way, and met the *Warspite* and *Valiant* next morning. Most of the Taranto squadron, including the battleships *Andrea Doria* and *Caio Duilio* and two cruisers, sailed from its base for Malta on the 9th. On the way they passed the British squadron which was carrying troops to occupy their former base.[2] The last battleship from Taranto, the *Giulio Cesare*, came to Malta four days later, and was also met at sea by the *Warspite*. Meanwhile various lesser Italian warships, including a number of submarines, had arrived at other Allied bases.[3] Further-more 101 merchant ships totalling 183,591 tons came under Allied control, while 168 ships of 76,298 tons were scuttled to avoid capture by the Germans. On the 23rd of September an agreement concern-ing the employment and distribution of the Italian warships and merchantmen was signed by Admiral Cunningham, and thereafter those ships gradually began to render useful service on many stations in the cause of the nations which were endeavouring to free the whole of their country from the yoke which Mussolini's ambitious folly had laid upon it.

In all the annals of military history there can be few such dramatic events as the submission of an enemy navy. For the victors it is the culmination of the whole process of the application of maritime power; it is the consummation of all their hopes, and the fulfilment of all their purposes. For the vanquished it means, by its very com-pleteness, the abandonment of all ambitions. It is the final and

---

[1] These bombs, called the FX.1400, must not be confused with the wireless-controlled glider bombs (Hs.293) used mainly against shipping on the Gibraltar route (see p. 30). The FX was a 1,400-kilogram (about 3,000 lbs.) armour-piercing bomb, and could be guided towards the target by the parent aircraft. Unlike the Hs.293 it had no propulsion unit, but descended under the force of gravity only. Heights of release were between 12,000 and 19,000 feet, giving a terminal velocity of about 800 feet per second. The Germans experimented with the FX from February 1942 until mid-1943, when an operation was carried out against Malta by Do.217s working from Istres airfield near Marseilles. Little success attended this and later attacks against off-shore shipping in operation 'Husky'. Off Salerno, however, the FX proved a serious menace (see pp. 177 and 179 below).

[2] See pp. 170.

[3] The complete list of Italian warships in Allied control on the 21st of September 1943 is given in Appendix F. The ships which fell into German hands were the heavy cruisers *Gorizia* and *Bolzano* (both immobilised by earlier damage), the old cruiser *Taranto*, eight destroyers, twenty-two torpedo-boat destroyers, ten submarines, nine corvettes and 215 minor war vessels. Many of these were scuttled by their own crews before being seized. (See Bragadin, *Che ha fatto la Marina?* pp. 538–546.) Losses suffered by the Italian Navy between 10th June 1940 and 8th September 1943 are given in Appendix G.

irreversible admission of defeat at sea. To the British race, and especially to the Royal Navy, the significance of the drama of the 10th of September 1943 was enhanced by the fact that the Italian fleet met our forces in the very waters which, in so many wars, and not least from 1940 to 1943, we had struggled so arduously to control. There was, moreover, a remarkable coincidence to link the events of that day with the surrender of the German Navy after the 1914–18 war; for the *Warspite* and *Valiant* had both been present when, on the 21st of November 1918, the Kaiser's fleet had steamed across the North Sea into captivity. Rarely, if ever, in naval history can the same ships have witnessed two such events separated by almost exactly a quarter of a century. In the *Warspite's* case her Commander-in-Chief and many of her older officers and men remembered, more-over, how she had pursued and fought these same enemies in the action off Calabria, the Battle of Cape Matapan and in many other fights.[1] Deep emotions were stirred throughout the fleet, especially when Admiral Cunningham came out from Bizerta in a destroyer to view the *cortège*, and signalled to his former flagship his pleasure at seeing her 'in her appointed station' at the head of the line. Captain H. A. Packer, who had served two previous commissions in the ship and had been in her at the Battle of Jutland, wrote down these impressions in his diary:

> 'Presently they came in sight at about 15 miles, and we steamed towards each other at 20 knots. It was in November 1940 in the Battle of Spartivento[2] that I had last seen the Italian battleships. Our feelings were queer. Curtis, the Officer-of-the-Watch (a South African), was mumbling to himself "To think that I should be here to see this", and I felt the same. "Guns" was busy comparing their silhouettes with his cards, and remembering his many tussles with them. As they took station astern the Padre said "It's pathetic somehow"; and Pluto [the ship's dog] raced up and down the fo'c's'le barking . . . Anyhow we set off along the North African coast to Malta.'

On the evening of the 10th of September Admiral Cunningham instructed all ships and authorities within his command that 'the Italian fleet having scrupulously honoured the engagement entered into by their Government, officers and ships' companies are to be treated with courtesy and consideration on all occasions'; and next day he tersely informed the Admiralty of these great events in the words which head this chapter. By these two messages, the one chivalrous and the other showing that magnanimity in victory which Mr Churchill himself has recommended, he closed a chapter in

---

[1] See Vol. 1, pp. 298–299 and 427–431 respectively.
[2] Ibid. pp. 302–304.

British history which, but for the unscrupulous opportunism of a dictator, need never have been written.

It remains only to add that, even if it was mainly the Navy's day of triumph, the whole service realised that it could never have come to pass by its own unaided efforts. The contribution of the Royal Air Force to the defeat of Italian maritime ambitions had been immense; and had the Army not quite recently driven its opponents out of Africa and Sicily, and then invaded the Italian mainland, the submission of the fleet would certainly never have come to pass. Even though the basis of the strategy which had brought about the defeat of the junior Axis partner had unquestionably been maritime, the actual victory had been accomplished by the ever-increasing integration of all arms in great combined operations.

On the day of the announcement of the Italian armistice Admiral Cunningham ordered Vice-Admiral A. J. Power (Vice-Admiral, Malta) to hoist his flag in the battleship *Howe* and take the *King George V* and four destroyers under his orders. He was to meet the four ships of the 12th Cruiser Squadron, the American cruiser *Boise* and the fast minelayer *Abdiel*, which had been loading troops and equipment of the 1st Airborne Division at Bizerta, and proceed forthwith to Taranto. The intention was to seize that important base by a sudden descent, and to hold it only with light forces until reinforcements could arrive from the Middle East. The operation was entirely successful, and we captured the port and all its facilities virtually intact. The only serious mishap was that the *Abdiel* swung over and detonated a magnetic mine while at anchor in the harbour early on the 10th, broke in two and sank in a few minutes. There were heavy casualties among the 400 troops on board. Intensive sweeping was then carried out, and a considerable number of mines (which were probably of German origin) were exploded. The remainder of the 1st Airborne Division was, however, safely carried in from Bizerta by the 12th Cruiser Squadron, and on the 24th of September the 8th Indian Division arrived direct from Alexandria.[1] Gradually, and with the willing co-operation of the local Italian authorities, the port and dockyard of Taranto were restored to full use. Other ports in southern Italy also fell quickly and easily into Allied hands before the end of the month.

To return now to the Salerno assault forces, which we left just before 'H-Hour' on the 9th of September, the Commandos and U.S. Rangers, who had travelled in convoy TSF.1(X,)[2] arrived correctly

---

[1] This was the Division which had been held for operations in the Aegean, and was diverted by order of the Combined Chiefs of Staff. See p. 190.

[2] See Table 12 (pp. 160–161).

off their beaches at the northern end of the assault area and touched down on time. Though neither force encountered much opposition on landing, the Germans reacted strongly in the Commandos' sector at Vietri, and for a time the issue was in the balance.[1] Both assaults were, however, successful; and while the Rangers seized one pass on the heights overlooking the Bay of Naples, the Commandos held against heavy odds the defile through which the main road and railway passed. But the successful execution of this part of the plan did not prevent the Germans bringing down substantial re-inforcements to oppose the principal landings.

The main British assault took place in three sectors, called 'Uncle', 'Sugar' and 'Roger', each of which was divided into two beaches. The Senior Naval Officer for the 'Uncle' landings was Rear-Admiral R. L. Conolly, U.S.N., whose flag flew in the Headquarters Ship *Biscayne*. Captain N. V. Dickinson in the L.S.I. *Royal Ulsterman* was responsible for the landings in the 'Sugar' and 'Roger' sectors, but two 'Local Naval Commanders' worked under him to direct the actual assaults.

To deal with events in the 'Uncle' sector first, the ships came under fire even before they had reached the lowering position for the assault craft. However, the minesweepers went ahead to clear a channel, and the destroyers and support landing craft moved close inshore, firing all the time at enemy batteries and strong points, and on the landing beaches themselves. At 2.45 a.m. Admiral Conolly ordered the assault to proceed, and the first waves of landing craft formed up. On the 'Red' beach everything went according to plan, with almost perfect timing. The result was that, in spite of stiff opposition, the troops quickly established themselves on shore. Events on the adjacent 'Green' beach, however, show how easily a minor mishap or error can throw all the delicate mechanism of a combined operation into disarray. The trouble began when a support craft fired its salvo of rockets on to the wrong beach. The assault troops, not unreasonably, chose to land where the rockets had ex-ploded, instead of at their proper point. Considerable confusion and heavy casualties resulted, and although 'Green' beach was never lost, nothing could be unloaded there throughout D-Day. The destroyers, steaming up and down only a mile offshore, were constantly in action with enemy batteries, and even with his tanks and infantry. It is likely that this was the first time since the siege of Boulogne in May 1940 that a close-range action was fought between British destroyers and German tanks[2]; but, whereas in Boulogne the ships had been desperately striving to extricate a beleaguered garrison, on the present occasion their gunfire aimed to help our assault troops gain a

[1] See Map 13.
[2] See Vol. I, pp. 213–214.

foothold in enemy territory. The *Laforey, Loyal, Tartar* and *Nubian* and several *Hunt*-class ships all did excellent work on this day off Salerno. But because the Forward Observing Officers were not yet in position accurate shooting was difficult; and our own and the enemy's troops were sometimes so mixed up together that fire had to be withheld to avoid endangering the former. In spite of these troubles, and of the impossibility of using the 'Green' beach, unloading went ahead so fast that by 9 a.m. the assault craft had been rehoisted into their parent ships, and the first return convoy then sailed for Bizerta.

Meanwhile the minesweepers had been clearing the channel for the large ships to approach the lowering position for the assaults in the 'Sugar' and 'Roger' sectors, and they swept about a dozen mines while doing so. At 1.15 a.m. Commodore Oliver's *Hilary* and the L.S.Is arrived, and at once lowered their assault and support craft. On the two 'Sugar' beaches the 'touch-down' was about ten minutes late, but opposition was slight and the soldiers moved quickly inland. The second wave of assault craft all landed on the 'Green' beach, an error which derived from the incorrect landing made in the adjacent 'Uncle' sector. Considerable congestion resulted on that beach; but, as the enemy did not shell it while matters were being straightened out, the consequences were not serious. The L.C.Is and L.C.Ts of the third and fourth waves followed in, and the 'Sugar' sector was soon well secured. As dawn began to break, enemy batteries opened fire on the beaches and on the offshore shipping, and the destroyers moved in to engage them. While doing so the *Laforey* received five hits, and had to retire temporarily to carry out repairs. She, the *Lookout* and *Loyal* moved between the different beaches, wherever enemy gunfire was proving troublesome, throughout the day; and the grateful messages received from the Army provide as good evidence of the effectiveness of their support as the enemy's own records. At 6 a.m. the L.S.T. convoy for the 'Sugar' sector arrived, and the busy minesweepers swept it in.

In the 'Roger' sector the initial assault also took place almost on time, and without serious difficulty. The only error made was that the first wave of landing craft bound for the 'Green' beach landed their troops some 1,500 yards south of the correct position; but as a strong enemy battery, of whose presence we were unaware, was covering the proper beach the mistake was a fortunate one. The follow-up waves suffered some shelling and dive-bombing; but losses were slight, and by 10.30 the first L.S.Ts were coming inshore to beach themselves. During the next eleven hours no less than thirty-eight L.S.Ts were unloaded in the 'Sugar' and 'Roger' sectors, and before nightfall two convoys composed of these invaluable ships had sailed again south-bound. The easy gradients on all the beaches in the British assault area greatly facilitated the unloading of the L.S.Ts, because the use of pontoon causeways was rendered unnecessary.[1] The pontoons were later towed to the southern assault area, where unloading was proving far more difficult.

Soon after daylight the cruisers *Mauritius* and *Orion*, the monitor *Roberts* and two more destroyers took up their pre-arranged bombarding positions off-shore, where the *Uganda* was already engaging enemy positions. But, whereas the heavier ships actually received comparatively few calls for fire support on D-Day, the destroyers were constantly in action; and it was they who, in Commodore Oliver's words, 'filled the gap' until the Army's artillery could be deployed. The enemy's gunfire caused a few losses, mainly among the landing craft, and his air attacks continued by night as well as by day; but our smoke screens were very effective, and German claims to have inflicted heavy losses on the offshore shipping bore no relation to the truth.

The Seafires from Admiral Vian's escort carriers flew 265 sorties on D-Day, and the average strength of their patrols was about twenty aircraft. They, the long-range Lightnings of the Strategic Air Force, and single-seater fighters of the Tactical Air Force working from Sicily shared in the defence of the assault area to begin with; but after D-Day the strength of the escort carriers' patrols was bound to decline. We had originally hoped to dispense with the carrier aircraft by the 10th, when Montecorvino airfield should have been in use; but it was not captured on D-Day as had been planned, and in consequence Admiral Vian's force continued to provide a proportion of the necessary air cover until the 12th. By that time an emergency landing strip had been established at Paestum in the American sector, and Admiral Hewitt ordered the surviving Seafires to land on shore. During the afternoon of the 12th twenty-six of them landed safely, and Admiral Vian's ships then withdrew to Palermo, and thence to Bizerta. The protection of assault forces engaged on a combined operation by carrier-borne fighters until the shore-based aircraft could assume full responsibility had been a novel and valuable experience. Although on this occasion it was not an unqualified success, it was due to no fault of the Fleet Air Arm pilots that they engaged in few combats. The enemy attacks were generally made by fast fighter-bombers, and the Seafires could not compete with such 'tip and run' tactics. They probably shot down two enemies and damaged four others. Losses among the Seafires were, however, heavy. Ten of their number were lost, and thirty-two were damaged beyond repair, mostly through deck-landing crashes. The slow speed of the escort carriers, the flimsiness of the Seafire's undercarriage, and the

---

[1] Compare experience in operation 'Husky', in which L.S.Ts grounded some distance off-shore. See pp. 131–134.

light winds which prevailed throughout the operation certainly aggravated the pilots' difficulties; but there seems no doubt that many of them had received insufficient training to cope with such conditions.[1] On the 12th and 13th the surviving Seafires made several patrols from the landing strips on shore, but by the 15th the U.S.A.A.F. and R.A.F. fighters had matters well in hand, and the last carrier fighters were then withdrawn. On the 20th Admiral Vian hauled down his flag, and the escort carriers returned to Britain to prepare for other duties.

To return to D-Day in the British sector, by nightfall the beach-head was firmly held; but the Army's penetration inland was nowhere more than three miles, Montecorvino airfield had not been captured, and there was still a gap of about five miles between the British right wing and the American left. Plainly this dangerous situation could be exploited by a resolute enemy making a thrust down to the sea coast between the two Allied armies. But before telling how the Germans reacted to that opportunity we must briefly re-count the events of D-Day in the American sector, which lay to the south of the mouth of the River Sele. Here it was intended to assault simultaneously on four contiguous beaches, called 'Red', 'Green', 'Yellow' and 'Blue'. The assault convoy, which included three British L.S.Is and the three large L.S.Ts *Boxer*, *Bruiser* and *Thruster*, which were loaded with DUKWS, was in position by 1 a.m., and the hoisting out of the assault craft began immediately. Included in the convoy were a number of support craft fitted with rocket projectors, whose duty it was to fire their salvos on to the beaches if the first waves came under enemy gunfire. Though Admiral Davidson's heavy bombardment ships were in the offing to provide support for Admiral Hall[2], no arrangements had been made for destroyers to close the beaches behind the assault waves and engage the enemy defences.

Trouble began over the sweeping of the approach channel for mines. Too few minesweepers had been provided to clear the outer anchorage as well as the channel leading to the beaches; and the channel was not buoyed in the manner normally employed by British sweepers. The assault craft thus had to rely on radar to keep them in safe waters; and as the channel had in fact not been thor-oughly swept they were sometimes delayed by the presence of floating mines. No ships were, however, lost through striking mines. In con-

---

[1] See Admiral Cunningham's despatch (Supplement to the London Gazette No. 38899 of 28th April 1950) para. 19. In the invasion of southern France (operation 'Dragoon') in the following August, Fleet Air Arm fighters again worked from escort carriers, and although the wind was again very light the accident rate was far lower than at Salerno. This was almost certainly due to the pilots being better trained. (See Part II of this volume, Chapter XVI.)

[2] See p. 162.

trast with the trouble experienced over clearing the approach channels, all the beaches were correctly identified by the guide boats, and there was no case of troops being landed in the wrong place. This, however, did not save the assault waves from coming under heavy fire as they approached, or directly after the troops had landed. It was now that the lack of close support for the assault troops immediately after the touch-down, such as had been provided in the British sector, was severely felt by the American troops. Admiral Hewitt considered that this deficiency contributed greatly to the difficulty experienced in securing the beach-heads in the southern assaults; but he himself could presumably have divided the available vessels equally between the two landings had he so desired.

In spite of the strength of the opposition the assault troops fought their way steadily inland, and by daylight all except those on the southern flank were approaching their initial objectives; but the heavy fire directed on to the beaches and landing craft by tanks, guns, mortars and lighter weapons produced serious troubles; two of the four beaches had to be closed for several hours, and when craft were diverted from them to the other two beaches they became very congested. In the afternoon a new beach was opened two miles further up the coast, and this eased the situation; but difficulties were by no means over. Because the enemy's resistance was so stiff it was urgently necessary to get the tanks ashore as quickly as possible; but when, at about 6.15 a.m., the six L.C.Ts, which were all that had been allocated to the southern attack force, tried to land their thirty tanks they were heavily fired on and had to haul off temporarily. According to the operation orders some fifty L.C.Ts should have come from the northern sector as soon as they had unloaded; but this hope proved far too optimistic. Commodore Oliver himself possessed too few L.C.Ts to unload all his ships; some had broken down and, for lack of spare parts, could not be repaired, while others were damaged. The result was that only sixteen joined Admiral Hall on D-Day, and eleven more on the following day. Nor did the beaching and unloading of the thirty-two L.S.Ts (twelve of them British) which arrived in convoys FSS.2(X) and (Y) proceed smoothly. Unswept mines delayed the approach to the shore, only the 'Red' and 'Green' beaches could be used, and when the L.S.Ts did arrive incorrect loading and the acute congestion on shore made discharging very slow. None of the British L.S.Ts beached as had been intended on D-Day, and it was midnight on the 11th–12th before they were cleared. A number of factors—some unavoidable and some which could have been foreseen—thus combined to produce a difficult situation in the American sector. Air attacks were heavier than on the British front but, for all the large claims made by the Luftwaffe, they did very little damage. The main cause of the trouble unquestionably

was the very strong resistance offered to the assault troops by a determined enemy, whose defensive positions had been left virtually
undisturbed until the moment of the landing.

Soon after daylight on the 9th the monitor *Abercrombie*, the
American cruisers *Savannah* and *Philadelphia* and several destroyers of
Admiral Davidson's task force engaged the enemy's positions; and
there is no doubt that they helped greatly to stave off disaster. That
evening, however, the *Abercrombie* struck a mine and had to withdraw. By nightfall Paestum was in American hands, and most of VI
Corp's other initial objectives had been captured.

In the British sector the developments which took place on the
10th, when the town and port of Salerno were occupied, were
reasonably satisfactory; but next day the enemy's fire became so
heavy that the port had to be closed. This meant that we had to continue to unload all the stores and reinforcements for X Corps over the
beaches; and that was bound to delay the building up of the Army's
strength. On the 10th British troops captured Montecorvino, but as
enemy guns still commanded the airfield it could not be used by
Allied aircraft. Battipaglia was also captured on that day; but
enemy reinforcements arrived, strong counter-attacks took place,
and the position could not be held. After four days of heavy fighting
the British beach-head was nowhere more than five miles deep, and
considerable losses had been suffered. None the less no serious anxiety
was felt in the Headquarters Ship *Hilary*; for the Eighth Army was
approaching from the south, contact had by then been made with the
Americans on the right, and the follow-up convoys were pouring men
and stores ashore.

In the American sector, in spite of the handicap of the bad start
made in the initial assaults, progress on the 10th and 11th was rather
better than on the British front. On the night of the 10th–11th E-
boats attacked the transport anchorage and sank an American
destroyer; air attacks on the beaches and on off-shore shipping continued troublesome, and the beach-head was still far too shallow for
comfort. The American troop transports sailed after dark on the 10th,
and Rear-Admiral Conolly, U.S.N., then took over command of all
ships working in the southern sector from Rear-Admiral Hall, who
had sailed with the transports. His flag still flew in the small and
cramped Headquarters Ship *Biscayne*, and to that same ship Admiral
Hewitt transferred on the 12th when his own much larger Headquarters Ship the *Ancon* sailed for Sicily. This re-arrangement,
though it had always been intended, and followed the practice carried out in the invasion of Sicily, did result in overstraining the
capacity of the *Biscayne*. In combined operations satisfactory headquarters ships had been found to be quite essential, and it may be
that in the present instance it would have been better to defer the

The Landing at Salerno, operation 'Avalanche', 9th September, 1943

Top. Invasion shipping assembled in North Africa.
Bottom. A destroyer laying a smoke screen to cover L.S.Ts approaching the beaches.

The Landing at Salerno, operation 'Avalanche', 9th September, 1943

Top. An L.S.T. convoy approaching the beaches. (Note barrage balloons.)
Middle. H.M.S. *Mauritius* covering U.S. naval landing craft.
Bottom. Bombarding ships in action and the scene off the assault area on D-Day.
Taken from H.M.S. *Cadmus.*

departure of the *Ancon*. Meanwhile the supporting warships—
monitors, cruisers and destroyers—were constantly in action against
enemy gun positions, concentrations of tanks, road junctions and
bridges in both assault areas; and the British ships were far more
heavily engaged than the American. To give an idea of the scale of
their support, and its importance to the Army, about forty calls for
fire were answered in the British sector on the 10th, and between that
day and the 13th the cruiser *Mauritius* fired over 1,000 rounds from
her 6-inch guns. The bombardments were generally controlled by
shore observers, but air spotting was also sometimes used.

Between the 8th and 12th of September the Germans sailed three
U-boats from Toulon to the Gulf of Salerno; but on arrival they
found conditions little to their liking. So closely were the offshore
waters patrolled by surface ships and aircraft that it was very difficult
for them to get in an attack; and the bright moonlight deprived them
of the usual opportunities and benefits of the night hours. The sum
of their accomplishments was to sink an American merchantman and
a minesweeper of the same nationality.

Up to the 11th air attacks had been little more than a nuisance
and, thanks largely to the prompt and efficient use of smoke-making
apparatus, they had caused us few losses. On that day, however, the
enemy first used his new wireless-controlled (FX.1400) bombs
against the supporting warships and merchantmen.[1] The attacks
were made by the Luftwaffe formation which had sunk the *Roma*[2];
and at the beginning we had no counter to these novel weapons.
Only the Lightnings could reach up to and catch the parent aircraft,
gunfire was helpless to defend the ships, and as a bomb released at
18,000 feet was travelling at about 800 feet per second at the end of
its trajectory, no avoiding action could be taken by the ships—
especially in crowded anchorages such as those off Salerno. The first
to suffer were the American cruisers *Philadelphia*, which was badly
shaken by a near-miss, and *Savannah*, which received a direct hit and
was seriously damaged. On the afternoon of the same day, the 11th,
the *Uganda* was also hit and had to be towed to Malta. Admiral
Cunningham ordered up the *Aurora* and *Penelope* of the 12th Cruiser
Squadron to replace the damaged ships, and they and the U.S.S.
Boise (which had arrived to replace the *Savannah*) were soon in action.

On the 13th the crisis of the struggle came with a powerful German
tank attack down the valley of the River Sele, at the weakly-held
junction of the British and American armies. By the following morning the situation was precarious; for the enemy's penetration was so
deep that the American beaches had been brought under heavy

---

[1] See p. 168 fn. (1) regarding the FX bomb.
[2] See p. 168.

artillery fire. Admiral Hewitt now stopped all unloading in the American sector, ordered all ships to keep steam at short notice, and asked Admiral Cunningham for more and heavier naval support. The response was immediate. Three light cruisers at once sailed from Bizerta to Tripoli to embark additional troops and carry them to Salerno at high speed; the battleships *Valiant* and *Warspite*, escorted by six destroyers, left Malta that same evening; and Admiral Cunningham told Hewitt that if necessary the *Nelson* and *Rodney*, which he had ordered from Malta to Augusta to have them close at hand, would be sent as well. Meanwhile the cruisers and destroyers already off Salerno were heavily engaged with enemy troop and tank concentrations throughout the day, and the Strategic and Tactical Air Forces both made a very big effort. Their bombers and fighters flew over 1,900 sorties that day and during the following night; and the heaviest possible attacks were made on the enemy's spearhead, which was still pushing down the Sele River towards the beaches, and on his zones of concentration and lines of reinforcement. Fighter patrols were also strengthened, for the enemy's air attacks were still continuing; and emergency measures were taken to drop paratroops in the American sector and to rush in other reinforcements by sea. On the afternoon of the 14th Admiral Hewitt called for Commodore Oliver to come over to the *Biscayne*, where the Commodore found an atmosphere of grave anxiety. To his intense surprise and misgiving he was told that General Clark wanted two emergency plans prepared. One was to withdraw the British X Corps and disembark it through the American VI Corps' beaches, while the other was to withdraw VI Corps and transfer it to the British sector. The latter was stated to be the more probable requirement. Commodore Oliver protested that to re-embark heavily engaged troops from a shallow beachhead was certainly impracticable, and would probably prove suicidal. Even if the troops could be taken off, the whole of the stores and ammunition which had been unloaded during the previous day would be lost. As the Commander of X Corps, Lieutenant-General Sir R. McCreery, had apparently not been told of the proposal, Commodore Oliver at once got in touch with him. He also signalled to Admiral Cunningham to enlist his support against any such plan being carried out. By the evening, however, the situation, though still dangerous, had improved somewhat, and Admiral Hewitt ordered a partial resumption of unloading. Early next morning, the 15th, General Alexander, the Commander-in-Chief of the Allied armies in Italy, arrived in Salerno Bay in a destroyer, and Admiral Hewitt at once went aboard to meet him.[1] The Admiral remembers

---

[1] In Admiral Hewitt's report the arrival of General Alexander is stated to have been on 16th September; but General Alexander's despatch and many other sources make it plain that this is an error.

that, as soon as the withdrawal plan was mentioned, General Alexander expressed himself strongly against any such proposal. General Alexander then went ashore to the Fifth Army Commander's headquarters, after which nothing more was heard about withdrawal from the beach-head. Though General Clark has explained that he was only taking precautionary steps to meet a situation which might arise if matters became critical on VI Corps' front[1], in retrospect it is plain that the navies could never have re-embarked the embattled troops successfully. As was said earlier, the greatest danger to a combined operation will always arise when a strong counter-attack is launched before the build-up of the troops is complete. But once troops have been committed to a landing on a big scale, the issue must be fought out where they stand. Withdrawal in the face of heavy pressure could only result in utter disaster.

On the 15th the Allied Air Forces continued their attacks, and the situation had so far improved that full-scale unloading was restarted on the American beaches. Enemy gunfire and bombing, including wireless-controlled bombs, continued against the ships, and more losses were suffered. The *Valiant* and *Warspite* had now arrived, and at 5 p.m. the latter opened fire. The sight of her 15-inch shells bursting on the enemy positions must have been heartening to the hard-pressed soldiers. The other support ships, cruisers and destroyers, had another very busy day and were constantly answering calls for fire. Before nightfall it was plain that the dangerous enemy advance had been halted.

Next day, the 16th, the *Valiant* and *Warspite*, which had withdrawn to seaward during the night, returned to their bombarding positions, the *Ancon* arrived with a much-needed supply of 6-inch ammunition, and Admiral Hewitt re-hoisted his flag in her; and the light cruisers *Euryalus*, *Scylla* and *Charybdis*, now commanded by Admiral Vian, landed the troops they had fetched from Tripoli. The bombardments continued on much the same scale as during the preceding days; but early in the afternoon, just after the *Warspite* had successfully completed another shoot, three wireless-controlled bombs were aimed at her. Two were very near misses, but the third scored a direct hit which exploded in a boiler room. The ship lost all power and was badly flooded. American and British tugs took her in tow, and after an anxious passage through the Straits of Messina she arrived safely in Malta three days later. Meanwhile on the 16th the Fifth Army gained touch with the leading troops of General Montgomery's Eighth Army and, although the former did not resume the offensive until the following day, the crisis had plainly passed.

It is difficult to say at what precise moment the grave perils which

---

[1] See *Calculated Risk* (Harrap, 1951), p. 193.

for a time undoubtedly threatened the entire Allied expedition to Salerno began to recede; but the enemy's records show that it was on the 14th that the most dangerous thrust was halted, and the salient which they had driven towards the beaches began to shrink. It is also difficult to decide which were the main factors in restoring the situation. Admiral Hewitt in his report on the operation and Admiral Cunningham in his despatch both stressed the important part played by the bombarding ships. The German naval command's War Diary states that on the 15th 'our attack had to stop and reform because of the great effect of the enemy sea bombardment and continuous air attacks'; and again that 'the effect of the heavy ships' bombardment and the almost complete command [of the air] . . . by the far superior enemy air force has cost us grievous losses'. It therefore seems certain that the naval and air bombardments, taken together, played a very big part. Where contemporary judgments now seem to have been at fault is in attributing too great a share of the success to the heavy ship bombardments of the 15th and 16th. Heartening though these must have been to the soldiers, it is now plain that the crisis had in fact passed before they took place. It therefore seems more correct to attribute the major share of the credit for the undoubted success of the naval bombardments to the cruisers, monitors and destroyers which had worked so hard during the preceding days.

Before continuing to tell the story of the sequel to the successful holding of the Salerno beach-heads certain conclusions derived from a study of the difficulties which arose may be mentioned. Whereas all the units which took part in the northern assault, the great majority of which were British, had considerable previous battle experience behind them, hardly any of those who were first landed in the southern sector had been in action before. The most experienced American troops, brought from Sicily, only arrived in the follow-up and reinforcement convoys.[1] As to the curious manner in which General Clark's proposal to shorten the front by transferring one of the two Army Corps reached the naval commanders on the 14th, this may have occurred through inexperience on the part of some of his staff, all of whom were working at high pressure in very difficult conditions. On the other hand, whereas X Corps' two divisions were able to land simultaneously in the northern sector, shortage of assault ships restricted the initial southern landings to a one-division front; and that must have been a considerable handicap. The loading of American shipping at Oran certainly left something to be desired, and this aggravated the troubles on the beaches; while the

---

[1] Some elements of the U.S. 45th Division, from General Patton's experienced corps in Sicily, landed on the 10th. The remainder of that division did not arrive until the 13th. The U.S. 3rd Division, also from Patton's corps, arrived on the 18th.

unloading of the American L.S.Is, which were admittedly much larger than their British counterparts, was at first slow. Lastly both assaults were constantly handicapped by shortage of L.C.Ts. The difficulties experienced in the southern sector were probably caused by the cumulative effect of all these factors, but lack of experience was perhaps the greatest of them.[1]

Once the German counter-attacks had been halted the building up of the Allied armies proceeded rapidly, though not without hindrance from the enemy. The port of Salerno was under shell fire until the 25th of September, when it could at last be re-opened and used by Allied shipping; but the British beaches and anchorages were not freed from artillery bombardment until the 26th. None the less, stores and reinforcements were poured ashore over the beaches during this period, and the losses of ships and landing craft caused by the enemy were comparatively slight. On the night of the 28th–29th, however, a violent gale swept Salerno Bay. Many small ships and landing craft were driven ashore, especially in the American sector, and although most of them were salved later all unloading was stopped until the 30th. In passing it may be remarked that had such a gale arisen between the 10th and 15th of September, when the enemy's counter-attacks were producing a critical situation on shore, a major calamity would almost certainly have overtaken the Allied armies. Such are the inescapable hazards of an assault from the sea.

The build-up of the British army was accomplished mainly by L.S.Ts, and special mention must be made of the work of the three large ships of that type, the *Boxer, Thruster* and *Bruiser*. They displaced about 5,740 tons when fully loaded, compared with the 3,770 tons of a normal L.S.T., and could steam at nearly double the 9-knot maximum speed of the latter class; but their deeper draught made them more difficult to beach satisfactorily. In operation 'Avalanche' they came into their own, and between D-Day and the 1st of October they made no less than six trips to the beaches. Between them they carried in 6,000 troops and 1,345 guns and vehicles. They gained a special commendation from Admiral Hewitt, and immediately after the Salerno landings they sailed for Bombay to take part in the combined operations now being planned in the South-East Asia Command.[2]

As the German army withdrew slowly to the north, we were able to occupy and open the small ports on the southern shore of the Bay

[1] In an article entitled 'The Allied Navies at Salerno', published in the *U.S. Naval Institute Proceedings* for September 1953, Admiral H. K. Hewitt discusses this matter fully.

[2] These operations never took place (see p. 345), and the three L.S.Ts were recalled to the Mediterranean to take part in the Anzio landing in January 1944 (see p. 302).

of Naples, and a proportion of the Armies' stores and supplies was unloaded in them instead of in the Bay of Salerno. The supporting squadrons of warships stayed off the coast until the end of September, but calls for fire support declined as the Fifth Army fought its way inland. On the 1st of October British troops entered Naples and, although the great port had been very thoroughly wrecked, so promptly were steps taken to restore its facilities that the first ships were able to berth there two days later. The work of clearing the many obstructions and of rehabilitating the port fell to the Anglo-American salvage team which had gained much experience in similar circumstances at Bizerta and Palermo. But in the rapid restoration of Naples they surpassed all their previous accomplishments. By the 18th of October over 5,000 tons of cargo were being discharged there daily, and the total figures for that month were 155,134 tons of cargo and 37,013 vehicles.

While operation 'Avalanche' was actually proceeding the Mediterranean Fleet greatly improved its strategic situation by gaining the use of all the important bases in the south of Italy—a process in which the local Italian naval authorities generally co-operated cordially. The seizure of Taranto on the 9th of September has already been recounted[1]; but two days later we also occupied Brindisi and Bari[2], and quickly brought them into use as ports of entry for the Eighth Army's supplies, and as advance bases for the light naval forces which at once began to scour the Adriatic for enemy shipping. A Coastal Force base was established at Brindisi, and two destroyer flotillas were soon stationed at Bari to carry out patrols in the Adriatic. On the night of the 2nd–3rd of October the first combined operation took place on the east coast of Italy, when two Commandos were landed near Termoli and achieved complete surprise. They quickly linked up with an infantry brigade coming up overland from the south, and on the following night another brigade was landed from the sea; but stiff resistance from German troops was encountered, enemy aircraft attacked the offshore shipping heavily, and for a time the issue was in doubt. Two destroyers were sent up to support the assault forces, and on the 6th, after heavy fighting and bombardments from the sea and air, Termoli was firmly in our hands. This operation, taken with the fall of Naples, gave the Allies a grip over the whole of southern Italy. As more combined operations would probably be required, the Commander-in-Chief now appointed two 'Senior Naval Officers, Advanced Landings' for the east and west coasts of Italy, thus keeping the necessary nucleus of trained men constantly available; but in the period following the capture of

[1] See p. 170.
[2] See Map 12.

Naples in the west and Termoli in the east the main duty of the inshore forces on both coasts became the supply of the Fifth and Eighth
Armies.

At noon on the 6th of October the Western Naval Task Force was
dissolved, and Admiral Hewitt's appointment lapsed. Responsibility
for naval operations off the west coast of Italy was now vested in
Rear-Admiral J. A. V. Morse, who flew his flag ashore at Naples.

Thus, twenty-one days after the initial landings in Salerno Bay,
was the main object of operation 'Avalanche', the capture of Naples,
achieved. Considering that, for the first time since the Dieppe raid[1],
Allied assault forces had encountered an alert enemy established in
prepared positions, that the defenders were troops of the first quality,
and that the enemy was able to reinforce them quickly and counter-
attack vigorously before a satisfactory Allied lodgement had been
gained, the accomplishment may be considered remarkable. Italy
had been eliminated from the Axis partnership; the major part of her
Navy and many of her aircraft had joined the Allies, and our forces
of all arms were now well poised to regain control of the whole
Mediterranean, and to strike at the heart of the enemy's territory.
Nor had the cost been excessive. True the enemy had struck back
with all his weapons at the offshore ships, and the Allied invasion
fleet had suffered considerable loss and damage; but when the full
list of casualties is studied it seems today remarkably small in relation to the number of ships involved and the hazards encountered.
One British and three American destroyers, one American fleet minesweeper, two British L.S.Ts, two L.C.Is and seventeen L.C.Ts of both
nations, three American merchantmen and one British hospital ship
were the principal losses attributable to the enemy; and about
another seventy vessels, ranging from battleships and cruisers down
to landing craft, were damaged. Of all the lessons learnt perhaps the
most important concerned the need to neutralise the enemy's
defences by heavy bombardments before making an opposed landing.
Every important combined operation so far carried out, from the
failure at Dieppe to the successful assault on Sicily, had re-affirmed
that principle. In his report on 'Avalanche' Admiral Hewitt strongly
criticised the decision to sacrifice preliminary air and naval bombardments in the interests of achieving surprise. He pointed out that,
because the assembly of the assault convoys was bound to be noticed,
and Salerno was an obvious choice for their destination, we were in
any case unlikely to surprise the enemy; and today it seems undeniable that to land the assault troops in the face of prepared and
intact defences was to accept avoidable hazards. The emphasis
placed on preliminary bombardments in the reports on operation

---

[1] See Vol. II, pp. 240–252.

'Avalanche' did, however, ensure that they would be fully employed in the future. Finally, in Admiral Hewitt's words, these events 'marked the beginning of the end of Germanic military might'.

It was, perhaps, appropriate that on the same day that the Western Naval Task Force was dissolved Admiral Sir Andrew Cunningham's appointment as First Sea Lord should have been announced[1]; for he, who had brought the Mediterranean Fleet through its severest trials, had now seen not only the submission of the Italian fleet but the successful launching of the first great combined operations in Europe. He hauled his flag down on the 17th of October, and in his farewell message to his fleet he expressed the keen regret he felt over leaving it, as well as his pride in its great accomplishments. 'You have' he said 'taken a vital part in throwing the enemy out of Africa, in the capture of Sicily, and in the invasion of Italy'; but posterity may well judge that no man had played a bigger part in those high achievements than the naval Commander-in-Chief himself. He was succeeded by Admiral Sir John Cunningham from the Levant Command, which in turn was taken over by Vice-Admiral Sir Algernon Willis, of Force H. The latter struck his flag on the 13th of October, and a few days later Force H was disbanded. It had been brought into being at a moment of grave crisis in June 1940[2], and during the following three years and more, through many vicissitudes of fortune, it had remained the main instrument of British maritime power in the western Mediterranean and in the approaches to Gibraltar. To those who had served in it in the early days the great concourse of warships assembled for the recent operations would scarcely have been recognisable; yet throughout almost the whole of its long life Force H had maintained the form of a properly balanced, if sometimes small fleet[3]; and it may be that its outstandingly successful career owed much to the consistency with which all the varied elements of maritime power were included in it. By October 1943 it was plain that there was no further need for a battle fleet in the Mediterranean; and, as the ships of Force H were urgently needed, some to reinforce the Eastern Fleet and others to prepare for the invasion of Normandy, it was inevitable that the force should be disbanded. But its record throughout the war was, as Admiral Cunningham reminded its officers and men, a proud one.

As to the German U-boats, in September they continued to work against the convoys moving slowly along the North African coast, and sank the destroyer *Puckeridge* and three merchantmen in convoy; but

---

[1] See pp. 60–61 regarding the illness and death of Admiral Pound.

[2] See Vol. I, pp. 241–242.

[3] The only period during which Force H was virtually disbanded was when most of its ships were sent to the Indian Ocean to take part in the assault on Madagascar in April–May 1942. See Vol. II, pp. 185–192.

in the small hours of the 12th U.617 was damaged by a Wellington bomber and beached herself on the coast of Spanish Morocco. There she was destroyed by the gunfire of a British trawler—which caused considerable discussion on whether Spanish neutrality had been infringed or whether the doctrine of 'continuous pursuit' held good. In October nine U-boats were at sea, in widely spread areas; but it was only the four working off the Algerian coast which achieved appreciable success. During the month they sank between them the British minesweeper *Hythe*, an American destroyer and three merchantmen. In relation to the size of the traffic on the Mediterranean routes these were, however, small losses; and in November they declined still further.

It thus came to pass that by the autumn of 1943 Allied maritime control had been re-asserted over the greater part of the Mediterranean, and the fleet which had played so large a part in that accomplishment passed the peak of its strength. The changes in its composition which had come to pass since 1939 had been very far-reaching, and in order that posterity may be able to compare the strength available to hold the Mediterranean at the beginning of the war with that needed to regain what we so nearly lost, the state of the fleet when Admiral Cunningham gave up his command for the second time has been summarised in an Appendix.[1]

It will be convenient to insert here an analysis of the merchant shipping losses suffered by the Axis powers in the Mediterranean theatre between June and December 1943. In order to preserve the statistical basis used in previous volumes Table 13 (p. 186) treats losses inflicted before the Italian armistice separately from those inflicted after that event. In the former case the ships which fell under Allied control or were scuttled to prevent them falling into German hands at the time of the armistice have been excluded. But in the latter case ships which the Germans themselves scuttled in various ports as they retreated up Italy have been included under losses from 'other causes', even though some of them were subsequently salved and brought into service by the Allies.

While the main attention of the Allied naval authorities was focused on Salerno, concurrent events in Sardinia and Corsica had not escaped their notice. Apart from the Italian mainland it was perhaps in those two islands, and in Corfu and Cephalonia[2], that the Italian armistice gave the enemy the greatest embarrassment. The Germans started at once to transfer their forces from Sardinia to

---

[1] See Appendix E. The Mediterranean Fleet's strength in 1939 is given in Vol. I. pp. 48–49 and Appendix E of that volume.

[2] See Map 14.

Table 13. Italian and German (Mediterranean) Merchant Shipping Losses
June–December 1943

(1) Italian

No. of ships—Tonnage

Month	By Surface Ship	By Submarine	By Air Attack	By Mine	By other causes	Total
June . . .	—	12–23,652	19–31,418	1–1,413	6– 4,994	38– 61,477
July . . .	—	19–33,745	24–25,827	3–2,436	55–15,098	101– 77,106
August . .	—	8–12,091	27–32,153	1–1,416	11–16,063	47– 61,723
1st–8th September	—	5– 881	1– 61	1– 846	48–11,770	55– 13,558
Total . .	—	44–70,369	71–89,459	6–6,111	120–47,925	241–213,864

(2) German and German controlled (Mediterranean only)

Month	By Surface Ship	By Submarine	By Air Attack	By Mine	By other causes	Total
1st June–8th September	—	9– 39,925	4–16,637	1– 50	3– 2,077	17– 58,689
9th–30th September	3– 7,338	7– 22,907	6–15,294	6– 8,868	69–106,455	91–160,862
October . .	4–11,195	8– 21,231	6–13,646	2– 1,496	23– 38,638	43– 86,206
November .	2– 3,034	3– 8,848	8–10,368	1– 253	10– 10,459	24– 32,962
December .	6– 4,400	5– 21,688	9– 9,970	2– 676	14– 10,055	36– 46,789
Total . .	15–25,967	32–114,599	33–65,915	12–11,343	119–167,684	211–385,508

NOTES: (1) Of the 452 ships accounted for in the above tables 300 were of less than 500 tons.
      (2) Of the 104 ships sunk by air attacks 78 were destroyed in raids on harbours.
      (3) A considerable number of small vessels of various merchant ship categories such as tugs, coasters and Greek caïques were requisitioned for naval service as auxiliaries. These have been excluded from the tables.

Corsica, and they accomplished their purpose very successfully. Some 25,000 troops, 2,300 vehicles and 5,000 tons of supplies were safely ferried across the Straits of Bonifacio with virtually no interference from the Allied navies or air forces. Sardinia thus fell to the Allies as a natural consequence of the invasion of Italy, and with hardly a shot having to be fired. As, however, the enemy appeared likely to resist in Corsica, in the middle of September French troops were carried there from North Africa in the same country's warships. Meanwhile, on the 12th, Hitler had actually ordered the evacuation of the island. The withdrawal was carried out by air transport as well as by sea, and the latter traffic was organised by the same officer, Captain von Liebenstein, who had been instrumental in the successful evacuation of Sicily.[1] Although the enemy's records contain no confirmation of any losses to their evacuation fleet by Allied surface ships, our coastal craft were several times in action off Corsica by night, and it seems probable that damage was inflicted on at least one occasion. Our submarines certainly sank several ships, including a 10,000-ton tanker which was torpedoed off Bastia by the *Ultor* on the 24th of September. At the peak of the traffic the Germans employed fifteen steamers and about 120 ferry barges, landing craft and miscellaneous vessels. The majority of the troops and the greater part of the equipment were carried from Bastia in the north of Corsica to the Italian mainland at Leghorn, or to the island of Elba[2]; but the main port of embarkation received little attention from Allied aircraft until the 21st of September when American Liberators destroyed five merchantmen there. Seventy-five Wellingtons then followed up with a night attack, which increased the damage. Other aircraft worked against the evacuation route by night as well as by day, but their accomplishments were not enough to stop the traffic. By the evening of the 3rd of October, when the French were approaching Bastia and the enemy movements had to end, 6,240 troops, about 1,200 prisoners-of-war, over 3,200 vehicles and nearly 5,000 tons of stores had been transhipped by sea. The total cost to the German Navy of the evacuations from Sardinia and Corsica was eighteen ships and craft of all types (most of them small), totalling 16,943 tons. The enemy's air lift from Corsica, which had been running for the greater part of September, had meanwhile taken out 21,107 men and some 350 tons of stores; but to accomplish this a heavy price was paid, for fifty-five transport aircraft were destroyed, the majority of them as a result of bombing attacks on Italian airfields.

One cannot but admire the efficiency and determination shown by the enemy in these successful evacuations, and the high degree of

---

[1] See pp. 144–150.
[2] See Map 12.

flexibility which enabled him to switch his air and naval forces so rapidly from one duty to another—even at a time of acute difficulty. As regards the Allied failure to intervene effectively, it must be remembered that Naples did not fall until the 1st of October, two days before the evacuation of Corsica ended, and that throughout September operation 'Avalanche' had demanded the greatest possible effort by all the Allied services. Any appreciable diversion from the main operation would doubtless have been resisted to the utmost by the commanders of the embattled forces; and, bearing in mind the Allied high command's attitude regarding diversions to the Aegean at this time (about which we shall have more to say shortly), it seems likely that General Eisenhower and the three service Commanders-in-Chief would have regarded any considerable transfer of their forces to Corsica in similar light. Nor should it be forgotten that an attempt to dispute command of the waters between Corsica and Leghorn by night as well as by day for several weeks would have absorbed a big naval and air effort. In these circumstances it is not surprising that the Allied authorities, though fully aware of what was going on, limited their commitments to the transport of French forces to the island, and the deployment of submarines and coastal craft off the enemy's ports. These events did, however, reinforce the view that only by a carefully planned combined operation could a determined enemy be stopped from evacuating troops and equipment by sea. Heavy and repeated bombing and bombardment of the terminal ports and airfields, constant sweeps and patrols by light naval forces, and effective air cover for these latter were all once more shown to be essential.[1]

We will now take leave temporarily of the central Mediterranean to review the events which had meanwhile taken place in the eastern basin.

Even before the Italian armistice the Prime Minister's eyes had turned towards the islands of the Dodecanese, the seizure of which would, in his opinion, bring important strategic advantages for a relatively small expenditure of effort. Mr Churchill considered that the disorganisation in the enemy's camp following on the collapse of one partner in the Axis might produce the opportunity he sought —provided that we acted quickly. The principal key to control of the Aegean was the large Italian-owned island of Rhodes, which possessed a good harbour and two airfields.[2] It had proved a thorn in our flesh ever since the entry of Italy into the war; but we had

---

[1] See pp. 144–150 regarding the Messina evacuation.
[2] See Map 14.

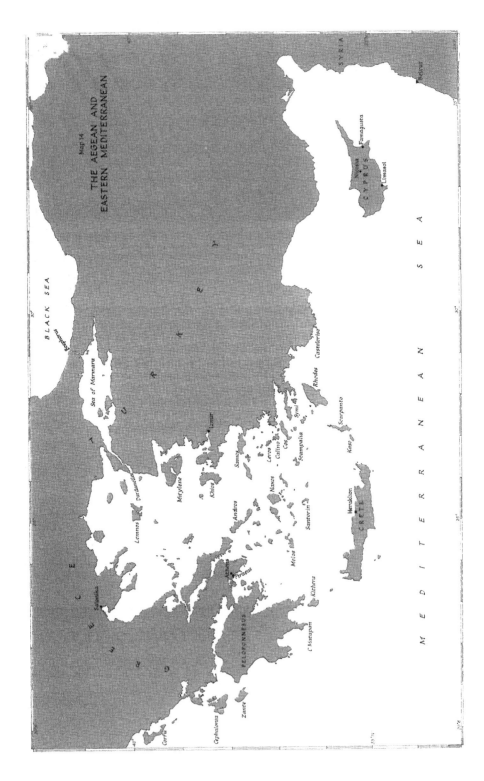

Map 14

THE AEGEAN AND
EASTERN MEDITERRANEAN

never possessed the forces necessary to neutralise it—let alone seize it
by assault from the sea. Next in importance to Rhodes were the
smaller islands of Leros, which possessed a seaplane base and a
harbour suitable for use by small warships but no landing grounds
for shore-based aircraft, and Cos, where there was an airfield from
which single-engined fighters could operate and on which it was
possible to construct other landing grounds. After the Germans
overran the mainland of Greece and captured Crete in the summer
of 1941 they rapidly extended the Axis hold over the Aegean by
occupying the more important of the Greek islands; and they also
reinforced the garrisons of those which belonged to Italy. Thereafter
not only was the Aegean virtually barred to Allied shipping, but
good use was made by the enemy of the island bases for offensive
purposes. Air attacks on our eastern Mediterranean convoys and
bases had often been mounted from the islands, German and Italian
submarines made regular use of their harbours, and the light forces
and aircraft stationed there were able to command the Aegean sufficiently to protect the enemy's coast-wise and inter-island shipping
traffic. Though our submarines had often worked in among the
islands, and had achieved occasional successes there, they alone
could not interrupt the traffic for prolonged periods. Surface ships
and air forces were also necessary; and to employ them effectively
a base much nearer than Beirut or Haifa, let alone Alexandria, was
a pre-requisite. But to the Prime Minister there were far weightier
reasons for seizing the initiative in the Aegean than considerations of
local advantage. The Dodecanese islands lay close off the coast of
Turkey and commanded the approach to the Dardanelles. Not only
would Allied control of those waters act as a convincing encouragement to Turkey to enter the war on our side, but once the Dardanelles
were open to our shipping Russia could be supplied through her
Black Sea ports as well as by the long and difficult Arctic and Persian
Gulf routes. Mr Churchill considered these potential gains so great
that the acceptance of serious risks was justified in order to achieve
them.[1]

Plans for a full-scale assault on Rhodes and Scarpanto had been
made as early as May 1943, and on several subsequent occasions the
assembly of a force to undertake the capture of the former was
actually put in hand; but the impact of other events in the central
Mediterranean prevented it ever sailing. By the early days of August,
when an Italian collapse appeared imminent, the shape of the plan
was changed somewhat. Instead of launching a big combined operation against Rhodes we now intended to hold ready such forces as
were necessary to make a quick descent on the island, should an

---

[1] See Churchill, Vol. V, Chapter XII and Ehrman, *Grand Strategy*, Vol. V (H.M.S.O.,
1956), pp. 88–105, for a full account of the strategic considerations involved.

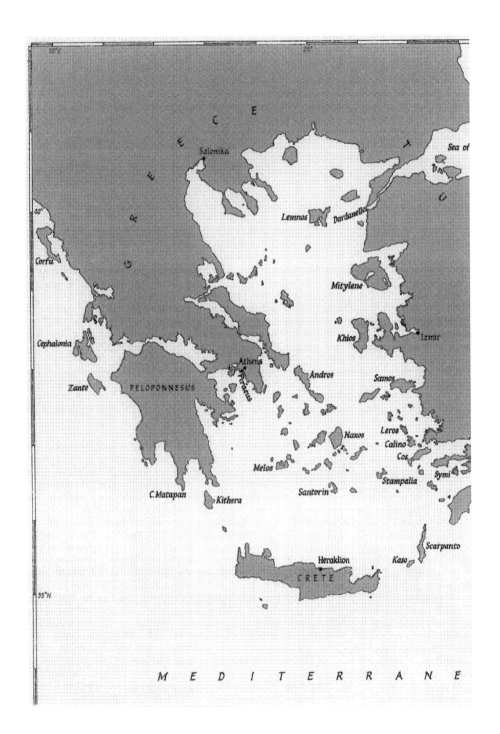

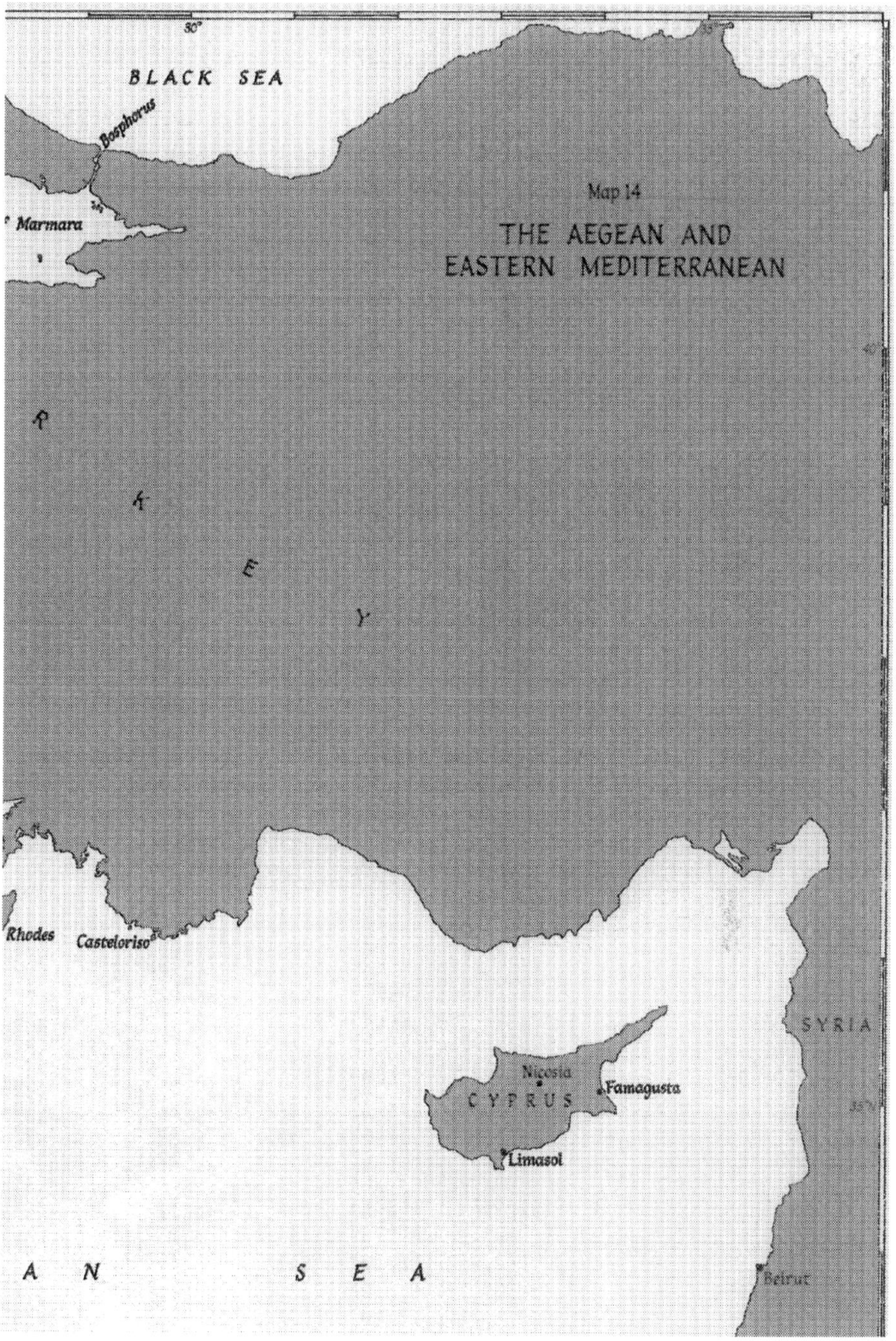
30°
35°
BLACK SEA
Bosphorus
Marmara
Map 14
THE AEGEAN AND
EASTERN MEDITERRANEAN
40°
R
K
E
Y
Rhodes
Casteloriso
SYRIA
Nicosia
Famagusta
CYPRUS
35°
Limasol
A N
S E A
Beirut

armistice with Italy produce an opportunity to win it at small cost. But even to carry out this more modest purpose the reinforcement of the Middle East commands from the central Mediterranean theatre was essential. In particular American Lightning long-range fighters, transport aircraft to carry paratroops, and certain types of landing craft were needed; but General Eisenhower could not spare the fighters[1], the transport aircraft or the landing craft from the main Allied campaign in Italy. The British Chiefs of Staff and the three Commanders-in-Chief on the spot were, however, still reluctant to abandon the whole enterprise, and so allow a possibly fleeting chance of achieving an important success to go by default[2]; but they had by no means yet reached the end of their difficulties. On the 26th of August the shipping which had been assembled was transferred to the South-East Asia theatre in accordance with an earlier decision of the Combined Chiefs of Staff. This, and the movement of the 8th Indian Division to the Italian theatre in mid-September[3], finally frustrated the possibility of launching a properly trained and organised expedition against Rhodes or any of the other islands. The only alternative to abandoning the whole enterprise which now remained to those who, headed by the Prime Minister, strongly desired action was to improvise from local resources. If today, with full knowledge of the heavy losses we finally suffered, it seems that abandonment would have been preferable, it should be remembered that failure to take any action in the Aegean would probably have been regarded by posterity as a serious reflection on the enterprise of the commands concerned.

Not long after the troops and shipping had been diverted to other purposes the expected opportunity did arise with the collapse of Italy. However, the German garrison in Rhodes, numbering 7,000 men, acted quickly and overpowered the far more numerous Italians. By the 11th of September, three days after the Italian armistice, Rhodes was firmly in German hands. It was now plain that, with the small resources left to the Middle East, there was no possibility of ejecting the enemy from the island. Instead it was decided to seize Leros, Cos and a number of smaller islands stretching up the Aegean archipelago from Casteloriso in the south to Samos in the north.[4] Mr Churchill, when shown these proposals, telegraphed to the

---

[1] In fact two groups of Lightnings, each of three squadrons, were lent to the Middle East Air Forces from 6th to 10th of October (see p. 196).

[2] The three Commanders-in-Chief in the Middle East theatre at this time were:
Admiral Sir John Cunningham until 14th October 1943, and thereafter Vice-Admiral Sir Algernon Willis (C.-in-C., Levant).
General Sir Henry Maitland-Wilson (C.-in-C., Middle East).
Air Chief Marshal Sir W. Sholto Douglas (Air Officer Commanding, Middle East).

[3] See p. 170.

[4] See Map 14. At least three different ways of spelling the names of the Aegean islands are available. In this narrative the spelling used in contemporary reports has been adhered to.

Commander-in-Chief, Middle East, 'Good. This is a time to play high. Improvise and dare.'[1]

Between the 10th and 17th of September the smaller islands mentioned above were all occupied; but it soon became apparent that, with Rhodes still in the enemy's possession, we could make little use of the new acquisitions, and might well find them expensive and difficult to hold. The Commanders-in-Chief therefore proposed to assault Rhodes at the end of October, and the British Chiefs of Staff approved the proposal. It will be told shortly how it came to pass that this decision was never implemented, for we must now retrace our steps to the early days of September to see how the forces allocated to the Aegean campaign had meanwhile fared. In the Levant command only eight destroyers, the submarines of the 1st Flotilla, and a number of small craft were at first available to support and supply the troops landed on Casteloriso, Cos, Leros and Samos. With no advanced base available for refuelling the ships it was inevitable that our maritime control should be very imperfect. To conserve fuel and conceal themselves from enemy aircraft, the ships often had to lie up by day in remote anchorages in the islands, or off the Turkish mainland. Much of the local traffic in among the island-studded waters of the Aegean had always been carried in Greek fishing schooners (called caïques); and a number of these vessels were requisitioned by the Levant Command and commissioned as the Levant Schooner Flotilla under Lieutenant-Commander A. C. C. Seligman, R.N.R. In September and October they made a large number of patrols among the islands, landing soldiers of the Long Range Desert Group, collecting intelligence, and carrying supplies to isolated garrisons. On the 19th of September Sir John Cunningham told the First Sea Lord that 'our policy is to put some 4,000 men into Leros, Cos and Samos and to stiffen the Italians in the smaller islands with British detachments'. He fully realised the difficulties of the supply problem, but he thought it could be done by destroyers and by aircraft—if the caïques failed to do all that he hoped. But, he added regretfully, 'if they had left us "Accolade" [i.e. the forces earmarked for the capture of Rhodes] for just a few days longer we could not have failed to take Rhodes, and the situation would then have been simple.' Unfortunately that was not to be. Sir John Cunningham's opinion regarding the ease with which that key island could have been captured is confirmed by the War Diary of the German Naval Group Command, South, in which an entry dated the 12th of September records that 'if the enemy had made full use of the moment of weakness [following on the Italian armistice] he could easily have taken Rhodes'.

---

[1] See Churchill, Vol. V, p. 182.

As there were Italian troops in many of the islands, and German patrols or landing parties were liable to arrive at any moment, it was to be expected that the schooners' cruises should produce some unusual situations. To quote only one, when His Majesty's Levant Schooner No. 8 (an ex-Greek caïque) was investigating conditions on Naxos in October her party suddenly met a car containing two German and one Italian officer. 'It is hoped' said the schooner Captain's report 'that the British officer present [presumably Seligman himself], who was dressed strictly in accordance with uniform regulations, will not be blamed for finding it necessary to remove his cap, for the purpose of scratching the back of his head, at this moment.' The report went on to describe the terrain of Naxos as 'the roughest yet encountered. . . . A Greek policeman in fear of his life will cover the ground at about $2\frac{1}{2}$ miles per hour; a mule, even when its rider sees two field-grey figures bearing down on him, will only make $1\frac{1}{2}$ miles per hour; while a sailor not aboard a mule is unable to progress at all.' But for all the daring shown by the crews of these small craft, such makeshifts could never be regarded as substitutes for well-organised maritime forces, provided with adequate bases and supported by the other services.

The problems facing the Air Force were at least as serious as the Navy's; for not only had much of the resources of the Middle East been transferred to the central Mediterranean, but it proved quite impossible to establish satisfactory advanced air bases on either Leros or Cos, both of which lay within easy range of the enemy's airfields on the Greek mainland, in Crete and in Rhodes. The Navy and Army thus found themselves once again committed to combined operations in a theatre where command of the air lay in the enemy's hands. The main burden of the defence of shipping in the Aegean against air attacks fell on No. 201 Naval Co-operation Group, but responsibility for protection of the islands lay with two groups of the Air Defences, Eastern Mediterranean Command. Two squadrons of Beaufighters and two of Hurricanes, all working from Cyprus, were allocated to this latter task; but they also helped to provide long and short-range cover for our ships.

The occupation of Cos was carried out mainly by air transport, while destroyers carried troops to Leros, from which some were ferried north to Samos in small craft. At first all went reasonably well, and the destroyers *Faulknor*, *Eclipse* and *Queen Olga* (Greek) carried out successful sweeps against enemy merchant ships, three of which they sank. But it was not long before the Germans reacted powerfully from the air, and it was then that serious troubles began. We now know that, at a conference held on the 24th of September, Field Marshal von Weichs, the C.-in-C. of the German Army in the Balkans, and Dönitz both recommended the immediate evacuation

Command of the Sea (*1*)

Troops embarking in Landing Ships Infantry (taken from the *Duchess of Bedford*).

Command of the Sea (2)

The *Queen Mary* crossing the Atlantic with about 15,000 Allied troops on board, August 1943.

of Crete and of the Aegean islands; but Hitler refused to entertain the idea 'on account of the political repercussions which would necessarily follow', and insisted that they should all be held. The policy of the local German commanders thus became to suppress the revolts which had broken out in Corfu and Cephalonia, from which a threat to their hold in the Adriatic might develop, and then to turn their attention to the Aegean. By the last week of September they had successfully accomplished the first part of that plan, and they then turned their full attention to the Aegean.

Meanwhile German air strength in Greece and Crete was being reinforced. At the beginning of September the Luftwaffe had only possessed 284 aircraft in that theatre, and there were no long-range bombers; but within a week of our occupation of the Aegean islands reinforcements started to arrive. By the 1st of October the enemy's strength had risen to 362 aircraft and included a substantial number of long-range bombers. Even more important than the advantage in numbers was the proximity of the enemy's airfields to the decisive points. Whereas Cyprus was 350 miles from Cos—far outside the range at which regular fighter cover could be provided—the enemy possessed two good airfields on Rhodes, some seventy miles from the island, and two more in Crete, which was only 150 miles away. The first serious setback occurred on the 26th of September, when the destroyers *Intrepid* and *Queen Olga* were sunk by air attacks while in Leros harbour. They had been ordered into the port on the understanding—which was actually erroneous—that the anti-aircraft defences were adequate for their protection.

Meanwhile the difficulties facing the Middle East commanders were being discussed in London. On the 29th of September Mr Churchill, referring to their latest report on the enemy's reinforced air strength in Greece, told the Chiefs of Staff that 'this looks serious . . . we should certainly make a strong effort to supply the necessary forces. There is only one German Air Force and the more rapidly it is diminished by fighting the better.' Next day the Chiefs of Staff considered the whole matter of future operations in the eastern Mediterranean, and the Chief of the Air Staff recorded his view that 'it was quite wrong to consider withdrawing from Cos and Leros because the enemy air threat to those islands had increased'. 'We had in the Mediterranean' Sir Charles Portal continued 'more aircraft than there were in the whole German Air Force, and our policy should be to fight the enemy wherever the opportunity offered.' There now followed a long series of messages from the Prime Minister to General Eisenhower and Air Chief Marshal Tedder, urging that every possible support should be given to the Aegean operations. In spite of the Supreme Commander's reluctance to accept a commitment which would divert some of his strength from the main task in Italy, which he had forcibly expressed in the previous August, he now promised Mr Churchill to 'examine resources carefully [in order] to give the Middle East the necessary support', and felt sure he could meet their minimum requirements. On the 4th of October Air Marshal Tedder reported that 'we are putting forth the maximum effort against the enemy in Greece, and I will do everything possible to help'. But in spite of these hopeful signs on the next day General Eisenhower signalled to the American and British Chiefs of Staff stating his serious concern regarding German strength in Italy, and his need to offset his inferiority on the ground 'by sustained and continuous attacks on enemy communications'. He regarded 'any material diversion to the Aegean as highly prejudicial to the prospects of success in Italy'. Plainly the hopes of the Middle East commanders for substantial aid were no better than before.

By the beginning of October German bombing had made one of the two airfields on Cos unserviceable, and the situation of the 1,300 British troops, encumbered as they were by some 4,000 Italians of doubtful morale, was plainly precarious. Endeavours were being made to prepare additional landing strips, but, as one tractor and a few oxen were the only motive power available, work was only proceeding very slowly. The prospect of being able to bring in the urgently needed fighter reinforcements was thus remote.

The number of *Hunt*-class destroyers in the Levant command had now risen to seventeen, but because of their short endurance they were by no means the ideal ships for the task in hand. On the last day of September we learnt that enemy shipping and landing craft were assembling at Piraeus and in Cretan harbours, and were embarking troops and equipment. In anticipation of a movement towards Rhodes or Leros three destroyers were sent from Alexandria to patrol to the east of Crete. On the evening of the 2nd of October a convoy was sighted by aircraft further north, off Naxos; but by that time the destroyers had been forced to return to refuel. Two submarines were ordered to intercept the convoy off Cos, which we now realised to be its most probable destination; but they did not arrive in time. On the island itself the reports of the enemy's movement were received from the naval authorities, but the local headquarters assumed that the convoy was bound for Rhodes. At 5 a.m. about 2,000 German troops started to disembark on Cos, covered by heavy air bombardments; and successful parachute landings quickly followed. The garrison was now heavily outnumbered, and to hold the harbour and the two airfields was beyond its strength. After the withdrawal of the surface ships the only counter-action immediately possible was long-range air strikes by Beaufighters from Cyprus. Many attacks were made on enemy shipping during the day; but they did not impede his landings, and substantial losses were suffered by the Beaufighters. By the evening of the 4th resistance on Cos had ceased.

The Germans were elated by their success in carrying their invasion force across the Aegean without loss, and were surprised over their quick progress after they had landed on the island. Nine hundred British and 3,000 Italians were captured; and, true to the Nazi habit of wreaking cruel vengeance, the victors at once shot ninety Italian officers. The Germans next began energetically to prepare to invade Leros; and as they had deprived us of the only airfields from which, poor though they were, single-engined fighters might have operated, the prospects of repeating their success were plainly favourable.

Reinforcements, consisting of four ships of the 12th Cruiser Squadron under Commodore W. G. Agnew in the *Aurora*, the A.A. cruiser *Carlisle* and eight more large destroyers, had meanwhile been ordered to the Aegean from the central Mediterranean; but they arrived too late to influence the struggle for Cos. It is now plain that the failure to intercept the invasion convoy and the enemy's overwhelming air superiority were the main factors in bringing about this set-back. Had the naval reinforcements been sent earlier, and had adequate fighter cover been available for them, it would have been impossible for the enemy to mount and transport this expedition.

The Prime Minister was reproachful over the failure to intercept the enemy convoy, and criticised the lack of heavy weapons on Cos. 'It is quite right to run risks' he told General Wilson 'but foresight and energy are all the more required.' The reply given was to the effect that the faulty deduction regarding the convoy's destination, combined with the *Hunt*-class destroyers' low endurance, had been the main causes of the failure to intercept the convoy; and that as the soldiers had been carried to the island in small craft or by air they could only carry their personal weapons. Mr Churchill himself had earlier on urged that 'caïques and ships' boats can be used between ship and shore' when proper landing craft were lacking.[1] But there was, as the Commander-in-Chief, Levant, later admitted in his report, another circumstance which had affected the naval strength available at a critical time. The battleships *Howe* and *King George V* arrived at Alexandria on the 16th of September, having escorted some of the larger Italian warships there from Malta. The six fleet destroyers which had accompanied them were at once sent to strengthen the forces operating in the Aegean; but when, on the 1st of October, the two British battleships returned to the west, four of the destroyers sailed with them as escorts. In view of the reports

---

[1] Churchill, Vol. V, p. 181.

of enemy shipping movements in the Aegean received on the 2nd of October it certainly now seems that the movement might profitably have been cancelled, and the ships recalled; but the Admiralty had stressed the urgent need for the battleships to return home as soon as possible.

The Middle East command now expected 'a seaborne attack on Leros at an early date', and that it would be 'preceded by heavy air attacks with a view to softening opposition'. Both anticipations were quickly proved correct; but before recounting the fate of Leros we must return to the high-level discussions, which we left at the moment when the British Chiefs of Staff had supported the Middle East Commanders' intention to assault Rhodes at the end of October. The really critical problem was the provision of the air forces needed not only for offensive action in the Aegean but to make possible the retention of the islands we still possessed. These could only come from Air Marshal Tedder's Mediterranean Air Command; but on the 6th of October General Eisenhower refused to accept any firm commitment to help the Middle East forces at the expense of his own campaign in Italy. None the less two groups (six squadrons) of U.S. Air Force Lightning long-range fighters were temporarily lent to the Middle East command at this time. On the 6th of October they started to work from Gambut airfield near Benghazi in defence of our Aegean shipping; but the distance to the waters where they were needed was so near the limit of their endurance that they could only stay on patrol for about twenty minutes. In any case the loan was of very short duration; for on the 10th they were ordered to return to the air bases in Tunisia because they were needed to escort the strategic bombers on their long-distance raids.

On the day before the Lightnings were recalled the Supreme Commander called a conference in Tunis. It was attended by all the service commanders concerned with operations in the theatre, including the Commander-in-Chief, Mediterranean (Admiral Sir Andrew Cunningham, who was about to take up the appointment of First Sea Lord), the Commander-in-Chief, Levant, Sir John Cunningham, who was about to relieve Sir Andrew Cunningham, and Vice-Admiral Sir Algernon Willis, who was to take over the Levant Command.[1] In spite of the disagreement of the Middle East commanders, the decision was taken that the slenderness of the resources available ruled out the Rhodes operation at the present time. On reading this Mr Churchill remarked that 'the fate of Leros is sealed' and told President Roosevelt that he intended to give General Wilson authority to evacuate the garrison.[2] General Eisenhower's conference

---

[1] These changes actually took place on 17th October. See p. 184.
[2] Churchill, Vol. V, p. 194.

decided, however, that we should try to hold the islands of Leros, Samos and Casteloriso and Sir John Cunningham and his successor both left the conference with the impression that the aircraft needed to support the operations in the Dodecanese would be forthcoming. But under the command organisation of those days, although the Commanders-in-Chief, Middle East, were responsible for the conduct of the Aegean operations, the disposition of forces in the whole Mediterranean theatre rested with the Supreme Commander. The compromise decision taken by General Eisenhower's conference was confirmed at a meeting held under the chairmanship of the Foreign Secretary at Cairo on the 12th. It meant that reinforcements had to be carried to Leros as soon as possible. As more warships had been promised by Sir Andrew Cunningham hopes were entertained that the movements could be carried out in time.

Success or failure in holding the remaining islands depended, however, more on air power than on any other single factor; and the decision to try to hold them brought out the disagreements which had in fact existed ever since Mr Churchill had begun to press for action in the Aegean. On the one hand stood General Eisenhower, with the authority of the President behind him, and supported by Air Chief Marshal Tedder; while on the other hand stood the Middle East triumvirate, supported by the British Chiefs of Staff and fully cognisant of the Prime Minister's views and purpose. The allocation of air forces to the Aegean had now become the critical issue. Air Marshal Tedder had protested strongly over operations being launched from the Middle East without consultation with himself and General Eisenhower; but the Chief of the Air Staff held that the air forces in the Mediterranean were ample to enable the Allies to afford the fighter aircraft and bomber support needed to maintain our position in the Aegean. Heavy bombers were, in fact, diverted to attack enemy airfields in Greece at this time. A wider diversion from the powerful air forces available in the central theatre was, however, rejected. In a letter to the Chief of the Air Staff Air Marshal Tedder argued that 'an attempt was being made to maintain garrisons and operate surface ships outside the effective range of the Allied fighter forces, and under the very noses of enemy shore-based aircraft'— which was the indisputable truth; but he also protested that the onus of failure was being placed by the other services on the Air Force, which he stigmatised as claiming 'a false alibi'. Air Marshal Douglas, however, refuted this latter assertion on behalf of his Middle East colleagues.

The enemy had meanwhile been building up his forces on Cos with the object of attacking Leros, on which the British garrison numbered only 1,100 men. On the night of the 6th–7th of October the cruisers *Sirius* and *Penelope* and two destroyers were operating in the Aegean, and early on the 7th they intercepted an enemy convoy, consisting of an ammunition ship and six ferry barges, off Stampalia. A battalion of troops intended to reinforce Cos was embarked in the convoy, but only one barge survived the British ships' attack. Over 400 men and the whole of the German battalion's equipment were lost. After achieving this success the squadron withdrew by the Scarpanto Strait[1], where it was heavily attacked from the air. At first U.S. Air Force Lightnings gave effective cover; but, when they had to return, the relief air escort failed to find the ships. The *Penelope* received a hit in a heavy attack by eighteen Ju.87s, and damage from several near-misses as well; but luckily the bomb that hit her failed to explode, and she got back to Alexandria safely.

Two days later the A.A. cruiser *Carlisle* and four destroyers (one Greek) were making a similar sweep. At first a single Beaufighter escorted them, but after she had left there was an interval with no air cover at all. Just after noon, again in the Scarpanto Strait, a mass attack by Ju.87s took place. The *Carlisle* was so badly damaged that she stopped, and the destroyer *Panther* was sunk—in spite of the fact that seven Lightnings had by that time arrived to protect the force. They did, however, destroy eight enemies during the ensuing chase back to Rhodes; and in addition to these defensive activities they made offensive sweeps over Crete and Leros, and attacked the enemy-held airfield on Cos. The recall of the Lightnings to the central Mediterranean on the 10th of October has already been mentioned, and the easement which they brought to the naval forces working in the Aegean, now left as naked as ever, had been very brief.

Meanwhile, with the much-discussed and long-deferred attack on Rhodes now finally abandoned, the staff in Cairo was planning to evacuate the islands which we still held; but the decision to try to hold Leros and Samos was finally adhered to. Mr Churchill even entertained hopes of recapturing Cos; but after the Foreign Secretary's conference on the 12th of October it was made plain to him that this was out of the question. Leros would, so the conference reported, now have to be supplied by submarines, aircraft and caïques.

By the middle of October the *Penelope* of Commodore Agnew's force and the A.A. cruiser *Carlisle* had been damaged; but the arrival from Malta of the *Phoebe* had restored his strength to four ships. On the 17th, however, the *Sirius* was hit by a bomb. There were eight fleet destroyers available for the Aegean, but of the seventeen ships of the *Hunt*-class in the Levant command only eight, for one reason or another, were available. A number of submarines and coastal

---

[1] See Map 14.

craft, and the heterogeneous collection of vessels of the Levant Schooner Flotilla, which had done good work carrying men and supplies between the various islands, or to and from the Turkish mainland, completed the naval strength. The larger surface ships continued to make forays into the Aegean from Alexandria, covered by such air strength as could be provided. On the 15th of October Vice-Admiral Willis, who had just succeeded Sir John Cunningham in the Levant Command, reported that naval patrols could not be continued by day without suffering prohibitive losses. Decision now depended, he said, on air power; and 'unless the enemy could be trounced in that element the prospects were grim'. A few days later Air Marshal Douglas also reported on the situation. He considered that the enemy had enough forces in the vicinity of Leros to mount an attack in the near future. 'Our task in attempting to provide cover for naval forces' he continued 'is not an easy one'; for his strength was inferior to the enemy's, and he was hampered by having no air bases near at hand. He was doing all that he could with his limited resources, but could not provide the Navy with strong enough air cover to enable its ships to operate near Rhodes in daylight.

In spite of the justifiably pessimistic view taken by the Naval and Air commanders the decision to hold on was not modified, and stores and reinforcements were carried to Leros by destroyers and submarines. The intention was to build up our strength in this manner sufficiently to hold the island throughout the winter, and then to maintain the garrison by caïques working from Samos. In October the destroyers *Jervis, Penn, Pathfinder* and *Petard* each made two successful trips to Leros, and six other British or Greek destroyers completed one each; but heavy losses were incurred in the process. On the 22nd the Greek destroyer *Adrias* struck a mine in a field recently laid by the enemy off Calino[1] with the express purpose of catching our patrolling warships. She was badly damaged, and when the *Hurworth* went to her assistance she too was mined, and sank with heavy loss of life. The *Adrias* managed to beach herself on the Turkish coast, and finally reached Alexandria under her own steam, but minus her bow, on the 6th of December—long after the rest of our forces had withdrawn from the Aegean. Two days after the *Hurworth* and *Adrias* were mined the *Eclipse*, with 200 soldiers on board, including a high military mission on its way to review the whole matter of the defence of Leros and to urge on the garrison the need to take the most energetic measures to prepare against invasion, fell victim to another mine in the same waters. Survivors, including the senior Army members of the mission, were picked up by the *Petard*; but Captain P. Todd, the Commodore of the Levant

---

[1] See Map 14. Also written Kalino, Kalymnos, Kalymno, etc.

destroyer flotillas, whose war service had been highly distinguished, was not among them. On the 24th a supply ship was bombed and sunk in the harbour at Samos, and four days later an L.C.T. carrying guns and troops was also sunk; nor were these the end of our losses. It is not surprising that on the 27th of October Admiral Willis sent the First Sea Lord what he described as 'a rather gloomy letter about the Aegean situation'. After analysing the difficulties of the troops on Leros, and the even greater difficulty of running in supplies, let alone the reinforcements they so badly needed, the Commander-in-Chief told how, with the capture by the enemy of the smaller islands, 'the ring is closing in on Leros'. 'I fully appreciate the importance of hanging on to this island if we can' he continued ' . . . but the enemy has practically everything in his favour—distance, adjacent islands, good air reconnaissance and complete air superiority'. All of which was perfectly correct, both in diagnosis and in prognosis. Furthermore, continued Admiral Willis, the destroyers which, if a crisis arose, he would have to use regardless of the certainty of heavy bombing attacks and the paucity of air cover were beginning to feel the strain.

On the 30th of October the *Aurora* and three destroyers from Alexandria entered the Aegean to make another offensive sweep against enemy shipping. Air attacks started very soon and, although protecting Beaufighters did their best, the cruiser was hit and damaged, with heavy casualties. She managed to reach Alexandria safely, escorted by one destroyer, while the other two carried on into the Aegean. Next the *Belvoir* was hit, but luckily the bomb did not explode. The experience of this squadron had not been happy; for no successes had been gained to compensate for the losses suffered; and the naval forces available in the Levant were now so reduced that it was hardly possible for the survivors to carry on with the reinforcement of Leros, let alone continue the offensive sweeps and patrols. The Chiefs of Staff now represented that the use of cruisers and destroyers was too expensive, and Sir John Cunningham was reluctant to release more from the central Mediterranean. The operations in the Gulf of Salerno were still demanding considerable strength, the Adriatic had become a profitable field for the employment of light forces, and a new combined operation was in view in Italy.

By the beginning of November it was apparent that, quite apart from the serious troubles encountered in the Aegean, the system of command was unsuitable to the task in hand. We had in fact embarked on a combined operation without an integrated command organisation, such as had been found essential in the far bigger, but basically similar, invasions of North Africa, Sicily and Italy. The Naval C.-in-C's Headquarters were in Alexandria, and No. 201

Naval Co-operation Group's staff worked in the same building; but there integration ended. The Corps Commander appointed by the Army was in Cairo, as was Air Vice-Marshal R. E. Saul, who commanded the Air Defences, Eastern Mediterranean; but the latter had his operational headquarters in Cyprus.

On the 1st of November Major-General H. R. Hall was appointed General Officer Commanding, Aegean, and four days later he arrived in Leros, saw to the organisation of the defences, and then set up his headquarters for the control of operations in Samos. Brigadier R. A. G. Tilney, who had been appointed Fortress Commander of Leros, arrived there with General Hall, and at once prepared the garrison to meet the expected attack; for by that time it was clear that the enemy was about to mount a new expedition from Piraeus, and his heavy air attacks on Samos indicated that island or Leros to be his next object. Between the 5th and 10th of November enemy landing craft moved gradually to the east from Greece. Many air strikes were made against them; but the Beaufighters were by no means ideally suited for such work. They did little damage, and themselves suffered heavy losses. Nor were the destroyers sent to intercept the convoy any more successful. In daylight the enemy vessels lay up in various harbours under strong air cover, and when they moved by night they were very hard to find. By the 10th of November the Germans had successfully assembled a substantial fleet of some two dozen small craft at Cos and Calino. Two naval squadrons, each of three destroyers, bombarded the harbours of those islands on the night of the 10th–11th; but the effects were not significant and the enemy was not deterred from his intention. As usual daylight brought heavy air attacks while the destroyers were withdrawing, and the *Rockwood* was hit by a glider bomb.[1] One of the two destroyer forces had anchored off the Turkish coast on the 11th and its three ships remained there all the next day, in spite of having received air reports of enemy small craft steering towards Leros very early that morning. These were actually carrying the German invasion forces, which were to land on the north side of Leros. Even though the senior officer of the destroyers was troubled by shortage of fuel, and knew that more destroyers could not arrive until the next night, it now seems that he should have taken his ships on patrol earlier. Not until after dark on the 12th did he sweep the waters around Leros; but by that time the enemy had landed. Nor did the naval Commander-in-Chief's operation room, where the air reports had also been received, deduce that the invasion forces were approaching the threatened island, and order the destroyers to sea. It thus came to pass that, although we had watched

---

[1] See p. 30 regarding these weapons, called Hs.293. Early in November it was known that Do.217 aircraft, which the enemy used to control them, had arrived in Greece.

this convoy's passage all the way across the Aegean from Piraeus to Cos, we failed to intercept it on its final stage. The enemy had boldly discounted any effective threat to the convoy by day, and by night he had concealed his vessels very skilfully; yet it seems undeniable that it should not have reached its destination virtually unscathed. Early on the 12th the Germans successfully landed about 500 men in a bay on the north side of Leros, and made some progress inland. In the afternoon 800 enemy paratroops were dropped on the high and rocky neck of land in the centre of the island, where we had believed it impossible to carry out such an operation. Though they suffered some losses they cut the garrison in two, and so greatly added to the difficulties of the defence.

In London these developments caused grave anxiety, and on the 12th the Chief of the Air Staff urged on Tedder that, now the battle for Leros was being fought, the Mediterranean Air Command should do all it could to help. Leros was, in Sir Charles Portal's view, 'more important at the moment than strategic objectives in southern France or north Italy'. But by that time it was, in fact, too late to switch our forces—even had the Supreme Commander been prepared to accept a considerable diversion of his air strength.

On the night after the first German landings on Leros (12th–13th of November) destroyers and M.T.Bs swept the adjacent waters for enemy reinforcements; but they found none. Three other destroyers were now on the way to the Aegean, but very early on the 13th one of them, the *Dulverton*, was hit by a glider bomb and sunk. The other two lay up in Turkish waters before sweeping around Leros and bombarding shore targets after dark. On the 13th the enemy managed to reinforce his assaulting troops by sea and air, and he continued to strike heavily at the defending troops with his bombers. On our part endeavours were made to reinforce the garrison on Leros from Samos, but very bad weather frustrated the first attempt. On the night of the 13th–14th, however, three more destroyers arrived in the Aegean, and during the next two nights the *Echo* and smaller vessels managed to carry 500 troops—all that were available—from Samos. They also caught and sank three enemy landing craft which were approaching Leros full of troops; but the experience of these ships had followed the earlier pattern. By night they could find few targets, and by day they were constantly bombed. The garrison of Leros too was repeatedly under the lash of the enemy's air power. Signal delays and slow reaction by one of our destroyers prevented enemy reinforcements being intercepted on the night of the 15th–16th, and by daylight on the 16th the situation on Leros had become critical. In the evening it was known in Cairo that the island had fallen. Admiral Willis reported that 'overwhelming air superiority was the deciding factor in a grim and close struggle'; which was unquestionably true. But other factors, such as the faulty command organisation, had also contributed to the failure. The enemy's records show, however, that the margin of his success was exceedingly narrow; for they described the condition of their forces on Leros on the 15th as 'critical'. It is plain that had we been able to send the garrison quite modest reinforcements the scales might well have been tilted in our favour.

The last hours on Leros were vividly described by Lieutenant-Commander L. F. Ramseyer, R.N.V.R., who had originally been sent to organise the sea transport needed for all the various clandestine operations in the Aegean, but soon found himself collecting scattered groups of men and stimulating them to further resistance. The surrender of the garrison took him by surprise, and he himself finally escaped to a neighbouring island where, aided by a Greek with the singularly unhellenic name of John Paradise, he arranged the rescue of isolated groups of men from Leros. He then resumed his raiding activities, and quickly proved a thorn in the flesh of the scattered German garrisons.

Immediately after the fall of Leros orders were given to evacuate the British and Greek troops remaining on Samos, and this was successfully carried out during the night of the 19th–20th of November. The greater part of the garrison of Casteloriso was withdrawn on the 28th, and in neither case did the enemy interfere.

So ended a series of fruitless operations the cost of which was not light. The British and Greek navies had four cruisers damaged (one, the *Carlisle*, beyond repair), six destroyers sunk and four others damaged. Two submarines and ten coastal craft and minesweepers were also lost; and many warship crews had been subjected to ordeals which can reasonably be compared with those undergone off Norway and Crete several years earlier. At the end of October Admiral Willis had told the First Sea Lord that ships' companies were beginning to ask why we had to go on trying to hold an island which was costing such heavy losses; and why, at that stage of the war, they could not have better support from the air. Today it seems that the questioning doubts which had reached the Commander-in-Chief's ears were not unreasonable. Nor was the Navy alone in suffering heavy losses. The Army suffered 4,800 casualties, the equivalent of an expanded Infantry Brigade Group—but many of them were taken prisoner; and the Royal Air Force lost 115 aircraft in these Aegean endeavours. Even today it is difficult to assess the price exacted from the enemy for his success. In October and November twelve of his merchant ships totalling nearly 21,000 tons were sunk in those waters, and his records also show the loss of over twenty ferry barges, landing craft and miscellaneous vessels. Although the actual assault on Leros only cost him 520 casualties it is likely that his losses in the whole

Aegean campaign were over 4,000 men.[1] The final balance sheet of men, ships and aircraft lost may therefore not have been very greatly in the enemy's favour; but it none the less remains true that he had frustrated our strategic purpose.

It may, perhaps, be justifiable to attempt to summarise the lessons of this unhappy failure. The consequences of the dependence of the Middle East on a different command to supply many of the forces needed has already been commented on, as has the lack of an integrated command system to conduct the actual operations. There are, however, two other points which we should remember. The first is that, in spite of the heavy price exacted in the Aegean, the attempt to seize the islands did cause the enemy to divert considerable air strength and an appreciable number of troops, who might otherwise have been added to his forces in Italy. It is reasonable therefore to suppose that the Aegean operations caused some weakening of the enemy's effort in the main theatre. The prospect that this would be the case was repeatedly stressed by Mr Churchill when he urged on the Commanders-in-Chief the importance of the benefits to be gained. The second point is that the strategic advantages might, as Mr Churchill clearly realised, have been substantial; and bearing in mind the small strength initially needed we may regret that his pressure to provide adequate forces did not prevail. At the same time we should take account of the fact that every peripheral operation inevitably grows in size as it progresses, with ever-increasing demands on resources; and the dislike of the American Chiefs of Staff, and of General Eisenhower and his subordinate commanders, for such enterprises, what time the major campaign which they had on their hands still had to be decided, is readily to be understood. But, even if we accept the possibility of achieving substantial gains from the plans as first conceived, the decision to go ahead after we knew that the main part of the original plan—namely the capture of Rhodes— could not be attempted must surely remain open to criticism. In any theatre of combined operations there is always one position, generally an island, which, because of its geographical position and because it possesses harbours and airfields, is the key to control over a wide area. In the central Mediterranean Malta was such a key: in the Solomon Islands it was Guadalcanal; and in the Aegean it was, as everyone realised, Rhodes. Yet we went ahead with operations well knowing that the key was to be left in the enemy's hands; and we persisted in them long after it was plain that the enemy intended to exploit to the utmost his continued possession of the key. No commander likes

---

[1] For example when our aircraft sank the *Sinfra* on 18th October, nearly 2,000 German and Italian soldiers are known to have been lost.

to withdraw from an undertaking he has launched; and when its most powerful advocate is his own Prime Minister the commander's reluctance will certainly be increased. In the Aegean the moment to withdraw was when it had become clear that we could not exercise adequate maritime control over the disputed waters—and that unpleasant fact was abundantly plain after the fall of Cos on the 3rd of October, if not earlier. In many campaigns, from Norway in 1940 to Malaya in 1942, we had learnt that an attempt to maintain garrisons in theatres where the enemy held command of the air was bound to end in a costly failure. Yet similar conditions were reproduced in the Aegean in 1943.

We must now return from the Aegean to the central Mediterranean, and review the campaign which had meanwhile started in the Adriatic. To understand the significance of the maritime operations in those waters it is necessary to retrace our steps to the previous September, when the collapse of Italy and the occupation by the Allies of all the principal ports in the south of that country made the supply of the German armies in Italy, Yugo-Slavia and the Balkans much more difficult.

To hold on in Italy, as Hitler had insisted, a proportion of the German army's supplies had to be carried by sea down the east coast to be disembarked at such ports as could be developed for the purpose; but in Yugo-Slavia the enemy's situation was far more precarious, for land communications were so bad, and the resistance groups were so active in the interior, that the troops needed to hold down that country and Greece had to be supplied mainly by sea. As the Germans finally had no less than eighteen divisions in the Balkan countries the problem which now faced them was formidable. Moreover they initially had hardly any naval forces in the Adriatic, and such merchant shipping as remained to them was by no means all suitable for the task in hand. Thus the larger ships, which they assembled in Venice, were better suited to work in the Aegean than in the Adriatic; but, when in mid-October six cargo vessels and three tankers tried to break out by the Straits of Otranto in order to reach Greek ports, they were very severely handled by Allied surface ships, aircraft and submarines.[1] Only two reached Piraeus safely. For the Adriatic the Germans needed small ships, motor-driven barges and landing craft; and to provide them they acted with characteristic energy, transporting vessels in sections from Germany to ports on the Adriatic coast, where they were assembled. The collection of a considerable fleet of small craft in this manner was, indeed, a remarkable

---

[1] Originally nine cargo vessels were detailed, but two did not sail, and one was destroyed by Yugo-Slav Partisans.

feat of improvisation by the Germans. By the end of September they had seized all the most important Dalmatian ports except Split, which was in Partisan hands, and between the middle of October and the end of November they further strengthened their position by clearing the irregulars from the northern offshore islands. Th Germans thus gained a reasonably firm hold over the whole Dalmatian coast from Fiume to Split.[1] Next they embarked on a series of operations to clear the larger islands in the central Adriatic, and on the 24th of December they recaptured Korčula. Thus by the end of the year, although still faced by serious difficulties and shortages, the enemy had gained a reasonable measure of control over the inshore shipping routes on which supply of his Balkan armies greatly depended.

But the Allies had meanwhile not been idle. Their policy was to support the Yugo-Slav Partisans with weapons, equipment and supplies, which at this stage were mainly sent by sea, and to hinder the enemy's purpose by making offensive sweeps with destroyers and coastal craft. The air forces assisted by bombing his ports and bases, and attacking any ships they might encounter. In September the Headquarters Ship *Vienna* came to Brindisi to act as a floating base for our coastal craft, and two flotillas of M.T.Bs (about fifteen boats) joined her there. In the following month the base ship and her flotillas moved north to Bari. Two flotillas of destroyers, consisting on an average of seven 'fleets' and four or five of the *Hunt* class, were allocated to support the light forces working in the Adriatic.

The most important island still in Partisan hands was Vis (Lissa), about half-way down the Dalmatian coast[2], and in mid-October Commander A. E. P. Welman, who commanded the coastal forces in those waters, went there to investigate the possibility of using it. The result was that advanced bases were set up on Vis and at Termoli in Italy, and the light craft were thus able to maintain themselves much nearer to the scene of operations. There now began a long and highly original campaign of hide-and-seek operations, with the coastal craft dodging in and out of the narrow channels seeking enemy vessels, engaging shore positions, landing Commandos and Partisans to carry out raids, making cutting-out expeditions into enemy harbours, and generally causing the Germans as much discomfort as possible.[3] The reports rendered by such officers as Lieutenant-Commander M. Minshall, R.N.V.R., who held the unusual appointment of naval liaison officer to the Partisans, and of

---

[1] See Map 12.

[2] See Map 12.

[3] A full account of the work of the British Coastal Forces in the Adriatic is to be found in *Flag 4* by Dudley Pope (Kimber, 1954).

Lieutenant-Commander M. C. Giles, who became Naval-Officer-in-Charge of Vis early in 1944, provide the historian with more entertainment than he derives from the vast majority of wartime annals. The records of the whole campaign make it plain that the individualism and courage of the young R.N.V.R. officers, leavened by a small number of more senior regulars, here found abundant opportunities for a type of warfare to which they were singularly well suited, and which they obviously enjoyed. Allied purposes were not, however, made easier of accomplishment by the discord which prevailed between the various Yugo-Slav political factions.[1]

During the last months of the year the British destroyers and coastal craft made repeated sweeps far up into the Adriatic, and Allied tactical bombers carried out many raids on the enemy's ports. The most important success scored by the M.T.Bs was when two of them totally disabled the small cruiser *Niobe* (ex Yugo-Slav *Dalmacija*) after she had run ashore during a German assault on one of the islands on the 22nd of December. In the same month heavy damage was done by air raids on Sibenik and Zara (Zadar), and in the latter port a large ship (8,446 tons), which had previously been damaged by a mine, was destroyed. The favourable effect of all these activities is shown by the fact that less than half of the cargoes which the Germans despatched from the north was safely discharged at this time. At the end of the year the German naval authorities were becoming increasingly pessimistic about the prospects of meeting the army's needs. Although they held the Italian coast as far down as Pescara, and were also in possession, if somewhat precariously, of the Dalmatian coast and of most of the islands, they were finding their air and naval forces increasingly inadequate to meet the many duties falling to them. On the other hand Allied strength was steadily rising, air raids were becoming heavier and more frequent, the coastal craft more numerous and more active, and the Commandos and Partisans bolder. It was becoming plain that the maintenance of the German armies in the Balkans was likely sooner or later to become impossible; and the strategic possibilities which a collapse in that theatre would open up were clearly appreciated in British circles, and especially by Mr Churchill.

The last two months of 1943 were, for the Mediterranean Fleet, a period of readjustment to the changed strategic circumstances brought about by the clearance of Sicily and the invasion of Italy. It has already been told how the heavy ships of Force H were

---

[1] See John Ehrman, *Grand Strategy*, Vol. V (H.M.S.O., 1956), regarding the intricacies of the negotiations with Mihailovic's 'Cetniks', Tito's 'Partisans' and the Royal Yugo-Slav party. Finally all Allied support was given to Tito.

dispersed to other stations[1]; but the cruiser strength on the station was also reduced and by the beginning of December consisted of only seven ships (including two A.A. cruisers); and all landing ships and craft which could be spared from the duty of keeping the armies in Italy supplied soon returned to Britain or were transferred to the Eastern Fleet. On the other hand, the escort and minesweeping commitments continued heavy, because the flow of shipping from Gibraltar to the newly acquired bases in Italy still required protection against submarine and air attacks and the Germans were constantly mining the approaches to those ports.

At the beginning of November there were thirteen German U-boats inside the Mediterranean, working generally from Toulon or Pola. One of the latter (U.453) made three sorties at this time to lay mines off Brindisi and Bari. The British destroyer *Quail* struck one of these mines on the 15th of November, and was lost while in tow; the fleet minesweeper *Hebe* was sunk by another a week later, and several smaller vessels were damaged. In general the successes achieved by the U-boats were now not substantial, though by their mere presence they prevented any reduction of our escorts. Using the new acoustic homing torpedo[2] they did, however, sink two destroyers and damaged a frigate from the escort of convoy KMS.34 on the 11th and 12th of December; but in the ensuing hunts U.593 and U.73 were both sunk. These two successes are of particular interest, for they were obtained by a new technique, which had been developed in the Mediterranean by the Coastal Air Force and the naval authorities and was only used on that station. On the 14th September Air Marshal Sir Hugh Lloyd, commander of the Coastal Air Force, wrote to Admiral Sir Andrew Cunningham stressing the need for naval and air forces to work together in locating and attacking U-boats. 'We cannot by ourselves carry out a successful hunt after an attack on a convoy' he wrote. More surface ships were needed to maintain contact once the enemy had submerged and to pursue him if he tried to escape on the surface in darkness. The naval Commander-in-Chief cordially agreed, and promised to make the necessary anti-submarine vessels available. Joint operation orders were issued to the naval and air authorities directing that, whenever a U-boat was detected, a succession of aircraft was to be sent out to 'swamp' the air in its vicinity, by night as well as by day. The object was to keep the enemy down until the surface escorts could regain contact and complete its destruction. The new tactics were eminently suited to the conditions which prevailed on the Mediterranean convoy routes, since the U-boats generally worked compara-

---

[1] See p. 184.
[2] See pp. 17 and 40–41 regarding this weapon.

tively close inshore, and the aircraft could therefore be quickly reinforced. Although the first attempts, made in November, were not
successful, the plan worked to perfection in the following month; and
the destruction of U.593 and U.73 by British and American surface
escorts owed much to the fact that the patrolling aircraft kept in
touch with them for long periods (thirty-one hours in the case of
U.593), and so enabled the surface ships to regain asdic contact.

On the 24th of November a heavy air attack was made on the
U-boat base at Toulon. Considerable havoc was wrought on shore,
and five U-boats suffered damage which prevented them going on
patrol for several weeks. Attacks on Marseilles, Pola and Fiume, all
of which were also used by U-boats, followed; but none succeeded
in actually destroying an enemy submarine. Soon after the Germans
had taken possession of 'unoccupied France' in November 1942 they
started to construct bomb-proof U-boat shelters at Marseilles, similar
to those which had proved successful in the Bay of Biscay bases.
The construction work was revealed by Allied air reconnaissance,
and on the 2nd of December the site was bombed by 118 American
Fortress aircraft. The damage caused such serious seepage of water
into the excavations that work could not progress, and the shelters
were never completed. This experience proved how vulnerable the
shelters were to bomb damage while in the early stages of construction—a weakness of which we had failed to take advantage in the
case of the Bay of Biscay bases.[1]

Air attacks on the Mediterranean convoys, generally made by
torpedo-bombers at dusk, were now a more serious menace than the
U-boats. In November we lost seven ships, including two transports
which were carrying Canadian troops to Italy. One of these was the
fine Dutch liner *Marnix van St. Aldegonde* (19,335 tons), which had
done excellent work on many stations since 1940. Happily on this
occasion the loss of life was small; but when convoy KMF.26 was
attacked in the Gulf of Bougie by about thirty aircraft at dusk on the
26th of November the British troopship *Rohna* was hit by a glider-
bomb and sank half-an-hour later. Rescue work was seriously impeded by darkness and the heavy swell, with the result that over
1,000 American soldiers (more than half the total embarked) lost
their lives. This was one of the very few instances in which the
sinking at sea of a troop transport resulted in heavy casualties among
the soldiers; and the fact that the ship was British and the escort
consisted mostly of Royal Navy ships made it the more regrettable.
In general, however, our counter-measures against the German

---

[1] See Vol. I, p. 459 and Vol. II, pp. 351–352.

wireless-controlled bombs were by this time becoming more effective, and they achieved few important successes. The most serious blow of the period to Allied shipping was struck on the night of the 2nd–3rd of December when the crowded port of Bari was heavily raided. The warning system broke down, and the defences were caught unprepared. An ammunition ship blew up, and fires spread so rapidly that sixteen merchantmen and 38,000 tons of cargo were lost. Over 1,000 casualties were suffered, most of them by the crews of the ships in harbour; and control of the fires which broke out was made more difficult by the escape of poison gas from a ship which was loaded with gas bombs. She had been brought to Bari because the Germans had threatened to use gas against their former Ally; and the British and American governments had announced that, if that was done, they would retaliate against Germany itself using the full weight of their air power. It was several weeks before the full capacity of the port of Bari was restored.

In spite of the depredations of enemy aircraft and U-boats the vast majority of the ships which started out to pass through the Mediterranean now got through safely. The increase in this traffic is shown by the fact that whereas only 357 ships had passed through in June 1943, the December figure reached 1,012; and at the end of the year sailings in Mediterranean convoys actually exceeded those in Atlantic convoys. Early in December the famous 10th Submarine Flotilla moved from Malta to Maddalena in Sardinia. Many patrols were made by the submarines and by the coastal craft working from their new base at Bastia in Corsica; but few targets could now be found in the western Mediterranean.

As the Army fought its way north towards the River Sangro, across difficult country and in very bad weather, the destroyers worked in support off the east as well as the west coast of Italy. Bombardments and feint combined operations were several times carried out to divert the enemy's attention when the Army was about to take the offensive; but the only actual assault from the sea made at this time was by a Commando, which was landed in the enemy's rear north of the Garigliano River on the night of the 29th–30th of December.[1]

As the fighting moved north the bases in North Africa and Sicily lost their former importance, and they gradually reverted to the full control of the French and Italians. The smaller ships of those two nations had now been formed into escort groups and minesweeping flotillas and had taken their place in the great pattern of Allied maritime control. The larger ships were not needed, so the Italian battleships remained in Egypt or Malta with reduced crews, while

---

[1] See Map 12.

the French *Richelieu* returned to Britain, and later joined the Eastern Fleet.[1]

At the end of the year the Mediterranean naval commands were completely reorganised. The Levant Command was abolished, and the whole station was placed under Admiral Sir John Cunningham, the Commander-in-Chief, Mediterranean. Four sub-commands, at Gibraltar, Algiers, Malta and Alexandria, were established and the fleet thus reverted to an organisation very similar to that which had been in force in 1939.[2] This return to an earlier tradition may be taken as a measure of the great successes achieved in the Mediterranean during the second half of 1943.

---

[1] See p. 355.

[2] The sub-commands were (a) Gibraltar and Mediterranean Approaches (Vice-Admiral Sir H. M. Burrough), (b) Western Mediterranean (Rear-Admiral C. E. Morgan), which was held in abeyance while the Commander-in-Chief was at Algiers, and was cancelled in January 1944, (c) Malta and Central Mediterranean (Vice-Admiral L. H. K. Hamilton), (d) Levant and Eastern Mediterranean (Vice-Admiral H. B. Rawlings).

CHAPTER VIII

THE PACIFIC
AND INDIAN OCEANS

1st June–31st December, 1943

> 'It is only the offensive that can produce positive results, while the strength and energy which are born of the moral stimulation of attack are of a practical value that outweighs almost every other consideration.'
>
> J. S. Corbett, *Some Principles of Maritime Strategy* (Longmans, Green, 1918) p. 27.

AT the beginning of the period now to be discussed the situation in the Indian Ocean and on the Burma front was depressing. The first attempt to take the offensive against the Japanese in Arakan had just ended in failure[1], and nothing had so far happened to loosen in any great degree the firm grip which the enemy held on the whole vast area of his conquests from north Burma, through Malaya and the Dutch East Indies, to New Guinea. Though small naval forces had been assembled at Chittagong to support the Army in the Arakan, Japanese domination of the Bay of Bengal was still virtually undisputed; and the Allied command organisation was as unsatisfactory as the strategic situation. While the Army and Air Forces in Burma were under General Wavell, the Commander-in-Chief, India, the naval forces responsible for the safety of the shipping on which all the services depended for their supplies and reinforcements were controlled by the Admiralty through Admiral Sir James Somerville, the Commander-in-Chief, Eastern Fleet; and his headquarters were at Kilindini in East Africa, several thousand miles away from the only front on which fighting was taking place. In July the Prime Minister commented bitterly on 'the welter of inefficiency and lassitude which has characterised our operations on the Indian

---

[1] The first Arakan campaign started in September 1942 with the object of capturing Akyab, but was held up in February 1943, and by May the British forces were back where they had started from. Light naval forces, mostly M.Ls and landing craft, supported the Fourteenth Army by working off-shore, but were not present in sufficient numbers to influence the decision on land. See S. Woodburn Kirby, *The War against Japan* (H.M.S.O., 1958), Vol. II, Chapters XV and XX.

front', and urged the need to establish a unified command.[1] The principle of placing all Allied forces in the theatre under one commander had been accepted at the 'Trident' conference in Washington in May 1943; and at the 'Quadrant' conference at Quebec in the following August the appointment of Captain (Acting Vice-Admiral) Lord Louis Mountbatten as Supreme Allied Commander, South-East Asia, with the temporary rank of Admiral, was approved.[2] His area of responsibility was to include India, Burma, Ceylon, Siam, Malaya and Sumatra. Subject to the strategic directions of the Combined Chiefs of Staff, he was made responsible to the British Chiefs of Staff, from whom he would receive his orders. The directive issued by the Prime Minister to the new Supreme Commander on the 23rd of October placed the Commanders-in-Chief of all three services under him, but so far as the naval Commander-in-Chief was concerned certain important reservations were made. These will be referred to again shortly. As regards the naval forces to be provided, the directive stated, somewhat optimistically, that the British Government would make available to Mountbatten, at least four weeks prior to his first major amphibious operation, a battle fleet of sufficient strength to engage any force which the Government considered the Japanese might be in a position to disengage from the Pacific theatre. The base of this battle fleet was to be Ceylon. Admiral Sir Andrew Cunningham, who had not yet taken over the office of First Sea Lord when the directive was issued, considered later that the paragraph quoted should not have been accepted by the Admiralty; and the reference to a 'battle fleet', which certainly did not exist in the Indian Ocean at the time and could not quickly be conjured into existence, does now seem somewhat rhetorical. It is not surprising that the paragraph aroused apprehensions in the mind of the naval Commander-in-Chief. The need for the Admiralty to make certain reservations derived from the fact that Somerville's responsibilities extended far beyond the limits of the new South-East Asia Command. To the north they included Aden and the Persian Gulf, and to the south Madagascar; and almost the whole of the East African coast, along which ran the convoy route to Suez, was also within his responsibility. Amplifying instructions from the British Cabinet therefore laid down that, in all manners affecting support of the land campaigns and combined operations Somerville was subordinate to Mountbatten; but where the security of shipping and offensive action against enemy naval forces, both within and outside the South-East Asia Command, were concerned, Somerville remained directly responsible to the Admiralty, which department

---

[1] Minute of 24th July 1943 to General Ismay for Chiefs of Staff Committee. Quoted Churchill, Vol. V, pp. 576–577.

[2] See Churchill, Vol. V, pp. 70, 79 and 109.

could communicate with him without the Supreme Commander's knowledge. Here was a possibly fruitful source of difficulty; for the instructions quoted could reasonably be regarded as limiting the powers of a Supreme Commander, who not unnaturally felt it essential that he should exercise full control over all the forces in his theatre.

There is no doubt at all that, in spite of the fact that in his permanent rank the new Supreme Commander was much junior to him, Somerville at first sincerely welcomed Mountbatten's appointment. But difficulties none the less soon arose between them. In the first place Somerville expected to find himself in a position analogous to that occupied by Admiral Cunningham in the inter-Allied organisation set up by General Eisenhower for the prosecution of the Mediterranean offensives.[1] In that theatre the Naval, Military and Air Commanders-in-Chief worked in intimate collaboration with the Supreme Commander, but were regarded by him more as deputies, expert advisers, and operational commanders within their individual fields, than as subordinates; and they retained a wide degree of personal and independent responsibility for the direction and control of their own forces. But it soon appeared to Somerville that the organisation through which his Supreme Commander intended to work more closely resembled those established by General MacArthur and Admiral Halsey, U.S.N., the Supreme Commanders of the South-West and South Pacific theatres[2], than that which had proved so successful under General Eisenhower's leadership in the Mediterranean. The conditions in that theatre were, however, by no means identical to those which prevailed in the South-East Asia Command, where Admiral Mountbatten had to weld an inter-Allied team, which included some American officers whose loyalties were plainly divided and whose personalities were by no means always tractable, into a smoothly working command organisation capable of prosecuting the war more effectively than hitherto; and it was his view that this could only be accomplished by means of a command system more analogous to that of General MacArthur than that of General Eisenhower.[3] It may be that Somerville was too concerned with the purely naval aspects of the command problem,

---

[1] See Vol. II, pp. 312–313.

[2] See Fleet Admiral W. F. Halsey, U.S.N., *Admiral Halsey's Story* (McGraw-Hill Book Company Inc., 1947), p. 138:
'I emphasize "Supreme Commander" to establish the realization that MacArthur and I commanded everything in our respective spheres—Army, Navy, Marines, and Allies; troops, ships, planes and supplies.' After 29th March 1943, however, Halsey became subject to the strategic directions of MacArthur for operations in the Solomons. (See Vol. II, p. 418.)

[3] In 1959 Admiral Mountbatten told the author that when he consulted the American Chiefs of Staff on the form that his command organisation should take, General Marshall had been strongly in favour of following the MacArthur model.

and took too little account of the inter-Allied aspects, which were of course the primary concern of the Supreme Commander.

In mid-November 1943 the Supreme Commander made it clear by messages to the Prime Minister and First Lord that his interpretation of the directive already quoted was that the naval Commander-in-Chief was 'under his command at all times and for all purposes'; but that the authorities at home would not accept. The Prime Minister and First Sea Lord therefore tried to define the position of the two commanders more clearly, by considering what their positions would be if certain hypothetical circumstances should arise. The matter was discussed with the Supreme Commander when he was in Cairo for the Inter-Allied Conference in November, and it was believed that a satisfactory solution had been reached. This, however, was to prove too optimistic.

In December the First Sea Lord replied to the misgivings which Somerville had expressed by saying 'Your forces working in the area of the South-East Asia Command in operations arranged by the Supreme Commander are definitely under him, and in so far as they are concerned you are under him as well; but as Commander-in-Chief, Eastern Fleet, you are responsible to the Admiralty for the Eastern Fleet area'. He also said that a request by the Supreme Commander to have 'the whole Eastern Fleet area placed under him' had been rejected. Another difficulty arose through the Supreme Commander having set up his own planning staff, in preference to utilising the staff officers already serving the three Commanders-in-Chief, as did General Eisenhower. The Admiralty had recommended against this separate staff from the beginning, and it rapidly proved a fruitful source of friction; for Somerville lacked confidence in the uses to which his fleet might be put in accordance with recommendations made by the Supreme Commander's own 'War Staff'.

The First Sea Lord, to whom these matters were constantly referred, replied to Somerville's doubts and enquiries expressing considerable sympathy over the acutely difficult problems facing the Supreme Commander of a vast theatre where forces of many nations, arms and services had to be integrated into a closely-knit team. He also pointed out to Somerville how important it was for the Supreme Commander to exercise a large measure of authority over the British Fleet if the Americans were to be whole-heartedly convinced of the need to place their own land and air forces under him. But Admiral Cunningham adhered firmly to the principle that the Admiralty should, as on all other stations, retain its authority to direct the operations of the Eastern Fleet when it was not acting under the Supreme Commander in accordance with the terms of his directive. Nor was that principle ever amended, let alone rescinded.

Early in June 1944 Somerville wrote to Mountbatten representing that the Commanders-in-Chief should be responsible for producing all operational plans, and should only submit them to the Supreme Commander when all details had been worked out; and he expressed the opinion that the Supreme Commander was constitutionally bound to accept the advice of the Commanders-in-Chief. In Mountbatten's eyes, however, the first of these proposals would have reduced his status to that of chairman of a Commander-in-Chief's committee; and there was no precedent for a commander being obliged to act on the advice of his subordinates.

It was, perhaps, natural that as long as an important problem in command structure remained unresolved lesser differences between the two commanders should arise. In themselves these now seem trivial, and it is surprising that such questions as visits by the Supreme Commander to the ships of the Eastern Fleet, and the issue of *communiqués* to the press about its operations should have been allowed to assume such a magnified importance in Admiral Somerville's eyes. The upshot of the whole controversy was that in June 1944 Admiral Mountbatten referred the substance of his disagreements with the naval Commander-in-Chief to the Chiefs of Staff. Meanwhile the First Sea Lord had recommended to the Prime Minister that Admiral Somerville should succeed Sir Percy Noble, who was pressing to return home, as head of the mission in America; and Mr Churchill had finally agreed to this change. It thus came to pass that in August 1944 Somerville was appointed to Washington, and Admiral Sir Bruce Fraser, lately in command of the Home Fleet, took over command of the Eastern Fleet. It is fair to record that the difficulties experienced by the Supreme Commander in achieving a satisfactory working arrangement with the naval command in his theatre thereafter evaporated.

These disagreements have only been referred to here because they may contain an important lesson in command organisation. The advantages of appointing a Supreme Commander for South-East Asia in 1943—and even the imperative need to do so—seem as clear today as they were to the Prime Minister and Chiefs of Staff at the time. Ideally he should unquestionably have been given a fleet commanded by a flag officer who was directly and solely responsible to him, much as Admiral Kinkaid of the U.S. Seventh Fleet was responsible to General MacArthur.[1] But we did not possess the ships and aircraft needed to meet the Supreme Commander's maritime needs in addition to providing for the security of sea transport in all adjacent seas and oceans. One fleet had to serve both purposes; and it was from that inescapable dilemma that the larger disagreements seem to have arisen. On the lesser issue of the internal organisation

---

[1] See p. 340.

of the Supreme Command, it does seem to this historian that there was much to be said for Admiral Somerville's belief that, as long as his planning staff was available to work between the Supreme Commander's Headquarters and his own flagship, an additional staff directly under the Supreme Commander made matters unnecessarily complex. Indeed it appears that Admiral Mountbatten himself ultimately came to accept such a view; since in November 1944, after he had accomplished his long-standing purpose of making the commanders of the Air and Land Forces *Allied* (as opposed to only British) Commanders-in-Chief[1], he decided to abolish his 'War Staff'. The experience of these matters gained in the South-East Asia Command in 1943–44 suggests that, even if other countries have successfully employed a staff which was divorced from any responsibility for the execution of the operations which it had planned, in the British services such a system is not workable. Though the Mediterranean and South-East Asia Commands cannot be regarded as exactly comparable, there is no doubt that similar difficulties never arose in the former theatre. It is true that the Mediterranean Commanders-in-Chiefs' staffs were frequently overloaded by the dual responsibility of conducting one great combined operation whilst planning the next one[2]; and the difficulties which beset them for that reason were serious. Yet it still seems that a system which places responsibility for execution on the shoulders of the officers who prepared the plans is greatly to be preferred to the alternative.

Before leaving the question of command organisation it should be mentioned that Admiral Sir Geoffrey Layton, to whom exceptional powers had been given at the time of the crisis of April 1942[3], was still serving as Commander-in-Chief, Ceylon. In the autumn of 1943, when the Supreme Commander's headquarters were still at Delhi but their move to Ceylon was being contemplated, the question arose whether Admiral Layton's functions should be transferred to the Supreme Commander. Admiral Mountbatten, however, was strongly opposed to the proposal, as he had no wish to carry the additional responsibility for the civil administration of Ceylon, and for the organisation and expansion of the many bases and installations then in progress on the island. In July 1944, after Supreme Headquarters had moved to Kandy, the First Sea Lord raised a similar proposal;

---

[1] On Admiral Mountbatten assuming command only the naval C.-in-C. (Somerville) was an Allied Commander-in-Chief. At the Cairo conference (November 1943) Mountbatten obtained approval for the Air Forces to be integrated under Air Chief Marshal Peirse; but it was not until the summer of 1944 that General Leese was appointed Allied Land Forces Commander-in-Chief.

[2] For example, the assault at Salerno in September 1943 had to be planned while the conquest of Sicily was still commanding much of the attention of the Commanders-in-Chief and their staffs. See pp. 155–156 and 158.

[3] See Vol. II, pp. 24–27.

but after Admiral Layton had represented the arguments against it he did not pursue the matter. It thus came to pass that Admiral Layton's position remained unchanged until he returned home in January 1945. His services to the Allied cause in the Indian Ocean theatre were of great importance, and rarely can a British naval officer have been entrusted with such wide powers over the civil as well as military authorities.

To turn now to the actual work of the Eastern Fleet, in the middle of 1943 no less than forty-eight of its ships were detached to the Mediterranean to take part in the invasion of Sicily. This left Somerville with inadequate strength even to protect merchant shipping within his command. But after the end of the Sicilian campaign and the submission of the Italian fleet a few of his ships returned to him[1], while a small flow of reinforcements began to arrive from Britain.

In June there were seven U-boats in the southern Indian Ocean, and at the end of the month they all managed to refuel from the tanker *Charlotte Schliemann* at a rendezvous off Madagascar. They then moved to the north and north-east, to seek the traffic passing through the Mozambique Channel and ships steaming between the Cape of Good Hope and India or Ceylon. Whereas in June our losses in this theatre had amounted to twelve ships (67,929 tons), two of which were victims of the raider *Michel*[2], in July we lost seventeen totalling 97,214 tons, almost all of which were sunk by German U-boats. With the forces available to Admiral Somerville it was very difficult to organise an effective convoy system on all the many routes which crossed this vast theatre; but ships sailing on the more important ones, such as Durban to Aden, Aden to Bombay, and Colombo to Bombay and Calcutta, were quickly organised into convoys. Escort vessels, of which the Eastern Fleet was still woefully short, were sent up from South African waters, which were now quiet, while the Royal Indian Navy made an important contribution to safeguarding shipping on its own coasts and in the Persian Gulf.

The air co-operation required by the Eastern Fleet was mainly supplied by the R.A.F's No. 222 Group (Air Vice-Marshal A. Lees), whose headquarters were at Colombo, where the two services worked alongside each other in a combined operations room; but the Air Headquarters in East Africa, in India and at Aden were also involved in maritime operations at various times—particularly when enemy submarines appeared within their spheres of responsibility. To simplify the control of maritime aircraft, and enable them to be quickly concentrated where most needed, a common pool of flying

---

[1] See p. 208.

[2] See Vol. II, p. 411.

boats was established to cover the whole theatre at this time; and
No. 222 Group delegated its responsibility for operational control to
the other Air Headquarters whenever the latter were required to
carry out such duties as anti-submarine searches. By this means the
flying boats could be quickly switched to any of the many bases now
established on the mainland of the continents bordering the Indian
Ocean and in the islands. In practice, though not in name, No. 222
Group thus acted as a 'Coastal Command' to work with the naval
forces of the Eastern Fleet. By the autumn of 1943 Air Marshal Lees
had under his control thirteen long-range reconnaissance squadrons,
eleven of which were equipped with Catalinas. Working from a large
number of different bases they provided air escort to many convoys,
at any rate during the most dangerous parts of their journeys; they
conducted far-ranging searches whenever an enemy submarine was
reported, and they provided all the shore-based air co-operation
needed by Admiral Somerville's main units. Towards the end of the
year the Chiefs of Staff issued a new directive with the object of
eliminating certain ambiguities which had previously existed in the
arrangements for the control of maritime aircraft. The principle that
the air commander should decide the best way of meeting the needs
of his naval colleague was re-affirmed, and command of all such
aircraft was vested in the Air Commander-in-Chief, South-East Asia,
who would work in close collaboration with the Naval Commander-
in-Chief; but operational control continued to be exercised through
the commander of No. 222 Group.

In spite of the improving air co-operation and the slowly rising
strength of the surface escorts, losses continued in August, when
seven ships (46,401 tons) were sunk—all of them by German U-boats.
The reader will remember how, early in June, Dönitz had ordered
nine more U-boats and two supply submarines to these waters, and
how they were severely handled by Coastal Command's Biscay
patrols and the American escort carriers, while southward-bound.[1]
At the end of August the five survivors of this group reached the
Cape of Good Hope, while the boats which they were to relieve were
beginning to withdraw westwards. On the 20th of August, however,
U.197 was sunk by R.A.F. aircraft flying from Madagascar. Early
in September the new group fuelled from the tanker *Brake* south of
Madagascar, after which they steered north and scattered over a
wide area. It is likely that the six ships (39,471 tons) sunk in this
month mostly fell victims to Japanese submarines, of which eight
were then working in the Indian Ocean.

In the month of October there were two German U-boats off the
Arabian coast, and others patrolling singly off Mombasa, Colombo

---

[1] See pp. 23–28.

and Bombay; but a Bisley aircraft sank U.533 in the Gulf of Oman on the 16th, and our losses for the month fell to six ships of 25,833 tons. By the beginning of November the surviving German U-boats were all moving towards Penang to replenish and, although Dönitz had ordered out three more, two of them had been sunk off the Azores.[1] The phase thus ended with the Indian Ocean almost entirely clear of German U-boats; but the depredations of their Japanese colleagues continued, and in the last two months of the year it was mainly they who caused us the loss of nine more ships (60,321 tons). With the temporary withdrawal of the Germans from the theatre the Admiralty considered the threat to be so diminished that they pressed Admiral Somerville to relax his precautions by restarting independent sailings on some routes, because they considered that the turn-round of shipping would thereby be expedited. The Commander-in-Chief accordingly cancelled certain convoys; but the continuation of losses, and the return of the German U-boats in the following year, were soon to show that the step had been premature.[2]

To sum up this phase of the U-boat war in the Indian Ocean, a comparatively small number of submarines—never more than seven German and eight Japanese—had caused us considerable dislocation; and it was they who contributed the major share of our total shipping losses of fifty-seven ships of 337,169 tons. We were very vulnerable to U-boat attack at such focal points as the entrances to the Red Sea and Persian Gulf, where much of the heavy and extremely valuable traffic was sailing independently; but only five of the ships lost in this phase were sunk in convoy. In retrospect it seems that the damage might well have been even worse than it was.

To return to the main body of the Eastern Fleet, in September, although still far too weak to undertake any offensive operations, it moved from Kilindini back to Colombo. This was at least a step in the right direction; but nothing more than this first step could then be undertaken, for Somerville's strength was still small and his fleet was seriously unbalanced in composition. He had only one battleship, the old *Ramillies*, and, until the escort carrier *Battler* reached Bombay in October, he had no aircraft carriers at all. His cruisers included four modern ships, but no more than five old ones and a few armed merchant cruisers were available for convoy duties. His one submarine flotilla was being strengthened by detachments from the Mediterranean, and would soon receive other reinforcements from home. Offensive patrolling had, however, been started off the enemy's Malayan bases. One of the earliest submarines to enter those

---

[1] See p. 44.
[2] See pp. 348–349.

waters, the Dutch O.24, complained that a promising attack had been frustrated by a total eclipse of the moon on the 15th August. By a curious coincidence the Polish submarine *Sokol* reported an exactly similar experience thousands of miles away in the southern Adriatic on that night. Possibly the goddess Phoebe had taken umbrage over her eclipse, and temporarily transferred her allegiance to the Axis. On the 12th of November, however, the *Taurus* suffered from no such handicap, when she torpedoed and sank the Japanese submarine I.34 in the approaches to Penang. Though it was satisfactory that our submarines were beginning to reach out into waters over which the enemy had exercised virtually undisputed control since the early days of 1942, the acute shortage of destroyers in Somerville's fleet still made it impossible to mount more ambitious operations. The three flotillas which he theoretically commanded comprised only thirteen ships; and all of them had normally to be employed as convoy escorts between Capetown and Aden or on the routes crossing the Indian Ocean. The shortage of frigates, sloops and corvettes for escort duty was also acute, and the use of destroyers in substitution for them immobilised the larger ships. Not until the spring of 1944, by which time more escort vessels had arrived, could the destroyers return to fleet work. Luckily the Japanese regarded the Indian Ocean as secondary to the Pacific theatre. They had a cruiser squadron of five ships at Penang and a few others at Singapore; but they did little to dispute the command of waters which, at that time, was almost theirs for the asking. It is certain that we owe the comparative immunity of this large and vulnerable theatre to the success of the American offensives in the south Pacific, and to the threat of new combined operations westwards across the central Pacific now developing. It is therefore to those theatres that we must turn.

Readers of our second volume will remember that in the spring of 1943 Allied strategy aimed at breaking through the chain of island defences, called the 'Bismarck barrier', which blocked the road towards Japan from the south Pacific.[1] To achieve this object two offensives were launched. The first was directed by General MacArthur from the south-west Pacific along the north coast of New Guinea, while the second drove up the Solomon Islands chain and was commanded by Admiral Halsey, U.S.N. The first fruits were the capture of Buna and Gona in New Guinea at the end of 1942 by General MacArthur's forces, and the expulsion of the Japanese from Guadalcanal by Halsey's in February 1943.[2] Both campaigns had been extremely arduous, and in prosecuting them the Allied land,

[1] See Vol. II, pp. 413–418.
[2] Ibid. p. 417 and Map 15 of this volume.

sea and air forces had suffered substantial losses. The succeeding months were therefore marked by a pause to allow the forces which had been engaged to recuperate, the newly-arrived reinforcements to be trained and acclimatised, and the necessary base and 'logistics' organisation to be expanded and prepared for the next move.

By the middle of 1943 the Allied forces of all arms stood poised and ready to resume the offensive. In the air their superiority, which had been decisively demonstrated in the Battle of the Bismarck Sea in March[1], was now very marked, both in numbers and in the quality of the aircraft and aircrews; but sufficient well-placed airfields from which this superiority could be decisively exploited were still lacking. Until the Americans had seized islands north of Guadalcanal and gained the use of their airfields, fighters could not accompany the bombers sent to attack the key enemy position at Rabaul in New Britain; and this was bound to reduce the effectiveness of the air offensive. The Japanese, on the other hand, possessed an excellent chain of airfields stretching south from New Britain to New Georgia in the Solomons, and west to Lae, Salamaua, Madang and Wewak on the north coast of New Guinea.[2] It was plain that command of the air over Rabaul could never be gained until the enemy had been driven from at least some of these positions. As so often in the Pacific campaigns the strategic advantage in a large area was decided by possession of a few landing strips levelled out of the jungle.

In the Central Pacific theatre, by June Admiral Nimitz had assembled at Pearl Harbour a great fleet of aircraft carriers, together with the necessary battleships, cruisers and destroyers to form balanced task forces, and the transports, landing vessels and auxiliaries essential to carry out combined operations. For the first time the fruits of America's vast industrial capacity, and her dynamic energy in organising and training the people of a peace-loving democracy for war, were coming to harvest. On the 20th of May 1943 the plan to launch an offensive against the Marshall and Caroline Islands was approved by the Combined Chiefs of Staff.[3] Its objects were to protect the northern flank of the offensives conducted by MacArthur and Halsey against the Bismarck barrier, to make the enemy divide his defending forces, and to produce uncertainty in his mind regarding the direction from which the main Allied thrust would develop. The Combined Chiefs of Staff had originally included in their plans

---

[1] See Vol. II, p. 422.

[2] See Map 15 (facing p. 225.)

[3] See Map 16 (facing p. 237). These islands were German colonies until 1918. Thereafter they were administered by Japan under a mandate. Though not allowed by the terms of the mandate, the Japanese had no compunction in turning them into strongly fortified military bases.

an offensive by the British forces in India against Burma and Malaya, with the ultimate object of regaining control of the South China Sea. In August the heads of the British and American governments and their advisers met again at the first Quebec conference, and discussed these plans.[1] The two-pronged offensive against the Bismarck barrier was then confirmed, and extended to include the capture of Wewak in New Guinea and of the Admiralty Islands.[2] In the Central Pacific theatre an assault on the Gilbert Islands was now given first priority, and Admiral Nimitz was instructed to carry it out in November 1943. The next step, to the Marshall Islands, would follow in January 1944. Only in the British strategic zone were the original plans substantially modified. The ships, aircraft, men and stores needed for a major assault in Burma could not be provided while we were still heavily committed in the Mediterranean and were also preparing for the invasion of northern Europe. That part of the Allies' grand strategy had therefore to be abandoned.

The Allies were not alone in refurbishing and adapting their plans at this time, for the Japanese had been going through a similar process. But whereas the Allies aimed at striking a number of offensive blows the enemy's plans were now recast in a purely defensive mould. The Japanese hoped to defend a vast perimeter stretching from the Aleutian Islands in the north-east to the Andamans in the Indian Ocean and including Wake Island, the Gilberts and Marshalls, the Bismarck archipelago, Timor, Java and Sumatra. The main strength of the Japanese Navy, the 'Combined Fleet', now commanded by Admiral Koga and based on Truk in the Caroline Islands, was to act as a mobile force and sail at once to any point on the defended perimeter which might be threatened. But hardly had this plan been brought into force before it became clear that, in face of the mounting Allied pressure, it provided no firm basis for the defensive strategy which its creators had visualised. By the end of June 1943 almost the whole of the Combined Fleet had withdrawn to the homeland. This move was forced on the Japanese mainly by the acute shortage of naval aircrews from which they were now suffering; and that state of affairs had come about through the profligate waste of trained men in the abortive offensive undertaken by Yamamoto against Allied bases in the Solomons and New Guinea in the preceding April.[3] But the Japanese were also becoming apprehensive regarding Russian intentions, and in particular by the fear that they might allow the Allies to make use of their naval and air bases in the maritime provinces of Siberia. In fact this latter fear

---

[1] See Churchill, Vol. V, pp. 72–87.

[2] See Map 15 (facing p. 225).

[3] See Vol. II, p. 423.

Map 15

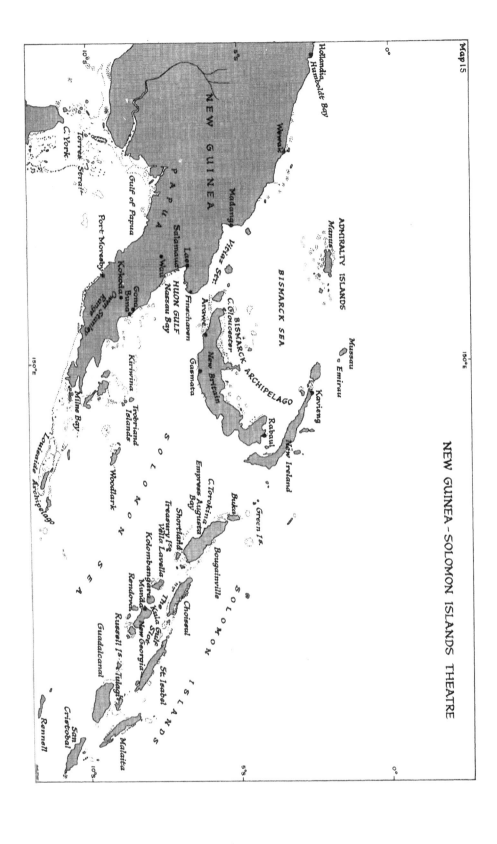

NEW GUINEA – SOLOMON ISLANDS THEATRE

proved groundless, and by the end of July the Combined Fleet was back again at Truk, though some of its carriers still had no aircrews. In the same month the Japanese evacuated the last of the Aleutian Islands[1]; and in August they decided, somewhat paradoxically, that although they would not abandon the Marshalls and Gilberts retention of those islands was no longer essential to their defensive strategy. Thus did fissures quickly begin to appear in the plan to defend the long perimeter enclosing their ill-gotten gains. By August they admitted it to have shrunk to the line of conquest reached in April 1942, before they had embarked on their further plan of aggrandisement.[2] Soon the fissures were to be widened into gaping chasms through which Allied forces would drive west from Pearl Harbour and north from New Guinea towards the Philippines.

The offensive thrusts by Admirals Nimitz and Halsey and by General MacArthur now to be described were in fact complementary to each other and took place simultaneously enough to distract and divide the enemy's forces. On the 29th of June forces of the South-West Pacific Command occupied the Woodlark and Kiriwina Islands off the Papuan peninsula unopposed; and on the same day a landing was made at Nassau Bay on the New Guinea coast some fifteen miles south of Salamaua.[3] This greatly eased the problem of supplying the Australian troops who were fighting their way forward from Wau towards the Huon Gulf, and aggravated the threat to Salamaua by enabling a thrust to be started northwards along the coast from Nassau Bay. The Japanese now became justifiably alarmed over the increasingly dangerous pressure against their New Guinea bases. These operations afford, in fact, an excellent example of the skilful and effective use of maritime power to support the seaward flank of an army, and to ease the difficulties of the land forces by carrying reinforcements and stores forward to points close up to the enemy's positions.[4] In fact all these offensives against a stubborn enemy would have been immeasurably more difficult, if not impossible, had Allied maritime control of the coastal waters not been effectively secured and imaginatively used.

In New Guinea the Japanese had concentrated their main forward defences around the ports of Lae, Salamaua and Finschaven, all of which lay in or near the Huon Gulf; but ever since the Battle of the Bismarck Sea they had been finding it very difficult to supply

---

[1] See Vol. II, p. 42 regarding the Japanese seizure of Attu and Kiska, and p. 424 regarding the American recapture of the former.

[2] Ibid. p. 21.

[3] See Map 15.

[4] Compare the work of the Mediterranean Fleet's Inshore Squadron in support of the Army of the Nile. See Vol. I, pp. 422 and 520 and Vol. II, pp. 311–312, 436, etc.

and strengthen these positions, and the traffic by small barges on which they had chiefly to rely was never really adequate to the needs. But while the Japanese, far from showing any intention of withdrawing from Lae and Salamaua, were struggling to reinforce their garrisons and were also developing new bases at Madang and Wewak further along the coast to the north-west[1], the Allies were finding it exceedingly hard to make further progress. Throughout July and August heavy air attacks were carried out, preliminary to a combined assault on Lae, and on the 17th and 18th of August a bomber force, which had assembled on airfields secretly built in the interior, struck at Wewak as well. This surprise attack achieved excellent results. No less than 120 of the enemy's aircraft were destroyed, and his air strength in the New Guinea theatre was virtually annihilated. The condition of the Japanese garrisons around Huon Gulf was meanwhile being made increasingly precarious by the American patrol crafts' campaign against the barges running from New Britain.

By the early days of September all was ready for the assault on Lae, and on the 4th an Australian division landed fifteen miles to the east of the town. Next day the Americans carried out a remarkable reinforcement of the Australian troops, who had been struggling towards the Huon Gulf from the west through very difficult country, by dropping 1,700 paratroops to capture a little-used enemy airfield some twenty miles inland from Lae. An Australian brigade was then flown in, and the advance from both directions towards Lae now became faster. On the 16th the Australians captured the town. The speed and economy with which this success was finally achieved owed a great deal to the manner in which the Americans exploited the mobility of their air power to seize, develop and supply an advanced base which outflanked the strong Japanese position on the coast.

Meanwhile the Allied forces around Salamaua had struck again, and had captured their objective on the day before Lae fell. On the 22nd of September assaults from the sea were made on either side of the last of the enemy's defences in Huon Gulf, at Finschaven, and on the 2nd of October Allied forces entered the town. Control of the Huon Gulf, on the flank of the main enemy positions in the Bismarck Islands, thus passed into Allied hands. It was an important step towards breaking the 'Bismarck barrier'; and it was achieved by combined operations in the fullest sense of the definition. While the Fifth Air Force of Major-General G. C. Kenney, U.S.A.A.F., had secured, retained and exploited command of the air, the Seventh Amphibious Force of Rear-Admiral D. E. Barbey, U.S.N., had

---

[1] See Map 15.

landed the troops wherever they were needed, and thereafter kept them supplied; and the Australian and American land forces had fought their way forward undismayed by the difficulties of some of the worst country in the world and undeterred by as bad a climate as can be found anywhere.

While the Allies were thus securing a firm grip on eastern New Guinea, a remarkably bold and successful penetration into the harbour of Singapore was made by a small band of fourteen British and Australian officers and men, working for the organisation known a the 'Special Operations Executive' (S.O.E.). They sailed on the 2nd of September from Exmouth Gulf in Western Australia in an ex-Japanese fishing vessel called the *Krait*, which had been one of the very few small craft to survive both the flight from Singapore and the evacuation of the Dutch East Indies. The expedition was organised and commanded by Major I. Lyon of the Gordon Highlanders, and its object was to attack Japanese ships by attaching limpet mines to their hulls. The *Krait* proceeded by a devious route, and arrived within thirty miles of Singapore without once being challenged. She then launched three canoes, each with a crew of two men, to make the final approach to the targets and carry out the attack, while the parent ship made herself scarce by proceeding towards Borneo. The canoeists made their attacks on the night of the 24th–25th of September and achieved some success. Though the contemporary claim that seven ships of 37,000 tons were sunk or damaged now appears to have been far too high, Japanese records confirm the sinking of two ships (8,740 tons) on that date; and a third one, of 2,197 tons, listed as lost through an unknown cause, may also have been attributable to the *Krait's* expedition. Major Lyon described in his report how, while he and his companion, Able Seaman A. W. G. Huston (a Royal Australian Naval Reserve rating) were actually attaching their mines to the hull of a large tanker 'Huston drew my attention to a man who was watching us intently from a porthole ten feet above. He continued to gaze until just before we left, when he withdrew his head, and lighted his bedside lamp . . .' The canoeists stayed in their place of concealment long enough to witness the explosions, and then set off for the rendezvous with the *Krait*. The passage back to Australia was anxious, but they survived a close scrutiny by a Japanese patrol vessel in the Lombok Strait and reached Exmouth Gulf safely on the 19th of October. The cruise had lasted forty-eight days, and covered 4,000 miles.

In September 1944 Major Lyon undertook a second expedition of a similar nature, but that time the canoeists were carried by the submarine *Porpoise*. It is sad to relate that, after they had landed, the gallant band was trapped and captured. Though they were all service men, and were undertaking a perfectly lawful operation of war, they were put to death by the Japanese.[1]

To return to the South-West Pacific theatre, after the capture of the Huon Gulf bases General MacArthur decided that before he could advance further north-west, towards Madang and Wewak, he must gain full control of the Vitiaz Straits between New Britain and New Guinea. This necessitated occupying the western end of New Britain. On the 15th of Decmeber the first Allied landings on New Britain therefore took place at Arawe on the south coast, against only slight opposition.[2] The preparations for the main assault, at Cape Gloucester, including very heavy air bombardments, were meanwhile going ahead; and for the three days before the landings shore-based aircraft from the Solomons, which were under Admiral Halsey's control, attacked enemy installations around Rabaul. Next, a strong supporting force of Australian and American warships bombarded the assault beaches, and on the 26th of December some 12,500 troops landed on Cape Gloucester. By the last day of the year the whole promontory was in Allied hands; but the retreating Japanese garrison continued to contest any further advance bitterly. If, as the American historian has pointed out, the whole operation now seems to have been a superfluous insurance, because 'it was not necessary in order to make use of the Vitiaz Strait to control both sides of it'[3], there is no doubt that it secured the increasing number of Allied bases in the theatre from the possibility of interference by the Japanese Combined Fleet coming down from the north-east.

While General MacArthur's South-West Pacific forces were thus steadily extending their grip on the western flank of the Bismarck archipelago, those of Admiral Halsey, which were working under MacArthur's strategic direction, had timed their assaults on New Georgia and adjacent islands in the Solomons to coincide with the re-opening of the New Guinea offensives in June. On the last day of that month a powerful combined assault was made on the island of Rendova, across a narrow strait from Munda in New Georgia, where there was an important Japanese airfield.[4] At the same time troops landed at four points on New Georgia itself, and on adjacent islands. By this time the Americans had six airfields on Guadalcanal and the Russell Islands in use, so the landing forces could be effectively covered. Except at one point resistance was slight, and easily overcome. The Allied air forces had in fact neutralised the bases at

---

[1] A personal account of these expeditions, told by the widow of one of the officers who took part in them, is to be found in *Winning Hazard* by Noel Wynyard (Sampson Low, Marston & Co., 1949). They are also mentioned in Willoughby and Chamberlain, *MacArthur 1941–51* (Heineman, 1956), pp. 152–160.

[2] See Map 15.

[3] Morison, Vol. VI, pp. 369–372.

[4] See Map 15.

Munda and on adjacent Kolombangara Island before the assault, and the enemy could therefore only reply by sending striking forces from Rabaul, 400 miles away. This, and Japanese concern with the New Guinea operations, accounts for the slowness of their reaction to the new landings in the Solomons. It was the 2nd of July before the Japanese Navy appeared on the scene, and by that time the American assault troops had been reinforced and were holding a satisfactory beach-head. On the night of the 2nd–3rd a Japanese cruiser and destroyer force bombarded Rendova, but did no damage at all.

Admiral Halsey's main strength had been giving distant cover to the landing forces, while two groups of cruisers and destroyers commanded by Rear-Admirals A. S. Merrill and W. L. Ainsworth, U.S.N., gave support closer inshore. It was on these latter ships that the brunt of the new phase of close-range night fighting in the narrow waters of 'the Slot' mainly fell. Indeed the situation in the central Solomons now became very similar to that which had prevailed off Guadalcanal nearly a year earlier.[1] Allied command of the air was so complete that the enemy did not dare to use his surface forces by day, but after night had fallen the waters off New Georgia were hotly disputed; for the Japanese repeatedly attempted to run in reinforcements, and the Allied cruisers and destroyers as often tried to intercept them.

Rear-Admiral R. K. Turner, U.S.N., who commanded the landing forces assaulting New Georgia, next determined to land troops in Kula Gulf to take the Japanese positions around Munda in the rear. On the night of the 4th–5th of July this was successfully carried out with the support of Admiral Ainsworth's ships. These latter were returning to Tulagi after bombarding enemy positions, when an enemy destroyer force was reported steaming south towards Kula Gulf. It actually consisted of ten destroyers, seven of which were carrying reinforcements for the garrison on Kolombangara. Admiral Ainsworth, who had three cruisers and four destroyers, at once reversed course, and gained contact with the enemy at the entrance to Kula Gulf. In a very confused action, later called the Battle of Kula Gulf, the cruiser *Helena* was torpedoed and sunk.[2] The Japanese lost one destroyer, while another ran aground when landing her troops and was destroyed by bombing next day. Once again, and not for the last time, was the deadliness of the Japanese torpedo convincingly demonstrated; but the action also showed that the Americans had not yet developed effective tactics for use by a mixed force of cruisers and destroyers in the inevitably confusing conditions of a fast-moving night encounter. The Royal New Zealand Navy's cruiser

---

[1] See Vol. II, p. 227.
[2] See Morison, Vol. VI, pp. 160–175.

Leander now came up from the New Hebrides to replace the lost *Helena,* and exactly a week after the Kula Gulf battle Ainsworth, with three cruisers and ten destroyers, was searching the same waters for another Japanese squadron reported to be bringing more reinforcements south. Soon after midnight on the 12th–13th of July an air report placed one enemy cruiser and five destroyers off Vella Lavella, about twenty-six miles ahead of Admiral Ainsworth.[1] The enemy squadron actually consisted of the cruiser *Jintsu* and a number of destroyers, some of which were carrying reinforcements for Kolombangara. The Japanese, who by this time had been equipped with a device for detecting radar transmissions, were well aware of the presence of Ainsworth's force. They therefore detached the troop-carrying destroyers to make their landings, while the other ships stood on ready to give battle. Just after 1 a.m. contact was made, and Ainsworth ordered his destroyers to attack with torpedoes. Then the cruisers opened fire in radar control, all concentrating on the *Jintsu,* which was soon overwhelmed and sunk. But the Japanese had already fired their torpedo salvos and, just as the American Admiral was turning his ships a half circle to engage on the other side, the *Leander* was hit by a torpedo and came to a standstill. This and the failure of some ships to receive the signal to turn caused confusion in the Allied line. The three leading American destroyers lost touch after they had finished off the sinking *Jintsu;* while Ainsworth, now with only two cruisers and five destroyers, had turned north again to pursue the retiring enemy. When, just before 2 a.m. the flagship *Honolulu* obtained a new radar contact, the Admiral's uncertainty whether it might not be his own missing destroyers caused some minutes' delay in engaging; but the Japanese had already sighted him and had again fired torpedoes. Before the Americans had opened fire the *Honolulu,* her sister ship the *St. Louis* and a destroyer were all struck. Luckily the cruisers were both hit right forward and escaped serious damage, but the destroyer had to be scuttled. Although this Battle of Kolombangara was, from the Allied point of view, not a success, the Japanese had again learnt that a heavy price would be exacted from each attempt to reinforce the New Georgia garrisons.[2] They therefore gave up using destroyers and had recourse to motor barges; but these latter were so constantly harassed by American aircraft in daylight and by patrol craft at night that the Japanese gained little or nothing from the change. None the less the capture of Munda airfield was not achieved until the 5th August, and only after bitter resistance had been overcome.

With Munda at last secured Rabaul was within range of American

---

[1] See Map 15.

[2] See Morison, Vol. VI, pp. 194–196, for an account of the reasons why this encounter was so unsatisfactory.

light bombers and fighters; but the Japanese remained stubbornly determined to hold on to Kolombangara Island, and it was the despatch of reinforcements for its garrison which brought about the next battle. Allied intelligence had given warning that another of these 'Tokyo Express' operations was likely to take place on the night of the 6th–7th of August; and as Admiral Merrill's force was too far away at the time, and Admiral Ainsworth's was in no condition to fight another battle, a special group of six American destroyers sailed north from Tulagi at noon on the 6th. It thus happened that for the first time in these waters a destroyer force was able to fight unhampered by forming part of a composite squadron, including larger ships. Shortly after midnight the Americans gained radar contact off Vella Lavella[1], fired their torpedoes too quickly for the Japanese to take avoiding action, and hit and sank three destroyers transports which were carrying 1,500 troops between them. Only one of the Japanese squadron escaped. After two unsatisfactory encounters, the employment of normal destroyer night fighting tactics thus turned the tables on the enemy in this Battle of Vella Gulf.

The campaign in and around the Solomon Islands had now been in progress for exactly a year, and both sides had suffered heavy naval losses. If the fighting off New Guinea and the Bismarck archipelago be included, the Japanese had lost two battleships, three heavy and three light cruisers, one small aircraft carrier and thirty-six destroyers. Moreover their naval air arm had suffered so severely that the fleet carriers could no longer all be manned. In the middle of 1943 the tale of losses was swollen by the destruction of the battleship *Mutsu* after an internal explosion; and their fleet was further depleted by the withdrawal of two other capital ships for conversion to a hybrid type of 'battleship-carrier' with a flight deck built over the after end of the ship. Moreover losses were not being replaced by new construction. No more battleships or heavy cruisers were being built, and less than half of the destroyer losses were being made good. Not only had the Japanese fighting fleet, which had at first scored such sweeping successes, become a wasting asset, but their merchant navy was also dwindling fast. By August 1943 two million tons had been lost, much of it sunk by the far-ranging American submarines; and little had been done to replace the losses. Not until the autumn of 1943 was the significance of the situation brought home to the Japanese High Command, which then took measures to conserve what was left, and at last started to sail their merchantmen in convoy. But the remedial steps were taken too late. Not only were the Japanese so desperately short of escort vessels and maritime

----

[1] See Map 15.

aircraft that the convoys could not be properly defended, but American submarine strength was now increasing rapidly; and with better trained crews and improved weapons their accomplishments continued to rise. In the last four months of 1943 they sank a further 622,000 tons of shipping, out of a total Japanese loss of 855,000 tons. It will thus be seen how, by this stage of the war, the Japanese condition had become parlous in two out of the three elements on which maritime power depends—fighting strength and transport capacity.[1] In the third element—the provision of well-placed and adequately defended bases—their prospects were steadily deteriorating; for the bases seized in 1941–42 lacked equipment and supplies, and more and more of them were coming within the reach of American shore-based and carrier-borne aircraft. With her maritime power now crumbling, Japan's hold on the whole vast Pacific theatre was bound ultimately to disintegrate. The process was delayed by the stubborn fanaticism with which her cut off garrisons continued to fight; but it was none the less ultimately inevitable.

On the Allied side losses had also been severe, but they had been replaced many times over by the stream of new ships and aircraft coming from American yards and factories; and the equipment now being provided was, thanks to American industrial genius and production capacity, greatly superior to that with which our principal Ally had started the war. Of particular importance was the fleet of new aircraft carriers, large and small, now assembling in the Central Pacific, whose share in the campaign soon to be opened was to be of the utmost importance. But before telling that story we must return briefly to the Solomon Islands theatre.

Admiral Halsey had originally intended to follow up the capture of New Georgia by attacking the neighbouring Kolombangara Island[2]; but the new strategic idea of 'leap-frogging' over one unsubdued garrison to attack another nearer to the final objective—in this case Rabaul in New Britain—was now gaining favour. By capturing Vella Lavella further to the north a sea and air blockade could be enforced against Kolombangara, thereby reducing its powerful garrison to impotence. Moreover, whereas Kolombangara was strongly defended, and to capture it a long and costly campaign would probably be necessary, Vella Lavella was known to be far more lightly held. Even before New Georgia had been completely occupied preparations for the first 'leap frog' in this theatre were accordingly put in hand.[3] At dawn on the 14th of August Rear-

---

[1] See Vol. I, pp. 5–7, for a discussion of the elements on which a maritime strategy depends.

[2] See Map 15.

[3] The earliest example of the 'leap frog' strategy may be said to have occurred in the Aleutian Islands, where the capture of Attu in May 1943 unexpectedly caused the Japanese to evacuate the more easterly island of Kiska. See Vol. II, p. 424.

The Campaign in the Solomon Islands, 1943

Above. U.S. Marines approaching Rendova Island, central Solomons, 30th June 1943.

Below. The assault on Bougainville, northern Solomons, 1st November, 1943.

(*Photographs U.S. Navy Department*)

Above. Empress Augusta Bay, Bougainville. The assault beaches, June 1943.

Below. Tanks disembarking from an L.S.T. at Cape Gloucester, New Britain, 26th December, 1943.

(*Photographs U.S. Navy Department*)

Above. Landings at Lae, New Guinea, September, 1943.

Below. The U.S. Navy's fleet type submarine *Blackfin*.

(*Photographs U.S. Navy Department*)

Landings at Cape Gloucester, New Britain, 26th December, 1943

Above. U.S. Marines building a causeway for unloading.

Below. U.S. Marines disembarking from L.S.Ts.

Admiral T. S. Wilkinson, U.S.N., who had succeeded Admiral Turner as commander of the South Pacific Amphibious Forces a month previously, sailed north from Guadalcanal with an assault force, including a New Zealand brigade, which landed next day on Vella Lavella almost unopposed. None the less six weeks were needed to subdue the garrison and occupy the whole island.[1]

Because the strain on their resources had become excessive the Japanese had actually decided in the middle of August to evacuate all the islands of the Solomons chain except Buka, Bougainville and the Shortlands.[2] Thus the capture of Vella Lavella caused them concern only because it lay on the flank of the route by which the garrison of 10,000 men on Kolombangara would have to withdraw. Their fears were well grounded; for the Americans at once blockaded the island. None the less 9,000 Japanese troops were successfully evacuated from Kolombangara, mostly by motor barges moving at night. A few skirmishes took place in August and September between the blockading light forces and the enemy's transports, but no important action was fought until the night of the 6th–7th of October, by which time the Japanese were withdrawing the remnants of the Vella Lavella garrison. Three American destroyers then engaged a superior enemy squadron, and each side lost one ship; but both the other American ships were badly damaged.[3] Once again the Japanese evacuation was successful.

Halsey's next object on the road towards Rabaul was the large island of Bougainville, on the extreme north and south of which the Japanese had constructed airfields. These were known to be strongly defended, but the centre of the island's long western coastline offered prospects of an easier assault. By gaining the use of airfields in Bougainville Allied shore-based fighters would be able to accompany and defend the bombers raiding Rabaul, only some 200 miles away. After making very thorough reconnaissances Halsey decided to land at Empress Augusta Bay.[4] Heavy bombing attacks were made on the airfields around Rabaul and on Bougainville in October, and on the 27th, as a curtain raiser to the main assault, the Treasury Islands were seized. Supported by Admiral Merrill's cruisers and destroyers and by heavy carrier strikes against the airfields, the assault forces landed on Bougainville soon after dawn on the 1st of November. By nightfall they had established a firm foothold. The Japanese Navy's reaction to the threat developing against their whole position in New Britain was delayed by the movement of the Combined Fleet, including such aircraft carriers as they were able to man, from Truk

---

[1] See Morison, Vol. VI, pp. 225–239, for a full account of the assault.
[2] See Map 15.
[3] See Morison, Vol. VI, pp. 244–252, for an account of the Battle of Vella Lavella.
[4] See Map 15.

to Eniwetok in the Marshall Islands in October[1], to deal with a westward movement by Admiral Nimitz which they had wrongly anticipated. It was the 24th of October before the Combined Fleet returned to Truk, and it thus happened that the carrier air group, which Admiral Koga had intended to disembark at Rabaul in imitation of Yamamoto's offensive of the previous April[2], did not arrive there until the day of the American landing on Bougainville. Throughout the whole of October Halsey's forces thus encountered no opposition from the enemy's carrier planes. The incorrect intelligence which caused the easterly movement of Admiral Koga's main forces undoubtedly helped the assaults in the Solomons. But the Japanese realised that they could not afford to ignore the landing in Empress Augusta Bay. On the 1st of November they therefore sent south from Rabaul a force of four cruisers and six destroyers, with the object of making a surprise descent on the American transport anchorage and so repeating the success obtained off Savo Island in August 1942.[3] Their hope was quickly proved vain. The Japanese squadron was soon reported by reconnaissance aircraft, and Admiral Merrill was ordered to intercept it. Having sent the transports south, clear of danger, his four cruisers and eight destroyers took up a position west of Cape Torokina. Radar contact was gained at 2.30 a.m. on the 2nd, and fifteen minutes later the battle began. In a long series of confused encounters the Japanese lost the cruiser *Sendai* and one destroyer; but no American ships were sunk. At daylight the surviving Japanese ships returned whence they had come, having wholly failed in their purpose.[4]

This attempt did not, however, mark the end of the Japanese reaction to the invasion of Bougainville; for Halsey quickly learnt that a strong force, including seven heavy cruisers, was being detached by Admiral Koga from the Combined Fleet to join the squadron stationed at Rabaul. As Halsey possessed no ships comparable to the enemy heavy cruisers this development had to be taken seriously, so on the 5th of November he attacked Rabaul with the carrier air groups from the *Saratoga* and *Princeton*. Six days later he repeated the blow with even greater strength, for carrier reinforcements sent to him by Admiral Nimitz had just arrived. The American carriers were themselves attacked by many shore-based aircraft, but survived unscathed; and by the damage done to nearly all the enemy ships in the harbour the threat from the reinforced Rabaul squadron was eliminated. Perhaps even more important than this success was the

---

[1] See Map 16.
[2] See Vol. II, p. 423.
[3] Ibid. pp. 224–225.
[4] Morison, Vol. VI, pp. 305–322, contains a full account of the Battle of Empress Augusta Bay.

lesson then learnt that the carrier task forces could now stand up to and repulse strong shore-based air attacks—exposure to which had previously been considered unacceptable. The significance of this was not lost on Admiral Nimitz, whose staff had now completed the plans for the first assaults in the Central Pacific.

One more of the long series of fiercely contested night encounters took place in the South Pacific theatre before the end of the year. On the 25th of November five American destroyers intercepted an equal Japanese squadron off the southern end of New Ireland and sank three of its number.[1] Furthermore the air groups disembarked from the Japanese carriers had suffered heavily for a negligible return. For all the optimistic claims made at the time not one major Allied warship was sunk by them; and very few ships of any class were even hit. Of the 173 Japanese naval aircraft which had disembarked early in November only fifty-two remained when they were recalled to Truk to rejoin their carriers twelve days later. Admiral Koga's misuse of his irreplaceable carrier aircrews by sending them to operate as a shore-based striking force had produced identical results to the similar mistake made earlier by his predecessor Yamamoto.[2]

By the end of the year Halsey had satisfactorily expanded his beach-head on Bougainville, and had completed the construction of the bomber and fighter airfields from which he hoped to dominate Rabaul decisively. The Japanese garrisons meanwhile remained entrenched and comparatively inactive around their own airfields, use of which was becoming increasingly difficult and expensive.

While Admiral Halsey's forces were steadily fighting their way up the Solomon Islands chain towards Rabaul, those of Admiral Nimitz were assembling and training for the first westward offensive from Pearl Harbour towards the distant Philippine Islands. In the South and South-West Pacific theatres strategy was conditioned greatly by geography, and especially by the fact that the islands around which the campaigns were being fought were about 3,000 miles from the assembly bases in Australia and New Zealand, which in turn were some 6,000 miles from the main supply ports on the west coast of America. In the Central Pacific similar conditions prevailed; for the advanced base at Pearl Harbour was over 2,000 miles from the western United States, and the Gilbert and Marshall Islands lay about the same distance further to the west. The innumerable atolls of those two groups stretched across some 1,200 miles of ocean[3], and

[1] See Map 15. This action is known as the Battle of Cape St. George.
[2] See Vol. II, p. 423.
[3] See Map 16.

the Allied bases recently constructed in the New Hebrides were 1,500 miles away to the south of them. Moreover, as the American offensive gathered momentum and moved westwards, the distance from the home bases on which it would largely depend for supplies and reinforcement would widen; and, apart from what might be captured from the enemy, nothing whatever could be supplied by the islands themselves. Every item of food, ammunition and equipment needed not only for the assault but throughout the period of occupation would have to be carried there across thousands of miles of ocean. In the case of petrol and oil fuel, on which the land, sea and air forces all depended for their mobility, they would have to come even further—from the oil fields and refineries in the Caribbean. As repair facilities would at first be totally lacking in the islands which Nimitz hoped to capture, a mobile repair organisation also had to be created and carried along with the fleet; and, because wastage from damage and breakdowns was likely to be large, a very liberal number of landing craft was allowed for. The problems of 'logistics' were second in importance only to the planning of the actual operations; and were probably still more intricate and complex. The Americans tackled them, as was their wont, with enormous energy and, confident in the knowledge of vast and largely untapped industrial power behind them, on a scale which to austerity-bound Britain appeared unduly lavish.[1] However just or unjust contemporary feeling on that matter may have been, it is certainly the case that the Pacific offensives were a triumph of supply, as well as of strategy and tactics.[2]

The enemy had occupied certain of the Gilbert Islands, south-east of the Marshall group, early in the war, and the American Chiefs of Staff decided that the assault on the latter could not be safely launched until Tarawa and Makin Island in the former had been secured.[3] In September and October far-reaching carrier aircraft raids were made on Marcus Island, which was only 1,000 miles from

---

[1] See Vol. II, pp. 420–422. C. B. A. Behrens, *Merchant Shipping and the Demands of War* (H.M.S.O., 1955), Appendix LXVII, deals with the wasteful use of shipping by the American military authorities.

[2] On the matter of 'austerity' Rear-Admiral E. M. Eller, U.S.N., head of the U.S Navy Department's Office of Naval History, made the following comment in 1959:

'Shortages in the Pacific were far greater, at least throughout 1943, than I think was ever realised by our own people in the Atlantic. For example, you mention DUKWs in the Sicily landings [see p. 132]. I do not remember any of these craft in the Pacific, except an experimental one, until well into 1944. In the Gilberts operations we used a battleship for a command ship [compare the specially fitted headquarters ships used in the Mediterranean combined operations of 1943, see pp. 121 fn. (1) and 176]; and even in the Marshalls campaign we had few small amphibious-type craft. We were, like everybody, always short of destroyers.'

As Admiral Eller served in the Pacific theatre throughout the war his views are based on first-hand experience and must command respect.

[3] See Map 16.

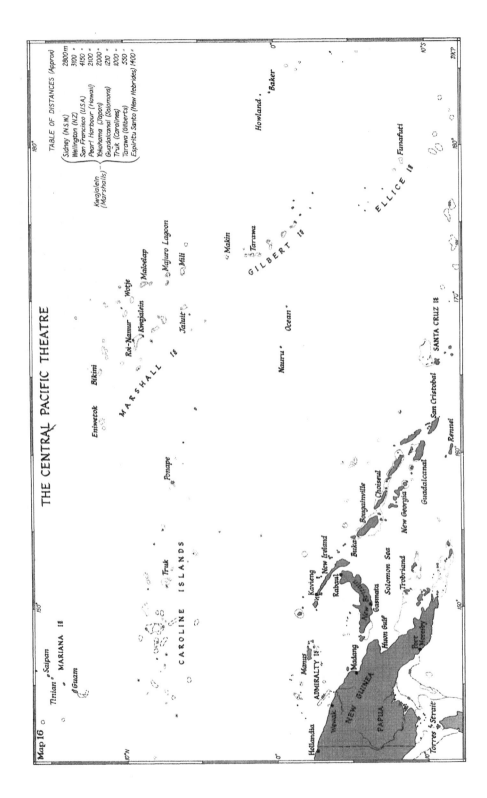

THE CENTRAL PACIFIC THEATRE

Map 16

TABLE OF DISTANCES (Approx)

Sidney (N.S.W.) .... 2800 m
Wellington (NZ) .... 3100 "
San Francisco (USA) .... 4150 "
Pearl Harbour (Hawaii) .... 2100 "
Kwajalein   Yokohama (Japan) .... 2000 "
(Marshalls)   Guadalcanal (Solomons) .. 1210 "
Truk (Carolines) .... 1000 "
Tarawa (Gilberts) .... 550 "
Espiritu Santo (New Hebrides) .... 1400 "

MARIANA I.S
Tinian · Saipan
Guam

CAROLINE   ISLANDS

Truk

Ponape

Eniwetok   Bikini

MARSHALL   I.S

Roi-Namur   Wotje
Kwajalein   Maloelap
Jaluit   Majuro Lagoon
Mili

Makin
Tarawa
GILBERT   I.S

Nauru ·   Ocean ·

ELLICE   I.S
Funafuti

Howland ·
· Baker

Manus
ADMIRALTY I.S

Hollandia

Wewak
Madang

NEW   GUINEA

PAPUA

Torres · Strait

Port Moresby

Huon Gulf

Kavieng
New Ireland
Rabaul
New Britain
Gasmata

Solomon Sea

Trobriand

Buka
Bougainville
Choiseul
New Georgia
Guadalcanal

San Cristobal

Rennel

SANTA CRUZ I.S

DX7

10°N

0°

10°S

150°   150°   170°   180°

Japan, on Wake Island and on the Gilberts. It was the attack on Wake which caused the Japanese Combined Fleet to move from Truk to Eniwetok with, as was mentioned earlier, fortunate results to Halsey's embattled forces in the Solomons.[1] By the end of October Nimitz was ready. The naval forces under his command comprised a formidable array of thirteen battleships (six of them modern), six fleet carriers (the veterans *Saratoga* and *Enterprise*, and four of the new *Essex*-class), five light fleet carriers, eight escort carriers and fifteen cruisers. Behind these main units lay numerous transports and auxiliaries, and also the flotillas of landing craft, whose crews had recently completed a period of intense training for the assaults. The larger part of this fleet and the forces which were to attack Makin Island sailed from Pearl Harbour on the 10th of November. Vice-Admiral R. A. Spruance, U.S.N., whose name had been made famous as an exponent of carrier air warfare in the Battle of Midway[2], was in general command of the operation; but responsibility for the actual assault rested with Rear-Admiral R. K. Turner, U.S.N., who had led the 'amphibious forces' in the Solomons campaign.[3] Two days after the ships from Pearl Harbour headed to the west the other arm of this great strategic pincer was set in motion by the departure northwards from the New Hebrides of the forces which had been assembled and trained in New Zealand and were to attack Tarawa. The two arms came together at a rendezvous about 400 miles south-east of Tarawa on the 19th.

On the 16th of November heavy air attacks were launched against the Gilbert Islands by shore-based aircraft working from the adjacent Ellice group. They continued daily until the assault; but in spite of this, and of the size of the forces now on the move, it was not until the 19th, when carrier aircraft struck at Nauru and a Japanese reconnaissance plane sighted Admiral Turner's ships, that the enemy suspected what was afoot. Though Admiral Koga had planned for the Combined Fleet to put to sea from Truk and engage the Americans, he was caught unprepared and in no condition to intervene effectively. Japanese records state that Koga had formed the opinion that the Allied counter-offensive in the Central Pacific would be deferred for a time on account of aircraft losses suffered by the Americans in the northern Solomons, which he had actually much over-estimated. Moreover the depletion of Koga's naval air groups in the futile Bismarck operations had been so severe that all his carriers except one had returned to Japan to re-equip; and the one carrier with him, the *Zuikaku*, had no organised air group on board. This weakness was not offset by the presence of six battleships, including

---

[1] See pp. 233–234.
[2] See Vol. II, pp. 37–42.
[3] Ibid. pp. 222–226 and 414, and this volume, p. 229.

the great 64,000-ton ships *Yamato* and *Musashi*. His cruiser strength had also been bled by the attempt to reinforce Rabaul[1], and he could muster only nine of that class of ship fit for sea. With such a force Koga could hardly hope successfully to challenge Spruance to a fleet action. All that he could do was to send his eighteen submarines out to find targets, and order his shore-based aircraft to attack. Apart from despatching cruisers hither and thither in the Marshall and Caroline Islands his surface forces remained inactive.

At dawn on the 20th of November the Americans assaulted Tarawa and Makin Island. On the latter the defenders were heavily outnumbered and were overcome comparatively easily; but Tarawa proved a very different proposition. Though the defences were strong the garrison actually numbered only 5,000 men (2,000 of whom belonged to the naval construction service); and nearly half of the fighting troops were put out of action by the preliminary bombardments. Furthermore a direct hit on the command post killed the garrison commander and most of his staff, and destroyed all centralised control. None the less the survivors fought fanatically to the end, and by the time that they were finally subdued on the 23rd under 150 prisoners (most of whom were Koreans) had been captured, and the assault forces had suffered about 3,000 casualties.[2]

The submarines sent to the scene by Admiral Koga accomplished no more than the sinking of one escort carrier, and four of their number were probably destroyed. Post-war enquiry suggests that the immunity enjoyed by the large American fleet owed much to excessive caution by Japanese submarine captains; but, however that may be, one of the lessons learnt off the Gilbert Islands was that, given good air cover and anti-submarine protection, a fleet could work in comparative safety close off an enemy-held coastline. This was very different from the experiences of the early combined expeditions in the Mediterranean, where German U-boats and bombers exacted a heavy toll.[3] The Japanese shore-based aircraft did no better than their submarines. Their own bases were constantly attacked, and when a striking force did manage to reach the American fleet it was met by a curtain of anti-aircraft fire through which few aircraft managed to penetrate. Their only success was to damage a light fleet carrier with a torpedo.

After the centre of resistance on Tarawa had been broken, the rest of the Gilbert group soon fell into American hands. Spruance's fast carrier striking force had meanwhile been unleashed against the main enemy base at Kwajalein in the Marshall Islands. With the airfields

---

[1] See p. 234.

[2] See Morison, Vol. VII, pp. 121–135 and 153–174, for a full account of the assaults on Makin Island and Tarawa.

[3] See Vol. II, pp. 333–334 and 429–430.

on Tarawa and Makin now in Allied hands the threat to the Marshalls could be driven home; and before the American carrier striking force had returned to Pearl Harbour on the 9th of December preparations were in hand to launch an offensive on an even greater scale early in 1944.

Towards the end of 1943 discussions took place between the Combined Chiefs of Staff whether the greatest possible Allied naval effort should be made in the Pacific, or whether the strength of the British Eastern Fleet should be built up with the object of striking across the Bay of Bengal against Malaya and Sumatra. For a complete study of these discussions the reader must be referred to the volumes of this series devoted to Grand Strategy.[1] Here we need only note that, although many points of detail remained to be settled at the 'Sextant' conference in Cairo in November 1943, it had become plain to the Admiralty before the latter meeting that the proponents of the Pacific strategy would win the day. The matter was of great importance to that department, because of the need to plan well in advance of sending a substantial British fleet to the distant Pacific. As early as September the Combined Chiefs of Staff had told the Navy Department and the Admiralty to examine the possibility of sending a powerful force from Britain through the Panama Canal. As most of the Italian fleet had by that time come under Allied control[2] and the *Tirpitz* had been put out of action by our midget submarines[3], the situation was, from the Admiralty's point of view, easier than at any time since the beginning of the war. Our mission in Washington had reported that the U.S. Navy 'had a definite operational requirement' for cruisers and destroyers, and the Admiralty accordingly reported that by the 1st of December they could send out a balanced force consisting of three capital ships, one or two fleet carriers, three cruisers and sixteen destroyers. This force was to be called the 'British Pacific Ocean Force', and although the movement was not carried out its planning is of interest because it demonstrates British readiness to share the burden of the Pacific war at the earliest possible moment. It was the recall from Britain of the U.S. Navy's task force, including the carrier *Ranger*[4], the decision to restart the Russian convoys in November and to run them monthly[5], and the need to strengthen the Eastern Fleet by February 1944 for offensive blows against the Andaman Islands and Sumatra which made this

---

[1] See Ehrman, *Grand Strategy*, Vol. V (H.M.S.O., 1956).

[2] See pp. 167–169.

[3] See pp. 65–69.

[4] See pp. 72–73.

[5] See p. 76.

plan abortive.[1] The discussions between the Admiralty and the Navy Department did, however, arouse for the first time doubts whether the Americans really desired to see the White Ensign in the Pacific; nor were these doubts resolved until, at the second Quebec Conference in September 1944, Mr Churchill's proposal to send out the British Pacific Fleet was 'no sooner offered than accepted' by President Roosevelt.[2] But that runs ahead of the stage now reached in our story.

---

[1] These operations, called 'Buccaneer' (Andaman Islands) and 'Culverin' (Northern Sumatra), were not actually carried out as planned for 1944. See pp. 344–346.

[2] Churchill, Vol. VI, pp. 134–135 and 136–137.

CHRONOLOGICAL SUMMARY
OF PRINCIPAL EVENTS
JANUARY 1944–MAY 1944

1944	Atlantic	Arctic	Mediterranean	Indian Ocean	Pacific	Europe
January	U-boats return to the Western Approaches	12–28. JW.56A 21–1 Feb. JW.56B	22 Allied landings at Anzio. Main Allied offensive held up on the Garigliano and Rapido rivers		31 Allied landings in the Marshall Islands	27 Russians raise the siege of Leningrad
February	Air and surface escorts and support groups sink many U-boats in the Western Approaches	20–28. JW.57	16 German counter-attacks at Anzio finally repulsed 18 Heavy fighting before Cassino	Shipping losses begin to rise again	17 Eniwetok captured 29 Allied landings in the Admiralty Islands	3 Russians cross the Estonian frontier
March	Sea and air escort and support groups continue to claim many victims	27–5 Apl. JW.58		12 Japanese offensive begins against central front in Burma		6 Russians begin spring offensive in the Ukraine

242

April	Germans abandon attacks on North Atlantic convoys until new types of U-boats become available	3 Fleet Air Arm attack and damage *Tirpitz* in Altenfiord Arctic convoys suspended		Japanese offensive held on Assam frontier 16 Eastern Fleet attacks Sabang No shipping losses during the month	22 Allied landings in the Humboldt Bay area, New Guinea	11 Russians enter the Crimea
May	North Atlantic almost completely clear of U-boats		11 Allied offensive begins in Italy 18 Monte Cassino taken 25 Junction of troops from Anzio with 5th Army advancing northwards	17 Eastern Fleet air attack on Soerabaya, Java	25 Allied landings at Biak in New Guinea	9 Russians re-capture Sebastopol

CHAPTER IX

THE BATTLE OF THE ATLANTIC
1st January–31st May, 1944
The Second Campaign in the
Western Approaches

> 'The Battle of the Atlantic was the dominating factor all through the war. Never for one moment could we forget that everything happening elsewhere, on land, at sea, or in the air, depended ultimately on its outcome.'
>
> W. S. Churchill, *The Second World War*, Vol. V, p. 6.

THE distant waters off the African and American coasts were clear of U-boats at the beginning of 1944, but in late January and early February a few arrived off West Africa and Newfoundland. They accomplished very little. In February a new group of six set out on the long journey to the Indian Ocean, the last theatre in which they had recently achieved any substantial success[1]; but an American Liberator from Ascension Island destroyed one of them, U.177, on the 6th of February. On the 13th of March there took place a particularly bad case of inhuman conduct by a U-boat crew towards survivors from a ship which they had sunk. U.852, while on passage to the Indian Ocean, encountered the Greek ship *Peleus*, which was sailing independently from Freetown to Buenos Aires, to the north-east of Ascension Island. Not until three survivors landed in Portuguese West Africa six weeks later did the merchantman's fate become known. They made it plain that, after sinking their ship, the U-boat crew had done their best to exterminate the survivors, and believed that they had done so. The three men who reached shore escaped by shamming death.[2]

Towards the end of February the U-boat Command made another attempt to arrange for mid-ocean refuelling, on which the fate of the

---

[1] See pp. 219–221.

[2] In October 1945 the Captain of U.852, Heinz Eck, three of his officers and one rating were tried by a military court in Hamburg on charges of murdering the crew of the *Peleus*. Eck and two other officers were sentenced to death, and the others to long terms of imprisonment.

245

distant operations greatly depended.[1] The 'milch cow' U.488 was sent from France to a position west of the Cape Verde Islands to replenish outward-bound boats; but American escort carriers, strongly escorted by destroyers, were again working near the Atlantic islands. On the 16th of March the U.S.S. *Block Island* sank U.801, which was bound for West Africa, and three days later repeated the success against U.1059, one of the Indian Ocean boats. Both had been seeking the 'milch cow', to fuel from her.

Next, off Cape Cod, American destroyers sank U.856 and U.550 on the 7th and 16th of April, while off the Canary Islands the U.S.S. *Guadalcanal's* aircraft caught two others (U.68 and U.515) steering for the refuelling rendezvous, and sank them both. Finally the destroyers with the American escort carrier *Croatan* caught and sank the 'milch cow' herself on the 26th. This success left one boat, U.66, in mid-ocean without fuel or provisions; but her fate was soon settled by the *Block Island's* aircraft. Thus did Dönitz's new attempt to conduct protracted operations in the remote parts of the Atlantic end in utter disaster; and in return for the very heavy losses he had suffered few Allied ships had been sunk.

For a time the enemy was more successful in reinforcing the U-boats inside the Mediterranean. The Straits of Gibraltar had always produced very difficult asdic conditions, and our air patrols were not yet dense enough to prevent a determined enemy slipping through submerged, generally by night. In the first week of January 1944 two boats ran the gauntlet and reached Toulon safely. They were followed by four more later in that month and early in February. Then an American Catalina squadron fitted with a device called the 'Magnetic Air Detector' (M.A.D.) arrived at Port Lyautey and started to work over the Straits. This instrument, which enabled a submerged U-boat to be tracked from a low-flying aircraft, was well suited to conditions in those waters; but the presence of surface ships to co-operate with the aircraft was soon shown to be essential. On the 24th of February U.761 was destroyed by British and American air and sea patrols with the help of M.A.D.

In March three U-boats got through, one was sunk (U.392 on the 16th) and one turned back. The solitary Allied success in the Straits was again achieved by the joint use of sea–air weapons. But the fact that, of the twelve U-boats which attempted the passage in the first three months of the year, nine got safely through was, from the Allied point of view, hardly satisfactory. It was left to the anti-submarine forces inside the Mediterranean to restore the balance, and by the beginning of April they had again reduced the U-boats' numbers to fifteen.[2]

---

[1] See pp. 26–27 and 31–32.

[2] See pp. 312–313.

It will be convenient to carry the story of the Gibraltar Straits passages on to the end of the period covered by this chapter. The decline of U-boat strength in the Mediterranean caused Dönitz to send out more reinforcements in April. The first boat passed in safely, but on the 15th of May U.731 was detected by an M.A.D. aircraft, which called up surface ships. Two of the latter destroyed her after a long pursuit. The U-boat Command thereupon recalled the last reinforcements, and so ended the many attempts made to build up their numbers in the Mediterranean. Since September 1941 the Germans had despatched ninety-five U-boats. Twelve were recalled, or returned early in their passages, and five were sunk in the Atlantic on the way south. Of the seventy-eight which actually reached the Straits, six were sunk, another six were damaged and withdrew, and four gave up the attempt. Sixty-two got through; but the effective work of the Mediterranean anti-submarine forces, and especially the convoy escorts, prevented the enemy's strength ever rising above twenty-six. Furthermore, once we gave a high priority to the Gibraltar Straits escorts and patrols, and were employing modern ships and aircraft, it became very hard for U-boats to pass in undetected. The statistics regarding their passages for the entire campaign are shown in Table 14 below.

Table 14. German U-boat Passages into the Mediterranean, 1941–1944

Year	No. of U-boats ordered out	On Passage in Atlantic				Gibraltar Straits Area (Europa Point to 6° West)					
		Sunk	Damaged and Returned	Defective and Returned	Cancelled	Sunk	Damaged and Returned	Gave up Attempt	Got Through	Sunk inside Mediterranean	Total in Mediterranean at end of year
1941 . .	36	2	1	1	Nil	1	5	Nil	26	5	21
1942 . .	23	Nil	Nil	6	Nil	Nil	Nil	1	16	14	23
1943 . .	22	3	Nil	1	3	2	1	2	10	20	13
1944 . .	14	Nil	Nil	Nil	Nil	3	Nil	1	10	23	Nil
TOTALS .	95	5	1	8	3	6	6	4	62	62	—

NOTES:

(1) Of the five sunk on passage in Atlantic, 4 were sunk by air attacks and 1 by surface ships.

(2) Of the six sunk in the Gibraltar Straits, 1 was sunk by air attack, 1 by surface ships and 4 were shared between aircraft and surface ships.

In the North Atlantic there were thirty U-boats at sea at the beginning of the year. Twenty of them were disposed in small groups of two or three to the west of Ireland and the south of Iceland, while ten more were patrolling about 500 miles north-east of the Azores, with the object of attacking convoys passing to and from Sierra Leone (OS-SL) and Gibraltar (KMS-MKS); but the shore-based aircraft in the Azores and surface support groups were available in strength to cover and escort convoys in those waters. On the 7th of January a support group located the enemy patrol line; but it was actually U.305 which scored the first success, by sinking the frigate *Tweed*—one of the ships then employed on searching for enemy blockade runners. The U-boat escaped unharmed.

On the 8th the surface escort of the combined south-bound convoy OS.64–KMS.38 gained contact with a U-boat, and after a very long hunt the enemy was heard trying to blow his tanks, after which the asdic contact faded. We now know that U.757 was then sunk by the frigate *Bayntun* and the Canadian corvette *Camrose*. Next day enemy aircraft reported a large convoy, probably MKS.35–SL.144, to the west of Gibraltar, homeward-bound. The U-boat group, which was already moving in that direction, prepared to attack; but German reconnaissance aircraft totally failed to keep in touch with the convoy, which passed on its way unharmed; while the supporting American escort carrier *Block Island* severely damaged U.758. On the 13th of January a Leigh-Light Wellington from the Azores, flying in support of a convoy, sank U.231 about 465 miles north-east of those islands. Most of her crew were picked up next day by the *Block Island*.

After this very bad start to his operations on the Gibraltar route the enemy sent the five survivors from the southern group of U-boats to join those which were working further north, and even dispersed the small groups into which the latter had been organised. Instead they stationed them singly, about thirty miles apart—a policy which was most unlikely to achieve success against strongly defended convoys. By the middle of January two dozen boats were available, and the U-boat Command shifted them to positions stretching over a wide arc from the Faeroes down to Brest, some 250 miles west of the British Isles. Their orders were to maintain diving patrols, and to surface only to recharge batteries. Luftwaffe aircraft were to search for and to locate our convoys, whose positions would then be signalled to the U-boats. This was the first serious attempt to work in the Western Approaches since the U-boats had been driven from those waters, and forced further out into the Atlantic in the spring of 1941.[1] But conditions were now far less favourable to the enemy than

[1] See Vol. I, Chapters XVI and XXI.

three years earlier; for our maritime air strength was much greater, and support groups were constantly available to assist any threatened convoy.

The period continued very unhappily for the U-boats. Two (U.377 and U.972) disappeared without trace in the North Atlantic at this time, and it is still uncertain whether Allied forces had any hand in their loss. On the 17th of January U.305, which had sunk the frigate *Tweed* ten days earlier, was accounted for by the *Wanderer* and *Glenarm* on their way home after a search for blockade-runners. That same day enemy aircraft reported another convoy, probably the south-bound OS.65–KMS.39, off north-west Ireland, and all U-boats in the vicinity were ordered to attack. Once again, however, the German long-range reconnaissance aircraft failed to keep in touch, with the consequence that most of the U-boats searched for their quarry in vain. Moreover one of their number, U.641, which did gain touch on the 19th, was promptly sunk by the corvette *Violet*, one of the surface escort. The U-boats next moved still closer to the coast of Ireland, between 15° and 17½° West; but they did not do so undetected. Coastal Command's No. 15 Group was rapidly reinforced by the neighbouring No. 19 Group, additional Liberator and Leigh-Light Wellington squadrons moved to the airfields in Northern Ireland, and support groups steamed to the waters where convoys appeared likely to be endangered. It was a fine example of the rapid and flexible redisposition of our forces made possible by the centralised control system established between the Admiralty and Coastal Command. Meanwhile two loosely organised groups of eight and eleven U-boats ventured to within 270 miles of Malin Head to wait for our convoys passing in and out of the North Channel from the Irish Sea.[1]

On the 27th our listening wireless stations heard a German aircraft report the positions of two large convoys (probably the outward-bound ON.221 and OS.66–KMS.40). No. 19 Group promptly intensified its sweeps, and a Beaufighter squadron moved to Northern Ireland to tackle the enemy's long-range Ju.290s and BV.222 reconnaissance planes. The escort carriers attached to the support groups normally carried six Fleet Air Arm fighters as well as a dozen Swordfish, and the former were now used to intercept German shadowers. Meanwhile the enemy had sent the U-boats in pursuit of ON.221 on the surface. They persisted in this somewhat rash measure on the 28th, in spite of the Luftwaffe having lost touch once more; and it gave Coastal Command a chance which the aircrews were quick to seize. U.271 was sunk by a U.S. Navy Liberator, and U.571 by a Sunderland of No. 461 Squadron. Next day the enemy gave up

---

[1] See Map 17.

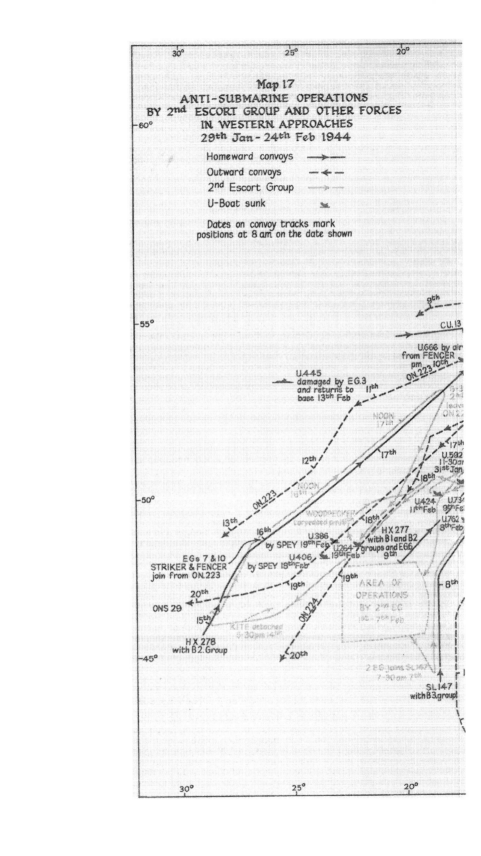

Map 17
ANTI-SUBMARINE OPERATIONS
BY 2nd ESCORT GROUP AND OTHER FORCES
IN WESTERN APPROACHES
29th Jan – 24th Feb 1944

Homeward convoys ——→——
Outward convoys — ←— —
2nd Escort Group ·····→·····
U-Boat sunk

Dates on convoy tracks mark
positions at 8 am on the date shown

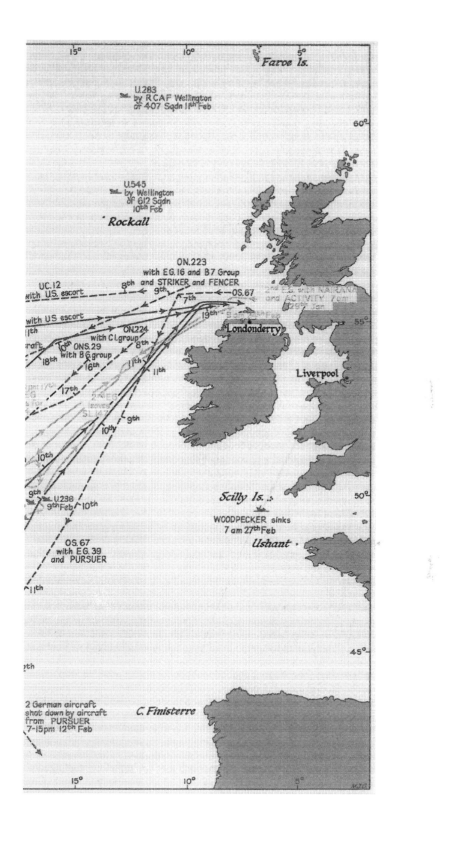

15°   10°   5°

Faroe Is.

U.283
by R.C.A.F. Wellington
of 407 Sqdn 11th Feb

60°

U.545
by Wellington
of 612 Sqdn
10th Feb

Rockall

ON.223
with E.G.16 and B7 Group
and STRIKER and FENCER

8th   9th   7th   OS.67

UC.12
with U.S. escort

with US escort
11th

with U.S. escort

2nd E.G. with NAIRANA
and ACTIVITY 7am
29th Jan

55°

19th

ON.224
with CI.group 8th

Londonderry

craft

10th ONS.29
with B.6 group 11th

18th 16th

Liverpool

11th

17th

9th

10th

9th

U.238
9th Feb 10th

Scilly Is.

50°

WOODPECKER sinks
7 am 27th Feb

Ushant

OS.67
with E.G. 39
and PURSUER

11th

45°

9th

2 German aircraft
shot down by aircraft
from PURSUER
7-15pm 12th Feb

C. Finisterre

15°   10°   5°

the chase, blaming the failure on the German Air Force, and moved the U-boats further to seaward; but they were not to escape retribution for their appearance in the focal area of all our Atlantic shipping. The escort carriers *Nairana* and *Activity*, screened by five sloops of Captain Walker's 2nd Escort Group, rounded Malin Head early on the 29th, and set course to the south-west to work in support of convoys off western Ireland.[1] Captain R. M. T. Taylor of the *Nairana* was in command until the carriers parted company on the afternoon of the 7th of February, after which Captain Walker conducted the operations now to be described. Early on the 31st the five sloops were steaming in line abreast with the carriers zig-zagging two miles astern, when the *Wild Goose* (Lieutenant-Commander D. E. G. Wemyss) obtained a contact.[2] She quickly warned the *Nairana* which, in course of operating her aircraft, was steering towards the danger spot; and, in order to discourage the U-boat from firing torpedoes at the carrier, carried out an attack without delay. Walker's *Starling* now joined in, and the *Wild Goose's* contact was, in the group commander's words, 'handed to him on a plate'. He at once manœuvred astern of the U-boat to fire a creeping pattern.[3] After fourteen charges had been dropped a violent explosion shook the ships, and wreckage soon began to rise to the surface. It marked the grave of U.592, which had actually been trying to return home after being damaged in an earlier air attack. The support group then continued the patrol, moving south and operating aircraft whenever the weather permitted, until the afternoon of the 7th of February when Walker joined the combined convoys SL.147–MKS.38. Enemy aircraft had reported this convoy in 41° North 16° West, and also two others (probably the Caribbean tanker convoy UC.12 of twenty-six ships and the combined convoys OS.67–KMS.41) which were both close off the north-west corner of Ireland outward-bound. On receiving these reports Dönitz divided his forces, and sent half of the twenty-two boats he had available against the north-bound SL.147–MKS.38, and the other half to find the two south-bound convoys. Aircraft from Nos. 15 and 19 Groups swept the waters ahead of the former on the night of the 7th–8th and made two attacks; but neither did any damage. Luftwaffe planes were still shadowing the convoy, and the carriers' fighters had tried to intercept them, though without success.

At 10.30 p.m. on the 8th the *Wild Goose's* alert lookouts sighted a U-boat, asdic contact was soon gained and held, while the *Starling*

---

[1] See Map 17.

[2] See D. E. G. Wemyss, *Walker's Groups in the Western Approaches* (Liverpool Post and Daily Echo, 1948, republished as *Relentless Pursuit* by William Kimber, 1955), Chapter V, for a graphic account of these operations by the 2nd Escort Group.

[3] See pp. 48–49.

and *Woodpecker* (Commander H. L. Pryse, R.N.R.) closed in. At 11.17 the *Woodpecker* fired a twenty-two charge barrage. It was so well placed that no further action was required. 'Come over here' signalled Walker to Commander Pryse 'and look at the mess you have made.' That was the end of U.762.

Enemy aircraft were again over the convoy during the next night; but the only consequence of their efforts to 'home' U-boats to the scene was to bring two more of them into the deadly clutches of Walker's little ships. The enemy actually called the operation off early on the 9th, because the U-boats could not face such strong air cover in daylight; but the escorts' offensive still continued.

At 6.15 a.m. on the 9th, only a few hours after the sinking of U.762, the *Wild Goose* detected another U-boat about ten miles on the port beam of the convoy, turned towards and picked her up by asdic soon after the radar contact had faded. The sloop dodged an acoustic torpedo, attacked with depth charges, and then held on until the *Starling* had joined her. Walker went ahead with his well-tried tactics of a creeping attack, followed by a barrage. The results strongly suggested that the enemy was damaged, but the harmless explosion of two more acoustic torpedoes showed that he was not yet finished. At 9.40 a.m. Walker repeated the same tactics, and that time U.734 must have disintegrated; for ample evidence came to the surface. The two sloops then set off to join the *Kite* and *Magpie*, which had been sent ahead of the convoy soon after dawn to search for another U-boat, whose presence had been indicated by direction-finding wireless. The *Kite* had obtained a radar contact at 6.40 a.m., just after the *Wild Goose* had first detected U.734, and soon afterwards she sighted her quarry at 800 yards range, coming out of a patch of mist. She dropped one charge to counter-mine any acoustic torpedoes which might have been fired—and an adjacent explosion suggested that the precaution had been very necessary—and then moved in to attack. Five patterns of charges were fired, and when the *Magpie* arrived the *Kite* directed her creeping attack. The *Kite* herself followed up with twenty-six more charges; but the U-boat survived them all. By noon the *Starling* and *Wild Goose* were on the scene, Walker took over the contact, and directed the *Kite* in two more creeping attacks. Again the 'wily enemy' escaped. The *Kite* was now short of depth charges, so her place was taken by the *Magpie*. Once more Walker directed the attack, and at about 3 p.m. the combination of a hedgehog salvo, a creeping attack and the follow-up barrage at last proved lethal to U.238. It had taken eight hours and the expenditure of 266 depth charges to accomplish her destruction. The *Kite* was now sent to replenish with depth charges from a merchantman in the approaching Halifax convoy HX.277, while the other ships of the group rejoined SL.147–MKS.38, with which they remained until the 10th.[1] Early that day U.256 fired an acoustic torpedo at one of the Halifax convoy's escorting destroyers, and claimed, erroneously, to have sunk her. By that evening both convoys had passed through the danger zone.

The support group next patrolled independently under the *Woodpecker*, since Walker's *Starling* had also gone to seek more depth charges. At 1 a.m. on the 11th, when steaming in line abreast one-and-a-half miles apart, the *Wild Goose's* highly experienced asdic team obtained another contact. She and the *Woodpecker* made three attacks, the last of which produced unmistakable evidence of success. U.424 had been sunk.

To add still further to the busy scene in the waters west of Ireland, ON.223 had meanwhile come out by the North Channel, and was crossing to the south-west. The escort carrier *Fencer* was with the escort, and on the afternoon of the 10th her Swordfish sighted and sank U.666. The south-bound OS.67–KMS.41 was next sighted and reported by the U-boats, which trailed it for twenty-four hours and fired several acoustic torpedoes at the escorts. In spite of the usual prodigal enemy claims being made none was damaged. Coastal Command sent out very strong air cover, and during the night of the 10th–11th of February a Leigh-Light Wellington of No. 612 Squadron damaged U.545 so seriously that her crew abandoned ship and scuttled her in a position some 200 miles to the west of the Hebrides. Another aircraft from the same squadron was, however, shot down by U.283 late that night; but she was not long unavenged, for at 4 a.m. on the 11th an R.C.A.F. Wellington of No. 407 Squadron, which was supporting the convoys off Ireland, sank her.

Convoy OS.67–KMS.41 had with it the escort carrier *Pursuer*, and her fighters drove off an attack by long-range He.177 bombers on the evening of the 12th, and shot down one enemy. They also destroyed a shadowing FW.200 that day. Meanwhile the Commander-in-Chief, Western Approaches, had ordered Walker's group to go to the support of convoy HX.278, which was approaching from the south-west. The sloops set off, joined the convoy on the 15th and replenished again with fuel and depth charges. We will return to it shortly, for it is time to see how this protracted operation appeared to the enemy. Although Dönitz's headquarters were aware that the U-boats were meeting very strong opposition, they had little idea of the severity of the losses they had so far suffered. They did, however, shift the boats 150 miles further west on the 13th. That day German reconnaissance aircraft were seeking the next outward-bound convoy off Northern Ireland. U.445 claimed, quite wrongly, to have sunk a

---

[1] See Map 17.

destroyer in the evening; but she was heavily counter-attacked by the ships of the 3rd Escort Group, damaged, and had to return home.

Late on the 15th another outward-bound convoy, actually OS.68 though the enemy believed it to be ON.224, was reported by aircraft off north-west Ireland. No less than twenty U-boats were ordered to close towards it; but, as had happened so often before, the Luftwaffe found it impossible to keep in constant touch with their quarry. The first two Ju.290s to be sent out on the 16th were shot down by Fleet Air Arm fighters and Coastal Command's interception patrols, and the result was that the convoy was not reported again until late in the afternoon. The enemy thereupon decided to attack during the night of the 17th–18th and concentrated a score of U-boats in lines three deep across its path. As, however, their night air reconnaissance failed, the U-boats did not receive the expected homing signals. In fact there were two convoys approaching the enemy concentration, for ONS.29 was about 150 miles south-west of ON.224, and the latter was overtaking the former. The threat to them both had not gone unobserved in London; strong air cover was being continuously provided by Coastal Command, and three escort groups had been diverted from HX.278, which had now reached safe waters. The 2nd and 7th Escort Groups, with Walker in command, were sent to reinforce ON.224, while the 10th Group joined up with ONS.29. The former convoy was also diverted further to the south during the night of 17th–18th; but all this remained hidden from the enemy until late on the 18th, because his air searches had once again failed. When the German wireless-interception service revealed ON.224's diversion on the afternoon of the 18th, they sent the U-boats in pursuit. At 3.20 p.m. the 10th Escort Group obtained a contact near ONS.29, and the frigate *Spey* sank U.406. Among the forty-five survivors was a party of scientists embarked to investigate radar counter-measures, and from them we gained valuable information on enemy progress in that technique.

By the small hours of the 19th the two convoys ON.224 and ONS.29 were not far apart, and the U-boats were still pursuing them. Liberators forced several of them down that night. At daylight Walker decided to sweep back along the convoy track to seek enemies whose presence had been detected earlier. At 10 a.m. the *Woodpecker* obtained a contact, and after a seven-hour hunt she and the *Starling* forced U.264 to surface and abandon ship. It was the group's sixth success in this remarkable operation, and it was perhaps appropriate that this further victim of Walker's deadly tactics was the first U-boat fitted with the new 'Schnorkel' to operate at sea.[1] That same afternoon the 10th Escort Group, which was on its way to join ON.224,

---

[1] See p. 18 and fn. (1).

added to the score by sinking U.386. Walker's ships meanwhile continued to search the scene of their latest success. But it was the enemy who got in the final blow. At 10 p.m., while following up another wireless report, the *Woodpecker's* stern was blown off by an acoustic torpedo fired by U.764, which escaped unharmed. The stricken sloop was taken in tow, firstly by the *Starling* and then by tugs. Unhappily, after nearly seven days of agonisingly slow progress, she capsized off the Scilly Islands early on the 27th. Miraculously not a man of her company was lost.

Thus ended an operation which had, for the 2nd Escort Group, lasted twenty-seven days. It marked the climax not only of Captain Walker's achievements but of the whole long-drawn, bitter offensive by the convoy escorts against their cunning and ruthless enemies. It cost the Germans eleven U-boats, of which six were sunk by Walker's ships—three of them in under seventeen hours; and in return for those losses all that the U-boats could show was the torpedoing of the *Woodpecker*, the shooting down of two Coastal Command aircraft, and the sinking of one straggler from a convoy coming home from Iceland on the 8th of February. Twelve large Atlantic convoys passed safely in and out of the Western Approaches in that period, and at least two of them were saved from heavy attacks. The 2nd Escort Group had repeatedly refuelled and replenished with depth charges (of which its ships expended no less than 634) at sea, and not for one hour of the day or night during those four weeks was the vigilance and instant readiness of the group relaxed. Under Walker's leadership they had become a perfectly trained team 'like a well drilled three-quarter line, passing and inter-passing in a way which was a pleasure to watch'.[1] Very few signals were made, for every ship knew exactly what was expected of her; and confidence in their leader and in each other was complete. Rarely can such a welcome have been given to men returning from 'the dangers of the sea and the violence of the enemy', or have been better earned, than the ringing cheers of the whole Liverpool base when the *Starling, Wild Goose* and *Magpie* berthed in Gladstone Dock on the 25th of February 1944.[2]

Dönitz attributed his defeat to the repeated failures of the German air reconnaissance, especially on the night of the 17th–18th of February; but he remained convinced that success could be achieved in this type of operation, and declared his intention of persisting in them. At Hitler's conference on the 26th he demanded more long-range aircraft and higher priority for the new Type XXI boats.[3]

---

[1] D. E. G. Wemyss, *Walker's Groups in the Western Approaches*, p. 134.

[2] The *Wren* missed this welcome because she had been standing by the stricken *Woodpecker*, and the *Kite* had returned to harbour earlier with condenser trouble.

[3] See pp. 17–18.

Meanwhile he dissolved the groups off western Ireland, and sent the eighteen boats with full fuel tanks 700 miles out into mid-Atlantic, to individual patrol positions far apart from each other. It will be told later how they fared.

Turning now to the Bay of Biscay, the reader will remember how, at the end of 1943, U-boats crossing it submerged had again achieved a high degree of immunity from air attacks.[1] This, and the fact that by the early days of 1944 many of them were fitted with a new 3·7-centimetre (1·4-inch) anti-aircraft gun and an efficient receiver to detect our short-wave radar transmissions, had restored their confidence somewhat; and they thus became less careful over surfacing by night only for the minimum time needed to charge their batteries. Dönitz also gave permission for boats fitted with the new gun to surface by day. Coastal Command, however, had a new squadron of Leigh-Light Liberators (No. 224) ready for operations. Night sightings and attacks thus increased in January, and four U-boats were damaged by night-flying aircraft. Furthermore when U.426, which had the new gun, was sighted in daylight by a Sunderland of No. 10 (R.A.A.F.) Squadron and tried to fight it out, she was sunk. After another boat had been damaged Dönitz cancelled his permission to surface by day. This and the diversion of No. 19 Group's main strength to the waters off Ireland[2], caused a decline in actions in the Bay during the latter part of January. Coastal Command next shifted its patrols further inshore, to the swept channels which the U-boats had to use to approach or leave the Biscay bases.[3] Several attacks followed, and U.364 was sunk on the 30th by a Leigh-Light Wellington of No. 172 Squadron which, unfortunately, was herself shot down and lost with all hands. Of the sixty-six U-boats which crossed the Bay in January only two were sunk and four damaged. February proved even less successful for No. 19 Group's patrols. In spite of an increase of flying effort, out of fifty U-boats which crossed the Bay none was even damaged; and the shooting down of a Liberator and a Halifax by U.763 during the night of the 4th–5th showed that the enemy could still hit back hard. In March the threat in the North-Western Approaches had subsided, and No. 19 Group's full strength was again devoted to the Bay patrols. Yet successes remained few and far between. On the 10th a fierce sea-air battle took place around a Japanese submarine sighted inward-bound off the north coast of Spain. She was escorted by four torpedo-boats and eight Ju.88s. Two of Coastal Command's 'Tsetse' Mosquitos, which had six-pounder guns, attacked the submarine, Liberators bombed the torpedo-boats, and fighter Mosquitos engaged the air escort. Four Ju.88s

---

[1] See pp. 29–30.

[2] See p. 249.

[3] See Map 1.

were shot down; but neither the submarine nor its surface escort was damaged. Coastal Command meanwhile continued the inshore sweeps at the entrances to the German approach channels, and on the 25th 'Tsetse' Mosquitos there sank U.976 with their guns—the first instance of such a success. In spite of more aircraft being employed than ever before, out of fifty-three U-boats which crossed the Bay in March only one was sunk and two damaged; and the patrolling aircraft suffered substantial losses from U-boat gunfire and at the hands of the German fighters. The results were not regarded as satisfactory at Coastal Command Headquarters, particularly with regard to the ineffectiveness of the night attacks. Once again the need for better training of the aircrews was stressed, and one of our submarines was therefore allocated to carry out intensive exercises with the aircraft in the Irish Sea.

At the end of March Dönitz was told to form a group of forty U-boats and keep them ready for inshore work in the event of an Allied invasion of Europe. This caused a big decline in passages across the Bay.

In the northern transit area there was not much activity on either side for the first two months of the year. No. 18 Group and the Iceland-based squadrons of No. 15 Group were, as has been told[1], fully engaged on convoy work to the west of Ireland; while the enemy was reinforcing his northern flotilla against our Arctic convoys, and also forming an inshore group in Norway similar to that in western France already mentioned. Not until late in March did they resume outward passages by the northern transit route; and when they did so the policy of staying submerged as much as possible was completely successful. Apart from one U-boat, which was sunk by the 2nd Escort Group while supporting an Arctic convoy on the 29th[2], all got through in March and April. Even after the Western Approaches had quietened down and air patrols could be fully resumed in the north, they accomplished no successes. On the convoy routes the sea and air escorts were able to tell a very different tale, and once again the superiority of convoy over patrolling as an offensive strategy was strikingly demonstrated.

U.257 was returning from a mid-Atlantic rendezvous with a blockade-runner when, on the 24th of February, she was detected by the 6th Escort Group, which was supporting convoy SC.153, and was promptly sunk by the Canadian frigate *Waskesiu*. On the following night three frigates of the 1st Escort Group, which was on anti-submarine patrol in 49° 45′ North, 26° 20′ West, despatched U.91. The *Gore* had detected her late on the 25th, but the enemy went

---

[1] See pp. 249-254.
[2] See p. 273.

Captain F. J. Walker, Commander of the 2nd Escort Group. By Stephen Bone.

(*National Maritime Museum*)

Off duty on an escort vessel's mess-deck (H.M.S. *Widgeon*, 1943).

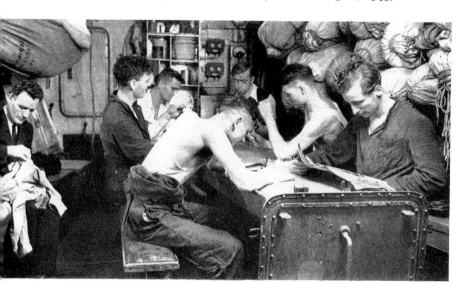

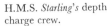
The 2nd Escort Group in action

H.M.S. *Starling's* depth charge crew.

An attack by H.M.S. *Kite*, February 1944.

H.M.S. *Magpie*, followed by other ships of the 2nd Escort Group, entering Gladstone dock, Liverpool, 25th February, 1944.

very deep, and it was not until the small hours of the next morning that she was blown to the surface. A 'free for all' gunfight ensued, after which the U-boat surrendered. On the 29th the *Garlies* of the same group obtained another contact. Repeated attacks with depth charges and hedgehogs were carried out by the *Affleck*, *Garlies* and *Gore* all that day, but at nightfall the enemy was still dodging about skilfully at a very great depth. The moon set at 2 a.m. on the 1st of March, and the escorts expected the U-boat to take advantage of the darkness and come to the surface; but he did no such thing. All that night the escorts held on to the contact, and at dawn they resumed their attacks. The enemy's cunning, however, seemed unimpaired, and he even survived a mass creeping attack by four ships, in which 104 depth charges were released. The effect was described, no doubt accurately, as a 'marine convulsion'; but it brought no results. The weather was now deteriorating, and after twenty-nine hours of cease-less hunting the ships' crews were becoming exhausted. At 4 p.m. the *Gore* and *Garlies* had to leave for Gibraltar, but the *Affleck* and *Gould* managed to hold on to the enemy, in spite of the asdic con-ditions having become very bad. Then at 7.20 p.m. the echo suddenly improved, and the *Gould* was hit by an acoustic torpedo. The *Affleck* sighted U.358 at 1,500 yards range, and finished her off with depth charges and gunfire. Only one survivor was picked up from the U-boat, because the *Affleck* had to rescue the crew of the sinking *Gould*. The hunt had lasted for thirty-eight hours, and was the longest continuous hunt of the war.[1] Tribute must be paid to the enemy's endurance, and to the fact that he fought to the end, rather than surface and surrender. On the same day American destroyers of the U.S.S. *Block Island's* group sank U.709 and U.603.

Next there took place another very long hunt. C2 Group was a mixed R.N. and R.C.N. group under Royal Navy leadership. It was escorting HX.280 when, on the 5th of March, the Canadian des-troyer *Gatineau* obtained a contact. Between 10.28 a.m. and 9.20 p.m. fifteen attacks, in which six ships took part, were made. Then there was a lull until shortly after midnight on the 5th–6th. The enemy was as clever and as determined as U.358 had been during the 1st Escort Group's prolonged hunt. He used every evasive trick, and every device which might confuse the hunters; but the ships held on, and at the end the enemy's morale collapsed. At 3.30 p.m., thirty hours after the first contact, U.744 surfaced and abandoned ship.

The surviving U-boats now moved further north, and on the night of the 8th–9th of March U.575 not only scored one of their rare

---

[1] The longest hunt of all was that for U.616 in the Mediterranean, which lasted for more than three days (May 13th–17th 1944, see p. 326); but that prolonged 'swamp operation' comes in a somewhat different category to the hunt for U.358, with which the pursuers maintained virtually continuous contact.

successes by sinking the corvette *Asphodel* from a group which was supporting convoy SL.150–MKS.41, but then survived an eighteen-hour hunt. On the 10th C1 Group, another mixed British-Canadian group, sank U.845 while escorting SC.154; and a few hours later a Sunderland of No. 422 R.C.A.F. Squadron attacked U.625 in face of heavy gunfire and injured her mortally. The enemy surfaced, signalled 'Fine bombing' to the circling Sunderland, and then sank. The U-boat Command sent two boats to search for the survivors' dinghies; but they were never found.

Next the enemy constantly shifted his patrol positions to prevent them being accurately fixed by our reconnaissance aircraft and intelligence organisation; but it was in vain. On the 13th U.575 was attacked by aircraft from the Azores, which also called the escorts of convoy ON.227 and the U.S.S. *Bogue* to the scene; and between them all they finished her off. On the following night Swordfish from the carrier *Vindex*, which was now working with the 2nd Escort Group, sank U.653, with the help of the *Starling* and *Wild Goose*. This was Captain Walker's thirteenth kill. His group next went to join the Arctic convoys, where we shall meet it again in another chapter.[1]

On the 22nd of March Dönitz, tacitly admitting defeat, evacuated a large area in the central Atlantic, the scene of his recent heavy losses, and cancelled all further operations against convoys. He told Hitler that they could not be renewed until the new types of U-boat and the improved defensive devices mentioned earlier were available; and the Luftwaffe's air reconnaissance also had to be improved. Meanwhile he would build up the strength of the inshore groups in Norway and western France in accordance with Hitler's plans to deal with an Allied invasion of Europe. But the truth was that the U-boats had again been heavily defeated by our sea and air convoy escorts. Never again were our convoys seriously threatened. Between January and March 1944 105 convoys of 3,360 merchant vessels crossed the northern ocean, and only three ships were lost. During this period thirty-six U-boats were sunk in the theatre, and no less than twenty-nine of them met their end on or near the main convoy routes. Surface vessels sank eighteen of them, shore-based aircraft nine and carrier-borne aircraft four. By the 1st of May only five U-boats remained scattered about in the North Atlantic; but the convoy escorts soon made what was virtually a clean sweep of the ocean.

U.302 sank two ships in convoy SC.156 on the 6th of April, but was then sunk by the frigate *Swale* of the escort. Other surface escorts despatched U.962, U.448 and U.986 during the month, while Coastal Command aircraft added U.342 and U.311, and the large

---

[1] See p. 273.

1,600-ton 'U-Cruiser' U.851, which was bound for the Indian Ocean, disappeared without trace at about that time. In May the surface escorts added two more to their tremendous total of successes, and Dönitz then abandoned all attempt at offensive operations. The last two U-boats were kept on weather-reporting duties only; and even so they were constantly and severely harried by aircraft. At the end of this phase there were precisely three U-boats left in the whole, vast ocean which had so long been their main battle ground.

While the enemy was suffering this decisive defeat we had carried out another re-organisation of the North Atlantic convoy system. The necessity for this measure arose through certain escort groups being withdrawn from the Western Approaches Command to take part in the invasion of Normandy. Greater economy of escorts could be achieved by re-classifying the convoys into three instead of two categories of speed, and by accepting the sailing of larger convoys. Thus the last slow west-bound convoy of the old series (ONS.32) sailed from Britain on the 28th of March, and the last of the corresponding east-bound series (SC.157) started its homeward journey from Halifax on the 13th of April. Thereafter the convoys in both directions were divided into Fast, Medium and Slow categories, with rated speeds of ten, nine and eight knots respectively.[1] Some of these convoys were very large. It was now nothing uncommon for a homeward-bound one to consist of more than a hundred ships, while outward convoys frequently contained about eighty. The risk of causing severe congestion in the arrival ports was reduced by detaching groups of the faster ships towards the end of the journeys. Many changes had been made in the Atlantic convoy system since September 1939[2], and the only two series which had run continuously since the beginning were those homeward-bound from Halifax or New York (HX), and from Sierra Leone (SL). The convoy system, the linchpin of Allied maritime strategy, was now virtually world-wide, and in April 1944 Britain and America were between them operating no less than 236 separate series of trade and military convoys.

To return to the more distant operations by the U-boats, ten more sailed for the Indian Ocean towards the end of April 1944, and on their way south they managed to sink three independently-routed ships; but neither the five stationed off West Africa nor the three off the eastern seaboard of America scored any successes at all in May. The end of that month did, however, bring the enemy a success

---

[1] The suffixes F, M and S were added to the identification letters HX and ON of these convoys.

[2] See Vol. I, pp. 92–93, 343–345, 451–457 and Maps 9 and 38. Also Vol. II, pp. 109, 214, etc.

against the hard-hitting American escort carriers, which had inflicted such heavy losses since they began to work on the central Atlantic convoy routes in June 1943. U.549, which was on her way to Brazilian waters, encountered the U.S.S. *Block Island* south-west of Madeira on the 29th of May, sank the carrier and damaged one of her destroyer escorts. Though the U-boat was quickly accounted for by the other destroyers present, it was a sad end to a ship with a splendid record.

At the end of this phase there were very few U-boats in distant waters. Four were still on the way to the Indian Ocean, but there were only two left in West African waters, and two others off eastern America. Since the 1st of September 1943 the enemy had sent forty-two U-boats to patrol in the remote parts of the Atlantic, where they still hoped to find lightly protected or unescorted targets. The sum of their accomplishments had been to sink twenty-seven Allied ships in those nine months; but twelve of their own number had succumbed to our various counter-measures. In addition, twenty-one boats had been sent to the Indian Ocean in the same period, but ten of them were sunk while on passage.

In the Bay of Biscay and on the northern transit routes, the need for intensive training of our aircrews in night attacks reduced the amount of flying carried out in April; but the retention of many U-boats for the new inshore groups had simultaneously reduced the numbers on passage.[1] On the 11th of April there was a fierce air battle above the Bay of Biscay, where U.255 was being escorted home by surface ships and Ju.88s. The 'Tsetse' Mosquitos did not damage the U-boat, but seven German aircraft were shot down for the loss of four Mosquito fighters. The only success obtained by the Biscay air patrols during the month was the sinking of U.193 by a Leigh-Light Wellington of No. 612 Squadron on the 28th. The traffic across the Bay declined still further in May, and the only important fight was against U.846, which was one of the ten boats bound for the Indian Ocean, mentioned above. She shot down a Halifax on the night of the 1st–2nd, was again unsuccessfully attacked next night, and was finally sunk in the early hours of the 4th by an R.C.A.F. Wellington.

The early days of May, however, produced a dramatic change in the far north. The thaw of ice in the Baltic permitted the sailing of U-boats from Kiel to the Atlantic and Arctic to be restarted, and Dönitz had decided to reinforce his flotilla stationed in north Norway to work against our Arctic convoys. Meanwhile the Home Fleet's aircraft carriers were carrying out sweeps against enemy shipping

---

[1] See Table 15 (p. 263).

moving along the Norwegian coast[1]; and to enable the U-boats to seize any chance of attacking the carriers the enemy ordered them to use a route well out into the North Sea, instead of passing up the Inner Leads. The hours of daylight were, however, now so long that to charge batteries in darkness was virtually impossible; and this added to the perils which the U-boats had to face. In the spring of 1940, during the Norwegian campaign, we ourselves had learnt to our cost the hazards of operating submarines in those waters under such conditions.[2] The rôles were now reversed.

As soon as the U-boats' northward movements were recognised, Coastal Command reorganised and strengthened the air patrols. It was appropriate that the first success to the new patrols fell to a Norwegian-manned Sunderland of No. 330 Squadron, which sank U.240 on the 16th of May. The Sunderland herself was, however, so severely damaged by A.A. fire that she only just managed to reach her base. Two days later U.241, which was outward-bound for the Atlantic, was sighted and sunk by one of No. 210 Squadron's Catalinas. Aircraft from No. 15 Group and from Iceland were now transferred to reinforce the patrols flying to the north-east of the Faeroes. U.476 was damaged by another Catalina on the 18th, and then, as had happened so often before in such circumstances, the Germans sent U-boats to her assistance, while Coastal Command despatched more aircraft to finish off the damaged enemy. U.476, however, was still defending herself stoutly, and shot down the Sunderland which next attacked. But the enemy could not save her, and after another U-boat had rescued her crew she was scuttled in the early hours of the 25th. Finally a Liberator sighted the rescuing U-boat (U.990) a few hours later, and sank her. The survivors of both crews were, however, picked up by a German patrol vessel. Meanwhile further to the south a Sunderland of No. 4 Operational Training Unit had sunk U.675 on the 24th. Still more of Coastal Command's strength was now diverted to these fruitful waters; and on the 27th U.292, on passage to the Atlantic, was sunk by one of No. 59 Squadron's Liberators. Next, on the 3rd of June a Canadian aircraft sank U.477 which, although fitted with 'Schnorkel'[3], had rashly decided to fight it out on the surface.

These successes were all the more welcome because they came to No. 18 Group's aircrews after many months of arduous but unrewarded flying, often in very bad weather, in these high latitudes. During the first four-and-a-half months of 1944 no results at all had been obtained. Then between the 16th of May and the 3rd of June, when there were thirty-two U-boats in the area, fifteen were

---

[1] See p. 279.

[2] See Vol. I, pp. 149 and 179.

[3] See p. 18.

attacked, seven were sunk, and four were compelled to return. These were by far the best results ever obtained in the northern transit area. The only disturbing feature was that all the boats fitted with Schnorkel, except the rash U.477 already mentioned, got through safely.

Meanwhile the enemy had sent five Schnorkel boats from the Biscay ports to the north coast of Brittany towards the end of May. They were intended to counter the inshore sweeps by which our surface ships and coastal forces were now making German traffic in the Channel more costly, and were also to gain experience of working in those waters against an invasion fleet. But No. 19 Group's aircraft were already scouring the western Channel for German shipping, and the air activity was so intense that the enemy quickly thought better of it, and recalled the boats.

As the month of May 1944 virtually marked the end of the Bay Offensive by Coastal Command, its results can conveniently be summarised here. It was almost entirely undertaken by No. 19 Group, whose aircraft, in forty-one months of flying, sank fifty U-boats and damaged another fifty-six out of a total of 2,425 which had passed into and out from the Bay of Biscay bases. The losses suffered by the Royal Air Force were, however, heavy. No less than 350 of No. 19 Group's aircraft failed to return from missions over the Bay.[1]

The accomplishments of the air patrols must not, however, be studied in isolation from the rest of the war against the U-boats, and the conclusion of the story of the Battle of the Atlantic up to the end of May 1944 offers an opportunity to compare them with the achievements of the convoy air escorts. It should not, of course, be assumed that had the air patrols been reduced the escorts could have been correspondingly strengthened. The former were in fact largely flown by short- and medium-range aircraft, which could have contributed nothing to meeting the urgent need for air escorts in mid-Atlantic. Until June 1943 few 'Very Long-range Aircraft' worked in the Bay, and at the time when such aircraft were allocated to patrol work the victories of the previous May in the North Atlantic had temporarily reduced the opportunities for convoy escorts to sink U-boats; for the few enemies still operating in the north were showing a marked tendency to avoid involvement in convoy battles. None the less, the contrast between the results shown in the two succeeding tables is striking. Taking the Bay patrols first (Table 15), it will be seen that until the end of May 1942 their accomplishments were negligible; and, for all that the flying hours increased enormously during the next eleven months, only one per cent of the U-boats on passage was sunk—and at the high cost of sixteen aircraft lost for

---

[1] See Table 15 (p. 263).

each of them. Then Dönitz cancelled the order to pass across the Bay on the surface at night.[1] So apprehensive was he regarding the increasing effectiveness of our night-flying radar-fitted patrol aircraft that at the end of April 1943 he ordered the U-boats to stay on the surface by day and fight it out with the aircraft. For just over three months, and in spite of heavy losses, he stubbornly persisted with these disastrous tactics. Such a rich harvest was then reaped by Coastal Command that the percentage of U-boats sunk on passage increased ten-fold compared with the preceding period, and at a far lower cost in aircraft losses. When Dönitz at last rescinded the fatal order we were faced with the same situation as had prevailed earlier; and the results achieved by the air patrols declined to approximately the previous figure. In fact it now appears that, but for Dönitz's error, the 'Bay Offensive' would only have achieved very moderate results throughout the whole war. In making a final assessment of the accomplishments of Coastal Command's patrols allowance must, however, be made for the severe strain which they undoubtedly imposed on U-boat crews. The War Diary of the U-boat Command makes it plain that the delays caused to boats on

Table 15. The Bay Offensive by Coastal Command of the Royal Air Force 1st January, 1941–31st May, 1944

| Period | Total Hours of Flying on Patrols (Day and Night) | Allied Aircraft Losses | Number of U-boats | | Number of U-boats on Passage | Percentage of kills to U-boats on Passage | Aircraft Lost per U-boats sunk | Hours Flown per U-boat sunk |
			Sunk	Damaged				
1st Jan.–31st Dec., 1941 (12 months) .	9,658	16	1	2	451	0·22%	16	9,658
1st Jan.–31st May, 1942 (5 months) .	5,041	6	Nil	2	265	Nil	—	—
1st June 1942–30th April, 1943 (11 months) .	65,744	148	9	20	959	1%	16	7,305
1st May–2nd Aug., 1943 (94 days) . .	32,243	57	28	22	270	10%	2	1,152
3rd Aug., 1943–31st May, 1944 (10 months) .	114,290	123	12	10	480	2½%	10	9,524
TOTALS . . .	226,976	350	50	56	2,425	—	7·0	4,540

[1] See Vol. II, p. 371.

passage, and the wear and tear on the nerves of their crews, materially reduced the efficiency of boats starting out on long ocean patrols. Although it is impossible to express these effects statistically, they undoubtedly gained substantial benefits for the Allies, additional to the toll of losses and damage actually inflicted on the enemy.

If we turn to Table 16, it will be seen that the aircraft employed on convoy duties were more effective as U-boat destroyers than those allocated to patrolling, and that their own losses were much smaller. If the last two columns of this table be compared with the similar columns in the preceding table the superior effectiveness of the escorts is strikingly illustrated. Furthermore no account is here taken of the merchant ships saved by the presence of air escorts. The fact, however, that during the entire war, in the Atlantic, British home waters, the Caribbean and the Arctic, only twenty-five ships (one per cent of our total losses) were sunk by U-boats *when both air and surface escorts were present* suggests that the saving of ships must have been enormous. Furthermore, study of the many convoy battles, which were such an outstanding feature of the Atlantic struggle, reveals two consistent features. The first is that, with only rare exceptions, U-boats broke off their attacks as soon as air escorts joined a convoy; and the second is that as soon as the air escorts left they pressed in once again. This makes plain the extent to which the complete integration of our sea and air escorts wrested the initiative from the enemy; and from that deduction it seems fair to claim that

Table 16. The Accomplishments of Convoy Air Escort and Support
1st June, 1942–31st May, 1944

Period	Total Hours of Flying on Convoy Escort and Support	Aircraft Losses	Number of U-boats		Aircraft Lost per U-boat Sunk	Hours Flown per U-boat Sunk
			Sunk	Damaged		
1st June, 1942–30th April, 1943	58,525	36	23	16	1·5	2,544
1st May, 1943–1st Aug., 1943	19,329	10	10 plus 2 shared	8	0·9	1,757
2nd Aug., 1943–31st May, 1944	43,534	24	25 plus 3 shared	15	0·9	1,643
TOTALS	121,388	70	58 plus 5 shared	39	1·1	1,927

the moral effect of the air escorts on the U-boat crews was every bit as great as that of the patrols which flew over the Bay of Biscay and northern transit areas. The matter is of cardinal importance, because it has often been suggested, and in the highest circles, that the strategy of convoy and escort is 'defensive' compared with allegedly 'offensive' hunting and patrolling.[1] Study of the results accomplished in the last war, and indeed those of the 1914–18 war as well, strongly indicates, however, that the opposite is the case; that convoy and escort is by far the most effective means of prosecuting the desired counter-offensive, not only against U-boats but against surface commerce raiders as well. Moreover this is as true of warship escorts as it is of air escorts.[2] It was told in our first volume how dangerously British naval escort strength was dissipated on hunting and patrolling in 1939 and 1940, and how long it took us to accept the merits of the convoy strategy[3]; and in our second volume we saw how slow the Americans were to institute convoy off their eastern seaboard in the early days of 1942, when comparatively few U-boats inflicted such heavy losses on independently-routed shipping.[4] It now seems that to some extent similar false reasoning was later applied to the allocation of our maritime aircraft. It may be hoped that the illusion that the convoy system is a wholly defensive measure may be finally dispelled by the experiences here quoted and by the statistics compiled since the war.

---

[1] See, for example, Churchill, Vol. I, pp. 362–363: 'I always sought to rupture this defensive obsession by searching for forms of counter-offensive. . . . I could not rest content with the policy of "convoy and blockade".'

[2] See Vol. II, pp. 376–377 and Tables 31 and 32.

[3] See Vol. I, pp. 10, 33–34 ,134–135, 357, 481, etc.

[4] See Vol. II, pp. 94–102.

CHAPTER X

HOME WATERS AND THE ARCTIC

1st January–31st May, 1944

> 'But the English temper, when once aroused, was marked by a tenacity of purpose, a constancy of endurance, which strongly supported the conservative tendencies of the race.'
>
> A. T. Mahan, *The Influence of Sea Power on the French Revolution and Empire*, Vol. II, p. 317.

WITH the *Tirpitz* still out of action in Altenfiord, as a result of the midget submarine attack of the 22nd of September 1943[1], and the *Scharnhorst* sunk, the strategic situation in the north had altered greatly in the Allies' favour; for the enemy now possessed no force of surface ships capable of threatening our Arctic convoys, and we were therefore able to reduce the strength needed to cover their passages. Moreover it was now possible to strengthen the Eastern Fleet, which the Admiralty had long been endeavouring to rebuild, at the expense of the Home Fleet.[2] It thus came to pass that, as so often in maritime war, a favourable development in our home waters produced favourable consequences in a remote theatre, where the commanders were at last able to consider turning to the offensive.

The Luftwaffe's strength in the far north was still at a low ebb, but about two dozen U-boats were stationed in northern Norway, and it was they who constituted the main threat to the Arctic convoys. On the other hand the forces available to escort the convoys were now far more powerful, and included a number of escort carriers; and the experience gained in 1943 had shown that a really strong surface escort, carrying its own air protection along with it, could provide a high degree of immunity from U-boat and air attacks.[3] This experience was put to full use in the next series of convoys, and to such good effect that, compared with some earlier ones, their passages were almost uneventful.

---

[1] See pp. 66–69.
[2] See Vol. II, pp. 47 and 236–237, and this volume, p. 89.
[3] See Vol. II, pp. 280–285.

The first Arctic convoy to sail from Britain after the sinking of the *Scharnhorst* was JW.56A of twenty ships, which left Loch Ewe on the 12th of January 1944. On the third day out it ran into a very violent gale off the Faeroes, and was forced to seek shelter at Akureyri in Iceland. Many ships were damaged, and five merchantmen had to return to the starting point. By the 21st repairs had been effected, and the rest of the convoy sailed again. The close escort now consisted of nine destroyers and two corvettes under Captain W. G. A. Robson in the *Hardy*. Vice-Admiral A. F. E. Palliser, flying his flag in the *Kent*, commanded a covering force of three heavy cruisers. The enemy had gained knowledge of the convoy's departure from an agent in Iceland, and although subsequent air searches did not locate it a patrol line of ten U-boats, which had been placed across its probable track through the Bear Island passage, gained contact on the 25th. Next day they managed to sink three ships; but the enemy then called off the pursuit and transferred his U-boats to the west to prepare to meet the next convoy (JW.56B of sixteen ships), which had meanwhile been reported by his search aircraft.

In view of the delay suffered by JW.56A, and the U-boat concentration which it had encountered, Admiral Fraser postponed the sailing of the next homeward convoy and sent its escort to reinforce that of JW.56B, which had left Loch Ewe on the 22nd and was then approaching the danger zone. By the 29th the enemy had massed fifteen U-boats against it, and had ordered them to attack that night. When they did so they encountered the reinforced escort, and Admiral Fraser's anticipation of the enemy's actions reaped its reward. 'The destroyers', noted the German command's War Diary, 'have forced the U-boats to submerge again and again, and have pursued them for periods up to seven hours . . . Owing to strong anti-submarine measures the U-boats did not again succeed in getting near the convoy.' On the 30th the destroyers *Whitehall* and *Meteor* sank U.314, but the flotilla leader *Hardy* was so severely crippled by an acoustic torpedo that she had to be sunk by our own forces. She was the second ship of her name to be lost during the war.[1] The enemy's northern U-boats had been ordered to use acoustic torpedoes, which had only reached them recently, against the escorts—and especially against the aircraft carrier, if one was present.[2] On this occasion no less than seventeen were fired (in addition to nine ordinary torpedoes), and it is surprising that more ships were not hit. The Germans actually claimed that in their attacks on JW.56A and JW.56B they had sunk seven destroyers and four merchantmen, with another four destroyers probably sunk and

---

[1] The previous *Hardy* was lost in the First Battle of Narvik. See Vol. I, pp. 173–175.
[2] See pp. 40–41 regarding the introduction of these weapons in the Atlantic battle.

six more merchantmen torpedoed. In fact JW.56A lost only three of its number, JW.56B suffered no losses at all, and the sinking of the *Hardy* and damage done to the *Obdurate* were the only successes achieved by the many acoustic torpedoes fired at the escorts.[1]

The early days of 1944 produced a series of storms which, even for the Arctic Ocean, were unusually ferocious. Rarely can war operations have been carried out in conditions which tried the crews of the merchantmen and of the smaller escorts so severely. Constant vigilance was essential to safety; but the weapons and equipment on which the crews depended for their lives were continuously covered in ice and snow, and if left unattended for any length of time rapidly became unserviceable. The state of the inside of the ships, where the men had to live, and where they tried to find rest during their short intervals off duty, beggars description. To give one example of a small ship's ordeal, during a storm the trawler *Strathella* lost touch with a convoy sailing from Britain to Iceland in mid-January, and was given up for lost. Five weeks later she was sighted adrift off the coast of Greenland by an American aircraft. All her crew survived.

To return to the Arctic convoys, after JW.56B had made its safe passage Admiral Fraser collected all the unloaded ships which were waiting to return home from Murmansk into one large convoy (RA.56 of thirty-seven ships). They sailed on the 3rd of February, protected by the combined escorts of the two recently arrived outward convoys, reinforced by three destroyers sent out from Scapa. An increase of Russian wireless traffic warned the Germans of the imminent departure of this convoy, and five U-boats which were on patrol off Murmansk were ordered to intercept it early in its passage and then shift to the Bear Island channel. The convoy slipped around to the east of the first patrol line safely and then turned west. On the 6th the German U-boat headquarters in Norway were astonished to receive an air report of a large convoy off Bear Island steering *east*. The sudden appearance of what they presumed to be another JW. convoy came 'as a complete surprise'. In fact the Luftwaffe aircrew must have been members of the community which in the Royal Navy is satirically described as the 'reciprocal club' and signals its enemy reports 180 degrees wrong; but many hours elapsed before the Germans realised that the convoy must in fact be RA.56, and that it was steering *west*. The resultant confusion in the enemy's camp probably helped the convoy to avoid the second U-boat concentration, and all its ships reached Loch Ewe safely on the 11th of February.

The speeding-up of traffic on the Arctic route shown by the short

---

[1] A U-boat picked up two survivors from a merchantman sunk in JW.56A, and they told the enemy that six ships of their convoy had gone down. Their information gave the U-boat command considerable encouragement.

interval between the departure of the two January convoys (JW.56A and B) led the German authorities in Norway to anticipate a new Russian land offensive. To stop or hinder the flow of supplies they demanded reinforcements for the U-boat flotilla, and also better co-operation from the Luftwaffe. Although U-boat strength in the far north was, in spite of heavy losses, maintained at a fairly steady level of twenty-five to thirty boats throughout this phase, the frequent appeals for more and better long-range aircraft met with little response; and there is no doubt that the indifferent performance of the Luftwaffe seriously handicapped the U-boats.

After the successful passage home of RA.56 the Commander-in-Chief, Home Fleet, decided to discontinue the practice of sailing outward convoys in two sections, which his predecessor had inaugurated to deal with somewhat different conditions[1], and instead to send large convoys with the strongest possible escorts. He had meanwhile arranged with the Western Approaches Command for the loan of support groups and escort carriers. Convoy JW.57, which thus consisted of forty-two ships and a tanker, sailed on the 20th of February. Vice-Admiral I. G. Glennie in the light cruiser *Black Prince* commanded the escort, which included the carrier *Chaser* (Captain H. V. P. McClintock) and no less than seventeen destroyers. Three other cruisers (the *Berwick*, *Jamaica* and the Polish-manned *Dragon*) covered the convoy as usual, and shore-based aircraft of Coastal Command gave fighter and anti-submarine protection during the first part of the passage.

The enemy made a determined attempt to intercept JW.57, and to score what he called 'a grand slam' against it. His whole available strength of fourteen U-boats was deployed in two patrol lines, one behind the other. On the 23rd the first shadowing aircraft gained contact, and several engagements with the *Chaser's* Wildcat fighters took place. No enemies were, however, shot down—partly owing to defects developing in the fighters' guns. By the 24th U-boats were in touch with the convoy, but the destroyer *Keppel* (Commander I. J. Tyson, R.N.R.), which, although an old ship dating back to the 1914–18 war, had a most distinguished record in Atlantic and Arctic convoy operations[2], sank U.713 with depth charges. Next day a Catalina of No. 210 Squadron, working at the extreme limit of its range from the Shetlands, sank U.601 by a very skilful attack. The following night, however, the enemy gained his revenge when U.990 torpedoed and sank the destroyer *Mahratta*. As so often happened when a ship went down in Arctic waters there were few survivors. The *Chaser's* Swordfish, though handicapped by very bad weather,

---

[1] See Vol. II, pp. 290–291.

[2] See pp. 38–40 regarding the *Keppel's* defence of ONS.18 and ON.202 in September 1943.

carried out many patrols and made several attacks; but none succeeded in sinking an enemy. The Germans called off the operation early on the 28th of February, the day that JW.57 steamed into Kola Inlet completely intact. The U-boat command noted in its war diary how 'the weather, depth charge and hydrophone pursuits, and enemy air activity' had scattered the U-boats and frustrated their attacks; and that the unsatisfactory result of the operation was attributable mainly to the exceptionally strong escort provided for the convoy.

The corresponding west-bound convoy, RA.57 of thirty-one ships, left Kola Inlet on the 2nd of March. Admiral Fraser expected, we now know correctly, that the U-boats whose efforts against the outward convoy had been thwarted would try to catch the homeward ships early in their passage. He therefore arranged for Russian air patrols to search the approaches to Kola Inlet, and ordered the convoy to make a wide detour to the east. These measures were successful, and the convoy was not located until it was two days out. As continuous storms made it impossible for the *Chaser* to work her aircraft until the 4th and the enemy had concentrated fifteen U-boats against the convoy, it was as well that the evasion was ordered. By the time that flying became possible the U-boats had gained touch, but they were very severely handled. On the 4th a rocket-firing Swordfish damaged U.472 badly and enabled the destroyer *Onslaught* to finish her off. Next day the carrier managed to continue working her aircraft in spite of the heavy motion on the ship, and she was rewarded by another Swordfish sinking U.366. Nor was that the end of her successes; for on the 6th U.973 was destroyed in like manner and two other enemies were damaged. The Swordfish continued their anti-submarine patrols on the 7th; but there were no more sightings, and three days later all the convoy except one ship, which had been sunk by a U-boat, arrived safely in Loch Ewe.

The Germans were highly dissatisfied with the results achieved against JW.57 and RA.57. Realising that the carrier-borne aircraft had been the main cause of failure, the naval authorities urged that long-range bombers and torpedo-bombers should return to north Norway from the Mediterranean, in order to attack the carriers; but the Luftwaffe refused to send the help asked for. In default of air reinforcements the U-boat command realised that its tactics must be altered. The U-boats would have to stay submerged by day, attack by night, and then quickly withdraw well clear of the convoys. The only alternative was to order them to work independently—which, in the Atlantic, had already proved futile.[1] As the period of virtually continuous daylight on the Arctic route (30th April–12th August)

---

[1] See pp. 258–259.

was approaching, they realised that the prospects of success were likely to decrease; but recent reinforcements had restored the strength of the northern flotilla to twenty-eight boats, and the enemy showed no sign of relaxing his efforts.

From the British point of view the recent double operation had been a substantial success. For the loss of five U-boats, and damage to several others, the enemy's only return had been one merchant-man and one destroyer sunk.

There now took place a meeting in London at which measures to improve still further the offensive capacity of the air and surface escorts were discussed. The result was that, for the next pair of convoys, two escort carriers—the *Activity*, a British conversion (Captain G. Willoughby), and the *Tracker*, a Lend-Lease ship (Captain J. H. Huntley)—and two Western Approaches support groups, one of which was Captain F. J. Walker's famous 2nd Escort Group, were made available. This was the most powerful and experienced opposition so far offered to the enemy in an Arctic convoy operation. The inclusion of two escort carriers not only went a long way towards overcoming the poor asdic conditions, which so often handi-capped the surface escorts in northern waters, but also enabled the aircraft to be specially organised to deal with enemy shadowers as well as U-boats. The *Activity* embarked three Swordfish and seven Wildcat fighters, while the *Tracker* had twelve American Avengers and seven Wildcats.[1] It was the first appearance of the Avengers on this route, and although not yet fitted to fire rocket-projectiles, they had many advantages over the Swordfish, such as greater speed and endurance and enclosed cockpits. The intention was that the fighters should subdue the U-boats' A.A. gunfire, and that the Swordfish and Avengers should then finish them off with rockets and depth charges.

JW.58, of forty-nine ships and the U.S. cruiser *Milwaukee*, which was being transferred to the Russians[2], sailed on the 27th of March. Once again a very strong escort was provided. It comprised in all twenty destroyers, five sloops of Captain Walker's group, four cor-vettes and the escort carriers *Activity* and *Tracker*. Rear-Admiral F. Dalrymple-Hamilton in the light cruiser *Diadem* was in command. Three days after the convoy's departure the first German recon-naissance plane found and reported it, and thereafter many battles took place between the shadowers and the carrier-borne fighters. The latter did splendidly, and shot down no less than six long-range

---

[1] Wildcat was the American name of the Grumman (F4F) fighter, which we called the Martlet, and which has been referred to by the latter name previously in this narrative (see, for example, Vol. I, p. 478). Similarly the American Avenger (TBF) torpedo-bomber was for a time called the Tarpon by the Royal Navy. As the English names fell into disuse at about this time they are henceforth referred to by their American names.

[2] See p. 280 fn. (1) regarding the transfer of British and American warships to the Russians at this time.

The Fleet Air Arm attack on the Tirpitz, *3rd April, 1944*

The *Tirpitz* inside net defences in Kaa fiord.

Barracuda bombers approaching the target.

Hits in the first attack.

Damage to the Tirpitz *in the Fleet Air Arm attack of 3rd April, 1944*

The aircraft hangar (Hit No. 8. See Map 18 facing p. 277).

Damage on the aircraft deck (Hit No. 7).

Bomb hole in upper deck (Hit No. 9).

aircraft during the convoy's passage—successes which the German authorities found very disturbing. As soon as his aircraft had located the convoy, the enemy moved the U-boats to a patrol line south-west of Bear Island. They were to attack on the last night of March, by which time sixteen boats were in position. 'This convoy' signalled the U-boat command 'must not be allowed to get through un-scathed.' The convoy escorts, however, decided otherwise. It was Captain Walker's well-tried *Starling* which drew first blood when, on the 29th of March, she sank U.961. Two days later the destroyer *Beagle* and aircraft from the *Tracker* accounted for U.355. On the 2nd of April the *Keppel* sank U.360 with her 'hedgehog' [1]; and, when a Swordfish sighted U.288 very early next day and summoned up a Wildcat and Avenger, between them the three aircraft blew the enemy up. The escorts thus achieved a splendid success, and the new air organisation and tactics had justified themselves abundantly. Apart from one ship, which was damaged by ice and had to return, the convoy arrived unscathed. As so often happened in the enemy's camp, especially when acoustic torpedoes were being used, his claims on this occasion bore no relation to the truth. His assessment of losses inflicted was 'nine destroyers sunk and four probably sunk'; but he admitted that 'strong enemy air cover had led to heavy losses' of his U-boats, and that he would have to discontinue shadowing our convoys in daylight.

After this substantial achievement by the escort forces with JW.58 it was hardly surprising that the corresponding homeward convoy (RA.58 of thirty-six ships) had a comparatively uneventful passage. It sailed on the 7th of April, and although sixteen U-boats were on patrol none of them found the convoy, which steamed through the dangerous waters off Bear Island unmolested. All its ships reached Loch Ewe safely on the 14th.

Before JW.58 sailed we had received indications that the repair of the damage done by the midget submarines to the *Tirpitz* in the previous September was approaching completion[2], and it was there-fore urgently necessary to put her out of action again. This it was planned to do by launching a strong force of carrier-borne bombers during the passage of JW.58. Admiral Fraser entrusted the prepara-tions to his second-in-command, Vice-Admiral Sir Henry Moore, who flew his flag in the battleship *Anson*. The fleet carriers *Victorious* (Captain M. M. Denny) and *Furious* (Captain G. T. Philip), under Rear-Admiral A. W. la T. Bisset, were to carry the two striking forces, each consisting of twenty-one Barracudas. The fighters which were to protect the air striking forces (forty with each) were to be

---

[1] See Vol. I, p. 480, regarding this ahead-throwing weapon.
[2] See pp. 65–69.

provided partly from the fleet carriers and partly from the three escort carriers *Emperor*, *Searcher* and *Pursuer*; and sufficient aircraft were to be kept on board the *Furious* and *Fencer* to provide fighter cover and anti-submarine protection for the surface ships. The Fleet Air Arm Wings forming the bombing force were Nos. 52 and 8, belonging to the *Victorious* and *Furious* respectively, commanded by Lieutenant-Commanders V. Rance and R. Baker-Faulkner; but in order to fly off each Wing at full strength at an interval of one hour, and with the minimum delay, one squadron from each carrier was exchanged into the other ship. Though there were disadvantages in this procedure Admiral Moore later considered that they had been worth accepting, in order that each Wing should work as a complete unit. Lastly four cruisers and fourteen destroyers provided the close screen, and also surface protection against the five large enemy destroyers known to be in Altenfiord.[1]

Meanwhile a great deal of preparatory work had been proceeding in north Russia, under the directions of Rear-Admiral E. R. Archer, the Senior British Naval Officer. Royal Air Force ground crews and photographic experts had been carried there in the *Chaser* at the end of February, and early in March a Catalina and three photographic-reconnaissance Spitfires reached Vaenga. On the 12th and 13th of March the Spitfires managed to take an excellent series of pictures of the *Tirpitz's* anchorage and defences, and the Catalina at once flew them back to England. Admiral Archer reported that her departure was witnessed by a large number of Russian Customs officials, who enquired if the Catalina's crew had anything to declare.

In view of the fact that on many previous occasions the Russian authorities had, as has been recorded elsewhere, proved themselves highly unco-operative[2], it is fair to record that, even if their methods sometimes appeared exceedingly strange, on the present occasion they did do their best to further the purpose in hand. They themselves had made a night bombing attack on the *Tirpitz* in the previous February, but only four aircraft found the target, and they inflicted no damage.

In spite of prolonged spells of bad weather a very careful watch was kept on the enemy battleship for the next fortnight. No developments which might affect the impending attack were, however, observed. The reconnaissance flights were noticed by the Germans, and they seem to have realised that something unusual was afoot; but they took no exceptional precautions.

To return to the Home Fleet, in order to provide heavy ship cover for the outward convoy (JW.58) Admiral Fraser, flying his flag in

---

[1] See Map 4.
[2] See Vol. II, pp. 127–128, 279 and 400–401.

the battleship *Duke of York*, took part of Admiral Moore's force under his command during the first stage of the 1,200-mile journey to Norwegian waters. Admiral Bisset with the remaining ships steered to meet the Commander-in-Chief at a rendezvous some 250 miles north-west of Altenfiord on the evening of the 3rd of April. Admiral Fraser intended then to return home, leaving his second-in-command to carry out the attack.

The Commander-in-Chief therefore left Scapa early on the 30th of March with the *Duke of York*, *Anson*, *Victorious*, *Belfast* and five destroyers (two of them R.C.N. ships). Admiral Bisset, in the light cruiser *Royalist*, sailed with the *Furious*, *Sheffield*, *Jamaica* and the four escort carriers the same evening; and after passing through a position off the Faeroes the two forces steered to the north-east. It soon became apparent to Admiral Fraser that the close escort of convoy JW.58 was giving a very good account of itself against enemy aircraft and U-boats, and that a sortie by the *Tirpitz* was improbable. In view of this, and of the unusually favourable weather, early on the 1st of April he decided that there was no need for him to continue covering the convoy, and that he could best seize a possibly fleeting opportunity by advancing the attack on the battleship by twenty-four hours. The necessary adjustments were made to the rendezvous with Admiral Bisset's force; but the change meant that, in order to reach the flying-off position in time, the escort carriers had to steam at their maximum speed of seventeen knots. The junction was, however, successfully effected on the afternoon of the 2nd of April. Admiral Moore then took command of the attacking force, while the Commander-in-Chief cruised about 200 miles to the north until the attack had been completed. Meanwhile final preparations were being completed in the carriers, and by the evening of the 2nd all aircraft had been fuelled and had received their bomb loads. At 1.30 a.m. on the 3rd the aircrews were called for the final briefing, and by 4 a.m. all were ready. In spite of the severity of the Arctic conditions there were hardly any failures of material in the carriers—a fine tribute to the work of the aircraft maintenance crews. Zero hour for flying off was 4.15 a.m., and the first of the escorting Corsair fighters took off from the *Victorious* exactly on time. The first Strike Wing, of twenty-one Barracudas, quickly followed; then the rest of the fighter escort (Hellcats and Wildcats) took off. By 4.37 they had all formed up, and set course for the target, about 120 miles distant. 'It was' wrote Admiral Bisset 'a grand sight, with the sun just risen, to see this well-balanced striking force departing.' The aircrews had, in Captain Denny's words, 'left the carriers' decks in the greatest heart, and brimful of determination'. At 5.25 the second striking force, also of twenty-one Barracudas and forty fighters, followed. One of the former failed to start, and one crashed into the sea, just after taking off, and was lost with all hands. Of the forty-two bombers which originally made up the striking force ten carried one 1,600-pound armour-piercing bomb, twenty-two carried three 500-pound semi-armour-piercing bombs each, and ten were armed with high-explosive[1] or anti-submarine bombs. The heavy bombs could penetrate the *Tirpitz's* main armour belt (except over the magazines, where it was thickest), provided that they were released above 3,500 feet; the semi-armour-piercing bombs could, if released above 2,000 feet, penetrate the ship's two-inch weather deck; and the high-explosive and anti-submarine bombs were included to cause damage to superstructures and exposed positions, and under-water damage from near-misses. The weapons finally chosen formed a compromise between the need to penetrate the ships vitals and the smaller proportion of hits which could be expected as the height of release increased.

While the second wave was winging its way towards the target the first wave carried out its attack, almost exactly as planned. No fighter opposition was encountered and, until the bombers had started their dives, there was no anti-aircraft gunfire. Plainly surprise had been complete. The fighters engaged gun positions, and sprayed the *Tirpitz* with their fire so effectively that 'her gunnery was undoubtedly spoilt'. The enemy started his smoke screen too late to obscure the pilots' view, and at 5.29 the bombs started to rain down on the battleship. Hits were at once seen, smoke and flames rose up from her decks, and in one minute the attack was over. All except one bomber and one fighter returned safely to the carriers.

About an hour later the second wave came in. Anti-aircraft fire was now heavier; but the smoke screen, though denser, did not handicap the bombers greatly. Again all attacks took place within a minute, more hits were observed, and by 8 a.m. all the striking force except one Barracuda, which was seen to be shot down by gunfire, had flown on safely. The attacks had been beautifully co-ordinated and fearlessly executed—a splendid tribute to the spirit of the aircrews and to the thoroughness of their training.

Let us now see what had meanwhile happened aboard the *Tirpitz*. Her steaming trials, which were to have been carried out on the 1st of April, had been postponed for forty-eight hours because of a bad weather forecast. Early on the morning of the 3rd she prepared for sea. The five destroyers had already proceeded down the fiord, the net defences were open and the ship was weighing anchor when, at 5.25, a warning that some forty aircraft were approaching was received. Her Captain at once ordered the anti-aircraft armaments to be fully manned and water-tight doors closed; but the attacks

---

[1] These were actually a new type called 'medium case' (M.C.) 500-pound bombs, but their purpose was similar to that of ordinary high-explosive (H.E.) bombs.

Map 18

HITS OBTAINED ON TIRPITZ IN ATTACK BY F.A.A. AIRCRAFT
OPERATION 'TUNGSTEN' 3RD APRIL 1944

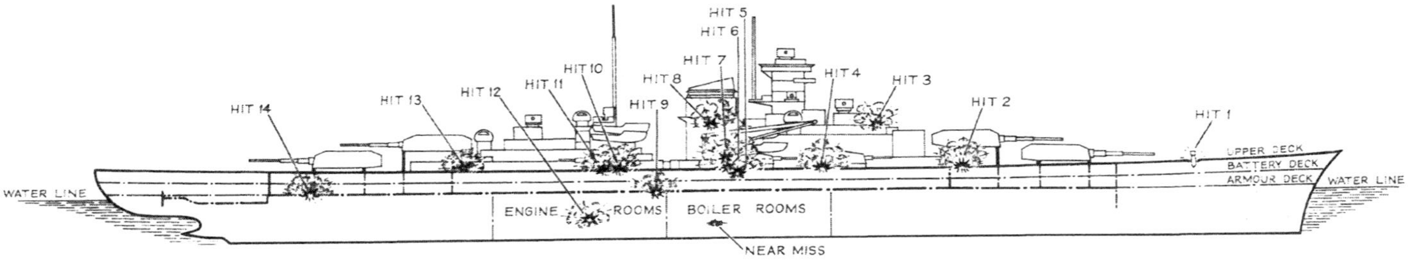

WATER LINE

HIT 14 HIT 13 HIT 12 HIT 11 HIT 10 HIT 9 HIT 8 HIT 7 HIT 6 HIT 5 HIT 4 HIT 3 HIT 2 HIT 1

ENGINE ROOMS   BOILER ROOMS

NEAR MISS

UPPER DECK
BATTERY DECK
ARMOUR DECK
WATER LINE

HIT	SIZE OF BOMB (Probable)	POSITION OF HIT
1	1600 lb. A.P.	Upper deck stbd side. (Failed to detonate)
2	500 lb. M.C.	Upper deck port side.
3	500 lb. M.C.	Superstructure stbd side
4	500 lb. S.A.P.	Upper deck port side.
5	500 lb. M.C.	Upper deck port side.
6	1600 lb. A.P.	Upper deck stbd side.
7	500 lb. S.A.P.	Upper deck stbd side.

HIT	SIZE OF BOMB (Probable)	POSITION OF HIT
8	500 lb. M.C.	Funnel
9	1600 lb. A.P.	Armour deck port side.
10	500 lb. M.C.	Upper deck stbd side
11	500 lb. S.A.P.	Superstructure & upper deck on the centre line.
12	1600 lb. A.P.	Stbd side armour plate.
13	500 lb. S.A.P.	Upper deck stbd side.
14	500 lb. S.A.P.	Armour deck stbd side.

NEAR MISS   500 lb. M.C. or S.A.P.   Close against stbd side.

A.P. = Armour Piercing   S.A.P. = Semi-Armour Piercing   M.C. = Medium Case

DXP

started before she was fully prepared to meet them, and well before the smoke screen put up by shore stations had covered her effectively. The tactics of the attacking planes were so skilful that very little opposition was put up. Most of her fire control was put out of action by the preliminary machine-gunning of the fighters, and the nine bomb hits (plus one very near miss) caused such damage and casualties that the fighting efficiency of the ship, though not her ability to steam, was considerably impaired. It is likely that in the first attack she was hit by five armour-piercing and four high-explosive bombs.[1] In addition one very near miss, probably with an anti-submarine bomb, caused some hull damage. Of the armour-piercing hits certainly two, and possibly three, were obtained with the heavy 1,600-pound bombs; but, for reasons to be discussed shortly, none penetrated the main armour protection of the ship.

As soon as the attack was over the *Tirpitz* started to shift back inside the net defences, but before she had resumed her former berth warning of the approach of the second wave of attackers was received. The smoke screen was by this time (about 6.30 a.m.) more effective, and all her guns were firing 'blind' through it; but the battleship probably received five more bomb hits in this attack.[2] Unfortunately the only heavy armour-piercing bomb to find the target did not explode. While the Barracudas were diving on the principal target the escorting fighters attacked the smaller vessels and auxiliaries lying in the fiord, and they set on fire a large tanker. The enemy, however, managed to save her and her cargo. The German destroyers did not return to the anchorage in Kaa fiord until after the attacks were over, and thus played no part in the defence of the *Tirpitz*.

The German accounts state that the height at which the Barracudas released their bombs was between 600 and 1,200 feet, and it seems unquestionable that, in their anxiety to obtain hits, the pilots did press in a good deal closer than had been intended. This undoubtedly decreased the chances of the armour-piercing bombs getting well inside the ship before they exploded—chances which in fact had never been very good. None of the bombs actually penetrated the battleship's main armour belt, and her vital compartments were therefore unaffected. Above the main deck, however, damage was widespread and she suffered 438 casualties, of whom 122 was killed. Although a high percentage of hits was obtained, the *Tirpitz* was only put out of action for about three months; and contemporary British estimates that up to six months would be needed to repair her were, in fact, too optimistic. In retrospect it is plain

---

[1] See Map 18.
[2] See Map 18.

that, with the weapons put into their hands, the Fleet Air Arm crews could hardly have accomplished more against such a very well protected target.

After the aircraft of the second wave had returned to the carriers the fleet shaped course to the north-west. Admiral Moore had intended to repeat the attack next morning; but on reconsideration he cancelled it, because he believed that the *Tirpitz* had been seriously damaged, and because of 'the fatigue of the aircrews and their natural reaction after completing a dangerous operation successfully'. As the weather broke during the night of the 3rd-4th of April the second attack would, in all probability, have been frustrated in any case. On the afternoon of the 6th the main body of the fleet re-entered Scapa, to be given a rousing welcome by the ships already in harbour.

When the First Sea Lord heard the results of the operation he signalled to Admiral Fraser stressing that, even though the *Tirpitz* could not be sunk with the bombs then available to the Fleet Air Arm, it was certain that the harder she was struck the longer she would be incapacitated. He therefore urged that another attack should be made as quickly as possible, before she had recovered from the damage to material, personnel and morale suffered in the first attack. It is indeed a sound and ancient principle that an injured enemy should be hammered and harassed relentlessly; and in that connection it is interesting to find that, in his report, the Captain of the *Tirpitz* remarked that, although the attack had been anticipated, it achieved 'considerable success'. He also said that 'we must expect a repetition, because of the *Tirpitz's* lessened powers of resistance'. Admiral Cunningham's views did not, however, appeal to the Commander-in-Chief, who represented that the favourable conditions enjoyed during the first attack were unlikely to be repeated. It was, he considered, optimistic to expect again to achieve surprise; for the nights were getting much shorter, and next time there would be no convoy at sea to divert the enemy's attention and draw off his submarines. He therefore preferred to revert to the policy of attacking enemy shipping off the Norwegian coast, on which a good deal of effort had lately been expended. After a considerable interchange of signals with London, Admiral Fraser did, however, finally agree to attack the battleship again, provided that he could find favourable weather and also achieve surprise. Since many of his destroyers were needed in the Channel at the end of April to take part in invasion exercises, he proposed to do so on the 23rd of that month. Should conditions frustrate his primary purpose he would attack shipping in Bodo and other Norwegian harbours used by the enemy's coastal traffic.

Admiral Moore accordingly sailed on the 21st of April with forces similar to those he had commanded on the previous occasion. He arrived in the flying-off position undetected, but the weather proved wholly unfavourable and, although he re-fuelled his destroyers at sea and held on to the prudent limit of his larger ships' endurance, he was finally forced to abandon the enterprise. On the 26th he flew off two striking forces from the *Victorious*, *Furious* and escort carriers to attack shipping in Bodo harbour and sweep the 'inner leads' to the south. The weather inshore proved far from ideal, and a misunderstanding of the operation orders caused some confusion in the striking forces. For this reason most of the aircraft attacked the same target, a south-bound convoy. Three ships totalling 15,083 tons (all loaded with iron ore) were sunk; but we lost six aircraft—considerably more than in the attack on the *Tirpitz*. That same afternoon the *Victorious's* aircraft reconnoitred the approaches to Narvik harbour, to give the impression that the Allies intended to make a combined assault in that neighbourhood. This was part of the deceptive plan now being implemented to mislead the enemy regarding the destination of the large invasion forces which were assembling in Britain. Several other similar operations were carried out by the Home Fleet in the spring of 1944, but it seems that Hitler's 'intuition' that we intended to invade Norway (which he had declared as early as the beginning of 1942[1]) played as great a part in misleading the enemy as any of the Allied ruses designed to achieve the same purpose.

Carrier aircraft attacks such as that made on Bodo in April now took a prominent place in the Home Fleet's activities. No less than three more were made in May. The first achieved no successes, but in the second and third two ships (2,667 tons) were sunk and three others, totalling about 12,500 tons, were damaged. These operations formed part of a big campaign now being waged by the Home Fleet's submarines and coastal craft and by No. 18 Group of Coastal Command, against the enemy's coastal shipping. We will return to the results they achieved in the next chapter; but here it must be mentioned that, after the *Scharnhorst* had been sunk and the *Tirpitz* put out of action, the Home Fleet's submarines were able to devote far more attention to the inshore shipping routes off Norway. Between January and May 1944 they sank in those waters, or caused to be beached, no less than fifteen ships (about 56,000 tons) and a U-boat (U.974). Considering that the conditions for submarine patrols off Norway were always difficult and hazardous this was a big accomplishment.

To return to the Arctic convoys, after JW.58 and the corresponding homeward-bound RA.58 had completed their successful passages in April the quota which we had agreed to run in the spring of

---

[1] See Vol. II, p. 100.

1944 was completed. A number of empty merchantmen were, however, still in Russian ports, the crew of the American cruiser *Milwaukee*, which had been transferred to the Russians, had to be brought back, and some 2,300 men of the Russian Navy were to come to Britain to take over the battleship *Royal Sovereign*.[1] Rear-Admiral R. R. McGrigor, flying his flag in the *Diadem*, therefore took out a powerful escort force consisting of the two carriers *Activity* and *Fencer* (Captain W. W. R. Bentinck), sixteen destroyers and four frigates, all of which reached Kola Inlet on the 23rd of April. During the next five days the maintenance crews of the carriers worked unceasingly to make every possible aircraft serviceable, and when convoy RA.59, of forty-five ships, sailed on the 28th the *Activity* and *Fencer* between them had ready thirteen Swordfish and sixteen Wildcats. As the *Tirpitz* had been put out of action no heavy covering force was provided on this occasion.

The weather lived up to its usual form, and the high seas, snow storms, and strong winds taxed the carrier crews severely. At one time there was six inches of snow on the flight decks; but they overcame all handicaps brilliantly. Some of the twelve U-boats concentrated in the Bear Island channel gained touch on the 30th of April, and one merchantman was sunk. But they paid heavily for that meagre success. The *Fencer's* Swordfish sank U.277, U.674 and U.959, all with depth charges, on the 1st and 2nd of May. She had very experienced aircrews on board, and there is little doubt that her outstanding success owed much to that fact.[2] Moreover the experiences of this convoy gave strong support to the view that, in waters where asdic conditions were bad, carrier-borne aircraft afforded the best protection to the convoys. On the 3rd and 4th May, by which time the U-boats had been left far astern, the carriers were detached to Scapa and the Clyde, and Coastal Command aircraft took over the protection of the convoy for the latter part of its journey. On the 6th the forty-four merchantmen dropped anchor safely in Loch Ewe. It was, perhaps, a happy chance that the Russian Admiral Levchenko and his staff were onboard the *Fencer* during the operation. They may well have been impressed by what the Senior Officer of the carriers described as 'the extremely high standard of her deck

---

[1] The transfer of the *Milwaukee* and *Royal Sovereign* formed part of the agreement made to compensate the Russians for our inability to hand over to them the proportion of the Italian fleet which they had claimed. (See Churchill, Vol. V, pp. 402–406.) In addition to those two ships, six of the '*Town*' class destroyers, originally transferred to Britain by the U.S.A. in 1940 under the 'destroyers for bases' agreement (see Vol. I, pp. 347–348), and four British submarines were taken over by the Russians in July 1944. Unfortunately one of the submarines (ex-*Sunfish*) was sunk in error by one of our own aircraft while on her way to Russia (see Part II of this volume, Chapter XVIII).

[2] The *Activity's* experienced aircrews were taken out of the ship just before this operation, because they were needed in connection with the preparations to invade France. Their relief by new crews greatly reduced the ship's efficiency.

landing operations . . . at times [carried out] with a great deal of movement on her'.

Thus did the series of Arctic convoys run during the spring of 1944 not only carry a huge quantity of stores, munitions and equipment safely to our Russian Ally, but also inflicted repeated and sharp repulses on the enemy's U-boats; and the main credit for these accomplishments must undoubtedly be given to the escort carriers and their Fleet Air Arm crews.

In May the Home Fleet made two more attempts to repeat the successful carrier air attack on the *Tirpitz*. Admiral Moore sailed again on the 12th, and reached the flying-off position two days later. The target was, however, completely shrouded in low cloud, and although the striking forces tried hard to get through, the operation had to be abandoned. On the next occasion no escort carriers were available, which limited the scope and increased the hazards of the undertaking. The fleet, which included the *Victorious* and *Furious*, was this time sighted by German reconnaissance aircraft well before reaching the flying-off position. As we knew that a number of U-boats were in the offing, and the weather again appeared unpropitious, Admiral Moore cancelled the attempt and switched his forces to make another attack on shipping off the Norwegian coast. On the 1st of June a convoy was found north of Stadlandet, and in the ensuing attack two ships (6,471 tons) were sunk, and two others damaged.

It remains to mention one more important duty which fell to the Home Fleet in the early summer of 1944, and that was to give special training to the many ships allocated to take part in the invasion of France. It has been told elsewhere how, as we and our American Allies gained experience of combined operations, more and more emphasis was placed on the support of the Army by bombardments from the sea.[1] It fell to the Home Fleet's main bases at Scapa and the Clyde to provide a large share of the training needed. In April and May four battleships, twenty cruisers, two monitors and many destroyers were given special 'working-up' practices. Even these great bases, which had played such an important part in both World Wars, can rarely have been more busy. Day after day the thunder of the guns of British and American warships, large and small, was heard off the bombardment ranges which had been established nearby; while other ships trained intensively against aircraft and E-boat targets. Gradually the various Task Forces formed and rehearsed together, until senior officers were satisfied that every ship in the whole vast organisation was ready to play its part. The staffs of naval bases rarely receive much recognition for their work behind

---

[1] See Vol. II, pp. 251, 330 and 332.

the stage on which move the operational fleets; but there is no doubt at all that those who laboured so long at Scapa, on the Clyde and at other bases contributed greatly to the success of the invasion of Europe. It was to them that Admiral Fraser paid his final tribute in concluding his despatch for this period.

CHAPTER XI

COASTAL WARFARE
1st January–31st May, 1944

'The vital British policy [is] that the coasts
of the enemy are the frontiers of England.'
Admiral Lord Fisher of Kilverstone
to Edward A. Goulding,
6th June, 1911.

D URING the first half of 1944 the campaign waged against the
enemy's coastal traffic followed the same general pattern as
in the preceding phase; but the momentum of Coastal Command's offensive was all the time rising, and other arms were now
making an increasing contribution towards stopping the flow of shipping along the Norwegian, Dutch and French coasts. The attacks
made by the Fleet Air Arm formations of the Home Fleet off Norway
were generally planned as part of other operations by that fleet, such
as covering the passage of Arctic convoys or striking at the German
squadron in Altenfiord. Although they had exactly the same object
as the blows struck by their colleagues of Coastal Command, in
order to preserve continuity in this narrative they were described
with the main fleet's other operations.[1] The Home Fleet submarines
were also now able to devote a bigger effort to the same purpose, as
were the coastal force flotillas of motor torpedo- and motor gunboats;
and all the time the minelaying aircraft of Bomber Command were
infesting the more distant waters, and in particular the Baltic, in
order to disrupt traffic to and from the Scandinavian countries and
hinder the U-boat training programme. Lastly the enemy's principal
naval and mercantile ports received a certain amount of attention
from the heavy bombers—generally those of the Eighth U.S. Army
Air Force—at this time. Though the number of ships actually sunk
or destroyed by these raids was small, the damage they caused to
port facilities probably contributed to the enemy's difficulty in
keeping his coastal traffic moving.

As to the German offensive against our own shipping, except for
a certain amount of rather sporadic minelaying, the Luftwaffe had
practically dropped out of the battle in the narrow seas; and it
failed conspicuously to protect its own side's coastal shipping,

---

[1] See pp. 279 and 281.

to hinder the assembly of the enormous forces needed to invade Europe, or to give warning of our movements and intentions by regular air reconnaissance. Even when, in April, a substantial number of German bombers attacked Portsmouth and Plymouth, and against the latter used the new radio-controlled FX bomb[1], the damage was remarkably slight. It was indeed during the critical months of the early spring of 1944 that the failure of the Germans to decide on and apply a consistent policy in anti-shipping operations reaped its inevitable harvest. Several good opportunities to embarrass us seriously by attacks on our coastal traffic had come the way of the Luftwaffe during the preceding years; but they had been frittered away by violent changes in strategy and in aircraft construction policy. The decline of the Luftwaffe in this, as in other aspects of the maritime war, must be attributed mainly to the direction of its efforts by Hitler's arbitrary and erratic 'intuitions', to the failure of his advisers to impose the need for consistency and stability, and to the increasing ascendancy of the Allied air forces over Europe.

Our chief troubles arose from the German E-boats which, though never more than about three dozen in number, could be switched rapidly from one convoy route to another; and, by choosing their own moment to attack, they occasionally brought off some unpleasant successes. In comparing the results achieved by the enemy and ourselves in this type of warfare it must, however, be remembered that, whereas Axis coastal traffic was by this time declining, our own was increasing rapidly. Moreover the preparations for the invasion of Europe necessitated frequent movements of ships and craft of many, and sometimes strange types along our coasts; and the convoys running along the east coast and in the Channel had reached a greater size and importance than ever before. The result was that, whereas it had become increasingly difficult for our own aircraft and light forces to find worth-while targets, the enemy could at any time take his choice from any one of perhaps half-a-dozen large convoys which were moving slowly along our coasts; and our escorts could never be as numerous as those that the enemy could provide to his fewer and much smaller convoys. Both sides still found the tactical conduct of night raids by fast-moving craft difficult; both experienced numerous accidents, such as collisions or engagements between friendly vessels; and we now know that both showed considerable optimism in the successes which they claimed. The advantage in equipment, and especially in radar, was however generally with our flotillas; but the E-boats proved skilful and stubborn fighters, and the German convoy escorts defended their charges with devotion,

---

[1] See p. 168 fn. (3) and p. 177.

and often with success. Their guns' crews were excellently trained and provided with good weapons, and it was mainly they who succeeded in keeping the enemy's coastal traffic moving, in spite of the unremitting and very varied offensive which we were now waging against it.

In considering the accomplishments of each arm of the coastal offensive in turn, it is first necessary to enlarge on the brief mention of the work of the Home Fleet's submarines made in our last chapter. In February the North Sea weather improved somewhat. This and the greater number of boats on patrol off Norway brought a sharp increase in successes. The *Taku* and *Stubborn* between them destroyed five valuable ships totalling over 18,000 tons between the 7th and 12th; but on the 13th the *Stubborn* was heavily depth charged, and had a very narrow escape. She struggled in damaged condition from 500 feet to the surface, and limped away from the hostile coast. Luckily the enemy did not find her again, and she was finally picked up by destroyers and towed safely into Lerwick a week later. In March substantial further successes were achieved by the *Venturer*, *Sceptre* and *Terrapin*; but the *Syrtis* was lost—probably in a minefield laid off Bodo[1]—on about the 28th. April produced two very successful patrols by the Norwegian submarine *Ula*, in the second of which she sank U.974, in spite of the presence of a strong escort. On the 14th of that month the midget submarine X.24 (Lieutenant M. H. Shean, R.A.N.V.R.) penetrated into Bergen after being towed across the North Sea by the *Sceptre*. The intention was to destroy the large floating dock in the harbour, and Shean believed at the time that he had done so. In fact he attacked the merchantman *Barenfels* (7,569 tons), which was lying close to the dock, and sank her. After a very long dive X.24 then got clear of the fiord, rejoined the *Sceptre*, and was towed safely home.[2] The enemy attributed the sinking of the *Barenfels* to sabotage.

By the end of April the lengthening hours of daylight had made inshore submarine patrols highly hazardous. The *Taku* and *Venturer* made an unsuccessful attempt to penetrate the mine barrage in the Skagerrak, in order to attack the traffic sailing between Germany and southern Norway; but it only resulted in the *Taku* being damaged, and that operation marked the end of the submarine campaign off Norway until the following autumn. Patrols continued, however, in the Bay of Biscay, and we will refer to their successes shortly.

In May the midget submarine X.20 carried out a close reconnaissance of the Normandy beaches, on which our assault forces were to land. It seems that the crews of the X-craft must be given

---

[1] See Map 4.

[2] See Warren and Benson, *Above us the Waves* (Harrap, 1953), pp. 158–170, for a vivid account of this attack.

a high place among the various claimants to the distinction of having been the first Allied forces to land on the enemy's coast.

To return to Coastal Command's offensive, because the enemy had diverted most of his traffic from Rotterdam to Emden[1], No. 16 Group was now suffering from a scarcity of targets in its sweeps along the Dutch coast. Although the aircraft were steadily reaching further to the east, they never managed to interfere appreciably with the traffic in the Ems and Elbe estuaries until after the land operations in Europe had gained us the use of more advanced bases. The Strike Wing technique, already described[2], was now being put to good use in both Nos. 16 and 18 Groups, each of which possessed two such wings. Though tactics were still fluid, and new experiments were constantly being tried, a typical operation would be carried out by between twenty and thirty Beaufighters. Some would be armed with cannon and machine-guns, to subdue the enemy ships' anti-aircraft fire, while others would carry the torpedoes or rockets with which to sink their targets. To protect the Beaufighters from the air escorts which accompanied the German convoys off the Dutch coast, a very strong force of single-seater fighters invariably accompanied No. 16 Group's Strike Wings; but No. 18 Group's wings could not be given similar protection off Norway; and in their case the Beaufighters armed with guns had to shield the strike aircraft as best they could. In all these operations a high standard of training and very accurate timing and co-ordination were essential to success. No. 18 Group's wings, working from Wick and Leuchars in Scotland, came into their own at this time. Between January and March they sank nine ships (21,317 tons) off Norway, which seriously affected the transport of much-needed coal from Germany.

In No. 16 Group's sphere an interesting development took place in this period. Day attacks off the Dutch coast were liable to be expensive, because of the strong escorts provided by the enemy, and successes had not been plentiful. Coastal Command therefore decided to try night attacks, using Wellington bombers to illuminate the targets with flares. The first attempts were not successful, but early in March a ship of nearly 2,000 tons was sunk by this means.

After a very fruitful three months at the beginning of the year, No. 18 Group's Strike Wings were brought south in April. In the invasion of Normandy they were to work on the flanks of the waters through which our convoys had to pass, to help protect them against enemy surface vessels. Operations off Norway thereupon ceased.

Throughout this phase No. 19 Group's aircraft were, as always, chiefly occupied with anti-U-boat operations in the Bay of Biscay

---

[1] See p. 91.
[2] See Vol. II, pp. 259–260 and 389–390.

and could devote hardly any attention to the enemy's surface ships. In March we learnt that iron ore shipments from Spain to German-occupied France had risen substantially; but it was our submarines which very soon reduced the shipments to a more normal figure. In May the *Sceptre* sank two iron ore ships (5,360 tons) on the Bilbao–Bayonne route, while the *Upstart* accounted for a third one in the Mediterranean.

In the Channel Fighter Command aircraft were still making constant sweeps against enemy shipping, and occasionally they destroyed a few small vessels; but the main contribution of the fighters was to harass the German E-boats. It is interesting to find that in May the German naval command noted with concern how its surface vessels were always attacked from the air as soon as they left harbour, and that they had thereby been prevented from laying a mine barrage in Seine Bay as a defence against invasion. Night patrols against E-boats, for which a comparatively slow aircraft was the most suitable, were generally made by the Albacores which the Admiralty had transferred to the R.A.F.[1] In May two Fleet Air Arm squadrons, equipped with Swordfish and Avengers, came to the R.A.F. station at Manston in Kent to join in the offensive, thus adding yet one more arm to the many-sided campaign for control of the coastal waters. Indeed not the least remarkable feature of this period is the high degree of integration achieved by the different arms and services in pursuit of the common purpose—an accomplishment which the Germans might reasonably have envied.

As the preparations to invade Europe advanced, the tempo of operations in those narrow waters, the scene of so many historic conflicts, was quickening.

The successes achieved by the R.A.F's offensive against enemy shipping in this phase, shown in Table 17 (p. 288), were the greatest so far accomplished; and it was particularly satisfactory that the rising effort should have brought greater successes without any appreciable increase in our own losses.

In order to complete the picture of the losses inflicted on the enemy's shipping by air attacks in this phase, it is necessary to add the results accomplished by the Home Fleet's carriers when their strike aircraft were launched against the *Tirpitz* and the Norwegian coastal traffic in the operations described in the previous chapter. In addition to the damage caused to the enemy battleship the Fleet Air Arm aircraft sank eight merchant ships of 30,027 tons (two of them by air-laid mines), and damaged a further eleven totalling 33,428 tons between the 3rd of April and 1st of June. Thus in five months the strike aircraft of both services together caused the enemy the

---

[1] See p. 93.

Table 17. The Air Offensive against Enemy Shipping by Direct Attacks at Sea

(All Royal Air Force Commands, Home Theatre only)

January–May 1944

Month	Aircraft Sorties	Attacks Made	Enemy Vessels Sunk		Enemy Vessels Damaged		Aircraft Losses
			No.	Tonnage	No.	Tonnage	
January .	942	123	4	15,659	2	2,379	14
February .	847	140	5	4,488			11
March . .	1,093	177	9	14,470	2	18,286	9
April . .	1,095	154	9	5,537	3	9,064	9
May . .	1,625	248	9	7,853			12
TOTALS .	5,602	842	36	48,007	7	29,729	55

NOTE: Included in enemy vessels sunk are 2 of 450 tons sunk in May by Fleet Air Arm shore-based aircraft, working under Coastal Command.

loss of forty-four ships of nearly 78,000 tons, and damage to eighteen more, totalling some 63,000 tons—a formidable combined achievement.

To turn to the offensive minelaying campaign, Bomber Command was now devoting an increased effort to waters stretching from the Baltic to the Bay of Biscay. More mines were being laid, and we now know that better results were achieved than during the closing months of 1943. In January the new technique of laying mines by radar control from heights up to 15,000 feet was brought into use. This made minelaying sorties far less hazardous to the aircraft, and enabled the bombers fully to exploit the new radar set with which they were now equipped[1]; but, to begin with, the 'high-level minelaying' produced large inaccuracies of its own, and after some mines had fallen in Sweden, thirty miles from their intended positions, Bomber Command realised that special training and more practice were essential to success with this technique, as with every other. None the less the proportion of mines laid from great heights increased steadily, until in May it amounted to more than two-thirds of the total.

At the end of March minelaying was extended, at the Admiralty's request, to the Gulf of Danzig, where a great deal of training and working-up of new U-boats went on. We know from the enemy's records that this caused a month's interruption to his U-boat training programme, and also seriously impeded the flow of his coastwise shipping. Moreover the mining of the Kiel Canal on the 12th of May by eleven Mosquitos held up important traffic through that water-

[1] This was the ten-centimetre radar set called 'H2S', originally designed to give bombers employed in attacks on land targets a clear picture of the zone over which they were flying.

way, and further strained the overtaxed German minesweeping service. The actual losses caused to the Baltic U-boats by mines between January and May 1944 were, however, only two.[1] In the Bay of Biscay our minelaying produced similar difficulties for the enemy; but the sinking of U.263 off La Pallice on the 20th of January was the only actual success scored. The comparatively small results which our minelaying sorties produced against the U-boats themselves can, however, be attributed largely to the highly efficient radar network established by the Germans on the western coasts of the Baltic to give warning of the approach of our aircraft, and to the special sweeping operations always undertaken to safeguard U-boats leaving or approaching their bases.

In April and May the laying of defensive minefields to protect the Normandy assault area against incursions by U-boats or surface vessels necessitated the diversion of a proportion of the air effort from offensive minelaying. None the less the resources now available were so great that the invasion preparations caused no appreciable decrease in offensive minelaying. Surface ships were also extensively used to lay minefields off the Normandy coast. The minelayers *Apollo* and *Plover* and no less than ten flotillas of M.T.Bs and M.Ls worked from our southern ports for this purpose, and between mid-April and early June they laid no less than 2,867 mines in the enemy's coastal waters. Admiral Ramsay later expressed high appreciation of the minelayers' contribution to the safety of the invasion fleets.

The accomplishments of the R.A.F's air minelaying campaign in this five-month period are shown below:

Table 18. The R.A.F's Air Minelaying Campaign

(Home Theatre Only)

January–May 1944

Month 1944	Aircraft Sorties	Mines Laid	Enemy Vessels Sunk		Enemy Vessels Damaged		Aircraft Losses
			No.	Tonnage	No.	Tonnage	
January	363	1,101	10	14,572	1	1,668	3
February	673	1,661	12	1,226	5	8,123	11
March	518	1,472	19	19,496	4	4,929	4
April	855	2,643	17	7,930	3	10,492	20
May	812	2,760	21	18,317	2	2,922	10
TOTALS	3,221	9,637	79	61,541	15	28,134	48

The surface ship operations in the narrow waters now differed

[1] U.854 sunk on 4th February, and U.803 on the 27th of April. See Appendix D, Table 1, for details.

from those of preceding phases in that destroyers, often supported by a light cruiser, were regularly working a 'Western Channel Patrol' from Plymouth. Our early experience with this type of offensive sweep had not been happy, for on one of the first occasions the cruiser had been sunk[1]; but experience had produced better tactics, and the benefits were soon reaped. In the early hours of the 5th of February four *Hunt*-class destroyers engaged a German force consisting of one torpedo-boat and two minesweepers off the Brittany coast, and damaged one of the latter so severely that she ran ashore and became a total loss. The following months produced a series of night encounters in the same waters. Very early on the 26th of April the light cruiser *Black Prince* and four destroyers (three of which belonged to the Royal Canadian Navy) were off the Ile de Bas on the Brittany coast[2], when they encountered three German fleet torpedo-boats.[3] After a running fight the *Haida* (R.C.N.) sank one enemy, the T.29. Two nights later the *Haida* and *Athabaskan* were covering a minelaying force in the same waters, when they detected two similar enemies. On this occasion, however, the Germans fired a torpedo salvo very quickly, and the *Athabaskan* was hit and blew up; but the *Haida* soon avenged her by driving the T.27 ashore, where air and M.T.B. attacks later completed her destruction.

On the night that this action was fought the French destroyer *La Combattante* and a British frigate encountered a force of E-boats, which had been sent from Boulogne on a reconnaissance designed to find out where Allied landing craft were concentrating. After a chase the French ship sank one enemy, the S.147. Shortly after midnight on the 13th of May *La Combattante*, which was again working with a British frigate, engaged some more E-boats, which were carrying out another reconnaissance, off Selsey Bill, and scored a second success by sinking S.141. From the survivors picked up we learnt that one of Admiral Dönitz's two sons, a German naval Lieutenant who was on board the E-boat in a supernumerary capacity, was among those lost.[4] *La Combattante* had certainly lived up to her name in these two fights. But her next engagement had a less happy outcome; for on the 28th of May she sank our M.T.B.732, whom she encountered in the same waters and mistook for an enemy.

The offensive sweeps by the Nore Command Coastal Forces off the Dutch coast and by those from Dover in the Channel followed a similar pattern to those of the previous phase. They made many night attacks against heavily escorted ships or convoys, and fierce

---

[1] See p. 100.

[2] See Map 8.

[3] See p. 98 fn. (2) regarding the classification of these ships, which were often, but erroneously, called 'Elbing-class' destroyers by the British.

[4] Dönitz's other son was killed when U.954 was sunk on 19th May 1943.

fights often developed between the attackers and the German escorts. But it was, we now know, a comparatively rare event to sink an enemy supply vessel, and contemporary claims of successes against the German escorts are often not substantiated by the enemy's records.

On the 15th of February five Nore M.T.Bs became engaged in a typical close-range *mêlée* with German patrol craft and E-boats off Ijmuiden.[1] Two E-boats were seriously damaged, as was M.T.B.444 on our side; but all the damaged craft of both sides reached harbour safely. In March our coastal craft made repeated forays off the Dutch coast and in the Channel, and there were many actions; but the losses inflicted on the enemy amounted only to one patrol vessel and one minesweeper; and we had two M.T.Bs sunk during the month. In the next two months, April and May, the pattern was the same. A small steamer was sunk by French M.T.Bs off Guernsey on the night of the 7th–8th of May, and a patrol vessel on the 19th–20th. Four nights later a minelaying operation was carried out by M.T.Bs in Seine Bay, and the covering forces became engaged with German torpedo-boats and minesweepers. After confused fighting the torpedo-boat *Greif* was sunk. A torpedo hit was claimed on her, but the enemy's records state that it was a bomb from an Albacore carrying out the normal night air patrol against E-boats which caused her loss. Her sister ship the *Kondor* was badly damaged by a mine, one minesweeper was sunk by a torpedo, and another damaged by mine. Altogether it was a satisfactory night's work, especially if we take into account that two more German craft, which were sunk a few nights later, were probably victims of the mines laid on this occasion.

Among the losses inflicted on the enemy at this time the sinking of the blockade-runner *Munsterland* (6,408 tons) by the Dover batteries on the 20th of January must be mentioned.[2] This was actually the third success achieved by the heavy weapons which we had been at such pains to mount on the cliffs in 1940.[3] In March the Germans tried to move two other large ships, the *Rekum* (5,540 tons) and the *Atalanta* (4,404 tons), from Boulogne to their home waters. On the night of the 20th–21st the former was sunk by the same batteries which had accounted for the *Munsterland*; but the *Atalanta* got through unscathed under very heavy escort during the succeeding nights, in spite of all that the big guns and coastal craft could do.

---

[1] See Map 8.

[2] See pp. 93 and 99–100 regarding the previous career of the *Munsterland*, which had sailed from the Gironde for Cherbourg on 8th October 1943. In December she moved to Dieppe, and on 1st January 1944 arrived at Boulogne.

[3] See Vol. I, p. 256, regarding the mounting of the Dover batteries. Their first success was obtained on 2nd March 1943 when a ship of 2,382 tons was sunk. Another ship (3,094 tons) was sunk on the 3rd–4th October 1943.

Although the actual accomplishments of the former had not been very substantial (four ships sunk in nearly four years) the German War Diary did at this time note that 'long-range bombardment is at present the enemy's most dangerous weapon against our large, slow ships'.

Mention must be made of one other operation carried out by our light craft at this time. Readers of our earlier volumes will remember how, on several previous occasions, special efforts had been made to bring particularly valuable cargoes home from Sweden, and with varying success.[1] During the winter of 1943-44 five specially converted motor gunboats ran the gauntlet of the enemy's patrols[2] and between them made no less than nine successful round trips from Hull to Gothenburg and back again. These operations, like the earlier ones, were planned and organised by Commander Sir George Binney, R.N.V.R., who was appointed Commodore of the flotilla and himself sailed several times to Sweden. The M.G.Bs flew the Red Ensign, and, except for the Chief Officers, were manned by volunteers from the Ellerman's Wilson Line, which operated them on behalf of the Ministry of War Transport. The picturesque names given to them—*Gay Corsair, Gay Viking, Hopewell, Master Standfast,* and *Nonsuch* need a Rudyard Kipling to commemorate them appropriately, and added to the Elizabethan atmosphere of the adventure on which they were engaged. In each ship's saloon hung a portrait of the Prime Minister, and in each Captain's cabin was a picture of Sir Francis Drake. One ship, the *Master Standfast,* was captured close off the Swedish coast by a German patrol craft, which seems to have deceived the M.G.B. into the belief that she was a Swedish vessel. The others, by employing many ingenious ruses, brought back to Britain 348 tons of valuable cargo and sixty-seven Norwegian refugees. The attitude of the Swedish Government now was, in Binney's words, 'entirely correct'; 'and', continues his report, 'we were given every facility to which the waning star of Germany entitled us'.

If we turn now to the enemy's offensive against our coastal shipping, throughout the early months of 1944 the German E-boats were very active on the east coast and in the Channel. They made the task of the defending escorts more difficult by constantly switching from one route to the other and by using mines as well as torpedoes, or a combination of the two weapons, in their numerous forays. Although

---

[1] See Vol. I, p. 391 and Vol. II, p. 125.

[2] These M.G.Bs had originally been ordered by the Turkish Government in 1938-39. After being taken over they were specially adapted by the Admiralty to carry 20 men and 40-50 tons of cargo. Their maximum speed was 28 knots, and they could maintain 14-16 knots continuously over the 1,000-mile journey from Hull to Gothenburg. Their engines were, however, conspicuously unreliable, and this was a cause of constant concern to the crews. The boats were fitted with radar and light A.A. armaments.

there were only two or three flotillas of E-boats based on Cherbourg and Ijmuiden they caused us considerable trouble; and on a few occasions they penetrated the escorts' screen and inflicted appreciable losses. None the less they did not seriously impede the building-up and training of the invasion fleets.

On the 6th of January seven E-boats attacked the Bristol Channel–Portsmouth convoy WP.457, and sank three ships totalling 3,801 tons and an escorting trawler. On this occasion bad weather had frustrated the air defence of the convoy, but several other attempts to attack shipping in the western Channel in that month were defeated. Then, on the 31st, six E-boats attacked the west-bound convoy CW.243 and sank two ships and another trawler. In February the enemy's main effort was transferred to the east coast; but an attack by thirteen E-boats on convoy FS.1371 off Yarmouth on the 24th was vigorously driven off by the destroyers *Vivien* and *Eglinton*, and only one merchantman was sunk.

February produced an encounter with a U-boat in our coastal waters such as had not taken place since 1940. U.413 had been ordered to attack the convoys sailing between Portsmouth and the Bristol Channel ports. Our intelligence had given warning that some such movement was afoot, and the old destroyer *Warwick*, which had been Admiral Keyes's flagship in the raids on Zeebrugge and Ostend in 1918, was sent to patrol off the north coast of Cornwall. Then, on the 20th of February, U.413, which had so far found no merchant shipping to attack, hit and sank the *Warwick* with an acoustic torpedo. The U-boat then moved to the North Channel, to make a reconnaissance of the inshore shipping routes in those waters; and it thus happened that the surface ships and aircraft sent to search where the destroyer had been sunk missed their quarry. But the indication that the Germans might be planning a major offensive against our coastal routes with 'Schnorkel'-fitted U-boats was not lost on the Admiralty, and preparations were made to deal with it.

The next month, March, saw many sorties by the E-boats, but no important results were achieved by either side. On the 26th a strong force of 358 Marauders of the U.S. Army Air Force attacked the concrete shelters at Ijmuiden. Two E-boats were destroyed, and construction of a new shelter was delayed by damage. The next month, April, produced an unpleasant success to the enemy when, in the small hours of the 28th, a convoy of American L.S.Ts, which was proceeding towards the Devon coast to take part in an invasion rehearsal, was attacked by nine E-boats, which had actually left Cherbourg to seek a convoy off Portland Bill. A destroyer which should have been with the L.S.T. convoy had suffered damage in a collision and had gone into Plymouth for inspection. By an error she was not sailed again to rejoin the convoy, as she could have been; nor was a replacement sent. The result was that only one corvette was with the convoy when it was attacked. Two L.S.Ts were sunk and one damaged, and the loss of life was heavy.[1] Destroyers pursued the retiring enemies, but they escaped without sustaining loss or damage. This encounter showed that, unless the escorts were numerous and alert, the E-boats could still be dangerous as well as elusive foes. We were now using a large variety of ships, aircraft and weapons against them; but the actual sinking of an E-boat was still a rare event, and in fact the German flotillas only lost seven of their number (two of which collided with each other) during this five-month phase. Though specially selected, comparatively slow aircraft now regularly patrolled the Channel by night, and our fighters made many daylight attacks on returning E-boats, in fact only one success —the destruction of S.87 by a Swordfish on the 19th of May—can be attributed to air action at this time. The losses which our own M.T.Bs sustained in their many sweeps and patrols on the other side of the Channel were about the same as the enemy's losses in our own waters; and an interesting feature of both sides' tale of casualties is the frequency with which they were caused by the bombs or gunfire of friendly forces, or by accident.[2] Such mishaps are indeed inseparable from high-speed, close-range night fighting of this nature. Notwithstanding the losses which we suffered and the number of indecisive encounters with the enemy, it seems certain that the combined efforts of our escort vessels and aircraft, and the ever-extending use of radar, imposed a good deal of caution on the enemy, and so saved us heavier losses. The E-boat Command's War Diary at this time summed up the matter by saying that 'Owing to the superior radar, strong escorts and air patrols of the enemy, and the German dependence on good visibility [because their boats still lacked radar], each success must be paid for by many fruitless attacks.'

The first five months of 1944 thus marked a very important stage in the development of our maritime control over the narrow waters; for it was then that we gradually established a sufficient ascendancy to ensure that, when the invasion fleets set sail for France, the Germans would not be in a position to molest them seriously. The degree of success accomplished could not, of course, be judged until the expedition actually sailed; but by the end of May there were solid grounds for believing that, even though the passage would undoubtedly be contested with all the means available to the enemy,

---

[1] Naval casualties were 197 and military casualties 441. Morison (Vol. XI, p. 66) says the loss of life was 'greater than the invasion forces suffered on D. Day at Utah beach'.

[2] M.T.B. 708 was destroyed by a friendly aircraft on 5th May, M.T.B. 203 probably blew up on one of the mines she had just laid on the 18th, and M.T.B. 732 was sunk on the 28th by the French ship *La Combattante* (see p. 290).

his worst efforts would not suffice to frustrate our purpose. Such was the measure of the accomplishment of the astonishingly varied forces of little ships and aircraft which had so long fought to gain control of our coastal waters, and to deny a similar measure of control to the enemy.

CHAPTER XII

THE MEDITERRANEAN CAMPAIGNS

1st January–31st May, 1944

> 'Armies go so slow, that Seamen think they never mean to get forward; but I dare say they act on a surer principle, although we seldom fail.'
>
> Nelson to Mrs. Nelson. Off Bastia, Corsica. February 28th 1794.

WHEN the Allied leaders dispersed from the Cairo conference early in December 1943, far-reaching decisions affecting the Mediterranean campaigns had been taken.[1] The British Prime Minister and War Cabinet, ever conscious of the importance of that theatre in deciding the control of central Europe, had reason to be satisfied with the decisions taken; for it had been agreed that the invasion of Normandy and of southern France, both of which the Allies intended to launch in May 1944, should not deprive the Mediterranean commands of the forces needed to bring the Italian campaign to a successful conclusion, nor stultify the hope of capturing Rhodes. This latter plan would rectify the failure in the Aegean of the previous autumn[2] and, so it was hoped, bring Turkey into the war on the Allied side. The whole programme for the future offensives in the theatre did, however, hinge on the capture of Rome in January 1944; yet hardly had the decisions been taken when it became clear that the premise on which they had been based would not be fulfilled. After the break-out of the Fifth Army from the Salerno beach-head in mid-September, and its junction with the Eighth Army coming up the 'toe' of Italy from the Messina Straits, the Allied advance to Naples had been rapid[3]; but after the capture of that port on the 1st of October stiff resistance was encountered to the north of it, and a pause was necessary before a new offensive could be launched.

The next blow, which was intended to breach the German defences

---

[1] See Ehrman, *Grand Strategy*, Vol. V (H.M.S.O., 1956), Chapters IV and V, for a full account of the Cairo and Teheran conferences 'Sextant' and 'Eureka' of November–December 1943.

[2] See pp. 189–204.

[3] See p. 182.

along the Sangro and Garigliano rivers known as the 'Gustav Line', and to carry the Allies to Rome and beyond, was to include an assault from the sea on the west coast of Italy between the small port of Anzio and the seaside resort of Nettuno, about thirty miles south of Rome and fifty-five miles north of the Garigliano River, which was the main obstacle on the Fifth Army's front.[1] General Alexander, the commander of the armies in Italy, relied on this flank assault to divert substantial enemy forces from the main front, where the country greatly favoured the defenders and a frontal attack on prepared positions was bound to be expensive. Unfortunately the assault shipping available in the Mediterranean limited the combined operation to the landing of one division and certain supporting troops. This being so, it was essential that the troops landed from the sea should link up quickly with the main forces coming up from the south; for failure to do so might well result in the extermination of so weak a force. The assault at Anzio (called operation 'Shingle') was accordingly fixed to take place on the 20th of December, the earliest date by which the shipping could be made available, and plans were made to lift 24,500 men and 2,700 vehicles to the beaches.

The Eighth Army's offensive on the eastern sector of the main front started in very bad weather on the 27th of November. After bitter fighting the passage of the River Sangro was forced; but little progress could be made beyond it. The experiences of the Fifth Army, which attacked in the western sector on the 1st of December, were similar to those of the Eighth Army, and before the end of that month it was obvious that the main assaults had failed. In such circumstances the landing of the single division at Anzio had plainly lost its purpose, and could only be carried out at very serious risk to the troops flung ashore. On the 18th of December General Mark Clark, the Fifth Army Commander, therefore recommended that the operation should be cancelled, and his view was accepted by General Alexander. Within a week, however, it was revived in a different form. At a conference held at Tunis on Christmas Day and presided over by Mr Churchill, it was decided to land a stronger force, of two divisions, without regard to the likelihood of an early junction with the Fifth Army, in the hope of easing the latter's next advance by drawing off enemy forces from the main front.[2] But the difficulty of providing the assault shipping for the stronger landing, and in particular the eighty-eight L.S.Ts needed, proved stubborn, chiefly because no postponement of the landings in Normandy and southern France was acceptable.[3] It was finally overcome only at the expense of depriving the South-East Asia Command of virtually all the ships

[1] See Map 12.
[2] See Churchill, Vol. V, pp. 378–387.
[3] See Ehrman, *Grand Strategy*, Vol. V, pp. 210–221.

which had been allocated to Admiral Mountbatten for the projected operations across the Indian Ocean[1], and by cancelling the intended attack on Rhodes. On the 7th–8th of January another conference took place at Marrakesh in Morocco, where Mr Churchill was recovering from an attack of pneumonia.[2] Half an hour before the discussions opened the Commander-in-Chief, Mediterranean, Admiral Sir John Cunningham, heard that the Chiefs of Staff had agreed to meet his minimum requirement for L.S.Ts, and he thereupon accepted the responsibility for landing two divisions at Anzio and for maintaining them ashore for fifteen days. The conference ended in agreement that the assault should take place on the 22nd of January. The commanders present fully realised the risks involved; but the prize—the early capture of Rome—was considered, especially by Mr Churchill, to justify accepting them. The chief hazards were, firstly, that supply of the Army over the beaches was bound to be very uncertain at that time of year; and, secondly, that the small port of Anzio was the only other entry for reinforcements and for all the vast quantities of stores needed after the assault. A new offensive was to be launched on the main front five days before the landing.

Early in the New Year, Admiral Cunningham set up an advanced naval headquarters in Naples, leaving only his administrative staff in Algiers. The planning of the assault from the sea was carried out mainly in the new headquarters, which were shared with the U.S. Navy. Although work did not begin until the last day of 1943, it was completed by the 12th of January 1944. Under the Commander-in-Chief the responsibility for the naval side of the undertaking was placed in the hands of Rear-Admiral F. J. Lowry, U.S.N.[3] He also had personal charge of the landing of the 3rd (American) Division in the southern sector, while Rear-Admiral T. Troubridge, who had just returned from India, was responsible for the assault by the 1st (British) Division in the northern sector. It was originally intended to land some U.S. Rangers in the British sector, to make a rapid lunge to the south and seize the enemy gun positions which commanded the port of Anzio; but the Ranger landings were finally shifted to beaches just south of the port. A paratroop drop on the Rome–Anzio highway, which also formed part of the original plan, was cancelled two days before the assault. We had learnt at some cost how difficult it was to synchronise airborne and seaborne

---

[1] These were operation 'Culverin' (against northern Sumatra and Malaya) and 'Buccaneer' (against the Andaman Islands). See pp. 344–346 regarding their cancellation.

[2] See Churchill, Vol. V, pp. 395–396.

[3] An interesting account by Admiral Lowry of the landing at Anzio is to be found in the *United States Naval Institute Proceedings* for January 1954 (pp. 23–31).

landings in a combined operation, and it seems that the commanders had no desire to accept the risks once again.[1]

Admiral Lowry paid a warm tribute to the speed with which Admiral Troubridge's experienced staff completed their share of the planning. It was, he said, 'reflected in the outstanding and seaman-like manner in which their landing was carried out'.

Difficulties, of which at any rate some could not have been fore-seen, are almost certain to arise while a large combined operation is being planned. In the case of 'Shingle' there was an acute shortage of the modern type of L.S.T. fitted with six pairs of davits for carrying assault landing craft. As only fourteen of this type could be provided (four for the British assault force and ten for the American), DUKWS were placed on board other L.S.Ts as substitutes for the assault craft which could not be carried. The DUKWS' slow speed (about five knots) made them, however, a poor alternative. A second and perhaps more serious trouble arose through the beach gradients being too gentle to allow landing craft to approach close enough to lower their ramps in shallow water, let alone on dry land. To avoid them beaching far offshore, restrictions had to be placed on the loads embarked in L.S.Ts and L.C.Ts.

Meanwhile photographic reconnaissance had revealed all that we needed to know about the assault area. In fact it was so successful that Admiral Lowry considered that the beach reconnaissances, which might have given away our plans, need not have been carried out. The naval operation orders were issued on the 16th of January, and the captains of all ships and craft, which had by that date assembled in the Bay of Naples, were at once briefed. Two days later Admiral Cunningham arrived there by air, and rehearsals of the assault then took place in the Gulf of Salerno. That by the British Task Force passed off reasonably well; but on the night of the 17th–18th of January the Americans encountered very rough weather, and lost a considerable number of DUKWS. Enquiry revealed that not only had some of the landing craft been incorrectly loaded, but their crews had been too inexperienced to cope with such difficult con-ditions. There was, however, no time for further practice landings.

The Air Plan had been issued on the 30th of December 1943, and divided the operations of the Strategic and Tactical Air Forces into three phases. From the 1st to the 14th of January their broad pur-poses were to disrupt the enemy's communications and to deceive him regarding our intentions by helping to carry out the cover plan (regarding which more will be said shortly). From the 15th to the 21st of January the assault area was to be isolated by bombing

---

[1] See pp. 135–136 regarding the fate of the airborne forces in operation 'Husky' (the invasion of Sicily). At Salerno the paratroop drop was cancelled (see p. 158).

attacks on road and rail communications north of Rome and on the Fifth and Eighth Armies' fronts. After the landings had taken place this policy was to continue, but in addition close support was then to be provided to the forces landed at Anzio. While the disruption of communications fell mainly to the Strategic Air Force, the Tactical Force's bombers would help to prevent the movement of enemy reinforcements towards the scene of the assault. Once the convoys had sailed from Naples the Coastal and Tactical Air Forces would protect the shipping by day and by night; and after the troops had landed the duty of supporting them from the air fell to the latter command. To help provide close air support for the beach-head, over 1,000 tons of expanded steel sheet was to be landed at a very early stage and laid to form an air strip; but in the event this extemporised landing ground could never be used, because it remained within range of enemy artillery fire. Air support therefore had to be provided from more distant airfields.

The cover plan was intended to mislead the enemy into expecting a landing further up the west coast of Italy near Civitavecchia[1], or on the south coast of France. Diversionary air attacks were accordingly carried out at both points, troops and landing craft were assembled in Corsica and Sardinia, and on the night of the 21st–22nd a cruiser and destroyer force bombarded targets at Civitavecchia, while coastal craft made dummy landings. In fact the enemy was so heavily engaged on the Fifth and Eighth Armies' fronts that he paid little attention to either our real or our simulated intentions.

While all these preparations were in train the new offensive was launched on the main front. In appallingly bad weather the British X Corps fought its way across the Garigliano River on the 17th of January, but could not make further progress. Two of the 15th Cruiser Squadron, which had been brought up to its full strength of six ships after the defeat of the enemy's blockade-runners in the Bay of Biscay[2], and four destroyers supported the attack by bombardments from the sea; but the enemy's stubborn resistance and the weather frustrated all attempts at a break-through. On the night of the 20th–21st the American II Corps forced the Rapido River, but had to abandon its bridgehead two days later. It thus became plain that the Gustav Line defences had held, and that an early junction between the main forces and those landed from the sea at Anzio was improbable.

In view of the long stalemate which followed on the landings at Anzio, it will be interesting to see how the operation was regarded at the time by the commanders concerned. General Alexander's

---

[1] See Map 12.

[2] See pp. 73–75.

instructions make it plain that he intended the assault force to break out of the beach-head as quickly as possible 'to cut the enemy's main communications in the [Alban Hills] area south-east of Rome'; but General Clark was less explicit in his orders to Major-General J. P. Lucas, the commander of the landing force (designated VI Corps). General Clark merely stated that his subordinate's main object was 'to seize and secure a beach-head in the vicinity of Anzio', whence he was 'to advance on the Alban Hills'. Nor did the orders issued by VI Corps headquarters to the American 3rd Division or the British 1st Division contain any instructions regarding the rapid exploitation of a successful landing. General Lucas himself appears to have been pessimistic about the whole undertaking from the outset, which could hardly improve the prospects of an operation 'of peculiar complexity and hazard'.[1] On the naval side the weather was the chief anxiety; for we needed five fine days to establish a firm beach-head, and at that time of year such a favourable break was unlikely. Admirals Cunningham and Lowry were confident that they could land the assault forces successfully, but felt less happy with regard to the subsequent support and supply of the Army.[2]

Admiral Troubridge's ships, which were to carry the British 1st Division and two Commandos to the 'Peter' sector about six miles north-west of Anzio[3], assembled outside the Bay of Naples on the afternoon of the 21st of January. The troops were embarked in three L.S.Is, in the three large L.S.Ts *Boxer*, *Bruiser* and *Thruster*, which had done such good work off Salerno and had just returned from the Indian Ocean[4], and in a number of other L.S.Ts and landing craft, both British and American.[5] The *Orion* and *Spartan* of the 15th Cruiser Squadron, now commanded by Rear-Admiral J. M. Mansfield, eight fleet destroyers and four of the *Hunt*-class were to escort the transports and support the landings; and there was the usual complement of minesweepers and anti-submarine vessels to clear and protect the anchorage.

Embarked in the cruiser *Spartan* was Rear-Admiral Frolov of the Russian Navy, who had come to witness a combined operation conducted by his country's two principal Allies. He made a very favourable impact on all who met him, and appeared to be deeply and genuinely impressed by what he saw. As he left the ship, after addressing her company and being cheered in return, he assured the *Spartan's*

---

[1] See Morison, Vol. IX, pp. 328, 352, 358 and 365, for extracts from General Lucas's diary.

[2] See article by Admiral Lowry in *United States Naval Institute Proceedings* for January 1954, p. 25.

[3] See Map 19 (facing p. 305).

[4] See pp. 174 and 181.

[5] See Table 19 (p. 304).

Captain that 'Britain is the best friend of Russia'. To read the report of his visit to the Royal Navy after the lapse of fifteen years is rather a saddening experience; for the good will which then prevailed on both sides is abundantly clear.

Admiral Lowry flew his flag in the headquarters ship *Biscayne*, and the ships for the southern assault (called 'X-Ray') also loaded in the ports of the Gulf of Naples and sailed on the 21st of January. The military forces consisted of the 3rd American Division, which was to land four miles to the east of Anzio, and three battalions of U.S. Rangers and a parachute battalion, who were to land near to that small port, seize it and clear the harbour works as quickly as possible.[1] The Ranger Group was embarked in three British L.S.Is, and the majority of the transport provided for the American infantry division was also British. The gun support ships for the 'X-Ray' landings were the cruisers *Penelope* and U.S.S. *Brooklyn*, and five American destroyers; while the escort group consisted of American, British and Greek ships. Lastly the submarines *Uproar* and *Ultor* were to serve as beacons during the approach of the assault forces to their anchorages. Table 19 (p. 304) shows the composition of the naval assault, covering and support forces. Ships of the British and American navies were intermingled in them, but all were under Admiral Lowry's command.

The convoys carrying some 50,000 men and 5,000 vehicles formed up outside the Bay of Naples on the 21st of January and then steered to the north-west. Their routes had been chosen to keep them clear of the enemy's minefields and to conceal our precise intention for as long as possible. The weather was fine and calm, and the passage of the expedition was uncontested and uneventful. The full extent of the failure of the enemy's reconnaissance is well demonstrated by the fact that no aircraft had reconnoitred Naples since the 11th of December 1943; and it is probable that it was the bombing of his airfields which thus gave the Allies the great advantage of secrecy in preparation. As the transports approached their lowering positions almost complete silence prevailed on shore.

The sweepers were meanwhile trying to clear the anchorages and the channels leading inshore; but our intelligence regarding the enemy's minefields was soon proved inaccurate and, as there was not enough time between the arrival of the sweepers and 'H-hour', which was at 2 a.m. on the 22nd of January, clearance had by no means been completed when the assault waves started to move towards the beaches.

Shortly before the first landing craft touched down two of the rocket craft successfully fired their spectacular salvos on to the

---

[1] See Map 19 (facing p. 305).

Table 19. The Landing at Anzio—Operation 'Shingle'—22nd January, 1944

Composition of Naval Forces
(British unless otherwise stated)

(Based on the operation orders of Naval Commander Force 'P'
dated 15th January, 1944) .

	Northern Assault ('Peter' Force)	Southern Assault ('X-ray' Force)
H.Q. Ships	1	1
L.S.Is	3 (1 Polish)	5
Cruisers	2	2 (1 U.S.)
A.A. Ships	1	1
Destroyers	11	13 (10 U.S., 2 Greek)
Gunboats	—	2 (Dutch)
Minesweepers . . .	16 (4 U.S.)	23 (U.S.)
Large L.S.Ts (*Boxer* class) . .	3	—
L.S.Ts	30 (4 U.S. 2 Greek)	51 (10 U.S.)
L.C.Gs and L.C.Fs . . .	4	4
L.C.Is	29	60 (54 U.S.)
L.C.Ts	17	32 (7 U.S.)
L.C.Ts (R)	1	2
Salvage & Repair craft (L.C.Ts & L.C.Is)	5 (3 U.S.)	6 (U.S.)
A/S—M/S Trawlers . . .	4	—
Beacon Submarines . . .	1	1
Tugs	3 (2 U.S.)	2 (1 U.S.)
M.Ls and Scout Craft . . .	17 (9 U.S.)	23 (U.S.)
Miscellaneous	1	2

beaches. They were so effective that Admiral Lowry recommended that in future the whole length of the shore on which a combined assault was to be launched should be drenched with rockets a few minutes before the troops arrived. At Anzio all the arrangements made to help accurate navigation and to identify the beaches worked excellently, the assault waves arrived almost exactly on time, and it was at once obvious that we had achieved complete surprise. The decision not to bombard or bomb the beaches before the assault was, in this case, abundantly justified.[1]

In Admiral Troubridge's 'Peter' sector the L.S.Is were quickly cleared and sent back to Naples under escort, and the only untoward incident in the assault occurred when the A.A. ship *Palomares* struck a mine. After daylight the shipping moved closer inshore to speed

---

[1] Compare Allied experiences in the Salerno operation (pp. 159 and 183), in which surprise was not achieved and the assault forces landed against alert and intact defences.

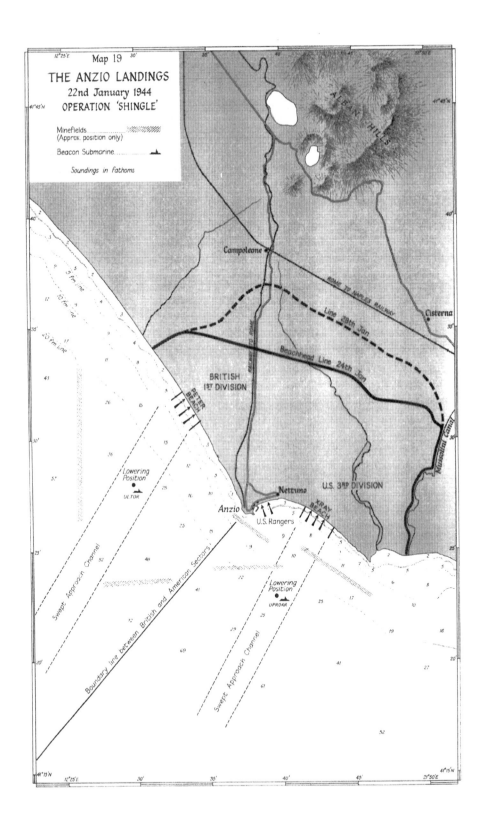

Map 19

THE ANZIO LANDINGS
22nd January 1944
OPERATION 'SHINGLE'

Minefields ....
(Approx. position only)

Beacon Submarine ....

Soundings in fathoms

ALBAN HILLS

Campoleone

ROME TO NAPLES RAILWAY

Cisterna

Line 28th Jan.

Beachhead Line 24th Jan.

BRITISH
1ST DIVISION

Mussolini Canal

U.S. 3RD DIVISION

PETER BEACH

Lowering
Position
ULTOR

Nettuno

X-RAY BEACH

Anzio

U.S. Rangers

Swept Approach Channel

Lowering
Position
UPROAR

Boundary line between British and American Sectors

Swept Approach Channel

up discharge, and a few enemy guns then opened fire on the anchorage; but little damage was caused. The only serious difficulties arose through the very flat gradient of the beaches and the off-shore sand bars, which prevented the landing craft discharging their men and vehicles quickly and dry-shod. The beaches were, said Admiral Troubridge, the worst he had ever encountered in a combined operation. Although pontoons were quickly launched and rigged into causeways, unloading was so difficult that ten L.S.Ts were transferred to the American sector, where the beaches were rather better. None the less by 6 p.m. on D-Day most of the men and the greater part of the 1st Division's vehicles had been landed. Enemy shelling and a raid by fighter-bombers during the afternoon caused no significant damage.

Meanwhile the U.S. Rangers had made their assault on the beaches between Anzio and Nettuno.[1] They encountered no opposition, quickly seized the port and by 8 a.m. Captain E. C. L. Turner, who had commanded the Rangers' transports, was established on shore as Naval Officer in Charge, Anzio. The first L.S.T. and two L.C.Ts entered the port at 5 p.m., and Turner then found that six of the former could be berthed at the same time against the mole. The prospect of keeping the Army adequately supplied, regarding which the naval command had been anxious, thus brightened considerably. No one could then have foreseen that the difficulties of supply, particularly through the port of Anzio, would mount as enemy bombing and artillery fire increased.

In the main American sector ('X-Ray') the assault and follow-up waves encountered little resistance, ships and craft were rapidly cleared, and by daylight it was plain that the landing had been wholly successful.

By midnight on the 22nd–23rd—only twenty-two hours after the first landing craft had touched down—no less than 36,034 men, 3,069 vehicles and a large quantity of stores had been landed[2]; the two assault forces were in touch with each other and were advancing slowly inland; casualties had been trifling, and there seemed to be nothing to prevent the seizure of the Alban Hills twenty miles away. In fact we know from the enemy's records that there was at that moment almost nothing to prevent the landing forces advancing right into Rome. Whether, had they done so, they could have supported themselves until reinforced is likely to remain a matter for dispute. What is certain is that the slowness with which VI Corps reacted to an apparently very favourable situation, combined with the speed with which the Germans moved towards Anzio to counter

[1] See Map 19.

[2] See *Report by the Supreme Allied Commander, Mediterranean (SACMED) to the Combined Chiefs of Staff on the Italian Campaign* (H.M.S.O., 1946), p. 22.

the threat, very soon lost an opportunity which was never to recur.[1] It thus came to pass that the remarkable accomplishments of planning the assault in its revised and strengthened form in less than a month, of assembling and loading the shipping, and of landing the armies on a hostile coast with scarcely any losses all went for naught; and the Allied Navies, which had carried out all their initial purposes with complete success, were thus condemned to the arduous and trying duty of supplying and reinforcing the beach-head in face of severe opposition for a long period.

The day following the assault brought a foretaste of what was to come; for the enemy's air attacks on our shipping increased in strength and in variety. Lightning raids by fast fighter-bombers, of which little warning was often received, and which were exceedingly difficult targets for the naval gunners, alternated with torpedo and glider-bomb attacks.[2] When torpedo-bombers came in at dusk that evening they hit the destroyer *Janus*, which sank with heavy loss of life; and a few minutes later her sister ship the *Jervis* was damaged by a glider-bomb. Admiral Troubridge now suggested to his colleague of the 15th Cruiser Squadron that, as most of the Army's artillery was ashore, and destroyers and gunboats were available to give close support, the cruisers *Orion* and *Spartan* should return to Naples. Admiral Lowry at once challenged this proposal from one of his subordinates, and it was finally decided that the U.S.S. *Brooklyn* should remain off Anzio and take command of all fire support ships. That night, as had been feared, the fine weather broke, and the first of many gales struck the shipping massed off the beaches. All landing craft were sent to shelter in Anzio harbour, and, as both the British sector's pontoon causeways, which were essential for unloading, broached to on the beaches, all shipping was transferred to the American sector on the 24th. With the concurrence of the Commander-in-Chief, who had arrived off Anzio in a destroyer, the British sector was then closed, and Admiral Troubridge sailed for Naples. While he was proceeding down the swept channel at dusk in the *Bulolo* a succession of severe air attacks took place, and an American destroyer was hit and damaged. Then, after dark, the

---

[1] Field-Marshal Alexander's Despatch (Supplement to the London Gazette of 12th June 1950, p. 2912) states, 'I considered that our progress in the first days of the landing had been rather too slow . . . VI Corps, with the resources available to it, would have found it very difficult both to be secure on the Alban Hills and at the same time retain the absolutely necessary communications with the sea at Anzio. There are too many hypotheses involved to make further speculation valuable . . . the actual course of events was probably the most advantageous in the end.'

[2] The type of glider-bomb used against shipping off Anzio was generally the Hs.293. See p. 30, for a description. The unit which employed them worked from Bergamo airfield near Lake Como. Many attacks were made on Allied shipping with these weapons, but although they proved troublesome and caused some losses the German unit concerned (11/KG.100) suffered heavily in the process.

Luftwaffe turned its attention to three British hospital ships, which had just sailed from the assault anchorage, and were brightly illuminated and unmistakably marked with Geneva crosses. One of them, the *St David*, was sunk, and the others were severely shaken by near-misses. In consequence of this further German disregard of international law concerning the immunity of hospital ships Admiral Cunningham decided to use specially converted L.S.Ts to evacuate casualties. Meanwhile the American destroyer *Mayo* had struck a mine and had been taken in tow to Naples. Admiral Lowry was thus deprived of four of his destroyers within twenty-four hours.

On the 25th Admiral Mansfield returned in the *Orion* to take over responsibility for fire support from the U.S.S. *Brooklyn*, and a large convoy of reinforcements also reached the assault area; but the day closed with the wind and sea rising again, unloading over the beaches had to stop, and severe damage was done to pontoon causeways and landing craft in the American sector. Had the port of Anzio not been in full use to unload L.S.Ts a crisis might well have arisen. The sweepers were striving all the time to extend the waters swept clear of mines; but there were a great many still about, and when the gale caused ships to drag their anchors, and so enter unswept waters, casualties were bound to occur. In the early hours of the 26th a British L.S.T. was mined, caught fire and sank, and an L.C.I. which tried to go to her assistance suffered the same fate. Next day, the 27th, the sea went down, unloading was resumed, and Admiral Cunningham sent his congratulations on 'the very successful conclusion of the first phase'. But, although by the 29th 68,886 men, 508 guns, 237 tanks and 27,250 tons of stores had been landed[1], the real troubles of operation 'Shingle' had not yet begun. The Allied armies had consolidated their beach-head; but by the 28th, on which day Hitler issued vehement orders for their extermination, they had only covered about half the distance to the Alban Hills. Nowhere was the beach-head more than ten miles deep, and, although by the 30th General Lucas's strength was equivalent to four divisions, the enemy had assembled approximately equal numbers facing Anzio; and yet stronger reserves were rapidly concentrating south of the Tiber. Not only had the chance of achieving a quick success vanished, but it was obvious that a strong counter-attack was now imminent.

As a first step the Germans increased the weight of their air attacks on our off-shore shipping, by night as well as by day. Dive-bombing, torpedo attacks and glider-bombs were all used; and the enemy generally made his biggest effort each day at dusk. Admiral Lowry asked for more anti-aircraft ships to be sent to him, and when

---

[1] SACMED Report, p. 22.

they arrived he stationed them close inshore to protect the ships and craft which were unloading. The fixed A.A. defences on shore were strengthened simultaneously, while the Tactical Air Force attacked the German airfields by night as well as by day. At night the Germans used flares to light up the transport anchorage, and we soon learnt that, in Admiral Lowry's words, 'smoke, silence and slow speed' then afforded the best protection. Strict fire discipline was again shown to be essential. Off Anzio it was not always good, and it was noteworthy that it was often ships which opened fire without authority which were hit. In daylight, smoke was found to be far less effective than at night, and its use was almost certain to handicap the anti-aircraft gunners.

It was the glider-bombs which did most of the damage. After the trouble experienced from wireless-controlled weapons off Salerno and elsewhere, we had taken energetic steps to fit ships with equipment for listening on the enemy's wave-length, and jamming the transmissions of the controlling aircraft. Three such ships had been included in the Anzio assault force; but their crews were not yet adequately experienced in their highly specialised task. On the evening of the 29th the light cruiser *Spartan*, which had been stationed close inshore to protect the vessels unloading on the beaches, was hit and capsized with heavy loss of life. A Liberty ship was also hit, caught fire, and blew up some hours later. Admiral Lowry now ordered the cruisers to steam clear of the transport anchorage each day at dusk, and to return the following morning. Destroyers only were to be kept inshore to give anti-aircraft protection during the hours of darkness.

That day, the 29th, the Army attacked at two points near the head of the salient formed by the beach-head, but was completely frustrated by strong German reinforcements. Generals Alexander and Clark both visited VI Corps headquarters at this time; but they can have gained little comfort regarding the prospects of operation 'Shingle'. The Fifth and Eighth Armies' main fronts were now static and, VI Corps' landing at Anzio having failed in its purpose, the Navies had to carry on with the arduous duty of keeping the beach-head supplied, no matter how bad the weather nor how open the anchorages. The small port of Anzio, the only sheltered entry for supplies, was now exposed to constant artillery fire and air attacks, and had become so encumbered with wrecked or damaged craft that no more than one L.S.T. at a time could reach the beaching ramp. Cruisers and destroyers had to be kept continuously offshore to protect the exposed shipping and answer calls for fire support from the Army, while other warships waited at short notice in Naples, five hours' steaming away.

So far there had not, as at Salerno, been many calls for bombardment.[1] The *Orion* had fired on a radar station on D-Day, the U.S.S. *Brooklyn* had engaged various targets, and on the 29th the *Dido* used her 5·25-inch guns against an enemy battery. We had found that British and American air and shore observers could control the indirect fire of the ships of either Navy; but off Anzio there were at first comparatively few opportunities for the bombardment teams to show their skill. Admiral Lowry considered that naval gunfire on road junctions and highways contributed greatly to delaying the concentration and arrival of enemy reinforcements; but the evidence from German records does not confirm that they were appreciably hindered. It was moreover the British view that naval fire was not employed to the best advantage during the first weeks off Anzio, because control was not centralised in a Headquarters Ship. This accordingly became the practice, and for the next three months the gun support ships were constantly in action with enemy batteries, or engaging his concentrations of troops and vehicles.

On the 2nd of February Admiral Cunningham directed Admiral Lowry to hand over control of the naval forces supporting the Anzio landing to the Flag Officer, Western Italy, Rear-Admiral J. A. V. Morse, whose flag flew ashore at Naples, and Lowry accordingly left the assault area in his flagship the *Biscayne*. He had been instrumental in launching a combined operation with exemplary efficiency.

The chagrin felt in naval circles over the apparent failure to exploit a favourable opportunity was widespread, and on the 11th of February Sir John Cunningham expressed his disappointment forcibly in a letter to the First Sea Lord in which he compared the situation at Anzio with that at Suvla Bay during the Gallipoli operation in 1915.[2] The First Sea Lord replied that he fully shared the Commander-in-Chief's feelings, but that it had not escaped notice in London that the naval side had been a great success. 'Now we are faced with a long and hard battle, and a fairly uncertain supply line ... Still we have a position on the enemy's flank which, if it can be maintained, will be a running sore. It has also had the effect of bringing down into Italy something in the neighbourhood of six [German] divisions, some of them from France.'[3]

We must now take temporary leave of the Anzio beach-head to review other events in the Mediterranean theatre.

---

[1] See pp. 176, 177 and 179.

[2] This refers to the flank landing at Suvla Bay on 6th–7th August 1915. The troops were put ashore virtually unopposed, but no attempt was made to exploit the opportunity. See Corbett, *Naval Operations*, Vol. III, Chapter V (Longmans, Green & Co., 1923), and Alan Moorehead, *Gallipoli*, Chapters XIII–XV (Hamish Hamilton, 1956).

[3] In fact the diversion of German strength to Italy at this time amounted to the equivalent of about eight divisions.

In addition to the through-Mediterranean convoys from Britain (KMS–MKS) and from America (UGS–GUS), a large number of local convoys had recently been organised to meet the needs of the Allied forces and of the civilian populations of territories wrested from the enemy. New series of convoys had been organised to run between the ports on the 'heel' of Italy to Augusta (HA–AH), between Augusta and Naples (NV–VN), from Naples to the North African ports (SNF–NSF), and between Algiers and Ajaccio in Corsica (AC–CA). Naples had now become one of the largest ports of discharge in the theatre. Three convoys arrived there in January, and in that month we started to sail the KMS convoys from Britain direct to Naples on a thirty-seven-day cycle. Outside the Mediterranean various changes were made to dovetail the Atlantic convoys with those entering or leaving the inland sea. The Sierra Leone to Britain (SL) convoys were, for instance, delayed to enable the homeward MKS convoys from Naples to unite with them off Gibraltar. Escorts had, of course, to be found for all this shipping, and, although French warships and a few from the Italian Navy now carried a small part of the burden, the greater share of it still fell to the British and American Navies and to the associated Allied air commands.

Although air attacks on coastal shipping in our home waters had virtually ceased in the autumn of 1943, the defence of the heavy traffic moving along the North African coast continued to be a major problem for nearly another year. At the beginning of 1944 the Germans had collected nearly 100 modern bombers in the south of France, and thereafter they steadily increased their numbers until, in spite of suffering considerable losses, they reached a peak of 125 in May. They consisted of Ju.88 and He.111 torpedo-bombers, and of He.177s fitted to use the new wireless-controlled bombs, which we had first encountered off Salerno.[1] Nor were we left long in any doubt regarding the serious threat which this force represented, and the difficulties involved in dealing with its sorties. In the first place the route which the convoys had to use, running about forty miles off the African coast, could not be varied. Secondly, by coming down the Spanish coast, or through the gap between Minorca and Sardinia[2], the German bombers could sometimes achieve a measure of surprise; for it was difficult to gain long warning of their approach from the north. Lastly it was always possible that, by attacking at dusk, they might catch the defenders at a disadvantage. Responsibility for the protection of the convoys was shared between the surface escorts, which were always numerous and generally included an A.A. cruiser, and the fighters of Air Vice-Marshal Sir Hugh

---

[1] See pp. 177 and 179.
[2] See Map 12.

Lloyd's Mediterranean Coastal Air Force. These latter maintained a continuous day and night patrol over the convoys, and always kept numerous other aircraft ready to take off as soon as warning of attack was received; and in addition a special effort was always made to intercept the shadowing aircraft, whose presence invariably indicated that attack was imminent. None the less we soon realised that our organisation for directing the fighters on to their targets left a good deal to be desired. Rear-Admiral Troubridge summed the matter up succinctly when, early in 1944, he reported to the Commander-in-Chief that 'Fighters alone did not constitute fighter cover, and were indeed almost valueless unless properly directed.' The air and naval authorities both recognised the urgency of the need to provide Fighter Direction Ships with modern radar equipment, and at the end of 1943 the Commander-in-Chief had represented the matter to the Admiralty; but the requirement had not yet been met.

In January only one convoy (KMS.37) was heavily attacked. Two ships were torpedoed at dusk on the 10th, and one of them sank; but the defenders probably destroyed some half-dozen of the thirty torpedo-bombers taking part.[1] Next, on the evening of the 1st of February, about forty bombers attacked UGS.30 off Oran. The long-range fighters broke up the enemy formations, and only seven torpedo-bombers got through; but they sank one ship and damaged a second. The enemy's next effort was made against a troop convoy on the 8th of March, and again his bombers were successfully intercepted at long range. This time they suffered several losses without inflicting any damage on the convoy. Air Vice-Marshal Lloyd had meanwhile stationed a long-range fighter wing in Sardinia, to catch the bombers as they came south; and this measure quickly proved its worth.

The Germans now switched to night attacks, using 'Pathfinders' to locate the convoys, and flares to illuminate them. On the 19th and 29th of March respectively two east-bound convoys (KMS.44 and KMS.45) were attacked in that manner. We countered these new tactics by putting up smoke screens from the escorts, and sometimes from the merchantmen as well; and this, combined with heavy A.A. gunfire, generally proved effective. No losses were suffered on either of these occasions; but we realised that we had by no means yet got the measure of the enemy, and that the co-ordination of our defences had to be improved before we could expect to repulse him decisively. We will return to the subject later, for it is time to consider the other threat to our convoys—that of the U-boats.

On the 1st of January 1944 there were still thirteen U-boats in the

---

[1] The German records for this period of the war are not complete enough for their losses always to be assessed with confidence.

Mediterranean, but only three were at sea, and they caused us no losses during the month. Our intelligence had, however, given warning that reinforcements were on the way, and a prolonged but fruitless search for them was made off the Spanish coast. Between the end of January and the 25th of March nine more U-boats attempted to pass through the Straits of Gibraltar. One gave up and returned to western France, and two were sunk by the combined efforts of M.A.D. aircraft and surface ships (U.761 on the 24th of February and U.392 on the 16th of March).[1] The six boats which got through did not, however, appreciably increase the enemy's operational strength inside the Mediterranean, because two (U.380 and U.410) were destroyed in a raid on Toulon by U.S. Army bombers on the 11th of March, and three others were accounted for in various actions which will be related shortly.

In February two U-boats worked against the ships carrying supplies to the Anzio beach-head. On the 16th U.230 sank L.S.T. 418, but two days later her colleague U.410 scored a more important success. She encountered the light cruiser *Penelope*, which was on her way back to Naples, hit her with three torpedoes and sank her. It was sad to lose in this manner a ship which had served so long, and with such distinction, on this station.[2] On the 20th the same U-boat torpedoed the American L.S.T. 348, which blew up. Both these enemy successes were obtained near Cape Circe, off which Homer may have placed the mythical island of Aeaea, where the goddess Circe drugged and degraded Odysseus' crew and tried to seduce their captain. It was, perhaps, appropriate that the U-boats should have found victims in the waters overlooked by the palace of that ruthless enchantress.

In March there were two U-boats in the Tyrrhenian Sea, and one of them sank a ship off Palermo on the 10th; but nemesis quickly overtook them both, for on the same day the trawler *Mull* sank U.343 off southern Sardinia and a combined effort by three British and one American destroyer disposed of U.450 after a ten-hour hunt. Another success to a force of British escort vessels, once again after a long and persistent search, was the sinking of U.223 on the 30th; but before she was despatched the U-boat torpedoed and sank the destroyer leader *Laforey*. The loss of life was heavy, and included the commander of the 14th Flotilla, Captain H. T. Armstrong, one of the Royal Navy's most distinguished destroyer captains. That these U-boats were tough and elusive enemies was shown by an attack on convoy SNF.17 off Bougie on the 17th. Two merchantmen (one

---

[1] See p. 246 regarding M.A.D. aircraft. Details of U-boat sinkings are in Appendix D.

[2] See Vol. I, pp. 159–161, 174–175, 532–533 and Vol. II, pp. 44, 48, 51–55, 58 and 430 regarding the fighting record of the *Penelope*. C. S. Forester's novel, *The Ship* (Michael Joseph, 1943), was built around her part in the 2nd Battle of Sirte.

*The Assault at Anzio,
operation 'Shingle', 22nd
January, 1944*

An L.S.T. approaching
the assault area, while
destroyers lay a smoke
screen.

General view of the
assault area, showing
L.S.Ts unloading.

Bombarding ships in
action. H.M.S. *Spartan*
in foreground.

The Assault at Anzio, operation 'Shingle', 22nd January, 1944

Above. L.S.Ts unloading in Anzio harbour.

Below. In Anzio town, 27th January, 1944. (Left to right in foreground are Captain E. C. L. Turner, Senior Naval Officer, Landings: Rear Admiral F. J. Lowry, U.S.N., Naval Assault Force Commander, and Admiral Sir John Cunningham, C.-in-C., Mediterranean.)

Above. A mine or bomb explodes among DUKWs carrying stores on to the Anzio beaches.

Below. Night bombardment by H.M.S. *Mauritius* in support of Fifth Army, February 1944.

Air Attacks on Enemy Shipping

R.A.F. Beaufighters blow up an ammunition ship in the Aegean.

R.A.F. Beaufighters sinking the German supply ship *Lisa* off Crete, 22nd February, 1944. One of the escorting destroyers was also damaged.

The destruction of a supply ship in the Adriatic by 'Kitty-bombers'.

of over 17,000 tons) were sunk, and although the 'swamp' technique described earlier was applied for three-and-a-half days U.371 got away safely, albeit badly damaged.[1]

In the eastern basin our maritime control was hardly disputed at all at this time; and, apart from the large flow of merchant shipping proceeding towards the Suez Canal, important reinforcements for the Eastern Fleet, including the *Queen Elizabeth, Valiant, Renown* and *Illustrious*, the French battleship *Richelieu* and a large floating dock, which was towed out in sections, all passed through under continuous air cover.

Of our own submarines, the 10th Flotilla was still based on Maddalena in Sardinia, while the 1st moved from Beirut to Malta in February. Neither flotilla was, however, at full strength. Patrols were maintained off Toulon and along the coastal route from that base to Genoa but, because targets were now hard to find, successes were comparatively rare. In February, however, the *Upstart* and *Ultor* each sank one ship.

Apart from the waters off Anzio perhaps the most active scene of naval operations at this time was the Adriatic, where our purposes were to hinder the supply of the German army in Italy by sea, to prevent the transfer of merchantmen and light naval forces to the Aegean, and to help the Yugo-Slav irregulars contain large German forces, which the enemy needed so badly on other fronts. But operations were constantly entangled in the intricacies of Balkan political feuds, and incidents more appropriate to comic opera than to war alternated with the human tragedies which are inevitable when a whole nation is in revolt against a barbaric enemy. Our main force consisted of the 24th Destroyer Flotilla, of about ten ships, based on Bari. They constantly bombarded targets in north-east Italy, Albania and Dalmatia, covered the landings of Commandos on various islands, and protected the lighter vessels during their frequent forays against the German supply traffic. But it was the coastal craft which played the greatest part in this piratical hide-and-seek type of warfare. In January Commandos occupied the island of Vis (Lissa), about thirty miles south-west of Split, which was almost the last off-shore position not to have fallen to the enemy.[2] We had used that island as an advanced naval base from 1812 to 1815, in order to deny control of the Adriatic to Napoleon's allies, and in 1944 the circumstances were remarkably similar. There were two good anchorages for medium-sized vessels, and a Coastal Force base was quickly established in one of them under Lieutenant-Commander M. C. Giles, who had been appointed Senior Naval Officer, Vis, and

[1] See p. 208 regarding the introduction of this new anti-U-boat technique.
[2] See Map 12.

commanded a heterogeneous collection of ships manned by curiously assorted crews. His must have been one of the most unusual commands ever given to a naval officer. Construction of a landing strip was also begun, but it was not until American engineers arrived in May and, with characteristic speed and energy, greatly improved and extended it, that it served as a satisfactory advanced air base. The Germans fully realised the importance of Vis, and in January made plans for its capture. Although they managed to assemble a considerable fleet of small craft they never launched an assault, and by April they had abandoned their intention. The main reasons were that Allied air patrols were making these waters prohibitively dangerous by day, while our coastal craft were becoming bolder and more vigilant at night. In March the German Naval Commander remarked in his War Diary that Allied air superiority had virtually stopped all movements by his surface ships. The Desert Air Force's Warhawks and Mitchell bombers, and occasionally the Strategic Air Force's Fortresses, attacked the enemy's ports all along the coast at this time.[1] Several quite large ships were sunk in Sibenik in January, a German U-boat (U.81) and the ex-Italian submarine *Nautilo* were both destroyed in Pola on the 9th, and losses of small craft were so heavy that the Germans began to construct concrete shelters for their E-boats at various points on the Dalmatian coast. Taken together, Allied sea and air activities in the Adriatic not only frustrated the enemy's offensive purposes but soon began to imperil his hold on the off-shore islands. Vis was the main hub of our activity; but it was, of course, within fairly easy supporting distance of the much bigger Allied naval and air bases in southern Italy. The operations gradually took the shape which we had vainly hoped to produce in the Aegean in the previous autumn; and a comparison of the failure in those waters with the successful campaign in the Adriatic may not be unprofitable.[2] Whereas in the case of the Aegean our main bases in Egypt had been too distant, our forward bases too ill-equipped and too weakly defended, and the necessary air support was not forthcoming, in the Adriatic no such handicaps existed. The enemy's island garrisons very soon began to experience precisely the same difficulties as had beset our own on Cos and Leros; and German reports on the Adriatic campaign in 1944 read remarkably like those of the British commanders on the Aegean operations of the preceding autumn.

Prominent among the Commandos on Vis, according to Com-

---

[1] The Desert Air Force formed part of the Allied Tactical Air Force, and worked mainly in support of the British Eighth Army. An Appendix to Part II of this volume gives the organisation and composition of the Mediterranean Allied Air Commands in June 1944.

[2] See pp. 189–205.

mander Giles, was to be found Admiral Sir Walter Cowan, thinly disguised as a naval commander. His age was now seventy-three, and since the early days of the war he had, although long since on the retired list, been determined to get into the thickest of the fighting. His was an astonishing character to meet in the twentieth century. Caring nothing for his personal safety, he positively throve on danger; and he undoubtedly enjoyed physical combat. Perhaps he is best described as a survival from the age of the first Elizabeth, with a strong spiritual kinship with Richard Grenville or Hawkins. After serving in the western desert in 1940 and being captured while on a raid, he was exchanged, only to join up again with the Commandos in the Adriatic. To them he was a much-loved mascot; but to keep him out of danger was a constant anxiety, and everyone knew that their efforts to do so would prove vain. His services with the Commandos were recognised by the award of a bar to the D.S.O. which he had gained no less than forty-three years earlier.

Late in February three large French destroyers joined the Adriatic flotilla. These ships were capable of at least 40 knots, which enabled them to leave Bari on the reports of our evening air reconnaissance and catch an enemy convoy before daylight next morning. They very soon proved their worth. On the last night of the month *Le Malin* and *Le Terrible* attacked a German convoy bound for the Aegean and sank both the principal ship and one of the escorting corvettes. In a similar operation on the 19th of March *Le Fantasque* and *Le Terrible* almost exterminated a convoy of small vessels making for Navarin. Three Siebel ferries and a barge were sunk, or so badly damaged that aircraft were able to finish them off next day. These were heartening successes to the rejuvenated French Navy.

While the Adriatic patrols were scouring the maze of channels on the Dalmatian coast for targets, other coastal craft, working from Bastia in Corsica, were very active against the enemy's supply traffic from southern France to north Italy; and yet others were reaching into the Aegean from Cyprus to intercept the small ships used by the Germans to supply their island garrisons. It is indeed interesting to find how the virtually complete disappearance of the big ships from the Mediterranean—because there were now no comparable enemy ships to oppose them—brought the small craft their greatest opportunities. Though our sea and air forces never managed to bring the enemy's coastwise traffic to a complete halt, there is no doubt that they greatly increased the difficulty of supplying the German armies in Italy and the Balkans, both of which depended to a considerable extent on sea transport. The Germans did not, however, remain idle in face of the rising threat to their coastal shipping. Late on the evening of the 22nd of April three ex-Italian destroyers left Porto Ferraio in Elba to bombard Bastia and to cover a minelaying operation which was to be carried out concurrently further to the south. The enemy had intended that Luftwaffe aircraft should co-operate by making a simultaneous bombing raid and should also drop flares to illuminate the shore targets; but, as so often happened, German air co-operation never materialised. The destroyers opened fire in the small hours of the 23rd, but neither their shells nor the torpedoes which they fired at the harbour entrance caused any damage. Our coastal craft searched for the enemy ships, but failed to find them.

By way of contrast with this abortive German raid, one of the most successful actions fought by the Allied light forces took place two nights later (April 24th–25th), when Commander R. A. Allan, R.N.V.R., took to sea from Bastia a mixed squadron of L.C.Gs (Landing Craft Gun), motor gunboats, and British and American motor torpedo-boats. The Senior Officer had trained and organised his sixteen vessels to work as a miniature battle fleet, in which the L.C.Gs were the capital ships; and he controlled them all by radar and radio from the torpedo boat in which he himself had embarked. The first encounter took place just after midnight against a south-bound convoy of three barges and a tug from Leghorn, and the entire German force was destroyed. Next there was an engagement with three armed barges which were patrolling in the vicinity and came to the assistance of the convoy. Two of them were sunk, and the third was badly damaged and driven ashore. A patrol vessel which formed part of a north-bound convoy from Elba to Leghorn also blew up and sank at about this time, and although it is uncertain whether this success can be attributed to our torpedo craft it seems likely that this was so. The last incident on this busy night took place shortly before 5 a.m., when Allan's scouting craft made contact with three enemy torpedo-boats which were out on a minelaying foray. Although the enemy avoided the torpedoes fired by the Allied vessels, one of their number, the TA.23 (ex *Impavido*), hit a mine, and had to be sunk by her consorts. The outcome of the night's work was extremely satisfactory, and a fine tribute to Allan's initiative and to his original tactical organisation.[1]

Successes such as the foregoing were, however, not obtained on every night, and we now know that, in spite of the heavy losses they suffered in the process, the Germans succeeded in transporting a monthly average of some 8,000–12,000 tons of military cargoes along the west coast of Italy to ports near the front line. Some 4,000–6,000 tons were also carried down the Adriatic coast each month, mostly from Venice to Ancona. It was our aircraft which inflicted the

[1] Full accounts of this action will be found in Dudley Pope, *Flag 4* (Kimber, 1954), pp. 196–202, and in J. Lennox Kerr and W. Granville, *The R.N.V.R.* (Harrap, 1957), pp. 199–203.

greatest proportion of the losses on both these coastal routes; and their raids on ports were more successful than their attacks on ships at sea.

To turn to the Aegean, after the bad check we had suffered in October and November 1943, culminating in our ejection from Cos and Leros[1], the Middle East Commanders once more framed plans to capture Rhodes; but the decision to land at Anzio in January caused them, as was told earlier, to be cancelled yet again.[2] While our Middle East air forces were being weakened to provide for the needs of the Italian campaign, the Germans had diverted all their own bombers from Greece to the same theatre. This placed the Luftwaffe, which was left with only about 100 aircraft of mixed types, on the defensive in the Aegean. The Commander of the German Naval Group, South, thus had to face a very difficult situation; but he responded energetically to the emergency. The policy adopted was to strengthen the defences of the islands and to reduce the supply problem by evacuating all unwanted persons, including the considerable number of recently captured prisoners. The German Navy therefore requisitioned and repaired every ship they could lay their hands on and started to send reinforcements and equipment to the islands. First of all large vessels were used, but when they proved too vulnerable smaller craft and caïques were substituted. In the final stages most of the traffic was carried by naval auxiliaries and transport aircraft.

Allied negotiations with Turkey, which aimed to bring that country into the war, had meanwhile reached a state of deadlock; and in January we stopped all supplies of military equipment. We were, moreover, very concerned over the passage allowed to German transports and naval auxiliaries from the Black Sea through the Dardanelles to the Aegean. No less than twenty vessels came through in January; and we claimed, with good reason, that the inspection carried out by the Turks under the terms of the Montreux Convention, to ascertain whether they were armed, had been extremely perfunctory. Our protests were, however, weakened by the fact that we could not deny that our own light naval forces had not shown too scrupulous a regard for Turkish neutrality when conducting operations, against the enemy's Aegean garrisons and shipping.[3]

The Middle East Air Force bombed Piraeus several times in January, but the attacks were not heavy enough to cause serious damage to the port or to the shipping in it. Nor did our attenuated air striking forces do better in their sweeps over the Aegean. It thus came to pass that the Germans were allowed a breathing space in

---

[1] See pp. 194–203.

[2] See p. 299.

[3] See, for example, pp. 191 and 201.

which to reinforce their island garrisons, with the help of the vessels newly arrived from the Black Sea.

In February, however, we did better, and were able to show the enemy that the employment of large supply ships would be made unprofitable. Four such ships, of tonnage between 2,500 and 5,350, were sunk during the month. Two were destroyed by air attacks, one was lost in a gale in Leros, and the submarine *Sportsman* sank the fourth, a ship of 4,785 tons loaded with troops and stores, off the north coast of Crete on the 7th. On the 28th of April she repeated her success by sinking another ship of about the same size which was approaching Candia under strong sea and air escort. Though the German supply traffic to the Aegean islands, which passed at the extreme range of our strike aircraft, suffered little during the first three months of the year, the supply of his Cretan garrisons was thus hard hit.

Meanwhile our raiding forces were being re-organised and were preparing to extend their activities. On the 1st of April all the former semi-independent flotillas were placed under one authority, named the Anglo-Hellenic Schooner Flotilla, with Lieutenant-Commander A. C. Seligman, R.N.R., still in command.[1] A measure of rationalisation of the various irregular forces had, indeed, become long overdue; and a central authority controlling them all was rendered the more necessary by the clashes of interest between, for example, those who wished to raid enemy-held islands and those who knew that we might thereby be deprived of valuable sources of intelligence. Nor did the highly independent characters of some of the very gallant men involved in this type of operation always smooth the work of the staffs in Cairo and Alexandria. Raiding was, however, restarted on a considerable scale early in the year, and no less than thirty-seven separate attacks, in which nearly a score of enemy caïques were destroyed, took place during the first three months.

Another re-organisation which took place at this time was that by which, on the 1st of February, No. 201 Naval Co-operation Group of the Middle East Air Force, the air command most concerned in assisting in the war at sea since the early days[2], was amalgamated with the Air Defences, Eastern Mediterranean Command, in order to simplify the administrative and operational structure. A new headquarters, combined with those of the Flag Officer, Levant and Eastern Mediterranean, was established in Alexandria.

We must now return to the struggle off Anzio, which we left at the beginning of February. Admiral Mansfield normally had four

---

[1] See p. 191. This included the Levant Schooner Flotilla, the Special Boat Squadron, and the Greek Sacred Squadron.

[2] See Vol. I, p. 422, and this volume, p. 107.

or five cruisers of his own 15th Cruiser Squadron, the American ships *Brooklyn* and *Philadelphia*, and about a dozen British and American destroyers for gun support duties; but the French cruiser *Gloire* and the A.A. ship *Delhi* also joined him during the month. Two cruisers and two destroyers were usually kept off the beaches, ready to answer at once any calls for fire from the Army, while the other ships lay in Naples Bay at short notice in case reinforcements were needed. An inshore route between Naples and Anzio, which had been swept clear of mines, was now used by all the supply ships which ferried to and fro; and destroyers and minesweepers patrolled its length continuously. The Germans, however, had installed a heavy gun battery on Cape Circe[1], which forced our convoys further out to sea and lengthened their passages. We attacked the battery repeatedly from the sea and air, but never succeeded in putting it permanently out of action. Off the beach-head unloading was constantly handicapped by gales, which sometimes put a stop to all work and forced us to rely entirely on the port of Anzio; but the total quantity of supplies landed none the less remained very impressive. Between D-Day and the 20th of February 97,669 tons were discharged and, in spite of two severe gales and constant enemy shelling, bombing and minelaying, the average daily figure for the month was 3,441 tons.

On the 3rd of February the expected counter-attack by the greatly reinforced enemy started, and for a fortnight the issue hung in the balance. Not until the 20th did VI Corps manage to check the German onslaught decisively, and throughout this anxious period of stubborn fighting in a very confined space the bombarding ships and the Tactical Air Force's bombers were almost continuously in action supporting the defenders of the beach-head. At the height of the battle the *Orion, Mauritius, Phoebe, Penelope*, the U.S.S. *Brooklyn*, the Dutch gunboats *Soemba* and *Flores*, and all available destroyers were called up to the assault area; and the enemy's War Diary makes it plain that their harassing fire on his concentrations of troops and tanks, and their engagements with his mobile batteries, contributed greatly to halting his drive towards the beaches. To give an idea of the scale of this naval support, Admiral Mansfield reported that up to the end of February his ships had fired 8,400 rounds of 6-inch, 7,800 of 5·25-inch and 3,500 of 4·7-inch ammunition at shore targets. Taking account of the hazardous nature of this inshore work, and the strength of the enemy's counter-measures, the losses suffered by the supporting warships might well have been heavier. Smoke screens and jamming generally succeeded in foiling the glider-bomb attacks; but on the 15th of February a Liberty ship loaded with ammunition was hit, caught fire, and became a total loss. On the 25th the

---

[1] See Map 12.

destroyer leader *Inglefield* was hit by a glider-bomb during the usual dusk air attack and sank with heavy casualties.[1] The loss of the *Penelope* and of two L.S.Ts to U-boat attacks between the 16th and 20th has already been mentioned.[2]

The enemy was not slow to realise the opportunity which the large quantity of Allied shipping lying off Anzio offered to fast assault craft. These had always been something of a speciality of the Italian Navy, and, as their training base on Lake Maggiore, and also the operational bases at Spezia and Leghorn, were now in the German-occupied part of Italy, and the Germans had temporarily gained the services of Prince Borghese, the Italian naval officer who commanded the special units, they set about organising their use against the supply traffic near Anzio.[3] Between January and March several sorties took place; but the results must have been disappointing to the enemy, for the only positive success achieved was the sinking of L.S.T.305 on the 20th of February. E-boats also sometimes joined in the attacks, but the Allied patrol craft were very alert and often inflicted losses on them and on the assault craft. We will return shortly to other attempts of this nature.

The month of February thus closed with VI Corps, now commanded by Major-General L. K. Truscott, U.S.A., who had relieved General Lucas, locked in a dour struggle with General Mackensen's Fourteenth Army. On the main front too there was a state of deadlock, which the bombing and destruction of Cassino monastery on the 15th had done nothing to break. Off Anzio the ships were still pouring supplies into the narrow perimeter, answering calls for fire and defending themselves and their charges against repeated attacks of every conceivable kind. The difficulties and dangers which beset our forces on land and sea were greatly increased by the cold and stormy weather. This and the constant calls for support from the Army on the main front prevented the Allied air forces from fully exploiting their superiority over the Anzio beach-head. It was plain that little could be done to break the stalemate until the weather improved.

Throughout the whole of March conditions on shore changed but little. The supply of the Anzio forces reached a peak on the 29th, when 7,828 tons of stores were landed. The total for that month reached the prodigious figure of 158,274 tons, in spite of some L.S.Ts being withdrawn for repairs. Congestion on shore was now so

---

[1] The Luftwaffe unit which operated the wireless-controlled bombs (II/KG. 100) only employed the Hs.293 (see p. 30) against our shipping off Anzio. The FX.1400 type, which had been used during the Salerno landings with some success (see pp. 177–179), was apparently going out of service by this time.

[2] See p. 312.

[3] Prince Borghese's account of his unit's operations is to be found in *Sea Devils* (Andrew Melrose, 1952). The assault craft used off Anzio were of the two-man variety, which displaced 3 tons, had a speed of 34 knots and carried one torpedo.

serious that, so noted the Commander-in-Chief's War Diary, 'the amount of material which it was possible to land . . . began to reach its limit'. Shelling of the transport anchorage was so persistent that merchantmen were moved further out, to a distance of six or seven miles off-shore. Air attacks, raids by E-boats, and minelaying were frequent; but losses were much less than in February. There were also fewer calls for supporting fire—probably because neither side was planning an early resumption of the offensive. On the 15th the Germans made a heavy air attack on Naples, but it caused only slight damage to shipping in the port. Three days later Mount Vesuvius suddenly erupted. It seemed as though Pluto, god of the underworld, wished to show that, if it came to creating physical upheavals in the vicinity of his volcano, he could do just as well as man. Dust and ashes put nearby airfields temporarily out of action and damaged many aircraft on them.

By April the recall of ships and landing craft needed for the invasion of Normandy could not be deferred any longer. The First Sea Lord had already warned Admiral Cunningham that most of his cruisers would be needed to join the bombardment forces being organised for 'Overlord'. Though he would leave the move as late as possible, 'because the Mediterranean cruisers are past-masters at bombardment and should require only three or four days working up', in no other way could he meet the requirements. It thus came to pass that the Headquarters Ship *Bulolo*, the cruisers *Orion* and *Mauritius*, four destroyers, forty-six L.S.Ts (about half of which were American), and many L.C.Ts and L.C.Is all left for Britain during the month. Admiral Mansfield transferred his flag to the *Dido*, and carried on the support of the Anzio beach-head with his reduced forces. The tonnage discharged during April was 97,658, which was considerably less than in March because, so noted the Commander-in-Chief, 'there was no longer any room for additional store dumps until an army offensive took place to use up some of what had already been landed'. The enemy's shelling of the port of Anzio and of the transport anchorage, and his air attacks, had now become a normal part of each day's work; but early on the 21st an attempt by the Germans to use their own version of the 'human torpedo' (called 'Marders') on a large scale introduced a note of novelty. We now know that early in April they sent to Italy no less than forty such weapons.[1] Allied intelligence had, however, gained knowledge of

---

[1] These were one-man electrically-driven contrivances. They weighed about 3 tons, and carried a torpedo slung beneath the main hull; but their speed was only 2½ knots. They were originally invented as a stop-gap until something better could be produced, but in spite of their total failure off Anzio they were used again off Normandy in July 1944, and off southern France in the following autumn. Details of all types of 'small battle units', as the Germans called these special craft, are given in an Appendix to Part II of this volume.

what was in the wind, and a special warning had been passed to all our patrols. At dusk on the 20th the Germans launched twenty-three 'Marders' in a position about eighteen miles from Nettuno; but several quickly came to grief on the off-shore sand banks and never reached the transport anchorage. Enemy aircraft were very active all night, but the human torpedo attack did not actually synchronise with the bombing, as had been intended. It was day-break before they arrived, and they then met fully alert defences. At least four were sunk by depth charges and gunfire, and one was captured intact. The Germans lost ten of the new weapons from all causes that night; and as not one Allied ship was even damaged the carefully planned operation proved a complete fiasco. The surviving 'Marders' thereupon returned to Germany, and attacks of this nature were left to Italian assault boats. But they too were severely handled and soon lost several more of their dwindling number. The enemy thus obtained a remarkably poor return for the substantial effort expended on these special weapons, and the whole series of attacks showed that, provided the defending patrol craft were alert and used depth charges liberally, off-shore shipping had little to fear from them.

In May the *Sirius, Ajax* and twelve more Mediterranean destroyers were recalled to Britain, which left only the *Dido,* the two American cruisers *Brooklyn* and *Philadelphia,* and an exiguous number of destroyers to support the Army. The French cruiser *Emile Bertin,* however, joined the bombarding forces for part of the month. The few ships left were kept very busy. From the 12th to the 19th they were in action almost every day, generally in the Gulf of Gaeta giving flank support to the new offensive which the Army had opened on the 11th.[1] In those eight days the *Dido* carried out seventeen shoots at shore targets, firing 1,865 rounds from her 5·25-inch guns, while the *Brooklyn* and *Philadelphia* added 1,735 rounds of 6-inch. The commander of the American II Corps sent his warm thanks for the support of the warships, which, so he said, had neutralised batteries and driven them out of position, had blocked roads, dislocated enemy traffic and produced 'a general state of demoralisation and dis-organisation in the rear areas'. When, on the 23rd, VI Corps began the offensive which was to succeed in breaking out at last from the Anzio perimeter, the bombarding forces transferred their efforts to that front, and from the 23rd to the 29th their guns were again constantly in action.[2]

In May there were fewer enemy air attacks off Anzio and shelling

---

[1] See Map 12.

[2] Between 23rd and 31st May off Anzio the U.S.S. *Brooklyn* fired 1,361 rounds, the French cruiser *Emile Bertin* 373, and American destroyers 1,656 rounds at shore targets.

was less heavy than in the previous month. Casualties to shipping were slight. The only serious incident was a collision between the U.S.S. *Philadelphia* and an American destroyer on the 22nd, which put both ships out of action at an unfortunate moment. The tonnage landed during the month was 131,424, which brought the total for the nineteen weeks since the first landing to no less than 523,358 tons.

By the end of May VI Corps' advance had taken it beyond the range of naval supporting fire, and although the destroyers continued to harass the enemy as he retreated up the coast towards the mouth of the River Tiber, the work of the Navies was now virtually completed. On the main front Monte Cassino was captured on the 18th, and the Germans fell back on the 'Hitler Line', their last prepared defences south of Rome. By the 25th that position had also been breached, and that day saw the long-awaited junction between the troops fighting their way south from Anzio and those of the Fifth Army coming north. On the last day of May the Alban Hills, which we had originally hoped to seize soon after the assault forces landed at Anzio on the 22nd of January, and towards which longing eyes had since been all the time raised, were at last in Allied hands. The Germans now disengaged all along the front. On the 4th of June Allied troops entered Rome.

It is unlikely that historians will ever be unanimous on the question whether operation 'Shingle' should have been launched before it was known that an early break-through could be expected on the main front. That it absorbed a far bigger Allied effort than was originally intended is plain, since the two divisions originally landed had swollen to seven (five American and two British) before the end came; and VI Corps suffered fairly heavy losses while holding the beach-head. On the other hand the equivalent of at least six good German divisions were absorbed in containing the forces landed from the sea, and it is hard not to believe that, had they been freed to reinforce the main front, the German defence against the Fifth and Eighth Armies would have been still more stubborn. To this historian however, it seems that, had we made no attempt to exploit Allied maritime power by a landing from the sea throughout the first five months of 1944, we should have been deliberately sacrificing one of the greatest advantages we possessed. The enemy's records are full of expressions of anxiety regarding the use which the Allies might make of their control of the sea; and there is no doubt at all that the prevailing uncertainty regarding our intentions, combined with knowledge of our ability to strike suddenly on one of his exposed flanks, greatly aggravated the problem of correctly disposing his reserves. To keep the enemy guessing for as long as possible, and then to strike suddenly at a point where he does not expect it, must ever be cardinal requirements of good strategic planning; and operation 'Shingle' fulfilled both those needs excellently. If that be accepted then the only criticism which can justly be levelled at the plan is that, after the assault, it did not work out as we had intended; and that can be said of many, if not of most operations of war. Though disagreement may well continue whether more energetic leadership on shore would have brought the hoped-for quick success, on three points there can surely be no argument. The first is that the naval side of operation 'Shingle' was faultlessly planned and executed; the second that the Army was safely put ashore on a hostile coast in conditions which augured extremely well for its success; and the third is that, after the failure to break out from the beach-head, the maritime services quickly adjusted themselves to the changed conditions, and throughout four long and exceedingly trying months nourished and supported the Army to the limit of its needs, and even beyond. Such accomplishments surely deserve a high place in the annals of the services concerned.

We must now return to the beginning of April, and review other events in the Mediterranean theatre. The defence of our convoys against the German bombers working from southern France still absorbed a big naval and air effort, and we were aware that we had not yet solved the problem of dealing with them decisively.[1] Night attacks on three convoys took place in April, and, although in the first two (against UGS.36 on the 1st and UGS.37 on the 11th and 12th) the smoke screens put up by the escorts gave the merchantmen such effective protection that only slight damage was suffered, comparatively few of the two dozen or so attackers were destroyed by the A.A. gunners or night fighters. Then, shortly after dusk on the 20th, UGS.38 was attacked off Algiers by some sixty aircraft, most of them Ju.88s. An American destroyer, the *Landsdale*, and two merchantmen (totalling 15,077 tons) were sunk, and two others of the convoy seriously damaged. The loss of life on our side was heavy, and another merchantman was sunk in a convoy approaching Algiers from Corsica at the same time. These were the greatest successes so far achieved by the German bombers, and Admiral Cunningham and Air Vice-Marshal Lloyd again reviewed the problems involved in the defence of the convoys. Both services recognised that the solution lay in providing Fighter Direction Ships with modern radar sets; but although the *Ulster Queen* was on the station her equipment was not fully up to date, and she was unable to cope

---

[1] See pp. 310–311.

satisfactorily with night attacks.[1] None the less, in May such ships accompanied all the larger convoys, and in addition Coastal Air Force extended its night fighter patrols to try to bar the enemy's approach routes from the north. These developments, and the manner in which the Navy and R.A.F. jointly tackled the problem, prompt a comment on how far we had travelled since the early days of the war, when the Navy had declared that warships alone could defend mercantile convoys adequately, and the R.A.F. had refused to consider the control of its fighters otherwise than from its own shore stations.[2]

It was not long before the new defensive measures were tested severely. On the 11th of May convoy UGS.40, consisting of no less than eighty-two merchantmen with sixteen flotilla vessels and the A.A. cruiser *Caledon* as escort, was off the Algerian coast. As German reconnaissance planes had been shadowing during the preceding day, Coastal Air Force had organised the strongest possible fighter protection. Nearly 100 single- and twin-engined fighters were allocated to this duty. At 9 p.m. a force of sixty-two Ju.88s, with strong fighter escort, came in to attack. There was no moon, and the enemy did not this time use flares; but conditions were perfect for screening the convoy with smoke, and this, combined with the excellent work of the A.A. gunners and night fighters, prevented any of the ninety-one torpedoes dropped from finding their marks. Moreover, although at the same time we claimed no more than ten enemy aircraft, we now know that no less than sixteen of the German striking force were shot down, mostly by the escort vessels' gunners. It was a sharp repulse for the Germans; but they none the less repeated the attempt, though on a smaller scale, on the last day of May, when one small merchantman in convoy KMS.51 was sunk for the loss of about four of the two score bombers which took part. That same month saw the last of the very large convoys enter the Mediterranean, for we realised that they were getting too unwieldy to defend effectively. UGS.42 consisted of 103 ships, but thereafter the total was restricted to ninety, and the qualifying speed for inclusion in such convoys was raised by one knot to nine-and-a-half knots.

To turn to the U-boats, in April one more passed safely into the Mediterranean, but the destruction of U.421 in a bombing raid on

---

[1] The *Ulster Queen* had recently controlled day fighters with marked success off Anzio. By September 1944 she had been fitted with the modern radar equipment needed to control night fighters as well, and she then made an outstanding contribution to stopping the evacuation of German troops from Crete by air. (See Part II of this volume, Chapter XVI.) The *Palomares*, which was the only other Fighter Direction Ship on the station, had been mined off Anzio in January (see p. 304), and was not ready for service until early 1945.

[2] See Vol. I, pp. 108–109.

Toulon on the 29th offset that reinforcement. The enemy was generally able to keep five boats on patrol during the month, but their
only important success was the destruction of two ships of convoy
UGS.37, which was attacked off Derna on the 16th. In the next
month, May, the U-boats suffered severely. U.371 torpedoed one
of the escorts of a GUS convoy off Bougie on the night of the 2nd–
3rd. The 'swamp' technique was at once applied[1], continuous air
patrols were flown, and after a relentless pursuit by aircraft and
surface ships lasting twenty-seven hours the enemy surfaced early
on the 4th, and was sunk by British and French escort vessels. Before
her destruction the U-boat managed, however, to torpedo the French
destroyer *Sénégalais*, and, as an American destroyer which formed
part of the same convoy's escort was torpedoed and sunk by a different U-boat a short time later, the pursuit of U.371 showed that the
enemy could still hit back hard. On the 14th the next convoy on the
same route, GUS.39, was also attacked; but the torpedoing of two
of its ships was avenged when, after a three-day 'swamp' operation,
surface ships and aircraft sank U.616 on the 17th. On the same day
torpedoes were fired at an American destroyer which was returning
to port with the U-boat's survivors; another 'swamp' was promptly
ordered, and on the 19th it was rewarded by the sinking of U.960.
That afternoon the Taranto–Augusta convoy HA.43 was attacked off
southern Italy. The U-boat was kept under by Italian naval escorts
until aircraft and three British destroyers arrived on the scene. It was
the latter who, in the early hours of the 21st, finally sank U.453.
Thus four enemies were destroyed in the Mediterranean in May—
all of them as the result of counter-attacks by forces carrying out
'swamp' tactics. As this was the last occasion on which that technique
was employed it will be appropriate to sum up the results. Between
October 1943 and May of the following year nineteen 'swamps' were
ordered, and they achieved the destruction of seven U-boats. Bearing
in mind that several of the hunts took place in waters where local
conditions were very difficult—notably off the Spanish coast, where
neutral fishing craft seriously handicapped the searchers—the results
are impressive. But perhaps the grounds on which this whole series
of joint operations against U-boats most merits attention, and pre-
servation for posterity, are that in them the sea and air forces were
completely integrated. Considerations such as the jealously guarded
autonomy of both services, dogmatic views on the correct employment of ships or aircraft, and recital of the limitations of both arms
were all, if not forgotten, totally subordinated to the single purpose of
destroying the enemy. It may be doubted whether in any other
theatre—not even excepting the Atlantic convoy battles—such

[1] See p. 208.

intimate harmony and such complete fusion was accomplished. The organisation needed to implement such a policy was, of course, only arrived at after a long process of trial and error; but the excellent results achieved in May 1944 were the reward for the patience and perseverance with which the air and naval commanders pursued their aim.

At the end of the period covered by this chapter only eleven U-boats remained in the Mediterranean. Their fate will be recounted later, but here we should note the rapid decline of the enemy's successes against Allied shipping. Whereas in 1943 the U-boats had sunk fifty-nine ships (241,215 tons) in this theatre, during the first five months of 1944 their score was only ten ships of 76,760 tons; and in the same period we lost only ten ships (61,217 tons) to air attacks.[1] Though it anticipates events, we may here note that after May 1944 not one Allied merchantman was sunk by a U-boat in the Mediterranean; and before the end of the year all the last eleven enemies had been accounted for. Yet it seems true to say that the margin of our success was narrow; for in May 1944 the U-boat Command gave orders that 'Schnorkel' equipment was to be fitted to all the Mediterranean boats[2], and there is little doubt that had the enemy managed to fulfil that intention we should have been faced with a renewal of the campaign which would have produced serious difficulties for us.

While the German U-boats were thus being severely handled in the central and western basins of the Mediterranean, the patrols by our own submarines based on Maddalena in Sardinia, and by the Coastal Forces working from Bastia against the enemy's traffic running to ports in north Italy, continued. On the night of the 23rd–24th of May coastal craft encountered two convoys between Elba and Leghorn. They sank one of the escort vessels which had come out of Spezia to cover the movement, badly damaged the other, and also destroyed two ferry barges in the north-bound convoy. The other convoy was also attacked, but escaped damage.

With the larger forces now available for the Adriatic the Allied position improved steadily during this phase. While the harassing of the German inshore traffic by our aircraft and coastal forces continued, substantial numbers of British troops and Partisans were being carried in landing craft to raid German-held islands or coastal garrisons. Thus on the 9th–10th of May a very successful attack was

---

[1] These figures exclude small vessels under 100 tons. For a complete analysis of Allied losses of merchant shipping see Appendix K.

[2] See p. 18 regarding the 'Schnorkel' equipment. Its effect on operations in our Home Waters is described in Part II of this volume.

made on the island of Solta, and a fortnight later no less than 1,000 British troops were embarked in landing craft at Vis to assault an enemy-held island near Dubrovnik.[1] On the 25th of May the Germans attacked and surrounded Marshal Tito's headquarters in Bosnia, and for some days the resistance leader was in serious danger. He and his staff were, however, rescued early in June by Allied aircraft and, to draw off enemy forces, a strong diversion was mounted from Vis against the island of Brac. About 3,500 British and Partisan troops were carried there; but the urgency of the occasion had not allowed time for the assault to be carefully planned, the enemy defences were strong, and adequate air support was not at once forthcoming. On the 4th of June the troops were withdrawn; but as a diversion the operation seems to have helped to restore the situation on the mainland.

In May the demands of the new offensive on the main Italian front caused a reduction in the air effort in the Adriatic, and sinking of enemy ships declined. None the less the losses inflicted on the enemy's coastal traffic by air attacks in this phase remain impressive[2]; and German records leave no doubt that, apart from the usual lack of co-operation by the Luftwaffe with the German Navy, it was Allied air superiority, combined with the energetic raids by our coastal craft, which so weakened the enemy's hold on the Yugo-Slav coast that by the end of this phase a complete collapse was becoming a distinct possibility; and once the Allies had gained a firm control of those coastal waters a direct drive up the Adriatic and into central Europe could become a practical strategy.

One other event which took place at this time in the eastern Mediterranean, and that an unhappy one, must here be mentioned briefly. With the increase of Communist influence on the mainland of Greece it was perhaps inevitable that some taint of that political doctrine should permeate the crews of the Greek warships, who had been exiled from their homeland since 1941. For some time the British authorities in Egypt had been aware that trouble was brewing in the Greek Army as well as in their Navy; and when, on the 8th of April, the crews of the old cruiser *Georgios Averoff* and of four escort vessels at Port Said and Alexandria broke into open mutiny, the cruiser *Ajax* was at once sent to the latter base. The mutineers demanded that representatives of the Communist-controlled E.A.M.[3] party should be included in the government-in-exile; and, after persuasion had failed to make them return to duty, loyal Greek elements carried out a boarding operation against the three ships in Alexandria on the night of the 22nd–23rd of April. Casualties were fortunately

---

[1] See Map 12.
[2] See Table 20 (p. 330).
[3] The Greek initials of the National Liberation Front party.

slight, and, as the crew of the *Georgios Averoff* at Port Said surrendered a few days later, the use of British arms to quell the mutiny proved unnecessary. To the Royal Navy, whose association with the Greek Navy had been long and intimate, in peace as well as in war, and who remembered how the two services had shared the severe trials and dangers of 1941, the whole episode was deeply distressing. With the appointment of Admiral Voulgaris as Commander-in-Chief we hoped that it would soon be forgotten. In fact, however, trouble recurred several times during the succeeding months; and, unfortunately, we soon learnt that the Communist attempt to gain control of Greece had by no means yet been defeated.[1]

On the 9th of May the Russians recaptured Sebastopol, and the Germans thereupon evacuated the whole Crimea. This led to the enemy renewing his efforts to pass ships from the Black Sea through to the Aegean. On the 26th a transport and five armed trawlers made the passage, and fifteen vessels (totalling over 7,000 tons) came south to reinforce and strengthen the enemy's supply traffic to the Aegean islands before, in mid-June, strong Allied protests to Turkey led to the movements being stopped. But the losses we had inflicted during the preceding months had by that time been made good, and the enemy at once ran more supplies into Cos and Leros. Then, on the last day of May, three ships with some 8,500 tons of vital cargo left Piraeus for Crete under very strong sea and air escort. The movement was reported by our reconnaissance aircraft, and on the 1st of June a striking force of thirty bombers was sent from Cyrenaica. Two of the escorts were sunk and two merchantmen damaged in the ensuing attacks. When the survivors from the convoy entered Heraklion our air attacks were switched on to the port. Another of the escorts, the former Italian torpedo-boat *Castelfidardo*, now known as the TA.16, and both the damaged merchantmen were sunk in harbour, and the whole of their cargoes was lost. Finally the single surviving merchant ship was sunk by the submarine *Vivid* on the 9th, while trying to return to Piraeus. This harsh experience, which may be compared with our own efforts to supply Malta in 1942 when we lacked adequate command of the air[2], convinced the Germans that it was futile any longer to try to pass convoys of big ships through our blockade. Thereafter they depended on small steamers, caïques and naval auxiliaries. In the first five months of 1944 we thus inflicted very serious losses on the German traffic to Crete, but vessels plying between Greece and the Aegean islands had so far suffered comparatively little, and the German garrisons thus remained in reasonably good shape. Although our submarines, aircraft and coastal forces had accounted for eighteen ships totalling

---

[1] See Churchill, Vol. V, Chapter XXX and Vol. VI, Chapter XVIII.

[2] See Vol. II, pp. 302–308, regarding operation 'Pedestal', for example.

28,300 tons in that period[1], a big proportion of these losses had been made good from the Black Sea. Before leaving the Aegean we may remark that the great effort made by the enemy to maintain his position in those waters suggests that the strategy of thrusting powerfully north towards the Dardanelles, which Mr Churchill had always favoured, but which had so far been frustrated by the concentration of forces on the Italian campaign, was viewed by the Germans with very considerable concern. They seem to have realised clearly that if we gained a firm grip on the long-contested islands a collapse in the whole Balkan theatre could scarcely be averted.

We may conclude this survey of the first five months of 1944 by analysing the extent and cause of the enemy's shipping losses in the Mediterranean. The table below shows that the monthly rate of loss was remarkably steady, and that the attrition of his sea transport had reached a level which would before long make it impossible for the land forces to be kept supplied. It was the attacks by the Tactical and Strategic bombers on the enemy's ports and bases which caused the greatest proportion of his losses at this time. Just as a great share of the Allies' land successes can confidently be attributed to the successful protection of our convoys and ports of loading and discharge against air attacks, so did the failure of the enemy adequately to protect his own shipping greatly aggravate the difficulties of his armies in this theatre.

Table 20. Enemy Merchant Shipping Losses in the Mediterranean

January–May 1944

No. of ships—Tonnage

Month	By Surface Ship	By Submarine	By Air Attack	By Mine	By other cause	TOTAL
January	10—1,231	1— 61	22— 12,657	2—3,623	10—16,163	45— 33,735
February	7—4,412	3— 8,253	28— 23,045	1—2,212	23— 9,289	62— 47,211
March	2— 101	3— 5,611	40— 48,771	—	18— 4,427	63— 58,910
April	—	2— 5,887	14— 9,930	1— 227	13— 2,086	30— 18,130
May	—	2— 5,102	26— 27,237	1— 142	20—18,317	49— 50,798
TOTAL	19—5,744	11—24,914	130—121,640	5—6,204	84—50,282	249—208,784

NOTES: (1) Of the 249 ships accounted for in the above table, 192 were of less than 500 tons.
(2) A large number of small vessels such as Greek caïques, ferry barges, etc., were also sunk in this period. These have been excluded from the above table as they were in service as naval auxiliaries.
(3) Of the 130 vessels sunk by air attack, 108 were accounted for in air raids on harbours.
(4) Of the vessels shown lost by 'other cause', 31 of about 38,000 tons were scuttled.

[1] These figures exclude small craft of less than 100 tons. The losses inflicted on the enemy in the Aegean cannot, however, be given with confidence, as so many different causes may have contributed to them, and it is also impossible to be sure whether certain vessels were or were not working under German control.

CHAPTER XIII

THE PACIFIC
AND INDIAN OCEANS

1st January–31st May, 1944

> 'The moral effect of an omnipresent fleet is
> very great, but it cannot be weighed . . . .
> against a main fleet known to be ready to
> strike, and able to strike hard.'
>
> Lord Fisher to Lord Stamfordham,
> 25th June, 1912.

A T the beginning of 1944 our American allies were very much on the offensive in the Pacific. In the central theatre the Gilbert Islands had been won, and plans were well advanced for the attack on the Marshalls[1]; while in the south Pacific Admiral Halsey's forces were firmly established on Bougainville, and the enemy's main base at Rabaul in New Britain was being heavily bombed. Further to the west, General MacArthur bestrode the Vitiaz Strait between New Guinea and New Britain, and his south-west Pacific forces were preparing for further advances along the northern coast of New Guinea, and to assault the Admiralty Islands.[2] Only in South-East Asia was there no progress; for in that theatre Admiral Mountbatten had not yet been given the forces necessary to take the offensive. We will return to his problems later.

While the Allies could therefore view the future with ever-growing confidence, the Japanese had less reason to be satisfied with the way things were going. Late in September 1943 they had recast their strategy, and had decided to establish and fortify a new and more modest 'defensive perimeter' in the Pacific, stretching from the Marianas through Truk in the Carolines and Rabaul to northern New Guinea, and thence west to Timor.[3]

From behind this line they hoped to deliver counter-attacks against the advancing Allies, whilst preparing for a large-scale offensive in the spring of 1944. The island garrisons left outside the perimeter were not to be withdrawn, but were to delay the Allied advance and wear down the attackers. It is significant that the rôle

---

[1] See Map 16.
[2] See Map 15.
[3] See pp. 224–225 regarding the original Japanese defensive perimeter.

331

allotted to the Japanese Navy was still that of bringing the American fleet to decisive action on terms of their own choosing, preferably when the Allies were committed to supporting an overseas expedition. The U.S. Navy was equally keen for a trial of strength; but this was not to occur until the middle of the year.[1] In the present phase the Japanese Navy never seriously interfered with American fleet movements.

At the beginning of 1944 the Japanese could claim that their basic plan still held firm. Their smaller defensive perimeter had not yet been pierced; but they were being pressed very hard. Their garrisons in the Gilberts had faithfully fulfilled their destiny by resisting the invaders almost to the last man. In the south, Rabaul was still the bastion on which their hopes rested; and although it had been subjected to heavy air attacks they were confident that it could be held. In northern New Guinea, after the loss of the Huon Gulf ports[2], they were making great efforts to construct airfields and to develop strong defensive positions further to the west before the Allied advance was resumed. On the far-away Burma–India frontier they were planning an offensive into Assam for the spring of 1944 and were well content that for the present relative quiet should prevail on that front.

Such then were the plans of each side at the beginning of 1944. It will be convenient to follow the course of events in each command separately, as has been done in previous chapters; but the reader should bear in mind that it was the combined pressure on all fronts which brought about the discomfiture of the enemy.

To consider first the central Pacific, by January American plans for the conquest of the Marshall Islands were nearly ready. This group of widely-separated atolls had been captured by the Japanese from the Germans in the 1914–18 war, and was mandated to Japan in 1920, together with the Carolines. The building of military bases on the islands was prohibited by the terms of the mandate[3]; but recent reconnaissances by American aircraft working from the newly-won bases in the Gilberts, and by American submarines, had revealed fortifications on Jaluit and Mili in the south, on Kwajalein, Wotje and Maloelap in the centre and east, and on Eniwetok, 330 miles to the north-west of Kwajalein.[4] Although the Marshall group lay well outside the defensive perimeter envisaged by the Japanese high command when its new strategic policy was established in September 1943[5], the defenders had been ordered to hold out as long as possible in order to gain the time needed to reinforce

---

[1] See Part II of this volume regarding the Battle of the Philippine Sea.
[2] See pp. 226–227.
[3] See p. 223 fn. (3).
[4] See Map 16.
[5] See p. 330.

and strengthen the new defence line running through the Mariana and Caroline groups.

One of the main problems confronting the American planners was the selection of the principal objective of the initial assaults. Would it be wiser to take the southern and eastern atolls first, or would it be safe to 'leap-frog' right into the heart of the group by descending on Kwajalein itself? What the Americans needed was an island on which an airfield capable of taking heavy bombers could be constructed, and it was doubtful whether Kwajalein could fulfil this requirement. On the other hand, if that island was captured first it should prove possible to cut off the outlying bases and thereby save both time and the expense of additional assaults. When, in December 1943, reconnaissance revealed that the Japanese had nearly completed an airfield on Kwajalein, that island was at once named as the next objective. The small undefended atoll of Majuro about 150 miles to the south-east of it was to be seized at the same time, so that its fine anchorage could be used by the large 'Fleet Train', which must accompany a combined expedition sent to such a great distance from the main supply bases. Over 40,000 American troops were allocated to the assaults.

During December and January shore-based naval and army aircraft in the Gilberts made daily reconnaissance flights and bombing attacks on the Marshalls, all the time whittling away Japanese air strength. Although these raids achieved substantial success, at the end of January there still remained some 150 enemy aircraft, most of them at Eniwetok and Kwajalein, to contest the landings.

'D-Day' for the assault on the Marshalls was set for the 31st of January 1944, and on the 29th the Fast Carrier Task Force, which had returned to Pearl Harbour in December for a brief period of recuperation, reappeared on the scene under the command of Rear-Admiral Marc A. Mitscher, U.S.N. It now consisted of six fleet and six light fleet carriers, eight battleships, and numerous cruisers and destroyers; and this formidable array was organised to work in four separate 'task groups'. Nearly 700 aircraft were embarked in the carriers, and the blows which they struck proved devastating. All the main atolls in the Marshall group, including Eniwetok, received such a hammering that, so it is reported, not a single enemy aircraft was serviceable when D-Day came; and no Japanese shipping remained afloat in the anchorages. The occupation of the Marshalls took place without one American ship being attacked from the air.

Meanwhile the main assault force, yet again under the experienced command of Rear-Admiral R. K. Turner, U.S.N.[1], was approaching its destination from Pearl Harbour. These expeditions

---

[1] See Vol. II, pp. 222–226 and 414, and this volume, pp. 229 and 237.

were now developing a standard pattern. After heavy carrier-borne air attacks, the islands to be captured would be subjected to a concentrated dawn bombardment by the escorting and covering warships. 'H-Hour' was fixed for about 9 a.m. on the 31st of January, and more aircraft gave tactical support before the actual landings. This differed from the policy adopted in the assaults on North Africa, Sicily and Salerno, where the landings were made shortly before dawn, in order that the forces might make their approach in darkness, and preliminary bombing and bombardments were sacrificed in the interests of achieving surprise.[1]

Kwajalein itself is the largest atoll in the Pacific. It consists of a chain of small islands protruding from a reef which encloses a lagoon covering some 840 square miles of water; yet the total land area is only just over six square miles. On this atoll the Japanese had about 6,800 men[2], mostly on the twin islands of Roi-Namur in the north and on Kwajalein itself, forty miles to the south. Although strong land defences had been built, the Japanese had, surprisingly, neither mined nor in any way obstructed the few entrances to the lagoon. The approach thus offered no difficulty.

The American historian gives a vivid and detailed description of the assault on the islands[3] on the 1st of February; here we can only pay tribute to the thoroughness with which the expedition was planned and executed. The issue was never in doubt. Overwhelming force was brought to bear, and the small islands were pulverised by the gunfire of the warships and the bombs of the planes. In spite of this, those enemies who survived the bombardments resisted fanatically for four days. Almost all the garrison were killed, and the few prisoners taken were mostly Korean labourers. On the American side losses were comparatively slight, under four hundred being killed.

With Kwajalein in Allied hands, mopping-up expeditions were sent to the smaller atolls; but the bigger ones of Jaluit, Mili, Maloelap and Wotje were left alone.[4] They were completely cut off from reinforcement, and were not worth the trouble of reducing. Those four islands remained in Japanese hands until the final surrender, but many of their garrisons had by that time died from starvation and disease.

Away to the north-west of Kwajalein, however, was Eniwetok, the capture of which was a necessary preliminary to progress westwards towards the Carolines and Marianas. Even before Kwajalein had

---

[1] See Vol. II, Chapter XIII and this volume, pp. 115, 159 and 183, for discussion on this matter.

[2] This figure includes about 2,000 civilians, some of whom were Koreans.

[3] See Morison, Vol. VII, pp. 225–278.

[4] See Map 16.

fallen plans were being made to occupy Eniwetok, and an expeditionary force, consisting of about 10,000 of the American marines and soldiers who had been engaged at Kwajalein, sailed from that newly-captured base on the 15th of February.

Ships of the Fast Carrier Task Force had made repeated raids on Eniwetok, and had effectively eliminated any chance of local air opposition; but, as the island was less than 700 miles from Truk, and the same distance from Rabaul, the enemy was expected to react energetically. Thus the rôle allotted to the U.S. Pacific Fleet was to neutralise Truk and, if possible, catch the Japanese fleet while in its usual advanced base. Rabaul was to receive the attention of aircraft from the other Pacific commands at the same time.

While one carrier group covered the landing at Eniwetok, Vice-Admiral Spruance's Fifth fleet of five large and four smaller carriers, six battleships, and many cruisers and destroyers, arrived undetected 100 miles to the north-east of Truk shortly before dawn on the 17th of February. The striking forces caught the enemy unprepared and virtually wiped out his air strength in the first attacks. Well over 200 aircraft were destroyed or damaged on the ground and about thirty more were shot down in combat.

The main body of the Japanese fleet was not, however, in the harbour; for it had withdrawn to Palau in the western Carolines when a preliminary American air reconnaissance made earlier in the month caused Admiral Koga to expect a heavy attack.[1] Nevertheless there was still much merchant shipping present, and twenty-four vessels of 137,091 tons were destroyed before the American fleet left two days later, some to return to the Marshalls and others to attack the Marianas. An outstanding feature of this operation was that about one-third of the Japanese losses were inflicted by night attacks by the carrier-borne aircraft. The success of this new technique led to 'night carriers', as they were called, forming an integral part of the American fleet in later offensives.

In addition to the merchant shipping sunk, the enemy lost the light cruisers *Agano* and *Naka*, the old training cruiser *Katori*, two auxiliary cruisers (one of which was the *Aikoku Maru* which had made raiding expeditions into the Indian Ocean in 1942[2]), four destroyers, and a number of auxiliary vessels. Some of these were sunk by American surface ships, and others by submarines. In contrast to these severe enemy losses, American casualties amounted to no more than twenty-five aircraft; and the only warship to be damaged was the carrier *Intrepid*, which was hit by a Japanese aircraft's torpedo.

Not since the Battle of Midway had such a resounding success

---

[1] In March it mostly withdrew to Singapore. See p. 347.

[2] See Vol. II, pp. 184 and 271–273.

been achieved; and like Midway, it was to prove a significant turning point in the war. Although the airfield and installations at Truk had not been completely destroyed, the usefulness of the island as an advanced base was ended; and the 'defensive perimeter' strategy of the Japanese was shown to be completely illusory. The base at Truk and, as we shall see, the bastion of Rabaul had not only failed to hold up the advancing Allies but were to become positive liabilities.

Five days after the raid on Truk Admiral Mitscher, with six carriers formed into two task groups, penetrated to within 100 miles of the Marianas. His primary purpose was to make a photographic reconnaissance of those islands, but the carrier aircraft again struck hard. They inflicted severe damage on the enemy's airfields and destroyed about 120 aircraft, many of them carrier planes which had been landed to reinforce the defences. Because the Japanese had no air-sea rescue service the loss of a plane generally meant the loss of its crew; and, as their organisation for training new pilots was quite inadequate, they could not be replaced. Japanese profligacy in expending their trained aircrews contributed much to their defeat; and the loss of the carrier planes on the present occasion forced them to employ incompletely trained pilots when the battle for the Marianas opened four months later.[1] In addition to the losses inflicted by the American carrier aircraft, the submarines on patrol around the islands scored several successes against enemy ships fleeing from the harbours. Indeed co-operation between the submarine and air arms was now becoming a marked feature of raids such as this one. The American submarines also did good work in rescuing the crews of aircraft which had come down in the sea. Indeed the care and thought given by the Americans to the problems of survival and rescue contributed greatly to the high morale of their naval air arm.

The Americans assaulted Eniwetok atoll on the 17th of February, and in five days all the islands were in their hands. There was no opposition from the sea or air, but the Japanese garrison once again fought to the end. Very few of the 3,000 troops on the island were taken prisoner. As American casualties amounted to no more than about 700 killed and wounded the price paid for the complete victory gained in the Marshalls may be regarded as surprisingly low.

Back in America the Joint Chiefs of Staff were meanwhile constantly recasting their plans for the prosecution of the war, not only in the central Pacific but also in the other theatres of the Far East. On the 12th of March, partly as result of the successful carrier raid on the Marianas, they decided to 'leap-frog' Truk and the rest of the

---

[1] See Part II, Chapter XX, of this volume.

Carolines, and to make the Marianas the next object of Admiral Nimitz's Central Pacific forces. They named Saipan, Tinian and Guam for assault in June.[1]

While the forces were being assembled and trained for the assault on the Marianas the central Pacific remained comparatively quiet; but the Fifth Fleet, including Admiral Mitscher's Fast Carrier Task Force, was meanwhile sent to support General MacArthur's advance in the south-west Pacific, and to strike at enemy bases in New Guinea. The exploits of this famous force in that theatre will be recounted later.[2]

In April Mitscher's carriers, which were then returning from New Guinea, made a second onslaught on Truk. They did much damage, and neutralised it for good.

We must now retrace our steps to December 1943 and turn to the south Pacific, where we left Admiral Halsey's land forces developing airfields and fortifying their foothold on Bougainville, in order to support the air offensive against Rabaul.[3] In January 1944 the tempo started to quicken. We have already seen how the Japanese were confident that they could hold Rabaul; and their confidence was, on the face of it, well justified. No other base in the theatre was so strongly fortified, or so well stocked with weapons of war. Four hundred anti-aircraft and coastal guns ringed the defences. About 50,000 well-trained men awaited the expected onslaught; and about 200 aircraft, many of them dispersed in underground hangars, were based on adjacent airfields. To the north lay the important naval base of Kavieng, and the Japanese still held, if precariously, maritime control of the local waters.[4] Lastly Truk lay within supporting distance from the north and, until it was knocked out, air reinforcements could be flown in from there.

The Americans were well aware of the formidable opposition which they were likely to encounter if they made a direct assault on Rabaul, and they had long since given up the idea. Instead they considered that it could be subdued and isolated by thrusts through the central Pacific and along the New Guinea coast. It thus came to pass that the main burden of neutralising the fortress fell upon the Solomon Island's air command, which carried out its task very effectively. Strike after strike was sent to pound the defences. At first they encountered severe opposition; but by the end of February fewer and fewer enemy fighters rose to meet the bombers, and less and less gunfire was put up. The defences were further weakened when, after the raid on Truk by the Fast Carrier Task Force on the

---

[1] See Map 16.
[2] See pp. 340–341.
[3] See pp. 234–235.
[4] See Map 15.

17th of February, the Japanese commander had to send most of his surviving aircraft there. The air bombardment of Rabaul continued throughout April and May, until the base had been reduced to impotence. While this was taking place maritime control of the waters around New Britain and New Ireland was easily wrested from the enemy. A carrier task group twice raided Kavieng in late December, and a third visit early in January proved to the Japanese that they could no longer protect their shipping in those waters. In February a small expeditionary force, mainly of New Zealand troops, took possession of the lightly-held Green Islands just to the north of Buka,[1] and a useful coastal craft base and airfield were developed there. In February, too, U.S. destroyers carried out several night bombardments of Kavieng and Rabaul harbours. The Americans had originally intended to occupy the former in March, as a further step towards isolating Rabaul; but other operations had been so successful that the plan was abandoned early in the month in favour of capturing yet another island, Emirau, between Kavieng and the Admiralties. This was accomplished on the 20th of March without encountering any opposition. The isolation of Rabaul was thus completed, without the Allies having made a direct assault on it. It was a brilliant strategic accomplishment.

At the beginning of the year, General MacArthur's forces of the South-West Pacific Command were pushing along the New Guinea coast, and consolidating their hold on western New Britain. The decision to leave Rabaul in Japanese hands had set the Allies the problem of finding an alternative naval and air base close to the scene of operations in New Guinea. None of the harbours so far captured could be easily developed to meet the requirements of the fleet. In the middle of 1943 the American Chiefs of Staff had, however, decided that the island of Manus in the Admiralties could fill the need. In that group lay one of the finest natural harbours in the south-west Pacific; and it was strategically well placed to dominate the theatre. The date originally set for its capture had been the 1st of January 1944, but the decision to enter New Britain first had caused a postponement. The enemy had not developed Manus for his own purposes, and only a relatively small garrison of some 3,000 troops occupied the islands. The Japanese authorities were much more concerned about barring the advance of General MacArthur's forces in New Guinea, which was part of their 'defensive perimeter', and they were energetically constructing fortified defences and airfields around Hollandia and Wewak.[2] They had good reason for this concern, for Australian and American troops were steadily pressing

---

[1] See Map 15.
[2] See Maps 15 and 20.

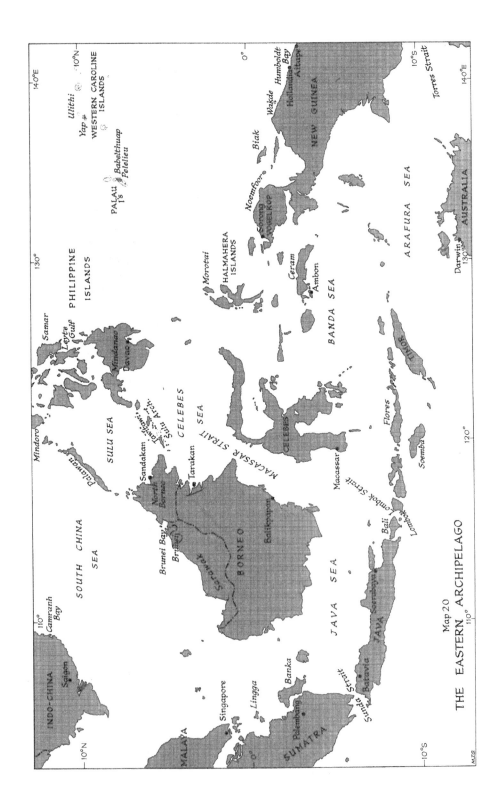

Map 20

THE EASTERN ARCHIPELAGO

up the coast towards Madang, greatly assisted by seaborne landings made behind the enemy's lines and by the complete dominance of the Allied air forces.

Towards the end of February, air reconnaissance had indicated that there were no considerable enemy forces in the Admiralties; so General MacArthur considered that it was worth the risk of carrying out a 'reconnaissance in force' to occupy them, instead of preparing for a full-scale assault. Accordingly on the 27th of February a small expedition of only about 1,000 troops sailed from New Guinea to attack the eastern tip of Manus, where lay a Japanese air-strip. On the forenoon of the 29th they landed against but slight opposition. The Japanese defenders had been taken by surprise; but it was not long before they reacted strongly. During the next few days and nights there was severe fighting around the air-strip, and the Americans found themselves greatly outnumbered; but reinforcements were on the way, and by the 9th of March the situation was well in hand. It was, however, the end of the month before all resistance was finally quelled. As had occurred in many other assaults from the sea which had run into trouble, the supporting fire of warships working close inshore helped greatly to overcome a period of difficulty.[1]

The absence of any interference with the assault on the Admiralties by the Japanese Navy gives a good indication of the extent to which maritime control of those waters had passed into Allied hands. Nor did a single enemy aircraft appear on the scene. With the group in Allied possession immediate steps were taken to develop Manus into one of the finest naval and air bases in the south-west Pacific.[2]

It will be appropriate to mention here the work of the U.S. Navy's Construction Battalions ('Seabees'), who earned many laurels in the Pacific. Their men often landed hard on the heels of the assault troops in order to level beaches, build roads and air-strips, and deal with every constructional problem which arose on islands which were often completely undeveloped. In several instances, notably at Manus, the 'Seabees' also proved themselves first-class fighting troops when the need arose. In the Royal Navy there was no counter-part to this American organisation.

The completion of the main objects of the Solomons campaign in February 1944, and the capture of Manus in the following month, marked the end of the phase of the Pacific war which had begun with the Allies' first counter-offensives in the Solomons and New Guinea in August 1942.[3] Though Admiral Halsey's main task in the south Pacific theatre was now fulfilled, and some of his ships were

---

[1] See pp. 177–180 regarding the effect of the supporting gunfire at Salerno.
[2] Part II, Chapter XXVI, recounts the use made of Manus by the British Pacific Fleet in 1945.
[3] See Vol. II, pp. 222–224 and 234–235.

accordingly transferred to the south-west or central Pacific forces, he himself remained in command of the south Pacific area until June 1944. We shall encounter him and his famous Third Fleet many times later in our story.[1]

The capture of the Admiralty Islands was only the first step in General MacArthur's drive; for his principal target was the system of defences and airfields which the Japanese were energetically building around their supply base at Hollandia in Humboldt Bay on the north coast of New Guinea[2], and from which they still hoped to strike offensive blows. They had already sent strong reinforcements of troops and aircraft to that district, using the Palau Islands as a staging point. As it was to that group that the Japanese fleet had withdrawn shortly before the attack on Truk[3], General MacArthur was anxious to strike hard at it before he embarked on his Hollandia campaign. It was, however, out of reach of the Fifth U.S. Army Air Force working from north Australia; and, as the pattern of operations in the south-west Pacific had not so far required the support of large naval units, Vice-Admiral Kinkaid's Seventh Fleet possessed no carriers. The Australian cruisers *Australia* and *Shropshire* under Rear-Admiral V. A. C. Crutchley, V.C., and three American cruisers were the largest ships on the station. The main strength of the Seventh Fleet lay in its small craft, which transported the Army in its many overseas expeditions and supported it after it had landed. General MacArthur therefore asked that Admiral Mitscher's Fast Carrier Task Force should strike at the islands in the Palau group, and this was readily agreed upon. Almost the whole of the Fifth Fleet sailed from the Marshalls on the 22nd of March under Admiral Spruance. The Americans hoped to catch the Japanese fleet in the Palaus, and planned to prevent its escape by laying many mines in the exits; but part of Spruance's force was sighted by enemy reconnaissance aircraft on the night of 29th–30th of March, and the main units of their fleet thereupon withdrew, mostly to Singapore. The giant (64,000-ton) battleship *Musashi*, Admiral Koga's flagship, was however hit by a torpedo fired by one of the American submarines ringing the islands; and on the last day of March the Admiral lost his life when the aircraft in which he was flying to the Philippines disappeared at sea. Admiral Toyoda was appointed Commander-in-Chief, Combined Fleet, in his place.

At the end of March the American carrier aircraft made a series of heavy attacks on the Palau group, and, although this time the Japanese were prepared and put up a strong fighter defence, thirty-

---

[1] The original South Pacific Force had been renamed the 'Third Fleet' on 15th March 1943 (see Vol. II, p. 413).

[2] See Map 20.

[3] See p. 335.

six ships totalling nearly 130,000 tons were sunk. The attempt to block the Palaus was the first and only minelaying operation carried out by American carrier aircraft. Although it failed in its primary purpose, the harbour was closed for twenty days, and the Japanese therefore abandoned the island as a base. As they had already been deprived of the use of Truk[1], their fleet was now forced to work from an ill-protected anchorage in the Sulu archipelago between Borneo and the Philippine Islands.

On the 13th of April, only a week after arriving back at its Marshall Island base in Majuro lagoon, the Fifth Fleet sailed again, this time with Hollandia in Humboldt Bay as its target. General MacArthur planned to carry out three separate landings on the 22nd of April, two off Hollandia and one off Aitape 125 miles down the coast to the east.[2] The fleet was asked to strike from the 21st–24th in support of these landings. In the meantime, from the end of March until the middle of April, the air forces of the south-west Pacific command had delivered several heavy raids on the enemy airfields in northern New Guinea. So effective were they that by the time the Fifth Fleet arrived on the scene little remained for its aircrews to do, except to support the Army. Japanese air strength had already been practically wiped out, and once again the Navy made no attempt to dispute the issue.

The Hollandia campaign was another excellent example of successful 'leap-frog' strategy. Though the Japanese had no clear idea where the next blow would fall, and their strength was too small to enable them adequately to defend more than one or two places, they had expected that Wewak would be one of the sites selected by the Americans for an assault from the sea. While therefore Aitape and the Humboldt Bay district were comparatively lightly defended, they had usually kept a garrison of one division (perhaps 15,000 men) in the neighbourhood of Wewak; and that comparatively strong force now found itself by-passed.

All three landings at Hollandia and Aitape achieved complete surprise, and after the customary dawn bombardments by cruisers and destroyers and air attacks on the beach defences the troops stepped ashore practically unopposed. Within four days they were in possession of all their immediate objectives, and the defeated enemy was retreating to the west.

Even before the assaults on Hollandia had been launched plans were being made for the next jump along the coast to Wakde Island, 120 miles to the north-west, on which the Japanese had built a coral air-strip capable of taking the largest aircraft. Its capture

[1] See pp. 335–337.
[2] See Map 20.

assumed even greater importance when it was discovered that none of the airfields around Humboldt Bay was suitable for the heavy bombers needed to reduce the Palaus. As one such field was not enough, American eyes were turned also towards Biak, 200 miles north-west of Wakde.[1]

Hollandia was used as an assembly point for the invasion forces; troops were embarked for Wakde in L.S.Ts and L.C.Is, and sailed after dark on the 16th of May. At dawn next morning Australian and American cruisers and destroyers bombarded the shore defences prior to the landings. Japanese resistance was once again fanatical; but it did not prevent the Americans capturing the island in two days. By the 21st the air-strip was fit for use.

On the 25th of May, the Biak invasion expedition also sailed from the Humboldt Bay ports. For several days the Fifth U.S. Army Air Force had been raiding the island, as well as other targets further to the west, and had done considerable damage; but the Japanese on Biak were fully expecting attack and had taken careful defensive precautions. The launching of the assault so shortly after the Wakde and Hollandia operations, however, caught them off balance. The initial landings on the 27th were virtually unopposed, and air opposition did not develop until the evening after the assault. This was a fortunate chance, as the fighter cover which should have been provided by aircraft working from distant shore bases did not prove effective; and that experience reinforced the Americans' strong preference for an assault force to be provided with fighter cover from carriers. The comparatively easy conditions encountered at first by the Biak assault force did not, however, last long. In June the enemy's reaction, especially by their Navy, was stronger than anything that had been experienced for several months. The fighting which then took place will be described in a later chapter.[2]

Before leaving the Pacific theatre some account must be given of the American submarine campaign, which in this period achieved greater successes than ever before. Ranging far and wide in the western Pacific, from the waters around Japan to the Malacca Straits, penetrating deep into the South China Sea, and patrolling the routes from Japan to all her scattered conquests, the submarines reaped a rich harvest. Attempts to convoy their dwindling merchant fleet, which the Japanese had tardily initiated in the autumn of 1943, still proved ineffective. In the first five months of 1944, 212 Japanese ships of 993,800 tons were sunk by submarines and many more were damaged. A large number of them were carrying troops and supplies which could ill be spared; but the loss of the ships themselves was even more serious, for they could not be replaced by new

---

[1] See Map 20.
[2] See Part II, Chapter XX.

construction, and the lack of shipping was slowly paralysing Japan's war economy.[1] Nor were merchant ships the only victims. In the same five-month period three cruisers (*Agano*, *Tatsuta* and *Yubari*), nine destroyers, four submarines and several escort vessels were also sunk. The price paid for these successes by the American submarine service was not unduly heavy; for only six of their number were lost during the same period.

On the other hand, the performance of the Japanese submarines remained as unimpressive as it had been earlier in the war. Although often sent to attack invasion expeditions they met with little success, and several of their number were sunk. They were still saddled with the defensive task of carrying supplies to by-passed Japanese garrisons in the central Pacific and the Solomons, and many were lost on such duties. In all, twenty-six Japanese submarines were sunk in the Pacific theatres during this period.[2] It was in the waters to the north-east of the Admiralty Islands that the American destroyer-escort *England* achieved the most remarkable anti-submarine success of any single ship in the whole war. One of a group of three vessels sent as a 'hunter-killer' group to search for submarines supplying the isolated Bougainville garrison, she found and sank her first victim on the 19th of May. Moving westwards to a position north-east of the Admiralty Islands, the group then ran into a Japanese patrol line, and during the short period from the 22nd to the 26th no less than four more enemies were despatched by her. On the 31st, when working with an escort carrier group, the *England* was instrumental in the destruction of yet another. In the short space of twelve days, no less than six Japanese submarines were thus sunk; and what made her achievement even more remarkable was that the *England* was a new ship with little more than ten weeks' anti-submarine experience.[3]

Thus by the end of May 1944, in the two great Pacific commands, the Central and South-West, the war against Japan was being waged everywhere with outstanding success; and the vigorously conducted offensive operations by all arms of the services of America and the British Commonwealth, under American command and direction,

---

[1] An interesting account of the devastating results of the American submarine campaign on Japan's war effort and economy is contained in the *United States Naval Institute Proceedings* for October 1956. The writer, a Japanese officer, concludes that the neglect of convoy was due to the high command's complete absorption in allegedly 'offensive' strategy. They regarded convoy as 'defensive' and therefore an undesirable measure. Belief in that fallacy was only very slowly dispelled in Japanese circles. It is fair to remark that at various periods in the war the same error appeared in certain Allied quarters, as has been remarked elsewhere in this history. (See, for example, Vol. I, pp. 33–34, and this volume, pp. 264–265.)

[2] See Appendix D, Table III.

[3] See Morison, Vol. VIII, pp. 224–228, for a full account of the *England's* remarkable exploit, and Appendix D, Table III of this volume for full details.

had been made possible by the overwhelming maritime and air superiority which the Allies had established.

In the South-East Asia Command (S.E.A.C.), to which we must now turn, the opening months of 1944 brought no parallel to the Pacific victories. Except in Burma, offensive operations had been almost brought to a halt by the strategic decision that supplies and shipping should be diverted to the European theatre and that no large-scale expeditions could be undertaken until after the defeat of Germany.

For a full account of Allied strategy in south-east Asia in 1944 the reader must refer to other volumes of this series[1]; but without some knowledge of the background the apparent lack of activity in the Indian Ocean cannot be placed in its proper perspective. The Supreme Commander, Admiral Lord Louis Mountbatten, had received his first directive on the 23rd of October 1943, shortly after taking up his appointment.[2] It gave him clear authority to plan combined operations on the understanding that the necessary ships and assault craft would be forthcoming. For several months the Supreme Commander had indeed been planning a major attack on the northern tip of Sumatra (operation 'Culverin'); but examination of the resources needed showed that it certainly could not be carried out in the spring of 1944 without prejudicing the invasion of Normandy and of southern France. As that condition was not acceptable the plans were scrapped, and a more modest alternative, aiming to recapture the Andaman Islands (operation 'Buccaneer'), was substituted. This operation was to coincide with a Chinese offensive in northern Burma, with an assault on the Arakan coast to capture Akyab, and with a big attack by the army on the Burma–India frontier.[3]

In November 1943 Admiral Mountbatten brought these plans to the 'Sextant' conference at Cairo. But the British and American Chiefs of Staff were by no means yet agreed over the correct strategy; and the Chinese were demanding that any offensive by them should receive diversionary support from a strong seaborne expedition across the Bay of Bengal. As President Roosevelt had already promised the Chinese that this would be done, the British Chiefs of Staff found themselves committed, against their will, to carry out 'Buccaneer' in March 1944. When the Cairo conference dispersed, the Prime Minister, the American President and their staffs went on to Teheran

---

[1] See J. Ehrman, *Grand Strategy* Vol. V, Chapters III, IV and V (H.M.S.O., 1956). Also Churchill, Vol. V, Chapters XXIII, XXXI, XXXII.

[2] See pp. 214–216.

[3] See Map 21.

for the 'Eureka' conference, where priorities and dates for the invasion of Normandy and southern France were settled. They then returned to Cairo for a continuation of the 'Sextant' conference in the light of decisions taken at Teheran, and to consider the impact of those decisions on Pacific and Indian Ocean strategy. But in the meantime the Supreme Commander, S.E.A.C., had sent revised plans for 'Buccaneer', which, he considered, should be conducted in greater strength. American experience in the Pacific had indicated that, if the capture of enemy airfields was to be achieved while air support from carriers was fully effective, the superiority of the assault forces in an amphibious operation should be greater than was at first believed. Admiral Mountbatten had at his disposal sufficient shipping and landing craft, and he proposed that, for the short period necessary to carry out the assault, all his available resources should be devoted to the purpose.

From the 3rd to the 6th of December 1943 the staffs of both nations argued the matter. Both were agreed that in no circumstances should the operations in Europe be prejudiced; but whereas the Americans were insistent that the Burma operations and 'Buccaneer' should take place as planned, the British were equally insistent that any seaborne expedition in the Indian Ocean would undoubtedly lead to a diversion of strength from Europe. Moreover they considered that many of the landing craft already in south-east Asia would have to be withdrawn to take part in Mediterranean operations. The deadlock was finally resolved by President Roosevelt giving way over 'Buccaneer'. Instead, plans were to be prepared to support the Burma operations with raids by carriers and amphibious forces. It was also agreed that the main effort against Japan should be made in the Pacific.

On the 7th of December 1943 Admiral Mountbatten was ordered to send back to Europe fifteen L.S.Ts and six L.S.Is—over half of his landing ships. But, still hoping to carry out some operations across the Bay of Bengal with those remaining, he submitted a new plan. This was to be a small seaborne landing on the Mayu Peninsula behind the Japanese positions in the Arakan.[1] But by this time the assault shipping needed for the landings at Anzio had increased, and the British Chiefs of Staff were combing all commands to meet the requirement.[2] Towards the end of the year the Prime Minister agreed that more ships should be withdrawn from S.E.A.C., because Chiang Kai-shek was unwilling to carry out his advance southwards from Yunnan against Burma after operation 'Buccaneer' had been cancelled. Thus the Chiefs of Staff considered it unnecessary to retain any landing ships in the theatre, and by the first week of January

---

[1] See Map 21.
[2] See pp. 298–299.

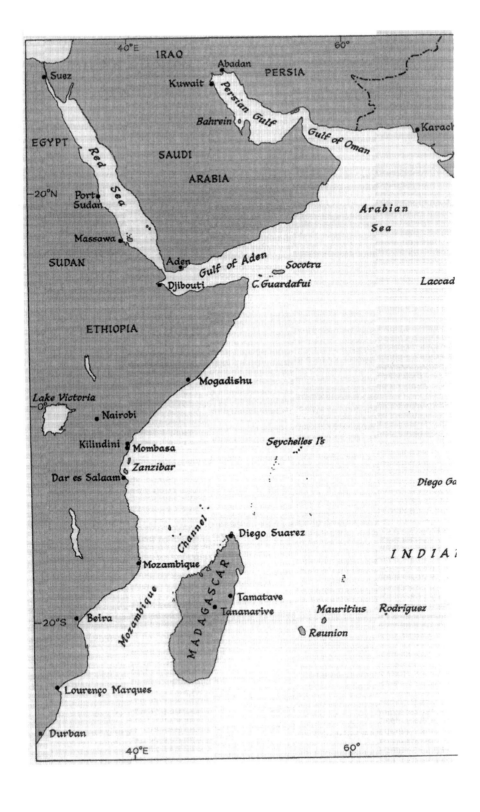

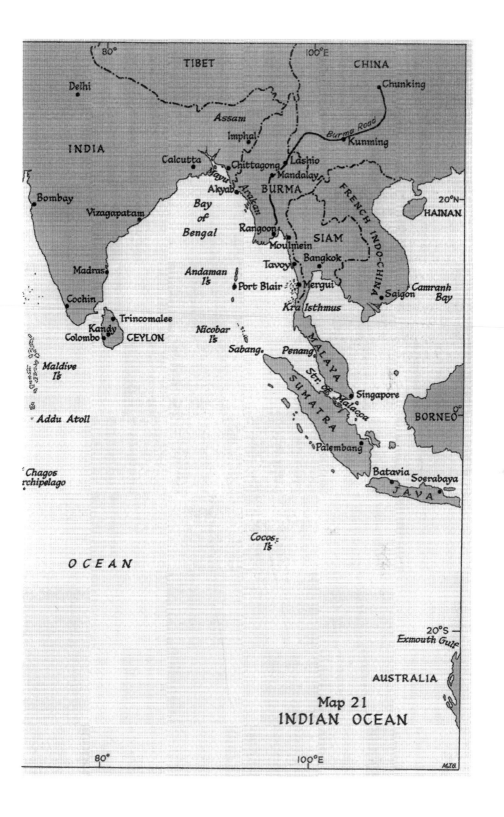

Map 21
INDIAN OCEAN

1944 Mountbatten was being deprived of most of his few remaining vessels. The Supreme Commander now had no alternative but to cancel his latest plan, and accept that no seaborne expedition could be carried out until the ships returned to him.

From this brief account of a complicated story the reader will see that Admiral Mountbatten did all that he could to launch an offensive in the Indian Ocean, but was stopped by considerations of high policy. Throughout the war every combined operation, in every theatre, hinged upon the availability of landing ships and assault craft; and the shortage of those types of vessels was never more acutely felt than in the early months of 1944. As long as the European theatres received over-riding priority, it was inevitable that offensive purposes in the Indian Ocean should suffer.

We have already seen how, in November 1943, the Cairo conference decided that 'the main effort against Japan should be made in the Pacific'. With regard to maritime operations in south-east Asia the conference recorded the view that 'Should the means be available, additional ground, sea and air offensive operations, including carrier-borne raids [are contemplated] with the object of maintaining pressure on the enemy, forcing dispersion of his forces, and attaining the maximum attrition of his air and naval forces and shipping'.[1] The conference then went on to establish the allocation of the British naval forces in the Far East to carry out these intentions. Enough strength was to be maintained in the Indian Ocean to protect the sea communications with the Andaman Islands, if they were re-captured, and to carry out operations and threats against Japanese positions in south-east Asia; but all other ships were to be concentrated in the Pacific. The combined Chiefs of Staff considered that a British Pacific Fleet could be assembled in Australia, and could work from advanced bases in the Bismarck and Solomon Islands, whence it could either cover operations in New Guinea, the Netherlands East Indies and the Philippines, or co-operate with the American fleet in the central Pacific. This decision marked the genesis of the British Pacific Fleet; but it also doomed all hopes of a large-scale combined offensive in the Indian Ocean.

Early in January 1944 the Prime Minister examined the implications of these decisions in detail and expressed himself at complete variance with them.[2] He considered that the correct strategy for the Navy was to remain based on India and Ceylon, and build up there to support an eventual drive by S.E.A.C. forces into Sumatra and Malaya. He reverted once more to his original project for the invasion of the northern tip of Sumatra (operation 'Culverin').

---

[1] See J. Ehrman, *Grand Strategy*, Vol. V (H.M.S.O., 1956), pp. 423–424.

[2] See Churchill, Vol. V, p. 504, and J. Ehrman, *Grand Strategy*, Vol. V, Chapters XI and XII.

Although the British Chiefs of Staff estimated that the assault shipping could not be made available until six months after the defeat of Germany (which they hoped would take place about October 1944), Mr Churchill considered that, with aid from the Americans, an attack could be launched in the autumn of 1944. The whole argument about strategy in south-east Asia was thus reopened, and for the next few months it was debated at length. The War Cabinet and, not unnaturally, Admiral Mountbatten were strongly in favour of the Indian Ocean policy; but the Chiefs of Staff produced convincing reasons against their view. The Americans too favoured the British Fleet remaining in the Indian Ocean, but for different reasons from the Prime Minister's. The question whether and when it should be sent to the Pacific was not finally resolved until the second Quebec Conference in September 1944.

The foregoing short summary supplies the background for the operations of the Eastern Fleet for the five months January to May 1944, now to be described.

It was told earlier how by the end of 1943 Admiral Somerville's strength had been run down until it consisted of little more than an escort and protection force of a few cruisers and destroyers.[1] But after the submission of the Italian fleet and the immobilisation of the *Tirpitz* in September of that year, and the sinking of the *Scharnhorst* in the following December[2], the Admiralty could look afresh at the problem of building up the Eastern Fleet. Early in January 1944 they promulgated their intentions for the next four months. No less than 146 ships, including the *Renown*, *Queen Elizabeth* and *Valiant*, the carriers *Illustrious* and *Victorious*, fourteen cruisers, twenty-four fleet destroyers, fifty-four escort vessels, twenty-seven minesweepers, seventeen submarines and five repair and depot ships, were to join Admiral Somerville's command.[3] Some of these substantial reinforcements were already on the way. The *Renown*, flying the flag of Vice-Admiral Sir Arthur J. Power, the second-in-command designate of the Eastern Fleet, arrived in Ceylon on the 27th of January 1944, together with the *Queen Elizabeth* and *Valiant* and the fleet carrier *Illustrious*. Cruisers, destroyers, escort vessels and submarines were also arriving from the Mediterranean, and Admiral Somerville thus at last possessed something like a fleet. No sooner had he been reinforced than the main strength of the Japanese Navy, consisting of five battleships, three carriers, eighteen cruisers and a number of smaller ships, concentrated at Singapore. Some of these ships had, as

---

[1] See pp. 219 and 221.

[2] See pp. 64–69 and 78–89.

[3] The *Victorious* did not arrive in the Eastern Fleet until July 1944. One of the repair ships was the *Unicorn*, which was fitted with a flight deck, and was to be used as an aircraft carrier until strength in that class of ship had been built up.

already told, come from Truk and the Palaus.[1] Should so powerful a force make an incursion into the Indian Ocean, Somerville felt that he was not yet strong enough to offer battle and, as in April 1942, might have to withdraw from Ceylon to the Maldives.[2] The Admiralty, whilst agreeing that he should avoid engagement with greatly superior forces, thought that even a temporary withdrawal to the westward would have a bad effect on morale generally and on prestige in India and the Dominions. There was no evidence, they said, that the move to Singapore was linked with any offensive intentions in the Indian Ocean. But as a precautionary measure one squadron of Beaufighters and one of Liberators were moved to Ceylon, and three fighter squadrons were rearmed with more modern aircraft. The U.S. Navy also agreed to send the carrier *Saratoga* with three destroyers from the Pacific to augment the carrier strength of the Eastern Fleet.[3]

The Japanese had indeed no large-scale offensive intentions. Their fleet had been sent to Singapore because the American carrier raids were making the bases in the Carolines and Marianas unsafe[4], and because Singapore possessed the only large dock outside Japan. Moreover, as they were finding it increasingly difficult to transport oil to their homeland, it was easier and more economical to replenish and refit ships at that base. Admiral Mountbatten was thus able to go ahead with his plans for the fleet to make carrier air attacks on Sumatra as soon as the American reinforcements arrived.

Meanwhile the depredations of the German and Japanese U-boats in the Indian Ocean were still a source of anxiety.[5] There were as yet nothing like enough escort vessels on the station to convoy shipping on all the many routes; and in the previous December the Admiralty had declared the delays which they expected to arise if a universal convoy system were established to be unacceptable. The Admiralty considered that what they described as 'the relatively modest and local risks' should be accepted, and that ships should only sail in convoy 'on routes actually or potentially threatened'. They even urged that escorts released from convoy should act 'as hunting groups in areas of known probability [of U-boat attack]'. It seems incredible that the hardly-learned lessons of the Atlantic Battle were thus regarded as inapplicable to the Indian Ocean; and that the old heresy of the hunting group should have been revived at this late

---

[1] See pp. 335 and 340.
[2] See Vol. II, p. 29.
[3] See p. 354 regarding the *Saratoga's* arrival in the Indian Ocean.
[4] See p. 340.
[5] See pp. 219–221.

date and in defiance of so much previous experience.[1] Delays to shipping in the Indian Ocean were indeed serious, but they were caused mainly by inadequate port facilities, and it may be doubted whether convoy contributed appreciably to them. None the less Admiral Somerville relaxed his protective measures, and for a time the Admiralty's view appeared justified. Then, in the last ten days of January, six independently-routed ships were sunk, and our total losses for the month were eight ships of 56,213 tons—the highest in any theatre of war for that month. Four German U-boats were working in the Gulf of Aden and to the north of the Maldives, and it was they who did most of the damage. A search was made to catch the tanker *Charlotte Schliemann*[2], which we believed to be waiting south of Mauritius to refuel the U-boats; but she had not yet arrived at the expected rendezvous. Her long and adventurous career was, however, brought to an end in February, when she was sighted by a Catalina flying boat from Mauritius and was finally sunk by the destroyer *Relentless*. As the *Schliemann* had only refuelled two U-boats when she was caught, the cruises of the others were bound to be curtailed.

Early in February Admiral Somerville re-introduced convoy on the routes where, in accordance with the Admiralty's wishes, he had suspended it. But some time was bound to elapse before it became effective, and most of the ten ships (64,169 tons) sunk during the month were still sailing independently. There were, however, three attacks on convoys. On the 11th the Japanese submarine Ro.110, which had damaged a ship in a Calcutta–Colombo convoy, was quickly destroyed by the escorts. Next day her colleague I.27 attacked a convoy of five troopships sailing from Kilindini to Colombo. She torpedoed and sank the *Khedive Ismail*, with the loss of over 1,000 lives —a rare disaster to happen to a troop convoy—but was herself sunk by the destroyers *Petard* and *Paladin*. They and the old cruiser *Hawkins* were the only escorts with the convoy at the time. In spite of the sinking of the troopship these two incidents showed once again how the convoy system must bring to the escorts the chance of counter-attacking and sinking an enemy who approaches their charges. But the truth was that Admiral Somerville still possessed far too few escorts to make the convoy system an effective U-boat killer on this station, and he at once protested to the Admiralty on that score. Moreover, because he had to use his fleet destroyers to supplement his meagre strength in escort vessels, the main units of his fleet were often immobilised. The Admiralty replied, not very helpfully, that risks would have to be taken; to which Somerville answered that

---

[1] See Vol. I, pp. 10, 134–135, Vol. II, pp. 97–102, and this volume, pp. 265–266.
[2] See Vol. II, pp. 178–182, 265 and 267, regarding the earlier career of this ship.

they were being taken, but that 'Mercator's projection was apt to cause erroneous conclusions to be drawn when considering the eastern theatre in relation to others more remote from the equator'. There was something in the Admiral's contention that the great distances between bases in his command were not always realised at home.

In March the U-boats achieved their greatest success in the Indian Ocean since July 1943, and sank eleven ships of 67,658 tons. This was about equal to the total losses inflicted by enemy submarines in all other theatres.[1] None the less the very heavy traffic on the station was not seriously interrupted. Searches were made to find another U-boat supply ship, and on the 12th of March aircraft from the escort carrier *Battler* sighted the *Brake* south of Mauritius, while she was actually fuelling two U-boats. The destroyer *Roebuck* closed the position and sank the supply ship. This success further curtailed U-boat operations in the Indian Ocean, and the survivors were forced to return to Penang prematurely.

To sum up the trend of the U-boat war in the Indian Ocean for the first three months of 1944, we lost twenty-nine ships of 188,040 tons in very widely dispersed attacks, and we only sank four enemies (including one off the Cape of Good Hope) in the same period—a comparatively poor return.[2] As Japanese as well as German submarines were working in the Indian Ocean at the time, it has proved difficult to distinguish which enemy was responsible for each merchantman sunk. In certain cases, however, callous brutality by the submarine crews towards the survivors has enabled the attacker to be identified as Japanese. The probability is that ten ships were sunk by them and nineteen by German U-boats. The distinction is only of importance because it emphasises how, at this stage of the war, it was only in the Indian Ocean that Dönitz's crews were still able to find unescorted or weakly escorted targets, and so achieve any significant results.

After the heavy sinkings of the first three months of 1944 in the Indian Ocean a lull followed in April and May, during which not one Allied merchantman was sunk in the whole theatre; and on the 3rd of May an R.A.F. aircraft of Aden Command hit U.852 off Socotra, damaging her so seriously that she scuttled herself. This loss seems to have discouraged the Germans from sending any U-boats into the Arabian Sea for three months, thus gaining a valuable period

---

[1] See Appendix K.

[2] These were:

Ro.110 (Japanese) on 11th February off the east coast of India.
    I.27 (Japanese) on 12th February south of the Maldives.
U-It.23 (German ex-Italian) on 14th February in the Malacca Straits.
U-It.22 (German ex-Italian) on 11th March south of the Cape of Good Hope.
See Appendix D, Tables I and III ,for fuller details.

of immunity for the heavy mercantile traffic passing through those waters. There is no doubt, however, that the main factors in the curtailment of Dönitz's campaign were the sinking of the two supply tankers, already mentioned, and the excellent work of the roving American escort carrier groups off the Azores.[1] But the enemy did not yet abandon the hope of finding easy targets in these remote waters, and in June there was a considerable revival of activity by both Japanese and German submarines. The losses then suffered, and the successes obtained by our anti-submarine forces, will be discussed in a later chapter.

One more incident in the enemy's campaign against our merchant shipping in the Indian Ocean remains to be described. Early in March three Japanese cruisers left Singapore on a raiding foray. On the 9th the *Tone* intercepted and sank the British India steamship *Behar* south of the Cocos Islands. Over eighty survivors were rescued but, in accordance with the orders of the squadron commander, Vice-Admiral Takasu, about sixty-five of them were massacred on board the *Tone*. It was one of the worst of all the many crimes committed by the Japanese against defenceless prisoners; and the captain of the *Tone* was later sentenced to serve a long term of imprisonment for his share in it. The *Behar* was, however, the last Allied merchantman to be sunk by an enemy surface raider.

In addition to the reinforcements already mentioned, more submarines were now reaching Admiral Somerville, and patrols in the Malacca Straits were therefore resumed. Their first success came on the 11th of January, when the *Tally Ho* (Lieutenant-Commander L. W. A. Bennington) sank the 5,100-ton light cruiser *Kuma*. On her next patrol she despatched the ex-Italian German-manned U-boat U-It.23 on the 14th of February, and, although six days later she was severely depth-charged and rammed by a Japanese torpedo-boat whom she fortuitously encountered in the dark, she continued her patrol and returned safely to Ceylon. The *Templar* torpedoed and severely damaged the light cruiser *Kitagami* off Penang on the 26th of January; but apart from these successes against warships the long and arduous submarine patrols were, for the most part, unrewarding. Few merchant ships of any size were seen, and most of the traffic consisted of small coasters and junks which the Japanese were now compelled to use to augment their diminishing merchant fleet. Such targets were difficult and dangerous to attack in the shallow coastal waters which they hugged as far as possible. In the five-month period from January to May 1944 only eight enemy merchant ships over 500 tons were sunk, the total amounting to 15,920 tons. Compared with the resounding successes of the American submarines in the

---

[1] See pp. 43–44 and 246.

Pacific[1], these results were a disappointing return for the effort expended. But in addition to the offensive patrols, our submarines carried out a number of special operations, such as landing agents on the enemy-held coasts[2]; and in March they also commenced mine-laying in the approaches to ports in the Malacca Straits. The *Stonehenge*, which became overdue in March, was our only loss from all these varied duties.

Air minelaying was not a new feature in the S.E.A.C. As far back as February 1943 Liberators of the Tenth U.S. Air Force, which were based on Calcutta, had laid mines in the Rangoon river delta; and later in the same year they repeated the operation several times. Although the tonnage of shipping sunk was not spectacular, the enemy's supply traffic was considerably disorganised—largely because the Japanese minesweeping service was ill-organised and its equipment primitive. The result was that their main port of entry for the supplies needed by their land forces in Burma was often closed for long periods, and during the last two years of the war very few iron-hulled ships dared to enter the river.

In December 1943 Admiral Mountbatten re-organised the structure of the air commands in his theatre. Air Chief Marshal Sir Richard Peirse became Allied Air Commander-in-Chief, with Major-General G. E. Stratemeyer, U.S.A.F., as his deputy; and air minelaying became the responsibility of the Strategic Air Force of General Stratemeyer's Eastern Air Command. At first it continued to be carried out only by the Tenth U.S. Air Force, but in January 1944 No. 231 Group of the Royal Air Force joined in the campaign. Early in 1944 the Supreme Commander established an inter-service committee to co-ordinate all minelaying (including by submarines), and during the year air minelaying was gradually extended to other ports on the Burma coast, such as Moulmein, Tavoy and Mergui.[3] The campaign was organised on the principle of obstructing regularly the ports most used by the Japanese, while complicating the enemy's minesweeping problems by using various types of British or American mines. Where distance or other factors prevented regular infestation of a harbour, long-delay mechanisms were introduced into the mine firing mechanisms.

On the night of the 10th–11th of January 1944 Liberators of the Tenth U.S. Air Force reached out to the South China Sea for the first time, and mined the harbour of Bangkok. The obstruction of Rangoon had increased the importance to the Japanese of the ports of entry on that coast, from which they could transport supplies

---

[1] See pp. 342-343.

[2] Edward Young, *One of our Submarines*, Chapter XVII (Hart Davis, 1952), contains a graphic account of one such operation off Sumatra in May 1944.

[3] See Map 21.

Attacks on Java and Sumatra by carrier aircraft of the Eastern Fleet

Above. Sabang, 19th April, 1944.

Below. Soerabaya, 17th May, 1944.

Above. The scene on Kwajalein after the assault, 31st January, 1944.

Below. The assault on Wakde Island, 17th May, 1944.

(*Photographs U.S. Navy Department*)

overland to Burma. During the six months following on the first operation against Bangkok we therefore set about mining other ports in the South China Sea as well. Here too, as in the Bay of Bengal, the Japanese minesweeping organisation proved inadequate; and in addition to the loss of several ships their seaborne traffic was seriously delayed. In June 1944 the Tenth Air Force's effort was transferred to carrying supplies over the Himalayan mountains ('the hump') to their colleagues of the Fourteenth U.S. Air Force in China; but in the summer the Americans formed two new bomber commands (the XXth and XXIst) to work from bases in India and China, and the former's long-range aircraft later joined with those of the R.A.F's No. 231 Group in the prosecution of the air minelaying campaign in south-east Asia.

The accomplishments of the minelaying aircraft and submarines will be summarised later, when we consider the campaign as a whole.[1] Here we need only note that during the first half of 1944 they caused very serious delays and dislocation to the Japanese sea-borne traffic on which their armies in south-east Asia depended, and that the cumulative effect of our minelaying was out of all proportion to the effort involved and the losses of aircraft we suffered.

Earlier in this chapter we saw how the Supreme Commander, S.E.A.C., was deprived of practically the whole of his landing ships and craft at the end of 1943. This decision vitiated his plans for the second Arakan campaign, which had opened in December. His aim had been to secure positions on the coast, from which he would eventually be able to capture the island of Akyab by a seaborne landing behind the enemy lines.[2] In January this project had to be cancelled, and the only naval forces remaining to support the Army were a few coastal craft, mainly motor launches, manned by men of the R.N., R.I.N., Burma, and South African Naval Forces. During the first three months of 1944, until the monsoon broke in April, the motor launches ranged up and down the Arakan coast seeking the enemy's supply vessels; but the Japanese were for the most part using inland waterways, and few targets were found.

Though the coastal craft performed many useful services, such as bombarding enemy positions, harassing his supply traffic, and land-ing Commandos and agents behind the lines, they could not act as substitutes for the assault landing craft which were almost entirely lacking in the theatre. The Army succeeded in halting the enemy's offensive on the Arakan front in February, but even then there was no prospect of a rapid advance towards Akyab; for, on the 22nd of

[1] See Part II, Chapter XXVIII.
[2] See Map 21.

March, the Japanese launched their attempt to invade India through Assam.

To return to the main Eastern Fleet, by March there were five naval air stations in Ceylon and southern India, capable of supporting thirty-four Fleet Air Arm squadrons, and possessing maintenance and repair facilities for 400 aircraft. Admiral Somerville still had, however, only one large carrier, the *Illustrious*; for the departure of *Victorious* from the Home Fleet had been delayed to enable her to take part in the attacks on the *Tirpitz*[1], and she was not due to arrive till July. He also expected the fleet carriers *Indomitable* and *Formidable* in due course; but meanwhile his carrier strength was to be augmented by the temporary loan of the U.S. Navy's *Saratoga*, which was on her way from the Pacific by way of Australia. In March, two escort carriers, the *Shah* and *Begum*, together with a welcome reinforcement of long-range escorts for convoy protection, joined the fleet; and some destroyers could now at last be freed to work with the big ships. On the 21st of that month the *Renown*, *Queen Elizabeth*, *Valiant* and *Illustrious*, four cruisers and ten destroyers sailed from Ceylon to sweep along the shipping route from Australia to the Middle East, which had recently been raided by a Japanese cruiser force[2], and to meet the *Saratoga*. Subsidiary purposes were to exercise the fleet as a body and to practise oiling at sea in preparation for making carrier aircraft strikes far from any base. From the 24th to the 26th the ships refuelled satisfactorily from a special force of tankers which had been sent to the south of Ceylon, and on the 27th they met the *Saratoga* and her escort of three American destroyers. Flying practices were carried out on the return journey to Trincomalee, where the fleet arrived on the 2nd of April.

On the Supreme Commander's orders Admiral Somerville now immediately planned a carrier air attack against Sabang, on the north-east tip of Sumatra, where there was a Japanese naval base guarding the entrance to the Malacca Straits[3]; but a request from the U.S. Navy Department for the Eastern Fleet to carry out a diversionary raid in the Indian Ocean caused a postponement. Admiral King asked that the operation should take place about the middle of April, so that Japanese naval aircraft, which were known to be mainly concentrated in southern Malaya, would not be diverted to New Guinea, where MacArthur proposed to assault Hollandia on the 22nd.[4]

It is interesting to note the Japanese attitude towards the Indian Ocean at this time. They were aware that the Eastern Fleet was not

---

[1] See pp. 274–279.
[2] See p. 351.
[3] See Map 21.
[4] See p. 341.

powerful enough to offer a serious challenge to their position in south-east Asia; nor did they expect any large-scale seaborne offensive. That they considered the Pacific to be the decisive theatre is clearly shown by a secret order issued by Admiral Koga on the 8th of March. 'The Combined Fleet' it stated 'is for the time being directing its main operations to the Pacific, where . . . it will bring to bear the maximum strength of all our forces to meet and destroy the enemy, and to maintain our hold on vital areas. . . . If during the course of these operations a strong enemy attack takes place in south-east Asia, should the situation in the Pacific permit, air reinforcements will be sent so that the occupation force and enemy fleet will be destroyed. . . . Consideration must be given to ensure that this diversion of strength . . . shall not gravely impede the disposition of forces for a decisive battle in the central Pacific.' Admiral Koga was, as mentioned earlier, killed when his aircraft disappeared at sea on the last day of the same month[1], but his successor as Commander-in-Chief of the Combined Fleet, Admiral Toyoda, saw no reason to adopt any different policy. Koga's order makes it plain that nothing short of a full-scale seaborne assault in the Indian Ocean would have caused any appreciable diversion of enemy forces. The Japanese naval aircraft in Malaya were there to prepare for the 'decisive battle in the central Pacific', and it seems clear that the raids by the Eastern Fleet, now to be described, made little impact on the enemy's strategy.

On the 16th of April Admiral Somerville sailed from Trincomalee flying his flag in the *Queen Elizabeth*. His fleet was a truly Allied force, for it included one carrier, two battleships, one battle cruiser, four cruisers and seven destroyers of the Royal Navy, the *Saratoga* and three destroyers of the United States Navy, the French battleship *Richelieu* (which had only arrived a week previously[2]), the cruiser *Tromp* and one destroyer of the Royal Netherlands Navy, the New Zealand cruiser *Gambia*, and four destroyers of the Royal Australian Navy. In the small hours of the 19th the fleet arrived undetected at the flying-off position, 100 miles to the south-west of Sabang. At 5.30 a.m. the carriers started to launch the striking force, which consisted of seventeen Barracudas and thirteen Corsair fighters from the *Illustrious*, and eleven Avengers, eighteen Dauntless dive-bombers and twenty-four Hellcat fighters from the *Saratoga*.

The air group from the *Saratoga* arrived over the target just before 7 a.m., and attacked immediately. The *Illustrious's* group followed **a** minute later, and attacked from a different direction. Surprise was complete, no enemy fighters were in the air, and the anti-aircraft

---

[1] See p. 340.

[2] See p. 73 regarding the earlier service of the *Richelieu* under Allied control.

guns did not open fire until after the first bombs had dropped. Oil storage tanks, shipping and installations in the harbour were the principal targets for the bombers, while the fighters attended to aircraft on the Sabang airfield and on another airfield twenty-five miles away on the mainland. Three out of the four oil tanks were set on fire and destroyed, and extensive damage was done to the harbour and airfield; but the port was practically bare of shipping. Only one small merchantman was sunk, and another forced ashore. Twenty-one aircraft were destroyed on the Sabang airfield, and three more on the more distant one. Our only loss was one fighter from the *Saratoga*, which was shot down; but the submarine *Tactician*, lying off shore on air-sea rescue duty, succeeded in rescuing the pilot, although under fire from a shore battery. As the fleet retired westward later in the day, fighters from the *Saratoga* intercepted and shot down three enemy torpedo-bombers which approached.

Satisfaction at the outcome of this raid, the first attempted by the Eastern Fleet, was tempered by a tragic disaster which occurred in Bombay on the afternoon of the 14th of April. The merchantman *Fort Stikine*, laden with ammunition and cotton, caught fire and blew up while she lay alongside the docks. Blazing cotton fell over a large area, the fire quickly spread, and it raged all the next night. The destruction on shore was widespread, 336 lives were lost and over 1,000 more persons were injured. In addition to the very extensive damage to store-houses and the dockyard, eighteen merchantmen (about 61,000 tons) and three warships of the Royal Indian Navy were involved. All but three merchantmen and one warship either became a total loss or were severely damaged. This was probably the most serious disaster of the whole war which could not be attributed to enemy action. It showed once again the very serious consequences which could arise if any mishap occurred in a merchant ship loaded with explosives while she was lying in a crowded harbour.[1]

On her arrival back at Ceylon on the 27th of April the *Saratoga* was ordered to the United States to refit, and Admiral King suggested that, supported by the Eastern Fleet, she should strike at Soerabaya on the way. Admiral Mountbatten readily agreed to the request. As Soerabaya was much closer to Australia than to Ceylon, the plan was to stage the raid from the Exmouth Gulf, and Somerville accordingly made arrangements to refuel his ships there. On the 6th of May he sailed with almost the same fleet as had carried out the raid on Sabang, to arrive in Exmouth Gulf early on the 15th. Because he anticipated stronger enemy reaction on this occasion, he fixed the

---

[1] The damage suffered at Bombay was comparable to that caused at Bari in Italy in December 1943, when the explosion of an ammunition ship brought about the loss of sixteen ships of 67,462 tons (see p. 210); but that disaster was attributable to an enemy air raid.

flying-off position at 180 miles from the target. As this distance was outside the radius of action of the Barracudas, the *Illustrious* embarked Avengers instead.[1] After refuelling quickly the fleet sailed from Exmouth Gulf the same afternoon and, once more undetected, arrived at the launching position due south of Soerabaya at 6.30 a.m. on the 17th.[2]

By 7.20 a.m. forty-five Avengers and Dauntlesses and forty Hell-cats and Corsairs, divided into two striking forces, had formed up and taken their departure. One force was to attack an important oil refinery, which was the only source of aviation petrol in Java, and an engineering works, while the other was to bomb the dockyard and shipping in the harbour. In spite of the striking forces having to fly overland for a considerable distance during the approach, they encountered no enemy fighters; and when they reached their targets anti-aircraft fire was slight and ineffective. The degree of surprise achieved is shown by a message sent by the Japanese Army head-quarters in Soerabaya, which was intercepted with amusement in the fleet. It asked whether the military organisation was concerned in the alert which had just been ordered.

At 8.30 a.m. both striking forces delivered synchronised attacks. Although at the time we believed that many of the ships in harbour had been sunk or damaged and that severe destruction had been done to the oil refinery and naval base, Japanese records do not confirm that either their shipping or the shore facilities suffered at all heavily. The loss of only one small ship (993 tons) is admitted, and the fires started on shore seem to have caused our aircrews to report too optimistically on the results of the raid.

After the striking forces, which only lost one aircraft, had landed on their carriers the fleet withdrew to the south-west. Admiral Somerville, in his report, regretted that he did not repeat the attack in the afternoon; but as he was not flying his flag in a carrier he was unaware that some targets had been left undamaged in the harbour until it was too late to order a repetition. It was the practice of the Royal Navy at this time for the senior officer to sail in a ship other than a carrier, because we considered that controlling a fleet would be easier if divorced from actual flying operations, and that the accommodation of the Admiral's staff and provision of the extra

---

[1] The Barracuda found little favour with Fleet Air Arm pilots as a strike aircraft. Although reasonably efficient as a steep glide-bomber, it was difficult to control as a dive-bomber using diving brakes, with consequent loss of accuracy. By the end of the year all British fleet carriers were re-equipped with American Avengers.

[2] There is a puzzling discrepancy between the times used in the Commander-in-Chief's report on this operation, and those shown on his flagship's track chart and used in the *Illustrious's* report. These latter give all times as two hours earlier than the Commander-in-Chief. It appears that they adhered to the Zone Time used in the operation orders (−6½ hours), whereas Admiral Somerville converted them to local times for the longitude of Soerabaya. In this account local time is used.

communications needed in a fleet flagship would overstrain the resources of a carrier. In the U.S. Navy the practice was for the commander of the Third or Fifth Fleet to fly his flag in a battleship, while the flag of the officer in tactical control of the main body—generally the Fast Carrier Task Force—was worn by a carrier. Any disadvantage which may have accrued from overcrowding in the latter ship was probably compensated by the advantage of the senior officer having complete knowledge of the progress of events instantly available to him.

Admiral Somerville gave high praise to the manner in which the *Saratoga* operated her aircraft, and he considered that in order to emulate it we should adopt the American carriers' flight deck organisation, and also certain aspects of our Ally's ship design. It is indeed certain that in the rapid operation of carrier aircraft we had at that time a great deal to learn from the Americans. On the afternoon of the 18th, the *Saratoga* and her escort parted company to return to America, and the Eastern Fleet steered for Ceylon, which it reached after steaming over 7,000 miles in three weeks. As had been the case when the *Victorious* was working with the U.S. fleet in the Pacific in 1943[1], co-operation between the two Navies had been excellent. In a farewell signal to the *Saratoga* Admiral Somerville thanked her for 'a profitable and very happy association'.

The phase thus ended with powerful and successful offensives in progress in both of the Pacific commands. In the Indian Ocean, on the other hand, the Supreme Commander's plans to strike offensive blows with the resources which he had on the station had been frustrated by the transfer of combined operation ships and craft to the Mediterranean; but it was at least certain that our control of the seas in that theatre had been re-asserted, and the assumption of the offensive by the Eastern Fleet so soon after it had been reinforced augured well for the future.

---

[1] See Vol. II, pp. 415–416.

Appendices

APPENDIX A

The Board of Admiralty

1st June, 1943–31st May, 1944

	Date of Appointment
First Lord: Rt. Hon. Albert V. Alexander	12.5.40
First Sea Lord and Chief of Naval Staff:	
Admiral of the Fleet Sir A. Dudley P. R. Pound	12.6.39
Admiral of the Fleet Sir Andrew B. Cunningham	15.10.43
Deputy First Sea Lord:	
Admiral Sir Charles E. Kennedy-Purvis	29.7.42
Second Sea Lord and Chief of Naval Personnel:	
Admiral Sir William J. Whitworth	1.6.41
Vice-Admiral Sir Algernon U. Willis	8.3.44
Third Sea Lord and Controller:	
Vice-Admiral Sir W. Frederick Wake-Walker	22.5.42
Fourth Sea Lord and Chief of Supplies and Transport:	
Vice-Admiral F. H. Pegram	8.5.43
Vice-Admiral A. F. E. Palliser	20.3.44
Fifth Sea Lord and Chief of Naval Air Equipment:	
Vice-Admiral D. W. Boyd	14.1.43
Vice-Chief of Naval Staff:	
Vice-Admiral Sir Henry R. Moore	21.10.41
Vice-Admiral Sir E. Neville Syfret	7.6.43
Assistant Chief of Naval Staff (U-boat Warfare and Trade):	
Rear-Admiral J. H. Edelsten	7.12.42
Assistant Chief of Naval Staff (Weapons):	
Rear-Admiral W. R. Patterson	8.3.43
Parliamentary Secretary:	
Lord Bruntisfield	4.4.40
Financial Secretary:	
Rt. Hon. G. H. Hall	9.2.42
Civil Lord:	
Captain R. A. Pilkington	5.3.42
Controller of Merchant Shipbuilding and Repairs:	
Sir James Lithgow	1.2.40
Permanent Secretary:	
Sir Henry V. Markham	5.12.40

Date of
Appointment

Assistant Chiefs of Naval Staff, not members of the Board:

Foreign:

Rear-Admiral R. M. Servaes	22.2.43

Home:

Rear-Admiral E. J. P. Brind	28.5.42

Air:

Rear-Admiral R. H. Portal	1.1.43

APPENDIX B

Coastal Command of the Royal Air Force

Establishment and Expansion, September 1943–June 1944

	1st September, 1943		1st January, 1944		1st June, 1944	
	Squadrons	Aircraft	Squadrons	Aircraft	Squadrons	Aircraft
Anti-U-boat						
Very long range .	4	61	4	60	3	45
Long range .	8	118	9	126	11	166
Medium range .	6	98	7	115	5½	81
Short range .	3	63	½	6	4½	56
Flying boats .	12½	140	8½	99	10½	127
Anti-Shipping						
All types of aircraft, including long-range fighters and those armed with torpedo, rocket projectiles, and cannon . .	7	142	8½	173	15	278
TOTAL . . .	40½	622	37½	579	49½	753

NOTE: The above Table excludes those squadrons which were not operational through re-equipment or training, and also excludes photographic reconnaissance, air-sea rescue and meteorological squadrons.

APPENDIX C

German U-boat Strength

July 1943–April 1944

Date	Operational	Training and Trials	Total	New boats commissioned in previous quarter
July 1943 .	207	208	415	71
October 1943	175	237	412	61
January 1944	168	268	436	78
April 1944 .	166	278	444	62

Principal characteristics of German U-boat Types IXC and IXC/40

These were Atlantic type U-boats of which a total of 141 were commissioned during the war.

Displacement:
    Surfaced: (IXC) 1,120 tons, (IXC/40) 1,144 tons
    Submerged: (IXC) 1,232 tons, (IXC/40) 1,257 tons

Maximum speeds (laden)
    Surfaced: 18·3 kts.
    Submerged: 7·3 kts. (for one hour)

Endurance:
    Surfaced: *IXC*
                  16,300 miles at 10 kts. (Diesel-electric)
                  13,450 miles at 10 kts. (cruising)
                  11,000 miles at 12 kts. (cruising)
                  5,000 miles at 18·3 kts. (maximum sustained)
                  IXC/40
                  16,800 miles at 10 kts.
                  13,850 miles at 10 kts.
                  11,400 miles at 12 kts.
                  5,100 miles at 18·3 kts.
    Submerged: 128 miles at 2 kts.
                  63 miles at 4 kts.

Diving Depth: 330 ft. (in emergency could be considerably exceeded)

Armament:
    Torpedo tubes: 4 bow, 2 stern
    Outfit   19 torpedoes (normal), 22 (maximum)
    Guns: 1–37 mm. Flak
                  2–20 mm. Flak
    Crew: 48

APPENDIX D

German, Italian and Japanese U-boats sunk

1st June, 1943–31st May, 1944

Note: All Ships and Air Squadrons are British except where
otherwise stated

Table I. German U-boats sunk, 1st June, 1943–31st May, 1944

Number	Date	Name and Task of Killer	Area
U.202	1 June '43	*Starling*—sea escort	North Atlantic
U.418	1 June '43	Aircraft of 236 Squadron—Bay air patrol	Bay of Biscay
U.105	2 June '43	Aircraft of French Squadron 141—air escort	Off Dakar
U.521	2 June '43	*U.S.S. PC.565*—sea escort	East coast of U.S.A.
U.308	4 June '43	*Truculent*—S/M patrol	Off Faeroes
U.594	4 June '43	Aircraft of 48 Squadron—Gibraltar air patrol	West of Straits of Gibraltar
U.217	5 June '43	Aircraft from *U.S.S. Bogue*—carrier air escort	North Atlantic
U.417	11 June '43	Aircraft of 206 Squadron—Northern Transit Area Patrol	West of Faeroes
U.118	12 June '43	Aircraft from *U.S.S. Bogue*—carrier air escort	North Atlantic
U.334	14 June '43	*Jed* and *Pelican*—sea escort	North Atlantic
U.564	14 June '43	Aircraft of 10 Squadron O.T.U.—Bay air patrol	Bay of Biscay
U.97	16 June '43	Aircraft of 459 R.A.A.F. Squadron—air patrol	West of Haifa
U.388	20 June '43	Aircraft of U.S. Patrol Squadron No. 84—air support	S.W. of Iceland
U.119	24 June '43	*Starling*—sea patrol	Bay of Biscay
U.194	24 June '43	Aircraft of 120 Squadron—air support	South of Iceland
U.200	24 June '43	Aircraft of U.S.N. Patrol Squadron No. 84—air support	South of Iceland
U.449	24 June '43	*Wren, Woodpecker, Kite* and *Wild Goose*—sea patrol	Bay of Biscay
U.126	3 July '43	Aircraft of 172 Squadron—Bay air patrol	Bay of Biscay
U.628	3 July '43	Aircraft of 224 Squadron—Bay air patrol	Bay of Biscay
U.535	5 July '43	Aircraft of 53 Squadron—Bay air patrol	Bay of Biscay
U.951	7 July '43	Aircraft of No. 1 U.S. Army A/S Squadron—air patrol	Western approaches to Mediterranean
U.514	8 July '43	Aircraft of 224 Squadron—Bay air patrol	Bay of Biscay
U.232	8 July '43	Aircraft of No. 2 U.S. Army A/S Squadron—air patrol	Off Portugal
U.435	9 July '43	Aircraft of 179 Squadron—air patrol	Off Portugal
U.590	9 July '43	Aircraft of U.S.N. Patrol Squadron No. 94—air escort	Off North Brazil

Table I. German U-boats sunk, 1st June, 1943–31st May, 1944 (Contd.)

Number	Date	Name and Task of Killer	Area
U.409	12 July '43	*Inconstant*—sea escort	Between Algiers and Bougie
U.506	12 July '43	Aircraft of No. 1 U.S. Army A/S Squadron—Bay air patrol	Outer Bay of Biscay
U.561	12 July '43	M.T.B.81—sea patrol	Straits of Messina
U.607	13 July '43	Aircraft of 228 Squadron—Bay air patrol	Bay of Biscay
U.487	13 July '43	Aircraft from *U.S.S. Core*—carrier air escort	North Atlantic
U.160	14 July '43	Aircraft from *U.S.S. Santee*—carrier air escort	North Atlantic
U.159	15 July '43	Aircraft of U.S.N. Patrol Squadron No. 32—air escort	Caribbean
U.135	15 July '43	*Rochester, Mignonette, Balsam*—sea escort	North Atlantic
U.509	15 July '43	Aircraft from *U.S.S. Santee*—carrier air escort	North Atlantic
U.67	16 July '43	Aircraft from *U.S.S. Core*—carrier air escort	North Atlantic
U.513	19 July '43	Aircraft of U.S. Patrol Squadron No. 74—air escort	Off South Brazil
U.558	20 July '43	Aircraft of No. 19 U.S. Army A/S Squadron—Bay air patrol	Bay of Biscay
U.662	21 July '43	Aircraft of U.S.N. Patrol Squadron No. 94—air escort	Off North Brazil
U.527	23 July '43	Aircraft from *U.S.S. Bogue*—carrier air escort	North Atlantic
U.613	23 July '43	*U.S.S. Badger*—sea escort	North Atlantic
U.598	23 July '43	Aircraft of U.S.N. Bombing Squadron No. 107—air patrol	Off Brazil
U.459	24 July '43	Aircraft of 172 Squadron—Bay air patrol	Bay of Biscay
U.622	24 July '43	U.S.A.A.F. air raid—bombing	Trondheim
U.759	26 July '43	Aircraft of U.S.N. Patrol Squadron No. 32—air escort	Caribbean
U.359	28 July '43	Aircraft of U.S.N. Patrol Squadron No. 32—air patrol	Caribbean
U.404	28 July '43	Aircraft of U.S. Army A/S Squadron No. 4 and of R.A.F. Squadron 224 —Bay air patrol	Bay of Biscay
U.614	29 July '43	Aircraft of 172 Squadron—Bay air patrol	Bay of Biscay
U.591	30 July '43	Aircraft of U.S.N. Bombing Squadron No. 127—air escort	Off Brazil
U.504	30 July '43	*Kite, Woodpecker, Wren* and *Wild Goose*—sea patrol	Bay of Biscay
U.43	30 July '43	Aircraft from *U.S.S. Santee*—carrier air escort	North Atlantic
U.461	30 July '43	Aircraft of 461 Squadron R.A.A.F. —Bay air patrol	Bay of Biscay
U.462	30 July '43	Aircraft of 502 Squadron—Bay air patrol	Bay of Biscay
U.375	30 July '43	*U.S.S. PC.624*—sea patrol	Central Mediterranean
U.199	31 July '43	Aircraft of U.S.N. Patrol Squadron No. 74 and Brazilian aircraft—air escort	Off South Brazil
U.383	1 Aug. '43	Aircraft of 228 Squadron—Bay air patrol	Bay of Biscay
U.454	1 Aug. '43	Aircraft of 10 Squadron R.A.A.F.— Bay air patrol	Bay of Biscay
U.706	2 Aug. '43	Aircraft of U.S. Army A/S Squadron No. 4—Bay air patrol	Bay of Biscay

Table I. German U-boats sunk, 1st June, 1943–31st May, 1944 (Contd.)

Number	Date	Name and Task of Killer	Area
U.106	2 Aug '43	Aircraft of 461 Squadron R.A.A.F. and R.A.F. Squadron 228—Bay air patrol	Bay of Biscay
U.572	3 Aug. '43	Aircraft of U.S.N. Patrol Squadron No. 205—air patrol	East of Trinidad
U.647	3 Aug. '43	Not known (probably mined)	Iceland–Faeroes
U.489	4 Aug. '43	Aircraft of 423 Squadron R.C.A.F. —Northern Transit Area patrol	West of Faeroes
U.34	6 Aug. '43	Accident—marine casualty	Baltic
U.615	6 Aug. '43	Aircraft of U.S.N. Patrol Squadrons Nos. 204 and 205, U.S.N. Bombardment Squadron No. 130 and U.S. Army Bombardment Squadron No. 10—air patrol	Caribbean
U.117	7 Aug. '43	Aircraft from *U.S.S. Card*—carrier air escort	North Atlantic
U.664	9 Aug. '43	Aircraft from *U.S.S. Card*—carrier air escort	North Atlantic
U.604	11 Aug. '43	Scuttled after attacks by U.S.N. Patrol Squadrons Nos. 107 and 129 and *U.S.S. Moffett* on 3rd August— air/sea escort	South Atlantic
U.468	11 Aug. '43	Aircraft of 200 Squadron—air patrol	Off Dakar
U.525	11 Aug. '43	Aircraft from *U.S.S. Card*—carrier air escort	North Atlantic
U.403	18 Aug. '43	Aircraft of Free French Squadron 697 and R.A.F. Squadron 200— air escort	Off Dakar
U.197	20 Aug. '43	Aircraft of 265 and 259 Squadrons— air patrol	Off Madagascar
U.670	21 Aug. '43	Accident—collision	Baltic
U.458	22 Aug. '43	*Easton* and *Pindos* (Greek)—sea escort	S.E. of Pantelleria
U.134	24 Aug. '43	Aircraft of 179 Squadron—Bay air patrol	Bay of Biscay
U.185	24 Aug. '43	Aircraft from *U.S.S. Core*—carrier air escort	North Atlantic
U.84	24 Aug. '43	Aircraft from *U.S.S. Core*—carrier air escort	North Atlantic
U.523	25 Aug. '43	*Wanderer* and *Wallflower*—sea escort	North Atlantic
U.847	27 Aug. '43	Aircraft from *U.S.S. Card*—carrier air escort	North Atlantic
U.634	30 Aug. '43	*Stork* and *Stonecrop*—sea escort	North Atlantic
U.639	30 Aug. '43	Russian S/M	Arctic—Kara Sea
U.669	7 Sept. '43	Aircraft of 407 Squadron R.C.A.F. —Bay air patrol	Bay of Biscay
U.983	8 Sept. '43	Accident—collision	Baltic
U.617	11 Sept. '43	Aircraft of 179 Squadron and *Hyacinth*, *Haarlem* and *Woolongong* (R.A.N.)—air/sea patrol	Western Mediterranean
U.341	19 Sept. '43	Aircraft of 10 Squadron R.C.A.F. —air support	North Atlantic
U.338	20 Sept. '43	Aircraft of 120 Squadron—air escort	North Atlantic
U.346	20 Sept. '43	Accident—marine casualty	Baltic
U.229	22 Sept. '43	*Keppel*—sea escort	North Atlantic
U.161	27 Sept. '43	Aircraft of U.S.N. Patrol Squadron No. 74—air patrol	Off Brazil
U.221	27 Sept. '43	Aircraft of 58 Squadron—Bay air patrol	Bay of Biscay
U.279	4 Oct. '43	Aircraft of 120 Squadron—air escort	S.W. of Iceland
U.336	4 Oct. '43	Aircraft of U.S.N. Bombing Squadron No. 128—air support	North Atlantic

Table I. German U-boats sunk, 1st June, 1943–31st May, 1944 (Contd.)

Number	Date	Name and Task of Killer	Area
U.422	4 Oct. '43	Aircraft from *U.S.S. Card*—carrier air escort	North Atlantic
U.460	4 Oct. '43	Aircraft from *U.S.S. Card*—carrier air escort	North Atlantic
U.389	5 Oct. '43	Aircraft of 269 Squadron—air support	North Atlantic
U.643	8 Oct. '43	Aircraft of 86 and 120 Squadrons—air escort	North Atlantic
U.610	8 Oct. '43	Aircraft of 423 Squadron R.C.A.F.—air escort	North Atlantic
U.419	8 Oct. '43	Aircraft of 86 Squadron—air escort	North Atlantic
U.402	13 Oct. '43	Aircraft from *U.S.S. Card*—carrier air escort	North Atlantic
U.470	16 Oct. '43	Aircraft of 59 and 120 Squadrons—air escort	North Atlantic
U.533	16 Oct. '43	Aircraft of 244 Squadron—air patrol	Gulf of Oman
U.844	16 Oct. '43	Aircraft of 86 and 59 Squadrons—air escort	North Atlantic
U.964	16 Oct. '43	Aircraft of 86 Squadron—air support	North Atlantic
U.631	17 Oct. '43	*Sunflower*—sea escort	North Atlantic
U.540	17 Oct. '43	Aircraft of 59 and 120 Squadrons—air escort	North Atlantic
U.841	17 Oct. '43	*Byard*—sea escort	North Atlantic
U.378	20 Oct. '43	Aircraft from *U.S.S. Core*—carrier air escort	North Atlantic
U.274	23 Oct. '43	*Duncan*, *Vidette* and aircraft of 224 Squadron—air/sea escort	North Atlantic
U.566	24 Oct. '43	Aircraft of 179 Squadron—Gibraltar air patrol	Off Portugal
U.420	26 Oct. '43	Aircraft of 10 Squadron R.C.A.F.—air escort	North Atlantic
U.220	28 Oct. '43	Aircraft from *U.S.S. Block Island*—carrier air escort	North Atlantic
U.282	29 Oct. '43	*Vidette*, *Duncan* and *Sunflower*—sea escort	North Atlantic
U.431	30 Oct. '43	*Ultimatum*—S/M patrol	Off Toulon
U.306	31 Oct. '43	*Whitehall* and *Geranium*—sea escort	North Atlantic
U.584	31 Oct. '43	Aircraft from *U.S.S. Card*—carrier air patrol	North Atlantic
U.732	31 Oct. '43	*Imperialist*, *Douglas* and *Loch Osaig*—Gibraltar sea patrol	Straits of Gibraltar
U.340	1 Nov. '43	*Fleetwood*, *Active*, *Witherington* and aircraft of 179 Squadron Gibraltar—air/sea patrol	Straits of Gibraltar
U.405	1 Nov. '43	*U.S.S. Borie*—sea patrol	North Atlantic
U.848	5 Nov. '43	Aircraft of U.S.N. Bombing Squadron No. 107 and U.S. Army Composite Squadron No. 1—air patrol	S.W. of Ascension Island
U.226	6 Nov. '43	*Starling*, *Woodcock* and *Kite*—sea escort	North Atlantic
U.842	6 Nov. '43	*Starling* and *Wild Goose*—sea escort	North Atlantic
U.707	9 Nov. '43	Aircraft of 220 Squadron—air escort	North Atlantic
U.966	10 Nov. '43	Aircraft of U.S.N. Bombing Squadrons Nos. 103 and 110 and of Czech Squadron No. 311—Bay air patrol	Bay of Biscay
U.508	12 Nov. '43	Aircraft of U.S.N. Bombing Squadron No. 103—Bay air patrol	Bay of Biscay
U.280	16 Nov. '43	Aircraft of 86 Squadron—air escort	North Atlantic
U.718	18 Nov. '43	Accident—collision	Baltic
U.211	19 Nov. '43	Aircraft of 179 Squadron—air support	North Atlantic

Table I. German U-boats sunk, 1st June, 1943–31st May, 1944 (Contd.)

Number	Date	Name and Task of Killer	Area
U.536	20 Nov. '43	*Nene, Snowberry* (R.C.N.) and *Calgary* (R.C.N.)—sea escort	North Atlantic
U.768	20 Nov. '43	Accident—collision	Baltic
U.538	21 Nov. '43	*Foley* and *Crane*—sea escort	North Atlantic
U.648	23 Nov. '43	*Bazely, Blackwood* and *Drury*—sea escort	North Atlantic
U.849	25 Nov. '43	Aircraft of U.S.N. Bombing Squadron No. 107—air patrol	East of Ascension Is.
U.600	25 Nov. '43	*Bazely* and *Blackwood*—sea patrol	North Atlantic
U.542	28 Nov. '43	Aircraft of 179 Squadron—air escort	North Atlantic
U.86	29 Nov. '43	Aircraft from *U.S.S. Bogue*—carrier air escort	North Atlantic
U.172	12 Dec. '43	Aircraft from *U.S.S. Bogue* and *U.S.S. Badger, Dupont, Clemson* and *Ingram*—carrier air escort	North Atlantic
U.345	13 Dec. '43	~~Mine~~ U.S. ARMY AIR RAID	~~Baltic~~ KIEL
U.391	13 Dec. '43	Aircraft of 53 Squadron—Bay air patrol	Bay of Biscay
U.593	13 Dec. '43	*U.S.S. Wainwright* and *Calpe* (R.N.)—sea escort	N.E. of Bougie
U.73	16 Dec. '43	*U.S.S. Woolsey* and *Trippe*—sea escort	Off Oran
U.850	20 Dec. '43	Aircraft from *U.S.S. Bogue*—carrier air escort	North Atlantic
U.284	21 Dec. '43	Scuttled	North Atlantic
U.645	24 Dec. '43	*U.S.S. Schenck*—sea escort	North Atlantic
U.426	8 Jan. '44	Aircraft of 10 Squadron R.A.A.F.—Bay air patrol	Bay of Biscay
U.757	8 Jan. '44	*Bayntun* and *Camrose* (R.C.N.)—sea escort	North Atlantic
U.81	9 Jan. '44	U.S. Army air raid—bombing	Pola
U.231	13 Jan. '44	Aircraft of 172 Squadron—air escort	North Atlantic
U.377	– Jan. '44	Unknown	Atlantic
U.544	16 Jan. '44	Aircraft from *U.S.S. Guadalcanal*—carrier air escort	North Atlantic
U.305	17 Jan. '44	*Wanderer* and *Glenarm*—sea escort	North Atlantic
U.641	19 Jan. '44	*Violet*—sea escort	North Atlantic
U.972	– Jan. '44	Unknown	North Atlantic
U.263	20 Jan. '44	Mine	Bay of Biscay
U.571	28 Jan. '44	Aircraft of 461 Squadron R.A.A.F.—air support	North Atlantic
U.271	28 Jan. '44	Aircraft of U.S.N. Bombing Squadron No. 103—air support	North Atlantic
U.314	30 Jan. '44	*Whitehall* and *Meteor*—sea escort	Arctic
U.364	30 Jan. '44	Aircraft of 172 Squadron—Bay air patrol	Bay of Biscay
U.592	31 Jan. '44	*Starling, Wild Goose* and *Magpie*—sea patrol	North Atlantic
U.854	4 Feb. '44	Mine	Baltic
U.177	6 Feb. '44	Aircraft of U.S.N. Bombing Squadron No. 107—air patrol	West of Ascension Is.
U.762	8 Feb. '44	*Woodpecker* and *Wild Goose*—sea escort	North Atlantic
U.238	9 Feb. '44	*Kite, Magpie* and *Starling*—sea escort	North Atlantic
U.734	9 Feb. '44	*Wild Goose* and *Starling*—sea escort	North Atlantic
U.545	10 Feb. '44	Aircraft of 612 Squadron—air support	West of Hebrides
U.666	10 Feb. '44	Aircraft of 842 F.A.A. Squadron from *Fencer*—carrier air escort	North Atlantic
U.283	11 Feb. '44	Aircraft of 407 Squadron R.C.A.F.—air support	North Atlantic
U.424	11 Feb. '44	*Wild Goose* and *Woodpecker*—sea escort	North Atlantic

Table I. German U-boats sunk, 1st June, 1943–31st May, 1944 (Contd.)

Number	Date	Name and Task of Killer	Area
U.738	14 Feb. '44	Accident—collision	Baltic
U-It.23	14 Feb. '44	*Tally-Ho*—S/M patrol	Malacca Straits
U.406	18 Feb. '44	*Spey*—sea escort	North Atlantic
U.7	18 Feb. '44	Accident—marine casualty	Baltic
U.264	19 Feb. '44	*Woodpecker* and *Starling*—sea escort	North Atlantic
U.386	19 Feb. '44	*Spey*—sea escort	North Atlantic
U.257	24 Feb. '44	*Waskesiu* (R.C.N.)—sea escort	North Atlantic
U.713	24 Feb. '44	*Keppel*—sea escort	Arctic
U.761	24 Feb. '44	Aircraft of U.S.N. Bombing Squadrons Nos. 63 and 127 and 202 Squadron (R.A.F.), *Anthony* and *Wishart*—Gibraltar air/sea patrol	Straits of Gibraltar
U.601	25 Feb. '44	Aircraft of 210 Squadron—air escort	Arctic
U.91	25 Feb. '44	*Affleck, Gore, Gould*—sea escort	North Atlantic
U.358	1 Mar. '44	*Affleck, Gould, Garlies* and *Gore*—sea escort	North Atlantic
U.709	1 Mar. '44	*U.S.Ss Thomas, Bostwick* and *Bronstein*—sea escort	North Atlantic
U.603	1 Mar. '44	*U.S.S. Bronstein*—sea escort	North Atlantic
U.472	4 Mar. '44	Aircraft of 816 F.A.A. Squadron from *Chaser* and *Onslaught*—carrier air escort	Arctic
U.366	5 Mar. '44	Aircraft of 816 F.A.A. Squadron from *Chaser*—carrier air escort	Arctic
U.744	6 Mar. '44	*St. Catherines, Chilliwack, Gatineau, Fennel, Chaudière* (all R.C.N.) and *Icarus* and *Kenilworth Castle*—sea escort	North Atlantic
U.973	6 Mar. '44	Aircraft of 816 F.A.A. Squadron from *Chaser*—carrier air escort	Arctic
U.450	10 Mar. '44	*Exmoor, Blankney, Blencathra, Brecon* and *U.S.S. Madison*—sea escort	Off Anzio
U.343	10 Mar. '44	*Mull*—sea patrol	South of Sardinia
U.625	10 Mar. '44	Aircraft of 422 Squadron R.C.A.F.	West of Ireland
U.845	10 Mar. '44	*Forester* (R.N.) and *St. Laurent, Owen Sound, Swansea* (all R.C.N.)—sea escort	North Atlantic
U-It.22	11 Mar. '44	Aircraft of 279 and 262 S.A.A.F. Squadrons—air patrol	South of Cape of Good Hope
U.380	11 Mar. '44	U.S. Army air raid—bombing	Toulon
U.410	11 Mar. '44	U.S. Army air raid—bombing	Toulon
U.575	13 Mar. '44	Aircraft from *U.S.S. Bogue* and aircraft of 172, 206 and 220 Squadrons (R.A.F.) *U.S.Ss Haverfield* and *Hobson* and *Prince Rupert* (R.C.N.)—carrier air/sea escort	North Atlantic
U.653	15 Mar. '44	Aircraft of 825 F.A.A. Squadron from *Vindex* and *Starling* and *Wild Goose*—carrier air/sea patrol	North Atlantic
U.392	16 Mar. '44	Aircraft of U.S.N. Patrol Squadron No. 63 and *Affleck* and *Vanoc*—Gibraltar air/sea patrol	Straits of Gibraltar
U.801	16 Mar. '44	Aircraft from *U.S.S. Block Island* and *U.S.Ss Corry* and *Bronstein*—carrier air/sea patrol	West of Cape Verde Island
U.1013	17 Mar. '44	Accident—collision	Baltic
U.1059	19 Mar. '44	Aircraft from *U.S.S. Block Island*—carrier air patrol	West of Cape Verde Island
U.976	25 Mar. '44	Aircraft of 248 Squadron—Bay air patrol	Bay of Biscay
U.961	29 Mar. '44	*Starling*—sea escort	Arctic

Table I. German U-boats sunk, 1st June, 1943–31st May, 1944 (Contd.)

Number	Date	Name and Task of Killer	Area
U.223	30 Mar. '44	*Laforey, Tumult, Hambledon, Blencathra*—sea patrol	North of Sicily
U.28	– Mar. '44	Accident—marine casualty	Baltic
U.851	– Mar. '44 or – Apr. '44	Unknown	Atlantic
U.355	1 Apr. '44	Aircraft of 846 F.A.A. Squadron from *Tracker*, and *Beagle*—carrier air/sea escort	Arctic
U.360	2 Apr. '44	*Keppel*—sea escort	Arctic
U.288	3 Apr. '44	Aircraft of 846 and 819 F.A.A. Squadrons from *Tracker* and *Activity*—carrier air escort	Arctic
U.302	6 Apr. '44	*Swale*—sea escort	North Atlantic
U.455	6 Apr. '44	Unknown (possibly German mine)	Off Spezia
U.856	7 Apr. '44	*U.S.Ss Champlin* and *Huse*—carrier sea patrol	S.E. of Nova Scotia
U.2	8 Apr. '44	Accident—collision	Baltic
U.962	8 Apr. '44	*Crane* and *Cygnet*—sea patrol	North Atlantic
U.515	9 Apr. '44	Aircraft from *U.S.S. Guadalcanal* and *U.S.Ss Pope, Pillsbury, Chatelain* and *Flaherty*—carrier air/sea escort	North Atlantic
U.68	10 Apr. '44	Aircraft from *U.S.S. Guadalcanal*—carrier air escort	North Atlantic
U.108	11 Apr. '44	U.S. Army air raid—bombing	Stettin
U.448	14 Apr. '44	*Swansea* (R.C.N.) and *Pelican*—sea escort	North Atlantic
U.550	16 Apr. '44	*U.S.Ss Gandy, Joyce* and *Petersen*—sea escort	E. coast of U.S.A.
U.342	17 Apr. '44	Aircraft of 162 Squadron R.C.A.F.—air support	S.W. of Iceland
U.986	17 Apr. '44	*U.S.Ss Swift* and *PC.619*—sea escort	S.W. of Ireland
U 974	19 Apr. '44	Norwegian S/M *Ula*—S/M patrol	North Sea
U.311	– Apr. '44	Unknown	North Atlantic
U.488	26 Apr. '44	*U.S.Ss Frost, Huse, Barber* and *Snowden*—carrier sea patrol	West of Cape Verde Island
U.803	27 Apr. '44	Mine	Baltic
U.193	28 Apr. '44	Aircraft of 612 Squadron—Bay air patrol	Bay of Biscay
U.421	29 Apr. '44	U.S. Army air raid—bombing	Toulon
U.277	1 May '44	Aircraft of 842 F.A.A. Squadron from *Fencer*—carrier air escort	Arctic
U.674	2 May '44	Aircraft of 842 F.A.A. Squadron from *Fencer*—carrier air escort	Arctic
U.959	2 May '44	Aircraft of 842 F.A.A. Squadron from *Fencer*—carrier air escort	Arctic
U.852	3 May '44	Aircraft of 621 Squadron—air patrol	Gulf of Aden
U.371	4 May '44	*U.S.Ss Pride* and *Joseph E. Campbell, Sénégalais* (French) and *Blankney* (R.N.)—sea escort	N.E. of Bougie
U.846	4 May '44	Aircraft of 407 Squadron R.C.A.F.—Bay air patrol	Bay of Biscay
U.473	5 May '44	*Starling, Wren* and *Wild Goose*—sea escort	North Atlantic
U.66	6 May '44	Aircraft from *U.S.S. Block Island* and *Buckley*—carrier air/sea escort	West of Cape Verde Island
U.765	6 May '44	Aircraft of 825 F.A.A. Squadron from *Vindex* and *Bickerton, Bligh* and *Aylmer*—carrier air/sea patrol	North Atlantic
U.731	15 May '44	Aircraft of U.S. N. Patrol Squadron No. 63 and *Kilmarnock* and *Blackfly*—Gibraltar air/sea patrol	Straits of Gibraltar

Table I. German U-boats sunk, 1st June, 1943–31st May, 1944 (Contd.)

Number	Date	Name and Task of Killer	Area
U.240	16 May '44	Aircraft of Norwegian Squadron 330—Northern Transit Area Patrol	Off S.W. Norway
U.616	17 May '44	U.S.Ss *Nields, Gleaves, Ellyson, Jones, Macomb, Hambleton, Rodman, Emmons* and aircraft of 36 Squadron R.A.F.—air/sea escort	N.W. of C. Tenes
U.241	18 May '44	Aircraft of 210 Squadron—Northern Transit Area Patrol	Off S.W. Norway
U.960	19 May '44	U.S.Ss *Niblack* and *Ludlow* and aircraft of 36 and 500 Squadrons (R.A.F.)—on passage	Western Mediterranean
U.1015	19 May '44	Accident—collision	Baltic
U.453	21 May '44	*Termagant, Tenacious* and *Liddlesdale*—sea escort	N.E. of Cape Spartivento, Italy
U.476	24 May '44	Aircraft of 210 Squadron—Northern Transit Area Patrol	Off S.W. Norway
U.675	24 May '44	Aircraft of No. 4 Squadron O.T.U.—Northern Transit Area Patrol	Off S.W. Norway
U.990	25 May '44	Aircraft of 59 Squadron—Northern Transit Area Patrol	Off S.W. Norway
U.292	27 May '44	Aircraft of 59 Squadron—Northern Transit Area Patrol	Off S.W. Norway
U.549	29 May '44	U.S.Ss *Eugene E. Elmore* and *Ahrens*—carrier sea escort	North Atlantic
U.289	30 May '44	*Milne*—sea escort	Arctic

Table II. Italian U-Boats sunk, 1st June–8th September, 1943

Name	Date	Name and Task of Killer	Area
Barbarigo	17 June '43 or 19 June '43	R.A.F. aircraft—air patrol or U.S. aircraft—air patrol	Atlantic
H.8	5 July '43	R.A.F. air raid—bombing	Spezia
Flutto	11 July '43	M.T.Bs 640, 651 and 670—sea patrol	Straits of Messina
Bronzo (captured)	12 July '43	*Seaham, Boston, Poole, Cromarty*—sea escort	Off Augusta
Nereide	13 July '43	*Echo* and *Ilex*—sea escort	S.E. of Messina Straits
Acciaio	13 July '43	*Unruly*—S/M patrol	N. of Messina Straits
Remo	15 July '43	*United*—S/M patrol	Gulf of Taranto
Romolo	18 July '43	Aircraft of 221 Squadron—air escort	E. of Augusta
Ascianghi	23 July '43	*Laforey* and *Eclipse*—sea escort	South coast of Sicily
Pietro Micca	29 July '43	*Trooper*—S/M patrol	Straits of Otranto
Argento	3 Aug. '43	U.S.S. *Buck*—sea escort	Off Pantelleria
Velella	7 Sept. '43	*Shakespeare*—S/M patrol	Gulf of Salerno

NOTE: *Topazio* was sunk in error south-east of Sardinia on the 12th of September 1943 by an R.A.F. aircraft, when she failed to establish her identity.

Table III. Japanese U-Boats sunk, 7th December, 1941–31st May, 1944

NOTE: As some of the sinkings recorded in Vol. II, Appendix J, Table III have been re-assessed in the light of more recent information, that table is here reprinted in its entirety.

Number	Date	Name and Task of Killer	Area
I-170	10 Dec. '41	Aircraft from *U.S.S. Enterprise* —on passage	Off Hawaii
RO-66	17 Dec. '41	Accident—collision	Off Wake Is.
RO-60	29 Dec. '41	Accident—wrecked	Kwajalein
I-160	17 Jan. '42	*Jupiter*—sea escort	Sunda Straits
I-124	20 Jan. '42	*U.S.S. Edsall* and H.M.A.S. *Deloraine*, *Lithgow* and *Katoomba*—sea escort	Off Port Darwin
I-173	27 Jan. '42	*U.S.S. Gudgeon*—S/M patrol	Central Pacific
I-23	– Feb. '42	Unknown	Off Hawaii
I-28	17 May '42	*U.S.S. Tautog*—S/M patrol	Caroline Is.
I-164	17 May '42	*U.S.S. Triton*—S/M patrol	S.E. of Kyushu
I-123	28 Aug. '42	*U.S.S. Gamble*—sea escort	Off Guadalcanal
RO-33	29 Aug. '42	*Arunta* (R.A.N.)—sea escort	Off Port Moresby
RO-61	31 Aug. '42	*U.S.S. Reid* and aircraft of U.S.N. patrol squadron 43—air/sea patrol	Aleutian Is.
I-30	13 Oct. '42	Mine	Singapore
I-22	– Oct. '42	Unknown	Solomon Is.
I-15	2 Nov. '42	*U.S.S. McCalla*—sea escort	Solomon Is.
RO-65	4 Nov. '42	Accident—wrecked	Kiska
I-172	10 Nov. '42	*U.S.S. Southard*—on passage	Solomon Is.
I-3	9 Dec. '42	*U.S.S. PT.59*—sea patrol	Off Guadalcanal
I-4	20 Dec. '42	*U.S.S. Seadragon*—S/M patrol	Off New Britain
I-1	29 Jan. '43	*Kiwi* and *Moa* (both R.N.Z.N.)—sea patrol	Solomon Is.
I-18	11 Feb. '43	*U.S.S. Fletcher* and aircraft of *U.S.S. Helena*—sea escort	Solomon Is.
RO-34	7 Apr. '43	*U.S.S. Strong*—sea escort	Solomon Is.
I-31	12 May '43	Unknown—possibly *U.S.Ss Edwards* and *Farragut*—sea patrol	Aleutian Is.
I-178	29 May '43	*U.S.S. SC.669*—sea patrol	Off New Hebrides
RO-102	– May '43	Unknown	New Guinea
I-9	10 June '43 or 13 June '43	*U.S.S. Frazier* or *PC.487*—sea patrol	Aleutian Is.
I-24	10 June '43 or 13 June '43	*U.S.S. Frazier* or *PC.487*—sea patrol	Aleutian Is.
I-7	22 June '43	*U.S.S. Monaghan*—sea patrol	Aleutian Is.
RO-107	12 July '43	*U.S.S. Taylor*—on passage	Off Solomon Is.
I-179	14 July '43	Accident	Inland Sea
I-168	27 July '43	*U.S.S. Scamp*—S/M patrol	Bismarck Archipelago
RO-103	July–Aug. '43	Probably mine	Solomon Is.
I-17	19 Aug. '43	Aircraft of U.S.N. Scouting Squadron 57 and *Tui* (R.N.Z.N.)—sea escort	Off Noumea
RO-35	25 Aug. '43	*U.S.S. Patterson*—sea escort (or *U.S.S. Ellet*, 3 Sept. '43, see below)	Off New Hebrides
I-182	1 Sept. '43	Probably *U.S.S. Wadsworth*—sea patrol	Off Espiritu Santo
I-25	3 Sept. '43	*U.S.S. Ellet*—sea escort (or *U.S.S. Patterson*, 25 Aug. '43, see above)	Off New Hebrides
RO-101	15 Sept. '43	Aircraft of U.S.N. patrol Squadron 23 and *U.S.S. Saufley*—sea escort	Off Ellice Is.

Table III. Japanese U-boats sunk, 7th December, 1941–31st May, 1944
(Contd.)

Number	Date	Name and Task of Killer	Area
I-20	1 Oct. '43	*U.S.S. Eaton*—sea patrol	Solomon Is.
I-19	– Oct. '43	Unknown	Gilbert Is.
I-34	13 Nov. '43	*Taurus*—S/M patrol	Off Penang
I-35	22 Nov. '43	*U.S.Ss Frazier* and *Meade*—sea escort	Off Gilbert Is.
RO-100	25 Nov. '43	Mine	Off Buin
I-40	25 Nov. '43	Probably *U.S.S. Radford*—sea escort	Off Gilbert Is.
I-39	Nov.–Dec. '43	Unknown	Gilbert Is.
RO-38	Nov.–Dec. '43	Unknown	Central Pacific
I-21	Nov.–Dec. '43	Unknown	Gilbert Is.
RO-37	22 Jan. '44	*U.S.S. Buchanan*—sea patrol	S.W. of the Solomon Is.
I-181	– Jan. '44	Unknown	Off New Guinea
RO-39	1 Feb. '44	*U.S.S. Walker*—sea escort	Off Marshall Is.
I-175	5 Feb. '44	*U.S.S. Charrette* and *Fair*—sea escort	Off Marshall Is.
RO-110	11 Feb. '44	*Jumna* (R.I.N.), *Launceston* (R.A.N.) and *Ipswich* (R.A.N.)—sea escort	Off east coast of India
I-27	12 Feb. '44	*Paladin* and *Petard*—sea escort	South of Maldive Is.
I-43	15 Feb. '44	*U.S.S. Aspro*—S/M patrol	East of Guam
RO-40	15 Feb. '44	*U.S.Ss Phelps* and *Sage*—sea escort	Off Marshall Is.
I-11	17 Feb. '44	*U.S.S. Nicholas*—sea escort	East of Marshall Is.
I-171	– Feb. '44	Unknown	Solomon Is.
I-42	23 Mar. '44	*U.S.S. Tunny*—S/M patrol	Off Palau Is.
I-32	24 Mar. '44	*U.S.S. Manlove* and *PC.1135*—sea patrol	Off Marshall Is.
I-169	4 Apr. '44	Accident—marine casualty	Truk
I-2	7 Apr. '44	*U.S.S. Saufley*—sea patrol	Off New Ireland
I-180	26 Apr. '44	*U.S.S. Gilmore*—sea escort	Off Alaska
I-183	28 Apr. '44	*U.S.S. Pogy*—S/M patrol	Off Kyushu
I-174	– Apr. '44	Unknown	Central Pacific
RO-45	(?) 1 May '44	Unknown	Caroline Is.
RO-501 (ex U.1224)	13 May '44	*U.S.S. Francis M. Robinson*—sea patrol	West of C. Verde Is.
I-176	16 May '44	*U.S.Ss Franks, Haggard* and *Johnston*—sea patrol	Off Solomon Is.
I-16	19 May '44	*U.S.S. England*—sea patrol	North of Solomon Is.
RO-106	22 May '44	*U.S.S. England*—sea patrol	N.W. of New Ireland
RO-104	23 May '44	*U.S.S. England*—sea patrol	N.E. of Admiralty Is.
RO-116	24 May '44	*U.S.S. England*—sea patrol	N.E. of Admiralty Is.
RO-108	26 May '44	*U.S.S. England*—sea patrol	N.E. of Admiralty Is.
RO-105	31 May '44	*U.S.Ss England, George, Raby, Hazelwood* and *McCord*—sea patrol	N.E. of Admiralty Is.

Table IV. Analysis of sinkings of German, Italian and Japanese U-boats by cause
1st June, 1943–31st May, 1944

Cause	1943 (1st June–31st Dec.)			1944	
	German	Italian	Japanese	German	Japanese
Surface ships . . .	30	5	8	37	18
Shore-based aircraft .	71	2	—	22	—
Ship-borne aircraft . .	22	—	—	10	—
Ships and shore-based air-craft	4	—	2	5	—
Ships and ship-borne air-craft	1	—	—	8	—
Shore-based and ship-borne aircraft . . .	—	—	—	—	—
Submarines . . .	2	4	2	2	3
Bombing raids . .	2	1	—	5	—
Mines laid by shore-based aircraft . . .	—	—	—	3	—
Mines laid by ships. .	—	—	2	—	—
Other causes . . .	8	—	1	6	1
Causes unknown . .	1	—	6	5	4
TOTAL . . .	141	12	21	103	26

APPENDIX E

The Mediterranean Station, Naval Strength on 1st October, 1943

(Includes the Levant Command and Allied ships under British control except those of the U.S.A. Ships refitting or repairing battle damage are also included)

1st Battle Squadron	Battleships: *Nelson, Rodney, Warspite, Valiant, King George V, Howe* Fleet Carriers: *Illustrious, Formidable*
12th Cruiser Squadron	*Aurora, Penelope, Sirius, Dido, Cleopatra*
15th Cruiser Squadron	*Mauritius, Orion, Sheffield, Euryalus, Uganda*
A.A. Cruisers and A.A. Ships	*Charybdis, Ceres, Delhi, Colombo, Carlisle, Alynbank*
Escort Carriers	*Hunter, Stalker, Attacker, Unicorn*
Monitors	*Abercrombie, Roberts*
Destroyers for Fleet Work	27 ships of 4th, 8th, 14th, 19th and 24th Flotillas
Levant Destroyers	11 of *Hunt*-class
Escort Vessels	44 destroyers, sloops, frigates, corvettes of 1st, B4, 36th, 46th, 48th and 50th Escort Groups 9 destroyers of 13th Flotilla 20 *Hunt*-class destroyers of 57th, 58th, 59th and 60th Divisions 6 unattached escort vessels Levant Escort Force—20 *Hunt*-class destroyers, corvettes, trawlers, etc.
Submarines	24 of 8th and 10th Flotillas and 9 French
Combined Operation Headquarters Ships	*Hilary, Antwerp*
Landing Ships Infantry	12
Landing Ships Tank	4
Fighter Direction Ships	*Ulster Queen, Palomares*
Fleet Minesweepers	26 ships of 12th, 13th, 14th and 17th Minesweeping Flotillas
Other Minesweepers	64

376

Anti-submarine Trawlers	9	
Rescue Tugs	15	
Harbour Tugs	12	
Gunboats	5	
A/S-M/S Trawlers	71	
Harbour Defence M.Ls	62	
Repair and Depot Ships	12	
Boom Defence Vessels	22	
Ocean Boarding Vessels	5	
Royal Fleet Auxiliaries	21	
Armament Issuing Ships	15	
Petrol and Water Carriers	24	
Salvage Vessels	4	
Miscellaneous craft	25	
Coastal Forces		7 Motor Launch Flotillas (16 M.Ls)
		6 Motor Torpedo-Boat Flotillas (39 M.T.Bs)
		2 Motor Gunboat Flotillas (13 M.G.Bs)
French Ships		2 cruisers
		7 destroyers
		9 minesweepers
		9 patrol vessels

APPENDIX F

Italian Warships in Allied Control on 21st September, 1943

Battleships (5):	*Vittorio Veneto, Italia* (ex-*Littorio*), *Giulio Cesare, Andrea Doria, Caio Duilio*
Cruisers (8):	*Luigi Cadorna, Raimondo Montecuccoli, Eugenio di Savoia, Duca d'Aosta, Giuseppe Garibaldi, Pompeo Magna, Duca degli Abruzzi, Scipio Africano*
Fleet Destroyers (11):	*Legionario, Velite, Granatiere, Camicia Nera, Oriani, Grecale, da Recco, Riboty, Euro, FR.23* (ex-French *Tigre*), *FR.31* (ex-French *Trombe*)
Escort and Local Defence Destroyers (22):	*Orione, Ariete, Aliseo, Animoso, Ardimentoso, Fortunale, Indomito, Clio, Calliope, Aretusa, Cassiopea, Sagittaria, Sirio, Fabrizi, Carini, Abba, Pilo, Libra, Mosto, Stocco* (sunk 25.9.43 while operating with the Allies), *Monzambano, Cosenz* (sunk 27.9.43 while operating with the Allies)
Aircraft Transport:	*Miraglia*
Escort Vessels:	20
Submarines:	34
Midget Submarines:	5
Miscellaneous:	15 including one sloop, one gunboat, three minelayers, one survey vessel, two sail training ships, two hospital ships, one tug, four fuel and water carriers
E-boats:	12

In addition to the above, the following ships were interned in the Balearic Islands: the cruiser *Attilo Regolo*, the fleet destroyers *Mitragliere, Fuciliere, Carabiniere* and the escort destroyer *Orsa*.

APPENDIX G
Italian Naval Losses
10th June, 1940–8th September, 1943

Date	Name	Cause	Area
BATTLESHIP			
12.11.40	*Cavour*	F.A.A. aircraft (subsequently salvaged and taken to Trieste. Never again operational)	Taranto
CRUISERS			
19.7.40	*Colleoni*	Surface action	Off Crete
22.1.41	*San Giorgio*	Disabled by aircraft (subsequently scuttled)	Tobruk
25.2.41	*Diaz*	Submarine	Off Tunisia
29.3.41	*Fiume*	Surface action	C. Matapan
29.3.41	*Zara*	Surface action	C. Matapan
29.3.41	*Pola*	Surface action	C. Matapan
13.12.41	*Da Barbiano*	Surface action	C. Bon
13.12.41	*Di Giussano*	Surface action	C. Bon
1.4.42	*Delle Bande Nere*	Submarine	Off Stromboli
15.6.42	*Trento*	Aircraft and submarine	Ionian Sea
4.12.42	*Attendolo*	Aircraft	Naples
3.1.43	*Ulpio Traiano*	Human torpedo	Palermo
10.4.43	*Trieste*	Aircraft	Maddalena
28.6.43	*Bari*	Aircraft	Leghorn
DESTROYERS			
28.6.40	*Espero*	Surface action	Ionian Sea
5.7.40	*Zeffiro*	Aircraft	Tobruk
10.7.40	*Pancaldo*	Aircraft (subsequently salvaged and sunk again by aircraft 30.4.43)	Augusta
20.7.40	*Ostro*	Aircraft	Tobruk
20.7.40	*Nembo*	Aircraft	Tobruk
17.9.40	*Borea*	Aircraft	Benghazi
17.9.40	*Aquilone*	Mine	Off Benghazi
12.10.40	*Artigliere*	Surface action	E. of Malta
21.10.40	*Nullo*	Surface action	Red Sea
28.3.41	*Alfieri*	Surface action	C. Matapan
28.3.41	*Carducci*	Surface action	C. Matapan
1.4.41	*Leone*	Wrecked	Red Sea
3.4.41	*Sauro*	Aircraft	Red Sea
3.4.41	*Manin*	Aircraft	Red Sea
3.4.41	*Battisti*	Beached and scuttled	Red Sea
3.4.41	*Pantera*	Scuttled	Red Sea
3.4.41	*Tigre*	Scuttled	Red Sea
16.4.41	*Tarigo*	Surface action	Kerkenah
16.4.41	*Lampo*	Surface action (subsequently salvaged, sunk again 30.4.43 by aircraft)	Kerkenah
16.4.41	*Baleno*	Surface action	Kerkenah
21.5.41	*Mirabello*	Mine	Off Cephalonia
9.11.41	*Fulmine*	Surface action	Ionian Sea
9.11.41	*Libeccio*	Submarine	Ionian Sea
1.12.41	*Da Mosto*	Aircraft	N.W. of Tripoli
23.3.42	*Lanciere*	Foundered	East of Malta
23.3.42	*Scirocco*	Foundered	East of Malta
29.5.42	*Pessagno*	Submarine	N.W. of Benghazi
8.6.42	*Usodimare*	Italian submarine	Sicilian channel

379

Italian Naval Losses (Contd.)

Date	Name	Cause	Area
DESTROYERS			
(Contd.)			
21.6.42	Strale	Wrecked	Off C. Bon
19.10.42	Da Verazzano	Submarine	South of Pantelleria
2.12.42	Folgore	Surface action	Sicilian channel
17.12.42	Aviere	Submarine	N. of Bizerta
7.1.43	Bersagliere	Aircraft	Palermo
9.1.43	Corsaro	Mine	N.E. of Bizerta
17.1.43	Bombardiere	Submarine	Off Marittimo
3.2.43	Saetta	Mine	Off Bizerta
1.3.43	Geniere	Aircraft	Palermo
24.3.43	Malocello	Mine	N. of C. Bon
24.3.43	Ascari	Mine	N. of C. Bon
1.4.43	Lubiana (ex-Yugo-Slav Ljubljana)	Wrecked	Gulf of Tunis
19.4.43	Alpino	Aircraft	Spezia
8.8.43	Freccia	Aircraft	Genoa
9.8.43	Gioberti	Submarine	Off Spezia
DESTROYER			
ESCORTS			
22.9.40	Palestro	Submarine	Southern Adriatic
12.10.40	Ariel	Surface action	S.E. of Sicily
12.10.40	Airone	Surface action	S.E. of Sicily
20.11.40	Confienza	Collision	Off Brindisi
5.12.40	Calipso	Mine	E. of Tripoli
23.12.40	Cairoli	Mine	N.E. of Tripoli
10.1.41	Vega	Surface action	Off Pantelleria
17.3.41	Andromeda	Aircraft	Valona
28.3.41	Chinotto	Mine	Off Palermo
4.4.41	Acerbi	Aircraft	Red Sea
8.4.41	Orsini	Scuttled	Red Sea
24.4.41	Schiaffino	Mine	Off C. Bon
3.5.41	Canopo	Aircraft	Tripoli
4.5.41	La Farina	Mine	Kerkenah
20.5.41	Curtatone	Mine	Gulf of Athens
27.9.41	Albatros	Submarine	Off Messina
14.10.41	Pleiadi	Aircraft	Tripoli
20.10.41	Altair	Mine	Gulf of Athens
20.10.41	Aldebaran	Mine	Gulf of Athens
11.12.41	Alcione	Submarine	N. of Crete
22.8.42	Cantore	Mine	N.E. of Tobruk
4.9.42	Polluce	Aircraft	N. of Tobruk
4.11.42	Centauro	Aircraft	Benghazi
27.11.42	Circe	Collision	Off Sicily
2.12.42	Lupo	Aircraft	Off Kerkenah
12.1.43	Ardente	Collision	Off Sicily
31.1.43	Prestinari	Mine	Sicilian channel
3.2.43	Uragano	Mine	Sicilian channel
8.3.43	Ciclone	Mine	Sicilian channel
1.3.43	Monsone	Aircraft	Naples
8.3.43	Ciclone	Mine	Sicilian channel
16.4.43	Medici	Aircraft	Catania
16.4.43	Cigno	Surface action	Off Sicily
28.4.43	Climene	Submarine	Off Sicily
4.5.43	Perseo	Surface action	Off Tunisia
7.5.43	Tifone	Aircraft	Off Tunisia
25.5.43	Groppo	Aircraft	Messina
28.5.43	Antares	Aircraft	Leghorn
28.5.43	Bassini	Aircraft	Leghorn
2.6.43	Castore	Surface action	Off C. Spartivento
5.8.43	Pallade	Aircraft	Naples
28.8.43	Lince	Submarine	G. of Taranto

Italian Naval Losses (Contd.)

Submarines	Eighty-four, and one ex-French. For details see Vol. I, Appendix K, Vol. II, Appendix J, and this volume Appendix D.
Escort Vessels (corvettes and sloops)	Four, and one ex-French
Minelayers	Two, and one ex-French
Minesweepers	Twenty-seven, and eight ex-French
Gunboats	Ten, and six ex-Yugo-Slav minelayers in service as gunboats
Coastal Forces (M.T.Bs and vessels of a similar type)	Fifty
Tugs	Forty-three
Fleet Auxiliaries (tankers, transports)	Fifteen
Miscellaneous small craft	about nineteen
Landing craft	Sixty-one

APPENDIX H

British Commonwealth Warship Losses
in the Mediterranean

10th June, 1940–8th September, 1943

(This table includes British ships on loan to Allied Navies)

Date	Name	Cause	Area
BATTLESHIP			
25.11.41	*Barham*	U.331	Off Egyptian coast
AIRCRAFT CARRIERS			
13.11.41	*Ark Royal*	U.81	Off Gibraltar
11.8.42	*Eagle*	U.73	South of Balearic Is.
CRUISERS			
12.6.40	*Calypso*	It. s/m *Bagnolini*	South of Crete
11.1.41	*Southampton*	Aircraft	Central Mediterranean
26.3.41	*York*	E-boat (Italian)	Suda Bay, Crete
31.3.41	*Bonaventure*	It. s/m *Ambra*	South of Crete
22.5.41	*Fiji*	Aircraft	Off Crete
22.5.41	*Gloucester*	Aircraft	Off Crete
1.6.41	*Calcutta*	Aircraft	Off Egyptian coast
14.12.41	*Galatea*	U.557	Off Alexandria
19.12.41	*Neptune*	Mine	Off Tripoli
11.3.42	*Naiad*	U.565	Off Egyptian coast
16.6.42	*Hermione*	U.205	South of Crete
12.8.42	*Cairo*	It. s/m *Axum*	Off C. Bon
13.8.42	*Manchester*	E-boat (Italian)	Off C. Bon
14.9.42	*Coventry*	Aircraft	Eastern Mediterranean
MONITOR			
24.2.41	*Terror*	Aircraft	Off Derna
AUXILIARY A.A. SHIP			
11.11.42	*Tynwald*	It. s/m *Argo* or mine	Bougie
29.1.43	*Pozarica*	Aircraft (capsized in harbour 13.2.43)	Off Bougie
SUBMARINE DEPOT SHIP			
30.6.42	*Medway*	U.372	Off Alexandria
FAST MINE-LAYERS			
25.10.41	*Latona*	Aircraft	Off Bardia
1.2.43	*Welshman*	U.617	Off Bardia
DESTROYERS			
11.7.40	*Escort*	It. s/m *Marconi*	East of Gibraltar
23.8.40	*Hostile*	Mine	Off C. Bon
22.12.40	*Hyperion*	Mine	Off C. Bon

British Commonwealth Warship Losses in the Mediterranean (Contd.)

Date	Name	Cause	Area
DESTROYERS *(Contd.)*			
10.1.41	*Gallant*	Mine (towed to Malta but became a total loss)	Off Pantelleria
24.2.41	*Dainty*	Aircraft	Tobruk
16.4.41	*Mohawk*	It. dest. *Tarigo*	Off Sfax
27.4.41	*Wryneck*	Aircraft	Off Greece
27.4.41	*Diamond*	Aircraft	Off Greece
2.5.41	*Jersey*	Mine	Off Malta
21.5.41	*Juno*	Aircraft	Off Crete
22.5.41	*Greyhound*	Aircraft	Off Crete
23.5.41	*Kashmir*	Aircraft	Off Crete
23.5.41	*Kelly*	Aircraft	Off Crete
29.5.41	*Imperial*	Aircraft	Off Crete
29.5.41	*Hereward*	Aircraft	Off Crete
29.6.41	*Waterhen* (R.A.N.)	Aircraft	Off Tobruk
11.7.41	*Defender*	Aircraft	Off Bardia
23.7.41	*Fearless*	Aircraft	North of Bone
19.12.41	*Kandahar*	Mine	North of Tripoli
17.1.42	*Gurkha*	U.133	North of Sidi Barrani
12.2.42	*Maori*	Aircraft	Malta
20.3.42	*Heythrop*	U.652	North of Bardia
24.3.42	*Southwold*	Mine	Off Malta
26.3.42	*Jaguar*	U.652	North of Sidi Barrani
26.3.42	*Legion*	Aircraft	Malta
6.4.42	*Havock*	Wrecked	C. Bon
8.4.42	*Kingston*	Aircraft	Malta
11.5.42	*Lively*	Aircraft	South of Crete
11.5.42	*Kipling*	Aircraft	South of Crete
11.5.42	*Jackal*	Aircraft	South of Crete
12.6.42	*Grove*	U.77	North of Sidi Barrani
15.6.42	*Airedale*	Aircraft	South of Crete
15.6.42	*Bedouin*	Surface action and aircraft	South of Pantelleria
15.6.42	*Hasty*	E-boat	North of Derna
15.6.42	*Nestor* (R.A.N.)	Aircraft	N.W. of Derna
16.6.42	*Kujawiak* (Polish)	Mine	Off Malta
12.8.42	*Foresight*	Aircraft	North of Bizerta
14.9.42	*Sikh*	Shore gunfire	Off Tobruk
14.9.42	*Zulu*	Aircraft	N.W. of Alexandria
8.11.42	*Broke*	Shore gunfire	Off Algiers
10.11.42	*Martin*	U.431	N.E. of Algiers
2.12.42	*Quentin*	Aircraft	Off Galita
11.12.42	*Blean*	U.443	West of Oran
18.12.42	*Partridge*	U.565	West of Oran
12.3.43	*Lightning*	E-boat	North of Bizerta
16.4.43	*Pakenham*	It. t. b. *Cassiopea* and m/s *Cigno*	North of Pantelleria
6.9.43	*Puckeridge*	U.617	Off Gibraltar
SUBMARINES			
13.6.40	*Odin*	It. dest. *Strale*	Gulf of Taranto
16.6.40	*Grampus*	It. t. bs *Circe, Clio, Polluce* and *Calliope*	Off Syracuse
19.6.40	*Orpheus*	It. dest. *Turbine*	Off Tobruk
16.7.40	*Phoenix*	It. t. b. *Albatros*	Off Augusta
1.8.40	*Oswald*	It. t. b. *Vivaldi*	East of Sicily
15.10.40	*Rainbow*	It. s/m *Toti*	East of Calabria
?.10.40	*Triad*	Unknown	Off Libyan coast
?.12.40	*Regulus*	Presumed mine	Strait of Otranto
?.12.40	*Triton*	Presumed mine	Southern Adriatic
?.5.41	*Usk*	Presumed mine	Off C. Bon

British Commonwealth Warship Losses in the Mediterranean (Contd.)

Date	Name	Cause	Area
SUBMARINES (Contd.)			
?.5.41	*Undaunted*	Presumed mine	Off Tripoli
20.7.41	*Union*	It. t. b. *Circe*	West of Tripoli
30.7.41	*Cachalot*	It. t. b. *Papa*	N.W. of Benghazi
18.8.41	*P.32*	Mine	Off Tripoli
23.8.41	*P.33*	Presumed mine	Off Tripoli
?.10.41	*Tetrarch*	Presumed mine	Sicilian channel
6.12.41	*Perseus*	Mine	Off Cephalonia
14.1.42	*Triumph*	Presumed mine	Gulf of Athens
13.2.42	*Tempest*	It. t. b. *Circe*	Gulf of Taranto
23.2.42	*P.38*	It. t. b. *Circe*	Off Tripoli
26.3.42	*P.39*	Aircraft	Malta
1.4.42	*P.36*	Aircraft	Malta
1.4.42	*Pandora*	Aircraft	Malta
14.4.42	*Upholder*	Probably It. t. b. *Pegaso*	S.E. of Malta
28.4.42	*Urge*	Presumed mine	Between Malta and Alexandria
8.5.42	*Olympus*	Mine	Off Malta
6.8.42	*Thorn*	Mine	Off the coast of Cyrenaica
16.9.42	*Talisman*	Presumed mine	Sicilian channel
24.11.42	*Utmost*	It. t. b. *Groppo*	West of Sicily
8.12.42	*Traveller*	Presumed mine	Gulf of Taranto
12.12.42	*P.222*	It. t. b. *Fortunale*	Off Naples
25.12.42	*P.48*	It. t. b. *Ardente*	Gulf of Tunis
31.12.42	*P.311*	Presumed mine	Off Maddalena
?10.3.43	*Tigris*	Presumed mine	Gulf of Tunis
14.3.43	*Turbulent*	Presumed mine	Off Maddalena
14.3.43	*Thunderbolt*	It. corv. *Cicogna*	Off the Messina Straits
18.4.43	*Regent*	Presumed mine	Southern Adriatic
21.4.43	*Splendid*	Ger. dest. *Hermes*	Off Capri
24.4.43	*Sahib*	It. corvs. *Gabbiano* and *Euterpe* and t. b. *Climene*	Off the Messina Straits
10.8.43	*Parthian*	Presumed mine	Off Brindisi
14.8.43	*Saracen*	It. corvs. *Minerva* and *Euterpe*	Off Bastia
SLOOPS			
25.5.41	*Grimsby*	Aircraft	North of Sollum
24.6.41	*Auckland*	Aircraft	N.W. of Sollum
27.11.41	*Parramatta* (R.A.N.)	U.559	N.W. of Sollum
10.11.42	*Ibis*	Aircraft	North of Algiers
CUTTERS			
8.11.42	*Hartland*	Shore battery	Oran
8.11.42	*Walney*	Shore battery	Oran
CORVETTES			
24.12.41	*Salvia*	U.568	N.E. of Mersa Matruh
9.11.42	*Gardenia*	Collision	Off Oran
9.12.42	*Marigold*	Aircraft	West of Algiers
19.12.42	*Snapdragon*	Aircraft	Off Benghazi
30.1.43	*Samphire*	It. s/m *Platino*	N.E. of Algiers
6.2.43	*Louisburg* (R.C.N.)	Aircraft	N.E. of Oran
9.2.43	*Erica*	British mine	Off Benghazi
FLEET MINE-SWEEPERS			
31.1.41	*Huntley*	Aircraft	Off Mersa Matruh
3.5.41	*Fermoy*	Aircraft	Malta
7.5.41	*Stoke*	Aircraft	Tobruk

British Commonwealth Warship Losses in the Mediterranean (Contd.)

Date	Name	Cause	Area
FLEET MINE-SWEEPERS (*Contd.*)			
20.5.41	*Widnes*	Aircraft	Suda Bay, Crete
5.7.42	*Abingdon*	Aircraft	Malta
9.11.42	*Cromer*	Mine	Off Mersa Matruh
15.11.42	*Algerine*	It. s/m *Ascianghi*	Off Bougie
2.1.43	*Alarm*	Aircraft	Bone
GUNBOAT			
12.5.41	*Ladybird*	Aircraft	Tobruk
L. S. I. (LARGE)			
12.11.42	*Karanja*	Aircraft	Bougie
SUPPLY SHIPS			
24.4.41	*Ulster Prince*	Aircraft	Nauplia
26.3.42	*Slavol* (R.F.A.)	U.205	N.E. of Sollum
27.3.42	*Breconshire*	Aircraft	Malta

SMALL MINESWEEPING AND ANTI-SUBMARINE VESSELS
(Trawlers, drifters, whalers, etc.)   Thirty-two

COASTAL CRAFT
(M.T.Bs, M.G.Bs, M.Ls, etc.)   Thirty-four

MISCELLANEOUS SHIPS AND VESSELS
(Cable ship, tugs, schooners, armed boarding vessels, mooring vessels, etc.)   Seventeen

NOTES: 1. In addition, Allied Navies (other than U.S.) lost the following warships of their own Navies in the Mediterranean while under British operational control between the same dates:

> Greek Navy—3 submarines
> French Navy—1 submarine, 2 patrol vessels
> Royal Netherlands Navy—1 destroyer

2. Losses of Landing Craft cannot be stated with exactitude as many were lost other than by enemy action (e.g. on training exercises). It appears, however, that between the 10th of June 1940 and the 8th of September 1943 about 200 British Landing Craft (mostly of the smaller types) were lost from all causes in the Mediterranean.

APPENDIX J

The Organisation of the Imperial Japanese Navy on 1st August, 1943

This appendix shows the principal units of the Japanese Navy allocated to the various Fleets. The term 'Fleet' was primarily an administrative title, and they were not organised to operate as balanced tactical units; task forces were formed as necessary for that purpose. The title Combined Fleet, in its full sense, embraced all the fleet shown below, only a few ships (including the flagship *Musashi*) being retained under the immediate control of the Commander-in-Chief, Combined Fleet. For the sake of simplicity these few ships have been included in the First Fleet.

The figures given for destroyers and submarines can only be taken as approximate. In addition to those shown below, about twenty were employed on guard, training and escort duties and were not allocated to the various fleets. Similarly about fifteen submarines were used for training, mostly in home waters.

FIRST FLEET—Tactical Title—Battleship Force

1st Battle Squadron	*Musashi, Yamato*
2nd Battle Squadron	*Nagato, Fuso, Yamashiro.* (*Mutsu* was sunk by explosion in the Inland Sea in July 1943)
11th Destroyer Flotilla	Light cruiser *Tatsuta* and about three destroyers
11th Submarine Flotilla	About six submarines
Attached	Escort carriers *Unyo, Chuyo, Taiyo* and about three destroyers

SECOND FLEET—Tactical Title—Diversion Attack Force

4th Cruiser Squadron	Heavy cruisers *Atago, Maya, Takao*
5th Cruiser Squadron	Heavy cruisers *Haguro, Myoko*
2nd Destroyer Flotilla	Light cruiser *Noshiro* and about fourteen destroyers

THIRD FLEET—Tactical Title—Striking Force

1st Carrier Squadron	Fleet carriers *Zuikaku, Shokaku* and light fleet carrier *Zuiho*
2nd Carrier Squadron	Fleet carriers *Junyo, Hiyo* and light fleet carrier *Ryuho*
3rd Battleship Squadron	*Kongo, Haruna*
7th Cruiser Squadron	Heavy cruisers *Suzuya, Kumano* and *Mogami*
8th Cruiser Squadron	Heavy cruisers *Tone, Chikuma*
Attached	Light cruiser *Oyodo*

386

| 10th Destroyer Flotilla | Light cruiser *Agano* and about fourteen destroyers |
| 50th Air Flotilla (Training) | Light fleet carrier *Hosho*, one destroyer and two air groups |

FOURTH FLEET—Tactical Title—Inner South Seas Force

| 14th Cruiser Squadron | Light cruisers *Kashima, Isuzu* and *Naka* |
| 2nd Escort Flotilla | About seven destroyers and torpedo-boats |

FIFTH FLEET—Tactical Title—Northern Force

21st Cruiser Squadron	Heavy cruiser *Nachi* and light cruisers *Tama* and *Kiso*
1st Destroyer Flotilla	Light cruiser *Abukuma* and about six destroyers
12th Air Fleet	Three air flotillas
Attached	Three submarines

SIXTH FLEET—Tactical Title—Advance Expeditionary Force

1st Submarine Flotilla	
3rd Submarine Flotilla	Light cruiser *Katori* and about 27 submarines
8th Submarine Flotilla	

EIGHTH FLEET—Tactical Title—Outer South Seas Force

| 6th Cruiser Squadron | Heavy cruisers *Chokai, Aoba* and light cruisers *Yubari, Nagara* |
| 3rd Destroyer Flotilla | Light cruiser *Sendai* and about ten destroyers |

SOUTH-WEST AREA FLEET

16th Cruiser Squadron	Heavy cruiser *Ashigara* and light cruisers *Oi, Kitagami, Kinu* and *Kuma*
Attached	Light cruiser *Kashii*, two destroyers, three submarines
1st Escort Flotilla	About fourteen destroyers and frigates
23rd and 28th Air Flotillas	Five air groups

SOUTH-EAST AREA FLEET

7th Submarine Flotilla	About nine submarines
11th Air Fleet	Three air flotillas and two destroyers
1st Air Fleet	Three air groups
Battleships	*Ise, Hyuga* being converted into battleship aircraft carriers and did not rejoin the fleet until July 1944
Light Fleet Carriers	*Chitose, Chiyoda*
Light Cruiser	*Natori*

APPENDIX K

Table I. British, Allied, and Neutral Merchant Ship Losses from Enemy Action, and Causes—

1st June, 1943–31st May, 1944

1943 (June to December)

(Tonnage–Ships)

Month	Submarines	Aircraft	Mine	Warship raider	Merchant raider	E-boat	Unknown and other cause	TOTAL
June	95,753 (20)	6,083 (3)	4,334 (3)	—	17,655 (2)	—	—	123,825 (28)
July	252,145 (46)	106,005 (13)	72 (1)	—	7,176 (1)	—	—	365,398 (61)
August	86,579 (16)	14,133 (5)	19 (1)	—	—	—	19,070 (3)	119,801 (25)
September	118,841 (20)	22,905 (4)	4,396 (3)	—	9,977 (1)	—	300 (1)	156,419 (29)
October	97,407 (20)	22,680 (4)	19,774 (5)	—	—	—	—	139,861 (29)
November	66,585 (14)	62,452 (7)	6,666 (3)	—	—	8,538 (4)	150 (1)	144,391 (29)
December	86,967 (13)	75,471 (17)	6,086 (1)	—	—	—	—	168,524 (31)
TOTAL	804,277 (149)	309,729 (53)	41,347 (17)	—	34,808 (4)	8,538 (4)	19,520 (5)	1,218,219 (232)

1944 (January to May)

(Tonnage–Ships)

Month	Submarines	Aircraft	Mine	Warship raider	Merchant raider	E-boat	Unknown and other causes	TOTAL
January	92,278 (13)	24,237 (4)	7,176 (1)	—	—	6,420 (5)	524 (3)	130,635 (26)
February	92,923 (18)	21,616 (3)	—	—	—	2,085 (1)	231 (1)	116,855 (23)
March	142,944 (23)	—	7,176 (1)	—	—	—	—	157,960 (25)
April	62,149 (9)	19,755 (3)	—	7,840 (1)	—	468 (1)	—	82,372 (13)
May	24,424 (4)	2,873 (1)	—	—	—	—	—	27,297 (5)
TOTAL	414,718 (67)	68,481 (11)	14,352 (2)	7,840 (1)	—	8,973 (7)	755 (4)	515,119 (92)

388

Table II. British, Allied, and Neutral Merchant Shipping Losses from Enemy Action, according to Theatres

1st June, 1943–31st May, 1944

1943 (June to December)
(Tonnage–Ships)

Month	North Atlantic	United Kingdom	South Atlantic	Mediterranean	Indian Ocean	Pacific	Total
June	18,379 (4)	149 (1)	11,587 (3)	24,533 (7)	67,929 (12)	1,248 (1)	123,825 (28)
July	123,327 (18)	72 (1)	64,478 (11)	80,307 (14)	97,214 (17)	—	365,398 (61)
August	10,186 (2)	19 (1)	15,368 (2)	43,351 (11)	46,401 (7)	4,476 (2)	119,801 (25)
September	43,775 (8)	—	10,770 (3)	52,426 (11)	39,471 (6)	9,977 (1)	156,419 (29)
October	56,422 (12)	—	4,663 (1)	45,767 (9)	25,833 (6)	7,176 (1)	139,861 (29)
November	23,077 (6)	13,036 (7)	4,573 (1)	67,846 (10)	29,148 (4)	6,711 (1)	144,391 (29)
December	47,785 (7)	6,086 (1)	—	83,480 (18)	31,173 (5)	—	168,524 (31)
TOTAL	322,951 (57)	19,362 (11)	111,439 (21)	397,710 (80)	337,169 (57)	29,588 (6)	1,218,219 (232)

1944 (January to May)
(Tonnage–Ships)

Month	North Atlantic	United Kingdom	South Atlantic	Mediterranean	Indian Ocean	Pacific	Total
January	36,065 (5)	6,944 (8)	—	31,413 (5)	56,213 (8)	—	130,635 (26)
February	12,577 (2)	4,051 (3)	—	36,058 (8)	64,169 (10)	—	116,855 (23)
March	36,867 (7)	—	4,695 (1)	40,900 (5)	75,498 (12)	—	157,960 (25)
April	34,224 (5)	468 (1)	13,539 (2)	34,141 (5)	—	—	82,372 (13)
May	—	—	17,277 (3)	10,020 (2)	—	—	27,297 (5)
TOTAL	119,733 (19)	11,463 (12)	35,511 (6)	152,532 (25)	195,880 (30)	—	515,119 (92)

Index

INDEX

(The suffix letter 'n' denotes a footnote)

Wt. 2500. K64. 7/60. B. & T. Ltd. Gp. 51/3509.   S.O. Code No. 63-111-23-41*

19770376R00298

Printed in Great Britain
by Amazon